Sourcebook on Parenting and Child Care

SOURCEBOOK ON PARENTING AND CHILD CARE

by
Kathryn Hammell Carpenter

Oryx Press
1995

The rare Arabian Oryx is believed to have inspired the myth of the unicorn. This desert antelope became virtually extinct in the early 1960s. At that time several groups of international conservationists arranged to have 9 animals sent to the Phoenix Zoo to be the nucleus of a captive breeding herd. Today the Oryx population is over 800 and nearly 400 have been returned to reserves in the Middle East.

© 1995 by The Oryx Press
4041 North Central at Indian School Road
Phoenix, Arizona 85012-3397

Published simultaneously in Canada
Printed and Bound in the United States of America

∞ The paper used in this publication meets the minimum requirements of
American National Standard for Information Science—Permanence of Paper
for Printed Library Materials, ANSI Z39.48, 1984.

Library of Congress Cataloging-in-Publication Data
Sourcebook on parenting and child care / edited by Kathryn Hammell
Carpenter.
    p.   cm.
Includes bibliographical references and index.
ISBN 0-89774-780-1 (alk. paper)
    1. Parenting—Bibliography. 2. Child care—Bibliography. 3. Child rearing—
Bibliography. I. Carpenter, Kathryn Hammell.
Z7164.C5S56
[HQ755.8]
016.649'1—dc20   94-39012
                                                                      CIP

This sourcebook is dedicated to all parents and organizations who work to make the world a better place for the children entrusted to their care. May the information it provides guide their decisions, confirm their experience, and support them when the responsibility they shoulder seems daunting.

CONTENTS

LIST OF TABLES

PREFACE

"Trust yourself . . . you know more than you think you do" reads the opening sentence of the sixth edition of *Dr. Spock's Baby and Child Care*, as if to convince parents that this is the most important principle in child rearing.[1] Once they actually find time to read "Dr. Spock" and to sample the excellent general and specialized guides to parenting and child care reviewed here, parents will find that indeed this is the case—their judgment, intuition, and unadorned common sense have already provided them with the same answers given by the experts. In a recent *Cathy* comic strip in the *Chicago Tribune*, Andrea and her husband used the books in their parenting library to build a fortress between a rambunctious toddler and an active infant. Simply having the books on hand to advise on discipline puzzles, feeding battles, symptoms that signal danger, and developmental variations is enormously reassuring to new or perplexed parents.

Penelope Leach, another prominent parenting author, is succinct in her advice to parents: she counsels them to provide care and nurturing "by the baby," that is, according to the needs the child communicates rather than according to a program an expert deems best for all children. As she emphasizes in the revised edition of *Your Baby and Child*, "rearing a child 'by the book'—by any set of rules or predetermined ideas—can work well if the rules you choose to follow fit the baby you happen to have."[2]

PURPOSE

Spock, Leach, and other authors promoting parental common sense and confidence do so to reassure parents. The information they provide, however, educates parents about techniques and tasks they may otherwise have no idea how to perform. With increased mobility of families, outside employment for a majority of women, and later childbearing, new parents are less likely to learn child care skills within the family. Toni Burbank of Bantam, an active publisher in the field, maintains that parents require information to cope with modern-day circumstances; she says, "it's a myth that the previous generation's knowledge could adequately guide us . . . much more is known now about parenting; and many people do not want to parent the way they were parented."[3] Add to this educational need the evaluation of options and informed selection of what is best for their children that characterize consumer-oriented baby boomer parents, and the outcome is a defined need and strong demand for quality guides on child rearing. There is also a demand for access to other resources, such as organizations and reference materials that help parents to be most effective in raising their children.

Parents and professionals seek concise, up-to-date, accurate information for the best reasons—out of love for children and concern for their healthy development and happy, productive lives as adults. Steven P. Shelov, editor of an influential handbook from the American Academy of Pediatrics, best articulates what rewards parents for their efforts: "Although simple, your child's gifts to you—unqualified love, absolute trust, the thrill of discovery, the heights of emotion—are powerful enough to change your life."[4]

SCOPE

The 940 annotated entries in this text cover the best U.S. titles published during 1990–93, both professional and popular; a few 1994 titles that were available for review; and classic titles. Although a distinction was made between popular and professional titles, entries in the professional section may also be useful for general readers interested in a more specialized treatment of a topic. Likewise, professionals may identify titles helpful in advising or instructing their clients in the popular section.

Titles selected from the universe of publications on children and parents address the *practical* aspects of child care. Professional titles that met this criterion were handbooks or clinical guides for practitioners who work directly with children, including physicians, nurses, psychologists, teachers, and social workers. Titles targeted to a popular audience were selected because they provided parents and other care givers with how-to advice. Journals selected emphasize practice rather than theory or research. Titles reviewed were obtained either directly from publishers as review copies or borrowed via interlibrary loan. Some potentially appropriate titles were inaccessible through these channels and therefore were not included.

Books were excluded if they addressed children but not child rearing, or parents but not parenting. Many titles for a professional audience were not included because they focused on theory without noting practical applications, they outlined research methodologies and results without indicating applications for clinicians, or they presented material too specialized for general practitioners in the field. The professional literature in the fields of psychology, education, and medicine is extensive, so the titles selected were chosen from a number of competing works. Titles that cover rare conditions were not included in order to limit the size and scope of this work.

Titles for a popular audience were not included if their contents were out-of-date or they contained inaccuracies. Many topics, particularly religious training, sex education, and school-age children, are not covered as well as might be hoped in the current literature. Titles with "thin" or insubstantial contents were rejected in favor of better quality works on the same topic. Other titles of potential interest were rejected because of poor organization, awkward prose, inadequate references, or messy illustrations, all indications of inferior quality. The best popular books in each subject area are marked with an asterisk (*). These titles share an unusually intelligent, even wise perspective, exceptionally fluid, lucid writing, and comprehensive contents in an attractive format, often enhanced with color photographs.

Agencies selected for the directory section also focus on the practice of child care. Professional societies were included if they advise clinicians and other practitioners who work directly with children on techniques, skills, or child care issues. Parents' groups were selected because they instruct parents or support them in caring for children, especially children with challenging conditions. Each agency listed here was sent a questionnaire covering focus, programming, publications, educational initiatives, and other relevant activities. Missing or incomplete data were supplemented with data from other published sources, if available, and, in selected cases, direct calls to the agency in question.

Audiovisuals were difficult to evaluate because of inaccessibility. Time after time, promising titles were held at no more than one or two OCLC libraries and were not available on interlibrary loan. However, some titles were widely held and therefore accessible to local consumers seeking a videotape on child care. A list of relevant video titles is located in Appendix A. Notes on many of these are drawn directly from producer blurbs and so may not represent an unbiased evaluation of their contents.

Public and private agencies are the source of a vast array of statistical data addressing children and parents. National data for the time period covered that assist parents or practitioners in caring for children or that illustrate issues and concerns in child rearing are included. In some areas, data as current as 1990 have not been tabulated, so the most recent data available on the topic were substituted. State or local-level data were rejected, as were data that were too specialized in scope or format. While much of the data were drawn from government sources, the information has been completely reformatted to reduce the complexity of tables, to eliminate data for age groups other than children or adolescents, and to present only the most up-to-date figures. The data are presented in Appendix B.

ARRANGEMENT

Part 1 contains general publications on parenting, including materials that highlight the humorous side of raising children. Parenting concerns that relate to family characteristics, such as single or working parents, racial diversity, and adoptive families, and approaches to child care are covered in part 2. Considerations in parenting children and youths according to age characteristics are addressed in part 3. Children's growth—physical, psychological, and cognitive—and their health and fitness are the focus of part 4. In part 5, the parents' responsibilities to discipline their children; to teach them and to ensure that, no matter what their capabilities, they are educated; and to guide their spiritual development are addressed. Part 6 covers children in crisis because of abuse of various sorts. Part 7 discusses reference tools.

In general, the bibliographic information given for each entry includes author or editor, title, series title, publisher, year of publication, number of pages, LC card number and ISBN, and price. If a resource includes a bibliography, an index, illustrations, or photographs, this is indicated. Each entry also includes an annotation, which notes point of view, approach, intended audience, special or unique features, and a summary of contents.

A dual interest in social science and bibliography prompted me to compile a guide to both the parenting literature and child care resources. After four years of reading the self-help guides, statistical data, and scholarly tomes that make up the contemporary literature of child rearing, I developed an additional motivation for my work.

The materials presented here guide those who in good faith attempt to raise, discipline, educate, heal, and otherwise help children to develop to their fullest potential. Most people, if not everyone, involved with children profess this goal. But the condition of many children in the United States today does not reflect the ideals parents and professionals espouse. Poverty, homelessness, low birth weight, lack of immunizations, abuse, and even the threat of homicide are obstacles that many children must face. The resources in this book do not directly address these concerns because the materials focus on child rearing, not child advocacy. But for parents, teachers, doctors, psychologists, social workers, and even authors and editors, advocacy for children underlies concern for the growth of an individual child. Helping one child helps every child in some small way.

REFERENCES

1. Benjamin Spock and Michael B. Rothenberg, *Dr. Spock's Baby and Child Care*, 6th rev. ed. (New York: NAL-Dutton, 1992), 1.

2. Penelope Leach, *Your Baby and Child*, rev. ed. (New York: Knopf, 1989), 8.

3. Elinor Siegel, "Bringing Up Baby by the Book," *Publisher's Weekly* 238, no. 26 (June 14, 1991): 19.

4. Steven P. Shelov, ed. *Caring for Your Baby and Young Child: Birth to Age Five* (New York: Bantam in association with American Academy of Pediatrics, 1990), xx.

ACKNOWLEDGMENTS

Over the course of the past four years, I discovered that compiling a reference book on child rearing is similar to parenting itself: you don't know what you're getting into until it's too late. Like new parents, I experienced the joy of creating and the satisfaction of guiding, along with the weariness of discipline and the nagging fear that, despite all my efforts, my progeny would not turn out right after all. After four years my issue is ready to make its own way in the world, and, unlike my counterparts raising real children, I can soon relax in a house cleared of files, piles, and other paraphernalia of the growing manuscript.

Before I settle into enjoyment of my newly found free time, I have the pleasure of acknowledging with gratitude the support I received from many others in compiling this text. I appreciate the administrative support in time and money provided by the University of Illinois at Chicago (UIC), where I served as bibliographer for the Health Sciences. I acknowledge the encouragement of my colleagues on the library faculty there, who awarded funds to support postage and literature searches, and who freely provided advice and assistance. Many thanks to the UIC circulation staffs, who provided friendly, efficient service in spite of the sheer volume of loans I requested.

Most recently and most generously, my secretary at Valparaiso University, Marguerite Reinhertz, struggled daily with the intricacies of word processing to format the tables and many of the annotations presented here. I also appreciate the support and encouragement of Valparaiso University administration during my first year on the job while I completed my manuscript.

Publishers who kindly sent gratis review copies of the texts annotated here deserve a special thanks for helping to bring this sourcebook into creation. I also appreciate the assistance of my editors at Oryx, Sean Tape and Kristan Martina.

More than ever, I appreciate the dedication with which my parents raised me. I could not have completed this project without the help of my sister, Patricia Hammell, who completed much of the inputting. As a new home owner, graduate student, and hospital administrator, she had more than enough work of her own, and I am deeply grateful for her generous assistance. My husband, John Carpenter, is a musician and producer who understands creative focus, even obsession, but I am unceasingly grateful that he also knows about laundry, dishes, food shopping, and other key components of home management. The fact that he is blessed with a calm disposition also helped in my completion of this text. Thanks too to my friends who put up with a grumpy scholar for many, many, many months.

Many new parents undoubtedly experience what I as a new author encountered: a spiritual rebirth. The miracle of life and love is so magnificent! And when all other motivations pale, faith provides enough strength to continue.

LIST OF ABBREVIATIONS

A	annual	M	monthly
bibliog.	bibliographical references	pbk.	paperback
B-M	bimonthly	photog.	photographs
illus.	illustrations	Q	quarterly
LC	Library of Congress card number	S-A	semiannual

PART

1

AN INTRODUCTION
TO PARENTING

CHAPTER

1

General Guides

Parenting is abrupt.
A person must become a good parent
because parenting skills are not automatic.
Celia A. Decker. *Children—The Early Years*

Parenting is no less than the daily process of caring for children, monitoring their health and protecting their safety, stimulating their thinking, and promoting their self-esteem. It is preparing children for productive lives as adults through example, instruction, and love. The relationship of parent to child incorporates elements of other relationships, such as teacher and student, nurse and patient, social worker and client, coach and athlete, and lover and beloved. The parent functions unofficially but with the highest authority in these roles.

According to the most recent decennial census, there were 65,049,428 households in the United States in 1990, 48.2 percent with children under 18, either by birth, marriage, or adoption.[1] Typical parents want to be perfect and "... good parents know they can never know enough about parenting."[2] The materials reviewed here give parents a place to begin their study of how to be an effective, if not perfect, parent. Ninety-seven percent of women and 94 percent of men consider their family life very important, and general parenting guides give them knowledge and confidence in their ability to carry out their most significant adult responsibility.[3]

An asterisk (*) indicates a specially recommended title.

POPULAR TITLES: BOOKS

Ames, Louise Bates. *Questions Parents Ask: Straight Answers.* Delacorte, 1990. 306p. bibliog. index. LC 87-29078. ISBN 0-385-29902-8. $9.95.

The behavior of any child is influenced by individuality, age, and the environment in which that child exists. Despite changes in the outside world, human behavior development is largely patterned and therefore predictable given the experience of previous generations. Topics that interest new parents, such as spoiling infants, preschoolers' imaginary companions, shyness and other personality traits, and toilet training, have not changed much over the years. This text by a well-known developmental psychologist presents basic information for parents on these and other issues in a question-and-answer format. Divorce, grandparents, bonding, learning problems, adoption, preteens, and numerous other topics are also discussed.

Artlip, Mary Ann, James A. Artlip, and Earl S. Seltzman. *The New American Family.* Starburst, 1993. 259p. LC 92-81392. ISBN 0-914984-44-6. $9.95.

Personal experience supplements information gathered in a national survey of over 500 respondents, including 50 in-depth interviews about being stepparents, actual problems encountered in stepparenting, causes of problems and solutions devised, and positive aspects of stepfamily living. Using a behavioral approach that emphasizes learning positive strategies and helpful living skills, the authors explore expectations, family beginnings, the creation of a parental united front, and "the little things" during the first months together, always providing factual data, survey results, and practical advice for resolving problems. Interacting with the other parent, handling holidays, integrating extended families, disciplining, and keeping love alive are all covered in detail in separate chapters.

* Barrett, Kimberly. *Stress Strategies for Parents.* Berkley, 1993. 194p. LC 93-223946. ISBN 0-425-13626. $4.99.

This text by a professor of psychology supplies strategies and techniques to help parents cope with children's misbehavior in the everyday life of a busy contemporary family. Planning activities, using discipline, and encouraging a spirit of cooperation are techniques applicable to the pressure points of daily life such as mealtime, grocery shopping and running errands, evening rituals, traveling, outings with family members, and holidays. A final chapter counsels parents on how to better care for themselves and meet their own needs. This concise guide addresses day-to-day situations that cause parents stress.

* Brodkin, Margaret, and Coleman Advocates for Children and Youth. *Every Kid Counts: 31 Ways to Save Our Children.* Harper San Francisco, 1993. 201p. bibliog. illus. LC 91-56412. ISBN 0-06-250213-1. $8.00.

Colorful and upbeat, this sourcebook of facts and data, practical tips for action, organizational resources, and publications puts advocacy for children within the grasp of every parent. Grass-roots and individual techniques are emphasized to combat key obstacles in children's development: excessive television viewing, child abuse, disability, poverty, teen pregnancy, racial prejudice, drugs, alcohol and cigarettes, homelessness, running away, AIDS, inadequate health care, and unsafe living conditions, among others. Hundreds of practical tips and strategies for turning concern into action are presented: for example, to make neighborhoods safe, parents are encouraged to make their own house safe for children, join a neighborhood watch group, join a community conflict resolution program, volunteer to be a school hall monitor, or encourage a local "gang summit."

Cline, Foster, and Jim Fry. *Parenting with Love and Logic: Teaching Children Responsibility.* NAV Press, 1990. 227p. index. LC 90-61765. ISBN 0-8910-9311-7. $14.99.

The love and logic approach advocated by the authors, a psychiatrist and an educator, encourages children to mature in an empathetic way by letting them make mistakes and live with the consequences. After describing the concepts involved, which include building self-image, modeling mature behavior, offering choices, asking questions, controlling anger, and displaying empathy, the authors apply these concepts to problems parents commonly encounter, such as bedtime battles, discipline in public, poor table manners, sassing, messiness, and sibling rivalry. Interspersed throughout are "Love-and-Logic" tips, mini case studies of the approach in action. Love and logic parenting is appealing because of its emphasis on consequences rather than punishment to guide children's decisions and the assertive, rather than angry, way it advocates parents correct misbehavior. While the authors counsel from a Christian perspective, religion is downplayed in the text, making their advice applicable to others as well.

Drescher, John M. *Seven Things Children Need.* 2nd ed. Herald Press, 1988. 144p. LC 88-10173. ISBN 0-8361-3475-3. $5.95.

Minister and teacher John Drescher has assembled significant evidence from psychology to support his approach to parenting in this readable, down-to-earth guide. Each of the seven factors, which include significance or self-esteem, security, acceptance, love, praise, discipline, and God, is explored in detail. Ways in which a healthy approach to parenting is discouraged as well as encouraged are reviewed and practical steps to positive expression outlined. Each chapter contains a quiz suitable for parents' groups or individuals or to generate discussion. The warm tone and emphasis on case studies to illustrate the points being made enhance the value of this how-to book.

* Einon, Dorothy. *Parenthood: The Whole Story.* Paragon/Athena, 1991. 351p. photog. illus. index. LC 90-300085. ISBN 1-55778-374-8. $12.95.

Written to reassure new parents, to help them understand their feelings, and to instruct them in the basics of caring for a child through age two, *Parenthood* is an encyclopedic review of pregnancy, birth, adjustment, and child care. Because paragraphs are numbered sequentially, they are easily cross-referenced even though the book is arranged by topic. Many illustrations and detailed sidebars provide specific guidance on how to deal with diapering, breastfeeding, emergencies, home births, and diet. The text also contains a number of appealing photographs of infants, toddlers, and their parents. As with any how-to book, parents must determine which advice they will accept and which they will reject, e.g., the author, a British psychologist, advocates a family bed, a practice rejected by many child care professionals.

Galensky, Ellen. *The Six Stages of Parenthood.* Addison-Wesley, 1987. 364p. bibliog. index. LC 87-1800. ISBN 0-201-10529-2. $13.41.

Based on survey research, this text by an educator presents predictable stages of adult development as parents. Over 200 parents were interviewed about their preparations for having children, raising them, and letting them go, and their experiences are categorized into six stages, beginning with the image-making stage, as individuals prepare for their roles as parents, and ending with the departure stage, in which parents evaluate themselves, their decisions, and the ways in which their children turned out. In between, parents focus on nurturing, establishing authority, interpreting the world and its realities to their children, and developing interdependent relationships with their almost-adult children. Extensive case studies and quotations personalize the text, and much practical information is embedded in the anecdotes compiled here.

Gallagher, Patricia C. *Raising Happy Kids on a Reasonable Budget.* Betterway, 1993. 129p. bibliog. index. LC 92-40297. ISBN 1-55870-271-7. $10.95.

For growing families living on stable or decreasing budgets, frugality is a key technique for survival as well as peace of mind. In this guide, a former corporate business woman turned stay-at-home mom compiles hundreds of money-saving tips from the "experts"—other parents. Strategies such as bulk buying, coupon use, and home gardening stretch food dollars, and similarly effective methods pertaining to the purchase of clothing, education and entertainment, health and grooming, and children's rooms are given and can be easily adopted by parents. Flexibility in bartering, swapping, making or doing it yourself, and simple repairs and maintenance is also encouraged in this down-to-earth guide.

* Ginott, Haim. *Between Parent and Child: New Solutions to Old Problems*. Avon, 1969. 256p. ISBN 0-380-00821-1. $4.95.

First published in 1965, this enduring classic provides suggestions for daily living and solutions for common psychological problems affecting children, such as jealousy and anxiety. Practical advice on communication with children, praise and criticism, encouragement of independence and responsibility, and discipline techniques is provided, as is help for parents in avoiding self-defeating parenting practices such as bribes, sarcasm, or inviting misbehavior. When parents need to seek professional help is described. While the chapter on sex education is timely, as are the others noted above, the chapter on guiding development of proper gender and social roles is obviously dated and contradictory to contemporary concepts of equal opportunity and individual temperament.

Gordon, Thomas. *Parent-Effectiveness Training: The "No-Lose" Program for Raising Responsible Children!* Random, 1993. 352p. index. ISBN 0-679-26080-3. $18.00.

At the heart of the parent effectiveness philosophy (PET) is the successful management of conflict between child and parents through nonevaluative listening and honest communication. Using techniques such as "I-messages" rather than advice or put-downs, problem ownership, changing the immediate environments, and mutual agreement and negotiation, parents will establish and maintain good communication with their children. Even though this text is 20 years old, its practical message and goal of mutual respect are appropriate for today's families.

Guarendi, Raymond. *Back to the Family: Proven Advice on Building a Stronger, Healthier, Happier Family*. Villard Books, 1990. 254p. LC 91-16361. ISBN 0-671-74599-9. $10.00.

Drawn from the responses of 100 "excellent" families nominated by state teachers of the year, Guarandi's text is a meditation on the characteristics of good parents and healthy kids. Though it will be most valuable as a guide for parents to reflect on their values, how they express them, and areas where they may need to make a greater effort, the book also contains many practical tips for individual situations. Readers will be reassured to learn that excellent parents are not perfect parents; they make mistakes and lose their patience, but they rely on common sense (interestingly, most did not read the experts or follow their advice) and an absolute commitment to family life in order to rear happy, healthy children.

Keeshan, Robert. *Growing Up Happy: Captain Kangeroo Tells Yesterday's Children How to Nurture Their Own*. Doubleday, 1989. 224p. LC 89-32502. ISBN 0-385-24909-8. $17.95.

Using incidents from his own life experience to illustrate, Bob Keeshan gives advice to parents on how to raise children in contemporary times. Among the concerns he raises are encouraging financial responsibility from an early age, helping children grieve, and an unusual emphasis on the schools as a source of help for children whose parents cause or cannot help them with their problems.

Kutner, Lawrence. *Parent and Child Getting Through to Each Other*. William Morrow & Co., 1991. 248p. index. LC 90-40865. ISBN 0-688-10310-3. $9.00.

Noting that parents who find child rearing frustrating are those who are unfamiliar with the natural history of childhood, this practical handbook attempts to explain behavior from a child's perspective. By integrating this perspective with the results of research, clinical experience, and case material, the author, a child psychologist, offers fresh advice on transitions, early education, discipline, behavior problems, school, conflicts between children, sibling rivalry, money, puberty, and entering adulthood.

Lansky, Vicki. *Practical Parenting Tips: Over 1,500 Helpful Hints for the First Five Years*. Meadowbrook, 1992. 186p. illus. index. LC 92-17149. ISBN 0-88166-192-9. $8.00.

Over 400 new tips for parents supplement the tried-and-true ideas carried forward from the first edition of this guide, which was published in 1980. Gleaned from comments received in response to the author's "HELP! Family Circle" column and "Practical Parenting" column in *Sesame Street Parents' Guide*, the practical advice presented here covers new baby care, child care basics, health and hygiene, coping with kids at home and on the go, child's play, family traditions, and parenting challenges such as manners, tantrums, and sibling rivalry. In this new edition, outdated tips such as shag rug rakes are eliminated and contemporary items, such as juice boxes are included. An index provides additional access points to the often ingenious techniques that make a parent's job a little easier.

Lott, Jane. *Children's Rooms: A Mothercare Book*. Prentice Hall, 1990. 143p. photog. illus. LC 89-22814. ISBN 0-13-132234-6. $19.95.

Designing a special room for a child is one of the pleasures of child rearing for parents, and well-designed rooms enhance children's confidence and well-being, according to the author of this interior decorating book on children's rooms from infancy to school age. Photographs, floor plans, and line drawings illustrate chapters on planning for the child's needs throughout their "ages and stages"; selecting flooring, lighting, wall surfaces, etc.; using specific decorating techniques; and creating or assembling furnishings and fittings. The text has a practical tone as it is filled with tips and advice on safety, budgeting, storage, involving children in decisions, and accommodating their developing needs, such as collections, overnight guests, and study space. Special approaches for children of various ages sharing rooms are also provided.

McMahon, Tom. *It Works for Us: Proven Child Care Tips from Experienced Parents across the Country*. Pocket, 1993. 263p. illus. index. LC 92-40080. ISBN 0-671-77733-5. $9.00.

"Field-tested" tips that save time or make an everyday task easier were selected and compiled in this guide from among 1,500 ideas submitted in response to a media campaign. The 900 ideas presented here emphasize the most creative approaches to playtime, feeding, bathing, health and safety, sleep, travel, chores, and celebrations, among other topics. Each tip was reviewed in light of safety considerations by consulting pediatrician Remo Carruti. Dr. Carruti also provides commentary on the possible hazards of selected tips, such as the danger of younger children ingesting marbles.

* Neifert, Marianne R. *Dr. Mom's Parenting Guide: Commonsense Guidance for the Life of Your Child*. Dutton, 1991. 274p. index. LC 91-10035. ISBN 0-525-93373-5. $19.95.

While it includes much useful advice, this book focuses on teaching parenting skills and nurturing techniques that foster the development of high self-esteem in a child. Providing unconditional love, instilling values, managing misbehavior, and enriching family life through traditions are some of the parenting techniques Neifert, a pediatrician and mother of five, explores in an informative and understanding manner. She also presents ways to deal positively with the effects of divorce, manage sibling jealousy, and accept the unexpected when death or illness occur, as well as tips on how to manage the stresses of parenting and avoid being a victim to the myth of the superparent. Additional readings supplement each chapter. The combination of empathy and knowledgeable advice is both appealing and useful.

Rosemond, John K. *Parent Power! A Commonsense Approach to Parenting in the '90's and Beyond*. Andrews and McMeel, 1991. 332p. LC 90-28239. ISBN 0-8362-2808-1. $8.95.

The author advocates a commonsense approach to parenting in this overview of the tasks of child rearing. Emphasizing the need for parents to be authoritative, Rosemond advises on how to discipline children, including a description of how spanking can work, in the first section. The second section, a brief review of developmental stages from birth to age 19, is solid and informative, as is the third section, which provides techniques for dealing with little problems, such as tantrums and food fights, before they develop into bigger ones.

Rosemond, John K. *Six Point Plan for Raising Healthy, Happy, Children*. Andrews and McMeel, 1991. 191p. LC 89-30316. ISBN 0-83622-806-5. $8.95.

In this how-to manual, blunt, controversial family psychologist John Rosemond advocates a direct, practical approach to parenting, which he summarizes with six recommendations, plus a seventh—love the children enough to adopt the first six points. Rosemond advises parents to put the marriage above the needs of any individual, expect children to obey, guide development of a sense of responsibility in children, enable them to learn through frustration and creativity, and eliminate, or at least drastically limit, their exposure to TV. To persuade parents who may be unsure of these directives, he offers ample evidence of their success and much detailed advice on how to carry them out in practice. Each chapter concludes with questions and answers. The lack of an index makes it necessary to read the entire text for guidance.

Ross, Julie A. *Practical Parenting for the 21st Century: The Manual You Wish Had Come with Your Child*. Excalibur, 1993. 147p. bibliog. illus. index. LC 92-55103. ISBN 0-9627226-6-9. $10.95.

Consistency and respect are the key components of effective parenting according to the author, an active parenting instructor and family counselor. The text is full of practical tips , illustrated by personal anecdotes, parents can use to develop child rearing skills that supplement and strengthen their instincts and love for their children. The author's approach is based on effective listening via eye contact, body posture, verbal acknowledgment, and acceptance of the child's feelings. Keeping up with a child's development, applying a series of disciplinary techniques, encouraging good behavior, and managing tantrums are among the topics addressed. Sample dialogues and case studies demonstrate how the recommended parenting techniques actually work. The warm tone and positive message will appeal to parents.

Samalin, Nancy. *Love and Anger: The Parental Dilemma*. Viking, 1991. 242p. bibliog. index. LC 90-50602. ISBN 0-670-83136-0. $18.95.

Samalin explores common triggers for anger in the parent-child relationship as well as ways to express anger in a positive manner. Drawing on the experiences of parents enrolled in her parent guidance workshop, she reviews trivial anger triggers, spillover anger, power struggles, unreasonable expectations, and irritating but normal behavior such as crying and testing limits in order to help parents recognize and understand why they get so upset. She reinforces that anger is a normal emotion and outlines acceptable ways to express and acknowledge it. This clear, concise account is a fascinating study of an issue about which many parents feel deep shame and helplessness.

Schwartzman, Michael. *The Anxious Parent*. Simon & Schuster, 1990. 352p. LC 90-9513. ISBN 0-671-67920-1. $19.45.

To help parents understand their own emotional reactions to common child care issues, Schwartzman outlines how family background, social environment, and adult personality shape who parents are. To help them handle problems related to food and feeding, cleanliness, sleep, child development, elimination and toilet training, discipline, and relationships, the author provides a seven-step program for change. This approach, which includes identifying what is really bothering the parent, making a connection with the past, getting all the facts, understanding the child's point of view, grounding oneself, stepping back to reflect, and establishing a new pattern, is carefully explained with many examples and case studies. Schwartzman provides much practical advice for readers on controlling fears and using their self-knowledge to become better parents.

Spock, Benjamin. *Dr. Spock on Parenting: Sensible Advice from America's Most Trusted Child Care Expert*. Simon & Schuster, 1988. 224p. index. LC 19-88-15792. ISBN 0-671-63958-7. $17.95.

Without going into too much detail, Dr. Spock provides concise descriptions and guidance on many common issues facing parents, such as infant care, sleep problems, discipline, developmental stages, difficult relationships and behavior problems, health and nutrition, and personality and attitudes. Carefully outlining his own views and responding to criticism, he also takes on issues such as the father's role, the effect of divorce and remarriage, and sources of the anxiety that contemporary parents feel. Spock's emphasis on a flexible, individualized approach will help parents develop their own perspective on the tasks and responsibilities of a parent and weigh the advice they receive from other sources.

Taffel, Ron, with Melinda Blan. *Parenting by Heart: How to Connect with Your Kids in the Face of Too Much Advice, Too Many Pressures, and Never Enough Time.* Addison-Wesley, 1991. 302p. LC 91-11957. ISBN 0-201-57772-0. $18.95.

The concept of an empathic envelope, a child's sense of belonging and knowing what to expect, is invoked by the author as an effective approach to raising children. He begins by debunking five basic myths of parenting that limit how well parents connect to their children: the overinvolved mother and underinvolved father, absolute control by parents, unflagging harmony between parent and child, child development occurring without corresponding parental development, and the influence of communication by the parent, such as anger. Taffel applies the new framework that emerges to a number of everyday myths, suggesting skills for resolving the difficulties they present. The content includes parenting myths about sensitivity, quality time, consistency, wisdom, fairness, anger, and self-sufficiency. The how-to handbook closes with a chapter on the importance of spiritual faith and traditional values in family life.

POPULAR TITLES: JOURNALS

Family Life. Wenner Media. B-M. 1993. illus. $12.97.

This oversize, heavily illustrated magazine for parents who are intent on providing a vital and educational family life for themselves and their children promises to focus on real issues of interest to real people leading busy lives. According to letters to the editor, it delivers on that promise. In a recent issue, feature articles addressed fathering, family camps, gardening for children, ball games, schools that work, and pesticide hazards in food. Drawing on the insights of experts, these pieces were thoughtfully written. Regular columns focus on money; helping others; family matters (in one case, an analysis of X-Men comics); sports; kitchen activities; reviews of software, books, and music; and a biographical sketch of a child. Numerous advertisements for upscale products dot the text, and several articles with tie-ins to products also appear.

Growing Parent. Dunn & Hargitt. 1975. M. ISSN 0193-8037. $20.00.

Issued as a supplement to *Growing Child,* this newsletter focuses on the issues, problems, and choices parents face as their children grow and supports and encourages parents' own development to meet these challenges. Positive articles help parents cope with stresses, such as fatigue, in an upbeat manner. The results of recent research on child development are summarized.

Ladies' Home Journal Parent's Digest. Meredith Corp. 1991. S-A. ISSN 1060-9598. $7.00.

Reprints from well-known parenting books and reminiscences by prominent authors are the focus of this appealing how-to magazine. Feature articles address physical and psychological health, developmental issues according to age, parenting, and media reports. Humorous pieces are also included.

Parenting. Time Publishing Ventures. 1987. M. ISSN 0890-247X. $18.00.

Articles on nutrition, learning, safety, child care, travel, toys, and related concerns make up this journal for parents of children from birth to age 10. Book excerpts, investigative reports, personal accounts, news, humor, reviews, and opinion pieces are the formats in which practical information is conveyed.

Parents: On Rearing Children from Crib to College. Gruner & Jahr. 1926. M. ISSN 0195-0967. $20.00.

This upbeat, glossy magazine for parents focuses on development, behavior, and care of children from infancy to adolescence. A special section in each issue focuses on practical issues relevant to significant developmental stages, including birth to 6 months, 6 to 12 months, 1 year olds, 2 year olds, and so on. Feature articles offer professional insights into family relationships and report on new trends and important research in education, psychology, and health care. Food and crafts for kids are also covered. Letters, a parents' exchange, and answers to common questions promote dialogue with readers.

Sesame Street Parents' Guide. Children's Television Workshop. 1971. 10/yr. ISSN 0049-0253. $10.95.

For parents, this attractive magazine features practical articles about play, learning, family relations, behavior, child care, and other parenting issues. Guidance for readers on balancing work and family life, managing finances, controlling anger, and working with teachers is also included. The journal publishes regular columns on health, nutrition, safety, discipline, news, and parenting tips. Videos and books are evaluated.

PROFESSIONAL TITLES: BOOKS

Ambert, Anne-Marie, ed. *The Effect of Children on Parents.* Haworth, 1992. 308p. bibliog. index. LC 91-8366. ISBN 1-56024-117-9. $29.95. ISBN 1-56024-118-7 pbk. $19.95.

The effect that children have on parents, usually downplayed in parenting books, is mediated by parents' temperaments, the child's temperament, and their social environment. This anthology examines how children affect parents, how parents are vulnerable to children, and societal effects in enhancing the positive and minimizing the negative impact of children on parents. Information is drawn from interviews as well as the published literature. Contents include areas of parents' lives that may be affected, such as health, employment, values, life plans, and financial security; effects on mothers of multiracial families; how divorce affects parents; and the impact on their parents of children who are delinquent, emotionally disturbed, difficult, or chronically ill.

Bigner, Jerry J. *Parent-Child Relations: An Introduction to Parenting.* 4th ed. Macmillan, 1993. 546p. photog. bibliog. illus. index. LC 93-16111. ISBN 0-02-309841-4. Price not available.

Family systems theory is used in this textbook to explain how the contemporary family operates and how it evolves as its various members go through developmental changes over their life spans. In the first section, the nature of parent-child relationship is reviewed, the theoretical perspectives noted above are explained, and strategies for contemporary parenting are explored. The concepts of nurturing and structure are also used as the means of explaining how parents shape their own behavior and guide their children's socialization. In the second section, these concepts are applied to developmental interactions between parent and child from infancy through young adulthood. In the final section, the author turns to challenging issues, such as adolescent parenting, single-parent family and stepfamily systems, adoption, special needs, and child abuse, to complete a thorough review of historical and contemporary parenting. Numerous references, sidebars, case studies, statistics, and pedagogical aids supplement the text.

Cowan, Carolyn Pape, and Philip A. Cowan. *When Partners Become Parents: The Big Life Change for Couples.* Basic, 1992. 246p. bibliog. index. LC 91-55457. ISBN 0-465-01595-6. $24.00.

Drawing from their pilot study of 16 expectant couples, and a 10-year longitudinal study of 72 expectant couples and a control group of 24 couples without children, the authors conclude that for a majority of couples, the transition to parenthood was a difficult one that often resulted in reduced satisfaction with their marriage and less warmth and responsiveness to their child's needs. Cowan and Cowan examine why this transition is so stressful, what changes in parent's sense of self take place after a child is born, and specific reactions of a randomly chosen group of parents from among those recruited for the study in California. Written for couples who are thinking of starting a family, researchers investigating family life, and clinicians treating families in distress, the text emphasizes the negative aspects of life as a new parent in order to balance a largely positive, romantic view of parenthood in the popular media. In addition, the authors' findings on the effectiveness of the Becoming a Family Project illustrate for mental health professionals the usefulness of preventive strategies to ease the difficulty of the transition to parenthood.

Demick, Jack, Krisanne Bursek, and Rosemarie DiBlase, eds. *Parental Development.* Erlbaum, 1993. 282p. bibliog. index. LC 92-29724. ISBN 0-8058-1192-3. $29.95.

This scholarly anthology of papers, originally presented at a 1991 symposium on adult development, addresses theoretical concepts and research results in a relatively new area of study—parental development. The early chapters introduce relevant theories, and the final chapter looks at similarities and differences among the authors' theoretical perspectives and suggests useful directions for future research. In between, contributors look at such concerns as cognitive development in parents, their moral and empathetic development, effects of friendships and social networks on parenting, and periodicity of adult change in response to child-rearing challenges. Extensive references supplement the text.

Eshleman, J. Ross. *The Family: An Introduction.* 6th ed. Allyn and Bacon, 1991. 594p. illus. LC 90-37625. ISBN 0-205-12629-4. $32.25.

Eshleman's introductory textbook on marriage and the family is a concise but thorough review of theoretical principles, factual data, and results of research on all aspects of family life today. In its sixth edition, the book is divided into six sections, which cover understanding marriage and the family, family lifestyles, premarital structures and processes, sexual norms and relationships, marital and family relationships throughout the life span, and the effects of marital crisis, divorce, and social policy on the family. The writing style is lively and clear, and there are many sidebars that point to issues of the day, such as gay marriage, demise of the empty nest syndrome, and the desirability of punishing parents if their children break the law. There are numerous tables and graphs to support statements in the text as well as supplemental readings for each chapter.

Hamburg, David. *Today's Children: Creating a Future for a Generation in Crisis.* Times Books, 1992. 376p. bibliog. index. LC 91-50188. ISBN 0-8129-1914-9. $25.00.

This review of the current state of childhood in the United States, by a psychiatrist and former president of the Institute of Medicine, focuses on solving social and developmental problems in children using policies based on research results. Taking as his theme the question "Are we doing all we can do?" the author reviews why children, especially those living in poverty, are at risk of educational underachievement, poor health, and abuse due to social changes that have not been addressed by adequate program development. He identifies risks and ways to prevent them in the child's course of life from prenatal care through infancy, preschool, school age, and adolescence, looking at the potential for improvement in the family, schools, health care services, and social services. The text provides background on challenges facing children today for those who care for or educate them and for those professionals and parents who are concerned with shaping local, state, and national policies to improve children's lives.

Jaffe, Michael L. *Understanding Parenting.* William C. Brown, 1991. 412p. index. LC 89-81451. ISBN 0-697-07890-6. $25.85.

Based on a review of over one thousand recently published articles and experiences found in clinical practice, this undergraduate textbook gives a remarkably comprehensive, accurate, and accessible overview of the parenting process. Among the topics covered in detail are personality development; discipline and communication styles; family relationships; the development of self-concept, self-esteem, and sexual identity; emotional growth; adolescents; nontraditional family structures; special needs children; and family violence, abuse, and neglect. Each section includes a study guide that focuses on the main point discussed. An epilogue summarizes the major conclusions of the book. Nicely illustrated and readable, the book can serve parents as well as social service and health care professionals as a sourcebook to understanding, guiding, and enjoying child development.

Pillemer, Karl, and Kathleen McCartney, eds. *Parent-Child Relations Throughout Life.* Erlbaum, 1991. 292p. illus. LC 91-8539. ISBN 0-8058-0822-1. $45.00.

Drawn from the papers presented at a 1989 interdisciplinary conference on parent-child relations during different points in the life span, this anthology takes a fresh look at such concepts as attachment, transitions and their impact, relationships within families, and the effects of social-structural factors such as social norms and the economic system. Each contributor reviews the relevant literature, reports the results of original research, and presents recommendations for future research. Some of the topics addressed are the parents' view of attachment and the degree to which adult children are and remain attached to elderly parents, the ambiguous nature of the transition to parenthood, how siblings' expectations of the family environment may diverge, and the degree to which positive family interaction influences an adolescent's happiness and willingness to perform complex tasks such as household chores or studying.

Ryder, Verdene. *Parents and Their Children*. Willcox, 1990. 376p. illus. index. LC 89-30204. ISBN 0-87006-743-5. $29.00.

Suitable for use as a textbook for young adult parent education classes, this survey of parenting takes a thorough but concise look at what goes into the choice to have children, birth, development of children from infancy to adolescence, discipline and guidance, child care, and education concerns. Many color illustrations of diverse families enliven an already readable text, divided into brief chapters with clear headings and subheadings. Review questions and suggestions for enhancing information with observations, individual research, discussions, role-plays, and displays are helpful instructional tools. Bibliographical references are not included.

PROFESSIONAL TITLES: JOURNALS

Family Relations: Journal of Applied Family and Child Studies. National Council on Family Relations. 1952. Q. ISSN 0197-6664. $42.00.

Addressed to an audience of professionals serving families through community programs, counseling, or education, the articles in this journal examine health, social policy, and legal issues; link theory and research results to practice; and describe methodologies for program evaluation. As the official journal of the National Council on Family Relations, this title includes information on association activities. Issues have addressed maternal employment, parent education, marriage, and sources of stress in daily life.

DIRECTORY

Family Resource Coalition (FRC)
200 S. Michigan Avenue, Suite 1520, Chicago, IL 60604
(312) 341-0900 Fax (312) 341-9361 Handsnet HN1738
Judy Langford-Carter, Executive Director
Founded: 1981
Members: 2,300
Mission/Goals: To provide support to local groups concerned with parenting, child development, and family issues; to encourage the development of family resource programs that support family and community life through information and resources; to educate public, government, and corporate leaders about family needs and the means by which family support programs may assist families
Audience/Clientele: Parents, parent support groups
Budget: $2,000,000
Services: Advocacy through Parent Action, a national parent advocacy program; resource and referral service to parents; computerized mailing list and program database
Education and Outreach: In-service training, library
Publications: *FRC Connection*, a bimonthly newsletter containing information on conferences, new materials, and research; *FRC Report*, a journal issued 3 times a year with brief descriptions of family resource and support programs; a directory of programs titled *Programs to Strengthen Families: A Resource Guide*; other publications
Programs: Semiannual conference

Family Service America (FSA)
11700 W. Lake Park Drive, Milwaukee, WI 53224
(414) 359-1040 Fax (414) 359-1074 Hotline (800) 221-2681
Geneva Johnson, President and CEO
Founded: 1911
Members: 290 agencies
Mission/Goals: To influence society and its institutions to encourage, protect, and promote healthy family life in North America; to ensure a level of excellence in providing services to families through programs directed to member agencies; to maintain research programs that aim to improve service to families; to increase public awareness of the importance of healthy family life for a healthy society
Audience/Clientele: Social service agencies and their staffs
Budget: $3,307,000 Funding: Private sources, fund-raising, fees for services or products, donations, grants, dues
Services: Referral
Education and Outreach: Seminars, library, publishing
Publications: *Families in Society: The Journal of Contemporary Human Services*, 10/yr; *Directory of Member Agencies*, annual
Programs: Biennial conference

Informed Homebirth/Informed Birth and Parenting
P.O. Box 3675, Ann Arbor, MI 48106
(313) 662-6857
Rahima Baldwin, President
Founded: 1977
Members: 1,000
Former Name: Informed Homebirth
Mission/Goals: To provide information on alternatives for giving birth, parenting, and early childhood education
Audience/Clientele: Pregnant couples, parents of young children, childbirth educators, and midwives
Staff: 6 professionals, 5 nonprofessionals, 2 volunteers
Budget: $150,000 Funding: Fees, donations, dues
Languages: Russian, Spanish, German
Services: Counseling, referral

Education and Outreach: Continuing education courses, seminars, library, archives, publishing
Publications: *Special Delivery*, a quarterly journal; *Openings*, a quarterly newsletter for childbirth educators; monographic titles
Programs: Annual conference

National Institute for the Family (NIF)
3019 Fourth Street, N.E., Washington, DC 20017
(202) 269-3461
Dr. Donald B. Conroy, President
Founded: 1980
Mission/Goals: To strengthen families in the United States by providing education on issues related to family life
Audience/Clientele: Families, family life groups
Services: Compiling statistics
Education and Outreach: In-service programs, seminars, life cycle education services on intergenerational communication, library

REFERENCES

1. *1990 Census of Population and Housing: Summary Social, Economic, and Housing Characteristics*. U.S. Department of Commerce, Bureau of the Census, 1992, 1.

2. James Windell, *Discipline: A Sourcebook of 50 Failsafe Techniques for Parents* (New York: Collier Macmillan, 1991), 7–9.

3. George Gallup Jr. and Frank Newport, "Baby Boomers Seek More Family Time," *The Gallup Poll* 307, no. 37 (April 1991).

CHAPTER

Mothering

Women mother.
Nancy Chodorow. *The Reproduction of Mothering*

Motherhood is earned, first
through an intense physical and psychic rite
of passage—pregnancy and childbirth—then through
learning to nurture, which does not come by instinct.
Adrienne Rich. *Of Woman Born*

Being a mother differs from being a parent! At one level an appointment based on a customary division of labor between the sexes, mothering also expresses a child's individual experience of the mother who cared for him or her. Mothering reflects gender and personality but does not define parenting exclusively; fathers and other care givers may mother a child, but that child has only one mother. Contemporary egalitarian relationships contradict unquestioning historical assumptions of mothers as primary caretakers. In 1991, over 4 million women gave birth, so these issues concern many Americans! [1]

An asterisk (*) indicates a specially recommended title.

POPULAR TITLES: BOOKS

Barrett, Nina. *Playgroup: Three Women Contend with the Myths of Motherhood.* Simon & Schuster, 1994. 206p. bibliog. LC 93-39170. ISBN 0-671-74710-X. $21.00.

Three new mothers form a suburban play group in order to ease their own loneliness, boredom, and, in one case, emotional disturbance as stay-at-home care givers. Their stories are the focus of the text. Journalist Barrett speaks from the heart as one of the subjects who belatedly realized that making the "choice" to stay home with children was not as okay as she imagined it would be. Covering childbirth, marriage, career, and voice as subjects, the stories she recounts are painful, frustrating, depressing, and absolutely absorbing.

Comport, Maggie. *Surviving Motherhood: How to Cope with Postnatal Depression.* 2nd ed. Avery, 1991. 336p. LC 89-8074. ISBN 1-85398-013-7. $11.95.

Acknowledging that there is disagreement over what constitutes postpartum mental illness and its causes, Comport offers an exhaustive review of factors involved and many practical techniques for friends and family, and even the afflicted mother herself, to use in providing support and improving the situation. Differentiating among the blues, postpartum depression, and puerperal psychosis, the author addresses in detail how the quality of the birth experience itself and social factors such as giving up work, social isolation, and exhaustion affect the new mother. Conflicts in the marriage or lack of a partner, personal immaturity or childhood difficulties, and physical factors including hormones and poor nutrition all can add to the stress of being a woman in contemporary society. The author concludes, in a harrowing statement, that postpartum depression is universal, not because women have faulty wiring, but because "within most societies . . . women get a raw deal in terms of the value set on them and their needs, the amount of grinding, unremitting work they do, the quantity and quality of food they get . . . and opportunities to receive emotional support . . .," problems that have socioeconomic causes and potential solutions.

* Debold, Elizabeth, et al. *Mother Daughter Revolution: From Betrayal to Power.* Addison-Wesley, 1993. 299p. bibliog. index. LC 93-24502. ISBN 0-201-63277-2. $22.95.

Contemporary mothers balance how they encourage their daughters' potential with how they betray it by teaching feminine skills, such as niceness, silence, and attractiveness to men, attributes valued in women in Western culture. The three authors propose an alternative to the myths of romance, beauty, and perfection through counseling women to resist cultural messages, reclaim individuality, listen and talk back, express desire, and join forces in a close and supportive relationship with their maturing adolescents. This thoughtful, even heartfelt, guide addressed to mothers is soundly based in research as well as written in a style accessible to the educated reader.

Ginzberg, Ruth Szold. *Children and Other Strangers*. Transaction, 1991. 108p. LC 91-17362. ISBN 0-88738-445-5. $21.95.

This compact, witty autobiography by Ruth Ginzberg has as its thesis the belief that parenthood, specifically motherhood, is unnecessary for fulfillment and is a disadvantage for those who have other goals to accomplish. Through letters to her children and friends, reminiscences about her husband, well-known physician Eli Ginzberg, and conversations with her friends, this 71-year-old mother nicely, if negatively, examines the issues that characterize the lifelong giving of a mother and wife as a "one-way street." This account contains no footnotes or advice but is a thought-provoking essay on insights gained over a lifetime.

* Sanders, Darcie, and Martha M. Bullen. *Staying Home: From Full-Time Professional to Full-Time Parent*. Little, Brown, 1992. 239p. bibliog. LC 92-2839. ISBN 0-316-77061-2. $19.95.

For mothers who are considering leaving the workplace to devote their full attention to their children or who want to understand better why other mothers are making this decision, this comprehensive guide provides a wealth of information in an objective but reaffirming manner. The authors, two homemakers, present in a well-organized fashion the results of their survey of 600 women and their advice to those mothers who make the choice to stay at home with their children. The results include a woman's determining her own job description, acknowledging and applying her skills, validating herself as a person, and considering herself a feminist, that is, a person who makes life choices and views her own needs as important. Advice on preparing financially and emotionally for this lifestyle change, creating a new self-image, putting the marriage on a new footing, networking, forming support groups, and advocacy will be well received by contemporary mothers who consider full-time child care a "sequence" in their lives and who do not equate it with housekeeping.

Schap, Candace. *Sometimes I Don't Like My Kids*. Pacific Press Pub. Association, 1991. 124p. LC 90-20963. ISBN 0-8163-1037-8. $7.95.

An account of how one Christian woman faced the challenge of mothering six children by relying on her faith in God and psychotherapy, Schap's book reveals how easily home responsibilities may overwhelm and anger and how quickly resentment or disappointment may become part of daily life. Developing a more assertive attitude and improving her problem-solving skills enabled this harried, depressed mother to improve her situation. She distributed chores more equitably, accepted help from friends, adopted a more flexible approach to housekeeping, and simply became more willing to take ac-

tion once she identified a problem. Too realistic to be upbeat, this account is nonetheless moving and affirmative in the author's effective resolution of serious problems.

Thevenin, Tine. *Mothering and Fathering: The Gender Differences in Child Rearing*. Avery, 1993. 200p. bibliog. index. LC 93-13760. ISBN 0-89529-569-5. $9.95.

Down-to-earth and practical, this text by a popular author and mother explores emotional and biological differences between men and women that lead to differences in caring for children and examines the place that each parent's perspective has in child rearing. Thevenin cites personal experience, popular literature, and scholarly research to explain men's emphasis on independence and women's concern with connecting and nurturing. Ultimately, this insightful text finds the two parenting styles complimentary and essential.

POPULAR TITLES: JOURNALS

Mothering. Peggy McMahon. 1976. Q. ISSN 0733-3013. $22.00.

As an advocate for children and for support for parents, *Mothering* publishes experts' views on children's physical and psychological health, family interaction, learning, and mothering skills. Pregnancy and birth are also addressed in practical feature articles that generally list additional resources on the topic covered.

PROFESSIONAL TITLES: BOOKS

Berry, Patricia, ed. *Fathers and Mothers*. Spring, 1990. 259p. LC 90-39373. ISBN 0-88214-344-1. $17.50.

Rather than a research study or review of the literature, this anthology is an exploration of the myths, images, purposes, and predicaments of mothering and fathering from a Jungian perspective. Among the authors included are Robert Bly, James Hillman, Ursula LeGuin, Patricia Berry, Erich Neumann, and Carl Jung. Taken together, their essays provide an unusual view of the child and the parent from the deeper level of the imagination.

Dixon, Penelope, comp. *Mothers and Mothering: An Annotated Feminist Bibliography*. Garland, 1991. 219p. bibliog. LC 90-24981. ISBN 0-8240-5949-2. $26.00.

According to the compiler, the majority of the articles and books annotated in this bibliography are from the perspective of white, middle class, heterosexual women. Entries, which are primarily for U.S. publications since 1970, cover mothers and mothering; mothers' relationships with daughters, sons, children, and family; single, working, lesbian, and black mothers; and feminism, psychoanalysis, and reproduction issues as they relate to mothering. Items excluded include articles in popular magazines, historical and fictional treatments, books on how to mother, psychological literature on infant-mother relations, and theses/dissertations.

Gieve, Katherine, ed. *Balancing Acts: On Being a Mother.* Virago, 1990. 207p. LC 91-155645. ISBN 0-86068-968-9. $13.95.

In this anthology, 13 mothers explore the twin themes of what it means to be a mother and how to maintain independence and a place in the world. Each solution is as different as the individual who wrote it, as these women come from diverse cultural, racial, and economic backgrounds and face varying demands and degrees of support for their efforts. Their deeply personal essays offer remarkably moving insights into the push-me pull-you relationship of mother, child, and in some instances, father. In no way a practical guide to parenting, this text deciphers the psyche of the woman and mother.

Lowinsky, Naomi. *Stories from the Motherline: Reclaiming the Mother-Daughter Bond, Finding Our Feminine Souls.* St. Martin's, 1992. 229p. bibliog. LC 92-2537. ISBN 0-87477-680-5. $19.95.

According to this Jungian approach to woman's spiritual and psychological development, to reclaim the feminine soul requires a search for feminine continuity, both personal and cultural, and the desire for a sense of wholeness. Listening to one's own mother, seeking the voices of never-known ancestors, and participating in old female religious practices help a woman along her personal, unique, meandering path to individual wholeness. Other aspects of reclaiming the feminine self that are explored include the impact of the women's movement; images associated with bearing, bonding with, and breast-feeding children; generational change and the influence of the times; and acknowledgment of the importance of continuity of female identity from maiden to crone. To illustrate these themes, the author, a Jungian psychologist and faculty member at the Pacifica Graduate Institute in Santa Barbara, draws on her personal search for female roots, case material, research results, and literature.

O'Barr, Jean F., ed. *Ties That Bind: Essays on Mothering and Patriarchy.* University of Chicago, 1990. 306p. bibliog. index. LC 90-011070. ISBN 0-226-61545-6. $34.95.

O'Barr's anthology of 12 reprints from *Signs* explores the many facets of mothering from a feminist perspective. Among the topics addressed are how psychological research portrays mothers and mothering, models of mothering in children's literature, women as maternity case studies, and blame of the mother in incest cases. According to an insightful introduction, which analyzes and relates each essay to the others, "the greatest impact of feminist scholarship on concepts of mothering has been . . . to demonstrate the importance of understanding mothering within a dynamic, interactive context of social, political, historical, and sexual factors" (p. 3). Complex and thought-provoking, this anthology avoids repeating sentimental poems to motherhood that ignore the true degree of its impact on women.

DIRECTORY

American Mothers, Inc. (AMI)
6145 Jochums Drive, Tucson, AZ 85718
(602) 299-0666 Fax (602) 299-9133
Mary Dorr, President
Founded: 1935
Mission/Goals: To strengthen the spiritual and moral foundations of American families
Audience/Clientele: Mothers, families
Services: Counseling, support group
Education and Outreach: Publishing
Publications: *The American Mother*, quarterly newsletter; *American Mothers, Inc.—Yearbook*; *Mothers of Achievement in American History*
Programs: Annual conference

Mothers at Home
8310-A Old Courthouse Road, Vienna, CA 22180
(703) 827-5903
Cathy Myers, President
Founded: 1983
Mission/Goals: To support mothers who choose to raise their families by staying at home; to improve the morale and image of mothers who stay at home; to provide a forum for exchange of information among stay-at-home mothers
Audience/Clientele: Mothers, homemakers
Services: Lobbying, compiling statistics
Education and Outreach: Seminars, speakers' bureau, research
Publications: *Welcome Home*, a monthly newsletter; *What's a Smart Woman Like You Doing at Home?*

Mothers Matter
171 Wood Street, Rutherford, NJ 07070
(201) 933-8191
Kay Willis, President
Founded: 1975
Members: 5,000
Mission/Goals: To support and educate mothers who view motherhood as a profession in and of itself; to increase the enjoyment of parenting through the development of skills and confidence
Funding: Fees for services or products
Services: Support group
Education and Outreach: In-service programs, continuing education courses, seminars, publishing
Publications: *Memo for Mothers*, a bimonthly newsletter

REFERENCE

1. *Health United States 1993.* U.S. Department of Health and Human Services, National Center for Health Statistics, 1994, 68.

CHAPTER

Fathering

Fathering is not a spectator sport.
The prospect of fatherhood, with all its ramifications
and responsibilities, can faze, deter, daunt, and
disconcert even the most stable of the male species.
Connie Marshall. *The Expectant Father*

Nurturing the newborn infant, interpreting and caring for the baby's daily needs, and providing a model of masculinity are as essential to fathering as are play and discipline. Devoting enough time to infant care from the outset establishes a father as an involved caretaker of his child, one to whom the child will turn to satisfy needs. Unlike mothers, fathers may have to fight for the opportunity to fulfill their potential. "What [men] are hearing, from their bosses, from institutions, from the culture around them, even from their own wives, very often comes down to a devastating message: we really don't trust men to be parents, and we don't really need them to be." [1]

An asterisk (*) indicates a specially recommended title.

POPULAR TITLES: BOOKS

Levant, Ronald F. *Between Father and Child: How to Become the Kind of Father You Want to Be.* Penguin, 1991. 236p. LC 90-20942. ISBN 0-14-015261-X. $8.95.

Composite studies from the Fatherhood Project at Boston University illustrate how men may develop open and loving relationships with their children by improving their communication skills. Using techniques such as listening to content, understanding hidden messages, identifying the real problems, and improving self-awareness and self-expression enables fathers to better understand their children, resolve conflicts, discuss sensitive topics like sex and drugs, and prevent common forms of acting out. In part 1, these skills are presented, and in part 2 they are applied to moral growth, academic achievement, and sex-role identification (an egalitarian approach is advocated). The final section illustrates their usefulness when family circumstances involve divorce, stepfathering, and dual-career families.

Lindsay, Jeanne Warren. *Teen Dads: Rights, Responsibilities, and Joys.* Morning Glory Press, 1993. 190p. bibliog. photog. index. LC 93-4450. ISBN 0-930394-77-6. $15.95. ISBN 0-930934-78-4 pbk. $9.95.

Lindsay's easy-to-understand overview of fathering is illustrated with numerous photographs of a diverse mix of teen fathers. Interviews with 40 young fathers offer insights and informative quotes on such topics as what it means to be a father, coping with a partner's pregnancy, prenatal development, birth, and caring for a newborn. Other contents include care of babies, nutrition for babies and toddlers, safety and health, discipline and guidance, deciding to have a second child, and sharing the future with one's child.

Osherson, Samuel. *Wrestling with Love: How Men Struggle with Intimacy with Women, Children, Parents and Each Other.* Columbine Fawcett, 1992. 371p. bibliog. index. LC 91-57970. ISBN 0-449-90550-0. $20.00.

Osherson's thorough examination of male psychology explores why men have difficulty with becoming intimate, that is, responsive and able to connect emotionally with those with whom they share their lives. Using insights drawn from case studies, myth, fiction, and poetry, as well as psychological research, Osherson traces the dilemma between preserving manliness and connecting to another despite the obstacles of shame and anger. Also covered are issues of separation from the mother and identification with the father, marriage, parenthood, work relationships, and men's groups. To become "wholer," he advises men to risk connecting with and exploring the parts of the self that are new and do not fit the "manliness mold." So many insights and affirmations are presented that the book itself takes on a mythological, timeless tone.

* Sears, William, M.D. *Keys to Becoming a Father*. Barron's, 1991. 152p. LC 90-23988. ISBN 0-8120-4541-6. $5.95.

How fathers can participate in child rearing by nurturing their wives, juggling career and family, and bringing a "unique" approach to child care is the focus of this practical guide by William Sears, a well-known parenting author. Sears presents techniques that permit fathers to be more supportive and involved before birth, during labor and childbirth, and in the postpartum period. He also addresses nighttime fathering skills, special approaches to high-need babies, and single parenting.

Shapiro, Jerrold Lee. *The Measure of a Man: Becoming the Father You Wish Your Father Had Been*. Delacorte, 1993. 364p. index. LC 92-46154. ISBN 0-385-30773-X. $22.95.

Oral and written surveys completed by 1,100 men, case material, the scientific literature, and personal experience are integrated by the author into this helpful and compassionate guide to effective fathering. In the opening chapters the author, a clinical psychologist and family therapist, addresses what it means to be a father, why fathers are not like mothers, and fathering in contemporary society. Shapiro explores characteristics of good and poor fathering, concluding with a "declaration of interdepence" that states what a man may aspire to as a father within a family. The special requirements and challenges of being a single father or stepparent are explored. The final chapters review helpful sources of support and present a series of answers to questions frequently posed at the author's lectures and workshops.

* Sullivan, S. Adams. *The Father's Almanac*. Rev. ed. Doubleday, 1992. 391p. bibliog. photog. index. LC 91-42801. ISBN 0-385-49625-9. $16.00.

Patterned after *The Mother's Almanac*, this handbook for fathers supplements the on-the-job training fathers get in caring for a new baby. The text provides fathers' insights on preparing for a baby, caring for an infant, balancing work and parenting roles, parenting in nontraditional families, and providing financial support for the family. Sullivan offers tips on managing daily concerns such as bathing children; coping with special events; teaching and discipline; and learning, playing, and working with children. The final chapter discusses keeping a record of the child's life. Photos of a diverse group of fathers and their children illustrate this well-written text.

Yablonsky, Lewis. *Fathers and Sons: The Most Challenging of All Family Relationships*. Simon & Schuster, 1990. LC 90-3515. ISBN 0-89876-171-9. $11.95.

Survey data, in-depth interviews, clinical practice, and personal experiences are the source of insights Yablonsky, a sociologist and psychotherapist, brings to an exploration of the father-son relationship. Because of the intense attachment of this bond, most men's personalities are greatly influenced,

positively or negatively, by their fathers. Among the areas the author addresses are the father's role in his son's life, advantages and disadvantages of various fathering styles, life phases of father and son interaction, influence of other family members, and special problems such as delinquency and substance abuse. Guidelines on how to father summarize information presented in detail throughout the text. Many case studies and examples illustrate the theoretical points being made.

PROFESSIONAL TITLES: BOOKS

Biller, Henry B. *Fathers and Families: Paternal Factors in Child Development*. Auburn, 1993. 325p. bibliog. index. LC 92-18361. ISBN 0-86569-208-4. $59.95. ISBN 0-86569-227-0 pbk. $19.95.

From the perspective of an entire lifespan, this monograph integrates biological, psychological, and social influences on the father's role in child development. Both mental health professionals and parents will find advice for improving the quality of the father's involvement. Among the specific topics addressed are the advantages of shared parenting, the development of the father-mother-infant relationship, the father's role in guiding his child's development of moral standards, self-control, gender identity and self-image, school and educational issues, circumstances such as divorce that make family life difficult, and the effect of community factors and social change on parents and their children.

Bozett, Frederick W., and Shirley M. Hanson, eds. *Fatherhood and Families in Cultural Context*. Springer, 1991. 290p. LC 90-9955. ISBN 0-8261-6570-2. $35.95.

How cultural variables mediate men's approach to fathering is the theme of this scholarly anthology, edited by two nursing professors, one now deceased. Individual contributors review previous research on their topic, point out its significance, and suggest fruitful areas for study. Among the subjects covered are legal views of fathering; effects of religious beliefs; the impact of the environment, family culture, and ethnic culture on fathering; and how employer organizational culture shapes fathering behavior. General introductory chapters define the components of culture, fatherhood, and family; review historical change; and look at the influence of ethnicity to place later, more specialized chapters in context. In a concluding essay, the editors note that the women's movement, particularly women's participation in the workplace, has encouraged greater involvement of fathers in family life and has advocated the desirability of a future men's mental health movement. This anthology provides essential background information for health care and social service professionals to use in designing the individual interventions required by their diverse clientele.

Corneau, Guy. *Absent Fathers, Lost Sons: The Search for Masculine Identity*. Shambhala, 1991. 186p. LC 90-53373. ISBN 0-87773-603-0. $11.00.

Drawing on clinical observations, this text by a Canadian psychoanalyst explores how the lack of proper fathering prevents sons from developing a solid masculine foundation for an individual identity. Fathers who are absent, silent, or uninvolved deprive their sons of their physical and emotional presence and so contribute to negative complexes in relating to men. Corneau explores the impact that fear of intimacy and repressed aggressions have on the lives of men and urges healing through a beneficial depression that enables men to accept their own imperfections and accept assistance through therapy, male friendships, men's groups, and active inner dialogue. Because the unfamiliar stresses of fatherhood in turn cause many of the problems sons had with their fathers to flare up in their own lives, this material has applications for professionals helping new fathers better understand their role as parents through their own upbringing.

Gould, Jonathan W., and Robert E. Gunther. *Reinventing Fatherhood*. TAB, 1993. 277p. bibliog. index. LC 93-8026. ISBN 0-8306-4219-6. $10.95.

The authors give a philosophical discourse that integrates concepts from the men's movement into contemporary views of fatherhood. This self-help book for fathers enables them to develop new fathering ideas and behaviors through detailed exercises. The material presented here is drawn from clinical practice, interviews with expectant fathers participating in a Lamaze class, and the professional literature on the psychological development of men. In a light-hearted tone with humorous anecdotes throughout, the authors present the difficult realities of memories of their own absent fathers, overworked spouses, fatigue, and significant new responsibilities that parenting a child involves. Among the specific topics addressed are adjustments during each trimester of pregnancy, commitment, division of labor, sex and intimacy, stress, time management, moral development, and connecting with one's child.

Scull, Charles, ed. *Fathers, Sons, and Daughters: Exploring Fatherhood, Renewing the Bond*. Tarcher, 1992. 266p. LC 91-45075. ISBN 0-87477-681-3. $12.95.

Thirty-four brief selections, most excerpted from longer works, illustrate the pain, difficulty, satisfaction, and rewards of being a father in contemporary society. Analytical introductions open the five sections, which are organized around themes of the evolving father, father-son relationships, father-daughter relationships, new family structures for fathers, and reconciliation with the internal father. Among the innovative approaches to the issues of fathering are parenting as a spiritual discipline, nurturing self-development through nurturing children, initiation rituals for daughters, and midlife reconciliation as a rite of passage. Most of the essays reprinted here are moving personal accounts and several are amusing, with an occasional didactic lecture rounding out the collection.

Vogt, Gregory Max. *Like Son, Like Father: Healing the Father-Son Wound in Men's Lives*. Plenum, 1991. 285p. LC 91-20164. ISBN 0-306-43970-0. $22.95.

This book is designed to help men work out their relationships with their sons, their families, their own fathers, and themselves. Written from a psychological perspective, each chapter addresses a specific aspect of relationships, such as dependence on the mother; the father's role in imparting masculinity to the son; work; friendships and relationships with women; mentors; healing; and reconciliation. Vogt explores the problems that may arise and ways to resolve them, including specific exercises designed to effect change. While targeted to the public, the material covered is quite complex, so the text might more appropriately be used by therapists to gain insights in understanding and counseling their male clients. A final section explains therapy and identifies groups that may provide additional assistance to men seeking to reinvent their relationships with others.

DIRECTORY

Dads Against Discrimination (DADS)

P.O. Box 8525, Portland, OR 97207

(503) 222-1111

Victor Smith, President

Founded: 1977

Mission/Goals: To provide a forum for fathers to discuss family problems; to inform the public about issues of domestic relations; to provide support to fathers barred from their homes by court restraining orders

Audience/Clientele: Fathers, general public

Budget: $100,000

Services: Housing, medical and legal referrals, support group, statistics compilation

Education and Outreach: Produces programs for cable television, seminars, library, speakers' bureau, publishing

Publications: *Father's National Review*, quarterly

Programs: Annual conference

Fatherhood Project (FP)

c/o Families and Work Institute, 330 Seventh Avenue, 14th Floor, New York, NY 10001

(212) 268-4846 Fax (212) 465-8637

James A. Levine, Director

Founded: 1981

Mission/Goals: To examine the future of fatherhood and find ways to increase and support men's involvement in child rearing

Audience/Clientele: Corporations and other employers, schools

Services: Consulting, referral

Education and Outreach: In-service programs, research, publishing

Publications: *Fatherhood U.S.A.*, a guide to programs for fathers in all types of families and listing of book, films, and other resources related to men and child rearing

REFERENCE

1. Nancy R. Gibbs, "Bringing Up Father," *Time* 141, no. 26 (June 28, 1993): 26.

C H A P T E R

Humorous Side of Parenting

I am a shadow of my former self in all but size.
Are you working now? Or just
staying home having fun with the kid?
Kathryn Grody. A Mom's Life

If only to maintain a balanced perspective in the face of unrelenting demands, many parents relish the comic side of child rearing. Sleep deprivation, the physical changes of pregnancy, lack of privacy, defiant toddlers, and high-decibel road trips are all the stuff of parental irony. Many authors inject a light tone to make a serious instructional message more palatable, but some books are written solely to provide comic relief.

An asterisk (*) indicates a specially recommended title.

POPULAR TITLES: BOOKS

Burkett, Michael. *The Dad Zone: Reports from the Tender, Bewildering, and Hilarious World of Fatherhood.* Simon & Schuster, 1993. 222p. illus. LC 93-2816. ISBN 0-671-79890-1. $17.00.

Irony and a wry wit are evident in these brief (two- to three-page) ancedotes drafted by a father and former writer for the Arizona *New Times.* Previously published pieces from the author's syndicated column "The Dad Zone" have been compiled along with poems for a hilarious look at such universal concerns as feeding and changing the baby, selecting a pet, taking family vacations, bribing children to behave, calming a crying baby, dealing with a second child, and hosting birthday parties.

Cosby, Bill. *Childhood.* Putnam, 1991. 188p. LC 91-16722. ISBN 0-399-13647-9. $14.95.

Bill Cosby compares his childhood to that of his own children in this hilarious review of how children act and how parents try to make them behave. He looks at stealing, fighting, lying, playing, learning manners, disciplining, and learning the value of a dollar and an education. How he recognized as a child his interest in comedy and performance is one of many interesting and amusing tales recounted here.

* Grody, Kathryn. *A Mom's Life.* Avon Books, 1991. 123p. LC 90-23118. ISBN 0-380-76361-3. $7.95.

This personal account of a hectic day in the life of a mother of two young boys mixes social commentary with the antics and comments of two active children and one concerned but, on that particular day, largely unavailable father. While the author, an actress and wife to actor Mandy Patinkin, does not provide practical advice on how to rear children, her comments are insightful and the issues she raises, such as staying in a diverse urban neighborhood, selecting a school, regulating TV viewing, and choosing safe foods to eat, are interesting and relevant to most parents. The comical antics of the children also make for fun reading.

Heller, David. *Growing Up Isn't Hard to Do If You Start Out As a Kid.* Villard Books, 1991. 263p. LC 90-43575. ISBN 0-394-58713-8. $18.00.

Heller, the author of a number of books revealing how children feel about life, surveyed children on several issues of potential interest: marriage and dating, parenthood, food, adult possessions, work, the process of growing up, and differences between adults and kids. As the following comments illustrate, the kids' candid pronouncements are predictably hilarious: "When you get married you get arranged with a man, and you find a person with rings, and then you hire a flower child" and "If there was no kids, who else would eat the baby foods?"

Lansky, Bruce. *Dads Say the Dumbest Things*. Simon & Schuster, 1990. 99p. LC 89-29067. ISBN 0-88166-131-7. $5.95.

When they're pushed beyond their limits, dads can and do say funny, ironical, even dumb things. Aphorisms collected from a number of sources, including television programs, are listed in brief chapters organized by theme, including being the boss, the king of his castle, threats, games, quality time, holidays, and when dad was a kid, each prefaced by an amusing photo of a famous TV dad. The final chapter provides space for a photo of the reader's dad and a listing of his favorite pronouncements. This collection is by a well-known parenting author.

Leonard, Joan. *Tales from Toddler Hell: My Life As a Mom*. Pharos Books, 1991. 110p. LC 91-7601. ISBN 0-88687-542-0. $14.95.

A wry wit enlivens Leonard's lighthearted anecdotes about the daily hassles of raising young children and the guilty satisfaction of stolen moments devoted to simple adult pleasures such as exercise, conversation, shopping, and dancing. No true horror stories are reported here, just the bittersweet transformation of the beach-town romantic hideaway to a place for family outings and a flight from wine and *Vogue* to spit-up and apple juice.

Pierson, Stephanie. *"Because I'm the Mother That's Why!" Mostly True Confessions of Modern Motherhood*. Delacorte, 1994. 125p. illus. LC 93-5917. ISBN 0-385-31096-X. $16.95.

A business executive and contributing editor for *Metropolitan Home* describes in a series of wry essays what being a modern urban mother involves, from taking the commuter train with a cranky child to the realization that her life is not, and cannot be, well-organized, presented as a series of letters to Martha Stewart. Especially entertaining are a section on the facts of life, which explains, for example, why people say what they say, and useful information such as never wake a sleeping baby.

Schimmels, Cliff. *Oh No, Maybe My Child Is Normal!* Shaw, 1991. 160p. LC 90-43474. ISBN 0-87788-616-4. $7.95.

A clever treatment of daily life with a child, this humorous look at child rearing instructs parents on the broad range of normal behavior. The author, a professor of education, considers this the type of book that any mother would write if she were not so busy raising her children, an affirmation of the special and amusing character of daily life. Among the topics Schimmels tackles are managing expectations, cultivating a perspective, playing by the rules, fostering responsibility and self-esteem, supporting creativity, and liking as well

as loving one's children. This book is not a how-to manual but a fun look at the joys of parenting.

Schnur, Steven. *Daddy's Home*. Crown, 1990. 188p. LC 89-25273. ISBN 0-517-57775-5. $12.95.

The desire to leave something of his thoughts and a sense of the past for his children guided Steven Schnur's choice of topics in this series of essays revealing the joys and challenges of parenting. Much of the subject matter is serious, as he describes anticipating his first child after years of infertility, changing his lifestyle, and coping with twins. Housekeeping, moving, shopping for groceries, and accumulating 97 teddy bears are also covered in his witty, sensitive essays, several of which were previously published in the *New York Times*.

Zarnow, Teryl. *Husband Is the Past Tense of Daddy: And Other Dispatches from the Front Lines of Motherhood*. Addison-Wesley, 1990. 221p. LC 90-30796. ISBN 0-201-51801-5. $15.95.

Based on columns published previously in the *Orange County Register* (California), this collection of amusing essays recounts one mother's humorous experiences with her three children. Zarnow offers wry advice on common parenting issues, such as having more than one child, getting the father to do his share, coping with sibling rivalry, and managing daily stress. Wise and funny observations on losing all modesty during delivery, learning to be a mother, learning to love discount stores and family restaurants, and losing track of childless friends reflect the difficulties of child rearing without making them seem overwhelming. The pace is brisk and the writing style provides many quotable comments to share with others who have an interest in parenting.

PROFESSIONAL TITLES: BOOKS

Markel, Howard, and Frank A. Oski, eds. *The H.L. Mencken Baby Book*. Hanley and Belfus, 1990. 194p. LC 89-20104. ISBN 0-932-88322-2. $18.95.

Factual information about infant care during the early 1900s was transformed by noted journalist and editor H.L. Mencken into an acerbic series of articles published in *The Dilineator*. These were compiled in *What You Ought to Know about Your Baby*. The entire text is reprinted here, with commentaries and current views contributed by two contemporary pediatricians. Their contributions make the text informative as well as amusing for parents and physicians.

PART

2

PARENTING IN THE CONTEXT OF FAMILY LIFE

CHAPTER

New Families

*The family, whomever it may
include, is still the center of our daily lives.*
Benjamin Spock and Michael B. Rothenberg.
Dr. Spock's Baby and Child Care

*To children, divorce does not mean the
second chance that it so often means to one or
both parents. To children it is the loss of their family.*
Genevieve Clapp. *Divorce and New Beginnings*

American families are remarkably diverse in structure. In 1990, 36.9 percent of families were made up of married couples with children, compared with 10.2 percent of families headed by women with children and 1.8 percent headed by men with children. Other family types constituted 9.4 percent of the total, leaving married people without children as 41.7 percent of total families.[1] To understand contemporary family dynamics, it is important to acknowledge that many single-parent families and stepfamilies are born of loss. In an oft-cited study, Judith Wallerstein and Sandra Blakeslee discovered that 10 years after a divorce, many children and adults were still suffering. Young women developed a high level of anxiety about betrayal, young men were emotionally constricted without realizing it, and children were burdened with more responsibilities and felt less cared for.[2]

During any two-year period in the mid-1980s, 8 percent of married-couple households dissolved.[3] Many guides exist for parents to help them support their children through the losses of divorce and prepare themselves for the demands of single-parent lifestyles and the challenges of stepfamily formation. Over 27 percent of single-mother households discontinued during any two-year period in the mid-1980s, generally because of remarriage and stepfamily formation.[4]

Although they lack the emotional burdens borne by families that have broken and re-formed with new members, families in which both parents work outside the home face many demands. From 1969 to 1989, the annual hours of work of employed Americans rose by 140 hours. Taking into account the rise in commuting time and decrease in paid leave, the actual increase was 158 hours, the equivalent of an additional month of work a year. To accommodate this shift of mothers' time to the workplace, fathers' time is slowly being reallocated to housework and child care.[5] In a widely publicized study, Arlie Hochschild discovered that only 20 percent of the husbands of working mothers performed 50 percent of the housework. Ten percent performed less than 30 percent of the housework, with 70 percent performing between 30 and 50 percent.[6]

Even among married-couple families, unique structures have evolved to accommodate the birth of several children, particularly twins and other multiple births. According to mothers who have large families, having more than two children also requires stamina, a sense of humor, and a willingness to discipline constantly.[7]

An asterisk (*) indicates a specially recommended title.

POPULAR TITLES: BOOKS

Albi, Linda, et al. *Mothering Twins: From Hearing the News to Beyond the Terrible Twos.* Simon & Schuster, 1993. 414p. bibliog. index. LC 93-10244. ISBN 0-671-72357-X. $11.00.

In this chronological guide to raising twins, five mothers discuss the challenges of being pregnant with and giving birth to twins, special considerations in caring for them, and ways to balance their needs with those of their parents. Brief autobiographies are included in the introduction, and each chapter concludes with personal reflections on the textual material. The father's perspective is explored in the final chapter. Among the specific issues these mothers address are ambivalence at hearing the news, prematurity, the establishment of support systems, outings with twins, child care, and older siblings' concerns. A resource directory supplements the text.

Alexander, Shoshana. *In Praise of Single Parents: Mothers and Fathers Embracing the Challenge.* Houghton Mifflin, 1994. 404p. bibliog. LC 94-2063. ISBN 0-395-57436-6. $22.45. ISBN 0-395-66991-X pbk. $12.95.

In this volume of essays on becoming and being a single parent, Alexander views the single parent as a pioneer building a new dream. Drawing on personal experience and many conversations with other single parents, Alexander explores issues of chance versus choice in becoming a single parent; meeting the challenges of single parenthood as victim or victor; being oneself; doing all the work of parenting as one parent; and, perhaps as a response to guilt, trying harder to parent well. Other issues addressed are managing finances, arranging child care, love and its limits in a parent's relationship with his or her child, seeking a partner and dating, finding support from other parents, and extending the family.

Alexander, Terry Pink. *Make Room for Twins.* Bantam, 1987. 408p. photog. illus. LC 85-48050. ISBN 0-553-34207-X. $14.50.

Alexander's concise, practical handbook covers every aspect of twins from conception through preschool years. Simple drawings and graphic photos illustrate information on the biological basis for twinning, labor and delivery, and growth of the premature or low birth weight infant. Advice on breastfeeding, infant equipment, and developmental stages from infancy to preschool age is accompanied by appealing photos of several sets of twins and their parents. Information on the postpartum period, the mother's and father's roles, and how to encourage nurturing between twins and between siblings and twins is also given.

* Anderson, Joan. *The Single Mother's Book: A Complete Guide to Managing Your Children, Career, Home, Finances, and Everything Else.* Peachtree, 1990. 352p. LC 89-28640. ISBN 0-934601-84-4. $12.95.

This guide covers new turf in its advice on raising a child, running a home, and having a life—relations with the ex-husband and his extended family, the creation of new family customs and roles, and home security and repair—as well as more familiar ground, such as unconditional love, discipline, and sex education. For their own benefit, mothers should consider the text's advice on time management, job seeking, social life, romance, and just taking care of oneself. Much of the material is drawn from discussions of the Single Mother's Group sponsored by Vanderbilt University's Women's Center, but the advice presented is transferable to other women bringing up children on their own.

* Bloomfield, Harold H., with Robert B. Kory. *Making Peace in Your Stepfamily: Surviving and Thriving as Parents and Stepparents.* Hyperion, dist. by Little, Brown, 1993. 284p. bibliog. LC 93-35074. ISBN 1-56282-885-1. $19.95.

Exercises, anecdotes, and advice are presented in this helpful handbook whose purpose is to teach stepparents specific skills for recognizing, understanding, and healing conflicts that challenge their families. Written by a prolific author, the text emphasizes three steps to a more loving, accepting, harmonious family life: identifying conflicts and exploring their causes, considering alternative ways to respond, and practicing exercises that help resolve each conflict and promote better communication. Recognizing that stepfamilies are born of loss, avoiding obstacles to becoming a good stepparent, and learning to discuss concerns within the family are among the topics discussed. Strengthening the remarriage that supports the stepfamily, healing losses through communication, and growing via the resolution of conflict help stepparents create a warm, loving home for their new families.

Brazelton, T. Berry. *Families: Crisis and Caring.* Ballantine, 1989. 251p. bibliog. photog. index. LC 89-91493. ISBN 0345344561. $8.95.

Brazelton presents five case studies on family crises, with transcripts of parental visits to his office, his analysis, questions raised, and concrete suggestions for others coping with the same issues. Divorce and remarriage, infertility and adoption (including cross-cultural adoption), and life-threatening illness in a child are some of the topics covered. Brazelton describes how each event affects the family's stability, how each family member copes, and how a balance is eventually regained. He also addresses the need to consult professionals.

Brooks, Andree Aelion. *Children of Fast-Track Parents: Raising Self-Sufficient and Confident Children in an Achievement-Oriented World.* Penguin, 1990. 272p. LC 89-29929. ISBN 0-14-011800-4. $8.95.

Based on interviews with affluent parents, their children, and health professionals, along with insights gained in the scholarly and popular press, this detailed account by a journalist explores the impact that high achievement and its accoutrements have on children born to successful, affluent parents. Beginning with a sociological analysis of the origins of the "fast-track" lifestyle, Brooks then looks at its impact on children from infancy through young adulthood. In addition, much practical advice on such topics as selecting care givers; competitiveness; transferring management skills to the home; obtaining emotional support from grandparents, religion, and family rituals; making educational choices; coping with different family structures; and developing financial responsibility is offered. This survey of high achievers and their children, well written and organized, provides a wealth of information for parents, educators, and mental health professionals.

* Brown, Beth E. *When You're Mom No. 2.* Servant, 1991. 202p. bibliog. LC 91-18653. ISBN 0-89283-719-5. $8.95.

A guide to stepparenting, written by a mother with experience, this book offers practical information on issues that emerge in the blended family. Brown, who declares herself a Christian, covers the stepmother's need to acknowledge the loss, either through divorce or death, of the child's mother, uphold primacy of the marriage, and choose where to live and examines the myth of "instant love," discipline, and the changes a new baby brings. The author is warm, compassionate, and optimistic without minimizing problems that may occur. The text is an effective blend of personal experience, interview data, and academic research.

Bryan, Elizabeth M. *Twins, Triplets and More: Their Nature, Development and Care.* St. Martin's, 1992. 138p. index. LC 92-1095. ISBN 0-312-07876-5. $17.95.

Written by a pediatrician who has worked since 1973 in Great Britain with several thousand twins and their families, this slim volume covers fundamental facts about the nature and development of twins and higher-level births. Bryan also addresses common fears of parents of twins, triplets, and other multiples about birth defects, infertility, inability to tell their children apart or love each equally, and unhealthy dependence. Also covered in this reassuring guide are the biology of twinning, considerations in multiple pregnancies, unusual demands of caring for two or more infants, preschool twins, school issues at primary and secondary levels, disability or death of one twin, and long-term growth and development.

* Clapp, Genevieve. *Divorce and New Beginnings: An Authoritative Guide to Recovery and Growth, Solo Parenting, and Stepfamilies.* Wiley, 1992. 377p. bibliog. LC 91-27824. ISBN 0-471-52631-2. $14.95.

The author, a family and divorce mediator, gives practical guidance based on current research on divorce, solo parenting, and stepfamilies. Most ex-marrieds have not resolved divorce-related issues and carry them into new relationships even years after the separation took place. Divided into five sections, addressing what is known by researchers and those who have experienced divorce, the text provides practical advice on successfully coping with a divorce, helping children through the divorce process, building a rewarding single life, parenting without being the custodial parent, and adjusting to the stepfamily. Clapp thoroughly documents what is known about such aspects of divorce as stress, depression and anger, letting go of the marriage, and the child's perspective and long-term adjustment, along with ending conflict with the ex-spouse, disciplining as a single parent, and recognizing stepfamily myths. Literally hundreds of practical techniques for effectively working through the issues raised by these circumstances are offered. Two appendixes cover ways to make changes and stick to them and a deep relaxation technique. This volume is equally appropriate for men and women, mothers and fathers, because it addresses issues faced by both participants in a marriage coming apart.

Clubb, Angela. *Love in the Blended Family: Step-Families: A Package Deal.* Health Communications, 1991. 191p. bibliog. LC 90-23157. ISBN 1-55874-135-6. $9.95.

Alternately inspirational and painful, this is an intensely personal account of life in the extended, blended family. The author explores the reality of remarrying and forming a new family. She tackles practical issues such as the establishment of new traditions; cooperation and competition with the ex-spouse; links that connect the two households, both positive and negative; and balance between individual freedom and family ties and between work and motherhood, as well as the more abstract concerns of favoritism, honesty, trust, and commitment to love. The author is quite open about problems in her own blended family; it is clear the adversity is one source of her many insights on how to successfully negotiate life in this extended family setting.

Crosby, Faye J. *Juggling: The Unexpected Advantages of Balancing Career and Home for Women and Their Families.* Macmillan, 1991. 269p. LC 91-19534. ISBN 0-02-906705-7. $19.95.

While this is a review of the social science literature on the costs and benefits for women of balancing work and family roles and not a how-to book, the author does make three recommendations: women who juggle, or carry out, multiple roles should not blame themselves when they have difficulty meeting career and home demands; they should not let these problems prevent them from continuing to combine roles; and they should consider ways to effect societal rather than personal change. To support her proposals, Crosby looks closely and critically at studies identifying the costs and benefits of mothers working, including the effects on children and husbands, as well as media images that illustrate and influence understanding of the true impact of working mothers. Among the many instructive insights the author draws from her critiques are those related to the fate of children in dual-career households. The first conclusion is that experts do not agree among themselves; the second is that there is no conclusive evidence that men cannot nurture children as well as women can, despite allegations that women are more relational; and, third, greater involvement with their fathers brings practical benefits to children, such as intimate contact with the father, greater knowledge of the work world, and positive self-regard and initiative. Men's reluctance to assume home and child care responsibilities and women's unwillingness to push them to or to speak of the struggle publicly looms as the source of the greatest stress in American families today.

Friedrich, Elizabeth, and Cherry Rowland. *The Parent's Guide to Raising Twins.* St. Martin's, 1990. 304p. bibliog. LC 89-24105. ISBN 0-312-03906-9. $9.95.

This detailed account of how to care for twins, triplets, and more covers the period from conception to starting school. The authors review the biology of multiple births and offer concrete advice on the unusual aspects of pregnancy, birthing, the first months at home, and the toddler stage when two or more children are involved, including greater weight gain, hospitalization of premature infants, how to get outside help, and slower verbal development. The effects of increased involvement of the father and less attention from mother are also addressed in this how-to parent manual, along with the sibling bond and how to parent twins with disabilities.

Grief, Geoffrey L. *The Daddy Track and the Single Father: Coping with Kids, Housework, a Job, an Ex-Wife, a Social Life, and the Courts.* Lexington, 1990. 245p. LC 89-13611. ISBN 0-669-19849-8. $17.95.

Grief's book fulfills its purpose as a descriptive review of single parenting by fathers and a self-help guide with practical advice for fathers who are raising children on their own. An introductory section summarizes the history of single- father families and debunks a number of myths, e.g., these fathers were more involved with their children, had a unique bond with them from birth, or were raised themselves by fathers in single-parent families. The text then covers concerns in daily life, such as housekeeping, relating to the children, establishing a social life, balancing work with home life, and relating to the noncustodial mother. Special concerns of fathers who are widowers or in joint-custody arrangements are reviewed. Each chapter concludes with practical tips for fathers who are confronting these issues for the first time.

Johnson, Laurene, and Georglyn Rosenfeld. *Divorced Kids: What You Need to Know to Help Kids Survive a Divorce.* Nelson, 1990. 224p. bibliog. LC 90-37931. ISBN 0-8407-3174-4. $8.95.

Personal experience, survey data, and published research inform the advice that this therapist and professional writer offer parents about reducing the negative effects of divorce on their children. While they acknowledge the depth of the parent's feelings about the end of their relationship, the authors encourage active attempts at recovery through grieving, dumping "garbage," and forgiveness, because parental hostility can mar visitation, inhibit communication, and impede the healthy development of children. Each chapter includes many practical suggestions on how to defuse the problems addressed and implement the recovery goals sought. Though this text is billed as a Christian perspective to divorce recovery, the Christian approach is a low-key one that is easily ignored by those who do not respond to it.

Kite, Patricia L. *The Suddenly Single Mother's Survival Guide.* Mills & Sanderson, 1991. 168p. LC 90-25144. ISBN 0-938179-27-6. $9.95.

Using an upbeat, humorous tone, the author advises single-again women on coping methods for caring for their children, relating to their former in-laws, and dealing with the children's father. She covers practical issues that single mothers must confront, such as job hunting, thrifty practices, and family recreation, as well as more personal concerns of divorced women, like dating and friendships.

Krueger, Caryl Waller. *Working Parent—Happy Child: You Can Balance Job and Family.* Abingdon, 1990. 320p. LC 89-18266. ISBN 0-687-46191-X. $13.95.

A major feature of this useful parenting handbook is practical advice on how to connect with your child in a meaningful way throughout the busy work week through "touch-base" points at breakfast; during the commute; at work; before, during, and after dinner; and at bedtime. In addition, guidance on making family time a priority on weekends, participating in culturally enriching activities, managing after-school activities, and tips on stretching time will help busy parents provide

the attention, affection, instruction, and discipline their children need. The positive tone and wealth of information are appealing.

Leder, Jane Mersky. *Brothers and Sisters: How They Shape Our Lives.* St. Martin's, 1991. 257p. bibliog. index. LC 91-20035. ISBN 0-312-06312-1. $19.95.

Prompted by the death of her brother to explore what in contemporary society is perhaps the longest and most stable family tie, Leder reviews the mysterious, ambiguous, contradictory territory of sibling relationships throughout the stages of the life cycle. She notes that childhood insecurities and problems can continue even in adulthood, and marriage and divorce, death, incest, and family problems can create special circumstances. Many sibling relationships pass through predictable stages of rivalry, support and reconnection, forgiveness, and renewed family closeness as siblings age. The evolution of the sibling relationship is one of the important, though largely unacknowledged, mirrors of an individual's identity and a model for relationships with others.

Marston, Stephanie. *The Divorced Parent: Success Strategies for Raising Your Children After Separation.* Morrow, 1994. bibliog. index. LC 93-15847. ISBN 0-688-11323-0. $21.00.

Effective "survival strategies" for divorced parents and their children are the focus of this guide from a child and family counselor. Drawing on her personal and professional experience, Marston advises about helping kids cope with the transition to a new family lifestyle, avoiding negative interactions with an ex-spouse, resolving emotional conflicts, building a stable parenting partnership, and keeping both parents involved in their children's lives. Anecdotes and case studies not only reveal how challenging the author's advice is for children and adults, but also how effectively it helps children avoid the long-term, negative impact of divorce reported by other authors, most notably Judith Wallerstein in *Second Chances.* Marston criticizes Wallerstein's book as being based on an unscientific and invalid study. Other issues addressed in Marston's book include dealing with difficult ex-spouses, money and financial support, healing after divorce, and building a life of one's own.

Noble, Elizabeth, with Leo Sorger. *Having Twins: A Parent's Guide to Pregnancy, Birth, and Early Childhood.* Houghton Mifflin, 1990. 430p. photog. LC 90-38969. ISBN 0-395-51088-0. $24.95. ISBN 0-395-49338-2 pbk. $12.95.

Noting that today 1 in 45 people is statistically a twin, the author of this revised edition of a popular handbook on pregnancy, delivery, and infant care of twins and higher sets (supertwins) focuses on the realities, positive and negative, of multiple births to help parents prepare for the challenges they face. After reviewing images of twins throughout history and among various cultures, the author, a childbirth educator, examines the biological basis for multiple births, detection, potential hazards, nutrition, labor, and delivery options. She also covers bonding with more than one infant, caring for two, dealing with prematurity and special needs, and the emotions relating to the loss of one twin. A final chapter covers supertwins. The text, which is sensitive to the feelings of new parents of twins, is lavishly illustrated with appealing photographs, including some unusual prints of quadruplets. Insights from "New Age" approaches, such as regression and primal therapy, are presented along with results from medical and demographic studies. This edition, which has been significantly revised and expanded over the first edition of 1980, includes new information on prenatal communication and bonding, prenatal testing, nutrition, and experiencing loss, as well as updated statistics.

Olds, Sally Wendkos. *The Working Parents' Survival Guide.* Prima, 1989. 404p. bibliog. index. LC 88-38558. ISBN 0914629824. $10.95.

Olds advises parents on how to balance work, home, marriage, children, and self and gives an overview of issues that affect working mothers and fathers. Choosing child care is the single most important topic covered in the book.

Schlaerth, Katherine. *Raising a Large Family.* Macmillan, 1991. 304p. LC 90-54755. ISBN 0-02-607061-8. $18.95.

To supplement the knowledge of the issues, problems, and logistics of the contemporary large family, this pediatrician and mother of seven interviewed 60 diverse parents. She inquired about their decision to have more than two children, integrating the third child into the family, economics and strategies, daily life, handling chores and TV viewing, discipline, and sibling interactions. How to provide each child with individual time, deal with high-maintenance children, organize home life when both parents work, define the role of fathers, and finally, avoid the daily stresses and "going crazy" are also covered. The author's knowledge, based on her training and experience, makes this an informative text on both the theoretical and practical levels, and the warm but objective and concise writing style makes it readable. Parents with fewer than three children will also find the issues addressed and advice provided helpful.

Shapiro, Barbara A., with Vicki Konover and Ann Shapiro. *The Big Squeeze: Balancing the Needs of Aging Parents, Dependent Children, and You.* Mills & Sanderson, 1991. 228p. illus. LC 91-18195. ISBN 0-938179-29-2. $12.95.

Two gerontologists and a sociologist joined forces to provide a method for sons and daughters to balance the needs of their aging parents, their own dependent children, and themselves. Called "The Balancing Act," this method of problem solving is an eight-step process that emphasizes individual responsibility and cooperation. The steps are fully explained in individual chapters that include case studies and exercises as well as theoretical explanations and practical advice. Beginning with being aware of the people involved and their needs, this method also involves acknowledging expectations and determining their validity, identifying needs, communicating, reviewing resources, defining a balance, delegating and acting, and maintaining. If there is backsliding, the authors advocate looping back to an earlier point in the process. The readable and informative text provides the kind of advice and support that members of the "sandwich generation" will find enlightening. An appendix provides a checklist for evaluating a continuing care facility.

Smith, Donna. *Stepmothering.* St. Martin's, 1990. 146p. bibliog. LC 90-32771. ISBN 0-312-04792-4. $29.95.

Interviews, personal experience, clinical practice, and a command of a wide range of literature on stepmothering provide the background for this fascinating manual for new stepmothers by a family therapist. Images from mythology, folk and fairy tales, popular literature, and the findings of scholars usually portray the stepmother in a bleak light, but Smith has located affirming stories to create a self-esteem improvement manual. She looks at the issues arising in the creation of a stepfamily; expectations for a stepmother, the reaction of the stepchildren, and the transformation from outsider to insider in the intimate life of the family.

Wallerstein, Judith S., and Sandra Blakeslee. *Second Chances: Men, Women, Children a Decade after Divorce: Who Wins, Who Loses, and Why.* Ticknor and Fields, 1989. bibliog. index. 329p. LC 88-23320. ISBN 0-89919-648-9. $19.95.

Data from a longitudinal study of 60 families after divorce reveal that many adults and children continued to suffer 10 years later, despite the promises of a new chance at life and better parenting. The authors reached several conclusions, presented in a series of case studies, about the effects of divorce: a pattern of winners and losers emerges, young women develop a high level of anxiety about betrayal while young men become emotionally constricted and do not recognize it, children are burdened by greater responsibility but feel less cared for, and many ex-spouses still feel intense anger and bitterness about a divorce 10 years later. An outline of the psychological tasks for adults, such as mourning the loss, reclaiming oneself, resolving or containing passions, and venturing forth, can guide recovery from divorce. Similar advice for children is provided as well.

Zwieback, Meg. *Keys to Preparing and Caring for Your Second Child.* Barron's, 1991. 149p. index. LC 91-6571. ISBN 0-8120-4698-6. $5.95.

This concise but substantial guide organizes practical advice on planning for and adjusting to life with a second child into 48 keys, or brief chapters. Information is organized chronologically, from preparing for the child through birth, the first weeks at home, the first three months, the following years, and special situations, such as adoption, blended families, and child care. The author, a nurse practitioner, counsels parents on handling their own feelings as well as those commonly experienced by first children and advises parents on logistical matters such as managing their time, setting schedules, and simply juggling the work load of two or more children. Solid advice from an expert.

POPULAR TITLES: JOURNALS

Single Parent. Parents Without Partners. 1958. B-M. ISSN 0037-5748. $15.00.

The official publication of Parents Without Partners, this journal publishes constructive, upbeat articles on single parenting, family life, legal issues, divorce, widowhood, and child care. Useful information on managing finances, sexual abuse, travel, discipline, remarriage, drugs, and other issues of daily life is presented. Book reviews, information about association activities, and humorous pieces are also published.

Stepfamilies. Stepfamily Association of America. 1980. Q. ISSN 0195-5969. $14.00.

Practical advice, results of research, and commentaries, poems, and letters from readers make up the contents of this magazine covering issues and concerns of step-parenting. Topics addressed have included untangling conflict in stepfamilies, the impact of "step" terminology, marital relationships in stepfamilies, and communication in stepfamilies.

Twins. Twins Magazine. 1984. B-M. ISSN 0890-3077. $19.98.

Personal experience and how-to articles, interviews/profiles, and humor provide multiples, their parents, and the professionals who care for them with current information on twin facts and research. Regular columns address prematurity, family health, development from infancy through adolescence, first-person accounts, father's perspective, and humorous photos. Issues have addressed such topics as singletons' attitudes toward multiples, a parent's adjustment to a special needs child, and a stroller buying guide.

Working Mother Magazine. Lang Communications. 1978. M. ISSN 0278-193X. $7.97.

Articles in this magazine help mothers balance the demands of a career with the concerns of a parent. Feature articles detail trends and problems and provide solutions or resources on children from infancy to adolescence. The content also includes information on beauty, health, fashion, nutrition, financial planning, new products, and social policy affecting family life. Information on where to purchase books noted by the authors is also provided.

PROFESSIONAL TITLES: BOOKS

Beer, William R. *American Stepfamilies: A Sociological Report.* Transaction, 1991. 243p. illus. index. LC 91-8924. ISBN 0-88738-436-6. $29.95.

This layperson's account of the lives of stepfamilies explores the qualities that separate them from intact nuclear families, such as complex roles, unclear boundaries, people joining and leaving, a highly sexualized environment, unfinished grieving, and guilt. Rather than a how-to book, the text provides detailed information, supported by research studies, to describe how a second marriage differs from the first, key issues for different stepfamily configurations, the biological parent's role in a stepfamily, and sibling relationships and explains how the increase in stepfamilies grew out of social change. Liberal use of case studies makes for interesting reading in an insightful, informative text.

Carp, Frances M., ed. *Lives of Career Women: Approaches to Work, Marriage, and Children.* Plenum, 1991. 321p. bibliog. index. LC 91-10866. ISBN 0-306-43960-3. $23.95.

Sixteen autobiographical essays by women who have achieved career success are presented as guides for contemporary young men and women. When children are mentioned, it is clear that they were a welcome component of their mother's life;

most mothers also mention the use of live-in help to assist with child care. Despite different experiences of women in diverse fields, these essays are alike in that they emphasize the role of parents' expectations for their daughters, high-energy levels, a willingness to ignore illness, significant levels of drive and determination, the value of luck, and flexibility in making choices and taking advantage of career opportunities.

Depner, Charlene E., and James H. Bray, eds. *Nonresidential Parenting: New Vistas in Family Living.* Sage, 1993. Focus Edition Series. 218p. bibliog. index. LC 92-37537. ISBN 0-8039-5050-0. $46.00. ISBN 0-8039-5051 pbk. $23.95.

A dramatic increase in the number of children who live with one parent as a result of their parents' divorce or because of birth outside of marriage challenges scholars and policymakers to understand and support these youngsters' emotional and financial needs. In this anthology of essays, a multidimensional approach is employed to examine the de facto living arrangements of children and the factors that encourage a nonresidential parent to develop and maintain close emotional and financial ties with children. The first section reviews what is currently known about nonresidential parenting and includes differences among ethnic groups and situations in which the mother is the nonresidential parent. Social service concepts, such as family systems theory, individual development theory, and social exchange theory, are used to explore such issues as financial implications, patterns of involvement, obstacles to ongoing relationships, and adjustment of children to divorce and remarriage. The final chapter comments on the recommendations for research and policy initiatives and promotes a multidimensional approach to future research.

Dunn, Judy, and Robert Plomin. *Separate Lives: Why Siblings Are So Different.* Basic Books, 1990. 210p. bibliog. index. LC 90-80254. ISBN 0-465-07688-2. $19.95.

After documenting the extent to which siblings differ in all personality traits, this insightful text explores the sources of those differences in nature, nurture, treatment by the parents and other siblings, experiences outside the family, and chance events. Because the effect of similar environmental factors would be similarity in the siblings, they are discounted. The extent to which experiencing, witnessing, and reacting to the differential treatment of parents and siblings have an impact on development is explored. Implications for clinicians and parents on how an individual develops within a family are reviewed, and recommendations for treatment are outlined. The authors recommend that parents be aware of how sensitive to real or imagined differences in their relationships to parents children are, attempt to minimize differences in treatment by becoming sensitive to the ways in which children monitor them, and to decrease hostility in how the dominant "top dog" sibling treats the others because it has such a marked effect on self-esteem. While many of the insights here are drawn from an understanding of the scholarly literature, biographical information from celebrated siblings such as Henry and William James illustrates how profound individual differences and perceptions are.

Ehrensaft, Diane. *Parenting Together: Men and Women Sharing the Care of Their Children.* University of Illinois Press, 1990. 288p. LC 90-10768. ISBN 0-252-06137-3. $12.95.

Drawing on insights gained in clinical practice and in interviews with 40 couples who chose to have both father and mother perform primary child care, psychologist Ehrensaft reveals the impact that shared parenting has on the child, individual parents, and the marriage itself. She initially provides a profile of the parents, who were influenced by the women's movement, political movements of the 1960s, a desire to be fair in sharing both financial burdens and career opportunities, and a belief in the enhanced well-being of the child. How these parents surmount biological and temperamental hurdles, organize day-to-day distribution of duties, and express gender-based differences in their emotional reactions to child care is explored, as is how they bond to their child. The impact of this style of parenting on their marriage and on the psychological development of their child is explored in detail that illustrates clearly the multiplicity of issues and perspectives involved. Special risks of this parenting style, e.g., jealousy over the spouse's relationship to the child, risk of overparenting, or wall-to-wall parenting, are explored, along with the benefits.

Folberg, Jay, ed. *Joint Custody and Shared Parenting.* 2nd ed. Guilford, 1991. 380p. bibliog. index. LC 91-20289. ISBN 0-89862-768-0. $45.00. ISBN 0-89862-481-9 pbk. $19.95.

This anthology brings together a variety of mental health and legal professionals, researchers, and economists to look at the questions and issues raised by joint custody. Part 1 provides a historical overview, followed by chapters examining the benefits of joint custody, how it fulfills the best interests of the child, what needs children of divorced parents have, problems in shared parenting, who can make it work and who cannot, and reasons for professional resistance to the concept. Part 2 presents a number of research studies, with some results indicating that joint custody at its best is a better alternative to sole custody at its best and that joint custody is not detrimental to the economic interest of women and children, provides benefits to parents that sole custody does not, and requires a low conflict, cooperative approach from parents. In the third part, various laws and statutes are reviewed. Appendix A provides a chart of legal decisions to date, and appendix B provides a sample joint custody agreement with alternative provisions as well as a bibliography. In its second edition, this comprehensive handbook covers all aspects of shared parenting in a well-organized, readable format.

Furstenberg, Frank F., and Andrew J. Cherlin. *Divided Families: What Happens to Children When Parents Part.* Harvard University Press, 1991. 142p. LC 90-048171. ISBN 0-674-65576-1. $18.95.

Insights drawn from research in all fields in the social sciences form the basis of this brief survey of divorce, remarriage, and stepparenting by two sociologists intent on linking what is known and what to do about it for an audience of policymakers, practitioners, and the public at large. The authors review cultural reactions to divorce, how the process of uncoupling

affects children, the economic dip of mothers and children after divorce, how children's psychological well-being is affected, remarriage, and adjustment to the stepfamily. The authors draw two conclusions: children's welfare after divorce depends on how well the custodial parent, usually the mother, can continue to function as a parent and on how insulated children are from continuing conflict between the divorced parents. A third conclusion, that children's welfare depends on continuing contact with the nonresidential parent, usually the father, is valid in commonsense terms but surprisingly not supported by empirical research. The final section of this book outlines how these three goals can be best met. To help parents, the authors advocate assuring a minimum level of child support, reorganizing the workplace to be more responsive to parenting concerns, and providing mental health interventions to help parents adjust to divorce. Conflict can be minimized through parallel parenting, which results in reduced contact, and making joint legal custody the standard arrangement. This book is notable for the graceful, moderate style of writing as well as the vast amount of social science research that has been distilled and organized.

Goldscheider, Frances K., and Linda J. White. *New Families, No Families? The Transformation of the American Home.* University of California Press, 1991. 303p. bibliog. index. LC 91-15452. ISBN 0-520-07222-7. $34.95.

The National Longitudinal Survey provided the data on which these two demographers based their analysis of changes in adult lifestyles in the United States, changes that encompass new roles for men and women within marriage and a new emphasis on remaining single. To account for both of these rather startling developments, the authors look at how work-life is valued over home-life and how experiencing parental divorce has made young adults reluctant to enter marriages of their own. A fascinating variety of data is presented in a review of family life since 1950 and an examination of how adults approach and enter marriage and allocate roles within it. Interesting findings include a shift to less egalitarian divisions of labor in the home once a child arrives, with the wife's role becoming more demanding and stressful, the husband being left out, and children taking on very few of the household chores unless the family is a single-parent or stepparent family. This sociological treatise provides useful background reading on family dynamics for professionals working with individual families.

Kissman, Kris, and Jo Ann Allen. *Single Parent Families.* Sage, 1993. 159p. bibliog. index. LC 92-35502. ISBN 0-8039-4322-9. $44.00. ISBN 0-8039-4323-7 pbk. $21.95.

In this guide for social workers and professionals in related fields, special treatment methods for single-parent families that reflect differences in gender, ethnicity, sexual orientation, and parental age are described. The authors emphasize mother-headed households because mothers who head households face additional burdens in the form of economic hardship and negative expectations from society about their ability to head families. The authors propose techniques for communicating with single mothers and for easing transitions in family life cycles. Sources of support from family, partners, and others are explored as ways to help single mothers meet their challenging dual roles as wage earners and care givers. Ethnic families, adolescent parents, single father–headed households, and noncustodial parenting are also considered in this concise handbook.

Lerner, Jacqueline V., and Nancy L. Galambos. *Employed Mothers and Their Children*. Garland, 1991. 295p. bibliog. index. LC 90-25897. ISBN 0-8240-6344-9. $33.00.

This scholarly anthology surveys the psychological literature, particularly the studies focused on attachment and cognitive development, to identify the true impact on children from infancy through adolescence of mothers working and to provide guidance to policymakers concerned about children's welfare as well as the burden that working parents bear. The results of separate new studies on maternal employment are also reported in chapters devoted to the effect of day care on infants; the impact of mothers' employment on cognitive development, family setting, and adolescents, including self-care; the influence of mothers working on the division of household labor; the impact of fathers' employment; and how dual-career marriages function. The final chapter reviews intervening factors, such as education; income; attitudes; the child's age, sex, and temperament; and the quality of child care. Examining these moderating factors is the approach that the editor considers most fruitful for future research. Each chapter contains a brief annotated bibliography, a lengthier reference list, and resources for parents.

Mendelson, Morton J. *Becoming a Brother: A Child Learns about Life, Family, and Self*. MIT Press, 1990. 249p. bibliog. LC 90-5905. ISBN 0-262-13260-5. $24.95.

Hours of taped conversations, entries in a daily log, formal interviews, and behavioral checklists, compiled by a psychologist observing his son, contributed to this intensive case study of how a preschooler adapts to the arrival of a new baby. The author looks at and analyzes the child's psychological understanding of the biological facts of life, reaction to separation from the mother while she is in the hospital, reaction to the baby's arrival, and attitudes toward and interaction with the new sibling. Concluding that rivalry between the two is not necessarily an outcome, Mendelson points out that tension and stress do result from the anxiety of separation from the mother during her confinement and the frustration when comfortable routines enjoyed by the first child are disturbed.

Spurlock, Jeanne, ed. *Women's Progress: Promises and Problems*. Plenum, 1990. 258p. LC 90-7175. ISBN 0-3064434-229. $39.50.

Opportunities available to contemporary women and barriers that prevent them from achieving their goals are the underlying themes of Spurlock's survey of women's lives in a variety of settings, which is targeted to a professional audience of clinicians, educators, physicians, nurses, social workers, and behavioral scientists. This anthology is organized into sections that address family structures, adoption, parenting, women with extraordinary problems, and sexual issues. Each chapter explores a different issue of importance in understanding the circumstances of women today, such as foster mothering, adoption of children from other cultures, working mothers, mothers of children with mental disabilities, mothers who abuse their children, and lesbian mothers. The approach taken by the contributors is often a personal as well as scholarly one; many of the selections also include case study material. Some chapters deal with women outside their role as mothers, but the majority of the text explores circumstances having an impact on child rearing.

Stacey, Judith. *Brave New Families: Stories of Domestic Upheaval in Late Twentieth-Century America*. Basic Books, 1990. 328p. bibliog. index. LC 90-80244. ISBN 0-465-00746-5. $22.95.

An extended ethnographic study of 30 relatives in two white working-class Silicon Valley families provides insights into conditions of divorce, remarriage, and division of roles that others will recognize. The introductory chapters provide an interesting summary of the history of the family in the United States.

Stewart, Robert B. *The Second Child: Family Transition and Adjustment*. Sage, 1990. 251p. bibliog. LC 90-43949. ISBN 0-8039-3519-6. $38.95. ISBN 0-8039-3520-X pbk. $18.95.

The transition to parenthood is not completed when the first child is born, as data from this longitudinal study of 41 families expecting their second child in three to six months reveal. In addition to an observational session, each parent was interviewed five times, and scales assessing satisfaction with parenting, role division, sources of stress in parenting, temperament, and use of outside support were administered at various points throughout the study. Interviews with the first-born child were also conducted. The results indicate that mothers experience more stress from the "pileup" of demands in caring for a second child, especially in the area of role restriction and coping with difficult behavior by the first-born. Fathers took on more responsibility for child care tasks, especially for the first-born child. Parents both tended to view the second child's birth as a positive growth experience, however, and the mother in particular derived great satisfaction from being a parent. The theoretical basis of this study is systems theory, which is described and its connections to the family explicated thoroughly in the first chapter.

Yarrow, Andrew L. *Latecomers: Children of Parents over 35*. Free Press, 1991. 244p. bibliog. index. LC 90-45944. ISBN 0-02-935685-7. $19.95.

Data for this study of older parents from the child's point of view were obtained via interviews with 70 voluntary survey respondents. The text provides a historical overview of older parents, describes how their children feel different from their peers, and outlines the special problems that these children face. While this text does not provide older parents with practical advice on what to do, it does explore issues that their children may confront, such as having parents from another era, growing up fast, and facing mortality at an early age. Appendixes list birthrates and medical issues related to late childbearing as well as the text of the questionnaire.

DIRECTORY

Children's Rights Council (CRC)
220 I Street, N.E., Washington, DC 20002
(202) 547-6227 (202) 546-4272

David L. Levy, Esq., President
Founded: 1985
Members: 1,500
Affiliates: 22 state groups
Former Name: National Council for Children's Rights
Mission/Goals: To strengthen families, especially families of separation and divorce; to reduce hostilities between parents; to promote mediation, conciliation, and shared parenting; to strengthen the intact family through family instruction and family preservation
Audience/Clientele: Mental health professionals, custody reform advocates, researchers, writers, grandparents
Staff: 1 nonprofessional, 30 volunteers
Budget: $75,000 Funding: Private sources, fees for services or products, dues
Services: Referral, advocacy
Awards: Healer Award; Best in Media Award; Positive Parenting Award
Education and Outreach: Seminars, publishing
Publications: *Conference Proceedings*; *Speak Out for Children*, quarterly newsletter; *The Best Parent Is Both Parents*; *Catalog of Resources*, periodic; audiovisuals, posters, T-shirts, and gifts for kids
Programs: Annual conference

Committee for Mother and Child Rights (CMCR)

210 Ole Orchard, Clear Brook, VA 22624
(703) 722-3652
Elizabeth Owen, Coordinator
Founded: 1980
Members: 6,000
Mission/Goals: To help mothers with child custody problems
Audience/Clientele: Mothers who have lost child custody, mothers going through contested custody, mothers with visitation
Languages: French, Spanish
Services: Counseling, support group, social service/case management, referral, networking

Fathers for Equal Rights (FER)

P.O. Box 010847, Flagler Station, Miami, FL 33101
(305) 895-6351
Sam Ross, Executive Director
Founded: 1973
Former Name: National Society of Fathers for Child Custody and Divorce Law Reform
Mission/Goals: To educate the public about the impact of loss of a father figure in the family; to promote the establishment of minimum standards for attorneys in child custody litigation; to help families avoid making children the victims of divorce and custody cases
Audience/Clientele: Parents and grandparents involved in divorce or child custody disputes, general public
Services: Lobbying, referrals
Education and Outreach: Clearinghouse on issues of child custody litigation, research, publishing

Publications: *Fathers Winning Child Custody Cases*; *Pro Se* and *Pro Per* kits for members unable to afford an attorney; videos, audiotapes, booklets, and other educational materials related to child custody or divorce

International Youth Council (IYC)

8807 Colesville Road, Silver Spring, MD 20910
(301) 588-9354 Fax (301) 588-9216 Toll-free (800) 637-7974
Sean Thompson, President
Founded: 1962
Affiliates: 70 local groups; affiliated with Parents Without Partners
Mission/Goals: To bring members of local groups of youths from single-parent homes together to exchange ideas, address common problems, and provide mutual support; to foster leadership through respect, trust, and honesty; to promote active participation in school and community
Audience/Clientele: Youths ages 12 to 17 from single-parent homes
Services: Organizes weekend trips, social events, community projects; sponsors competitions; compiles statistics
Education and Outreach: Maintains speakers' bureau, library
Publications: *Bulletin*, issued monthly; *The Single Parent*
Programs: Annual international conference

Men International, Inc.

2639 Knoll Street E, Palm Harbor, FL 34690
(813) 786-6911
Kenneth R. Pangborn, President
Founded: 1977
Affiliates: 143 local groups
Former Name: United States Divorce Reform (USDR), Coalition of Divorce Reform Elements (CADRE), and subsidiary of Parents and Children's Equality (PACE)
Mission/Goals: Education, support, and advocacy for male parents; concerned with divorce, child custody, visitation, rape, spouse abuse, child abuse, marriage
Audience/Clientele: Divorced fathers, male parents
Staff: 6 volunteers
Funding: Donations, grants, dues
Services: Counseling, support group, referral, lobbying, compiling statistics, legal strategy assistance
Education and Outreach: Seminars, database development, publishing
Publications: *The Liberator*, monthly newsletter
Programs: Annual conference

Mothers without Custody (MWOC)

P.O. Box 27418, Houston, TX 77227-7418
(713) 840-1622
Jennifer Isham, National President
Founded: 1979
Members: 500
Affiliates: Varying number of local and state groups
Mission/Goals: To enhance the quality of life for their children by strengthening the role of the noncustodial parent in regard

to custody, child support, visitation, and parenting; to provide a self-directed network and outlet for noncustodial mothers to share their experiences; to educate and inform the public about issues affecting the noncustodial mother and her children; to serve as liaison between organizations and individuals that promote the health and well-being of children and mothers
Audience/Clientele: Mothers who have surrendered or are denied custody of their children
Staff: 20 volunteers
Funding: Dues
Services: Support group, referral
Education and Outreach: Publishing
Publications: *Mother-to-Mother*, a bimonthly newsletter
Programs: Annual convention

National Organization of Mothers of Twins Clubs (NOMOTC)
P.O. Box 23188, Albuquerque, NM 87192-1188
(505) 275-0955
Lois Gallmeyer, Executive Secretary
Founded: 1960
Members: 17,500
Mission/Goals: To increase understanding of how being a twin changes traditional concepts of child rearing; to accomplish this via communication among parents, educators, and physicians; to make information about twins more accessible to the general public; to increase awareness of the individuality of each twin
Audience/Clientele: Twins clubs members
Services: Publishing
Education and Outreach: Maintains speakers' bureau
Publications: *MOTC's Notebook*, quarterly newsletter
Programs: Annual conference

North American Conference of Separated and Divorced Catholics (NACSDC)
80 St. Mary's Drive, Cranston, RI 02920
(401) 943-7903
Dorothy J. Levesque, Executive Director
Founded: 1975
Members: 2,000
Mission/Goals: To provide divorced and separated Catholics and their children lay ministry and peer support
Audience/Clientele: Regional representatives of separated and divorced Catholics
Education and Outreach: Retreats, workshops, educational and training programs, speakers' bureau, publishing
Publications: *Jacob's Well*, quarterly; other resource packets, tapes, books, and training modules
Programs: Annual international conference with leadership workshop

Parents without Partners (PWP)
401 N. Michigan Avenue, Chicago, IL 60611-4267
(312) 644-6610 Toll-free (800) 637-7974
K.M. Bell, President
Founded: 1957

Members: 112,000
Affiliates: 90 regional groups, 750 local groups
Mission/Goals: To provide a support group for single parents; to support the welfare and interests of single parents and their children
Audience/Clientele: Single parents
Budget: $2,000,000 Funding: Dues, fees for services or products
Services: Support group, recreation, advocacy
Awards: Programming awards to chapters; Single Parent/ Youth of the Year Awards, college scholarships
Education and Outreach: Continuing education courses, seminars, library/resource center, publishing
Publications: *The Single Parent*, a bimonthly newsletter; *PWP Insider*, a publication about PWP activities
Programs: Annual conference

Rainbows
1111 Tower Road, Schaumburg, IL 60173-4305
(708) 310-1880
Suzy Yehl Marta, Executive Director
Founded: 1983
Members: 300,000
Affiliates: 4,500 state groups, 600 local groups
Former Name: Rainbows for All God's Children
Mission/Goals: To provide effective peer support groups for children, adolescents, and adults who are grieving a death, divorce, or other painful transition in their family; to offer training and curricula to assist in establishing peer support groups in churches, schools, or social agencies
Audience/Clientele: Children, adolescents, and adults who are grieving a death, divorce, or abandonment in their families
Staff: 10 professionals, 60,000 volunteers
Budget: $468,000 Funding: Fund-raising
Services: Support group
Education and Outreach: In-service programs, publishing
Publications: *Rainbows, Bumblebees, 'n Me*, a semiannual newsletter

Single Mothers by Choice (SMC)
P.O. Box 1642, Gracie Square Station, New York, NY 10028
(212) 988-0993
Jane Mattes, Chairperson
Founded: 1981
Members: 2,000
Affiliates: 20 state groups, 2 local groups
Mission/Goals: To provide support and information to single women in their thirties and forties who are considering motherhood or who are single mothers by choice
Audience/Clientele: Single women considering childbearing or adoption as single parents
Staff: 1 professional, 1 nonprofessional, many volunteers
Budget: $12,000 approximately Funding: Dues, fees for services or products
Services: Counseling, support group, recreation, referral

Education and Outreach: Seminars, library, database development, speakers' bureau, publishing
Publications: *Single Mothers by Choice*, quarterly; a collection of articles from back issues of the newsletter called *Highlights of Newsletters*
Programs: Periodic meetings

Stepfamily Association of America (SAA)
215 Centennial Mall South, Suite 212, Lincoln, NE 68508-1813
(402) 477-7837 Toll-free (800) 735-0329
William F. Munn, Executive Director
Founded: 1979
Members: 1,600
Affiliates: 2 state groups, 70 local groups
Mission/Goals: To provide information and advocacy for stepfamilies
Audience/Clientele: Stepparents, remarried parents, and their children
Staff: 2 nonprofessionals, 1-3 volunteers
Budget: $300,00 Funding: Private sources, fund-raising, donations, fees for service or products
Services: Support group, referral
Education and Outreach: Seminars, library, publishing
Publications: *Stepfamilies*, a quarterly newsletter; *Stepfamilies Stepping Ahead: An Eight-Step Program for Successful Family Living*, a bibliography of books, articles, and research findings on stepfamily issues; *Learning to Step Together*, a manual

Stepfamily Foundation (SF)
333 West End Avenue, New York, NY 10023
(212) 877-3244 Fax (212) 362-7030 Hotline (800) SKY-STEP
Jeannette Lofas, President
Founded: 1975
Members: 5,000
Mission/Goals: To gather information on stepfamilies and stepfamily relationships; to provide counseling and other support to individuals, couples, and groups
Audience/Clientele: Remarried persons with children, divorced couples, interested professionals
Services: Counseling, statistics compilation, support group
Education and Outreach: Seminars, library, publishing, research, speakers' bureau
Publications: *New American Family*, quarterly; *Step News*, quarterly newsletter; *Stepfamily Statistics*; various pamphlets, videos, audiotapes
Programs: Semiannual conference

The Twins Foundation (TF)
P.O. Box 6043, Providence, RI 02940-6043
(401) 274-TWIN Fax (401) 353-9223
Kay Cassill, President
Founded: 1983
Members: 2,000
Mission/Goals: The Twins Foundation is an international, non-profit organization established to collect, preserve, and communicate information about twins and twins research; serve as a primary educational and informational resource on twins and research involving twins; maintains the Voluntary National Twin Registry
Audience/Clientele: Twins (adult and young adult), parents and significant others of twins, researchers, the media and general public
Funding: Private source, fund-raising, donations, grants, dues, fees for services or products
Services: Search services, referral
Awards: Founding Member Certificates; Awards for Exceptional Volunteers and Donors; in process of developing the Foundation's Hall of Fame Awards
Education and Outreach: Seminars, library, archives, database development, publishing
Publications: *The Twins Letter*, quarterly newsletter; handouts and brochures

United Fathers of America (UFA)
595 The City Drive, Suite 202, Orange, CA 92668
(714) 385-1002
Marvin Chapman, Vice President
Founded: 1976
Mission/Goals: To promote equal rights for fathers in establishment of child custody in divorce cases; to encourage the best possible environment for children in divorced families
Audience/Clientele: Persons experiencing disruption in family life due to divorce
Services: Support groups, counseling, referrals
Education and Outreach: Monitoring and informing the public about legislation addressing divorce and custody, research, seminars, speakers' bureau

REFERENCES

1. Dennis A. Ahlburg and Carol J. DeVita, "New Realities of the American Family," *Population Bulletin* 47, no. 2 (August 1992): 7.

2. Judith S. Wallerstein and Sandra Blakeslee, *Second Chances: Men, Women, Children a Decade after Divorce: Who Wins, Who Loses, and Why* (New York: Ticknor and Fields, 1989), 62, 67, 184.

3. *Studies in Household and Family Formation: When Households Continue, Discontinue, and Form.* Current Population Reports, Special Studies P23-179. U.S. Department of Commerce, Bureau of the Census, 1992, 12, 2.

4. Ibid.

5. Laura Leete-Guy and Juliet B. Schor, *Great American Time Squeeze: Trends in Work and Leisure, 1969–89* (Washington, DC: Economic Policy Institute, 1992), 1–2.

6. Arlie Hochschild, *The Second Shift* (New York: Avon, 1989), 3.

7. Katherine Schlaerth, *Raising a Large Family* (New York: Collier Macmillan, 1991), 4–5.

CHAPTER

Celebrating Family Diversity

As Black parents
we face a unique and formidable
challenge preparing our children for
the race consciousness and outright racism
that still pervade American society while helping
them remain positive, productive, and self-respecting.

Darlene Powell-Hopson and Derek S. Hopson.
Different and Wonderful

Families differ in how they are organized and in who their members are; these differences in some ways reflect voluntary choices. Families are also diverse in terms of racial and ethnic background, religious affiliation, and sexual orientation of the parents. The gay liberation movement enabled gay men and women to form open, stable, long-term committed relationships conducive to child rearing. Through adoption, foster parenting, and high-tech conception techniques, more and more gays and lesbians are becoming parents. [1] In culturally or socially diverse families, typical parenting considerations, including emotional, financial, and time commitments, are coupled with specific concerns, such as maintaining a positive racial identity or developing "rules" for co-parenting.

An asterisk (*) indicates a specially recommended title.

POPULAR TITLES: BOOKS

* Bell-Scott, Patricia, et al., eds. *Double Stitch: Black Women Write about Mothers and Daughters.* Beacon, 1991. 271p. bibliog. LC 91-10284. ISBN 0-8070-0910-5. $19.95.

    Poems, short stories, personal narratives, and scholarly essays, many reprinted from two special issues of *SAGE: A Scholarly Journal on Black Women*, focus on the many guises that the relationship between African-American mothers and their daughters may take. The volume is shaped to reflect several themes: beginnings, identities, histories, tensions,

generations, and separations, with selections from 47 authors, including Alice Walker, Bell Hooks, Lois Lyles, Johnetta B. Cole, Paula Giddings, and Maya Angelou. In a perceptive introduction, Patricia Bell-Scott, one of the editors of this volume, notes that the essays reveal the remarkable diversity of African-American mother-daughter relationships, the need to acknowledge the effects of sexism in order to understand these relationships, and the recognition that the participants must work on growing positively within this intimate bond.

Comer, James P., and Alvin F. Poussaint. *Raising Black Children: Two Leading Psychiatrists Confront the Educational, Social and Emotional Problems Facing Black Children.* Plume, 1992. 436p. LC 92-5363. ISBN 0-452-26839-7. $12.00.

    A revision of *Black Child Care*, this practical reference guide for African American parents addresses how children mature and how that growth affects their emotional, psychological, and social development. Using a helpful question-and-answer format, the authors cover stage-by-stage development of black children from infancy through adolescence. They emphasize specific concerns that black parents have, such as strictness, street gangs, self-esteem and physical image, racism, racial pride, school busing, swearing, interracial dating, black colleges, and employment.

Corley, Rip. *The Final Closet: A Gay Parents' Guide for Coming Out to Their Children.* Editech, 1990. 176p. bibliog. LC 89-82740. ISBN 0-945586-08-6. $8.95.

    Lengthy, absorbing case studies personalize this approach to coming out to one's family, devised by a therapist who focuses his practice on this process. Because heterosexuality is assumed, he recommends that gay parents conquer their fear of rejection and risk of change and reveal themselves to their children, arguing that each child has a right to know, the pain of not knowing the reason for emotional distance is more damaging than the truth, and, in many instances, children are already aware of their parent's orientation. Advice on age-appropriate language is provided, as is information on legal issues such as co-parenting, guardianship, artificial insemination and paternity, and AIDS. An appendix lists self-help groups for adults and children. This author's approach to a challenge for gay parents is encouraging, supportive, and instructive.

Fricke, Aaron, and Walter Fricke. *Sudden Strangers: The Story of a Gay Son and His Father.* St. Martin's, 1991. 112p. LC 90-27344. ISBN 0-312-05869-1. $15.95.

A heterosexual father and his gay son recount the conflict that needed to be resolved before each could accept and respect the other. In the first few chapters, son Aaron summarizes the cycle of support and conflict that he and his father went through as came out, successfully sued the Rhode Island School System for approval to take a gay date to the senior prom (reported in *Reflections of a Rock Lobster* [Alyson Publications, 1981]), and clashed over values and lifestyle issues. Later chapters from both Walter and Aaron's perspectives address such issues as coming out and praying for change. Brief but insightful, this memoir will provide both parents and adolescents with guidance and support in accepting and living with, if not celebrating, homosexual orientation.

Hopson, Darlene Powell, and Derek S. Hopson, with Thomas Clavin. *Raising the Rainbow Generation: Teaching Your Children to Be Successful in a Multicultural Society.* Simon & Schuster, 1993. 205p. bibliog. index. LC 93-28075. ISBN 0-671-79806-5. $10.00.

Numerous anecdotes illustrate the challenges parents face from the media, schools, family and friends, their child's peer group and even themselves in raising children who accept and are comfortable with people of races other than their own. The authors, a husband and wife team of clinical psychologists who wrote *Different and Wonderful*, discuss the changing demographics of the U.S. population, why the melting pot is "simmering," and how to start explaining about other races to children as early as age three. The final section of the book consists of folk tales from several different cultures that emphasize universal concerns. In addition to anecdotes, this text provides practical tips, exercises, and age-specific problem-solving techniques to help parents, teachers, and other care givers prevent or combat prejudice in their children 12 years of age and younger.

* Martin, April. *The Lesbian and Gay Parenting Handbook: Creating and Raising Our Families.* Harper Perennial: HarperCollins, 1993. 352p. bibliog. index. LC 92-54782. ISBN 0-06-096929-6. $15.00.

Based in part on the author's personal experience as a mother and professional experience as a therapist, this handbook for prospective and current gay and lesbian parents provides a thorough introduction to parenting concerns at all levels from the practical to the legal, logistical, emotional, and social. Interviews and stories from 57 families throughout the country personalize the detailed information presented on the decision to become a parent, becoming pregnant, donors and coparents, surrogacy, adoption, and the legal ramifications of these approaches to starting a family. Advice on making a family work addresses issues involved in raising children; changes in daily, social, and sex life brought about by adding a child to the family; and coping with breakups, crises, or tragedy. The impact of coming out is also explored in this comprehensive handbook on gay and lesbian parenting. A resource section containing sample sperm donor-recipient and coparenting agreements, a list of groups and organizations, and a donor screening form supplements the insightful and informative text.

Parker, Matthew, and Lee N. June, eds. *The Black Family: Past, Present, and Future.* Zondervan Publishing House, 1990. 239p. LC 90-19567. ISBN 0-310-45591-X. $12.95.

African-American Christian leaders from various walks of life provide background data, insights, and practical advice on how to use resources of the black community, in particular the organized church, to strengthen the family in this anthology, prepared under the auspices of the Institute for Black Family Development of Detroit, Michigan. The chapters provide scriptural documentation for the grass-roots solutions these authors propose. Among the topics covered suitable for both lay and professional audiences are the history of the African-American family, extended and single-parent families, ways to strengthen male-female relationships, marital counseling, the role of the home in children's spiritual development, the role of the church in the educational development of children, sex and sexuality, and money management, all incorporating a biblical perspective. While much of practical use may be found here, particularly for families who choose a Christian approach to beliefs and behaviors, the opportunity for community and church leaders and counselors to develop a more informed approach to programs is the most likely application of this carefully organized, comprehensive, and well-written volume. The inclusion of additional readings in each chapter contributes to the potential usefulness of the ideas of these Christian leaders.

* Powell-Hopson, Darlene, and Derek S. Hopson. *Different and Wonderful: Raising Black Children in a Race-Conscious Society.* Prentice Hall, 1990. 272p. bibliog. index. LC 89-70909. ISBN 0-13-211509-3. $19.45.

Two clinical psychologists specializing in treating children and families instruct parents on building self-esteem and positive racial identity in their children. The techniques of modeling, positive reinforcement, role playing, and open discussions are covered for addressing racial issues. The authors trace the development of racial identity through childhood and examine attitudes such as a preference for white skin that can interfere with positive self-image. The text includes a lengthy resource guide that lists books, games, dolls, and educational materials to support healthy development in African-American children.

Rafkin, Louise, ed. *Different Mothers: Sons and Daughters of Lesbians Talk about Their Lives.* Cleis, 1990. 174p. LC 90-2529. ISBN 0-939416-40-9. $24.95. ISBN 0-939416-41-7 pbk. $9.95.

> While it is not a self-help book, this collection of essays from 38 sons and daughters of lesbian mothers provides helpful insights and, in some cases, pointed advice on how gay parents should relate to their children. The stories vary in sophistication, as some were contributed by young children, some by middle-aged adults, and all ages in between, but each addresses how the family began, how the children represent their family to the world at large, what they share with their mothers, and their feelings about their mother. Despite nearly universal secrecy about their mother's orientation, frequent hostility from fathers who are ex-spouses, and occasional rejection of boys by separatists, most of these offspring report close relationships and a happy home-life with their mothers.

Stewart, Julia. *African Names: Names from the African Continent for Children and Adults.* Citadel, 1993. 171p. bibliog. illus. LC 93-9441. ISBN 0-8065-1386-1. $9.95.

> More than 1,000 African and Muslim names, with greater emphasis on Swahili and East African terms, are compiled in this guide. Each alphabetical entry provides a guide to pronunciation and a brief history of the name and its meaning. The entries are organized by gender. The names compiled here were chosen according to the beauty of their sound when spoken as opposed to their significance. The text emphasizes simple, easily pronounceable names but suggests nicknames for the longer monikers. An informative introduction explores the cultural, legal, and emotional issues involved in assuming an African name.

POPULAR TITLES: JOURNALS

The Black Child Advocate. National Black Child Development Institute. 1971. Q. $12.50.

> From the National Black Child Development Institute (NBCDI), this newsletter is directed to all persons who are committed to positive development of African-American children and adolescents through education, research, service, and advocacy. Information on pending legislation, upcoming conferences and continuing education opportunities, results of recent research, and work of the NBCDI is covered. One issue addressed health hazards, such as lead poisoning, prenatal exposure to drugs, and the safety of day care facilities.

PROFESSIONAL TITLES: BOOKS

Barret, Robert L., and Bryan E. Robinson. *Gay Fathers.* Lexington, 1990. 196p. bibliog. LC 90-32417. ISBN 0-669-19514-6. $18.95.

> This guide to counseling gay fathers describes their concerns, conflicts, and actions using lengthy case studies and reviews of the literature. After outlining the challenges gay fathers face, including rejection and isolation from their families and the gay community, lack of social support, and internal-

ized homophobia, the authors examine evidence that refutes myths that gay fathers have disturbed relationships with their parents, will transmit the "germ" of homosexuality to their children, and are sex fiends. They describe gay family configurations and their effects on children, how gay fathers relate to their parents and ex-spouse, and the impact that HIV has had. Each chapter concludes with specific practical tips for counselors addressing these issues. Further, there is a lengthy list of books, audiovisual resources, and self-help organizations that provides additional information on a difficult-to-study, elusive topic.

Weston, Kath. *Families We Choose: Lesbians, Gays, Kinship.* Columbia University Press, 1991. 261p. LC 90-049349. ISBN 0-231-07288-0. $35.00.

> The emergence of gay families, made up of lovers, friends, supportive parents and other relatives, ex-lovers, and, in an increasing number of cases, children, is a dramatic historical shift in U.S. culture, according to anthropologist Kath Weston. In interviews with 80 respondents of diverse racial, ethnic, and economic backgrounds, she reviews the development of kinship bonds among gays and lesbians and explores their coming-out stories, investigating issues of identity and the desire for continuing relationships with blood or adopted relatives. Ten stories of gay families illustrate kinship bonds of a new sort, families organized around symbolic representations of love, shared history, and material or emotional assistance. Images of continuity versus incompleteness are explored in the life of lovers of the same sex. The author also examines childbearing and parenting by gays, noting that the availability of artificial insemination provided the historical spark that led to the recent "Lesbian Baby Boom."

DIRECTORY

Custody Action for Lesbian Mothers (CALM)
P.O. Box 281, Narberth, PA 19072
(215) 667-7508
Rosalie E. Davies, Coordinator
Founded: 1974
Mission/Goals: To provide free litigation support services for lesbian mothers in the Delaware Valley and consultation nationally
Audience/Clientele: Lesbian mothers facing custody/visitation problems
Staff: 1 professional, 60 volunteers
Budget: $35,000 Funding: Private sources, fund-raising, donations, grants
Services: Counseling, referral, legal services, networking

Gay and Lesbian Parents Coalition International (GLPCI)
P.O. Box 50360, Washington, DC 20091
(202) 583-8029
Tim Fisher, Administrator
Founded: 1979
Members: 1,500

Affiliates: 60 local groups
Former Name: Gay Fathers Coalition; Gay Fathers Coalition International
Mission/Goals: To act as a clearinghouse for information concerning gay and lesbian parenting; to encourage acceptance of parenting and homosexuality as compatible by educating professionals and the general public
Audience/Clientele: Gay and lesbian parents and parent groups
Services: Lobbying, support group
Education and Outreach: In-service programs, seminars, speakers' bureau, library, archives, publishing
Publications: *Bibliography of Books for Children of Gay and Lesbian Parents*, annual; *Annual Report*; *Confidential Directory of Affiliates and Area Contacts*, annual; *Gay and Lesbian Parents Coalition International—Network*, bimonthly newsletter covering issues, association news, and reviews
Programs: Annual conference

Interracial Family Alliance (IFA)

P.O. Box 16248, Houston, TX 77222
(713) 454-5018
Jane Archie, President
Founded: 1981
Members: 85
Mission/Goals: To affirm, through education, the dignity and equality of every racial group; to support and serve the interracial family and multiracial individual; to strengthen the bonds among groups in our multiethnic society
Audience/Clientele: Families and couples who are interracial through marriage or adoption
Staff: 15 volunteers
Funding: Fund-raising, donations, grants, dues, fees for services or products
Services: Support group
Education and Outreach: In-service programs, seminars, library, publishing
Publications: *Communique*, quarterly newsletter

Lesbian Mothers' National Defense Fund (LMNDF)

P.O. Box 21567, Seattle, WA 98111
(206) 325-2643
Jenny Sayward, Director
Founded: 1974
Members: 450

Affiliates: starting local groups
Mission/Goals: To support lesbians' choices in parenting legally, financially, and emotionally; to combat discrimination against lesbian and bisexual mothers; to educate lesbians, professionals, and the general public about lesbian mothers' rights and needs
Audience/Clientele: Lesbian mothers, co-parents, prospective mothers
Staff: 6 volunteers
Budget: $2,000 Funding: Private source, fund-raising, donations, grants, dues, fees for services or products
Services: Counseling, support group, referral, legal support
Education and Outreach: Seminars, library, publishing
Publications: *Mom's Apple Pie*, quarterly newsletter

National Black Child Development Institute (NBCDI)

1023 15th Street, N.W., Suite 600, Washington, DC 20005
(202) 387-1281 Fax (202) 234-1738
Evelyn K. Moore, Executive Director
Founded: 1970
Mission/Goals: To improve the quality of life for African American children and youth; to promote and advocate for health, child welfare, education, and child care; to analyze policy and legislative decisions and administrative regulations to identify their impact on African American children
Former Name: Black Child Development Institute
Audience/Clientele: Community groups, parents, government officials, professionals, the general public
Services: Lobbying, advocacy, networking
Education and Outreach: In-service training, seminars, publishing publications: *Black Child Advocate*, a quarterly newsletter discussing public policy, providing legislative updates, and reports on community services; *Child Health Talk*, quarterly newsletter; *Calendar of Black Children*, annual; other guides and reports

REFERENCE

1. Louise Rafkin, ed., *Different Mothers: Sons and Daughters of Lesbians Talk about Their Lives* (Pittsburgh: Cleis, 1990), 9.

CHAPTER

7

The Adoptive Family

Being "chosen" in this special
way is a two-edged sword for the adoptee.
The telling unfolds a story of decisions and
details that is of lifelong significance to the adoptee.
Miriam Komar. *Communicating with the Adopted Child*

Outcomes in many adoption custody battles publicized in the mass media display increasing recognition of the rights of the child as opposed to the rights of adoptive or biological parents. Only a small portion of adoptions are contested, yet these capture the public eye because they force us to rethink traditional adoption principles and practices. In 1986, 104,088 adoptions were finalized, with 52,931 of the children being adopted by relatives.[1] In 1991, 9,008 adoptions were of children from other nations, including 2,552 from Romania and 1,817 from Korea.[2]

Adopted children and adoptive parents in any setting face issues of abandonment, loss, belonging, and identity, and these concerns become even more pronounced when children do not physically resemble their parents. Encouraging ethnic pride and avoiding cultural insensitivity are key components in foreign adoptions. Working with children with physical, mental, or emotional difficulties, or those who have been adopted only after years of turmoil and crisis in birth families, requires particularly strong parental support and understanding.

In addition to covering the legal and psychological sequelae of adoption, the resources examined here describe the adoption process (including the parents' acceptance of infertility in most cases today) and compare and contrast the features of different types of adoption, including agency, independent, and open adoptions.

Adoption terminology is defined. To provide balanced coverage of the issues involved, the viewpoint of birth parents who have released their children for adoption is also presented.

An asterisk (*) indicates a specially recommended title.

POPULAR TITLES: BOOKS

Michelman, Stanley B., and Meg Schneider. *The Private Adoption Handbook*. Villard, 1990. 220p. bibliog. index. LC 88-17281. ISBN 0-394-56629-7. $12.50.

In this detailed introduction to independent adoption practices in the United States, alternate sections are written by an experienced adoption attorney and a former client of his, an adoptive mother. The attorney's contributions include an overview of the steps involved, how to select a lawyer, how to advertise and screen calls from prospective birth parents, how to choose a baby, and decisions necessary in the final months before the baby's birth. He also includes samples of many documents and forms required in the independent adoption process, as well as a chart detailing legal regulations of independent adoption in each state. The adoptive mother describes how going through all the procedures specified actually feels.

While attorney Michelman is clearly an advocate of private adoption and emphasizes its major advantage, the opportunity to adopt a healthy white infant within a few months of beginning the search, he does make an effort to point out potential problems, including higher and uncertain costs, and he is careful to include the advantages of adopting through an agency as well as the disadvantages of this route.

Pohl, Constance, and Kathy Harris, eds. *Transracial Adoption: Children and Parents Speak.* Franklin Watts, 1992. 143p. index. bibliog. photog. LC 92-10991. ISBN 0-531-11134-2. $8.95.

Parents, children, and siblings tell their stories in this anthology exploring adoptions in which the parents and the children they adopt are of different races. For many families discussed here, the parents are white and their children are black. Issues common to all adoptive situations, such as abandonment, attachment, anger, and special needs, are explored, with an emphasis on those concerns in the context of multiracial families. The racial mix of a family means that its members cannot hide from adoption, nor can they avoid related concerns such as racism and the search for cultural identity. Also covered are selecting a congenial neighborhood and participating in parent groups that not only give parents guidance and assistance but also provide children with peers. Photographs of the families interviewed enhance the realistic portrait of problems, challenges, successes, and satisfaction recounted here.

Rappaport, Bruce M. *The Open Adoption Book: A Guide to Adoption without Tears.* Macmillan, 1992. 195p. index. LC 91-42800. ISBN 0-02-601105-0. $20.00.

The psychological aspects of open adoption, the process in which birth parents and adoptive parents select each other and have ongoing contact over the years, are explored in this handbook. Written by the founder and director of an independent agency, the text examines the impact of infertility, birth parent stereotypes and realities, the initial bond and ongoing relations between adoptive parents and birth parents, the impact of open adoption on the adopted child, and the role of counseling. Procedural steps in the adoptive process are briefly outlined, but the emphasis is on what open adoption feels like, not how to carry it out. An appendix lists agencies that perform open adoptions.

* Register, Cheri. *Are Those Kids Yours?: American Families with Children Adopted from Other Countries.* Free Press, 1990. 240p. bibliog. index. LC 90-37734. ISBN 0-02-925750-6. $22.50.

Register provides a guide to family life for adoptive parents, especially those adopting children from South American nations, India, and Korea. The psychology of the adoption process is analyzed in detail, including the difficulties arising from combining cultures. The author addresses making the match, coming together, becoming a family, and developing a new family identity, including the new identity as a minority family. This guide informs prospective parents of the realities of international adoption. Accounts of adoptive parents and adoptees illustrate the truth behind the images presented in the media.

Schaefer, Carol. *The Other Mother: A Woman's Love for the Child She Gave Up for Adoption.* Soho, 1991. 295p. LC 90-39201. ISBN 0-939149-41-9. $19.95.

The emotions behind the facts of adoption are revealed in this memoir from a once unwed mother who in 1965 was persuaded, and not very sympathetically, to give up her child for adoption by her parents, boyfriend, and religious advi-

sors. From the vantage point of contemporary standards, her parent's desire for secrecy, her confinement in a Catholic home for unwed mothers, the reluctance of hospital personnel to allow contact with the baby, and the finality with which she was to resume her life as a carefree college student sound particularly harrowing. The lifelong process of longing, the search, eventual contact, and ultimately joyous reunion capture the impact of adoption on the lives of all who are involved but most deeply the feelings of a mother who loves and yet may not raise her child.

* Schaffer, Judith. *How to Raise an Adopted Child: A Guide to Help Your Child Flourish from Infancy through Adolescence.* Plume, 1991. 310p. LC 90-46612. ISBN 0-452-26560-6. $8.95.

Schaffer reviews the stages of growth and development that each child passes through from infancy to adolescence, concentrating on the complications that adopted children and their parents may experience. She begins with an overview of adoption issues, such as degree of openness, questions about the past, and rejection, and concludes with advice for adoptive parents in special circumstances, including multiracial families, single parents, and parents of special needs children. Each chapter provides questions and answers about topics of interest to adoptive parents, such as obtaining family support, telling teachers, and searching for an adolescent's birth mother. An appendix lists agencies that provide help.

Siegel, Stephanie. *Parenting Your Adopted Child.* Prentice Hall, 1990. 204p. bibliog. index. LC 88-19711. ISBN 0-13-815325-6. $17.95.

Siegel's personal experience as an adoptive mother of three and professional expertise as a family therapist specializing in infertility and adoption information enhance the practical advice and psychological approach of this self-help parenting handbook. Pointing out that infertility is the motivation for many couples' desire to adopt, the author incorporates material on acknowledging and accepting infertility and its effect throughout the course of parenting children from infancy to adolescence in addition to information on parenting the adopted child through those stages. Issues that all parents must face in raising their children are summarized, and special issues relating to adoption are described in greater detail. How to cope with issues of rejection, abandonment, defectiveness, and identity on the child's part and inadequacy and also rejection if the child wishes contact with the birth parents on the parents' part throughout the life span is an important focus of this parenting manual.

Stephenson, Mary. *My Child Is a Mother.* Corona, 1991. 253p. LC 91-70759. ISBN 0-931722-87-X. $16.95.

The practice of open adoption is explored in this autobiographical account from the birth grandmother who supported her teenage daughter's pursuit of this option. Drawn from memories recorded in a personal journal, her narrative covers learning of the pregnancy, accompanying her daughter to pre-adoption counseling, reviewing resumes, meeting the prospective parents, and observing the bond that developed between them and her daughter. The details of the birth, postpartum depression, and healing are carefully recorded, including much dialogue. Her daughter's continued contact with the baby and her adoptive family is a positive outcome enjoyed by all participants in this unusual adoption triangle. The text includes a foreword by the adoptive family.

Van Gulden, Holly, and Lisa M. Bartels-Rabb. *Real Parents, Real Children: Parenting the Adopted Child*. Crossroad, 1993. 279p. bibliog. illus. index. LC 93-27784. ISBN 0-8245-1368-1. $22.95.

Developmental theory guides this exploration of issues that parents may need to address when adopting children at various ages, from birth to adolescence. The first few chapters focus on general concerns such as bonding, loss and grief, pre- and post-placement stress, an adopted child's sense of identity and the desirability of timing the move to a new household. The bulk of this handbook features detailed discussions on adoption issues specific to each age group, including typical developmental milestones at each age, family cycle issues, the process of moving the child, and what to do if the parent-child relationship does not develop well. The final chapters address, in general terms, such concerns as school, adoption issues in adulthood, and qualities of a healthy family.

* Watkins, Mary, and Susan M. Fisher. *Talking with Young Children about Adoption*. Yale University, 1993. 256p. LC 92-44529. ISBN 0-300-05178-6. $27.50.

A psychologist and a psychoanalyst, both adoptive mothers, team up to provide parents and adoption professionals with advice on how to discuss adoption with children whose understanding of it evolves over time. Recognizing that the meaning of adoption varies depending on how a child is told and when, as well as how that child's reactions are shared and respected, the authors recount stories of concrete family life to reveal what open discussions sound like, the contexts in which they take place, and how parents and children experience them emotionally. The longest section of the book presents these stories; the psychological work that parents must do to prepare for satisfactory conversation, adoption research and how to interpret it, and children's conceptions of adoption are also covered.

POPULAR TITLES: JOURNALS

Adoptalk. North American Council on Adoptable Children. 1976. Q. ISSN 0273-6497. $25.00.

An important focus of this newsletter from the North American Council on Adoptable Children is providing reviews of recent books and summaries of research on adoptions. Brief articles address special needs and international adoption, foster care, federal legislation, and parents' experiences. The newsletter lists upcoming conferences and covers news about the association's work.

Adoptive Families. (Formerly *OURS Magazine*). Adoptive Families of America. 1994. B-M. ISSN 1076-1020. $16.00.

Adoptive Families, a new magazine (July/August 1994) from Adoptive Families of America, a parent support group, provides adoptive parents with in-depth information, anecdotes, and advice on adoption issues that is based on experience. Greater emphasis is given in the new magazine to parenting tips, stories by and about adoptive families, and developmental information provided by experts. Each issue will provide an article targeted

to families waiting to adopt, a feature focusing on birth parent issues, and biographical profiles. Regular columns giving advice, book reviews, pen pal connections, and information for single adoptive parents are also included in each full-color issue.

PROFESSIONAL TITLES: BOOKS

Adamec, Christine A. *The Encyclopedia of Adoption*. Facts on File, 1991. 382p. LC 91-4629. ISBN 0-8160-2108-2. $45.00.

Arranged alphabetically, the entries in this single-volume encyclopedia cover concepts, practices, associations, and participants related to adoption and focus on how adoption demands a different perspective on topics such as discipline, counseling, or media. The entries themselves define the concept of adoption, provide related statistical or legal data and bibliographic references, and are cross-referenced to related entries when appropriate. They note when a term, such as adoption triangle, has a negative or pejorative cast. The book opens with an informative survey of adoption from the beginning of recorded history through the current state of the adoption system in the United States. The volume summarizes current knowledge on adoption from a variety of perspectives and provides much statistical and directory information in a series of appendixes.

Brodzinsky, David M., and Marshall D. Schechter, eds. *The Psychology of Adoption*. Oxford University Press, 1990. 396p. bibliog. index. LC 89-2902. ISBN 0-19-504892-X. $39.95.

This anthology provides a state-of-the-art review of the mental health dimensions of adoption as it affects birth parents, adoptive parents, and the adoptees themselves. Divided into four sections, the essays examine theoretical perspectives on adoption, including stress and coping and psychoanalytic and biologic approaches; results of a variety of studies on such aspects of adoption as outcome, identity formation, interracial adoption issues, and disruption; clinical issues in counseling adoptive family members; and social policy issues, such as the impact on the birth mother of surrendering an infant, open adoption, and adoption by foster parents. Each contribution is organized to provide a concise summary of the issues to be addressed, a brief history, a literature review, and conclusions. The text, a scholarly examination of the changing nature and impact of adoption, is intended to inform and assist mental health professionals in their practice.

Brodzinsky, David M., Marshall D. Schechter, and Robin Marantz Henig. *Being Adopted: The Lifelong Search for Self*. Doubleday, 1992. 240p. bibliog. index. LC 91-30849. ISBN 0-385-41402-1. $22.00.

Erik Erickson's model of the life cycle is used to explore how adoptees' reactions to being adopted affect their lifelong search for self-identity. Using clinical experiences, interview data, and the scholarly literature, the authors examine the impact of adoption on anticipated developmental tasks in infancy, toddlerhood and the preschool years, middle childhood, and late adulthood. For example, because they are the featured characters, children enjoy their adoption story; once they develop logical thinking skills, they realize that to be "chosen" they first had to be given away. The authors provide similar insights, accompanied by case histories and illustrative quotes, for the other stages of the life cycle. They point out in a final chapter on the future that increased prevalence of nontraditional families and reproductive technology will make it more acceptable to have two sets of parents or unknown parents. This is a readable account for social service and mental health practitioners and adoptees as well.

Glidden, Laraine Masters, ed. *Formed Families: Adoption of Children with Handicaps.* Haworth, 1990. 242p. LC 90-4295. ISBN 0-86656-914-6. $29.95.

The essays in this anthology review the history and current status of adoption of children with mental, physical, and emotional disabilities. Contributors examine the characteristics of these adoptions, the process of forming a family when adoptive children have handicaps, factors that affect positively or negatively their placements, and the results, generally positive, of these adoptions. Among the specific topics addressed are who places children with disabilities and why; laws, including those related to terminating parental rights; barriers; sources of national data on who selects special needs children to adopt; and follow-up services for families whose bonding process has stalled or broken down. A small amount of case material personalizes this scholarly review of the practice of special needs adoptions today.

Hoffmann-Riem, Christa. *The Adopted Child: Family Life with Double Parenthood.* Transaction, 1990. 305p. bibliog. index. LC 89-4609. ISBN 0-88738-241-X. $32.95.

The author, a professor of sociology at the University of Hamburg, interviewed 30 German families to identify how adoptive families differ from "normal" ones and to explore how issues of identity, stigma, secrecy and disclosure, and public versus private life affect contemporary adoptive families. Most of the couples in her sample married in order to have children and chose adoption to "feel like a family" when infertility prevented them from doing so. The lengthy and uncertain placement process replaces the course of nature with the procedures of a social bureaucracy, but parents regain their autonomy when they choose and establish rapport with a child. Adoptive families achieve emotional normalization through naming the child, reconstructing their past, and constructing physical resemblances. In concluding her study of the impact of adoption, Hoffmann-Riem notes that the skill with which adoptive families deal with differences may provide guidelines for other types of families, such as stepfamilies, that are not based on biological ties.

Komar, Miriam. *Communicating with the Adopted Child.* Walker, 1990. 282p. LC 90-38340. ISBN 0-8027-1124-3. $21.95.

Adapted to the needs of the adoptive family, basic guidelines on communicating with children are provided here. The author, a social worker, advises parents on common issues such as being chosen, timing the moment of telling, nurturing self-esteem, dealing with two cultural heritages, and sex and commitment in and outside of marriage. Lots of anecdotal information is provided to clarify the guidelines presented and give examples of their application.

Reitz, Miriam, and Kenneth Watson. *Adoption and the Family System: Strategies for Treatment.* Guilford, 1992. 340p. bibliog. index. LC 91-44266. ISBN 0-89862-797-4. $30.00. ISBN 0-89862-033-3 pbk. Price not given.

For mental health professionals, this handbook explores in detail the issues and complications involved in counseling members of adoptive families, the birth parents, adoptees, and adoptive parents. Affiliation problems in adoption, therapy for adoptive families with young children and those with adolescents or young adults, the adoptee as spouse and parent, issues in the search and reunion process, open adoptions, and adoption issues in divorced, stepfamilies, or single-parent families are some of the areas covered. Reactions to secrecy about the adoption, parent-child mismatch conflicts, and obesity/eating disorder problems are also addressed. The introductory chapter, which discusses myths of adoption, therapeutic assessment skills, and general treatment strategies, provides context and explores fallacies about birth parents, providing services to birth parents, and, in the context of forming an adoptive family, marital therapy for infertile couples. The authors draw heavily from the results of prior research to substantiate their insights and advice and liberally use case studies to illustrate the complexity and subtlety of the issues that may motivate adoptive families to seek intervention. Both sources of data confirm the validity of the authors' perspective that adoption links birth and adoptive families into a lifelong kinship network.

Roles, Patricia. *Saying Goodbye to a Baby, Volume 1: A Book about Loss and Grief in Adoption.* Child Welfare League, 1989. 92p. ISBN 0-87868-387-9. $12.95. *Saying Goodbye to a Baby, Volume 2: A Counselor's Guide to Birthparent Grief and Loss.* Child Welfare League, 1990. LC 89-25451. ISBN 0-87868-393-3. $10.95.

Though grief is a normal reaction to loss, the grief of birth parents who relinquish a child for adoption has not been recognized, due in part to the social stigma of unwed pregnancy and in part to the belief that adoption satisfactorily meets the needs of all three parties in the adoption triangle. This sensitive guide from a social worker who as a youth relinquished her child covers the emotions birth mothers experience in pregnancy and birth. The birth mother's decision to relinquish her child for adoption and the feelings of loss and grief that adoption generates, both immediate and lasting, are covered in the first volume. The content also includes interactions with friends and family, the reunion process, and sources of outside assistance. In the second volume, much of this material is summarized in the first chapter. Additional information on interventions at the community and individual levels, suggestions for counseling clients, and worksheets that summarize these issues are also provided in volume 2.

Rosenthal, James Aaron. *Special Needs Adoption: A Study of Intact Families.* Praeger. 1992. 240p. LC 91-30278. ISBN 0-275-93790-9. $42.95.

To normalize adoptive family functioning, inform practitioners, make recommendations for policymakers, and compile baseline data for a field that is only 20-odd years old, the authors conducted a detailed investigation of 800 adoptive families of special needs children. They looked at a sample, from the caseloads of state agencies in Illinois, Oklahoma, and Kansas, of families who adopted children who were older, had a history of being abused, physical or mental disability, or behavioral disturbances. In their examination of rewards and differences from the parents' perspective, family functioning, and specific settings such as single-parent families, they discovered the majority of adoptive parents were satisfied and felt rewarded in their adoptions. The results are organized to provide first an overview of the issues in special needs adoptions, followed by the study design and methodology, an examination of parents' perceptions, and special topics such as family dynamics and behavioral problems. The text concludes with a summary of the findings and recommendations for practice.

Samuels, Shirley C. *Ideal Adoption: A Comprehensive Guide to Forming an Adoptive Family.* Plenum, 1990. 263p. bibliog. index. LC 89-28116. ISBN 0-306-43312-5. $20.95.

Defining an "ideal adoption" as one that meets the needs of the adoptive parents, adopted child, and birth parents, this handbook for social service and legal professionals provides a concise overview of adoption practices, past and present, and a review of issues that affect adoptive and birth families. It opens with a review of adoption history and major current issues, such as a decreased number of white infants and an increased number of special needs children, followed by an exploration of the stages of the adoption process and the emotions, problems, and needs of birth parents, adopted children, and the adopting family. Current trends in adoption, including open adoption, the search movement, and special parents, are covered. Appendixes list clearinghouses, parent support and search groups, agencies for intercountry and special needs adoptions, as well as additional readings.

DIRECTORY

Adoptee-Birthparent Support Network (ABSN)
3421 M Street, N.W., Suite 328, Washington, DC 20007-3552
(202) 686-4611 Fax (301) 774-1741
Robyn S. Quinter, Board Member
Founded: 1986
Members: 425
Mission/Goals: To provide support, information, and education to those who have been touched by adoption; to provide guidance in understanding adoption and its effects
Audience/Clientele: Adult adoptees, birthparents, adoptive parents, siblings, adoption professionals, including agency social workers, counselors, attorneys, and physicians
Staff: 12 volunteers
Budget: $8,400 Funding: Dues, donations
Languages: Spanish, sign language
Services: Support group, search services
Education and Outreach: Seminars, publishing
Publications: *The Network News*, a monthly newsletter

Adoptive Families of America (AFA)
333 Highway 100 N, Minneapolis, MN 55422
(612) 535-4829
Susan Freivalds, Executive Director
Founded: 1967
Members: 15,000
Local Groups: 250
Mission/Goals: To provide assistance in problem solving and information about adoption and its challenges to members of adoptive and prospective adoptive families; to encourage successful adoptive placement; to promote the well-being of children without permanent families
Audience/Clientele: Adoptive parents, parents by birth, adoptees, and adoption professionals who share a concern for the welfare of children
Staff: 9
Services: support groups, advocacy, help line, financial aid
Education and Outreach: Publications
Publications: *Adoptive Families*, a bimonthly magazine; *Adoption: How to Begin*, a 156-page booklet for prospective adoptive families; *Adoptive Parent Support Group Leader*, quarterly newsletter; *Parenting Resource Catalog*, an annotated listing of books, games, and audiotapes on adoption, multicultural issues, parenting, special needs, and self-esteem, sources for multicultural dolls, and books for children; educational brochures and flyers
Conference: Annual, with exhibits

American Adoption Congress (AAC)
1000 Connecticut Avenue, N.W., Suite 9, Washington, DC 20036
Toll-free (800) 274-OPEN
Kate Burke, President
Founded: 1978
Mission/Goals: To promote understanding of adoption and the issues it raises through study, teaching, and research; to act as a national clearinghouse and collect, publish, and disseminate information
Audience/Clientele: Adoptive parents, birthparents, and adoptees, organizations interested in adoption
Services: Referrals, speakers' bureau, compiling statistics
Education and Outreach: Seminars, publishing
Publications: *Decree*, quarterly; *Legislative Report*, annual; *Regional Directors' Directory*; *Special Services Directory*
Programs: Annual conference

American Foster Care Resources (AFCR)
P.O. Box 271, King George, VA 22485
(703) 775-7410 Fax (703) 775-7410
Jacob R. Sprouse, Jr., Director
Founded: 1981
Mission/Goals: To educate the public regarding foster care; to recruit and educate foster families
Audience/Clientele: Families, foster families, the general public
Budget: $300,000 Funding: Fees for services or products, grants

Education and Outreach: In-service programs, continuing education courses, seminars, publishing
Publications: *Foster Care Journal*, monthly
Programs: 24 symposia per year

Committee for Single Adoptive Parents (CSAP)

P.O. Box 15084, Chevy Chase, MD 20825
(202) 966-6367
Hope Marindin, Executive Director
Founded: 1973
Members: 350
Former Name: Single Parents Committee
Mission/Goals: To serve as an information service to prospective and actual single adoptive parents; to support the right of adoptable children to loving families, regardless of any difference in race, creed, color, or national origin, or of any disability the children may have; to inform public and private agencies of legislation and research applying to single-person adoption
Audience/Clientele: Unmarried women and men, adoption agencies
Staff: 1 nonprofessional, 1 volunteer
Budget: $6,000 Funding: Fees for services or products
Awards: Biennial award to individuals who have contributed to adoption
Services: Referral
Education and Outreach: Publishing
Publications: *Source List*, a biennial list of children awaiting adoption, updated every six months; *The Handbook for Single Adoptive Parents*

Concerned Persons for Adoption (CPFA)

P.O. Box 179, Whippany, NJ 07981
(201) 595-6929
JoAnn Tatz, President
Founded: 1972
Members: 350
Mission/Goals: Volunteer support group dedicated to the belief that every child deserves a family and whose objective is to offer support to the adoptive community
Audience/Clientele: Adoptive parents, adoption agencies, professionals in the field
Staff: 24 board members
Budget: $7,000 Funding: Fund-raising, grants, donations
Services: Support group, recreation, lobbying, fund-raising, advocacy, gathers and distributes to orphanages food, medicine, clothing, etc.
Education and Outreach: Seminars, publishing
Publications: *Adoption Today Newsletter*, monthly September-June; fact sheets and brochures
Programs: Annual conference, monthly meetings

Concerned United Birthparents (CUB)

2000 Walker Street, Des Moines, IA 50317
(515) 263-9558 Toll-free (800) 882-2777
Janet Fenton, President
Founded: 1976
Members: 2,000

Affiliates: 15 state groups
Mission/Goals: To provide mutual support for birthparents, both men and women, who have surrendered children to adoption; to help them cope with the ongoing pains and problems of adoption; to work for adoption reform in law and social policy, preventing unnecessary family separations; to assist adoption-separated relatives in searching for family members; to educate the public about adoption issues and realities
Audience/Clientele: Birthparents, adoptive parents, professionals, and others affected by adoption
Staff: Numerous volunteers
Budget: $45,000 Funding: Donations, dues
Services: Support group, search services
Education and Outreach: In-service programs, publishing
Publications: *Concerned United Birthparents—Communicator*, a monthly newsletter; *Birthparents' Perspective on Adoption*; brochures and booklets
Programs: Annual conference

Families Adopting Children Everywhere (FACE)

P.O. Box 28058, Northwood Station, Baltimore, MD 21239
(301) 239-4252
C. A. Tolley, Executive Director
Founded: 1975
Mission/Goals: To provide support to adoptive parents and families; to collect and disseminate information about adoption
Audience/Clientele: Prospective and current adoptive families, adoption agencies and personnel, adoptive parent support groups
Services: Support group, advocacy, compiling statistics
Education and Outreach: Research, library, seminars, publishing
Publications: *FACE Facts*, bimonthly newsletter; *The FACE Adoption Resource Manual*; booklets
Programs: Monthly meetings

Families for Private Adoption (FPA)

P.O. Box 6375, Washington, DC 20015
(202) 722-0338
Bunny Bart, President
Founded: 1984
Members: 400
Mission/Goals: To assist people who are considering private adoption; to provide them with information on adoption procedures and legal issues
Audience/Clientele: Individuals interested in or who have already adopted children through private adoptions, attorneys, physicians, and social workers
Services: Support group, referral
Education and Outreach: Workshops, publishing
Publications: *FPA Bulletin*, quarterly newsletter; *Successful Private Adoption*, a handbook

Independent Search Consultants (ISC)

P.O. Box 10857, Costa Mesa, CA 92627
Patricia Sanders, Executive Director
Founded: 1980

Members: 80

Mission/Goals: To maintain a network of independent search consultants who specialize in adoption issues; to offer a referral service for searchers

Audience/Clientele: Adoptees, birthparents, adoptive parents, children of divorce, social work professionals

Staff: 2 volunteers

Budget: $12,000 Funding: Fees for services or products, dues

Languages: Spanish

Services: Counseling, search services, referral, certification of search professionals

Education and Outreach: In-service programs, seminars, database development, publishing

Publications: *Searching in New York*, one of a series of publications on searching by state; *The Directory of ISC Consultants*; *The ISC Searchbook*

International Concerns Committee for Children (ICCC)

911 Cypress Drive, Boulder, CO 80303

(303) 494-8333

Anna Marie Merrill, Treasurer

Founded: 1979

Mission/Goals: To acquaint the concerned public with various ways to provide assistance to homeless children; to educate those interested personally and professionally about procedures for adoption; to inform prospective parents about the availability of "waiting children" in the United States and abroad

Audience/Clientele: Prospective adoptive parents, adoption professionals, general public

Staff: 3 volunteers

Budget: $37,000 Funding: Fees for services or products, donations

Services: Counseling, support group, referral

Education and Outreach: Publishing

Publications: *Report on Foreign Adoptions*, annual; *Listing Service*, updated monthly; *Newsletter*, quarterly

Programs: Annual conference

National Adoption Center (NAC)

1500 Walnut Street, Suite 701, Philadelphia, PA 19102

(215) 735-9988 Fax (215) 735-9410 Toll-free (800) TO-ADOPT

Carolyn Johnson, Executive Director

Founded: 1972

Mission/Goals: To promote adoption opportunities for children with special needs, including those who are older or have disabilities, racial minorities, or siblings seeking placement together

Audience/Clientele: Prospective adoptive parents, adoption agencies

Services: Referrals, consultation

Education and Outreach: Library, speakers' bureau, training, publishing

Publications: *National Adoption Center News*, semiannual; *Photolisting*, quarterly; videotapes of waiting children;

bibliography of books for children; brochures and pamphlets

National Adoption Information Clearinghouse (NAIC)

11426 Rockville Pike, Suite 410, Rockville, MD 20852

(301) 231-6512 Fax (301) 984-8527

Debra Smith, A.C.S.W., Director

Founded: 1987

Mission/Goals: To maintain the nation's most comprehensive library of adoption materials in order to answer Americans' questions about adoption; to strengthen adoptive family life

Audience/Clientele: Adopted persons, prospective adoptive parents, adoptive and birth family members, women experiencing a crisis pregnancy, adoption practitioners, students, researchers, the media

Staff: 3 professionals, 3 nonprofessionals

Budget: $250,000 Funding: Federal government, fees for services or products

Services: Counseling (minimal), referral, compiling statistics

Education and Outreach: Library, database development, publishing

Publications: *Adoption Laws: Answers to Most-Asked Questions*; *National Adoption Directory*, with biannual updates; *National Directory of Pregnancy Crisis Centers*; *National Adoption Training and Education Directory*; *Catalog of Audiovisual Materials on Adoption*; variety of fact sheets on adoption issues; directories of adoption-related services

National Coalition to End Racism in America's Child Care System (NCERACCS)

22075 Koths, Taylor, MI 48180

(313) 295-0257

Carol Coccia, President

Founded: 1984

Members: 1,000

Mission/Goals: To ensure that all children needing out-of-home placement, whether foster care or adoption, be placed at the earliest available home most qualified to meet that child's needs; to coordinate efforts of individuals and groups to avoid delays in recruitment and avoid removal of children at a later date to match color or culture; to educate the public and policymakers via the media and other legal means to assure that no child is denied services on the basis of race

Audience/Clientele: Prospective foster and adoptive parents, child care agencies, politicians, attorneys, government agencies, multiracial families, and support groups

Funding: Donations

Services: Referral

Education and Outreach: Workshops, speakers' bureau, publishing

Publications: *The Children's Voice*, a quarterly newsletter covering court decisions, laws, and civil rights regarding issues of race in adoption

National Council for Adoption (NCFA)
1930 17th Street, N.W., Washington, DC 20009
(202) 328-1200 Fax (202) 332-0935 Hotline (202) 328-8072
William Pierce, President
Founded: 1980
Members: 500 individuals, 60 agencies
Former Name: National Committee on Adoption
Mission/Goals: To promote sound, ethical adoption and maternity service practices; to provide information and advocacy for adoption; to monitor legislation; to inform the public that adoption is a loving, natural way to build families
Audience/Clientele: Adoption agencies and maternity homes, adoptive parents and adopted children, adoption practitioners, social workers, and attorneys
Staff: 7 professionals, numerous nonprofessionals and volunteers
Budget: $600,000 Funding: Fund-raising, donations, dues, grants
Services: Referral
Education and Outreach: Continuing education courses, seminars, publishing
Publications: *National Adoption Reports*, bimonthly newsletter; *Memo*; *Legal Notes*, periodic; *Unmarried Parents Today*, a periodic newsletter on pregnancy counseling services; *Annual Report*; *Adoption Factbook*; various pamphlets
Programs: Annual conference

National Foster Parent Association (NFPA)
226 Kilts Drive, Houston, TX 77024
(713) 467-1850 Fax (713) 827-0919
Gordy Evans, Director
Founded: 1972
Members: 3,300
Affiliates: 44 state groups, 71 local groups
Mission/Goals: To enhance the role and position of foster parents in the foster care system; to provide a coalition of all parties in the system; to network with other national organizations addressing children's issues; to communicate via a national newsletter developments of interest in the national program
Audience/Clientele: All parties in the child welfare system, with emphasis on foster parents
Budget: $100,000 Funding: Dues
Services: Support group, referral
Awards: Three or more scholarships a year to youngsters in foster homes; annual awards for foster family of the year and social worker of the year; merit awards
Education and Outreach: Seminars, library, publishing
Publications: *National Advocate*, a bimonthly newsletter; various monographs on foster care issues
Programs: Annual conference

North American Council on Adoptable Children (NACAC)
1821 University Avenue, Suite N498, St. Paul, MN 55104
(612) 644-3036 Fax (612) 644-9848
Joe Kroll, Executive Director
Founded: 1974
Members: 2,500
Mission/Goals: To advocate on the behalf of special needs children in need of adoption and the families who eventually adopt them
Audience/Clientele: Adoptive parents, professionals from law, child welfare, public policy
Staff: 4 FTE professionals, 1 nonprofessional
Budget: $500,000 Funding: Federal government, private sources, fund-raising, fees for services or products, donations, grants, dues
Services: Referral, lobbying, compiling statistics
Awards: Annual awards for outstanding work in the field of special needs adoption
Education and Outreach: Continuing education courses, seminars, publishing
Publications: *Adoptalk*, a quarterly newsletter; various monographs
Programs: Annual conference

Orphan Voyage
2141 Road 2300, Cedaredge, CO 81413
(303) 856-3937
Edwina Hill, Secretary
Founded: 1953
Previous Name: Life History Study Center
Mission/Goals: To encourage the elimination of the sealed record policy; to assist in any way healing from the destructive effects of this policy in the lives of all who have suffered its influence
Audience/Clientele: Any individual or group affected by adoption
Budget: $2,000 Funding: Donations, fees for products
Services: Counseling (informal), search services
Education and Outreach: Library, archives, publishing
Publications: *Orphan Voyage News*, monthly; various books and pamphlets

REFERENCES

1. *Statistical Abstract of the United States*, 12th ed., U.S. Department of Commerce, Bureau of the Census, 1992, 373.

2. Ibid.

CHAPTER

Child Care Options

*No one is able to take your place—your goal is to
find someone who will do a good job in your absence.*
Sonja Flating. *Child Care*

*A child's temperament is
as important a factor to consider as his
age when deciding on appropriate child care.*
Dian G. Smith.
Parents' Guide to Raising Kids in a Changing World

The percentage of mothers employed full-time whose youngest child was 3–4 years of age was 39 percent in 1990; an additional 19 percent of mothers with children this age were employed part-time.[1] Many options for child care are available, including in-home care, family care homes, and child care centers, but the demand far exceeds supply. When choosing between family day care homes and centers, parents questioned in the 1990 Profile of Child Care Settings Survey emphasized warm, loving care, group size, homelike atmosphere, and care givers known to the family. In contrast, training, safety, school preparation, promotion of development, and religious instruction were important considerations for parents who selected a child care center.[2]

Consistent, accessible, reliable, and affordable services are essential components regardless of the type of care chosen.[3] Advice on how to begin the search, conduct interviews, define criteria, evaluate the physical facility and social environment, and prepare one's child for care is readily available for parents' review. Parental guilt, particularly concern about the long-term effects of child care on their children, may be reduced by careful investigation, evaluation, and follow-up on child care choices.

An asterisk (*) indicates a specially recommended title.

POPULAR TITLES: BOOKS

Auerbach, Stevanne. *Keys to Choosing Child Care*. Barron's, 1991. 152p. LC 91-2165. ISBN 0-8120-452-7-0. $5.95.

Brief topical chapters provide parents with checklists, practical tips, and answers to common questions to aid them in understanding types of child care and choosing from among them with a minimum of time and effort. Written by a child care professional, the text covers such issues as qualities of good child care, program characteristics, the search, data gathering techniques, and criteria for evaluating the facility, learning, social environment, and emotional tone.

* Berezin, Judith. *The Complete Guide to Choosing Child Care*. Random House, 1990. 258p. illus. index. LC 90-45487. ISBN 0-6797-310-0-8. $12.95.

Berezin provides a step-by-step guide to determining the type of child care a family needs, locating and evaluating child care services, and making a selection. Child care advocates present the pros and cons of each type of care as well as qualities to look for in in-home care, family day care, child care centers, and camps. The process of screening, interviewing, and visiting providers is thoroughly covered. Numerous checklists for organizing and evaluating information are provided to help parents in making a decision.

The Family Guide to Child Care. Family Service America, 1990. 56p. LC 90-154225. ISBN 0-87304-246-8. $5.95.

Though concise, this booklet from Family Service America, which even a busy parent will have time to read, provides a comprehensive overview of child care options and choices. Among the topics covered are factors in determining what type of care is best for an individual child, how to judge quality, regulations, costs, how to begin the search, criteria for the decision, preparation of the child for starting child care, agreements with the provider, and parental involvement. Special concerns such as abuse, illness, and child care for special needs or school-age children are also addressed. This booklet provides support to unsure parents as well as factual information; for example, parents are advised that the best care available is the care that best meets their needs and values, and that the decision on when to return to work is based on what's best for a particular family.

* Flating, Sonja. *Child Care: A Parent's Guide*. Facts on File, 1991. 173p. bibliog. index. LC 90-40850. ISBN 0-8160-2232-1. $18.95.

Flating's comprehensive guide approaches the child care decision from a mother's perspective, with frequent references to managing guilt, quieting fears, explaining the mother's motivation, and justifying the need for child care. Various options for child care are reviewed, and checklists for judging providers and facilities are provided. The author advises parents how to prepare a child for child care. Lists of national and state referral agencies are included. This guide is thorough and informative but also personal in places, even anecdotal.

Pelletier, Elaine S. *How to Hire a Nanny: A Complete Step-by-Step Guide for Parents*. Andre and Lanier, 1993. 96p. LC 93-0072335. ISBN 0-9635575-7-2. $9.95.

This concise guide assists parents in selecting a live-out nanny as care giver for their child. Based on experience gained by the author and advice from other parents, it provides a simple approach to defining the job, determining the cost, locating the right nanny, ongoing management, and terminating the relationship when circumstances change. Sample interview questions, job descriptions, lists of responsibilities, and work agreements add to the usefulness of the text in helping parents create a safe and stimulating environment for their child. Specific information about IRS and other governmental regulations will reassure parents who are uncertain about their responsibilities as employers.

PROFESSIONAL TITLES: BOOKS

Beardsley, Lyda. *Good Day, Bad Day: The Child's Experience of Child Care*. Teachers College, Columbia University, 1990. 176p. LC 90-040611. ISBN 0-8077-3040-8. $29.00.

Drawing on many years of experience as a consultant, educator, parent, and director of a child care center, Beardsley knowledgeably portrays a day in the life of 15 children at two fictionalized centers, one mediocre, one good. She uses observations, reports from her own children, and research results to demonstrate what differences in several indicators of quality, such as staff training, working conditions, ratio and group size, relations with parents, curriculum, and physical environment, might be. Reality from the child's point of view is portrayed vividly in these two scenarios. In conclusion, she notes that differences in the two programs were largely due to money, that is, to higher wages, better adult work environment, lower staff turnover, a better educated and trained staff, and a lower ratio of staff to children. Knowing that these two programs are fictitious is not reassuring because they are based on stories compiled by the author from real child care settings.

Chehrazi, Shahla S., ed. *Psychosocial Issues in Day Care*. American Psychiatric, 1990. 292p. index. LC 90-561. ISBN 0-88048-310-5. $39.00.

Targeted to a diverse professional constituency, this anthology provides an overview of the developmental, psychological, and social implications of substitute child care. The text is organized into sections that address developmental issues (particularly attachment) and day care, the relationship between providers and parents, and the issues of separation, health and safety concerns, child abuse, and national policy and child care. Other sections address pediatric issues, child abuse, and national day-care policies. The chapters outline clearly the results of research, discuss their implications, and provide explicit conclusions. This comprehensive overview of child care in the United States illustrates how highly charged the issues are and how complex the problems requiring solutions.

Click, Phyllis. *Caring for School Age Children*. Delmar, 1993. 213p. bibliog. photog. illus. index. LC 93-28413. ISBN 0-8273-5411-8. $19.95.

Activities, approaches, and the type of personnel appropriate for providing after-school care for a diverse audience of school-age children are topics explored in this textbook. Much of the text is devoted to curricula, such as indoor and outdoor games, art, music, drama, and science activities, but there is also information on budgets, facilities, community involvement, and other issues of interest to teachers and care givers who administer programs for school-age children. Photographs, boxed information, and illustrations contribute to a useful guide on a topic poorly covered in the popular and professional literature.

Decker, Celia Anita, and John R. Decker. *Planning and Administering Early Childhood Programs*. 5th ed. Macmillan, 1992. 580p. bibliog. index. LC 91-20961. ISBN 0-02-327965-6. Price not given.

Organized to structure the thinking of early childhood administrators as they plan for local programs, this text is divided into three parts that address the framework and rationale, operational considerations, and program services for children and parents. A number of appendixes provide supplementary information such as site licensing and certification agencies, professional organizations, suppliers, sources for federal and philanthropic assistance, tests, and a sample parents' handbook. New to the fifth edition are a balanced focus on all types of early childhood programs, a discussion of the growing need for affordable, quality programs for children from infancy through the primary grades, and identification of the psycho-philosophical perspective the center will follow in making decisions.

Denholm, Roy Ferguson, and Alan Pence, eds. *Professional Child and Youth Care*. Haworth, 1990. 371p. illus. LC 90-4051. ISBN 0-86656-891-3. $34.95.

This sourcebook on the current state of child and youth care is compiled from the contributions of 39 leaders in the field on topics of their choosing. Though the 27 chapters address many themes, including professionalism, supervision and staff relations, administration, practice skills, teamwork, worker roles, education and training, future developments, and public awareness, the unifying principle is an explication of "the child care perspective," a way of understanding the world that evolves solely out of day-to-day care of children.

Donowitz, Leigh G., ed. *Infection Control in the Child Care Center and Preschool*. Williams & Wilkins, 1991. 364p. bibliog. LC 90-12957. ISBN 0-683-02611-9. $32.00.

Preschool children are the age group most susceptible to infectious diseases because they lack prior exposure to them, play in close contact with one another, and often ignore basic hygienic practices. To avoid infectious epidemics in day care, this sourcebook for center administrators provides background information on how infections are spread, proposed policies for staff to minimize transmission, and detailed guidelines for a number of common infections, such as roundworm, thrush, hepatitis A and B, HIV/AIDS, influenza, lice, and measles. These chapters cover cause, epidemiology, diagnosis, treatment, infectious period, and infection control. Special guidelines for protecting children at risk are covered.

Dowd, Frances Smardo. *Latchkey Children in the Library & Community: Issues, Strategies, and Programs*. Oryx, 1991. 232p. bibliog. index. LC 91-3580. ISBN 0-89774-651-1. $24.50.

As the results of surveys conducted by the author in 1988 and 1990 demonstrate, most sizable public libraries are forced to address the presence of unattended, or latchkey, children after school hours. Based on numerous suggestions from respondents, the author recommends that libraries draft explicit policy statements, educate their staffs, organize and cooperate with other community organizations, and design traditional library programs, such as homework and reading assistance or arts and crafts opportunities, for the children who are there. In presenting the survey results, the author also reviews the incidence of factors contributing to the situation, what impact lack of supervision has on latchkey children and their parents, what dilemmas the public librarian faces, and many helpful examples of national and local programs with creative solutions to this problem. An appendix includes the questionnaires and reading lists for children and adults.

Fox, Nathan, and Greta G. Fein, eds. *Infant Day Care*. Ablex, 1990. 215p. bibliog. illus. LC 90-425. ISBN 0-89391-587-4. $35.00.

Originally published in 1988 as a special issue of *Early Childhood Research Quarterly*, the papers in this anthology are divided into two parts. The first part presents the reworking of an influential and controversial review by Jay Belsky that links insecure attachment in infants or later socioemotional difficulties to entering day care under one year of age and spending more than 20 hours a week there, along with the responses of several notable scholars to this finding. The second part includes several specialized studies on infant day care, among them an investigation of the relationship of infant day care to preschool social behavior, a comparison of attachment to mother and to care giver, and an examination of social orientation to peers and adults in an infant care setting. These selections illustrate how complex, how contextual, and, finally, how inconclusive the results of

prior research on this topic are and provide many insights into potentially fruitful topics for investigation.

Hayes, Cheryl D., John L. Palmer, and Martha J. Zaslow, eds. *Who Cares for America's Children: Child Care Policy for the 1990s*. National Academy Press, 1990. 362p. index. LC 90-5813. ISBN 0-309-04032-9. $24.95.

Detailed results and recommendations from a two-year study of U.S. child care services and policies by a panel of experts are presented in this report from the National Research Council. The panel examined available research on the need for services engendered by social change, the effect of child care on children, the quality of that care, the impact of care on physical and psychological development, types of care services, and current governmental and private policies and programs. Summarizing the results obtained, the report emphasizes that existing services are inadequate to meet current and future needs; care is difficult, stressful, and time-consuming for parents to arrange; programs are diverse; and, most disturbing, poor-quality programs threaten children's development. Policy goals and conclusions drawn from this data support enhancing affordability, improving accessibility, and achieving quality through a combination of federal and state subsidies, programs, regulations, and parental leave. Appendixes provide a chart of current regulations for family day care and center care arranged by state and a chart of several current professional standards arranged by criterion.

Hildebrand, Verna. *Management of Child Development Centers*. 2nd ed. Macmillan, 1990. 347p. bibliog. photog. illus. index. LC 88-36888. ISBN 0-02-354522-4. $27.95.

Basic and fundamental principles of management are applied to the administration of child care centers in the second edition of this textbook, which was designed for use in college courses, in courses leading to the Child Development Associate (CDA) competency in administration, and by individuals seeking to improve management skills and knowledge in order to advance. New to this edition is information on accreditation by the National Association for the Education of Young Children (NAEYC), corporate-sponsored child care services, and management theories applicable to child care administration. Hildebrand provides an overview of the management process and then reviews in detail the components of planning, organizing, staffing, leading, monitoring, and controlling for quality. She also looks at the specific child care management tasks of managing financial and special resources, child care safety needs, food service, and instructional programs and communicating with parents and the community. The information provided is concise and clear and is supplemented with additional readings, sample documents, photographs, and exercises.

Miller, Angela Browne. *The Day Care Dilemma: Critical Concerns for American Families*. Plenum, 1990. 316p. bibliog. photog. index. LC 89-26664. ISBN 0-306-43435-0. $23.95.

Though the author of this study of the quality of six different day care settings presents her results within a complex context of philosophical, social, economic, and political issues and implications, what stand out are the results themselves. Despite the fact that the day care centers had many serious deficiencies in terms of their social, psychological, educational, physical, and environmental quality, some clearly documented in the text by photographs, the respondents in a survey of 241 parents who use these services gave them high rankings, leading to the conclusion that parents either have low standards or that they do not understand that the child care service they chose is deficient, or both. While parents uniformly ranked warmth of the staff as their greatest concern, they were clearly uniformed about what constitutes high versus low quality service. Even parents with higher education, parents with higher incomes, and parents who paid higher costs were only slightly more critical, a result that is not surprising when the heterogeneity of services, limited options, and lack of information about services is considered.

Miller introduces the study with a lengthy review of the philosophical, economic, and political underpinnings of the desirability of function versus feeling in child care, the lack of consensus on child care policy for the United States, and the economics of time, money, and options in choosing care. She concludes the book by making a number of policy recommendations, including increased regulation of care, support for parenthood, incentives for workplace care, legal limits on the ratio of care givers to children, and, most importantly, a public rating system for child care settings whose results could be publicized to inform parents just what to request and expect in primary care for their children.

Nelson, Margaret K. *Negotiated Care: The Experience of Family Day Care Providers.* Temple University Press, 1991. 305p. bibliog. index. LC 90-10860. ISBN 0-87722-728-4. $34.95.

By means of extensive interviews and a survey of several hundred current and former family day care providers, a number of their spouses, and a handful of the mothers who employ them, Nelson has assembled an impressive amount of data on the life and times of people who care for children in their homes. She notes that most of the providers studied were married, with one or more children and a commitment to being home to care for their own children. She also explores the tension between a market perspective and informal, reciprocal relationships with the children's mothers, as well as the difficulty in maintaining a "detached attachment" with the children in their care. The problems that such a home-based business can create for the care giver's family are addressed, as is the nature of the controversy over regulation and registration. Sources of turnover are listed. In closing, the author recommends organization of a family day care system that would reduce isolation of care givers, provide them with more reliable respite services than family or friends currently do, enhance income, and improve their training and skills. The methodology is explained in detail in an appendix.

Sciarra, Dorothy J., and Anne G. Dorsey. *Developing and Administering a Child Care Center.* 2nd ed. Delmar, 1990. 418p. bibliog. index. LC 89-16892. ISBN 0-8273-3666-7. Price not given.

Numerous sample forms and policy documents make this textbook on how to plan, set up, and operate a preschool a helpful sourcebook for experienced directors of ongoing programs as well as an introduction to the field. The authors emphasize effective interpersonal relationships with parents and staff as a basis for performing the management functions of a child care center administrator. The text covers assessing needs and establishing a program; licensing and certification; organizing and working with all advisory boards; budgeting and fund-raising; choosing equipment and staffing; selecting, grouping, and enrolling the children; managing food, health, and safety components; relating to parents, volunteers, and community; evaluating programs; promoting staff development; and choosing an effective management style. Changes from the first edition include expanded information on liability, infant care, sick child care, accreditation, and use of computers for administrative tasks. In addition to sample documents, the text also includes practical tips from practicing administrators in "director's corner" sidebars, exercises and assignments for students at the end of each chapter, and several appendixes that cover sources for materials, a bibliography, lists of professional regulations, information sources, and a list of periodicals and other media.

Shell, Ellen Ruppel. *A Child's Place: A Year in the Life of a Day Care Center.* Little, Brown, 1992. 272p. bibliog. LC 91-39218. ISBN 0-316-78376-5. $19.95.

This tale of a year in the life of a day care center in Cambridge, MA, highlights stories of the children, parents, and staff who make up its community. The narrative catalogs the emergence of issues such as prior difficult experiences with family day care, staff burnout, the role of licensing, allegations of abuse, the place of a rigorous curriculum in preschool, integration of families from different ethnic backgrounds, and fund raising. Transitions in the staffing, facilities, and philosophy of the center are described, as is the history of child care services in the United States. The memorable personal stories provide insights for parents into the hidden world of the day care center.

Zinsser, Caroline. *Raised in East Urban: Child Care Changes in a Working Class Community.* Teachers College, Columbia University, 1991. 187p. bibliog. index. LC 91-23654. ISBN 0-8077-3140-4. $17.95.

An ethnographic approach was used by the author to examine child care arrangements in a close community of first-, second-, and third-generation working- and lower-middle-class Italian Americans. After describing the community, Zinsser looks at individual cases that illustrate the strengths and weaknesses of nonregulated care; the impact of choices, cost, and quality of care on the parents; the motivation and experiences of "babysitters" or home day care providers; and conditions in several day care centers in the community used by families outside the majority immigrant group. This text illustrates the nature of day care options currently available to parents in the United States.

PROFESSIONAL TITLES: JOURNALS

Child and Youth Care Forum. Human Sciences Press. 1971. Q. ISSN 0893-0848. $87.00.

Aimed at child and adolescent care practitioners, supervisors, and educators, this independent scholarly journal covers practice, theory and research, selection and training, and other professional issues in day care and residential settings. Articles, some in topical issues, cover a broad range of subjects, including the developmental impact of heavy metal music, use of animals as therapeutic aids, and spatial arrangements in a family day care home.

Child Care Information Exchange. Exchange Press. 1978. B-M. ISSN 0016-8527. $25.00.

A news magazine targeted to directors of child care programs, this journal provides feature articles on staff development and training, communication with parents, and recommended books for children. Regular departments address practical management tips, biographies, continuing education announcements, health care information, products, and reviews. Each issue contains a "workshop" that may be copied for parents; topics addressed in past issues include ethnic culture and play.

Day Care and Early Education. Human Sciences Press. 1973. Q. ISSN 0092-4199. $49.00.

Practical articles designed to appeal to a broad range of care givers working with young children are the focus of this journal. Subjects covered include curricula, child care programs, administration, staff development, family-school relationships, facilities, child development, infant-toddler programs, and similar subjects. Innovative approaches with concrete examples drawn from the author's experience are preferred, as are pieces that advocate for the well-being of children.

Day Care U.S.A. Newsletter. United Communications Group. B-W. 1982. $229.00.

Tersely written but informative, this newsletter provides detailed accounts of federal legislation and regulations related to child care practices. Information on how to obtain resources such as catalogs and government publications and news on conferences and continuing education opportunities is provided in each biweekly issue. The newsletter is costly but substantive.

Early Childhood News. Peter Li, Inc. 1989. B-M. $24.00.

Administrators and owners of child care programs for children from six weeks of age will find this newsletter, which covers significant trends in the field, new products, and administrative issues, useful. Regular departments provide information on nutrition, equipment, legislative actions, news from the field, as well as editorials, book and media reviews, and advice to parents.

School Age Notes. School Age Notes. 1980. M. ISSN 0278-3126. $19.95.

This newsletter provides tips on curricula, guidance on administrative issues, and brief reports on recent research related to before- and after-school programs for children and youth. News items, resources, legislative updates, and announcements are also covered in this informative guide for child care professionals. One issue addressed summer projects, creative dramatics, and a summary of the National Study of Before- and After-School Programs released by the U.S. Department of Education.

DIRECTORY

Child Care Action Campaign (CCAC)
330 Seventh Avenue, 17th Floor, New York, NY 10001
(212) 239-0138 Fax (212) 268-6515
Barbara Reisman, Executive Director

Founded: 1983
Members: 3,500
Previous Name: Child Care Now
Mission/Goals: To stimulate and support the development of policies and programs that will increase the availability of quality affordable child care for the benefit of children, their families, and the economic well-being of the nation
Audience/Clientele: Parents, child care providers, educators, employers, corporate and government policymakers
Staff: 15 professionals, varying number of interns (average 4)
Budget: $1,100,000 Funding: Fund-raising, fees for services or products, donations, grants, dues
Services: Advocacy, research
Education and Outreach: Library, publishing
Publications: *Child Care Action News*, bimonthly newsletter for parents on developments in the field; *An Employer's Guide to Child Care Consultants*; summaries of 28 important family issues related to child care policy and advocacy, employers and child care, information for parents, and child care services
Programs: Annual conference

Child Care Employee Project
6536 Telegraph Avenue, Suite 201A, Oakland, CA 94609
(510) 653-9889 Fax (510) 653-8385 Hotline (800) 879-6784
Marcy Whitebook, Executive Director
Founded: 1982
Members: 1,200
Mission/Goals: To improve the quality of child care in America through raising the wages, status, and working conditions of child care providers
Audience/Clientele: Child care providers, directors, and parents
Staff: 5 professionals, 3 nonprofessionals, 12 volunteers
Funding: Private sources, fund-raising, fees for products, donations, grants
Services: Counseling, search services, referral, lobbying, fund-raising
Education and Outreach: In-service programs, seminars, library, archives, publishing, National Worthy Wage Day campaign
Publications: *Child Care Employee News*, quarterly newsletter; *National Child Care Staffing Study*; various brochures

The Children's Foundation (TCF)
725 15th Street, N.W., No. 505, Washington, DC 20005-2109
(202) 347-3300
Kay Hollestelle, Executive Director
Founded: 1969
Mission/Goals: To provide information to families on issues of critical concern, such as child care and child support
Staff: 3 professionals, 1 nonprofessional, 2 volunteers
Budget: $300,000 Funding: Fees for services or products, donations, grants

Services: Counseling, support group, search services, lobbying, compiling statistics

Education and Outreach: In-service programs, continuing education courses, publishing

Publications: *Directory of Child Care Support Groups*; *Family Day Care Bulletin*, quarterly newsletter; licensing studies on child care regulations

Council for Early Childhood Professional Recognition (CECPR)

1341 G Street, N.W., Suite 400, Washington, DC 20005
(202) 265-9090 Fax (202) 265-9161 Toll-free (800) 424-4310
Carol Phillips, Ph.D., Executive Director
Founded: 1975
Members: 40,000
Previous Name: Child Development Associate National Credentialling Program

Mission/Goals: To improve the quality of child care nationally; to accomplish this via a credentialing program for child care workers, the CDA, a nationally recognized credential based on performance

Funding: Federal government, fees for services or products

Services: Child care accreditation

Awards: CDA credential awarded after a candidate successfully completes the CDA assessment

Education and Outreach: In-service programs, seminars, publishing

Publications: *Competence* newsletter; CDA Information Brochure

National Association for Family Day Care (NAFDC)

725 15th Street, N.W., Suite 505, Washington, DC 20005
(202) 347-3356 Toll-free (800) 359-3817
Linda Geigle, President
Founded: 1982
Members: 2,500

Mission/Goals: To serve as a national voice for family day care providers; to promote quality standards for all day care operations

Audience/Clientele: Parents, advocates, and providers of family day care services

Services: National Assessment and Credentialling Program; compiling statistics

Education and Outreach: Speakers' bureau, publishing

Publications: *National Association for Family Day Care—National Perspective*, bimonthly newsletter

Programs: Biennial conference

National Coalition for Campus Child Care, Inc. (NCCCC)

P.O. Box 258, Cascade, WI 53011
(414) 528-7080
Jane Ann Thomas, President
Founded: 1980
Members: 450

Previous Names: Robert F. Kennedy Council for Campus Child Care; National Campus Child Care Council

Mission/Goals: To promote the existence of quality campus child care programs in diverse settings; to provide information on operating campus child care services; to advocate for the needs of children and families in the fields of education and public policy

Audience/Clientele: College and university campus children's centers' administrators and staff, which may include professionals in academic divisions, human resources, or student services, early childhood development faculty and administrators, parent support groups

Staff: 1 nonprofessional, governing board of 16

Budget: $35,000 Funding: Grants, dues, annual conference

Services: Support group, networking, compiling statistics, consulting for campuses starting child care centers

Education and Outreach: Continuing education courses, database development, publishing

Publications: *Newsletter*, semiannual; lists of campus child care centers, books, and bibliographies

Programs: Annual conference

Southern Early Childhood Association (SECA)

P.O. Box 56130, Little Rock, AR 72215
(501) 663-0353
Jane Alexander, Administrative Services Director
Founded: 1949
Members: 19,000
Affiliates: 14 state groups

Mission/Goals: To improve the quality of life for children and families who reside in the South

Audience/Clientele: Preschool teachers, program administrators, early childhood teacher educators, Head Start teachers, kindergarten and primary grade teachers, public school principals, infant and toddler care givers, parents, child advocates, and policymakers

Staff: 2.5 FTE professionals, 1 nonprofessional, 2 volunteers

Budget: $400,000 Funding: Fund-raising, fees for services or products, donations, grants, dues

Education and Outreach: In-service programs, seminars, publishing

Publications: *Dimensions on Early Childhood*, quarterly; various books and videos

Programs: Annual conference

REFERENCES

1. Barbara Willer et al., *Demand and Supply of Child Care in 1990* (Washington, DC: National Association for the Education of Young Children, 1990), 8.

2. Ibid.

3. Stevanne Auerbach, *Keys to Choosing Child Care* (Hauppage, NY: Barron's, 1991), 23.

PART

3

DAILY CARE ACCORDING

TO AGE

CHAPTER

9

Infants and Newborns

Your child is the greatest gift you will ever receive.
Steven P. Shelov, ed.
Caring for Your Baby and Young Child

It is not uncommon, as you gaze at
your sleeping newborn, to wonder when
his parents will arrive, because you do not
feel as though you are old enough to be a parent!
Jeanne Driscoll and Marsha Walker.
Taking Care of Your New Baby

The largest segment of self-help books on child rearing addresses the daily care and development of newborns and infants through the first year of life. Since 1989, the number of children born each year in the United States has risen above four million.[1] Adjusting to a new person in the home and learning how to care for the simple but relentless needs of a dependent little being are challenging tasks for new parents. What new parents do not know is astonishing, and though they learn what satisfies their baby through trial and error, a multitude of guides are available to help. Covering such topics as bathing, diapering, comforting, and other aspects of daily care, these books advise on developmental stages and milestones, provide reassurance, and simply commiserate with new parents shocked by the enormity of their responsibility and the rigors of a newborn's sleep and wake schedule. New parents whose babies are fussy and demand more attention are especially in need of reassurance about their child care skills.

An asterisk (*) indicates a specially recommended title.

POPULAR TITLES: BOOKS

* Brazelton, T. Berry, and Bertrand G. Cramer. *The Earliest Relationship: Parents, Infants, and the Drama of Early Attachment.* Addison-Wesley, 1990. 352p. LC 89-39839. ISBN 0-201-10639-6. $19.95. ISBN 0-201-56764-4 pbk. $10.95.

    A combination of research on infant psychology and behavior, this survey from Brazelton and Cramer addresses how attachment grows in the mother and father, from the initial desire for a child through birth. The authors look at how an infant participates and contributes to the parent-child relationship via its reflexes, sensory capacity, and states of consciousness, then review the methods and results of interaction studies, which reveal the psychological underpinnings of how individual parents interact with their children. The interplay between the infant's personality and the parents' reactions and fantasies is then thoroughly illustrated in nine case histories that present interdisciplinary treatment of troubled parent-infant attachments. The initial chapters on attachment are a remarkably thorough and moving account of this process, while the second section on how the infant plays an active role in the parent-child relationship is a clear, concise treatment and an important contribution to the popular literature on parenting.

Burck, Frances Wells. *Babysense: A Practical and Supportive Guide to Baby Care*. St. Martin's, 1991. 448p. LC 90-19119. ISBN 0-312-05055-0. $29.95.

This oversize sourcebook, written by a parent to provide support as well as practical information to other new parents, covers basic information on feeding, crying, sleeping, and other infant activities and confronts the issues of child care, getting acquainted, and adjusting to motherhood. The lively format includes numerous illustrations, sidebars, and recommended readings. The "we're-all-in-it-together" approach is reassuring to new mothers who are not yet confident of their knowledge or skills, but very little mention is made of the father or his role in child rearing.

Cooper, Grace C. *Parenting Curriculum*. Child Welfare League of America, 1973. illus. ISBN 0-87868-998-2. $24.95.

Six workbooks written in a style appropriate for adolescent parents cover basics about prenatal development; bathing infants, feeding them, and tending to other matters of daily care; bonding; understanding developmental stages; child care; and child-proofing the home. Advice to mothers on exercise, scheduling, dating, and marriage is also given. Numerous line drawings illustrate the text, which is formatted in short lines of uneven length for easy assimilation.

Cramer, Bertrand G. *The Importance of Being Baby*. Addison-Wesley, 1992. 203p. bibliog. illus. index. LC 91-33404. ISBN 0-201-57718-6. $17.95.

There is more than one patient in infant psychiatry: the baby and the mother, and, in some instances, the father too. Using case material, the author presents the family drama carried to an unhealthy extreme, with babies performing scripts from their parents' childhoods that render them ill, isolated, neglected, or worse. To alleviate such symptoms as regurgitation, anorexia, and aggressiveness requires the infant psychiatrist to cure the parents' conflicts, anxieties, and fantasies that determine the messages they convey to their infants on how to behave. Noting that new babies cause stress and upheaval, often unanticipated, in their parents, the author concludes by describing how discovering the real child and banishing the ghostly images from the past brings about harmony in the relationship of parents and infants.

* Driscoll, Jeanne Watson, and Marsha Walker. *Taking Care of Your New Baby: A Guide to Infant Care*. Avery, 1989. 162p. LC 89-6536. ISBN 0-89529-397-8. $6.95.

Concise and disarmingly cheerful, this sourcebook reviews basic information on infants and their care, such as feeding, elimination, crying, and bathing. Practical advice on postpartum adjustment in both the mother and father is also provided. The authors, two registered nurses, maintain a warm but professionally practical tone throughout. They emphasize that they are providing guidance, not rules, as each infant is unique and requires individualized care.

Eisenberg, Arlene, Heidi G. Muricoff, and Sandee E. Hathaway. *What to Expect the First Year*. Workman, 1989. 671p. illus. index. LC 87-40647. ISBN 0-89480-577-0. $12.95.

This encyclopedic companion to the popular *What to Expect When You're Expecting* (Workman, 1991) addresses common concerns of new mothers—daily care, health and safety, and development of the baby—on a month-by-month basis. Each chapter covers how the baby acts, what to expect at checkups, feeding concerns, and other important facts to know. Boxed information reviews developmental milestones achieved by 90 percent of babies at a certain age, also those that 25 percent to 75 percent of infants at those ages master. Introductory chapters cover buying for the baby and other preparations that need to be made. In the second section special concerns, such as seasonal issues, illnesses, adoption, developmental disabilities, and fatherhood, are covered. This easily accessible text also provides a ready-reference section of recipes, home remedies, common illnesses, and height/weight charts.

The Good Housekeeping Illustrated Book of Pregnancy and Baby Care. Morrow, 1990. 256p. photog. illus. index. LC 90-81176. ISBN 0-688-09667-0. $22.95.

Basic aspects of pregnancy and birth, infant and baby care, and health care/first aid are covered in this heavily illustrated textbook from *Good Housekeeping*. In the first section, explicit color photographs, drawings, and charts thoroughly illustrate information and advice on pregnancy, including planning the pregnancy, physical changes in mother and child, tests, relaxation and fitness, diet, labor aids, stages of labor, monitoring, and cesarean delivery. In the second section, the same approach is used to inform new mothers and fathers about the first weeks of life, feeding, sleeping, bathing, diapering, and other aspects of daily care. The third section covers health care, including safety, infectious diseases, injuries, first aid, and common symptoms such as fever. This is the best illustrated guide of its type.

Hill, Barbara Albers. *Baby Tactics: Parenting Tips That Really Work*. Avery, 1991. 160p. bibliog. index. LC 91-24672. ISBN 0-89529-489-3. $8.95.

Quick, practical solutions to a dozen common infant care problems, gathered from parents, professionals, and a few celebrities, form the content of this how-to guide. Sleeping, bathing, baby-sitters, play, and car travel are some of the topics addressed. Access is accomplished through the table of contents, which divides the material covered into two sections, newborn to eight months and nine to fifteen months.

Jones, Carl. *After the Baby Is Born*. Holt, 1990. 196p. bibliog. photog. index. LC 89-27386. ISBN 0-8050-1224-9. $8.95.

Covering the postpartum period of the first eight weeks after birth, this practical guide helps both parents adjust to the changes in themselves and their life together that a new baby brings. Jones, a popular parenting writer, gives advice on making the first hours after birth the most rewarding, understanding and monitoring physical changes in the mother, dealing with both parents' emotional reactions to their new responsibilities, and relieving minor postpartum discomfort. On sensitive topics that parents may be reluctant to bring up in a child care education class, such as natural body image, getting back into pre-pregnancy shape, father's jealousy toward the baby, and resuming lovemaking, this guide provides clear and sensitively presented information that will assist parents experiencing these challenging aspects of giving birth. The appendixes provide lists of additional readings and support groups, which supplement the practical advice provided in this text.

Landis, Dylan. *Checklist for Your New Baby*. Perigee, 1991. 109p. LC 90-25434. ISBN 0-399-51657-3. $5.95.

Landis's simple checklist of basic items required for infant care tells the best and worst features to watch out for; how to save money by improvising, foregoing unnecessary but attractive luxuries, and purchasing secondhand items that are safe; and how to be an informed shopper. Each chapter is devoted to a major type of product, such as car seats, clothing, diapers, strollers, carriers, and toys, and covers safety considerations, when multiples are needed, and what makes the items useful. Helpful lists provide a prenatal timetable for planning purchases, a gift list or "baby registry," and a selection of the best mail order catalogs. Only one shortcoming is evident in this comprehensive guide by a journalist: additional readings are mentioned in the text but full bibliographic information is not provided.

* Leach, Penelope. *Babyhood: Stage by Stage, from Birth to Age Two: How Your Baby Develops Physically, Emotionally, Mentally*. Knopf, 1983. 413p. bibliog. illus. index. LC 82-48881. ISBN 0-394-53092-6. $17.95. ISBN 0-394-71463-9 pbk. $14.95.

Though presented by Leach as "an easy overview" of how infants develop, this handbook is, in fact, a detailed review of research data that provides a comprehensive psychological and physical portrait of the infant at consecutive stages of development. Each stage has a theme that describes the major developmental tasks involved, such as settling into life in the first six weeks, establishing patterns from age six weeks to three months, and discovering other people from age three months to six months. This book is helpful to parents because it will provide them with an understanding of why their baby behaves as he or she does, and how the experts know that their theories are correct.

* Lief, Nina R., with Mary Ellen Fahs. *The First Year of Life: The Early Childhood Development Series*. Walker, 1991. 273p. bibliog. photog. index. LC 91-11501. ISBN 0-8027-1153-7. $24.95. ISBN 0-8027-7349-4 pbk. $12.95.

Small group discussions among participants in a parenting group form the basis of this handbook on a child's emotional and social development and the importance of parent-child interaction during the first 52 weeks of life. The material is organized into 12 chapters covering five-week intervals beginning with week four, each focusing on developmental highlights of the period followed by transcripts of the discussions on related topics and the parents' feelings about their roles. The approach is straightforward and accepting. The authors take particular care in exploring traditional child-rearing values, beliefs, and practices and replacing them with current information and new approaches.

Lindsay, Jeanne Warren. *Your Baby's First Year: A How-to-Parent Book*. Morning Glory, 1991. 190p. photog. LC 91-21513. ISBN 0-930934-53-9. $15.95. ISBN 0-930934-52-0 pbk. $9.95.

Parenting suggestions and comments from teen parents are emphasized in this simple, concise handbook that covers understanding, caring for, and enjoying infants during their first year of life. The material includes practical advice on keeping baby comfortable, nutrition and diet, health care, and

accident proofing the baby's environment, as well as guidance on issues involved in fathering, being a single parent, choosing child care, completing school, and money management. Adolescent readers will find the case material and photographs appealing, the tone and presentation of information supportive.

Lindsay, Jeanne Warren. *Your Pregnancy and Newborn Journey: How to Take Care of Yourself and Your Newborn if You're a Pregnant Teen*. Morning Glory, 1991. 191p. photog. LC 91-3712. ISBN 0-930934-50-4. $9.95.

Targeted to teenage mothers and fathers, this handbook reviews issues of concern to young parents, such as three-generation living and staying in school, as well as the basics every pregnant woman needs, including information about diet; prenatal care; how to stop smoking, drinking, or using drugs; and labor and delivery. Facts about the first months of life, feeding, and adoption are provided, as are data for fathers. The material, which is clearly and simply presented, is made more appealing to young readers by abundant quotations and photographs of teen parents.

Manginello, Frank P., and Theresa F. Digeronimo. *Your Premature Baby*. Wiley, 1991. 296p. bibliog. glossary. LC 91-10572. ISBN 0-4715-3587-7. $9.95.

This source on premature babies, organized by the degree of prematurity, provides parents with practical advice on routine daily care in the hospital and at home. Chapters on the reasons for prematurity, routine medical care, and common complications give parents a better understanding of their child's condition. Advice on managing their feelings and finances helps them cope with their new responsibilities. The book also includes a glossary, additional readings, and lists of suppliers and support groups.

Rafe, Stephen C. *Your New Baby & Bowser*. Denlingers, 1990. 64p. illus. LC 90-34674. ISBN 0-87714-138-X. $9.95.

Despite a cute title, this handbook from a leading expert on animal behavior is a concise, serious guide for dog owners on training a dog to accept the behavior of an infant or toddler. The content includes exchanging scents, investigating the baby's cries, socializing the dog, welcoming the baby, avoiding bites, and feeding the dog when the baby is present and ready to interfere. The second section provides owners with insight into the dog's signals and the influence an owner's personality has on dog behavior, especially in the case of dominant or overindulgent owners. Rafe explains how to establish leadership over the animal, offers alternatives to punishment to correct misbehavior, and suggests ways to help the shy or timid dog. At the outset, he cautions against any rough play with the dog as it encourages rough play with the child. Line drawings effectively illustrate the techniques described.

Samuels, Mike. *The Well Baby Book, Revised and Expanded for the 1990s*. Summit, 1991. 446p. bibliog. photog. illus. index. LC 90-26702. ISBN 0-671-73413-X. $27.95. ISBN 0-671-73421-1 pbk. $16.95.

Samuels's how-to guide to baby care differs from others in its focus on concepts of holistic medicine, such as relaxation and imagery techniques, to guide parents to understanding their infant's development and caring for its needs. The first section gives an overview of baby health which emphasizes understanding normal child development patterns, learning about common diseases and their treatments, and evolving a relaxed "family" style, all via the involvement of the whole parent and whole child. This approach is implemented in the second section, which addresses the baby before birth; the birthing process; and the essential aspects of newborn, toddler, and older baby development, growth, daily care, language, social skills, and child care concerns. In the third section, common medical problems are grouped by organ system, and symptoms, self-help approaches, guidelines on when to see the pediatrician, and prevention techniques are covered. Information on emergencies, rare diseases, immunizations, and common drugs are covered in the final chapter. Throughout the text are attractive photographs of babies and their parents and reproductions of paintings with child care as their theme.

* Sears, William. *Keys to Calming the Fussy Baby.* Barron's, 1991. 170p. index. glossary. LC 90-25343. ISBN 0-8120-4538-6. $5.95.

This practical book introduces parents to the concepts of temperament and high need in babies who are sensitive, intense, hyperactive, not easily satisfied, not cuddly, or discontent when they are not being held. Sears, a well-regarded author of many parenting guides, describes how to help such a child become better able to accept and control impulses by improving the sensitivity of the parents, primarily the mother. He introduces issues as they logically appear during the child's development and gives special attention to infants' sleep patterns. Much practical information is covered in an easy-to-read format.

Sears, William. *Keys to Preparing and Caring for Your Newborn.* Barron's, 1991. 170p. index. glossary. LC 90-25847. ISBN 0-81204-539-4. $5.95.

Sears's handbook of practical tips on infant feeding and sleeping and other routines of daily care also introduces new parents to the philosophy of "attachment parenting" from which these decisions naturally flow. The interaction between parent and newborn in a variety of family settings, newborn appearance, infant capabilities, premature medical care, infants with disabilities, and postpartum adjustment are examined in brief topical chapters.

* Sears, William, and Martha Sears. *The Baby Book: Everything You Need to Know about Your Baby—From Birth to Age Two.* Little, Brown, 1993. illus. index. LC 92-16085. ISBN 0-316-77906-7. $33.95. ISBN 0-316-77905-9 pbk. $18.95.

Veteran parenting authors William Sears and Martha Sears provide a comprehensive but undaunting guide to child care in the first few months of life to parents learning to become their own experts. Divided into five sections, the text tackles getting started, infant feeding and nutrition, contemporary parenting (e.g., attachment parenting, baby weaning, nighttime parenting, and parenting fussy babies—all principles previously promoted by the Searses), as well as infant development and behavior, and safety and health issues. The concise, simple, empathetic style reveals a wealth of authoritative information on child rearing in dual-career families.

Stern, Daniel N. *Diary of a Baby: What Your Child Really Sees, Feels, and Experiences.* Basic Books, 1990. 165p. bibliog. LC 90-80241. ISBN 0-465-01642-1. $18.95.

Organized to reflect the significant developmental leaps that occur in a baby's awareness of feelings, immediate environment, mindscapes, language, and stories from six weeks to four years in age, this invented diary of a baby is based on current research on infant perception, emotion, and memory. Stern, an infant psychiatrist and parent, addresses scientific concepts such as obligatory attention, attachment, and intersubjectivity as experiences in the daily life of a developing child in an absorbing, accessible narrative. A selective bibliography supports chapter by chapter the author's tale of a developing personality.

Stoppard, Miriam. *Day by Day Baby Care.* Ballantine, 1983. 343p. photog. illus. index. LC 83-48076. ISBN 0-394-53429-8. $13.50.

Originally published in 1983, this reprinted guide to infant care is heavily illustrated with diagrams that provide instruction to parents in matters such as equipping a nursery, feeding, diapering, and bathing the baby. The text is brief and informative, linking the baby's developmental capacity with down-to-earth advice. The author, a physician and parent, approaches the tasks of infant care by incorporating the father's role and advising parents how to fit the baby into the family. She also acknowledges contemporary family configurations as well as techniques for guiding the baby's development, health, and happiness. Safety considerations are emphasized, although small omissions in this area, such as a night light that looks like a toy, lack of gloves and mask on a dentist performing an examination, and barrier gates that attach by pressure rather than hardware, alert the reader that this text was compiled more than 10 years ago.

Taubman, Bruce. *Curing Infant Colic.* Bantam, 1990. 165p. LC 89-18516. ISBN 0-553-34903-1. $9.95.

Viewing colic as excessive crying (more than 30–90 minutes per day) for no apparent reason by a healthy infant, the author traces its appearance as the result of infants becoming agitated when parents misunderstand their attempts to communicate via their cries. After debunking colic myths, such as gas, immature nervous systems, or mother's diet, Taubman, a pediatric gastroenterologist, explores the many reasons why healthy babies cry and presents a trial-and-error method for parents to use to quickly identify the source of their infant's discomfort.

The five steps required are to rule out a separate health problem with a complete medical exam, maintain a behavior diary for the infant for several days, analyze the results, chart crying episodes, and try different approaches until the baby's need is met and crying ceases. Because babies cry to communicate their need to eat, sleep, suck, be held, or be stimulated, his approach focuses on simple techniques that satisfy and eliminate these needs in a brief amount of time. This well-organized and readable text from a recognized authority takes the mystery out of colic symptoms and helps parents relieve the agony that these symptoms impose on the entire family.

Thevenin, Tine. *The Family Bed.* Avery, 1987. 176p. illus. LC 86-28739. ISBN 0-89529-357-9. $7.95.

Believing that the most effective way to nurture independence in children is to pay total attention to their needs in the early years, the author proposes co-family sleeping as an extension of natural childbirth, breastfeeding, and immediate response to an infant's cries. A controversial work that is regularly cited, this text covers historical and cross-cultural antecedents for the practice of sharing sleep; reasons for and against it; issues related to infants, children past infancy, and siblings; and the special importance of sharing sleep with adopted children. The effects of co-family sleeping are also explored. The author cites personal experience and contributions from other parents rather than statistical data in providing support and encouragement for a shared family bed. Negative aspects, such as possible incest, smothering, or disturbed parental sleep, are noted.

* Ting, Rosalind Y., et al. *The Complete Mothercare Manual: An Illustrated Guide to Pregnancy, Birth, and Childcare through Age Five.* Fireside, 1992. 304p. photog. illus. index. LC 87-12556. ISBN 0-671-78978-3. $15.00.

Concise, easily accessible entries accompanied by colorful photographs and useful drawings comprise the contents of this handbook on the first five years of life. Following an introductory chapter addressing prenatal care and testing, complications in pregnancy or delivery, and the stages of labor, the chapters cover chronologically the common concerns of parents: feeding, bathing, sleeping, developmental milestones, play and toys, daily life, and family. Concerns specific to each age, such as diapering, independence, and childhood illnesses, are also covered. The simple and straightforward presentation, with its lavish use of photographs and its comprehensive approach to care of the young child, make this an attractive as well as useful guide for parents.

Todd, Linda. *You and Your New Baby: A Guide to the First Months After Birth.* Harvard Common, 1993. 134p. bibliog. illus. index. LC 92-47389. ISBN 1-55832-055-5. $11.95. ISBN 1-55832-054-7 pbk. $5.95.

This handbook provides new parents with an overview of changes in the mother's, baby's, and family's life in the first few months after an infant enters the family. Written by an experienced childbirth educator, this simple and sympathetic text addresses questions that parents have about themselves and their baby, such as how to settle into a "new normal" life and to acknowledge the need for support, how to cope with the blues or depression, infant health care and testing in the first days and beyond, newborn sensory and motor skills, infant feeding and patterns of sleep, and building a relationship with the baby. The book's summary alerts parents to situations in which they need to seek more in-depth information from other sources.

Van Pelt, Katie. *Potty Training Your Baby: A Practical Guide for Easier Toilet Training.* Avery, 1988. 144p. illus. index. LC 88-23681. ISBN 0-89529-398-8. $6.95.

Criticizing most toilet training as too late and too stressful, the author presents an alternative method for early training that may be completed by the time the child is one and a half to two years of age. Though she notes that training cannot be mastered until the child has sphincter control, she advises parents to begin training in the first year by teaching sensation recognition and connection to muscular function in order to achieve control. Instructions are modified for children one and two years of age to take advantage of their developmental needs. By making use of the toilet fun for children and a means of accomplishment that parents applaud, and by avoiding all negative responses or teasing, parents will contribute to their child's easily learning toileting skills without the tensions typically associated with this task.

* White, Burton L. *The First Three Years of Life.* Rev. ed. Prentice Hall, 1990. 380p. bibliog. illus. index. LC 89-23107. ISBN 0-1331-7678-9. $10.95.

The introduction to the new and revised edition of this detailed guide to raising children describes development in the first eight months, with an emphasis on parents giving the infant a feeling of being loved and cared for, helping the child develop specific skills, and encouraging its interest in the outside world. In the first section, chapters arranged chronologically cover general behavior patterns, apparent interests of infants in each phase, learning development, recommended child-rearing practices, language development, and practices not recommended. The second section takes a topical approach, covering the major issues of spoiling the child, sibling rivalry, hearing ability, developmental difficulties, benefits of breastfeeding, substitute child care, play, and toys. White is forthright about his opinions; what research results he endorses; and which results, despite the claims of others, he believes are inconclusive. A significant portion of the book is devoted to recommended readings, which he thoroughly evaluates and annotates.

Zahn, Laura. *Bringing Baby Home: An Owner's Manual for First-Time Parents.* Down to Earth Publications, 1993. 160p. illus. index. ISBN 0-939301-91-1. $8.95.

Unique aspects of this how-to guide on the care of infants are its exclusive focus on the first six weeks of life, a new mother's diary of this time period, and an unusually appealing approach that is direct, practical, and warm. Also useful for new parents is its coverage of feeding, bathing, skin care, and other basics including safety, laundry, interaction, and shopping lists. Advice on time management, choosing a pediatrician, handling visitors, and recovering from giving birth is presented in a concise manner suitable for a contemporary audience sophisticated in every area save infant care. The spiral format makes the text easy to prop, giving a new parent free use of both hands.

POPULAR TITLES: JOURNALS

American Baby. Cahners. 1938. M. ISSN 0044-7544. $12.00.

A monthly how-to magazine primarily aimed at expectant or new parents, this publication provides instructions on child care, solutions to common problems of raising children, and practical advice on psychological or emotional issues. Regular columns on products available for clothing, feeding, or playing with baby; personal experience; maternal and child health; and letters, book excerpts, and behavioral issues provide commonsense tips to mothers, and, increasingly, fathers. There are lots of photographs and advertisements in this magazine.

PROFESSIONAL TITLES: BOOKS

Hallett, Elisabeth. *In the Newborn Year: Our Changing Awareness After Childbirth*. Book Publishing Co., 1992. 219p. index. LC 91-42328. ISBN 0-913990-87-6. $10.95.

Using personal experience and stories shared by others as a guide, the author, a writer with a background in the health sciences, explores the emotional, physical, intuitive, psychic, even insane aspects of the bond between mother and child through the first year of life. The images she presents are arresting, and the transformations that these mothers profess are deeply moving, whether positive or negative. Because the writing is lucid, both the experience of parenting and the changes it brings are easily understood, even by neophyte parents. The material is organized into topical sections that reflect the impact of giving birth and caring for a child: bonding, daily life, changes that motherhood brings, and openness to change from other sources such as the subconscious. This book provides a mystical perspective on mothering that is not replicated in academic tomes or self-help handbooks.

Morris, Desmond. *Babywatching*. Crown, 1992. 214p. index. LC 91-43202. ISBN 0-517-58845-5. $15.00.

Morris, a zoologist, brings an observer's viewpoint to the reality of a baby—why it cries, how well it can see or smell, if it dreams, and why it likes being rocked. A baby is highly responsive to its environment right from birth, according to Morris, and has a well-developed ability to stimulate its parents and monitor their behavior. Presented in a question-and-answer format, the text covers social considerations such as baptism, birthday cakes, the role of the stork, and the source of the term "baby."

PROFESSIONAL TITLES: JOURNALS

International Journal of Early Childhood. World Organization for Early Childhood Education. 1969. 2/yr. ISSN 0020-7187. $10.00.

Providing information and practical advice to parents and teachers on the care, treatment, and environment of children from birth to age seven or eight is the focus of this journal. Articles are published in French and Spanish as well as English in this title, which is the official journal of the World Organization for Early Childhood Education (OMEP). Among the topics covered are health and nutrition, child psychology, preschool education, selection of toys and play materials, equipping playgrounds and play areas, and design of preschool institutions and homes to enhance their role in children's development.

Zero to Three. National Center for Clinical Infant Programs. 1980. 5/yr. ISSN 0736-8038. $18.00.

In brief articles for practitioners, this loose-leaf publication focuses on themes such as minor illnesses and community violence. Research reports, descriptions of service programs, case studies, and conference summaries are published. Reviews of new books and videos, funding opportunities, and information on conferences are also included.

DIRECTORY

Postpartum Support International (PSI)
927 N. Kellogg Avenue, Santa Barbara, CA 93111
(805) 967-7636
Jane Honikman, President
Founded: 1987
Members: 200
Mission/Goals: To increase awareness among public and professional communities about the emotional changes women often experience during pregnancy and following the birth of a baby; to provide current information on diagnosis and treatment, education about mental health issues of child bearing, and information about legal and insurance coverage issues
Audience/Clientele: All persons interested in the organization's goals, whether individuals or groups
Staff: 14 board members
Budget: $6,000 Funding: Donations, dues
Services: Support group, referral
Education/Outreach: Library, publishing
Publications: *Postpartum Equilibria*, quarterly; *PSI News*, quarterly
Programs: Annual conference

REFERENCE

1. *Health United States 1993*. U.S. Department of Health and Human Services, National Center for Health Statistics, 1994, 64.

C H A P T E R

Toddlers and Preschoolers

Having a toddler is a humbling experience.
Your preschooler may seem to be
in constant motion much of the time.
Steven P. Shelov, ed. *Caring for Your Baby and Young Child*

The care and feeding of toddlers may be even more challenging to parents than adjusting to a newborn, but they have far fewer resources to draw on. Fortunately, parents trailing an active and independent youngster do not have much time to read, nor as great an inclination to do so, as they have developed greater confidence in their parenting skills. During this stage of childhood, ensuring safety becomes a primary concern, along with establishing bedtime routines, coping with defiance, and encouraging instructive play.

Readiness for nursery school often occurs in the third year of life. By that time, many children are able to cope with separation, communicate in short sentences, interact positively with other children, and begin toilet training.[1] Setting consistent limits and disciplining children to follow rules assume increasing importance. Children become aware of gender and exhibit specifically masculine or feminine traits, often without coaching from parents, as though "gender traits are preprogrammed in the womb."[2]

An asterisk (*) indicates a specially recommended title.

POPULAR TITLES: BOOKS

Ames, Louise Bates, and Frances L. Ilg. *Your Five Year Old: Sunny and Serene.* Dell, 1981. 123p. photog. ISBN 0-385-29145-0. $8.95.

One of a number of books from the Gesell Institute of Human Development, this parenting handbook describes patterns of development that parents may expect of their children at approximately age five. The text covers what characterizes the child at age five; how five year olds relate to others; how routines, health, and tension function as emotional outlets at this age; effective approaches to discipline; cognitive development; how to determine school readiness; and what five year olds' interests and accomplishments are likely to be. While repeatedly reminding readers that each child is unique, this brief handbook provides a concise guide to what the authors term "one of the most rewarding periods in your entire relationship with your son or daughter."

* Brazelton, T. Berry. *Toddlers and Parents: A Declaration of Independence.* Rev. ed. Dell, 1989. 249p. bibliog. photog. index. LC 89-31336. ISBN 0-385-29787-4. $24.95. ISBN 0-385-29790-4 pbk. $13.95.

Thoroughly revised to address the issues faced by contemporary parents and day care providers, this collection of case studies examines the struggle for self-mastery and independence that every child experiences between the ages of one and three. The cases illustrate events at various ages, including 12, 15, 18, 24, and 30 months, and in diverse family and child care settings, such as single-mother families, single-father families, family day care, and day care centers. Each case is presented with commentary and references to relevant research. The cases are memorable and thought-provoking, and Brazelton's comments are helpful in identifying and clarifying the issues and tracing the consequences of behavior.

Goldstein, Robin, with Janet Gallant. *Everyday Parenting: The First Five Years.* Viking Penguin, 1990. 288p. LC 89-48027. ISBN 0-14-01-3345-3. $7.95.

A full range of options for parents to choose from in dealing with routine child care problems is organized topically in this quick reference guide to parenting tips. The coverage includes dependency, sleeping, eating, independence, limit setting, children's thinking, fears and imagination, toys and play, and preschools.

* Laskin, David, and Kathleen O'Neill Laskin. *The Little Girl Book: Everything You Need to Know to Raise a Daughter Today.* Ballantine, 1992. 287p. bibliog. index. LC 91-55503. ISBN 0-345-36802-9. $8.00.

The Laskins' handbook surveys the development of female children from infancy through the third grade. Content includes girls' psychological, physical, and social development, as well as parenting tips on father's involvement, relationship with siblings, and clothing and appearance. While the authors, backed by a detailed review of the scholarly social science literature, maintain that very few traits are sex-linked and temperament is more important than gender in influencing behavior, they do a thorough job of documenting just how girls develop. This text contains much practical advice, with a focus on ways that parents can avoid sexism in bringing up their daughters.

* Leach, Penelope. *Your Baby and Child: From Birth to Age Five.* Knopf, 1989. 553p. photog. illus. index. LC 89-1873. ISBN 0-394-57951-8. $29.95. ISBN 0-679-72425-7 pbk. $18.95.

Leach, an acclaimed and popular author of many parenting guides, offers here a detailed account of the developmental stages between birth and age five and how developmental accomplishments are expressed in the child's behavior. She gives advice that helps the parent and child develop a mutually satisfactory relationship through a flexible approach to care "by the baby," that is, according to the baby's needs and abilities. Without relying on the customary case studies and question-and-answer sections, Leach focuses on explaining in detail just what the infant's needs in each developmental stage may be. Illustrations aid in applying the techniques advocated by the author, and numerous attractive photographs of babies add to the appeal of this standard.

* Lieberman, Alicia. *Emotional Life of the Toddler.* Free Press, 1993. 244p. bibliog. photog. index. LC 93-8018. ISBN 0-02-919021-5. $22.95.

Current research, accepted theories of development, and clinical observations are synthesized in this masterful exploration of a toddler's fundamental struggle to reconcile the urge to become independent with the desire for parental protection and love. Themes of attachment, temperament, and the struggles of socialization are used to define how a child thinks, feels, and reacts to the demands of growing up. Common circumstances faced by contemporary parents, such as child care and divorce, are also explored in detail. A fluid writing style and interesting case material add to the quality of this handbook.

* Lief, Nina R., with Mary Ellen Fahs. *The Second Year of Life.* Early Childhood Development Center's Parenting Series.

Walker, 1991. 262p. LC 91-2852. ISBN 0-8027-1154-5. $24.95. ISBN 0-8027-7350-8 pbk. $12.95.

Small group discussions are the source of insights on child development and parental roles in this guide to the second year in a child's life. Divided into four-month intervals, the book covers age-specific issues, such as weaning, spacing of siblings, language development, temper tantrums, toilet training, manners, and birth of a sibling, as they commonly arise. Transcripts of parents' questions and the staff's answers follow presentations of the material. Particular attention is given to replacing traditional views with current practices.

Lief, Nina R., with Rebecca M. Thomas. *The Third Year of Life.* Early Childhood Development Center's Parenting Series. Walker, 1991. 205p. bibliog. photog. index. LC 91-13038. ISBN 0-8027-1155-3. $24.95. ISBN 0-8027-7351-6 pbk. $12.95.

The third in a series from the Early Childhood Development Center in New York, this volume summarizes the results of small group discussions with parents. Questions and concerns are linked to advice based on appropriate child-rearing methods and developmental theory, with special emphasis on the importance of parent-child interaction in fostering healthy development. The material is organized chronologically, but also topically, as developmental issues such as setting limits, sexual identification, transitional objects, and gender identity are addressed when group members bring them up. Particular attention is given to debunking outdated beliefs, such as "spoiling" an infant, and providing parents with information digested from current research that justifies their decisions and arms them against well-meaning but incorrect advice of family and friends.

Lindsay, Jeanne Warren. *The Challenge of Toddlers: Parenting Your Child from One to Three.* Morning Glory, 1991. 191p. LC 91-30316. ISBN 0-930934-59-8. $15.95. ISBN 0-930934-59-8 pbk. $9.95.

Practical information on toddlers' psychological and physical development, learning processes, and sleep and nutritional requirements as well as the challenges they present to young parents are thoroughly reviewed in this concise handbook. Parenting tips and advice on parental self-care supplement the practical instructions provided in the narrative. Lifestyle issues, such as the father's involvement, living with an extended family, and long-range planning, are also discussed.

Rosemond, John. *Making the "Terrible" Twos Terrific.* Andrews and McMeel, 1993. 183p. index. LC 93-24948. ISBN 0-8362-2811-1. $8.95.

An informative and enlightening handbook to guiding toddlers, this text by popular author and columnist John Rosemond emphasizes practical approaches based on personal experience over theoretical formulations. To make the toddler years tolerable, he explains the course of children's development, which behaviors are normal, how parents may guide their child, and the importance of discipline for parents as well as their offspring. Among the common problem areas of the toddler that are explored here are toileting, bedtime, territoriality, and the impact of day care. A breezy style, a parent-centered approach, and informative anecdotes characterize Rosemond's writing in this, his latest, parenting handbook.

* Shelov, Steven P. *Caring for Your Baby and Young Child: Birth to Age Five*. American Academy of Pediatrics. Bantam, 1990. 704p. illus. index. LC 90-47015. ISBN 0-553-07186-6. $32.95. ISBN 0-553-07186-6 pbk. $15.95.

A substantive contribution from the American Academy of Pediatrics, this handbook provides detailed information on specific health problems in young children, organized by bodily system or organ affected. The text opens with a section on developmental stages, which has a health care bent. Chapters organized by chronological age track physical, emotional, mental, and verbal growth, basic care, health watch, safety concerns, and family issues for each age group. Introductory chapters on how to parent and the emotional gifts that children and parents offer to each other, coupled with authoritative information on health care, successfully achieve the academy's intention to provide parents with quality information on children's health issues.

* Spock, Benjamin, and Michael B. Rothenberg. *Dr. Spock's Baby and Child Care*. 6th ed. NAL/Dutton, 1992. 832p. illus. index. LC 91-5105. ISBN 0-525-93400-6. $25.00.

In the latest edition of this American classic, Dr. Spock and fellow pediatrician Michael B. Rothenberg provide updated factual information on children's health care and address contemporary issues: divorce, step-parenting, AIDS, and open adoption. The approach is relaxed, as the authors urge parents to use their own good judgment and not to take the information presented literally because every child is unique. The counseling approach is evident in several chapters on how to be a parent. The guide is also a detailed sourcebook of factual information on equipment, medical care, feeding, and injury prevention and a handbook to developmental stages.

REFERENCES

1. Nina R. Lief, with Rebecca M. Thomas, *The Third Year of Life* (New York: Walker, 1991), 6–9, 12.
2. David Laskin and Kathleen O'Neill Laskin, *The Little Girl Book: Everything You Need to Know to Raise a Daughter Today* (New York: Ballantine, 1992), 8.

CHAPTER

School-Age Children

As your child grows up, he'll spend most of his time developing and polishing a variety of skills and abilities in all areas of his life.
Steven P. Shelov, ed. *Caring for Your Baby and Young Child*

Between the ages of 6 and 12, children mature physically, intellectually, socially, and emotionally as they proceed through a transitional period to adolescence. Much of what is written about children in this age group is focused on specific dimensions of children's lives, such as schooling, health care, or sports participation, rather than on general guides to their care. This approach is true for both professional and popular titles, journals as well as books.

An asterisk (*) indicates a specially recommended title.

POPULAR TITLES: BOOKS

* Ames, Louise Bates, and Carol Chase Haber. *Your Nine Year Old: Thoughtful and Mysterious.* Delacorte, 1990. 164p. bibliog. photog. illus. LC 89-39154. ISBN 0-385-29898-6. $17.95.

Like the others in this series, this handbook from the Gesell Institute of Human Development looks in detail at the identifying characteristics, relationships with others, routines and health, mental development, sense of self, interests, and abilities of children in a particular age group, in this case, nine year olds. The authors also examine how a nine-year-old child fares in school and at parties and provide a recommended approach to discipline. According to the authors, nine year olds tend to be independent, serious, critical, internally focused, and in general more individualized and unpredictable than other children. Common problems at this age are reviewed, including signs of

overplacement in school, learning disorders, and extreme tenacity in carrying out tasks. The text is readable and thought-provoking for parents who must confront their children's growing independence and autonomy outside the home.

* Ames, Louise Bates, Frances L. Ilg, and Sidney M. Baker. *Your Ten to Fourteen Year Old.* Doubleday, 1989. 364p. bibliog. index. ISBN 0-385-29631-2. $9.95.

Ames and her co-authors draw on replications of their 1956 study of adolescents conducted in the late 1970s and early 1980s to present the tasks of adolescence. These remain constant: to get free of parents, establish a sense of one's own personality, and gradually become interested and involved in a relationship with a life partner. The factors investigated are reviewed in the first section, and in the second, a series of maturity profiles and traits, such as activity level, self care routines, emotions, school life, and ethical sense, are examined as they change year by year. The final sections address developmental trends and provide a preview of development after age 14. This book is noteworthy in that it addresses many dimensions of behavior, both abstract and concrete, in a thoughtful tone that differs from the informal, practical tone found in other volumes in this series from the Gesell Institute of Human Development.

Brack, Pat, and Ben Brack. *Moms Don't Get Sick.* Melius, 1991. 106p. illus. LC 90-60228. ISBN 0-937603-07-4. $9.95.

This forthright, even blunt, account by a mother and her 10-year-old son of family life during her four-year battle with breast cancer reveals in intimate detail the difficulties that such a crisis can provoke. How the two solved their problems and coped with the disruption they faced during diagnosis, treatment, reconstruction, anniversary depression, and a second, unrelated cancer is revealed in their individual and sometimes contrasting versions of these events. Illustrations by Ben are also part of this touching and realistic account of the impact of serious illness on a mother and her child.

Durrell, Doris E. *Starting Out Right: Your Child's First Seven Years.* New Harbinger, 1989. 312p. LC 89-134775. ISBN 0-934986-59-2. $29.95.

Behavior modification guides this advanced approach to child rearing for parents who already understand the basics. The author translates research findings on promoting early language development, stimulating intelligence, encouraging creativity, fostering self-esteem, and curtailing aggressive behavior into practical advice for parents. Organized around developmental stages and principles of learning appropriate skills, the text suggests specific methods for guiding the child's development. Content on socializing the child includes such behavior modification techniques as modeling, using time-out to decrease undesirable behavior, and preventing fears. The opening chapter cautions parents to recognize and adjust to their child's unique temperament.

Editors of Time-Life Books. *Understanding Your School-Age Child.* Successful Parenting. Time-Life Books, 1988. 144p. bibliog. index. illus. photog. LC 88-4925. ISBN 0-8094-5962-9. $12.99. ISBN 0-8094-5963-9 lib bind. $12.99.

This heavily illustrated, upbeat guide tracks the middle years of childhood from age 6 to 12, describing normal physical, intellectual, moral, and emotional growth. A panel of expert consultants helps parents smooth the way for their child's development, covering such topics as making the most of elementary school, easing the transition from home to the outside world, becoming a good citizen, and advising on children's physical development and needs. Boxes and sidebars highlight more specialized concerns, such as difficulty paying attention, encouraging a scientific approach to learning, the impact of anxiety on a child's standardized test scores, and coping with depression. Developmental milestones are synthesized in a chart at the back of the book.

Goldstein, Robin, with Janet Gallant. *More Everyday Parenting: The Six-to-Nine-Year Old.* Penguin, 1991. 267p. LC 90-7805. ISBN 0-14-014729-2. $6.95.

As children grow, parenting issues become more complex, but few guides are available to assist the parents of an older child. Without going into the developmental basis for behavior or needs, this quick reference to tips and tactics helps busy parents set limits, discuss expectations, listen to their child, and be a positive role model. Goldstein covers such vexing problems as picky eating and clothes consciousness as well as serious concerns such as getting along with others, being home alone, and developing creativity.

* Kelly, Marguerite. *The Mother's Almanac II: Your Child from Six to Twelve.* Doubleday, 1989. 408p. bibliog. illus. index. LC 88-25650. ISBN 0-385-26283-3. $22.95. ISBN 0-385-13155-0 pbk. $14.95.

In a witty series of essays that are quite informative, Kelly, a journalist, looks at changes characteristic of the middle years of childhood through the lenses of developmental cycles, family life, and the outside world She provides year-by-year descriptions of physical, mental, and emotional development. Subsequent chapters address family relationships and school issues, also on a year-by-year basis. This text is a good introduction to issues; it gives parents sufficient background to pursue additional reading if they so choose. Though the approach is not at all academic, each chapter places the issues discussed in a developmental context.

Rincover, Arnold. *The Parenting Challenge: Your Child's Behavior from Six to Twelve.* Simon & Schuster, 1991. 220p. index. LC 91-20056. ISBN 0-671-68163-X. $9.00.

Rincover's how-to handbook focuses on children's behavior during the middle years, when significant nonphysical development occurs, such as moral development and the development of thinking and social skills. The purpose of the book is to help parents understand normal development, including many "strange and upsetting behaviors," identify when a problem exists and how often certain behaviors occur, and learn what they can do to help their child. Among the social, emotional, psychological, and intellectual concerns that the author examines are conduct problems, relationships, family problems, moods, school-related concerns, morals and values, and personality issues. The text begins with a review of specific anxieties and frustrations of parents, when parents themselves are part of the problem, and principles of effective parenting. Rincover excludes problems specific to older or younger children or related to physical, neurological, or genetic disabilities.

POPULAR TITLES: JOURNALS

Child. New York Times Magazine Group. 1985. B-M. ISSN 0894-7988. $12.00.

Features of interest to the contemporary family, such as articles on father-friendly companies; safety, nutrition, and clothing tips; and regular columns on education, health and family values, letters, and media reviews, are attractively presented in this upscale bimonthly. Maternal well-being and caring for the very young child are also covered. Articles and columns are color-coded according to the age of the child addressed, from infant to preteen, to enable parents to locate those that cover issues relevant to the age of their child. Glossy and sophisticated, this magazine also boasts articles by well-known child care experts.

C H A P T E R

Adolescents

As long as adolescents have existed, they
eventually have grown to adults, as yours will too.
Adolescence is a tremendous
opportunity, a beautiful chance for children
to be reassembled—largely by themselves—into
real, honest-to-goodness, decent adult human beings.
Jeanette Shalov et al. *You Can Say No to Your Teenager*

The years between childhood and adulthood are generally viewed as turbulent, if not downright troubled. The
voluminous literature on adolescence revolves in large part
around crisis—substance abuse, dropping out, unwed pregnancy, and suicide, all originating in rebellious disregard
for authority. One notable author, John W. Santrock, characterizes this emphasis as an "adolescent generalization
gap"[1] and notes the emergence of studies that recognize
adolescence as a period of evaluation, decision making,
and commitment. Old stereotypes are not easily aban-
doned, however, if the results of a recent Gallup poll are
considered. Sixty-seven percent of parents surveyed considered girls to be at their "worst" between ages 13 and
17, and 62 percent considered boys to be at their worst
during the same years.[2]

Physical changes, emotional maturation, peer influences, and academic responsibilities effect a transformation in school-age children that may be more or less
conflictual as parents and teens negotiate new relationships. For parents, "the tasks of parenting in the '90s are
the same as they have alway been: providing enough stability while encouraging enough independence to allow
a child to grow up. . . ."[3] John Bradshaw is even more
definite: "Letting our children separate is the most important task of parenting."[4] For those adolescents who
get caught up in drugs or alcohol, prematurely bear children, or attempt to end their lives, professional help as
well as parental support is required.

An asterisk (*) indicates a specially recommended title.

POPULAR TITLES: BOOKS

Anthony, Mitchel T. *Suicide: Knowing When Your Teen Is at
Risk.* Regal, 1991. 212p. bibliog. LC 91-9159. ISBN 0-8307-
1406-5. $9.95.

> Written by the executive director of Teens in Touch and the
> National Suicide Help Center, this self-help manual addresses
> causes, warning signs, prevention, counseling and caring, and
> "postvention" for parents, educators and others who work with
> youth. The content includes an examination of societal influ-
> ences, such as family breakdown and musical "invitations" to
> suicide, and psychological factors, such as low self-esteem, feel-
> ing unappreciated and misunderstood, relationship struggles,
> and neglect and loneliness, which make teens vulnerable to
> self-destruction. It also covers techniques to demonstrate car-
> ing, provide emotional first aid, and assist survivors, a neces-
> sary part of preventing cluster suicides by adolescents who have
> learned the reality of death and lost their fear of dying in the
> wake of a friend's death.

* Caron, Ann F. *"Don't Stop Loving Me": A Reassuring Guide for
Mothers of Adolescent Daughters.* Holt, 1991. 226p. bibliog.
LC 90-4273. ISBN 0-8050-1136-6. $19.95.

> A psychologist specializing in adolescent female development
> advises mothers on guiding teenage daughters through a con-
> temporary environment far different than the one in which
> they were raised. Mothers are encouraged to understand their
> daughter's concerns regarding body image, popularity and peers,
> limits and trust, sex, alcohol and drugs and their unique ways
> of thinking while continuing their efforts to guide and care for

them. Dad's role, or lack there of, is also explored in the voices of the female teens and mothers interviewed for this text.

DeSisto, Michael. *Decoding Your Teenager: How to Understand Each Other during the Turbulent Years*. Morrow, 1990. 203p. LC 90-41532. ISBN 0-688-08776-0. $16.95.

DeSisto, the founder and headmaster of a school for troubled teens, outlines his own approach to understanding and communicating with adolescents. He notes that the parental side of communication begins with caring and understanding one's own personal baggage and how it may interfere with open talk. He proposes seven rules for successful communication; these "secrets" include job descriptions for each family member, successfully playing family games, gaining expertise at the power play, and celebrating one's own shortcomings. The majority of the text is focused on DeSisto's schema for identifying and resolving the traits linked to various problems, such as the relationship addict, weak Romeo, angry child, runaway, weird dresser, wild child, and the clam. The book provides a unique commonsense approach to parenting teens that exhibit a selected set of problems.

Dumont, Larry. *Surviving Adolescence: Helping Your Child Through the Struggle to Adulthood*. Villard, 1991. 253p. index. LC 91-50066. ISBN 0-394-57405-2. $19.50.

The director of the Fair Oaks Hospital Adolescent Treatment Program advises parents on normal adolescent development, symptoms that signal problems, psychological disorders found in teens, their treatment and cure, and preventive strategies. The content includes a description of pain cues and coverage of such problems as depression, substance abuse, learning disabilities, conduct disorders, eating disorders, anxiety, and suicide. The pros and cons of treatment modalities such as medication, therapy, and hospitalization are reviewed. This text attempts to help parents recognize when teens have problems and assist in solving them in a positive manner and in a supportive environment.

Eagle, Carol J., and Carol Colman. *All That She Can Be: Helping Your Daughter Achieve Her Full Potential and Maintain Her Self-Esteem during the Critical Years of Adolescence*. Simon & Schuster, 1993. 252p. bibliog. index. LC 93-6791. ISBN 0-671-78948-1. $22.00.

Low self-esteem exacts a significant toll on adolescent girls. Girls with low self-esteem are at greater risk for developing emotional problems, are more likely to engage in unhealthy behavior, and are less prepared for the contemporary technology-intensive workplace. Figuring out when teenage girls are unhappy is difficult, and this book by a clinical psychologist is designed to help parents know what to expect as their daughter matures and become more sensitive to her needs and concerns by being advocates, accurately reading problems, improving communication, and becoming more creative parents. Case material and sample dialogues illustrate the very thorough text. After an insightful section exploring the legacy of the parent's own experience in adolescence, the author reviews the changes adolescents go through during their transition to adulthood. The second part of the text covers development from a daughter's perspective, including relationships

with mother, father, and siblings, changing looks, peers and friendships, academic decline, and dating and sexuality. A final section addresses both self-destructive behavior and divorce and stepfamilies, two special situations that increase the risk of lifelong problems.

* Greydanus, Donald E., ed. *Caring for Your Adolescent: Ages 12 to 21*. American Academy of Pediatrics. Bantam, 1991. 326p. LC 91-13801. ISBN 0-553-07556-X. $24.95.

The challenges of parenting an adolescent are many: preparing for change, being flexible, listening, understanding contemporary teen environments, and willingness to cut the cord. This handbook provides up-to-date information on physical growth, psychological development, sexual maturation, social skills, and education. Special issues such as obesity, sexually transmitted disease, learning disorders, organized sports, and chronic illness are also addressed.

Jester, Harold D. *Pulling Together: Crisis Prevention for Teens and Their Parents*. Mills and Sanderson, 1992. 178p. bibliog. index. LC 91-41371. ISBN 0-938179-30-6. $9.95.

Techniques for structuring family life by improving adolescent's understanding of their parents and vice versa is the focus of this psychological handbook. The first section, written for adolescents, covers issues that cause conflict in teenager-parent relationships, such as the need to be right, who's in charge, manipulation, expectations, trust, rights and duties, privileges and gratuities, and the particular difficulties of divorce and remarriage. The second section, for parents, provides commentary on the issues raised in the first, as well as addressing punishment and its risks. Both a means of being in charge and treating adolescents with respect, this handbook for parents is about working together with their teenagers to reach shared objectives.

Kirshenbaum, Mira, and Charles Foster. *Parent/Teen Breakthrough: The Relationship Approach*. NAL/Dutton, 1991. 320p. LC 91-13580. ISBN 0-452-26616-5. $11.00.

Because the central reality of teen life is to prepare to live on their own, adolescents will actively resist all parental efforts to control their behavior or individuality, whether they are direct attempts at control, such as rules, limits, and punishments, or indirect techniques like questions, hints, opinions, lectures, complaints, and expectations. Parents are more likely to succeed at living with, even guiding their adolescents, if they focus on improving the relationship they have with their offspring. By listening, asking questions, offering opinions only if invited to do so, revealing their feelings, cheering achievements, and having agreements, the authors, a husband and wife family therapy team, provide parents with a respectful and loving rather than controlling and angry approach to team parenting. The above material is presented in the first three sections; in the final section the authors apply the relationship approach to specific issues such as drugs, sex, single parenting, and friends. An annotated bibliography provides additional readings.

Lindsay, Jeanne Warren. *Schoolage Parents: The Challenge of Three-Generation Living*. Morning Glory, 1990. 222p. bibliog. index. LC 90-6039. ISBN 0-930934-37-7. $15.95. ISBN 0-930934-36-9 pbk. $9.95.

Who's in charge and who will parent when a teenage daughter returns home with her baby to live with her parents are key issue explored in this unusual parenting book. The content, which includes emotional, financial, medical, control and communication issues, is presented in the words of 28 families interviewed in depth. In discussing the transition to parenthood, outside support and help, daily chores, readjustment to living with a toddler, and moving to independence, the author also draws on 16 years of working with pregnant teens as coordinator of a Teen Mother Program for a California school system. By providing a close and personal look at the emotions and individual practical problems generated by teen pregnancy and three generations living in the same home, this text provides insights into the key elements involved in achieving solutions.

Newman, Philip, and Barbara Newman. *When Kids Go to College: A Parent's Guide to Changing Relationships*. Ohio State University Press, 1992. 166p. bibliog. glossary. LC 91-21700. ISBN 0-8142-0561-5. $37.50. ISBN 0-8142-0562-3 pbk. $17.95.

This text provides a guide for parents adjusting to the impact that their child's attending college has on themselves, their families, and the college-bound student. Among the issues covered are the dynamics of a changing relationship between parent and child, how the struggles and successes of college contribute to independence, the process of questioning values and development of mature, independent values, the role of educational culture on college life, impact of friendship and loneliness, personal problems students may encounter, role of gender in identity, and development of a sense of self as a worker with important contributions to make. Without directly surveying the literature, the authors incorporate scholarly insights into a simple, readable text and provide a bibliography at the end of each chapter as well as a list of additional readings. No index is included, however, the text opens with a glossary of college titles and terms that reduces some of the confusion a new language may cause parents.

Pedersen, Anna, and Peggy O'Marsa. *Teens: A Fresh Look*. Norton, 1991. 222p. bibliog. photog. index. LC 90-25425. ISBN 0-945465-54-8. $14.95.

Carefully crafted, thought-provoking essays and dramatic poems reprinted for *Mothering* magazine explore adolescence as a time of growth and opportunity for both parents and their offspring in this anthology. The contributors look at such concerns as career goals, drug and alcohol use, body changes, sex education, pregnancy, and character development. The content also includes the perspective of counselors, educators, and writers who are also parents on how to parent teens. Numerous photographs illustrate the text.

Reaves, John, and James B. Austin. *How to Find Help for a Troubled Kid*. Harper Collins, 1991. 384p. bibliog. index. LC 89-20042. ISBN 0-8050-0885-3. $9.95.

How to identify when a child is sufficiently troubled for parents to seek outside help and where to find it is the focus of this resource book from an educator and a child psychologist. To determine need, the authors provide a checklist as well as a description of what behavior is normal and what is not for adolescents. Support services are described in detail, including what their purposes are, advantages and disadvantages, costs, personnel involved, and questions to ask. The services reviewed range from professional evaluation and supplementary education, the least intrusive, to hospitalization and incarceration in the juvenile justice system, the most drastic. Other types of programs covered include counseling, self-help groups, boarding schools, group homes, and alcohol and drug treatment. The authors use a practical, no-nonsense approach, e.g. parents haven't "tried everything" if they haven't had their child evaluated by a professional, and empower parents to take action through a final chapter on putting knowledge to work and appendixes listing representative programs to contact.

Rowatt, G. Wade, Jr. *How to Talk with Teenagers*. Broadman, 1990. 168p. bibliog. LC 90-34772. ISBN 0-8054-5446-2. $9.95.

Using stories to communicate with teens is the focus of this pastoral guide to counseling adolescents in crisis. The text provides a "road map" for teaching teens, information on their situation in society, and examples of their struggles with religious faith under these circumstances. After reviewing the problems facing today's teens, most importantly a crisis in identity, loneliness, conflict with parents, substance abuse, and vocational choices, the author links resolving these concerns to effective use of stories dealing with ethics, daily life decisions, family settings, friendships, promotion and sustaining spiritual faith. Much substantive counseling information is provided to indicate the solutions to the problems appearing in settings where story telling will be helpful.

* Steinberg, Laurence D., and Ann Levine. *You and Your Adolescent: A Parent's Guide for Ages 10 to 19*. Harper and Row, 1990. 417p. LC 89-45720. ISBN 0-06-016241-4. $19.95.

For parents, this book is a comprehensive review of developmental changes by age group. It surveys psychological health and development, examines social relations, school, and reviews the transition to adulthood in the life of an average adolescent. The authors' review of issues such as balancing control with independence, intellectual development, sexuality, and search for identity make this text outstanding both as a reference book and a detailed overview of the teen years. The emphasis on normal developmental stages and solid foundation in contemporary developmental theory makes this an authoritative handbook for parents.

Weinhaus, Evonne, and Karen Friedman. *Stop Struggling with Your Teen*. Penguin, 1988. 96p. LC 87-7152. ISBN 0-9613736-2-8. $9.00.

This brief guidebook provides both a rationale and a practical four-step plan for parents, which will help them stop feeling responsible for their teen's behavior, develop a relationship based on respect and caring, and encourage responsible behavior by demonstrating faith in their teen's abilities and enabling him or her to learn from the consequences of actions. While the focus is on improving teen behavior through assertiveness, the text is implicitly a guide for parents who are unwilling to let go and let their adolescents lead independent lives. Parents are advised to state what they want the teen to do and negotiate an agreement, summarize teen comments and repeat what they want, take action, and, if the first three steps have not been effective, arrange a limited strike. The authors encourage both an assertive approach on the part of parents and independent behavior on the part of teens.

Wolf, Anthony E. *Get Out of My Life, but First Could You Drive Me and Cheryl to the Mall?* Noonday, 1991. 204p. LC 91-18261. ISBN 0-374-52322-3. $9.95.

The lighthearted tone of this text on adolescent development belies the seriousness of the issues it addresses: the struggle for separation with a childish need for dependency, the emergence of the sexual self, and fitting in. Wolf, a psychologist, draws on experience and interviews to construct realistic dialogue between elusive teenage sons and combative teenage daughters and their surprised and dismayed parents that illustrates his practical advice to parents on communicating, controlling, and resolving conflicts with their offspring. He also addresses issues that arise for teens facing the challenges of divorce, poor school performance, drug use and drinking problems, thoughts of suicide, and sexual decisions. Knowing when and how to intervene and when to let go will help parents realistically guide their adolescents and otherwise simply wait for them to mature.

POPULAR TITLES: JOURNALS

Adolescence. Libra. 1966. Q. ISSN 0001-8449. $50.00.

With an interdisciplinary focus on sociological, educational, psychiatric, psychological, and physiological aspects of the second decade of life, this journal publishes original research on topics as varied as depression in street youth, sexual abuse of male adolescents, premarital sexuality, eating disorders in female athletes, and gender differences in identity. The journal is notable for an extensive book review section.

Adolescence Magazine. A&D. 1988. B-M. ISSN 0001-8449. $26.00.

Practical articles emphasizing prevention and intervention are written by medical and social service experts for educators, counselors, and others who work with adolescents for this bimonthly journal. How to recognize behavioral disorders, abuse, and drug use, build self-esteem, work with parents and other family members, and specific treatment suggestions are covered in this topical magazine. One issue examined psychiatric hospitalization of adolescents, parent self-help programs, and first steps toward sobriety. Regular columns address such concerns as eating disorders, academic achievement, recovery, and parenting, as well as news from the field, reviews, calendar of events, and a referral directory.

PROFESSIONAL TITLES: BOOKS

Apter, T. E. *Altered Loves: Mothers and Daughters during Adolescence.* St. Martin's, 1990. 231p. bibliog. LC 89-49581. ISBN 0-312-04534-4. $24.95.

Case material from 65 American and British mother-daughter pairs illustrates the author's exploration of the positive side of this largely misunderstood relationship. Rather than accepting the conventional understanding that adolescents seek conflict to separate from their parents, she views this developmental stage as one requiring individuation and negotiation of a new relationship. The nature of adolescence, the myth of separation, developing an identity, confronting sex, envy and success, and the importance of peer relationships are addressed to validate and document this perspective.

Atwater, Eastwood. *Adolescence.* 3rd ed. Prentice Hall, 1991. 447p. bibliog. photog. illus. index. LC 91-23577. ISBN 0-13-007469-1. Price unreported.

A mediated-effects approach, one in which the primary physiological and cognitive changes of adolescence are influenced by the context in which they take place, is used in this survey of adolescent development. Drawing on current research, clinical data, and personal experience to prepare the third edition of this undergraduate textbook, the author looks at the larger societal and cultural context, including the impact of social change, to describe major aspects of adolescent psychosocial development, such as the development of personal identity, sexuality, moral development, transition to adulthood, and potential problems in delinquency, drug use, or psychological disorders. The content also includes an introduction to perspectives for viewing adolescent development and the primary biological and cognitive changes with a focus on the major settings in which they occur, such as the family, peers, school, and the workplace. Methods for studying adolescents are reviewed.

Berman, Alan L. *Adolescent Suicide: Assessment and Intervention.* American Psychological Association, 1991. 277p. bibliog. illus. index. LC 91-7968. ISBN 1-55798-107-8. $35.00.

Both a scholarly monograph and a practical guidebook, this examination summarizes current theory and provides advice for clinical practice on adolescent suicide. Each chapter provides illustrative case material, including copies of suicide notes, survey conceptual schemes, and supplements the findings and examples with an extensive bibliography. Three assumptions inform the content: a core body of empirical knowledge exists; clinical practice with suicidal adolescents is difficult and stressful; and there is no typical suicidal adolescent. To meet these challenges, the authors review and integrate research findings into guidelines for clinical practice, provide strategies for clinicians to use in assessment, treatment, prevention, and postvention, and preserve and integrate the data from which the art and science of suicidology is comprised.

Bosma, Harke, and Sandy Jackson, eds. *Coping and Self-Concept in Adolescence.* Springer-Verlag, 1990. 270p. illus. LC 90-32747. ISBN 0-387-51897-5. $49.00.

Two significant areas of research formerly conducted independently are linked in this anthology of empirical studies on adolescent self-concept, coping, and identity. Following an introductory chapter by the editors that examines potential areas of overlap, such as adolescents' perception of potential as a variable in coping, there are two separate chapters examining theory and research in coping and self-concept. The empirical chapters look at such issues as coping and development, ego strength development and social relationships, anxiety in adolescence, coping with difficult school situations and stress resistance, and identity formation in suicidal and non-suicidal youth.

Despite differences in their theoretical bases and methodologies, the editors note in a concluding chapter that the contributors display considerable agreement in how they view adolescent development. In this common perspective, the adolescent is seen as an individual who is competent in dealing with many conflicting demands and whose normal development is characterized by an increasing ability to control development rather than respond to crisis.

Bowser, Benjamin P., ed. *Black Male Adolescents: Parenting and Education in Community Context.* University Press of America, 1990. 352p. index. LC 90-45066. ISBN 0-8191-7975-2. $39.75.

Each selection in this anthology on guiding black male adolescent development was reviewed by a researcher, practitioner, and parent in order to balance academic soundness, experience, and advice for action. The text covers four areas: economic and social conditions that affect black communities, families, and teens; parenting concerns; educational options; and self-identity. In addition to an introduction, the editor provides an overview of the work and its implications. Among the topics explored are mother-son relationships, AIDS, home-based education, effect of powerlessness on sense of self, and self-exposure through language. Unlike most works of this type, this collection did not emerge from a scholarly perception that black teens should be investigated but from the ideas and concerns of a self-help collective of black men active in their communities and in the raising of their teenage sons.

Colten, Mary Ellen, and Susan Gore, eds. *Adolescent Stress: Causes and Consequences.* Aldine de Gruyter, 1991. 330p. bibliog. index. LC 90-47963. ISBN 0-202-30420-5. $42.95. ISBN 0-202-30421-3 pbk. $19.95.

Developmental and environmental aspects of stress are examined in this anthology of papers from a 1987 conference. The contributors examine how development and social stress interact, giving special emphasis to relationships as causing and mediating, the social world of adolescents and its inherently stressful nature, sources of variation in stress and response to stress, such as cumulative effects, protective-factors, and gender differences, and youth at high risk, such as the mildly retarded, youth abused in early childhood, teenage mothers, runaways, and male gay youth. Strategies for intervention are covered in the papers in the final section.

Consortium for Research on Black Adolescents and Velma McBride Murray, with assistance from Georgie Winter. *Black Adolescence: Current Issues and Annotated Bibliography.* G.K. Hall, 1990. 157p. bibliog. LC 89-26995. ISBN 0-8161-9080-1. $29.95.

A critical review of empirical and theoretical works on African-American adolescents published from 1975 and forward, this bibliography covers psychosocial development, psychological and physical health, drug abuse, suicide, teen parenting, academic performance, and employment. Each topical section is divided into three parts, an introductory summary, annotated references, and other references not exclusively focused on Af-rican-American adolescents. Each summary reviews trends and themes in the research literature, critiques methodology used, and identifies gaps in knowledge. The annotations describe the purpose, sample, and findings of the studies covered. The introduction to the volume includes a critique of problems, such as absence of a unifying theoretical framework and lack of controls of intra-group differences, that affect the results noted by these studies.

Feldman, Shirley S., and Glen R. Elliott, eds. *At the Threshold: The Developing Adolescent.* Harvard University Press, 1990. 642p. illus. index. LC 90-33784. ISBN 0-674-05035-5. $39.95.

The essays in this sourcebook emphasize research on normal development in the early adolescent aged 10-14. The contributors provide an overview of the basic processes of adolescence, contexts in which development occurs, and processes and outcomes in adolescence, with citations used to direct interested readers to more detailed information. All available research, including studies of minority youth, gender differences, and ethnicity, have been incorporated, as have a variety of methodological approaches. Among the topics addressed are the role of pubertal processes, adolescent thinking, peer groups and cultures, coming of age in changing family systems, leisure, work, and the adolescent, motivation and achievement, self and identity development, sexuality, and adolescent health. An overview by the editors introduces themes; their conclusion provides a number of recommendations for future research. These include: learning more about non-white youth and removing barriers to these studies, investigating normal development in minority youth, examining contexts and changing circumstances of today's youth, promoting longitudinal studies, and viewing adolescence as part of the normal life course.

Hardy, Janet B. *Adolescent Pregnancy in an Urban Environment: Issues, Programs, and Evaluation.* Urban & Schwarzenberg, 1991. 398p. bibliog. illus. index. LC 90-12908. ISBN 0-87766-519-2. $67.50. ISBN 0-87766-520-6 pbk. $39.50.

Model pregnancy prevention, prenatal care, and parenting programs conducted in Baltimore by Johns Hopkins Hospital are described and their impact charted in this review of adolescent pregnancy issues. Based on a random sample of pregnant adolescents receiving services in 1983, the study looks at problems and adverse consequences faced by these teens, their children, and their parents. The content also includes national and local data on the epidemiology of adolescent pregnancy, developmental issues in understanding and influencing adolescent behavior, medical management, nutrition, and social service guidelines, in addition to descriptions and evaluations of the Johns Hopkins programs. Adolescent childbearing is viewed as the end product of a process that begins with the initial sexual experience and the decisions teens make about contraception, conception and care, and the interventions required along the way. It points out the value of service programs that are comprehensive in scope, providing counseling, health care and parenting instruction, and medical care, all in a setting that is accessible, friendly, and supportive.

Hauser, Stuart T., with Sally I. Powers and Gil G. Noam. *Adolescents and Their Families: Paths of Ego Development.* Free

Press, 1991. 318p. bibliog. index. LC 90-25215. ISBN 0-02-914260-1. $29.95

The ways in which families influence adolescent ego development and self-esteem is explored in this three year study of 133 14-15 year olds and their parents. Beginning with the perspective of adolescence as a time of separation and reconnection to the family, the authors present data on ego development, family setting, and the particulars of their investigation in the first four chapters. They outline a theory of paths of ego development that identifies four types, arrested, conformist, progressive, and accelerated, and analyze the dialogue between adolescents and their parents in each category as they discuss moral dilemmas. The final chapter addresses how adolescent growth is sustained or endangered by family interactions. Appendixes include information on recruiting procedures and characteristics of the sample, the text of moral dilemmas used for family discussions, and instructions for using the constraining and enabling coding system.

Jones, Reginald L., ed. *Black Adolescents*. Cobb & Henry, 1989. 454p. LC 88-36427. ISBN 0-94539-01-3. $36.95. ISBN 0-943539-02-1 pbk. $25.95.

Providing an overview of contemporary black adolescence is the focus of this anthology. The content includes chapters on contemporary, historical, and comparative perspectives for understanding adolescents' lives, health care and mental health issues, education and underachievement, friendships, peer relations, role models, vocational development and the labor market, therapeutic interventions, and the "special topics" of pregnancy and parenting, substance use, and the criminal justice system. Two chapters look at black adolescents in white suburbs or rural areas, whereas most concentrate on urban youth. Most emphasize strategies for intervention, tying research to program development, and explaining statistical data with theoretical models, indicating an intense concern with advocacy for black adolescents on the part of the contributors.

Montemayor, Raymond, Gerald R. Adams, and Thomas P. Gullotta, eds. *From Childhood to Adolescence: A Transitional Period?* Sage, 1990. 308p. bibliog. illus. LC 89-28707. ISBN 0-8039-3726-1. $17.95.

To look at the development that occurs between childhood and adolescence is the purpose of this anthology of state-of-the art reviews of research advances. The twin themes of how children and adolescents are different and how they are similar and the degree to which early adolescence is a period of transition are explored in selections that address three topical areas: physical maturation and growth, development in a social context, and social cognitive development. The volume also contains a concluding chapter in which the editors look at differences between childhood and adolescence and the issues that emerge in investigating them, e.g., the difficulty in defining the transition period, the necessity of examining the process of change, and the importance of looking at development in social context.

Muuss, Rolf E., ed. *Adolescent Behavior and Society*. 4th ed. McGraw-Hill, 1990. 399p. illus. index. LC 89-13607. ISBN 0-07-044164-2. $17.95.

In this anthology of contemporary and classic readings about adolescent life and behavior, the emphasis is on the diversity that characterizes this developmental stage in the human life cycle. The contributors address the social meaning of adolescence, psychological aspects of physical changes during puberty, moral judgment and cognitive development, sex roles, family life, peers, dating, school adjustment, health, and disabilities. The authors digest contemporary scholarship on adolescence, demonstrating the uniqueness of this stage, and in the words of the editor, "document the present limited state of knowledge" in understanding adolescents, a condition noted even in an anthology that includes articles by Erik Erikson, Uri Bzonfenbrenner, Jean Piaget, and Carol Gilligan.

Nielsen, Linda. *Adolescence, a Contemporary View*. 2nd ed. Harcourt Brace Jovanovich, 1991. 580p. bibliog. illus. index. LC 90-46994. ISBN 0-03-032853-5. $32.00.

The author analyzes from an instructor's point of view the qualitative problems with textbooks in a thoughtful introduction to this 2nd edition of her survey on adolescent development. Her approach features observations on current research from the 1980s, accompanied by analysis of the shortcomings, discrepancies, and inconsistencies in available data. She focuses on adolescents aged 13-18, incorporating news articles and personal accounts as well as questions that demand self-examination in order to provoke interest. The text covers theories, physical and cognitive development, identity and personality, sex roles, minority cultures, schools, families, peers, sexuality, vocations, drugs, moral development, and atypical problems. The scope is broadened in the second edition by expanded coverage of divorce and blended families, poverty, father's influence, gender roles, and minority adolescents and the inclusion of information on such timely topics as steroids, date rape, codependency, incest, joint custody, and neo-nazism.

Noller, Patricia, and Victor Callan. *The Adolescent in the Family*. Routledge, 1990. 350p. bibliog. LC 90-33412. ISBN 0-415-01090-X. $14.95.

Part of the series Adolescence and Society, this volume endeavors to raise the profile of adolescence studies among practitioners and researchers as well as summarize the best research in an easily accessible format. The text addresses theory relating to family functioning, tasks of adolescent development, and the effect of family environments and explores the reasons behind a "generation gap" in attitudes toward responsibility, money, dress, appearance, and friendship. Other chapters focus on communication skills, family environment, including parenting style, sex role socialization, and family themes, leaving the family and dealing with separation, divorce, and remarriage.

Rogers, David E., and Eli Ginzberg, eds. *Adolescents at Risk: Medical-Social Perspectives*. Cornell University Medical College Seventh Conference on Health Policy. Westview, 1991. 168p. bibliog. index. LC 91-30506. ISBN 0-8133-8391-9. $34.50.

In its presentation of the results of the Seventh Cornell Conference on Health Policy, this anthology provides a broad perspective on what is known about adolescents at risk, what isn't known, and what approaches are most likely to fill this knowledge gap. Also covered are the extent to which current awareness influences policies and programs and recommendations for various groups on ways to intensify their efforts to advocate for America's teens. Following a substantive overview by Eli Ginzberg, the first two chapter provide conceptual frameworks for viewing adolescent risk behavior in terms of its roots in earlier life experience, incorporating social and psychological forces, and distinguishing between younger and older adolescents. These essays are followed by five chapters that focus, often with substantive statistical documentation, on the high risk behavior of violence, early sexual activity with exposure to AIDS, and substance abuse. In the final two chapters, one hundred programs to reduce high risk behavior are evaluated and recommendations for policy presented.

Sander, Joelle. *Before Their Time: Four Generations of Teenage Mothers.* Harcourt Brace Jovanovich, 1991. 190p. bibliog. LC 91-19965. ISBN 0-15-111638-8. $19.95.

The personal stories, childhood memories, economic, and psychological struggles, emotional needs of four generations of teenage mothers are carefully detailed in this oral history. In the first section, each woman, aged 20 to 83, provides an account of her individual history. The remaining two sections focus on the story of the youngest, first in her own words, followed by the reactions of the older generations to the difficulties of her daily life. Their stories convincingly demonstrate the hardship of early pregnancy for many teens, especially those who already endure problems brought on by poverty, poor schooling, loss of their fathers, and emotional neediness for male attention, companionship, and affection. With a foreword by Robert Coles.

Santrock, John W. *Adolescence.* 4th ed. Brown, 1990. 660p. bibliog. photog. LC 89-50280. ISBN 0-69-705950-2. $37.35.

The fourth edition of this textbook on adolescent biological, cognitive, and social development keeps up with the times by incorporating current research on sexuality, stress and health, dropouts, music videos, gender roles, pregnancy, sexually transmitted diseases, crack cocaine, and steroids. It includes additional cross-cultural and ethnic data, as well as a greater emphasis on the social worlds—family, peers, school, and U.S. culture—of adolescents. The writing style is lively, the photographs appealing. Pedagogical aids, such as chapter summaries, additional readings, and concept tables, make the information presented even more accessible. The detailed introduction provides a philosophical context for the material then presented.

Stinson, Kandi M. *Adolescents, Family, and Friends: Social Support after Parents' Divorce or Remarriage.* Praeger, 1991. 171p. bibliog. index. LC 90-7800. ISBN 0-275-93465-9. $39.95.

Thirty white teens between the ages of 13 and 17, along with their custodial parent(s), were interviewed in this study of the nature of adolescent support networks and how divorce and remarriage alters their effectiveness. Following a review of the literature on effects of divorce and remarriage and the characteristics of support networks, the author examines in separate chapters the impact of relationships with mothers, fathers, relatives, and friends on adolescents' ability to cope with changes in family relationships and structure. Data from married households is contrasted with results from divorced and remarried households. The author concludes this study by noting that

families must be viewed as systems of interaction where an event in one segment of the family affects all others, that reconceptualization is needed to determine the dynamic nature of social networks, and given the tremendous variety in contemporary family organization, the nuclear family should not be viewed as the norm against which all others are measured as such an approach yields distorted results.

Stuck, Mary Frances. *Adolescent Worlds: Drug Use and Athletic Activity.* Praeger, 1990. 179p. LC 90-34288. ISBN 0-275-93647-3. $42.95.

How adolescents view using drugs or drinking as well as their behavior related to these substances is investigated in this study of the relationship of drugs to participation in organized sports. One hundred adolescents, thirty-six of them female, were selected randomly from a larger sample drawn from another study and interviewed in depth about their social worlds, involvement in sports, drug taking behavior, and explanations for drug use and non-use. The results indicated that there was no difference in attitudes toward drugs between adolescents who were involved in organized activity and those who were not, and their incidence of using, though lower, was still quite high. Policy recommendations address the need for additional research on adolescent social worlds, increased opportunity for participation in organized sports, and more effective treatment of drug and alcohol users. The sample and methodology are covered in detail in an appendix.

Sugar, Max, ed. *Female Adolescent Development.* 2nd ed. Brunner/Mazel, 1993. 239p. bibliog. index. LC 92-41570. ISBN 0-87630-715-2. $30.95.

The revised edition of this scholarly anthology, first published in 1979, provides a state-of-the-art review of research and talks about pressing questions in the field. Written from a psychoanalytic perspective, the book emphasizes healthy development. The contributors examine issues such as the correlation of biological and social development; psychodynamic questions such as changing body image, superego development, and the development of femininity; and psychosocial issues such as cultural and ethnic factors in development, effects of secondary school and college experiences, the impact of motherhood on adolescents, and female delinquency. This text presents a basic introduction to psychoanalytic theory on the characteristics of normal adolescent development.

Voydanoff, Patricia, and Brenda W. Donnelly. *Adolescent Sexuality and Pregnancy.* Sage, 1990. 132p. bibliog. index. LC 90-8785. ISBN 0-8039-3385-1. $29.95. ISBN 0-8039-3386-X pbk. $14.00.

A volume in a series targeted both to undergraduates as a textbook and professionals as a resource, this book surveys adolescent sexuality from the decision to become sexually active to the long-term consequences of giving birth for the mother and her child. After outlining their approach in an introductory chapter, the authors examine recent trends and current levels of sexual behavior, pregnancy, and childbearing. They note that teens face challenges in the transition to adulthood, including diminished social disapproval toward sexual activity outside of marriage, decreased importance of religious beliefs, changes in family structure and relationships, increased peer pressure, and earlier biological maturity. Consequences of teen pregnancy, including living with family members, negative effects on educational and economic attainment, and high levels of welfare dependency, are outcomes for the mother; health risks, risk of maltreatment, and problem behaviors affect the child. Citations to research studies and statistics document these results. The text also covers intervention strategies.

Williams, Constance Willard. *Black Teenage Mothers: Pregnancy and Child Rearing from Their Perspective*. Lexington, 1990. 184p. bibliog. index. LC 90-41347. ISBN 0-669-24313-2. $24.95.

Thirty unmarried mothers who had their first child before the age of sixteen were interviewed for this study of black teenage childbearing by a social work professor and practitioner. Using the data gathered to develop the themes of importance to these respondents, the author looks at their socialization to motherhood, sense of responsibility and independence gained through giving birth, and reaction to resources outside the home, such as the school and health care systems. Introductory chapters examine African-American adolescent fertility in the context of African-American family structure and factors that contribute to the high incidence of teenage births. A review of the literature, a summary of the findings and their implications are also a feature of this study.

Zollar, Ann Creighton. *Adolescent Pregnancy and Parenthood: An Annotated Guide*. Garland, 1990. 244p. index. LC 89-25596. ISBN 0-8240-4295-6. $36.00.

Drawing primarily on the social and behavioral science literature, this bibliography addresses a broad range of research interests in adolescent pregnancy and parenthood in the U.S. Among the topics this scope includes are adolescent fertility, sexuality, and contraceptive behavior, sex education, social, psychological, medical consequences, and adolescent fathers. The annotations are detailed, including the methodology, subjects, major variables and findings, and viewpoints of the authors. The coverage is limited to the English language articles, books, and book chapters, most published in the 1970s to mid-1980s.

PROFESSIONAL TITLES: JOURNALS

Journal of Adolescence. Academic. 1978. Q. ISSN 0140-1971. $120.00.

Empirical research, clinical studies, and analytical reviews are combined in this periodical to provide information on adolescent development and disorders for a broad audience of professionals. Occasional topical issues, such as a special issue devoted to HIV/AIDS and adolescents, are published. Other topics considered in past issues are ethnic identity and self-esteem, interpersonal needs in middle adolescence, and preference for outdoor play in early adolescence.

Journal of Adolescent Research. Sage. 1986. Q. ISSN 0743-5584. $38.00.

With contributions from school counseling, public education, family therapy, social work, public health, and psychiatry, this interdisciplinary journal covers all aspects of adolescent development between the ages of 10 and 20. The journal published the results of empirical research and theoretical analysis of adolescent development, behavior, and reactions to social and cultural influences, giving professionals working in the field current, relevant information with practical applications. Refereed.

Journal of Early Adolescence. Sage. 1981. Q. ISSN 0272-4316. $35.00.

This scholarly journal brings an interdisciplinary perspective to the study of youth aged 10 to 14. Theoretical papers, state-of-the-art reviews, current research, and reviews of professional texts and movies and literature targeted to early adolescents are published. Among the topics addressed are creativity and problem solving, cognitive development, the adolescent and family, and middle school curricula.

Journal of Research on Adolescence. Society for Research on Adolescence. 1991. Q. ISSN 1050-8392. $39.00.

A multidisciplinary approach to issues important to understanding the second decade of life is the focus of this journal. The coverage is very broad, with basic research and applications, diverse methodologies, cross-cultural perspectives, and gender studies published here. Theoretical and review papers that address policy, methodological, or other issues relevant to how research on adolescence is conducted are also included.

Journal of Youth and Adolescence. Plenum. 1972. B-M. ISSN 0047-2891. $245.00.

Empirical research, review articles, clinical reports and theoretical papers addressing adolescence from a multidisciplincary perspective comprise the contents of this scholarly journal. Issues have covered such topics as attitudes toward abortion, academic success of Hispanic students, perception of the costs/benefits of health-compromising behaviors, family types and communication with parents, family interaction and sex role concepts, and factors related to cigarette smoking.

DIRECTORY

Center for Early Adolescence, School of Medicine, University of North Carolina at Chapel Hill
D-2 Carr Mill Town Center, Carrboro, NC 27510
(919) 966-1148 Fax (919) 966-7657
Frank A. Loda, M.D., Director
Founded: 1978
Mission/Goals: To promote the healthy growth and development of young adolescents in their homes, schools, and communities; to advocate for young adolescents; to provide information services, research, training, and leadership development for those who can have an impact on 10 to 12 year olds in the United States
Audience/Clientele: Youth workers, parent educators, policymakers, junior high educators, volunteers, health professionals
Staff: 10 professionals, 8 nonprofessionals
Budget: $1,000,000 Funding: Fees for services or products

Education and Outreach: In-service programs, continuing education courses, seminars, library, database development, publishing
Publications: *Common Focus*, periodic newsletter; books, resource lists, and monographs; pamphlets, parent education curricula, and program planning curricula

REFERENCES

1. John W. Santrock, *Adolescence*, 4th ed. (Dubuque, IA: William C. Brown, 1990), 23.

2. George H. Gallup Jr. and Frank Newport, "Virtually All Adults Want Children, but Many of the Reasons Are Intangible," *The Gallup Poll Monthly* 297, no. 11 (June 1990).

3. Jeanette Shalov et al., *You Can Say No to Your Teenager: And Other Strategies for Effective Parenting in the 1990s* (Reading, MA: Addison-Wesley, 1991), 6.

4. John Bradshaw, *Creating Love: The Next Great Stage of Love* (New York: Bantam, 1992), 219.

PART

GROWTH AND DEVELOPMENT

CHAPTER

13

Child Development Norms

Development follows a head-down-to-toes direction.
Theresa Caplan. *The First Twelve Months of Life*

*Each of us develops like all other individuals, like
some other individuals, and like no other individuals.*
John W. Santrock and Steve R. Yussen. *Child Development*

Development encompasses those processes, social, intellectual, emotional, and physical, that begin before birth and continue throughout the life cycle. After the prenatal period, child development is commonly viewed in terms of stages, starting with infancy, extending through early, middle, and late childhood, and followed by adolescence. A multitude of factors, including genetic inheritance, environmental influence, temperament, intellectual stimulation, and social interaction, influence a child's development.[1] Some conditions, such as infant day care, exposure to television violence, pressure to be thin, attention deficit-hyperactivity disorder, and gender differences, are controversial because people disagree about to what extent they affect development. According to Paul S. Kaplan, many such conditions are frequently discussed without an objective and complete understanding of the results of research on their true impact.[2]

The concept of developmental processes requires a time frame, with milestones marking developmental achievements. In terms of development, parents and other care givers must know how to identify what behavior to expect from children as they reach certain developmental stages. At the same time, parents must be aware of what kinds of behavior are normal in children who have yet to reach a certain point in their development. They must also be able to accept individual patterns of growth unique to each child.

An asterisk (*) indicates a specially recommended title.

POPULAR TITLES: BOOKS

* Brazelton, T. Berry. *Touchpoints: Your Child's Emotional and Behavioral Development.* Addison-Wesley, 1992. 400p. bibliog. photog. index. LC 92-23004. ISBN 0-201-09380-4. $22.95. ISBN 0-201-62690-X pbk. $14.95.

   In this new guidebook by Brazelton, the sequence of pediatric office visits is used to structure an introductory survey of the child's (and parent's) development during the first three years of life. This chronological review is followed by a topical section that addresses common emotional and behavioral problems such as crying, developmental disabilities, and sibling rivalry. The final section addresses the positive impact of parents, grandparents, friends, and outside care givers on the child and reviews problems that may affect these relationships. The author approaches both routine developmental concerns and problem areas in a calm, reflective manner.

Bruno, Frank J. *The Family Encyclopedia of Child Psychology and Development.* Wiley, 1992. 417p. LC 91-25322. ISBN 0-471-52793-9. $27.95.

   Bruno describes the thoughts, feelings, and actions of children and adolescents in brief subject entries arranged alphabetically. Biological impairments, mental and behavioral disorders, emotional problems, and learning disabilities are covered, including their signs and symptoms, causes, and options for treatment available to parents and other care givers. Included in the contents are entries on professionals who have made significant contributions to the study of child development. Among the other topics covered are genetic counseling, father ethology, developmental disorders, and coprolalia.

Caplan, Frank. *The First Twelve Months of Life: Your Baby's Growth Month by Month.* Rev. and updated ed. Putnam, 1993. 304p. photog. bibliog. index. LC 93-91. ISBN 0-399-51804-5. $14.95.

This updated edition of a popular guide to child development is not revised as much as supplemented. Much of the original text remains intact; information added since the book was first published in 1973 appears in boxes, in entirely new sections, and in an updated bibliography. Covering an infant's mental, physical, language, and social development from the first week of life through 12 months, this guide describes a sequence of events rather than a timetable. It also provides growth charts that summarize developmental milestones. Focusing on fathers as well as mothers, and supportive of diverse family types, this handbook will be helpful to first-time parents.

* Chess, Stella, and Alexander Thomas. *Know Your Child: An Authoritative Guide for Today's Parents.* Basic Books, 1987. 397p. bibliog. index. LC 86-47742. ISBN 0-465-03732-1. $12.95. ISBN 0-465-03731-3 pbk. $3.00.

In this handbook for educated parents, two eminent psychiatrists review and evaluate research studies on child development and select from among them useful information for parents about child development from infancy through adolescence. Results obtained from their New York longitudinal study, personal experience, and professional practice are also incorporated into their advice. Three major themes emerge: babies are human and capable of interaction from birth; babies are different, with different temperaments, from the start; and good parenting requires a good fit between parent and child rather than a prescribed list of behaviors. The authors pay special attention to debunking the idea that mothers are to blame for any problems their children exhibit. The first section of the book focuses on the developmental concepts noted above, the second on explaining child development from infancy through adolescence, and the third on special family issues such as children with special needs, adoption, divorce and remarriage, the effect of working mothers, and the role of the father. An exceptional work, this handbook integrates in clear prose the last century's worth of research on child development.

Fowler, William. *Talking from Infancy: How to Nurture and Cultivate Early Language Development.* Brookline Books, 1990. 236p. bibliog. LC 90-32791. ISBN 0-914797-71-9. $19.95.

Providing a language-enriched environment is an effective way to enhance an infant's cognitive ability and to have a positive impact on mental and social development, according to results of research conducted by the author. Techniques for improving language skills, which range from playing with sounds and words to constructing sentences and engaging in extended discourse, are simple for adults to learn and perform. According to Fowler, this approach is equally effective in home or day care settings and is not affected by the social, educational, or linguistic environment of the home. This how-

to manual examines principles and procedures, activities in which interaction may foster development, and evaluation methods. A chapter outlining procedures to use for moderately delayed infants is included. An accompanying videotape may be purchased separately.

Jacob, S. H. *Your Baby's Mind: How to Make the Most of the Critical First Two Years.* Rev. ed. Adams, 1991. 292p. bibliog. illus. index. ISBN 1-55850-137-1. $5.95.

Based on Piagetian stages of learning, this text examines how children learn from birth to 24 months and suggests practical techniques, games, and activities that parents may use to nurture their child's potential. Each chapter covers a stage, the type of learning accomplished therein, and how parents can match stage-appropriate materials and activities to their child's level of development. Appendixes provide information on risk factors affecting intellectual development, such as prenatal substance abuse and single parenting, as well as a list of recommended commercially available toys.

* Konner, Melvin. *Childhood.* Little, Brown, 1991. 451p. bibliog. photog. illus. index. LC 91-26458. ISBN 0-316-50184-0. $27.95.

Published in conjunction with the PBS series on childhood, Konner's text integrates new research results on child development with anecdotal and scholarly experiences of families from around the world. Rather than a textbook, scholarly monograph, or how-to guide, this is a review of the total experience of childhood. The author examines issues that emerge during pregnancy and childbirth, the development of attachment, the desire for mastery and separation in the second year, patterns of play, and language development. The experience of siblings, vulnerability to abuse and resilience in recovering from it, middle childhood, child culture and the metamorphosis of adolescents are also covered, among other topics. This text is notable for the author's reflective, concise, and humorous writing style and for the background in child development patterns that it provides parents.

Singer, Dorothy G. *A Piaget Primer: How a Child Thinks.* Penguin, 1978. 148p. bibliog. illus. index. LC 78-58483. ISBN 0-8236-4136-8. $11.50.

A reprint of the 1978 edition, this practical summary of Jean Piaget's theory of intellectual development uses examples from children's literature and comic strips to illustrate complex concepts. The basics of Piaget's theory, including observational methods, stages of development, and how intelligence develops within these stages, are presented first. The text then addresses Piaget's thinking on play and imitation; language development; the discovery of space, time, and numbers; and awareness of right and wrong. The authors comment briefly on applications of Piaget's theory in the final chapter. This book is a simple, concise introduction to the extensive writings of a significant twentieth-century theorist.

* Turecki, Stanley, with Leslie Tonner. *The Difficult Child: A New Step-by-Step Approach.* Rev. ed. Bantam, 1989. 259p. illus. index. LC 87-47568. ISBN 0-553-34446-3. $9.95.

Turecki and Tonner explore how aspects of temperament, such as activity level, distractibility, persistence, sensory threshold, and mood, influence how a child behaves and in turn how others react to that child. The authors then look in detail at how temperament makes a child difficult to handle and the effect that a difficult child has on family life. Case studies illustrate techniques for identifying behavioral traits and managing them within the context of family life. A chapter on coping with the difficult infant is included.

PROFESSIONAL TITLES: BOOKS

Beaty, Janice J. *Observing Development of the Young Child.* 2nd ed. Merrill, 1990. 386p. bibliog. illus. LC 89-60935. ISBN 0-675-21140-9. $19.95.

How to observe and record the development of children ages two to six is explained in this handbook. Each chapter covers a major aspect of child development, providing a checklist of behaviors, books and classroom activities that take developmental level into account, and coverage of recent research on these topics, and concluding with a sample observation and interpretation of the data that was gathered. The developmental areas covered include self-identity, emotional development, social play, cognitive development, language, art skills, and imagination.

Berk, Laura E. *Child Development.* Allyn and Bacon, 1991. 793p. bibliog. index. LC 90-1267. ISBN 0-205-12682-0. $48.00.

A detailed introduction provides a philosophical context for the topical material on child development presented in the text. Coverage includes theory and research perspectives, including historical precedent, modern theories, and dominant methods; development of foundations, such as genetic and prenatal influences; infancy; and physical growth. Similar to other textbooks in terms of content, currency, and engaging but scholarly style, this volume may be used with supplements that facilitate learning: an instructor's manual, transparencies, a test bank of 2,000 multiple choice questions, a student guide, and a media presentation on children's private speech.

Bowlby, John. *A Secure Base: Parent-Child Attachment and Healthy Human Development.* Basic Books, 1988. 205p. bibliog. illus. index. LC 88-47669. ISBN 0-465-07598-3. $13.00.

This compilation of lectures on attachment theory serves to introduce and clarify attachment theory and to emphasize important features for clinicians to use in treating disturbed patients. The lectures cover caring for children, origins of attachment theory, violence in the family, when parents disconfirm children's thoughts and feelings, the role of attachment in personality development, and attachment in the therapeutic process, as well as more general discussions of psychoanalysis and developmental psychology.

Bracken, Bruce A. *The Psychoeducational Assessment of Preschool Children.* 2nd ed. Allyn and Bacon, 1991. 573p. bibliog. illus. index. LC 90-43426. ISBN 0-205-12520-4. $47.95.

Bracken's handbook on preschool assessments is directed to an audience of psychologists, educators, speech and language pathologists, and other professionals who work with preschool children. The second edition provides comprehensive cover-

age of advances in the field since the late 1970s, including five chapters that examine individual assessment instruments, among them the McCarthy Scales of Children's Abilities, Wechsler Preschool and Primary Scale of Intelligence (revised), Stanford-Binet Intelligence Scale (4th edition), Differential Ability Scales, and Kaufman Assessment Battery for Children. New contributions on family assessment, preschool screening, and intervention design round out the thematic content, which also includes historical perspectives on assessment, assessment procedures, language, auditory, and visual processing, motor assessment, and assessment of special populations. While the anthology is organized to create and build on a hierarchical knowledge base, chapters are also accessible on an individual basis.

Decker, Celia Anita. *Children—The Early Years.* Goodheart-Willcox, 1990. 544p. photog. illus. index. glossary. LC 89-30203. ISBN 0-87006-747-8. $28.00.

With an emphasis on how children change as they grow, this textbook surveys physical, mental, social, and emotional development from birth through school age. Chapters on chronological development include theories, factual data, and illustrative examples. Pedagogical aids include review questions, a list of keywords, exercises in each chapter, and a glossary. The final chapters cover teaching via play activities, protecting children's safety and health, fostering development in group settings, and selecting a career in a child-related field. The writing style is very basic and many color photographs enliven the text.

Dixon, Suzanne D., and Martin T. Stein. *Encounters with Children: Pediatric Behavior and Development.* 2nd ed. Mosby, 1992. 483p. bibliog. illus. index. LC 91-27366. ISBN 0-8016-1432-5. $41.95.

Pediatricians can use this practical guide to upgrade their knowledge of developmental processes; better assess subtle developmental disturbances in such areas as language, cognitive, or social skills; and answer parents' questions about child development. Developmental milestones and stages from birth to young adulthood are emphasized in chapters 6-27. The initial chapters include an introduction to developmental theories and practical advice on organizing the office, interviewing, and establishing a relationship with the parents. Special concerns, such as family factors, reactions to illness or hospitalization, and use of drawings in diagnosis, also receive attention. The socially conscious and supportive approach enlivens the basic information presented. A foreword by T. Berry Brazelton is included.

Dworetzky, John. *Introduction to Child Development.* 4th ed. West, 1990. 612p. bibliog. photog. illus. LC 89-49613. ISBN 0-314-66761-X. $22.95.

Both the basic content on development presented in introductory courses and data on issues of current importance in the research literature are covered in this textbook. Typical chapters are arranged in rough chronological order, beginning with the history of development research and the genetic basis of development, followed by birth and infancy, language, cognition, and learning in the developing child and adolescent. An unusual feature is coverage of topics "at issue" in current research, such as genetics of behavior, children's understanding of adoption, birth order and intelligence, the pursuit of thinness, and the contagiousness of suicide. Numerous photographs, many of them striking, punctuate the text. Much of the information is presented in a question-and-answer format, a feature of the SQ3R (survey, question, read, recite, review) approach used in this text.

Goodnow, Jacqueline J., and W. Andrew Collins. *Development According to Parents: The Nature, Sources, and Consequences of Parents' Ideas.* Erlbaum, 1990. 190p. bibliog. index. LC 90-38263. ISBN 0-86377-160-2. $36.00.

Writing for educators and practitioners in child development and psychology, the authors have compiled not only a survey but a content analysis of several hundred references on the nature, sources, and consequences for both parents and children of the ideas that parents apply to child rearing. The scope is an international one and resources from sociology and cognition supplement the emphasis on developmental psychology. The authors go beyond simply reviewing the literature to present a research agenda that points out the most important gaps they have identified. The final chapter addresses techniques for improving the methodology of parenting studies and advises on a more complex theoretical approach, one that takes context or family relationships into account, for future studies.

Holt, K. S. *Child Development: Diagnosis and Assessment.* Butterworths, 1991. 232p. bibliog. illus. index. LC 90-2684. ISBN 0-7506-1035-2. $49.95.

The bases of development, patterns of normal development, and diagnosis of developmental difficulties are thoroughly covered in this handbook for pediatricians. In a summary of the bases of development, Holt covers neural development; major developmental theories introduced by Gesell, Piaget, and Erikson; and the process of receptive-expressive integration. Reflex activity, examination of the neonate, and developmental milestones in the first year and in years 1–5, 6–10, and 11–15 are covered, with summary charts and line drawings in the section on normal development. Delays or distortions in developmental patterns, developmental guidance, assessment of development, and developmental approaches to children with disabilities are topics addressed in the final section on developmental pediatrics.

Illingworth, Ronald S. *Basic Developmental Screening 0-4 Years.* 5th ed. Blackwell, 1990. 66p. ISBN 0-632-02905-6. $14.95.

A concise booklet to aid the busy practitioner in detecting all but the mildest forms of neurological or developmental disabilities, this guide covers only the essential screening tests. Contents include milestones of development, ages for screening, how to take a history, equipment needed, and specific tests for mental functioning, cerebral palsy, hip function, and vision and hearing defects. How to interpret the results, when to seek expert advice, the limits of screening, and mistakes to avoid are also addressed. This edition incorporates information on the pre-term baby.

Johnson, James H., and Jacquelin Goldman. *Developmental Assessment in Clinical Child Psychology: A Handbook.*

Pergamon, 1990. 289p. bibliog. illus. index. LC 90-6762. ISBN 0-08-36446-2. $45.01.

Experienced researchers and practitioners present in this anthology a state-of-the-art review of techniques to assess development in young children. Intended as a reference book for clinicians or a textbook for a developmental assessment course, this text covers the interview, reviews developmental screening measures, and addresses assessment of cognitive and motor development, speech and language, adaptive behavior, temperament and behavioral style, and the home environment. An overview of developmental assessment, normal development in infancy and early childhood, and factors contributing to deviation in development is also included. The authors also provide guidance on moving from assessment to intervention.

Kaplan, Paul S. *A Child's Odyssey: Child and Adolescent Development.* 2nd ed. West, 1991. 729p. bibliog. photog. illus. index. glossary. LC 90-20092. ISBN 0-314-80198-7. $49.25.

Physical, social, and cognitive development from infancy through adolescence is described chronologically in this textbook. Now in its second edition, the text includes cross-cultural data and controversial issues in addition to chapter updates on new studies, new perspectives, and new topics, such as the future of play, gene mapping, and prospects for non–college-bound teens. More extensive coverage of contemporary concerns such as day care, stepparenting, child abuse, and nutrition is provided. Numerous pedagogical aids, including reaction questions, a glossary, case studies, and true-false questions, are provided, along with ample photographs and tabular data.

Kohnstamm, Geldolph A., John E. Bates, and Mary Klevjord Rothbart. *Temperament in Childhood.* Wiley, 1990. 641p. LC 89-14788. ISBN 0-471-91692-7. $85.00.

Current scholarly research on temperament in childhood that emphasizes a developmental approach is reviewed in this anthology, which contains selections from 43 authors. The material is organized into six sections, each introduced by a major chapter, followed by shorter contributions from active scholars in the field. These sections discuss what temperament is and how it may be measured; the biological bases of difference in temperament; early development, temperament, and personality; applications of temperament in clinical and educational settings; effects of social class, ethnicity, and gender; and a historical and European perspective. Among the specific topics covered are temperament as an intervening variable, behavior-genetics approaches to temperament, temperament and cognition, sleep-loss stress and temperamental difficulties, and reviews of German, French, Italian, and Scandinavian scholarship in the field.

Lefrancois, Guy R. *Of Children: An Introduction to Child Development.* 6th ed. Wadsworth, 1990. 698p. bibliog. photog. illus. glossary. LC 88-25886. ISBN 0-534-09990-4. $32.00.

This undergraduate textbook provides a comprehensive chronological survey of development from infancy through adolescence. Themes addressed include history and methods, theories, genetics and environmental influences, prenatal influences and birth, physical development, language development, social and emotional development, cognitive development, and exceptionality. In this sixth edition, Lefrancois incorporates additional material on cognitive development and information processing approaches to development, AIDS and STDs, biological contributions to development, parent-infant interaction, infant perceptual development, gender roles, social cognition, and adolescent sexuality and drug use. Features of this textbook that make it a basic resource for understanding child development are chapter outlines, chapter summaries in point format, annotated lists of readings, and a glossary. The text is liberally illustrated with photographs, figures, and tables, with selective use of sidebars to cover material that would otherwise interrupt the flow of the chapters.

Levine, Melvin D., William B. Carey, and Allen C. Crocker. *Developmental-Behavioral Pediatrics*. 2nd ed. Saunders, 1992. 809p. photog. illus. index. LC 91-12323. ISBN 0-7216-3189-4. $120.00.

Following a perspective that acknowledges the influence development has on behavior and vice versa, this handbook of practical guidelines for clinicians emphasizes prevention, evaluation, and management rather than theory. The content includes normal patterns of development, influences of milieu and circumstances, biological factors that affect development and behavior, effects of illnesses and their treatment on development, negative outcomes during childhood, assessment, enhancement of development, and a review of legal and ethical issues. New to the second edition are the developmental effects of electronic media, day care, natural disasters, HIV infections, central nervous system diagnostic techniques, and social skills deficits.

Lively, Virginia, and Edwin Lively. *Sexual Development of Young Children*. Delmar, 1991. 198p. bibliog. illus. index. LC 90-20678. ISBN 0-8273-4198-9. $16.95.

The thoughts and reactions of children are revealed through case vignettes, drawings, and results of research in this study of the development of sexuality from infancy through the early school years. Defining sexuality as an individual's personal growth in all dimensions, the authors suggest that the task of parents, teachers, and all others who care for children is to encourage children to develop their sexuality in the most positive way possible rather than provide sex education per se. The authors, a kindergarten teacher and sociologist, discuss attitudes toward sexuality; complexities such as masturbation, sex play, and nudity in the home; gender identity; sexual abuse; current concerns such as AIDS; and the future of sexuality in light of such developments as technologically assisted reproduction, abortion, surrogates, and gay parents. This text is also intended for use in graduate level courses in child development, education, and family development.

Mussen, Paul Henry, et al., eds. *Child Development and Personality*. 7th ed. Harper & Row, 1990. 752p. bibliog. photog. illus. index. LC 89-27797. ISBN 0-06-044695-1. $42.50.

Reflecting increasing emphasis on applications in the study of child development, this textbook attempts to bridge basic knowledge and real world applications in four phases of development: the prenatal period, infancy, childhood, and adolescence. Now in its seventh edition, the material has been updated to incorporate new knowledge on behavior genetics, hazards in prenatal development, infant day care, temperamental differences in sociability, the transition from infancy to early childhood, the social interaction approach to language acquisition, ethnic group identity, minority children's self-concepts, peers as therapists, influences of television, economic influences on family life, and adolescent social problems such as pregnancy, parenting, work, running away, and drug use. Pedagogical aids have been added as well.

Pellegrini, Anthony D. *Applied Child Study: A Developmental Approach*. 2nd ed. Erlbaum, 1991. 242p. bibliog. photog. illus. index. LC 90-40649. ISBN 0-8058-0722-5. $60.00. ISBN 0-8058-0723-3 pbk. $30.00.

By reviewing a number of current theories of child development and methods for studying children, Pellegrini has created a sourcebook that outlines and integrates these two components of research on children. The interdisciplinary approach makes this title a relevant primer for parents as well as educators, psychologists, and other professionals. In each chapter, the author emphasizes the skills required to describe children, ways in which the context of a situation affects children, and underlying theories that make observable behavior understandable. The "action research" orientation encourages the use of research to solve everyday, practical problems. Within the general content of theories and methodologies, the author addresses such concerns as the ethics of studying children, outmoded concepts, school as a context, second language teaching, and the relationship between play and school performance, as well as tests, experimental and observational methods, learning and cognition, children's social competence, language, and play in general.

Santrock, John W., and Steve R. Yussen. *Child Development: An Introduction*. 4th ed. Brown, 1990. 572p. bibliog. photog. illus. LC 88-72247. ISBN 0-697-05951-0. $28.00.

Presently in its fourth edition, this textbook uses a topical, process-oriented approach to explore child development from the prenatal period through adolescence. Classic and cutting-edge research is cited in discussions of the nature of development, biological and perceptual development, cognitive development, social and personality development, and abnormal behavior, stress, and health. The text concludes with an epilogue integrating these themes into a chronological sequence. New content in this edition includes increased coverage of prenatal and infant development, pubertal processes, motivation, stress, and health. A "learning system" of teacher's aids and other pedagogical tools enhances access to information presented in the narratives.

PROFESSIONAL TITLES: JOURNALS

Advances in Child Development and Behavior. Academic. 1963. irreg. ISSN 0065-2407. Price varies.

The scholarly technical articles in this series serve as reference material in specialized areas of child development for practitioners and researchers. Issues are not organized around a theme, nor do they reflect new fads in treatment; rather, they reflect critical syntheses solicited from experts working in areas of current significant interest. Features are more speculative pieces that propose new ways to investigate a problem or encourage greater interest in an issue. For example, the lead article in one volume examined how developmental theories should be structured.

Advances in Motor Development Research. AMS. 1987. A. ISSN 0888-9287. $47.50.

Original research and reviews on current issues of interest to researchers investigating the biological, behavioral, and biomechanical aspects of human motor development are presented in this annual series. According to the editors, this is the only publication devoted solely to research in motor development and therefore supplements other journals and books. The scholarly standards for the theoretical, research, and review articles make the material published here references for researchers and studies.

Child Development. Society for Research in Child Development. University of Chicago Press. 1930. B-M. ISSN 0009-3920. $115.00.

This scholarly refereed journal covering all aspects of child development from a multidisciplinary perspective, publishes reports of empirical research and reviews articles and theoretical papers. Preference is given to articles that have important theoretical, practical, or policy implications and those that cover multiple studies, settings, or methodologies. This title is published by the Society for Research in Child Development.

Child Development Abstracts and Bibliography. Society for Research in Child Development. University of Chicago Press. 1927. 3/yr. ISSN 0009-3939. $53.00.

One of the publications of the Society for Research in Child Development, this serial publishes abstracts from professional journals and reviews books addressing all aspects of child development. Contributors are encouraged to submit abstracts from journals not routinely scanned; a list of these titles is published in the third issue of each volume. Among the areas reviewed are biology, health, medicine, cognition, learning, education, psychiatry, clinical psychology, history, theory, and methodology.

Child Study Journal. SUNY Buffalo. 1970. Q. ISSN 0009-4005. $32.00.

Original research and theoretical articles on the educational and psychological aspects of child and adolescent development are published in this scholarly journal. Issues have addressed such topics as development of argumentative writing, children's artwork and nonverbal communication, implications of attachment theory for day care professionals, social competence in depressed children, and friendship expectations in middle childhood. Most articles cover scholarly concerns without undue emphasis on jargon and academic prose.

Cognitive Development. Ablex. 1986. Q. ISSN 0885-2014. $35.00.

Critical reviews and empirical research on cognitive development, including pieces on the development of perception, memory, language, thought, problem solving, intelligence, and learning, make up this scholarly journal. Theoretical essays and methodological advances are also published. Articles have examined such topics as developmental shifts in the construction of verb meanings, category construction in preschool children, and assessment of memory for script-based narratives in young adults.

Developmental Psychology. American Psychological Association. 1969. B-M. ISSN 0012-1649. $100.00.

Theoretical and empirical articles addressing human development from infancy to old age are published in this scholarly refereed journal. Field research, cross-cultural studies, and research on ethnicity and gender are welcomed. Issues provide 15 to 20 articles grouped under such topics as early developmental processes, behavior problems and adjustment, cognitive development, personality and emotions, and social relationships, with the majority investigating children and adolescents as subjects. News about the association is also included.

Developmental Review. Academic. 1981. Q. ISSN 0273-2297. $74.00.

With an international focus, this interdisciplinary journal covers psychological development. Theoretical articles, critical reviews, program descriptions, reports of empirical studies, social policy analyses, book reviews, and historical or methodological analyses on development are published here. Future orientation in adolescents, father-child relationships in middle childhood, development of self in the first three years of life, and children's understanding of emotions are some of the topics covered in past issues.

Early Child Development and Care. Gordon and Breach. 1971. M. ISSN 0300-4430. Price varies.

Professionals in all fields who are concerned with research, planning, education, and care of infants and young children are the intended audience of this multidisciplinary international journal. The journal publishes experimental and observational studies and critical reviews on social, educational, and preventive medical programs for young children. In addition, coverage includes English translations of work previously published in other languages, book reviews, news items, and conference reports.

Early Human Development. Elsevier Scientific. 1977. M. ISSN 0378-3782. $630.00.

Original research on early human growth and development, particularly the continuum of fetal life with perinatal development and elements of postnatal growth affected by early events, is published in this scholarly multidisciplinary journal. The journal is a forum for practitioners and researchers with an interest in reproduction and fertility, fetology, perinatology, growth and development, epidemiology, nutrition, behavioral science, and teratology. Issues have addressed such concerns as breastfeeding and cognitive development and heart rate variability in healthy newborns and premature infants.

Infant Behavior and Development. Ablex. 1978. Q. ISSN 0163-6383. $39.50.

This journal focuses on original research that contributes to a better understanding of infancy. Review articles and theoretical analyses are also included. Content includes studies of temperament, mother-infant interaction, premature infant development, development in infants with disabilities, cognitive development, play, and responses to stimuli.

International Journal of Behavioral Development. Erlbaum. 1978. Q. ISSN 0165-0254. $57.00.

The official publication of the International Society for the Study of Behavioral Development, this refereed journal publishes original interdisciplinary research on developmental processes throughout the life span, from infancy to childhood, adolescence, adulthood, and old age. Theoretical reviews, book reviews, and news items on behavioral development are published, as are occasional state-of-the-art papers on development research within particular geographic areas and special topical issues.

Journal of Child Language. Cambridge University Press. 1974. 3/yr. ISSN 0305-0009. $99.00.

Scholarly research on all aspects of language development and use in children is published in this international journal. Vocabulary, grammar, sociolinguistics, pragmatics, semantics, phonology, and cross-cultural studies are covered. When they are concerned with issues of language development, articles on language disability, bilingualism, and acquisition of reading or writing ability are also published. Topics addressed have included use of nouns and noun bias, characteristics of maternal speech, bilingual studies, and computer methods in studying speech patterns.

Journal of Child Neurology. Mosby-Year Book. 1986. Q. ISSN 0883-0738. $75.00.

A scholarly refereed journal for physicians and psychologists, this publication provides an interdisciplinary forum covering all aspects of child neurology and developmental and behavioral pediatrics. Each issue contains 15 to 20 original research reports on topics such as spinal muscular atrophy, disorders of learning and lead neurotoxicity, emotional adjustment of parents whose child has hydrocephalus, and delayed myelination in Down's syndrome. A comprehensive topical review is provided, as are opinion pieces on controversial issues, correspondence, and book reviews.

Journal of Childhood Communication Disorders. Council for Exceptional Children. 1977. 2/yr. ISSN 0735-3170. $16.00.

Readers of this scholarly journal will find practical articles on clinical assessment and innovative programs for treating communication disorders in children. Reviews of books, software, and clinical tools are also published. The journal is the official publication of the Division for Children with Communication Disorders of the Council for Exceptional Children. Therapeutic strategies for children with language disorders and the effects of maternal conversations on the social development of deaf children were covered in past issues.

Journal of Developmental and Behavioral Pediatrics. Williams & Wilkins. 1978. Q. $115.00.

The official journal of the Society for Behavioral Pediatrics, this scholarly title for pediatricians, child psychologists, and special educators covers child behavior, learning disorders, and family dynamics. Reports of original research, case studies, preliminary research results, reviews, and opinion pieces are all included, as are news of the society, letters to the editor, and conference announcements.

DIRECTORY

Society for Research in Child Development (SRCD)
University of Chicago Press, 5720 Woodlawn Avenue,
 Chicago, IL 60637
(312) 702-7470 Fax (312) 702-0694
Barbara Kahn, Business Manager
Founded: 1933
Mission/Goals: To promote research in child development
Audience/Clientele: Educators, psychiatrists, psychologists, pediatricians, nutritionists, and others concerned with child development
Education and Outreach: Research, publishing
Publications: *Child Development Abstracts and Bibliography,* 3/ yr; *Child Development,* bimonthly; *Monograph of the Society for Research in Child Development,* 3 or 4/yr; *Society for Research in Child Development Newsletter,* periodic
Programs: Biennial conference, Annual conference

REFERENCES

1. John W. Santrock and Steve R. Yussen, *Child Development: An Introduction,* 4th ed. (Dubuque, IA: William C. Brown, 1990), 13–14.

2. Paul S. Kaplan, *A Child's Odyssey: Child and Adolescent Development,* 2nd ed. (St. Paul, MN: West, 1991), xx.

CHAPTER

Developmental Disabilities

*What kind of parent feels anger
toward a child who already has problems?*

Peggy Finston. *Parenting Plus*

**Being accepted enables slow
children to make the most of their abilities.**
Benjamin Spock and Michael B. Rothenberg.
Dr. Spock's Baby and Child Care

Children with developmental disabilities do not progress as fast or as far through the processes of biological, cognitive, or social development as other children. During 1986–88, the rate per 1,000 children of mental retardation was 14.2.[1] The parents of children with developmental disabilities defy the common interpretation of parenting as ". . . the job of slowly working themselves out of a job."[2] Instead, after spending many, often frustrating, years seeking an accurate diagnosis of their child's condition, they must determine, often on their own, which therapies and accommodations are required to provide the best possible life for their offspring. Educational assistance and special living arrangements may be lifelong concerns. Social isolation, financial vulnerability, family conflict, and unsettling emotions of guilt, shame, fear, and anger are particular problems parents in these circumstances must confront.

An asterisk (*) indicates specially recommended titles.

POPULAR TITLES: BOOKS

* Batshaw, Mark L. *Your Child Has a Disability: A Complete Sourcebook of Daily and Medical Care.* Little, Brown, 1991. 345p. index. LC 91-10580. ISBN 0-316-08369-0. $27.95. ISBN 0-3160-8368-2 pbk. $16.95.

    This guide is divided into five parts: the diagnosis, genetic and other causes of developmental disabilities, practical information on individual diseases and syndromes, approaches

to therapy, and social, legal, and educational decisions regarding a child with disabilities. The author presents a significant amount of material in a clear and concise manner that engages the reader. His approach is a responsible, capable, and supportive one for parents facing the challenge of caring for a child with greater needs.

* Beckman, Paula, and Gayle B. Boyes. *Deciphering the System: A Guide for Families of Young Children with Disabilities.* Brookline, 1993. 208p. bibliog. index. LC 92-7303. ISBN 0-914797-87-5. $21.95.

    Parents whose child is disabled will find in this guide advice on securing appropriate schooling and the value of early intervention. Drawing on personal experience and challenged by the difficulty in locating basic information on the services available for children with disabilities, the authors present an upbeat, sympathetic guide to developing a family "team" to face the challenges a disability brings to all members of the family. The text describes entitlements and rights under the law, how to work with multiple professionals, managing the information flow, educational assessment, responding to requests for family information, individual family service plans, due process, and how to handle transitions.

* Callanan, Charles R. *Since Owen: A Parent-to-Parent Guide for Care of the Disabled Child.* Johns Hopkins University Press, 1990. 466p. index. LC 89-24678. ISBN 0-8018-3963-7. $39.95. ISBN 0-8018-3964-5 pbk. $16.95.

    Callanan, whose son has disabilities, has written an informative handbook covering all aspects of caring for a child with developmental disabilities, using anecdotes from his life to illustrate. He briefly reviews the causes of developmental disabilities, prenatal tests, professionals, hospitalization, and the diagnosis. Dealing with emotions, finding support, managing finances, planning for the future, and other parental concerns are covered, as are child-focused concerns, including medical and dental care, special education, living arrangements, and sexual maturation. The text is notable for its comprehensiveness, including a particularly detailed review of how to secure specialized education services.

Lobato, Debra J. *Brothers, Sisters, and Special Needs: Information and Activities for Helping Young Siblings of Children with Chronic Illnesses and Developmental Disabilities.* Brookes, 1990. 213p. bibliog. photog. illus. index. glossary. LC 90-1518. ISBN 1-557-66043-3. $28.00.

Helping siblings adjust to their brothers' and sisters' developmental disabilities or chronic illnesses is the focus of this how-to manual suitable for parents and professionals. Based on research and clinical experience, the book covers the literature on siblings in general and how disability or illness may affect their relationships and provides background, step-by-step plans, and examples for conducting and evaluating a sibling workshop. Lobato notes that, when young, siblings do not understand their brothers' or sisters' disabilities but will still experience the gamut of emotions when relating to them. When older, siblings tend to become more nurturing and positive than is common in sibling relationships. Most important, there is no direct relationship between a child's disability and his or her siblings' psychological development. An annotated bibliography of children's literature and a glossary that defines disabilities in terms children can understand supplement the programmatic information provided.

Powers, Michael D. *Children with Autism: A Parent's Guide.* Quality, 1989. 368p. bibliog. index. glossary. LC 87-51322. ISBN 0-933149-16-6. $12.95.

The foreword by celebrity parent Beverly Sills and introduction by noted autism expert Bernard Rimland speak directly and optimistically to parents of an autistic child. The book covers current thought in the field of autism, including information on the causes of autism, methods for adjusting to the diagnosis, related medical problems and their treatment, daily routines, and adjustments to autism into family life. The content also includes information on charting developmental progress, evaluating educational programs, obtaining legally guaranteed rights, and caring for the adult with autism, as well as advice on becoming an advocate through individual and group action. The text, which is organized to provide detailed information in a logical and easy-to-read format, concludes with an extensive reading list and resource guide to national and state organizations.

Selikowitz, Mark. *Down Syndrome: The Facts.* Oxford University Press, 1990. The Facts Series. 205p. photog. illus. LC 89-15961. ISBN 0-19-261872-5. $18.95.

A current volume in a self-help health care series, this handbook provides background to help parents make more informed choices about their children with Down syndrome. Selikowitz discusses causes, diagnosis, development, health considerations, education, behavior management, and how to cope with the reactions of friends and family members.

Controversial treatments are also reviewed, as are services, adolescence and adulthood concerns, and school selection.

Smith, Romayne, ed. *Children with Mental Retardation: A Parents' Guide.* Woodbine, 1993. 437p. bibliog. photog. index. glossary. LC 90-50528. ISBN 0-933149-39-5. $14.95.

For parents of children with mild to moderate retardation, this book offers advice on helping a child achieve his or her potential and gives thorough background information on the causes of mental retardation, evaluation procedures, the importance of early intervention, and the legal rights of parents and children. Both parents and professionals contributed to the book, which includes empathetic chapters on getting the diagnosis, daily living, and family life. The final chapter on advocacy emphasizes parents' interest in obtaining the best for their children. The supportive and informative narrative is supplemented by reading lists, a resource guide of organizations, and a glossary of terms helpful in understanding health care professionals and in explaining specialized circumstances to family and friends.

Strom, Charles M. *Heredity and Ability: How Genetics Affects Your Child and What You Can Do about It.* Insight Plenum, 1990. 300p. bibliog. index. LC 90-37920. ISBN 0-306-43560-8. $22.95.

A practicing geneticist attempts to alert parents, educators, and others who work with children to the signs and symptoms that indicate a need for genetic testing, because parents' knowledge of a disorder will improve their understanding of their children and suggest new approaches to education. Strom advises parents in how to seek a diagnosis, accept a treatment plan, and work with the school system to see that their child receives an appropriate education.

The introduction covers the incidence of disabilities and elaborates on reasons for a diagnosis and annual follow-up evaluations. Succeeding chapters cover IQ and achievement testing, types of mental dysfunction, interaction and influence of nature and nurture, learning and attention deficit disabilities, diseases that cause specific behavior patterns or loss of developmental milestones, and inborn errors of metabolism. There is additional information on the mechanism of heredity, circumstances that indicate when parents should suspect a genetic cause for a disability, physical features associated with mental dysfunction, effective versus useless treatments, and nongenetic causes of disabilities. The textual material is supplemented by a lengthy bibliography of popular and professional literature and a list of references. A list of national support groups and voluntary organizations adds to the substantive information provided in this concise handbook.

Trainer, Marilyn. *Differences in Common: Straight Talk on Mental Retardation, Down Syndrome, and Life.* Woodbine, 1991. 231p. LC 90-50503. ISBN 0-933149-40-9. $14.95.

This collection of essays, some reprinted, illustrates what daily life with a child with disabilities is like. The individual accounts reveal the concerns of a mother whose child has Down syndrome and how a disabling condition may affect communication and influence family relationships. From the author's perspective, sharing her experiences is a way to advocate for her son Bennett and his friends, as well as a means of connecting with others in similar life circumstances. The essays address such concerns as mainstreaming, the "cringe factor," siblings' reactions, support from parents' groups, letting go, group activities, and sexual exploitation.

PROFESSIONAL TITLES: BOOKS

Bagnato, Stephen J., and John Nelsworth. *Assessment for Early Intervention: Best Practices for Professionals*. Guilford, 1991. 260p. bibliog. illus. index. LC 91-6540. ISBN 0-8986-2359-6. $40.00.

Child psychologists will find this sourcebook useful in planning and providing family-centered interventions. In the authors' view, early childhood assessment is not a test-based process, rather it is a collaborative and flexible process, drawing information from many sources and involving parents in the determination of children's changing developmental, educational, mental health, and medical needs. Bagnato and Nelsworth examine often neglected areas of assessment, such as curriculum-based assessment and the role of parents on the assessment team, as well as working with infants, predicting success in kindergarten, using the convergent assessment model, and evaluating programs. The material is presented in an engaging manner, with pedagogical aids such as issue summaries and illustrations, "guideposts" to assist in organizing the material, recommended instruments, and checkpoints for good practice.

Baroff, George S. *Developmental Disabilities: Psychosocial Aspects*. Pro-Ed, 1990. 259p. bibliog. index. LC 90-43702. ISBN 0-89079-412-X. $25.00.

Four major disabling conditions, mental retardation, cerebral palsy, autism, and, because it is often associated with them, epilepsy, are covered in-depth in this text. After discussing what it means to be a person, in terms of capacities and needs, Baroff examines what services are necessary to fulfill these human requirements. The bulk of the text is devoted to an explication of the disabilities themselves, including a description of each condition, its disabling aspects, prevalence and causes, and effect on those who live with it, the latter explored via autobiographical material obtained in interviews. How disorders such as autism or cerebral palsy influence children's development and their capacities, needs, and self-esteem from infancy to adolescence is revealed in this text.

Blackman, James A. *Medical Aspects of Developmental Disabilities of Children Birth to Three*. 2nd ed. Aspen, 1990. 292p. bibliog. illus. LC 89-17808. ISBN 0-8342-0107-0. $32.00.

Brief, factual entries provide health information on significant medical problems common in infants and young children with disabilities. In order to help early intervention and education professionals recognize health problems that affect the development of children with disabilities, the author conducted a survey of these professionals' information needs. Entries are arranged alphabetically and include several references and additional resources. Such topics as child abuse and neglect, congenital heart disease, floppy infant syn-

drome, autism, respiratory distress syndrome, congenital infections, cerebral palsy, problems with bowel and bladder control, Down syndrome, otitis media, seizure disorders, congenital heart disease, low birth weight, and fetal alcohol syndrome are covered.

Cantwell, Dennis P., and Lorian Baker. *Psychiatric and Developmental Disorders in Children with Communication Disorder*. American Psychiatric, 1991. 308p. bibliog. index. LC 90-14486. ISBN 0-88048-357-1. $32.50.

The results of this study of 600 children confirm findings that children with speech or language disorders have a higher incidence of psychiatric disorders common to the general population of children. Cantwell and Baker review the literature and the study, including sample selection, research methodology, and findings, and discuss clinical applications of study results to the treatment of emotional and behavioral problems in children with communication disorders. Appendixes chart the literature on childhood speech and language dysfunction and the link between both psychiatric and learning disorders and speech/language disorders in children. An extensive list of references is also appended.

Gerdtz, John, and Joel Bregman. *Autism: A Practical Guide for Those Who Help Others*. Continuum, 1990. 144p. LC 89-71247. ISBN 0-8264-0462-6. $17.95.

Promoting understanding and empathy in the treatment of people with autism within the context of their families is the focus of this brief guidebook for counselors, educators, and also parents, which reviews both historical and contemporary approaches to the disorder. The text covers the controversy about the diagnosis itself, theories about causes of autism, the use of medications in treating behaviors associated with autism, and advocacy for children with autism, including obtaining services authorized by PL 94-142. Gerdtz and Bregman also cover how to work with families who have an autistic member, adolescents with autism, and autistic adults. This text provides a brief, but thorough summary of issues related to diagnosing and treating autism as well as promoting awareness and sensitivity in working with families and individuals affected by it.

Meisels, Samuel J., and Jack P. Shonkoff, eds. *Handbook of Early Childhood Intervention*. Cambridge University Press, 1990. 760p. bibliog. LC 89-25312. ISBN 0-521-34371-2. $59.50. ISBN 0-521-38777-9 pbk. $27.95.

This anthology provides a state-of-the-art summary of research in early childhood intervention over the past 25 years. While scholars agree that early intervention for economically disadvantaged children has long-term effects, there is no agreement about the processes that influence this outcome. The contributions here come from many disciplines and integrate theory, research, and practical experience. They are arranged in seven sections: history and future challenges; biological, familial, and social sources of vulnerability; theoretical bases of early interventions; assessment instruments and strategies; modes of service delivery; research; and policy issues and programmatic directions. Conceived of as a core text for all professionals interested in young developmentally vulnerable children or young children with disabilities, the essays are guided by the assumptions that effective intervention requires the participation of an interdisciplinary team, that the needs of children can be understood only within a family context, and that programs are designed to enhance development, minimize delay, remedy existing problems, prevent further deterioration, limit additional disabling conditions, and promote adaptive family functioning.

Nelson, Donald C. *Practical Procedures for Children with Language Disorders: Preschool-Adolescence*. Pro-Ed, 1990. 94p. bibliog. LC 90-32276. ISBN 0-89079-235-6. $13.00.

Nelson's guide to clinical procedures for use with language-impaired children from preschool to adolescence is intended for the new or inexperienced clinician. The author, director of the Child Development and Rehabilitation Center of the Oregon Health Sciences University, explores first the characteristics of an outstanding clinician, then examines the use of informal language assessment techniques. The contents also include techniques for assessing hard-to-test children, such as those who are shy or mentally retarded; interaction and intervention; and strategies to use with preschool children, school-age children, and adolescents. Nelson makes no attempt to describe theoretical bases for these techniques because they are based on his own observations and improvisations as well as those of the clinical psychologists, speech-language pathologists, and occupational and physical therapists he interviewed in preparation for compiling this guide.

Rossetti, Louis M. *Infant-Toddler Assessment: An Interdisciplinary Approach*. College-Hill, 1990. 294p. bibliog. index. LC 90-9185. ISBN 0-316-75755-1. $34.50.

Appropriate for use as a textbook, this volume reviews the nature, purposes, selection, and evaluation of developmental tests for children at risk of developmental delay or disorders. Rossetti reviews the philosophy of testing; who should be tested; who performs such tests; issues in interpreting the results and collecting and reporting assessment data; language, motor, cognitive and family assessments; and administrative, research, and personnel considerations for the practitioner. The book is aimed at a wide audience of professionals who work with infants and toddlers. Two informative appendixes contain sample questionnaires and an annotated bibliography of assessment instruments.

Sloan, Christine. *Treating Auditory Processing Difficulties in Children*. Singular, 1991. 229p. illus. index. LC 85-17462. ISBN 1-879105-15-2. $39.35.

A reprint of the 1986 edition, this text provides both a review of the theoretical literature on auditory processing in children and a detailed description of a clinical program for identifying and treating auditory processing disorders. Because creation of clinical applications has not kept pace with advances in theoretical knowledge over the past decade, this book provides valuable information to practitioners in the field through its description of an auditory perceptual training and learning approach to treating disorders. Identifying such disorders is essential because auditory processing is one of the child's entry points to language development.

PROFESSIONAL TITLES: JOURNALS

Exceptionality. Springer-Verlag. 1990. Q. ISSN 0936-2835. $101.00.

Original research and review articles on persons of all ages with disabilities, as well as the gifted and talented, are published in this scholarly journal. The publication is directed to educators, physicians, psychologists, and other behavioral scientists concerned with exceptionalities of all types. Articles provide practical applications for working with persons having learning disabilities, behavior disorders, hearing and visual impairments, speech and language disorders, and mental retardation. Issues have addressed teachers with learning disabilities teaching students with learning disabilities, small-group instruction for students with moderate retardation, and recognition and development of academic talent in educationally disadvantaged youth.

Infants and Young Children. Aspen. 1988. Q. ISSN 0896-3746. $51.00.

This practice-oriented, refereed journal covers the clinical management of infants and young children from birth to three years of age with developmental disabilities and their families. It brings an interdisciplinary approach to the synthesis of research, theory, and opinion in psychology, health care, education, and support services related to the care of children with or at risk of developmental disabilities. Books related to practice in this area are briefly annotated.

Journal of Autism and Developmental Disorders. Plenum. 1971. M. ISSN 0162-3257. $210.00.

Original research, theoretical papers, critical reviews, and case studies on all severe psychopathologies in childhood are published in this journal. Contents include experimental studies of biochemical, neurological, and genetic factors in specific developmental disorders; analyses of the implications of normal processes for deviant development; and social factors in disordered behavior. Other topics within the journal's scope are revised diagnosis and classification of psychopathologies based on new knowledge and reports on applications of all types of case studies. Special issues, such as one on classification and diagnosis, are occasionally published.

Journal of Early Intervention. Council for Exceptional Children. 1979. Q. ISSN 1053-8151. $50.00.

The official journal of the Council for Exceptional Children's Division for Early Childhood, this title publishes research reviews, policy articles on interventions for children from birth to age eight with special needs or at risk of developing disabilities and their families. Because families assume a primary role in many intervention programs, research on family functioning, adaptation, and needs as they relate to a child with special needs is included in the journal's scope. Also of interest are articles that cover intervention issues for minority children or have an international focus. Selected articles on research methodology or reports on model-based innovative methods in a single classroom are included.

Research in Developmental Disabilities. Pergamon. 1981. 4/yr. ISSN 0891-4222. $145.00.

Original research that addresses remedying problems related to developmental disabilities is the focus of this scholarly journal. Interdisciplinary in scope, the journal publishes studies that examine all aspects of developmental disabilities, including occupational and speech therapy, traditional and behavioral assessment, and pharmacotherapy. Each issue has a software survey section of new products, as well as software and book reviews. Occasional topical issues, such as an issue on community-based treatment programs, are published.

DIRECTORY

Alliance of Genetic Support Groups

35 Wisconsin Circle, Suite 440, Chevy Chase, MD 20815
(301) 652-5553 Fax (301) 654-0171 Toll-free (800) 336-GENE
Joan O. Weiss, Executive Director
Founded: 1986
Members: 465 (172 organizations)
Mission/Goals: To strengthen collaboration and communication between consumers and providers of genetic services for the benefit of all affected by genetic disorders; to increase awareness of cross-disability similarities and resources by promoting communication among genetic support groups
Audience/Clientele: Consumers seeking genetic support groups, genetic counselors, nurses, social workers, researchers, educators, students, librarians, and other interested individuals
Staff: 5 professionals (part-time) and 18 board members and committee chairs
Funding: Federal government, donations, grants, dues
Services: Support group, referral, fund-raising
Awards: "Art of Listening" Award for professional who is nominated by a consumer or consumer group
Education and Outreach: Seminars, library, publishing
Publications: *Alert Newsletter*, monthly; *Alliance Resource Guide for Peer Support Training; Directory of Volunteer Genetic Organizations and Related Resources; Health Insurance Resource Guide*
Programs: Annual conference

Association for Children with Down Syndrome, Inc. (ACDS)

2616 Martin Avenue, Bellmore, NY 11700-3196
(516) 221-4700 Fax (516) 221-4311
Fredda Stimell, Executive Director
Founded: 1966
Members: 1,000
Former Name: Association for Special Children
Mission/Goals: To provide early intervention for children and continuing services to families to maximize each child's ability to become a contributing member of society; to assist parents in finding services for their children; to provide social and recreational programs for infants, toddlers, and preschool age children with Down syndrome; to promote and help strengthen the family; to provide psychological evaluation and counseling; to provide language and speech therapy and appropriate physical education
Audience/Clientele: People with Down syndrome and their families, professionals in the field
Staff: 51 professionals, 38 nonprofessionals, 60 volunteers
Budget: $2,000,000 Funding: Counseling, support group, social service/case management, recreation, substance abuse treatment, lobbying, fund-raising, compiling statistics
Awards: Annual local high school awards to students who have worked with persons with Down syndrome
Education and Outreach: In-service programs, seminars, library, database development, publishing
Publications: Journal, annual; *ACDS Newsletter*, bi-monthly; various videos, books, articles, and manuals; bibliographies; brochures
Programs: Periodic meetings

Association of Birth Defect Children (ABDC)

Orlando Executive Park, 5400 Diplomat Circle, Suite 270, Orlando, FL 32810
(407) 629-1466
Betty Mekdeci, Executive Director
Founded: 1982
Members: 4,000
Previous Name: Association of Benedictin Children
Mission/Goals: To serve as a national clearinghouse for information about birth defects
Audience/Clientele: Parents and professionals with an interest in birth defects
Staff: Numerous volunteers, professional advisory board, board of directors
Budget: $30,800 Funding: Dues, donations, grants
Services: Support group, compiling statistics, maintaining National Environmental Birth Defects Registry
Education and Outreach: Database development, publishing
Publications: *ABDC Newsletter*, quarterly; special reports on environmental illness and children of Vietnam veterans, aspartame, and Benedictin; *Birth Defect Fact Packs*, each 10-12 pages, including copies of newspaper, magazine, and medical articles; *Disabilities Fact Sheets*, brief articles on heart defects, skin disorders, learning disorders, and similar topics; *How-to Fact Sheets*, on learning more about a child's birth defects, advocacy, services, and related topics

Autism Services Center (ASC)

Prichard Building, P.O. Box 507, 605 Ninth Street, Huntington, WV 25710-0507
(304) 525-8014 Fax (304) 525-8026
Ruth C. Sullivan, Ph.D., Director
Founded: 1979
Mission/Goals: To assist families and agencies faced with the often difficult and unique needs of clients who are autistic; to operate a hotline for parents, educators, students, and others interested in obtaining information relating to the needs of autistic people and their families

Audience/Clientele: Autistic individuals and MR/DD (four counties in West Virginia), parents, educators, students, relatives, and others
Funding: Federal government, state government, donations, grants
Services: Social service/case management, residential facility
Education and Outreach: National Autism Hotline, library, compiling statistics, publishing
Publications: Newsletter, information packets

Autism Society of America
7910 Woodmont Avenue, Suite 650, Bethesda, MD 20814
(301) 657-0881 Fax (301) 657-0869 Hotline (800) 3-AUTISM
Veronica Zysk, Administrative Director
Founded: 1965
Members: 12,000
Affiliates: 186 local groups
Former Name: National Society for Children and Adults with Autism (NSAC)
Mission/Goals: To educate parents, professionals, and the general public regarding autism; to monitor and advocate for legislation and regulations affecting support, education, training, research, and other services involving the welfare of individuals with autism; to provide information and referral to members, professionals, and the general public
Audience/Clientele: Individuals with autism and their families, professionals, the general public
Staff: 1 professional, 3 nonprofessionals, 13 members of the board of directors
Budget: $1,400,000 Funding: Fund-raising, donations, grants, dues
Services: Support group, search services, recreation, referral, fund-raising
Awards: Various awards to chapters are given out at the annual conference
Education and Outreach: Seminars, database development, research, publishing
Publications: *The Advocate*, quarterly newsletter; various pamphlets
Programs: Annual conference

Division on Mental Retardation and Developmental Disabilities of the Council for Exceptional Children (MRDD)
245 Cedar Springs Drive, Athens, GA 30605
(705) 546-6132 Fax (706) 546-6132
Dr. Dana M. Anderson, Executive Secretary
Founded: 1963
Former Name: Division on Mental Retardation of the Council for Exceptional Children
Members: 8,000
Mission/Goals: To advance education, welfare, and research addressing persons with developmental disabilities and mental

retardation; to enhance public knowledge, promote legislation, and assure competency of teachers of mentally disabled youths
Audience/Clientele: Teachers and other professionals who work with students with developmental disabilities and mental retardation
Education and Outreach: Seminars, publishing, speakers' bureau
Publications: *Education and Training in Mental Retardation and Developmental Disabilities*, quarterly; *Best Practices in Mild Mental Retardation*; *MR Express*, newsletter, 3/year; *Education Programming for the Severely/Profoundly Handicapped*; other books
Programs: Semiannual conference

International Rett Syndrome Association (IRSA)
9121 Piscataway Road, No. 2B, Clinton, MD 20735
(301) 856-3334
Kathy Hunter, President
Founded: 1985
Members: 1,500
Former Name: International Rett's Syndrome Association
Mission/Goals: To support and encourage efforts to determine the cause of and cure for Rett syndrome, a progressive neurological disorder that causes severe physical and mental retardation in females; to increase public awareness of the disorder; to provide emotional support to families of children with Rett syndrome
Audience/Clientele: Parents, relatives, teachers, therapists, physicians, researchers
Staff: 1 professional, 1 nonprofessional, 25 volunteers
Budget: $200,000 Funding: Private source, fund-raising, fees for services or products, donations, grants, dues
Services: Counseling, support group, search services, referral, fund-raising, compiling statistics, parent networking
Awards: Outreach Award, for public awareness; Special People Award, for individual contributions; Community Service Award, for service; Outstanding Contributions, for major donors
Education and Outreach: Seminars, library, database development, sponsored research, publishing
Publications: *International Rett Syndrome Association*; various pamphlets and brochures
Programs: Annual conference

National Down Syndrome Congress (NDSC)
1605 Chantilly Drive, Suite 250, Atlanta, GA 30324
(404) 633-1555 Fax (404) 633-2817 Hotline (800) 232-6372
Michael Leonard, Executive Director
Founded: 1973
Members: 5,000
Affiliates: 500 local groups
Former Names: Down's Syndrome Congress, National Down's Syndrome Congress

Mission/Goals: To promote the interests of persons with Down syndrome and their families through advocacy, information dissemination, and support of families
Audience/Clientele: Persons with Down syndrome, parents, professionals concerned with Down syndrome
Staff: 2 professionals, 2 nonprofessionals
Budget: $300,000 Funding: Fund-raising, donations, grants, dues
Services: Support group, referral
Education and Outreach: Database development, publishing
Publications: *Down Syndrome News*, 10/yr, newsletter covering educational, research, and service programs; bibliographies of books, pamphlets, journals, articles, and films related to Down syndrome; position statements on treatments and education
Programs: Annual conference

National Down Syndrome Society (NDSS)
666 Broadway, New York, NY 10012
(212) 460-9330 Fax (212) 979-2873 Toll-free/Hotline (800) 221-4602
Donna M. Rosenthal, Executive Director
Founded: 1979
Members: 50,000
Mission/Goals: To promote a better understanding of Down syndrome and the potential of the individual with Down syndrome; to support research about this genetic disorder; to provide vital programs and services for people with Down syndrome; to provide information and referral to families and professionals
Audience/Clientele: Families, professionals, researchers, and concerned citizens with an interest in Down syndrome
Staff: 4 professionals, 2 nonprofessionals, 200 volunteers
Budget: $850,000 Funding: Private sources, fund-raising, fees for services or products, donations
Services: Referral, fund-raising, model programs for respite care, computer education, and mainstreaming
Awards: Science Scholar Award; Outstanding Physician; Special Recognition Award; Women's Humanitarian Award
Education and Outreach: Continuing education courses, seminars, library, publishing
Publications: *NDSS Update*, quarterly newsletter; *Directory of Parent Support Groups and Early Intervention Programs*, periodic; monographs, symposia proceedings, booklets, and fact sheets; video on children with Down syndrome
Programs: International Down Syndrome Science Symposium, periodic; Science Symposium, annual

The National Fragile X Foundation
1441 York Street, Suite 215, Denver, CO 80206
(303) 333-6155 Fax (303) 333-4369 Toll-free (800) 688-8765
Sabrina Jewell-Smart, Executive Director
Founded: 1984
Affiliates: 51 state groups
Mission/Goals: To promote education, diagnosis, treatment, and research for fragile X syndrome, the most common genetic disorder in humans and the leading cause of inherited mental retardation, also the cause for a wide array of learning disabilities and autism

Audience/Clientele: Families with members who display developmental delays or mental retardation of unknown causes, special education therapists, physicians, educators, the general public
Staff: 1 professional, 15 volunteers
Budget: $83,000 Funding: Private source, fund-raising, fees for services or products, donations, grants
Services: Social service/case management, referral
Education and Outreach: Continuing education courses, seminars, library, publishing
Publications: *National Fragile X Foundation Newsletter*, quarterly; *International Fragile X Conference Proceedings*; informational booklets
Programs: Biennial international conference

Pilot Parents (PP)
3610 Dodge Street, Omaha, NE 68131
(402) 346-5220 Fax (402) 346-5253
Annie Adamson, Coordinator
Founded: 1971
Members: 340
Mission/Goals: To provide factual information about disabilities and emotional support to new families who have recently learned that their child has a disability or special need; to promote positive attitudes about disabilities within our community
Audience/Clientele: Parents with children from birth to age 6 with disabilities
Staff: 1 professional, 30-50 volunteers
Funding: Private sources
Services: Support group, recreation, referral
Education and Outreach: In-service programs, continuing education courses, seminars, publishing
Publications: *Gazette*, monthly newsletter; booklets
Programs: Annual conference

The Sibling Information Network
The A.J. Pappanikou Center, 1776 Ellington Road, South Windsor, CT 06074
(203) 648-1205 Fax (203) 644-2031
Lisa Glidden, Coordinator
Founded: 1981
Members: 1,800
Mission/Goals: To act as a clearinghouse of information relating to siblings who have a brother or sister with disabilities
Audience/Clientele: Brothers, sisters, parents, grandparents, professionals, paraprofessionals, and the members of the general public with an interest in disabilities
Staff: 1 professional
Funding: Dues
Education and Outreach: Library, publishing
Publications: *The Sibling Information Network Newsletter*, quarterly; brochures and bibliographies

Support Organization for Trisomy 18, 13 (Soft 18/13) Related Disorders
c/o Barb VanHerrweghe, 2982 S. Union Street, Rochester, NY 14624

(716) 594-4621
Founded: 1980
Affiliates: 65 state groups
Mission/Goals: To provide support and information to families and medical professionals with an interest in trisomy 18 and 13, genetic disorders characterized by mental retardation and neurological, circulatory, and respiratory problems
Audience/Clientele: Families, health care providers, early intervention services
Staff: 100 volunteers
Funding: Donations, dues
Services: Referral, lobbying, compiling statistics
Education and Outreach: In-service programs, continuing education courses, seminars, library, database development, publishing
Publications: *The SOFT Touch*, bimonthly newsletter; *Directory*, annual; *Trisomy—A Book for Families*; various booklets
Programs: Annual conference

Williams Syndrome Association (WSA)

P.O. Box 3297, Ballwin, MO 63022-3297
(314) 227-4411
Dana Vouga, National Chairperson
Founded: 1982
Members: 1,900
Mission/Goals: To find all individuals affected by Williams syndrome; to disseminate timely and accurate information; to provide opportunities for families and professionals to meet, share their experiences, and support each other; to become an active and viable organization in the community; to actively encourage relevant research into educational, behavioral, and medical aspects of the syndrome
Audience/Clientele: Parents and professionals who are touched by individuals with Williams syndrome, individuals with Williams syndrome
Staff: 1 nonprofessional, 35 volunteers
Budget: $90,000 Funding: Private sources, fund-raising, fees for services or products, donations
Services: Support group
Education and Outreach: In-service programs, seminars, library, publishing
Publications: *Williams Syndrome Association National Newsletter*, semiannual, with research updates and forums for parents and professionals; brochures and videotapes
Programs: Biennial conference, regional meetings

REFERENCES

1. *Prevalence of Selected Chronic Conditions: United States, 1986–88*. Vital and Health Statistics, Series 10: Data from the National Health Survey, no. 182. U.S. Department of Health and Human Services, National Center for Health Statistics, 1993, 37.

2. John Bradshaw, *Creating Love: The Next Great Stage of Love* (New York: Bantam, 1992), 205.

CHAPTER

Physical Disabilities

As for the stares and pointing and whispered
remarks, the child with a noticeable handicap
has to get used to them, and the younger the easier.
Benjamin Spock and Michael B. Rothenberg.
Dr. Spock's Baby and Child Care

I have never seen a "handicapped" child
who has not developed other qualities, both emotional
and physical, to compensate for his or her special problem.
William Sears. *Keys to Preparing and Caring for Your Newborn*

Thousands of children under the age of 18 had a disabling condition in 1991, including 351,000 with visual impairments, 1,053,000 with hearing impairments, 1,093,000 with speech impairments, 158,000 with paralysis, and 1,648,000 with a physical disability.[1] Many of the issues that parents of children with developmental disabilities must face are likewise concerns of parents whose children are physically challenged: isolation, negative emotions, financial stress, and educational rights. For children who are affected, the difficulties they face may reflect more the treatments they undergo rather than the disability itself, in part because frequent therapy limits both their independence and their similarity to other children.[2] Finding the balance between accommodation for and disregard of a disabling condition is one of the greatest challenges these youngsters and their parents face.

An asterisk (*) indicates a specially recommended title.

POPULAR TITLES: BOOKS

Dickman, Irving R., with Sol Gordon. *One Miracle at a Time: Getting Help for a Child with a Disability.* Rev. ed. Simon & Schuster, 1993. 383p. index. LC 92-34040. ISBN 0-671-78934-1. $12.00.

Drawn exclusively from parents' experiences and advice, this handbook talks about the realities that parents with disabled children face, how they feel, and their techniques for successfully obtaining help, especially those ways in which they overcome obstacles in the health care and educational systems. The issues covered range from learning the diagnosis to getting on with living, receiving help from other parents, and choosing a physician or therapist. Other concerns include being an effective parent, learning about the disability and keeping detailed records on children, and avoiding being defined as a disabled family. Early intervention, assistive technology, and sexuality of the child are also discussed. This sensitively written text explores parents' emotions as well as their actions in caring for a child with a disability.

* Finston, Peggy. *Parenting Plus: Raising Children with Special Health Needs.* Penguin, 1992. 320p. bibliog. index. LC 89-28527. ISBN 3-525-24885-4. $19.95. ISBN 0-14-016837-0 pbk. $9.00.

Parents will find in this guidebook advice on helping their disabled children develop self-esteem, reduce bitterness at their condition, increase autonomy, and otherwise make the most of their life circumstances. The author also counsels parents on how to recognize and manage their own emotions regarding their child's disability. Parents are encouraged to set developmental goals for their children and determine how to pursue them. Some of the practical issues addressed include identifying an illness or disability and obtaining treatment, setting home routines, encouraging social skills in the child, and interacting with health care professionals.

Geralis, Elaine. *Children with Cerebral Palsy: A Parents' Guide.* Woodbine, 1990. 434p. LC 88-40660. ISBN 0-933149-15-8. $14.95.

Geralis brings together concise, accurate information from physicians, therapists, educators, and parents on all aspects of raising a child with cerebral palsy, which is the label given to a variety of disorders that affect a child's ability to move and maintain balance. Covering the years from birth to age five, the contributors address adjustment to the diagnosis; related medical conditions and treatment; daily care; family life and the child's self-esteem; child development; physical, occupational, and speech therapy; early intervention and special education; and legal rights. The text is notably comprehensive, substantive, and readable.

Krementz, Jill. *How It Feels to Live with a Physical Disability.* Simon & Schuster, 1992. 175p. photog. LC 91-43335. ISBN 0-671-72371-5. $18.00.

In this compilation, frank words and forthright photographs reveal how 12 young people have learned to live with a disabling physical condition brought about through an accident at birth. These courageous youngsters speak about how they learned they were different, their frustrations in adjusting to the physical challenges they face, how they cope with strangers' reactions, and the support they get from family and friends. Krementz, a photojournalist, personalizes in a few short pages the reality of physical disability.

Levin, Toby. *Rainbow of Hope: A Guide for the Special Needs Child.* Starlight, 1992. 192p. index. LC 91-67611. ISBN 0-9624680-1-0. $12.95.

Parents who are devastated by a diagnosis of disability may look to this how-to manual for guidance in regaining some control over their child's destiny. The book provides information on causes and therapies for common and rare disabilities, as well as information on support groups and other resources. Advice for parents on making informed life choices for their affected children and themselves is offered. Case studies personalize the data presented, and two informative chapters on the history of support, schooling, legislation, and parental activism and the potential of future genetic techniques will be welcomed by parents who may feel isolated by their situation.

Luterman, David, with Mark Ross. *When Your Child Is Deaf: A Guide for Parents.* York, 1991. 182p. LC 91-3239. ISBN 0-912752-27-0. $17.95.

Written by the founder of a nursery program for hearing impaired preschoolers, this handbook is parent-focused. It covers the emotional process of coming to grips with the diagnosis, the impact of a child's hearing loss on the parenting process and the extended family, and advice to parents from those who are graduates of the program. Current audiological practice, amplifying systems, and educational philosophies are also examined. The approach is empathetic; the author states that the best gift a professional can give parents is the gift of one another in a support group. By virtue of its approach and the material covered, this text will be an especially useful refer-

ence for parents whose child is newly diagnosed with a hearing impairment.

POPULAR TITLES: JOURNALS

ACCH Network. Association for the Care of Children's Health. 1982. Q. Free.

Supported in part by the Maternal and Child Health Bureau, U.S. Department of Health and Human Services, this quarterly newsletter reports on programs and research concerned with caring for children with physical, developmental, and cognitive disabilities. News items from the bureau are also published. The current focus of the newsletter appears to be family-centered health care, including the availability of training materials for professionals who work with families who have children with special needs and information on the new director of the National Center for Family-Centered Care.

Exceptional Parent. Psy-Ed. 1971. 8/yr. ISSN 0046-9157. $24.00.

Parents of a child with physical disabilities will find practical tips, resources, personal stories, and features in this magazine. Regular departments cover sources of help, new books, legislative updates, and updates on new technologies. Past issues addressed income tax tips, coping with incontinence, insurance claims, school bus safety, and residential versus at-home care. An annual guide to products and services is published in the January issue, covering such products as bedding, clothing, head gear, special foods, and schools, camps, and residences. Information on federal agencies, parent training and information centers, and wheelchair-accessible parks is also provided.

Our Kids Magazine. Alexander Graham Bell Association for the Deaf. 1982. S-A. $40.00.

From the parents' section of the Alexander Graham Bell Association for the Deaf, this substantive newsletter covers technological developments, educational techniques, social policy, biographies and personal accounts, and advice on child development. New to the newsletter are follow-up accounts on the adult success of children profiled earlier in the "OK Salutes" column.

PROFESSIONAL TITLES: BOOKS

Jackson, Patricia Ludder, and Judith A. Vessey. *Primary Care of the Child with a Chronic Condition.* Mosby, 1992. 564p. bibliog. photog. illus. index. LC 91-28012. ISBN 0-8016-2396-0. $37.95.

The impact of family relationships, child development, and health care financing on the provision of primary health care to children with chronic conditions is the subject of this handbook for nurses. After reviewing these broad issues, the authors examine primary care in children with 24 chronic conditions, among them asthma, cancer, cerebral palsy, Down syndrome, epilepsy, hydroencephalus, pediatric HIV and AIDS, and sickle cell disease. Each chapter on these conditions examines the etiology, incidence, clinical signs, treatment, associated problems, developmental issues, and special family concerns and concludes with a summary chart. Primary care of pediatric mental disorders is excluded.

Molnar, Gabriella E. *Pediatric Rehabilitation*. 2nd ed. Williams & Wilkins, 1991. 371p. bibliog. photog. illus. index. LC 91-7275. ISBN 0-683-06118-6. $45.00.

Directed to an audience of clinicians involved in physical rehabilitation, this anthology links principles of rehabilitation medicine with concepts of child development. In the first section, diagnostic and treatment methods are reviewed within the context of developmental needs and abilities; coverage includes history taking and examination, growth and development, psychological assessment, communication disorders, psychosocial issues, electrodiagnosis, and orthotics. In this edition, a chapter on pediatric rehabilitation nursing has been added and recent clinical and technological developments are identified under each topic. The second section addresses therapy for specific disabilities, including spina bifida, head injury, joint disease, spinal cord injury, limb deficiency, burns, and cerebral palsy. The chapters are thoroughly referenced and illustrated.

Northern, Jerry L., and Marion P. Downs. *Hearing in Children*. 4th ed. Williams & Wilkins, 1991. 418p. bibliog. photog. illus. index. LC 90-13107. ISBN 0-683-06574-2. $40.00.

Rapid advances in the diagnosis and treatment of hearing-impaired children have required extensive revision of this handbook since the previous edition was published six years ago. Every chapter has been rewritten to include such developments as real-ear measurements in pediatric hearing aid fittings, cochlear implants, screening protocols from the 1990 Joint Committee Position Statement for Infant and Newborn Hearing Screening, and the relationship of otitis media to hearing, speech, and language development. The auditory mechanism and hearing loss are introduced first, followed by medical sources of hearing loss, development of auditory behavior, behavioral and physiologic testing, screening processes, amplification, and education of hearing-impaired children. The appendix briefly reviews hearing disorders.

Rustin, Lena. *Parents, Families, and the Stuttering Child*. Singular, 1991. Far Communications Disorders Series. 125p. LC 91-15054. ISBN 1-879105-16-0. $19.50.

To understand stuttering, family dynamics are thoroughly appraised in a lengthy questionnaire (reproduced in the text) that assesses the child's general health, developmental history, current behavior, social functioning, school behavior, and family history to identify the problems present in a stuttering child's family. Rustin describes the results of the application of this survey to a data base of 200 clients, including clinical implications of their speech production, characteristics of parent and child verbal interactions, and ways in which parents need to change their behavior. Case studies are used to provide more detailed illustrations. This overview of contemporary approaches to treating children and adolescents who stutter and guiding the behavior of their parents is written in a concise, simple format designed to enhance the book's usefulness to speech pathologists in clinical settings.

Seligman, Milton. *The Family with a Handicapped Child: Understanding and Treatment*. 2nd ed. Allyn and Bacon, 1990. 412p. bibliog. index. LC 90-544. ISBN 0-205-12524-7. $41.95.

Seligman's anthology, intended for professionals in the fields of education, medicine, and mental health, focuses on the family, its adjustment to a child with a disability, and the support it requires to cope with the stress of disability. The author explores these issues from historical, philosophical, and developmental perspectives. The relationship that families have with social services and the effects of a child's disability on fathers and siblings are explored. The final chapters provide in-depth reviews of family responses to cystic fibrosis and autism and practical strategies for individual and family counseling.

Weisgerber, Robert A. *Quality of Life for Persons with Disabilities*. Aspen, 1991. 238p. bibliog. illus. index. LC 91-527. ISBN 0-8342-0221-2. $38.00.

Weisgerber focuses on ways to enhance the quality of life experienced by persons with disabilities throughout the four stages of the life span—birth, infancy, and early childhood, school years, productive years, and senior years. The author's approach encourages the most extensive development of skills and use of abilities possible for the individual affected by a disabling condition and also promotes the effective coordination of services within and at transition points across developmental stages by service providers aware of current trends in services and changing needs of persons with disabilities. Guidance on supporting the developing child, educating individuals with disabilities academically and vocationally, easing entrance into and productivity in the work force, and maintaining seniors' quality of life is included. An extensive list of references support the text, and a number of lists, charts, and graphs convey detailed information in a logical manner.

PROFESSIONAL TITLES: JOURNALS

Developmental Medicine and Child Neurology. American Academy for Cerebral Palsy and Developmental Medicine. 1958. M. ISSN 0012-1622. $110.00.

For an international audience, the official journal of the American Academy for Cerebral Palsy and Developmental Medicine includes scholarly articles on chronic disability in childhood. Much of the material published is readable enough to be of interest to parents. Each issue includes research results, case reports, and book reviews. The journal publishes an extensive topical bibliography of books and articles in an annual supplement.

Pediatric Physical Therapy. Williams & Wilkins. 1989. Q. ISSN 0898-5669. $37.00.

The official journal of the pediatrics section of the American Physical Therapy Association, this title provides practitioners with a forum on current issues of intervention and treatment, such as family involvement, cost containment, and ethical decision making. Original peer-reviewed research, new products, continuing education opportunities, and information about the association are included in its scope.

Physical & Occupational Therapy in Pediatrics. Haworth. 1980. Q. ISSN 0194-2638. $32.00.

Clinical research with practical applications for all therapists providing developmental or physical rehabilitation of infants and children is published in this refereed journal. Book reviews, thesis abstracts, and annotated bibliographies are also included.

DIRECTORY

American Council of the Blind (ACB)
1155 15th Street, N.W., Washington, DC 20005
(202) 467-5081 Fax (202) 467-5085 Toll-free/Hotline (800) 424-8666
Oral O. Miller, National Representative
Founded: 1961
Members: 40,000
Affiliates: 50 state groups
Mission/Goals: To improve the well-being of all blind and visually impaired people by serving as a representative national organization of blind people; to elevate the social, economic, and cultural levels of blind people; to improve educational and rehabilitation facilities and opportunities; to encourage and assist all blind persons to develop their abilities; to conduct a public education program to promote greater understanding of blindness and the capabilities of blind people
Audience/Clientele: Blind and visually impaired people
Staff: 6 professionals, 6 nonprofessionals, 125 volunteers
Budget: $800,000 Funding: Private source, fund-raising, fees for services and products, donations, grants, dues, thrift stores
Services: Counseling, support group, referral, lobbying, fund-raising, advocacy, consulting
Awards: Scholarship assistance to blind/visually impaired postsecondary students
Education and Outreach: Seminars, database development, publishing
Publications: *The Braille Forum*, bimonthly national magazine produced in braille, large print, cassette, and IBM-compatible computer disk, with articles on employment, legislation, sports and leisure activities, new products and services, and human-interest stories; *ACB Reports*, for radio reading information services; also TV and radio public service announcements highlighting the capabilities of blind people
Programs: Annual conference

American Deafness and Rehabilitation Association (ADARA)
P.O. Box 251554, Little Rock, AR 72225
(501) 868-8850 Fax (501) 868-8812 TTY/TDD (501) 868-8850
Deb Guthmann, Ph.D., President
Former Name: Professional Rehabilitation Workers with the Adult Deaf (PRWAD)
Mission/Goals: To assist and inform professionals and others who provide services, including rehabilitation, mental health, education, social work, speech therapy, medicine, psychiatry, and psychology, to persons who are deaf or hard-of-hearing; to provide opportunities for professional enrichment and improved communication among these groups
Audience/Clientele: Professionals and individuals who provide services to the deaf or hard-of-hearing
Services: Referral
Education and Outreach: In-service programs, seminars, publishing
Publications: *Journal of American Deafness and Rehabilitation Association*, quarterly; *ADARA Update*, quarterly newsletter; occasional special publications and monographs
Programs: Biennial conference

Blind Children's Fund (BCF)
8500 W. Capitol Drive, Milwaukee, WI 53222
(414) 464-3000 Fax (414) 464-5693
Sherry Raynor, President
Founded: 1978
Members: 1,300
Former Name: International Institute for Visually Impaired
Mission/Goals: To promote the health, education, and welfare of blind and visually impaired infants and young children; to encourage the development of activities and programs that enhance the growth, development, and education of visually impaired children
Audience/Clientele: Parents and teachers of visually impaired children from birth to seven years
Education and Outreach: Publishing
Publications: *VIP Newsletter*, quarterly; various pamphlets and books
Programs: Biennial convention

Division for Physical and Health Disabilities (DPHD)
c/o Council for Exceptional Children, 1920 Association Drive, Reston, VA 22091-1589
(703) 620-3660 Fax (703) 264-9494 TTY/TDD (703) 620-3660
Carolyn King, President
Founded: 1960
Former Names: Association of Educators of Homebound and Hospitalized Children; Division on Physically Handicapped, Homebound, and Hospitalized, Division for Physically Handicapped
Mission/Goals: To provide information and support to children with physical disabilities, multiple disabilities, or health impairments who are in classrooms, hospitalized, or homebound
Audience/Clientele: Professionals and teachers who work with children with disabilities or health impairments and their parents
Services: Support group
Education and Outreach: In-service programs, seminars, publishing
Publications: *DPHD Newsletter*, quarterly; *Journal of the Division for Physically Handicapped*, 3/yr, covering education and support services for handicapped, intended for teachers, administrators, and support personnel

Programs: Annual conference, in conjunction with Council for Exceptional Children

Division on Visual Handicaps (DVH)

c/o Council for Exceptional Children, 1920 Association Drive, Reston, VA 22091-1589

(703) 620-3660 Fax (703) 264-9494 TTY/TDD (703) 620-3660

Dr. Jane Erin, President

Founded: 1954

Former Name: Council for the Education of the Partially Seeing; Division for the Visually Handicapped

Mission/Goals: To support teachers, faculty, administrators, and others concerned with the education and welfare of visually impaired and blind children and youths

Audience/Clientele: Educators, administrators, parents

Services: Support group

Education and Outreach: Continuing education courses, database development, publishing

Publications: *DVH Quarterly*, providing news on current developments in the education of visually impaired children, legislative updates, and organizational news

Programs: Annual conference, held in conjunction with Council for Exceptional Children

HEAR Center (HEAR)

301 E. Del Mar Boulevard, Pasadena, CA 91101

(818) 796-2016

Josephine F. Wilson, Executive Director

Founded: 1954

Former Name: HEAR Foundation

Mission/Goals: To provide auditory and oral communication skills to reduce the effects of deafness and speech and language impairments; to prepare individuals for integration into the mainstream of society; to support early intervention, appropriate amplification, wide-range hearing aids, and educational mainstreaming

Audience/Clientele: For speech therapy, primarily children ages 2 to 21; for auditory and verbal therapy, hearing impaired children from birth to age 21; for diagnostic hearing tests, birth through any age

Staff: 5 professionals, 5 nonprofessionals

Budget: $320,000 Funding: Private source, fund-raising, fees for services or products, donations, grants

Languages: Sign language, Mandarin, Spanish

Services: Hearing testing, auditory verbal therapy, speech therapy

Awards: Glen H. Bollinger Award in recognition of volunteers

Education and Outreach: In-service programs, publishing

Publications: *The Listener*, bimonthly newsletter; *HEAR Center Proceedings*, periodic; other booklets

Programs: Annual board meeting

Human Growth Foundation (HGF)

P.O. Box 3090, 7777 Leesburg Pike, Suite 2025, Falls Church, VA 22043

(703) 883-1773 Fax (703) 883-1776 Toll-free (800) 451-6434

Deborah S. Swansburg, Executive Director

Founded: 1965

Members: 1,500

Affiliates: 50 state groups

Mission/Goals: To support and empower individuals with growth-related disorders, their families, and health care professionals through education, research, advocacy, and public outreach

Audience/Clientele: Families, children, and individuals affected with growth disorders, professionals in the area of growth and developmental genetics

Staff: 1 professional, 2 nonprofessionals

Budget: $300,000 Funding: Private sources, fund-raising, grants

Languages: Spanish

Services: Support group, referral, fund-raising, compiling statistics

Awards: Volunteers of the Year; Chapter of the Year; recognition of corporate sponsors

Education and Outreach: In-service programs, continuing education courses, database development, publishing

Publications: *Fourth Friday*, monthly; *Growth Series*, brochures

Little People of America, Inc. (LPA)

7238 Piedmont Drive, Dallas, TX 75227-9328

(214) 388-9576 Toll-free (800) 24-DWARF

Mary Carton, Contact

Founded: 1957

Members: 5,000

Affiliates: 12 state groups, 46 local groups

Mission/Goals: To unite individuals of short stature along with family and friends; to promote fellowship, education, awareness, medical referral, scholarship assistance, workshops, national, regional, and local gatherings; to provide emotional support for the little person and parents, siblings, and other relatives; to educate the public about dwarfism and its problems and characteristics; to work with families to help them adjust to and accept their child

Audience/Clientele: Dwarf population, people of short stature, medical and educational communities, news media, the general public

Staff: 2,500 volunteers

Budget: $25,000 Funding: Private sources, fund-raising, fees for services or products, donations, grants, dues

Languages: Spanish

Services: Counseling, support group, recreation, placement service, referral, fund-raising, compiling statistics

Awards: Annual distinguished service awards to regular, young adult, and auxiliary members

Education and Outreach: In-service programs, seminars, library, database development, publishing

Publications: *LPA Today*, quarterly newsletter; *My Child Is a Dwarf*; brochures and documentary about the association

Programs: Annual conference, with workshops

March of Dimes Birth Defects Foundation (MDBDF)
1275 Mamaroneck Avenue, White Plains, NY 10605
(914) 428-7100 Fax (914) 428-8203 Hotline (800) 288-BABY
Dr. Jennifer L. Howse, President
Founded: 1938
Affiliates: 131 chapters
Former Names: National Foundation for Infantile Paralysis;
National Foundation—March of Dimes
Mission/Goals: To improve the health of babies by preventing birth defects and infant mortality; to support via its Campaign for Healthier Babies research, community services, advocacy, and education
Audience/Clientele: Physicians, parents
Funding: Fund-raising, donations
Services: Support group, referral, lobbying, fund-raising, compiling statistics
Awards: Grants issued by chapters
Education and Outreach: Continuing education courses, seminars, publishing
Publications: *Genetics in Practice*, quarterly newsletter reporting current clinical research and practice in general; *Maternal/Newborn Advocate*, quarterly newsletter; *The Volunteer*, quarterly newsletter; *Birth Defects Compendium*, articles and reprints; *Annual Report*
Programs: Local chapter meetings

Muscular Dystrophy Association (MDA)
3300 E. Sunrise Drive, Tucson, AZ 85718
(602) 529-2000 Fax (602) 529-5300
Robert Ross, Executive Director
Founded: 1950
Affiliates: 193 field offices
Mission/Goals: To foster research and patient care for over 40 neuromuscular diseases; to provide patient services, clinical care, and professional and public health education
Audience/Clientele: Health care professionals, parents, scholars, general public
Staff: 14 professionals/nonprofessionals, 2,000,000 volunteers
Budget: $120,000 Funding: Donations, interest income
Services: Support group, orthopedic appliances, scholarships, research grants, recreation, fund-raising
Education and Outreach: In-service programs, continuing education, seminars, publishing
Publications: *MDA Newsmagazine*, quarterly; *Annual Report*
Programs: Annual conference; periodic international conferences

National Association for Parents of the Visually Impaired (NAPVI)
P.O. Box 317, Watertown, MA 02272-0317
(617) 362-4945 Fax (617) 972-7444 Toll-free/Hotline (800) 562-6265
Eileen Hudson, President
Founded: 1980

Members: 2,000
Affiliates: 16 state and regional groups
Mission/Goals: To provide information, support, and service to parents whose children are visually impaired; to provide emotional support and relief from feelings of isolation; to provide information for parents to decide on a child's care, education, and treatment; to provide training and assist in establishing local, state, and regional parent groups; to provide them with assistance in locating and using resources available to them
Audience/Clientele: Parents who have children that are visually impaired, blind with multiple disabilities, or dual sensory impaired
Staff: 2 nonprofessionals, 11 volunteers
Budget: $60,000 Funding: Fund-raising, fees for services or products, grants, dues
Services: Support group, referral, compiling statistics
Education and Outreach: Seminars, library, database development, publishing
Publications: *Awareness*, quarterly newsletter; handbooks for parents; fact sheets, videos, and audiotapes; other monographs
Programs: Annual board meeting, biennial National Parent Conference, regional conferences

National Easter Seal Society (NESS)
230 W. Monroe, Chicago, IL 60601
(312) 726-6200 Fax (312) 726-1494 TTY/TDD (312) 726-4258
James E. Williams Jr., President
Founded: 1919
Affiliates: 67 state groups, 98 local groups
Former Names: National Society for Crippled Children and Adults; National Easter Seal Society for Crippled Children and Adults
Mission/Goals: To design and carry out programs that assist people with disabilities; to work with other groups providing support services to this clientele; to collect and disseminate information on service gaps and medical programs related to rehabilitation; to offer therapies, vocational training, and recreational activities; to provide services for children
Audience/Clientele: Professionals, parents with children with disabilities
Services: Advocacy, fund-raising, lobbying, recreation, vocational evaluation and training, medical and rehabilitative care
Education and Outreach: Seminars, research, publishing
Publications: *AADC News*, quarterly; *Computer-Disability News*, quarterly; *Program Digest*, quarterly
Programs: Annual conference

National Gaucher Foundation (NGF)
19241 Montgomery Village Avenue, Suite E-21, Gaithersburg, MD 20879
(301) 990-3800 Fax (301) 990-4898 Toll-free (800) 925-8885
Karen Cohen, Executive Director
Founded: 1984

Members: 2,800
Mission/Goals: To provide support to patients and family members; to fund grants for Gaucher research; to increase awareness of the disorder
Audience/Clientele: Physicians, patients, family members and relatives, hospitals, Jewish community centers, medical centers, colleges and universities, congressional representatives
Funding: Private sources, fund-raising, donations
Languages: Hebrew
Services: Counseling, support group, social service/case management, referral, lobbying, fund-raising
Education and Outreach: Seminars, publishing
Publications: *Gaucher Disease Newsletter*, bimonthly, with reprints of recent research, legislative updates, and medical questions with answers; *Living with Gaucher Disease*; *David* brochure
Programs: Annual conference, regional meetings

National Hydrocephalus Foundation (NHF)
400 N. Michigan Avenue, Suite 1102, Chicago, IL 60611-4102
(815) 467-6548 Fax (312) 427-9311
James A. Mazzetti, Treasurer
Founded: 1979
Members: 500
Former Name: Know Problems of Hydrocephalus
Mission/Goals: To provide information about hydrocephalus to affected individuals, their families, the general public, and health care professionals
Audience/Clientele: Professionals, parents, and other caretakers of children with hydrocephalus
Staff: 10 volunteers
Budget: $2,000 Funding: Grants, dues
Services: Support group, networking
Education and Outreach: Publishing
Publications: *Reaching Potential: A Guide to Hydrocephalus*, videotape; *National Hydrocephalus Foundation Newsletter*, quarterly; bibliographies of articles on the disorder
Programs: Semiannual symposium

National Information Center for Children and Youth with Disabilities (NICHCY)
P.O. Box 1492, Washington, DC 20013-1492
(703) 893-6061 Toll-free (800) 999-5599 SpecialNet NICHCY TTY/TDD (703) 843-8614
Carol Valdivieso, Director
Founded: 1982
Previous Name: National Information Center for Children and Youth with Handicaps
Mission/Goals: To help children and youths with disabilities become participating members of the community; to provide responses to questions on disability issues, referral to other organizations, information packets on frequently asked questions, technical assistance to families and professional groups, and publications on current issues in disability

Audience/Clientele: Parents, educators, care givers, advocates, and others with an interest in disabilities
Staff: 17 professionals, 2 nonprofessionals, 25 volunteers
Budget: $1,000,000 Funding: Federal government
Languages: Sign language, Spanish, French
Services: Counseling, support group, search services, referral, compiling statistics
Education and Outreach: Seminars, library, database development, publishing
Publications: *News Digest*, a single-issue newsletter that provides research on current topics; *Transition Summary*, single-issue newsletter examining a single topic on the transition from school to adult life; general resources, including *Public Agencies Fact Sheet*, *National Toll Free Numbers*, parents' guides, disability information on specific disorders, and legal information
Programs: National symposia

National Information Center on Deafness (NICD)
Gallaudet University, 800 Florida Avenue, N.E., Washington, DC 20002
(202) 651-5051 Fax (202) 651-5054 TTY/TDD (202) 651-5052
Loraine DiPietro, Director
Founded: 1980
Mission/Goals: To respond to questions from any interested individuals about hearing loss and deafness or programs serving deaf and hard-of-hearing people either by providing specific information or referral to an appropriate resource
Audience/Clientele: Professionals, deaf or hard-of-hearing people, parents and relatives, members of the general public who are interested in hearing loss or deafness
Staff: 3.5 FTE professionals, 1 nonprofessional, 6 volunteers
Budget: $215,000 Funding: Federal government, fees for services or products, donations, grants
Languages: Sign language
Services: Referral
Education and Outreach: Resource center, research, publishing
Publications: Various publications and resource lists on related topics

National Marfan Foundation (NMF)
382 Main Street, Port Washington, NY 11050
(516) 883-8712 Toll-free (800) 862-7326
Priscilla Ciccariello, Chair
Founded: 1981
Members: 11,000
Affiliates: 15 state groups
Mission/Goals: To disseminate accurate and timely information about Marfan syndrome (an inherited disorder of connective tissue) to patients, family members, and physicians; to provide means for patients and relatives to share experiences, support one another, and improve their medical care; to support and foster research on the disorder
Audience/Clientele: People and families affected by Marfan syndrome and the medical community

Staff: 1 professional, 3 nonprofessionals, 100 volunteers
Budget: $220,000 Funding: Private source, fund-raising, fees
for products, donations, grants, dues
Services: Support group
Awards: Annual Antoine Marfan Award to person(s) who has
advanced knowledge of the Marfan syndrome
Education and Outreach: Seminars, research grants, publishing
Publications: *NMF Fact Sheet*, brochure; *The Marfan Syndrome*, booklet; *The Marfan Syndrome: Physical Activity Guidelines for Physical Educators, Coaches, and Physicians*, monograph; related brochures, booklets, video, and poster
Programs: Annual conference

National Rehabilitation Information Center (NARIC)

8455 Colesville Road, Suite 935, Silver Spring, MD 20910-
3319
(301) 588-9284 Fax (301) 587-1967 Toll-free (800) 34-
NARIC TTY/TDD (301) 588-9284, (800) 34-NARIC
Mark Odum, Director
Founded: 1977
Mission/Goals: To collect and disseminate the results of federally funded research projects on disability and rehabilitation
Audience/Clientele: Educators, allied health professionals, physicians, rehabilitation counselors, information professionals, and family members interested in disability and rehabilitation
Funding: Federal government
Languages: Spanish
Services: Referral
Education and Outreach: Library, database development (REHABDATA), database searches, publishing
Publications: *REHABDATA Thesaurus*; *NARIC Guide to Disability and Rehabilitation Periodicals*; *NARIC Directory of Library and Information Specialists in Disability and Rehabilitation*; *NARIC Quarterly*, free newsletter on disability and rehabilitation research and resources; free resource guides

North American Riding for the Handicapped Association (NARHA)

P.O. Box 33150, Denver, CO 80233
(303) 452-1212 Fax (303) 252-4610 Toll-free (800) 369-7433
William J. Scebbi, Executive Director
Founded: 1969
Members: 1,750
Affiliates: 450 operating centers
Mission/Goals: To promote equine activities for individuals with disabilities
Audience/Clientele: Equine and health professionals who provide therapeutic horseback riding services, individuals with disabilities and their families who participate
Staff: 5 professionals
Budget: $200,000 Funding: Fund-raising, fees for services or products, donations, grants, dues
Services: Recreation, referral
Education and Outreach: Continuing education courses, seminars, database development, accreditation reviews, publishing

Publications: *NARHA News*, bimonthly newsletter
Programs: Annual conference

Parents Helping Parents (PHP)

535 Race Street, Suite 140, San Jose, CA 95126
(408) 288-5010 Fax (408) 288-7943
Florene M. Poyadue, Executive Director
Founded: 1976
Mission/Goals: To help children with special needs receive services and achieve their full potential by strengthening families and professionals; to share PHP resources with other parent groups that want to begin a parent-directed organization, expand the number of services offered, or improve existing programs
Audience/Clientele: Families of children with special needs, professionals and other caretakers
Staff: 27 professionals
Budget: $486,000 Funding: Federal government, state government, local government, private source, fund-raising, donations, county government, grants
Languages: Spanish
Services: Support group, referral, consulting
Awards: Valley of Hearts for volunteer, educator, and physician of the year
Education and Outreach: In-service programs, continuing education courses, library, publishing
Publications: *Special Addition*, monthly newsletter with medical and legislative updates, association news, and calendar; how-to manuals for groups; booklets on specific programs, such as peer counseling and facilitating peer groups
Programs: Semiannual symposium

Parents' Section of the Alexander Graham Bell Association for the Deaf

3417 Volta Plaza, N.W., Washington, DC 22207
(202) 337-5220 TTY/TDD (202) 337-5220
Michael Hunter, Chairperson
Founded: 1957
Members: 8,000
Affiliates: 15 state groups, 6 local groups
Former Name: International Parent's Organization (IPO)
Mission/Goals: To provide parents of hearing-impaired children with the support they need to work for quality oral education for their children
Audience/Clientele: Parents, grandparents, and other relatives of hearing-impaired children
Staff: 1 nonprofessional, 18 board members
Funding: Private source, donations, dues
Services: Support group, referral
Awards: Honors Award every two years to parent who has made significant contributions to helping hearing-impaired children and their parents; award to teacher of regular classroom who has helped a hearing-impaired child to successfully integrate
Education and Outreach: Library, publishing
Publications: *Our Kids Magazine*, semiannual

Prader-Willi Syndrome Association USA (PWS)

2510 S. Brentwood Avenue, Suite 220, St. Louis, MO 63144

(314) 962-7644 Fax (314) 962-7869 Toll-free (800) 926-4797

Tere Schaefer, Executive Director

Founded: 1975

Members: 2,000

Affiliates: 25 state chapters

Former Name: Prader-Willi Syndrome Association

Mission/Goals: To provide parents and professionals with a national and international network of information, support services, and research endeavors to expressly meet the needs of affected children and adults and their families; to promote communication among parents, professionals, and others interested in the disorder

Audience/Clientele: Professionals and parents who have contact with individuals with Prader-Willi syndrome

Staff: 3 professionals, 100 volunteers

Budget: $100,000 Funding: Fund-raising, fees for services or products, donations, dues

Languages: Spanish

Services: Counseling, support group, residential facility for children, recreation via camps, emergency medical care, referral, compiling statistics

Education and Outreach: Seminars, library, continuing education courses, research grants, publishing

Publications: *The Gathered View*, bimonthly newsletter; *Handbook for Parents*, *Directions*, *Management of PWS*, and other booklets for parents; *Directory of Services*; bibliographies, brochures, and a variety of packets of information for parents; videos and cassette tapes; conference proceedings

Programs: Annual conference

Siblings of Disabled Children (SODC)

535 Race Street, Suite 140, San Jose, CA 95126

(408) 288-5010 Fax (408) 288-7943

Florene M. Poyadue, R.N., Executive Director

Founded: 1977

Members: 2,000

Mission/Goals: To address the needs of siblings of disabled or chronically ill children; to provide such children with information, support, and a forum for expressing and coping with feelings of resentment, guilt, anger, or jealousy; to provide a place for families to share and to learn about disability

Audience/Clientele: Parents and children with a disabled family member

Services: Support group, counseling

Education and Outreach: Library, publishing

Publications: *SODC Annual Calendar of Events*; *Special Addition*, quarterly

Programs: Annual symposium

The Sturge-Weber Foundation

P.O. Box 460931, Aurora, CO 80046

(303) 360-7290 Fax (303) 699-1406 Toll-free (800) 627-5482

Karen L. Ball, President

Founded: 1987

Members: 750

Mission/Goals: To improve the quality of life for individuals with Sturge-Weber syndrome and their families by serving as a clearinghouse for information, providing emotional support, and facilitating research on the disorder

Audience/Clientele: Professionals and parents with an interest in Sturge-Weber syndrome

Staff: 2 part-time professionals, numerous volunteers

Funding: Fund-raising, donations, grants

Services: Counseling, support group, referral, compiling statistics

Education and Outreach: In-service programs, seminars, database development, publishing

Publications: *Sturge-Weber Foundation Newsletter*, quarterly; various pamphlets

Programs: Annual conference

United Cerebral Palsy Associations (UCPA)

1522 K Street, N.W., Washington, DC 20005

(202) 842-1266 Fax (202) 842-3579 Toll-free (800) USA-IUCP

John D. Kemp, Executive Director

Founded: 1948

Former Name: National Foundation for Cerebral Palsy

Mission/Goals: To provide assistance to people with cerebral palsy and their families; to prevent cerebral palsy, minimize its effects, and reduce the isolation of individuals with cerebral palsy and their families; to support research and training for medical and allied health personnel

Audience/Clientele: Professionals, parents, children with cerebral palsy, the general public

Services: Support group, medical therapeutics, social services, recreation, special education services for parents, residential facility for children

Education and Outreach: Vocational training, publishing

Publications: *Word from Washington*, monthly newsletter, with news on federal legislation, programs, and policy

Programs: Annual conference

REFERENCES

1. *Current Estimates from the National Health Interview Survey, 1991*. Vital and Health Statistics, Series 10: Data from the National Health Survey, no. 184. U.S. Department of Health and Human Services, National Center for Health Statistics, 1992, 94.

2. Peggy Finston, *Parenting Plus: Raising Children with Special Health Needs* (New York: Viking Penguin, 1992), 135.

CHAPTER

16

Psychological Development

Self-esteem is self-regard.
It is . . . a composite picture of self-value.
Psychopathology is behavior which
once was but no longer can be considered
appropriate to the child's level of development.
Charles Wenar. *Developmental Psychopathology*

The realm of psychology is the development of normal psychological structures, individual temperament, emotional well-being, behavioral control, and high self-esteem in children. Encouraging healthy growth in these areas and seeking treatment for disturbances that occur are the concerns parents have regarding their children's psychological development. Much of this development is carried out in a social setting, as children grow and mature in response to interactions with their parents, their peers, and their environments.

Children are at risk for psychological disorders when they have difficult temperaments, low intelligence, poor coping strategies, poor self-esteem, or an external locus of control. Other risk factors for problematic psychological development in children are being male, suffering stressful life events, experiencing conflict in their parents' marriage, lacking adequate family support networks, and having parents who are unavailable, overly harsh in disciplining, or hypercritical.[1]

An asterisk (*) indicates specially recommended titles.

POPULAR TITLES: BOOKS

Doft, Norma, with Barbara Aria. *When Your Child Needs Help: A Parent's Guide to Therapy for Children.* Crown, 1992. 224p. index. LC 91-15576. ISBN 0-517-58046-2. $18.00.

This guide to child therapy by a child psychologist explains how to identify whether a child needs help, the nature of the

initial consultation, the results obtained in play therapy, and what to expect during successive phases of treatment. An important feature is the focus on parent-work, the translation of therapy into approaches a parent may take at home. Advice on adapting parenting to children's needs and helping children find new ways of coping is illustrated with numerous examples from the author's practice.

Elkind, David. *The Hurried Child.* Rev. ed. Addison-Wesley, 1988. 217p. bibliog. index. LC 88-7523. ISBN 0-201-07397-8. $10.53.

Revised in 1988 to update statistics and examples, this text explores the ways in which children are encouraged to mature more quickly than accepted developmental norms indicate that they should and identifies approaches for helping them cope with the stress that these pressures cause. The first section examines how children are hurried by parental expectations, school practices, and media messages; the second covers normal development as described by Piaget, stress sources and reactions, including responsibility and change overload, free-floating anxiety, school burnout, and learned helplessness. The author also addresses techniques, such as avoiding chronological or calendar hurrying, that parents may use to help children.

Gabriel, H. Paul, and Robert Wool. *The Inner Child: Understanding Your Child's Emotional Growth in the First Six Years of Life.* Times, 1990. 230p. index. LC 89-49560. ISBN 0-8129-1793-6. $18.95.

Consistency, structure, and discipline are essential qualities for parents to incorporate into their children's lives, according to the authors of this "psychological Dr. Spock," a pediatric psychiatrist and a professional writer and journal editor. Reassuring parents that a single disturbing incident does not create a serious disorder, they examine the influence of heredity, biology, environment, and parental behavior on children. Erickson's model of the five stages of development in the first six years of life is used to structure the material into chapters on dependency (birth–14 months), exploration (14–30 months), communication (30–48 months), separation (48–60 months), and early independence (60–72 months). The first section of each chapter covers what to expect during the period covered, followed by an application of this theoretical material to the "real world" of everyday problems and issues, such as toilet training, temper tantrums and breath holding, biting, food battles, working parents against each other, and television for children aged 14–30 months. A final chapter covers issues related to situations of divorce, sibling rivalry, adoption, and serious illness.

* Garber, Stephen W., et al. *Monsters under the Bed and Other Childhood Fears: Helping Your Child Overcome Anxieties, Fears and Phobias.* Villard: Random, 1993. 378p. illus. index. LC 92-56812. ISBN 0-679-40858-4. $20.00

Fear is a frequent emotion in a child's life, from the earliest fear of loud noises and falling to fear of animals, illness, weather, separation, social events, transportation, school, heights, crime, and death. This book helps parents understand and respond sensitively to typical children's fears. The authors—a behavioral psychologist, an educational consultant, and a former teacher—break down fear into its parts and outline techniques, such as relaxation, for combating each component of the fear response. To overcome fear, the authors present a four-part system for confronting and reducing fears: imagination, information, observation, and exposure. The down-to-earth tone and practical suggestions, recommended readings, and scripts for positive "self-talk" provide an appealing and workable system for parents who want to prevent or help their children overcome fears. An appendix advises parents seeking help for intractable fears.

Goldstein, Sam, and Michael Goldstein. *Hyperactivity: Why Won't My Child Pay Attention?* Wiley, 1992. 214p. bibliog. LC 91-24325. ISBN 0-471-53077-8. $19.95.

Understanding the numerous problems that hyperactive children face and finding ways to manage each of the problems effectively are the approaches that the authors, one a child psychologist and the other a child neurologist, recommend to parents who want to help their children succeed at home, in school, and in the community. Special attention is given in the first section to the latest scientific data on the diverse characteristics of hyperactivity and its causes, with an emphasis on refuting commonly held beliefs about the disorder. How hyperactive children behave at home and at school and as toddlers, school-age children, and teens and how to address the specific problems of each setting or age group are covered in the second section. Parenting strategies and treatment choices are reviewed in section three. Published resources are listed to further aid parents. The material is presented clearly and concisely in this detailed handbook.

Greenspan, Stanley I., and Nancy Thorndike Greenspan. *The Essential Partnership: How Parents and Children Can Meet the Emotional Challenges of Infancy and Childhood.* Penguin, 1990. 256p. LC 89-29928. ISBN 0-14-009374-5. $8.95.

Understanding and fostering a child's emotional health from birth through four years of age is the focus of this how-to guide to emotional development. Using a chronological perspective, the authors explore major areas of emotional development, covering healthy development, interaction to support it, problem areas, and how to resolve problems. Among the topics covered are mood and self-esteem; sexuality; pleasure and excitement; anger and aggressiveness; seemingly negative emotions such as separation anxiety, fear, sadness, and competition; capacity to concentrate, process information, and learn; and peer/group relationships. Interesting case material, an eloquent style, and an appropriate level of detail make this an unusually readable how-to manual for parents.

Herskowitz, Joel. *Is Your Child Depressed?* Warner, 1990. 224p. bibliog. LC 89-48152. ISBN 0-446-39160-3. $12.95.

Herskowitz describes how to recognize signs of depression in children who often seem "off" in their behavior or mood rather than sad, as well as how to obtain and prepare for a psychiatric consultation. This handbook explains the work of a psychiatrist; types of treatment for depression, including medication; causes of suicide and ways to prevent it; and genetic susceptibility to depression. The instructional material is illustrated with case histories and references provided at the end of the book. Appendixes contain checklists for related psychological disorders, such as manic syndrome.

Kerns, Lawrence L., with Adrienne B. Lieberman. *Helping Your Depressed Child: A Reassuring Guide to the Causes and Treatments of Childhood and Adolescent Depression.* Prima, dist. by St. Martin's, 1993. 283p. bibliog. index. LC 92-32926. ISBN 1-55958-275-8. $12.95.

Nearly 10 percent of the nation's children and youth suffer from depression according to Kerns, a psychiatrist specializing in the treatment of childhood depression. In most cases, the cause of depression is unknown. In this perceptive handbook for parents, the symptoms of depression and the masks that it hides behind—school failure, behavior problems, substance abuse—are described, using case material from the author's clinical practice. How parents can select a competent therapist, decide when hospitalization or medication is necessary, and use their own parenting skills to boost their child's self-esteem are thoroughly covered. Childhood depression puts children at risk for future bouts of depression and interferes with normal development. This text will help parents take prompt and informed action to treat this dangerous illness.

Leman, Kevin. *Bringing Up Kids without Tearing Them Down.* Delacorte, 1993. 369p. bibliog. index. LC 92-36596. ISBN 0-385-29945-1. $19.95.

Both positive and practical in tone, this general guide for parents focuses on the importance of healthy self-esteem and functional family life in raising children who are happy, successful, and responsible adults. Much of the author's advice is presented in memorable phrases such as the "A-B-Cs" (acceptance, belonging, and competence) of self-worth and "reality discipline," an accountability-based approach that uses consequences as a means of guiding behavior. Leman examines what children have to gain—such as attention and power—by misbehaving, and he emphasizes the importance of encouragement rather than either praise or criticism to guide children's maturation. The final chapters examine specific issues related to parenting toddlers, school-age children, and adolescents.

Narramore, Bruce. *Adolescence Is Not an Illness*. Revell, 1991. 203p. LC 91-23784. ISBN 0-8007-5416-6. $8.95.

By understanding why teens feel the way they do, communicating respect, choosing battles, enjoying their offspring, handling conflicts, and accepting their own imperfections, parents can make the most of the often turbulent teenage years. Such parenting skills are sorely tested by the psychosocial challenges facing adolescents: rapid physical growth, sexual awakening, mood swings, drive for independence, peer pressure, and the search for an identity. Dr. Narramore advises parents on how to "survive" the teen years through a combination of firmness, consistency, sensitivity, understanding, listening, and a willingness to rethink parenting as their child matures. He applies these skills to areas of conflict such as dating, sexual behavior, drug use, disinterest in religion, and general teen negativism.

Phillips, Debora, with Fred A. Bernstein. *How to Give Your Child a Great Self-Image*. Plume, 1991. 252p. LC 90-21282. ISBN 0-452-26589-4. $8.95.

This how-to manual provides step-by-step instructions in behavior modification for parents to follow to improve the self-esteem and self-image of any child, but especially those children who suffer from teasing, criticism, rejection, poor body image, and feelings of imperfection. Through positive reinforcement, empathy, repetition, modeling, rehearsing, and other techniques, parents can approach and resolve complex emotional problems one step at a time. Advice for nurturing a strong foundation of positive self-worth, accepting compliments, and sustaining effective communication through family "round table" discussions is also presented in this clear, practical text by a behavioral therapist.

Shore, Milton F., Patrick J. Brice, and Barbara G. Love. *When Your Child Needs Testing: What Parents, Teachers, and Other Helpers Need to Know about Psychological Testing*. Continuum, 1992. 192p. bibliog. index. glossary. LC 91-31652. ISBN 0-8264-0548-7. $18.95.

Written to take the mystery out of psychological testing and return responsibility for the child's future to the parents, this handbook covers in simple language what tests are, when they may be beneficial, how to interpret results, and how to use that information in decision making. The content also includes guidance in selecting a psychologist to conduct testing, informing the child and siblings, and ensuring that the legal rights of the child and parents are upheld. Fictionalized cases throughout illustrate how tests are used in assessing behavior problems and symptoms, distinguish the specific value and limitation of tests, and guide parents in negotiating the testing process and results, particularly if they disagree with the outcome reached. An appendix lists by name commonly used tests according to

type of information sought, and a glossary provides simple definitions of many psychological terms. An annotated bibliography of current books is included.

Youngs, Bettie B. *The 6 Vital Ingredients of Self-Esteem and How to Develop Them in Your Child*. Jalmar, 1991. 160p. bibliog. LC 91-19682. ISBN 0-915190-72-9. $19.95.

Written by a former educator who is now a personal and professional effectiveness counselor, this practical handbook outlines a plan of action to build a child's self-esteem in school. In introductory material, Youngs explores how self-esteem influences learning and affects behavior and provides an assessment for determining a child's level of self-esteem. Subsequent chapters are devoted to an in-depth exploration of the six dimensions of self-esteem she has identified—physical safety, emotional security, sense of identity, affiliation, competence, and mission. Case examples, practical techniques, and discussion questions increase the usefulness of this text.

POPULAR TITLES: JOURNALS

Pediatric Mental Health. Pediatric Projects. 1982. B-M. ISSN 0278-4998. $24.00.

This journal addresses services for parents whose children have mental disabilities, therapeutic play techniques for treating children, and psychological support for hospitalized, disabled, and ill children. The publisher, a nonprofit corporation, also distributes mental health publications and medically oriented toys that help children and their parents cope with health care. One issue covered magazines and books for children with diabetes as well as how to create and tell stories that promote healing.

Psychology Today. Sussex. B-M. ISSN 0033-3107. $17.95.

Family life and child development issues addressed from a psychological perspective are featured in this magazine. Brief articles on child health, sibling relationships, and panic attacks were published in a past issue.

PROFESSIONAL TITLES: BOOKS

Adan, Jane. *The Children in Our Lives: Knowing and Teaching Them*. State University of New York Press, 1992. 313p. LC 90-022958. ISBN 0-7914-0811-6. $34.00. ISBN 0-7914-0812-4 pbk. $19.95.

The impact of conflict in children's lives, including some incidents apparently trivial, like a disagreement over the type of bun used for a hamburger, and some devastating, like sexual abuse, is explored in this autobiographical account. Using first-person narrative and reflection, the author examines a disturbing experience in the lives of several children she knows. The opportunity for disagreement between the child's experience and the adult's interpretation of it is emphasized. In the first chapter, Adan introduces the group of children and adults discussed, and in the remaining five chapters she focuses on the issues illustrated by individual conflicts. The text illustrates how frequently adults overwhelm children through hasty reactions or decisions and insensitivity to their children's problems. Extensive autobiographical notes and comments are also included.

Algozzine, Robert, Kathy Rule, and Roberta Ramsey. *Behaviorally Disordered: Assessment for Identification and Instruction.* Council for Exceptional Children, 1991. 36p. bibliog. LC 91-8464. ISBN 0-86586-198-6. $8.50.

How to screen, identify, plan curricula for, and evaluate programs for behaviorally disordered children is the focus of this brief guide to assessment. Topics covered include clarifying the purpose of assessment decisions, determining eligibility, defining problem behaviors, examining the relationship between behavior and setting, and using a systematic screening approach. Other factors addressed include attitudes that occur with labeling, social behavior versus academic goals for the program, and modification of critical behaviors before the program begins. An extensive bibliography of current resources supplements the text.

Berlin, Irving N., ed. *Bibliography for Training in Child and Adolescent Mental Health.* 3rd ed. University of New Mexico Press, 1991. 731p. LC 91-11973. ISBN 0-8263-1275-6. $30.00.

With brief entries but nearly comprehensive coverage, this bibliography lists significant current and selected historical references for all areas of child and adolescent mental health, including historical and cultural perspectives, development, psychopathology, therapeutics, and community mental health. New to this edition (the first was published in 1976) are sections on divorce and custody, forensic psychiatry, borderline and narcissistic disorders, research and ethics, videotapes, and books for children, adolescents, and parents. Customary introductory analytical material is not included.

Blau, Theodore H. *The Psychological Examination of the Child.* Wiley, 1991. 279p. bibliog. illus. index. LC 90-39091. ISBN 0-4716-3559-6. $32.95.

Blau presents a method for examining children, the Basic Psychological Examination (BPE), and a rationale for its use. The BPE explores six areas, each of which is reviewed here in detail: environmental pressures on children, their behavioral response, intellect, neuropsychological status and response capabilities, academic achievement, and personality. The text also includes introductory material on the history of clinical child psychology, training and expertise needed to become a practitioner, the physical setting appropriate for conducting the BPE, and selecting the battery of tests to be administered. Follow-up material is also provided, including how to summarize the results in a psychological report and interpret them to parents. Appendixes contain a directory of test publishers and equipment manufacturers and sources for parent training material.

Breen, Michael J., and Thomas S. Altepeter. *Disruptive Behavior Disorders in Children: Treatment-Focused Assessment.* Guilford, 1990. 288p. bibliog. index. LC 90-3817. ISBN 0-89262-439-8. $30.00.

Three types of disruptive behavior disorders, attention deficit hyperactivity disorder (ADHD), oppositional defiant disorder, and conduct disorder, account for the majority of instances in which a psychotherapist is consulted. As a result, the authors have compiled a selective practical, research-based, and treat-

ment-focused clinical manual intended for practitioners of all types who treat children with these disorders. The content includes an overview of disruptive behavior disorders, interviewing to evaluate the disorder, questionnaires, laboratory measurements and observations, and treatment approaches. A chapter on integrating assessment techniques completes the text. Appendixes contain questionnaires that permit evaluation of medications and their side effects and assessment of development; parent, teacher, and family reactions; and home and school situations.

Campbell, Susan B. *Behavior Problems in Preschool Children.* Guilford, 1990. 270p. bibliog. index. LC 89-16838. ISBN 0-89862-395-2. $30.00.

Data from a longitudinal study conducted by the author and others are the basis for this long-term prognosis of behavior problems in preschool children. While causality of behavior problems is difficult to ascertain and the impact of environmental factors varies, she concludes that chronic problems are most clearly associated with provocative or aggressive child behavior, inadequate parenting strategies, and continuing family difficulties. The text opens with a review of theoretical issues, including a transactional view of development, developmental tasks, and clinical issues, such as epidemiology of disorders, diagnoses, and factors influencing referral, that contribute to an understanding of such symptoms in children. Later chapters address the influence of family, siblings, and peers, treatment issues, and the course, outcome, and prognosis for behavioral problems. A summary chapter with policy implications completes the text.

Chandler, Louis A., and Virginia J. Johnson. *Using Projective Techniques with Children: A Guide to Clinical Assessment.* Thomas, 1991. 128p. bibliog. illus. index. LC 90-20889. ISBN 0-398-5726-5. $25.75.

The use of expressive techniques for personality assessment in understanding and treating children is examined in detail in this clinical handbook by two psychologists. The four techniques examined are the Thematic Apperception Test, Children's Apperception Test, Sentence Completion Task, and Creative Drawings. For each, the authors review the recommended age groups and types of information the test is designed to elicit. Case studies are used to illustrate the knowledge that may be gained by content analysis of children's expressive products.

Collins, W. Andrew, and Stanley A. Kuczaj II. *Developmental Psychology: Childhood and Adolescence.* Macmillan, 1991. 710p. bibliog. photog. illus. index. LC 90-45609. ISBN 0-02-377010-4. $32.25.

Using topical and chronological approaches, this book addresses the biological, intellectual, psychological, and social development of youth from infancy through adolescence. Many pedagogical and supplementary aids are incorporated, such as boxed discussions of research focus and controversial issues, summaries and outlines, photographs, suggested readings, a study guide, an instructor's manual, and a test bank of multiple-choice questions. An unusual feature, a methodological chapter appendix explaining basic statistical and methodological points, is used with one chapter only. The authors note that their approach is characterized by an emphasis on process, attention to the environments of youth, and theoretical eclecticism.

Donovan, Denis M., and Deborah McIntyre. *Healing the Hurt Child: A Developmental-Contextual Approach.* Norton, 1990. 310p. bibliog. index. LC 89-49420. ISBN 0-393-70093-3. $34.95.

A developmental-contextual approach, based on understanding hurt children—those children who have experienced difficulties, such as abuse, learning disabilities, or physical handicaps—rather than establishing guidelines for diagnosing psychopathology, guides this manual, which is also a critique of the "modern biological approach" to psychiatry and psychology. After analyzing in detail flaws in the way contemporary psychiatry views the child, this text examines how children think, communicate, interact, and change. The developmental-contextual approach is reviewed, insights from the emerging field of traumatology considered, a detailed technique for history taking described, and the concept of the therapeutic space as a healing modality explained. How well the child can take advantage of therapeutic space to heal is reviewed using case examples of hurt children. A sample initial psychotherapy encounter is annotated to illustrate the problems evident in conventional child therapy, described in an earlier chapter.

Etezady, M. Hossein, ed. *The Neurotic Child and Adolescent.* Aronson, 1990. 435p. bibliog. LC 89-18246. ISBN 0-87668-808-3. $45.00.

Emphasizing a clinical approach, this anthology provides a state-of-the-art review of current concepts and treatment of neuroses in children and adolescents. The examples given here also support the traditional view that neurotic disorders, generated as a compromise between unconscious repressed urges and inhibitions that control them, are ideally suited for treatment with psychoanalytic and dynamic psychotherapeutic methods. The text is divided into three parts, which address the concept of neurosis in childhood, developmental and etiological considerations, and therapeutic issues. Coverage includes neurosogenesis, prevention, object relations, transference and trauma neuroses, neurosis in adolescence and in female children, art and play in treatment, dreams, and intergenerational considerations.

Feindler, Eva L., and Grace R. Kalfus. *Adolescent Behavior Therapy Handbook.* Springer, 1990. 459p. bibliog. index. LC 90-9448. ISBN 0-8261-6400-5. $48.95.

By integrating highlights of common adolescent behavioral problems and available assessment and intervention methods developed by prominent adolescent therapists, this anthology attempts to define the specialty area of adolescent behavior therapy. The text provides a review of adolescent development and psychopathology, as well as behavioral assessment, intervention methods that have proven effective, and long-term maintenance of behavioral gains. The case studies, which make up the bulk of the book, are organized to present overviews of specific disorders, assessment data from individual and family interviews, results of inventories, information on data collection methods, evaluation of treatment, and clinical issues. The disorders covered include depression, temper control problems, socialization problems, fears and phobias, substance abuse, medical problems, and sexual abuse.

Gardner, Richard A. *Psychotherapy with Children of Divorce.* 3rd ed. Aronson, 1991. 576p. bibliog. index. LC 90-14477. ISBN 0-87668-564-5. $50.00.

Gardner has written a detailed, readable survey of the stresses and traumas children experience during separation and divorce, the psychopathologies such stresses may produce, and specific ways to prevent or treat problems. This unique text covers how to advise separating parents on issues such as timing and approach in telling children about a separation, telling the teacher, and being honest about parents' behavior; criteria for determining whether therapy is needed; and specific techniques the author has developed for child therapy. He reviews reactions to separation and divorce that children may experience, including denial, grief and depression, abandonment fears, blame and guilt, anger, and preoccupation with reconciliation, and, using case material, he describes treatments. The final chapters include discussions of post-divorce advice to parents and the involvement of the therapist in custody litigation; a lengthy, 82-page case study; and concluding comments on social factors in divorce. An extensive bibliography adds to the usefulness of this work as a sourcebook on psychopathology in children of divorce.

Garfinkel, Barry D., Gabrielle A. Carlson, and Elizabeth B. Weller. *Psychiatric Disorders in Children and Adolescents.* Saunders, 1990. 569p. illus. index. LC 90-10683. ISBN 0-7216-2612-2. $55.50.

For health care practitioners, this clinical textbook provides an empirical approach to common internalizing, developmental, and disruptive behavior disorders encountered in children and adolescents. Each chapter systematically covers the definition of a disorder, its source and incidence, and the clinical picture, including illustrative case histories, differential diagnosis, prognosis, assessment, and treatment. Internalizing disorders covered include depression; bipolar, grief, and post-traumatic stress disorders; anxiety; eating disorders; and psychosomatic illnesses. Learning and communication disorders, autism, elimination disorders, tics, and mental retardation are some of the developmental disorders examined. Contributors also focus on special clinical issues such as child abuse, suicide, sleep disorders, and problems arising from the impact of adoption or divorce.

Gettinger, Maribeth, Stephen N. Elliott, and Thomas R. Kratochwill, eds. *Preschool and Early Childhood Treatment Directions.* Erlbaum, 1992. 268p. bibliog. index. LC 91-47582. ISBN 0-8058-0757-8. $27.50.

School psychologists will find in this anthology a series of state-of-the-art reviews on issues important in the treatment of preschool children identified as at risk for academic or developmental disabilities. The content focuses on early childhood service program models, their rationales, and implications for school psychology in terms of consultation, assessment, intervention, research, and training; treatment of children with disabilities; social environment issues in parental involvement;

stress and coping; and peer relations. The final chapter reviews theoretical and empirical findings on use of computers with preschool children. Common to these essays is the theme of exploring new roles for school psychologists.

Green, Wayne H. *Child and Adolescent Clinical Psychopharmacology*. Williams & Wilkins, 1991. 226p. bibliog. illus. index. LC 90-13131. ISBN 0-683-03766-8. $29.00.

Green's text is intended to guide practicing clinicians in selecting and prescribing drugs in the psychiatric treatment of children and adolescents. The author provides an overview of psychopharmacology with young patients, including the psychiatric diagnosis, developmental issues, medicolegal issues, baseline assessment, dosage determination, treatment monitoring, and supervision of the discontinuation of medication. Major classes of drugs, including sympathomimetic amines and central nervous system stimulants, antipsychotic drugs, antidepressants, and anxiolytics, are examined in detail. Coverage includes drug action, contraindications, interactions with other drugs, and side effects. Investigational reports for these products are included, as is an extensive list of references to the scholarly and clinical literature.

Greenspan, Stanley, with Nancy Thorndike Greenspan. *The Clinical Interview of the Child*. American Psychiatric, 1991. 245p. bibliog. index. LC 90-14571. ISBN 0-88048-420-9. $36.50.

Effective interviewing in psychotherapy involves being able to see, hear, and even sense all information that a child provides about their individual experiences and concerns. The Greenspans outline how clinicians may use the developmental structuralist approach, which is focused on how the child organizes experience at each stage of development, for systematic observation and interpretation. Categories that clinicians must examine are reviewed; these include physical and neurological development, mood, capacity to relate to others, affects and anxiety, use of the environment, and thematic development, as well as the subjective reactions of the therapist. How these vary according to developmental stage, along with how to conduct the interview and construct an interpretation, is examined using 18 case studies. The final chapter addresses issues to consider when interviewing parents.

Greydanus, Donald E., and Mark L. Wolraich, eds. *Behavioral Pediatrics*. Springer-Verlag, 1991. 417p. bibliog. index. LC 91-4845. ISBN 0-387-97547-0. $89.00.

This is the initial textbook on behavioral pediatrics, a subspecialty that emerged over the course of the last 20 years. Differing from child psychiatry in terms of the behaviors addressed, behavioral pediatrics reflects the efforts of the pediatrician to diagnose, treat, and prevent mental illness and problem behaviors in children. The first section of the text reviews basic concepts about psychological development and sexuality and gives an overview of assessment, including psychometric testing and reasons for seeking treatment for behavioral disorders. Background information on communication, family therapy, and psychopharmacology is also presented. The second section of the anthology addresses specific disorders in individual chapters, such as failure to thrive, behavioral aspects of chronic disease, anxiety disorders, psychological aspects of sexually transmitted diseases, chemical dependency in the adolescent, and tic disorders.

Hendren, Robert L., and Irving N. Berlin, eds. *Psychiatric Inpatient Care of Children and Adolescents*. Wiley, 1991. 330p. LC 90-13117. ISBN 0-471-51509-4. $45.00.

The effectiveness of inpatient hospital care for children and adolescents depends largely on the development of positive relationships with the staff. This anthology explores how to create good therapeutic relationships with patients from minority cultures and their families. After an introduction to the issues involved in providing culturally responsive inpatient treatment, the text examines assessment, treatment types, and administrative issues in providing this specialized kind of care. Among the topics addressed are working therapeutically with Hispanic and American Indian parents, considering multicultural aspects of countertransference when treating violent youth, recruiting staff for a multicultural setting, and evaluating treatment outcomes from a multicultural perspective.

Herbert, Martin. *Clinical Child Psychology: Social Learning, Development and Behaviour*. Wiley, 1991. 438p. LC 90-12947. ISBN 0-471-92907-7. $65.00.

For a broad audience of students and practitioners, this handbook focuses on assessment, diagnosis, and intervention for psychological problems in children from infancy to early adolescence. Herbert uses a developmental approach to explain problems presented by the child and the family. The text begins with a case history of a referral, which helps illustrate the nature of psychological problems in children within the wider context of family problems. Assessment of biological/physical problems and environmental problems is reviewed. A discussion of developmental tasks of preschool and school age children and adolescents is followed by a review of therapies. The book concludes with detailed analyses of five major clinical problems that are among the most difficult to treat: antisocial disruptive disorder, delinquency, fears and phobias, acute pain, and post-traumatic stress disorder. Appendixes provide additional information on recording and assessment, interviews of children and parents, and issues of race, gender, and creed in child psychology.

Hersen, Michel, and Cynthia G. Last, eds. *Handbook of Child and Adult Psychopathology: A Longitudinal Perspective*. Pergamon, 1990. 459p. bibliog. illus. index. LC 89-26673. ISBN 0-08-036101-3. $80.00.

Carefully organized sections covering the major psychopathologies contain chapters on childhood and adult manifestations of these disorders in this reference book for mental health clinicians. Depending on the chapter's focus, information given may include a description of a disorder's characteristics, its clinical presentation, epidemiology, natural history, impairment and complications, differential diagnosis, case examples, continuity and discontinuity with adult presentation, and childhood and familial antecedents. This approach, along with extensive lists of references, provides up-to-date, detailed information on major depression, bipolar disorder, schizophrenia, separation anxiety and agoraphobia, and social phobia. Other disorders examined are obsessive compulsive disorder, post-traumatic stress disorder, mental retardation, and obesity.

Ho, Man Keung. *Minority Children and Adolescents in Therapy.* Sage, 1992. 236p. bibliog. index. LC 91-41972. ISBN 0-8039-3912-4. $35.00. ISBN 0-8039-3913-2 pbk. $16.95.

Noting that no comprehensive theory-based treatment of the sociopsychological assessment and treatment of minority children was available, Ho compiled a text to guide mental health professionals working with minority clients. He provides data on understanding and treating mental health problems in four major groups: African Americans, Asian and Pacific Americans, Hispanic Americans, and American Indian and Alaska natives. After presenting a cultural framework on which assessment guidelines and treatment practices are based, the author examines in separate chapters each minority group noted. These chapters are arranged to cover historical background, including demographic and immigration data, native culture, family tradition, problems associated with relocation, and a number of variables related to personal beliefs, the family system, the school system, and societal issues. The remaining chapters link conventional to culturally specific assessment and treatment techniques in individual, family, and group therapy. An appendix provides the reader with a self-assessment tool addressing awareness of cultural considerations in the therapeutic process.

Hodges, William F. *Interventions for Children of Divorce: Custody, Access, and Psychotherapy.* 2nd ed. Wiley, 1991. 387p. LC 91-746. ISBN 0-471-52255-4. $45.00.

To guide mental health and legal professionals in decisions they make regarding custody, visitation, mediation, and therapy, this handbook reviews and integrates over 600 studies on the impact of divorce on children of every age group. The first three chapters provide the theoretical framework and a review of the literature on how children behave in response to specific circumstances of divorce such as reduced financial resources, high parental conflict, or multiple reconciliations. Remaining chapters cover techniques for helping children of divorce move successfully into new family organizations, mediation, custody, parental access and visitation, school-based programs, consultation, education, and individual/family therapy. Special problems of single-parent families and stepfamilies are also examined. Recommendations in highlighted type are interspersed throughout the text, and each chapter contains a concise summary for easy reference.

Hogarth, Christina R. *Adolescent Psychiatric Nursing.* Mosby-Year Book, 1991. 462p. bibliog. illus. index. LC 91-6888. ISBN 0-8016-3229-3. $22.95.

The author, a pediatric nurse, has compiled with selected contributors a handbook focused on practical interventions for the beginning adolescent psychiatric nurse. The first few chapters introduce the history of current adolescent problems, normal adolescent development, legal issues raised by caring for this clientele, disorders in adolescents, multidisciplinary assessment, and care systems. Remaining chapters cover adolescent inpatient units, psychotherapies and psychopharmacology, and specific nursing interventions for common adolescent problems such as anger, manipulation, and running away, and for crisis situations.

Horne, Arthur M., and Thomas V. Sayger. *Treating Conduct and Oppositional Defiant Disorders in Children.* Pergamon, 1990. 191p. bibliog. illus. index. LC 89-72168. ISBN 0-08-036438-1. $26.00. ISBN 0-08-036437-3 pbk. $20.95.

Horne and Sayger present a behavioral family approach to the treatment of conduct and oppositional defiant disorders, which account for the majority of psychological problems seen by child psychologists. After an overview of the disorders and their source, the process of assessing the child and the family, initiating treatment, modifying the family environment, teaching self-management skills and effective disciplinary skills, and maintaining progress is described in detail. Appendixes give examples of intake, assessment, monitoring, and therapist termination forms and a common problems checklist. Tables, charts, references, and case material illustrate the authors' instructions.

Husain, Syen Arshad. *Anxiety Disorders in Children and Adolescents.* American Psychiatric, 1992. 184p. bibliog. index. LC 91-22233. ISBN 0-88048-467-5. $28.50.

The practical clinical approach to anxiety disorders in youth suggested in this comprehensive handbook emphasizes current treatment methods and results of scholarly research. Husain gives a concise introduction to historical perspectives, animal models, epidemiology, diagnosis assessment, and treatment of anxiety disorders. Specific conditions such as separation anxiety disorder, avoidant disorder, overanxious disorder, panic and phobia disorders, and post-traumatic stress disorder are also reviewed. Also covered are issues of classification, commonality, developmental perspectives, and theories about the cause of these conditions.

Kernberg, Paulina F., and Saralea E. Chazan. *Children with Conduct Disorders: A Psychotherapy Manual.* Basic Books, 1991. 306p. bibliog. index. LC 90-55665. ISBN 0-465-01055-5. $26.95.

For clinicians refining and expanding their repertoire of treatment techniques for conduct and oppositional defiant disorders, this handbook covers three approaches: individual supportive-expressive play psychotherapy, parent training, and play group psychotherapy. The beginning, middle, and ending phases of each therapy are described, and phase-specific therapies are suggested. These approaches are for children who, despite their behavior, have the capacity for social relations and feelings of guilt or shame. Much case material, including dialogue, is used to illustrate the therapies described here.

Kratochwill, Thomas R., and Richard J. Morris. *The Practice of Child Therapy.* 2nd ed. Pergamon, 1991. 496p. bibliog. index. LC 89-78238. ISBN 0-08-036430-6. $32.50.

Detailed and systematic reviews of contemporary treatment techniques for childhood learning and behavioral disorders are the focus of this book, intended as a reference for practitioners and students who work with children. Childhood fears and phobias, depression, obsessive-compulsive disorder, academic problems, conduct disorders, autism, children medically at risk, psychopharmacotherapy, prevention, and professional, legal, and ethical issues in treatment, are covered, among other topics. Case material illustrates concepts in this behaviorally oriented sourcebook.

Lage, Gustavo A., and Harvey K. Nathan. *Psychotherapy, Adolescents, and Self Psychology*. International Universities Press, 1991. 448p. bibliog. index. LC 90-4924. ISBN 0-8236-5403-6. $55.00.

Case material from the psychoanalytic treatment of an adolescent is used to demonstrate significant aspects of psychotherapy with this age group for an audience of clinicians. Principles covered include the need to apply principles of self-psychology to understand the case, the difference between psychoanalysis and psychotherapy, and the modifications in techniques, functions, and responsibilities for treating an adolescent versus working with an adult. Basic concepts of self-psychology are reviewed in an introductory chapter, with the rest of the text devoted to revealing and discussing the natural history of this three-year case.

Lewis, Melvin, ed. *Child and Adolescent Psychiatry: A Comprehensive Textbook*. Williams & Wilkins, 1990. 282p. index. LC 90-12586. ISBN 0-683-04954-2. $120.00.

For the clinician, this textbook provides a complete syllabus of child and adolescent psychiatry. Content includes coverage of normal development, including biological factors; development of symptoms; etiological influences; diagnostic assessment; classification; syndromes; treatment; child psychiatry and allied professions; and research. Material on major syndromes and therapies is also provided. This anthology concludes with sections on psychiatric concerns that appear in the context of allied professions such as pediatrics, education, law, and public health and comments on recruitment, training, research, and the ethics of using children as subjects.

Mordock, John B. *Counseling Children: Basic Principles for Helping the Troubled and Defiant Child*. Continuum, 1990. 227p. bibliog. LC 90-39117. ISBN 0-8264-0487-1. $17.95.

A practical developmental approach to counseling children is the focus of this handbook, intended for professional counselors and others, such as parents and teachers, with responsibility for children. Mordock begins with a review of basic principles of counseling, interviewing and communication skills, and goals for counseling. Later chapters address such issues as play therapy; the development of mature defense mechanisms; interpretation, both empathetic and dynamic (dealing with unconscious material); and verbalization. The stages of the counseling process are also reviewed. Numerous examples and case studies illustrate the detailed instructions provided; the author, a clinical child psychologist, notes that they are drawn from the published literature rather than personal experience to permit the reader to examine the issues presented in-depth.

Oster, Gerald D., and Janice E. Caro. *Understanding and Treating Depressed Adolescents and Their Families*. Wiley, 1990. 228p. LC 89-37665. ISBN 0-471-60897-1. $34.95.

A multifaceted family therapy model for treating adolescents with mood disorders is presented in this handbook for clinicians. Organized into four sections, the text includes theoretical and case material on causes, diagnosis, and treatment, with a separate section on handling crisis situations. Specific topics considered are individual compared to family therapies, clinical tools for assessing the depressed adolescent, understanding suicidal behaviors in adolescents, and outpatient, residential, and brief hospitalization treatment.

Polsgrove, Lewis, ed. *Reducing Undesirable Behaviors*. Council for Exceptional Children, 1991. 33p. bibliog. LC 90-9005. ISBN 0-86586-201-X. $7.50.

Within the context of the controversy over the moral and ethical, effectiveness of aversive behavioral techniques, this concise guide reviews the empirical foundation of available procedures and offers guidelines regarding their appropriate use with youth with behavioral disorders. The text defines behavior reduction and reviews each technique, including differential reinforcement, time-out, overcorrection, aversive conditioning, and corporal punishment. These recommendations were approved by the Executive Committee of the Council for Children with Behavioral Disorders (CCBD). The council's policy statement on the use of these techniques is appended.

Reynolds, William M., ed. *Internalizing Disorders in Children and Adolescents*. Wiley, 1991. 336p. bibliog. index. LC 91-40212. ISBN 0-471-50648-6. $39.95.

Intended for the clinician or student with scholarly interest in and clinical practice involving the treatment of internalizing disorders in children and adolescents, this anthology provides an analysis of current thinking, reviews of recent research, and a summary of contemporary treatment practices. Individual chapters by experts cover anxiety disorders, obsessive-compulsive disorder, suicidal behavior, depression, and somatic disorders such as eating disturbances, elimination disorders, and asthma. An introduction to the nature and study of internalizing disorders and their taxonomy and classification is included.

Samuel, Susan K., and Susana Sikorsky. *Clinical Evaluations of School-Aged Children: A Structured Approach to the Diagnosis of Child and Adolescent Mental Disorders*. Professional Resource Exchange, 1990. 178p. index. LC 89-43664. ISBN 0-943158-44-3. $19.95.

This handbook provides a format for structuring data on major psychological disorders in childhood to aid therapists in making a diagnosis. Among the disorders considered are disruptive behavior disorders; anxiety; adjustment and autistic disorders; schizophrenia; depression; attachment and gender identity disorders; eating, elimination, and sleep disorders; and impulse control disorders. Demographic norms, case histories, and a checklist of symptoms are used to further clarify and confirm a diagnosis. The symptom checklist includes symptoms such as inattention, abnormal activity level, aggressiveness, anxiety, isolation, somatic complaints, and impaired cognition.

Schaefer, Charles, Karen Gitlin, and Alice Sandgrund, ed. *Play Diagnosis and Assessment*. Wiley, 1990. 718p. bibliog. LC 90-12661. ISBN 0-471-62166-8. $69.95.

A comprehensive collection of recent contributions on the assessment and diagnosis of children through play is presented in this sourcebook for clinicians. Various scales and techniques, including developmental play scales, diagnostic play scales, peer interaction and parent-child interaction scales, and projective play assessment and play therapy scales, are covered, accompanied by extensive bibliographies listing sources for applications of these scales with different populations. The editors note that techniques appropriate for a broad range of problems were selected for inclusion in this anthology.

Schroeder, Carolyn, and Betty N. Gordon. *Assessment and Treatment of Childhood Problems: A Clinician's Guide.* Guilford, 1991. 512p. bibliog. illus. index. LC 91-20201. ISBN 0-89862-565-3. $40.00.

This guide for a diverse audience of professionals who care for children outlines a comprehensive approach to assessment and treatment for a variety of common problems. The authors, both clinical child psychologists, review children's development, emphasizing those areas such as toilet training and autonomy that are most related to the development of childhood problems, including enuresis, encopresis, or negative behavior. They also examine child, parent, and family environment characteristics that may enhance children's development or put them at risk of stress. Three types of life stress, birth of siblings, divorce, and death of a parent, are discussed in detail. Brief reviews of the literature, guidance on comprehensive assessment, specific treatment options, and case examples for a number of psychological problems, such as elimination disorders, sexuality and sexual abuse, fears and anxieties, and sleep disturbances, are included. The Chapel Hill Pediatrics practice in which the authors participate is described as the basis for a model program. Appendixes include lists of books for parents and children, sample clinical forms, and assessment instrument descriptions.

Shafii, Mohammad. *Clinical Guide to Depression in Children and Adolescents.* American Psychiatric, 1992. 304p. index. LC 91-22112. ISBN 0-88048-356-3. $38.00.

Only in recent years have depressive disorders been studied systematically in infants, children, and adolescents; little is known about bipolar disorders in these age groups. This anthology summarizes and synthesizes significant advances that have occurred in the recognition, diagnosis, management, and treatment of depressive and bipolar disorders in children from infancy through adolescence; the role of the family is emphasized throughout the text. In the first part, contributors examine the clinical manifestations of depression; its epidemiology, etiology, and neurobiology; and how it relates to seasonal affective disorder and suicidal behaviors. Types of therapies, including dynamic psychotherapy, group therapy, and cognitive therapy, are reviewed in the second part, and, in the third part, bipolar disorders are discussed. The work is targeted to a broad audience of health and mental health care professionals.

Slomowitz, Marcia, ed. *Adolescent Psychotherapy.* American Psychiatric, 1990. 206p. bibliog. index. LC 90-871. ISBN 0-88048-181-1. $29.95.

Using a biopsychosocial framework, this handbook to clinical practice reviews theory and treatment for adolescent psychotherapy. Concepts are described and the organizational plan of the book reviewed in the opening chapter. Psychoanalytic theories, biological and neurodevelopmental factors, and the social context of adolescence are considered in the first sec-

tion. The second section reviews the psychotherapeutic process and emphasizes the value of group therapy for adolescents because of the importance of their peer group for promoting self-esteem and emancipation from the family. In the last section, the contributors examine psychotherapy with four specific disorders: neurotic conflicts, attention deficit disorder, behavior disorders, and unipolar/bipolar disorders.

Stiffman, Arlene Rubin, and Larry E. Davis. *Ethnic Issues in Adolescent Mental Health.* Sage, 1990. 360p. bibliog. illus. LC 90-8735. ISBN 0-8039-3984-1. $42.00. ISBN 0-8039-3985-X pbk. $18.95.

The essays compiled here make up a state-of-the-art review of the extent of social problems in various minority groups and their impact on mental health, ethnic-related barriers to treatment, and possible interventions that take ethnic considerations into account. The first section explores general mental health issues, such as psychological adjustment and ethnic identity development, in African American, Mexican American, and Asian American teens. Remaining sections address antisocial behavior/violence/delinquency, sexuality (African American teens only), substance use and abuse, and suicide among minority youth. Extensive references contribute to the usefulness of this text as a primer on ethnic issues in understanding and treating adolescent problems.

Trad, Paul V. *Conversations with Preschool Children: Uncovering Developmental Patterns.* Norton, 1990. 227p. bibliog. index. LC 89-2553. ISBN 0-393-70085-2. $19.95.

Guiding health care professionals to become more sensitive to and skilled at distinguishing adaptive responses to traumatic events from the beginnings of psychopathology in preschool children is the focus of this anthology on developmental processes. The intricacies of development and the various ways that children confront challenges in their lives are explored via case studies, each highlighting a major issue such as attachment, separation-individuation, focus of control, aggression, birth of a sibling, and divorce. Developmental theories are reviewed in general and noted in the discussion of each of the seven cases reviewed here.

Trad, Paul V., ed. *Interventions with Infants and Parents: The Theory and Practice of Previewing.* Wiley, 1992. 557p. LC 91-3043. ISBN 0-471-53229-0. $55.00.

In a practical and detailed manner, this handbook examines the practice and value of previewing, a technique whereby care givers rehearse for infants developmental skills that they subsequently perform, giving them in turn a sense of mastery over the environment and themselves. If the relationship between care giver and infant has not developed to the point that this degree of communication occurs, therapeutic intervention can either correct the dysfunction or minimize its effects on the infant's development. The text introduces previewing as a developmental tool, reviews assessment techniques, describes intervention strategies, and explains how to apply previewing in a number of therapeutic settings. The editor notes that this text is the first volume to provide comprehensive guidelines to psychiatrists for conducting this form of early life intervention.

Weiner, Irving V. *Psychological Disturbance in Adolescence*. 2nd ed. Wiley, 1992. 668p. bibliog. index. LC 91-18344. ISBN 0-471-82596-4. $49.95.

Clinicians and educators who are concerned with identifying and treating psychological problems in teens will find in this text comprehensive reviews of the major disturbances affecting youth, including schizophrenic, affective, and neurotic disorders; academic underachievement; and delinquent and suicidal behavior. New to this second edition are chapters on borderline disorders and substance abuse. In each chapter, the author reviews clinical and experimental literature covering origins, symptoms, causes, epidemiology, and treatment approaches. Introductory chapters provide a perspective from which to understand adolescent psychopathology, and the concluding chapter covers principles of therapy with disturbed adolescents.

Weisz, John R. *Effects of Psychotherapy with Children and Adolescents*. Sage, 1993. Developmental Clinical Psychology and Psychiatry Series. 119p. bibliog. index. LC 92-48962. ISBN 0-8039-489-X. $14.95.

This volume in the Developmental Clinical Psychology and Psychiatry Series evaluates the current state of research and practice in child and adolescent psychology. It examines who receives therapy, who drops out, the effects of treatment by age and gender, and factors that influence therapeutic change. More important, the authors examine the impact of psychotherapy on children and whether children who receive therapy benefit from it. The results of research demonstrate encouraging outcomes for youths participating in controlled experimental studies, but for the majority of children and adolescents receiving treatment in service-oriented clinics or community-based programs the results are not uniformly positive. The authors conclude that much remains to be done, and they encourage partnerships between scholars and practitioners to promote improvement in the field.

Wenar, Charles. *Developmental Psychopathology from Infancy through Adolescence*. 2nd ed. McGraw-Hill, 1990. 493p. index. LC 89-12794. ISBN 0-07-069269-6. $41.95.

This textbook views childhood psychopathology as normal development gone awry, an approach the author acknowledges is not universally accepted. He also notes the value of the multiple causal perspective in interpreting psychopathology across the life cycle from infancy through adolescence. The book includes an introduction to the developmental approach to psychopathology, normal development, theoretical "bridges" between normal and deviant development, the process of psychological assessment, prevention and treatment, and the consequences of brain damage, physical illness, abuse, and neglect. Major disorders covered include autism and childhood schizophrenia in infancy, depression, pathologies of initiative and early socialization in toddlers, learning disabilities, neuroses, conduct disorders, and mental retardation. A chapter on minority children was added to this edition.

West, Patricia, and Christina L. Sieloff Evans, eds. *Psychiatric and Mental Health Nursing with Children and Adolescents*. Aspen, 1991. 428p. bibliog. index. LC 91-26125. ISBN 0-8342-0240-9. $49.00.

Specific nursing interventions for treating children and adolescents with such psychiatric disorders as attention and motor disorders, communication difficulties, conduct problems, substance abuse, self-destructive tendencies, and eating difficulties are the focus of this comprehensive textbook, intended for all nurses who work with children and adolescents. Using the nursing process as the basis for organization, the text also provides an overview of psychiatric nursing with youth, nursing assessment, the role of developmental theory, cultural aspects of assessment, diagnosis and care plans, selection of treatment modalities, and the relationship between psychopathology and nursing problems. Legal issues, the environment in which treatment takes place, and preventive care are covered as well. The text includes the American Nursing Association standards for psychiatric practice with youth.

Wexler, David B. *The Adolescent Self: Strategies for Self-Soothing, Self-Regulation, and Self-Esteem in Adolescents*. Norton, 1991. 192p. bibliog. index. LC 91-1963. ISBN 0-393-70114-X. $22.95.

Viewing many adolescent problems, such as substance abuse, aggression, eating disorders, and destructive behaviors, as stemming from deficiencies in self-control, the author describes a program, PRISM (Program for Innovative Self-Management), that enables troubled teens to learn and practice self-management skills. In an engaging manner, PRISM integrates techniques based on a number of psychotherapies to help teens develop a cohesive sense of self, including self-esteem, self-regulation, self-control, self-soothing, self-stimulation, and self-efficacy. Several detailed case studies illustrate the narrative. The material is intended for anyone, including parents, who works with adolescents.

Wexler, William C., and Donald J. O'Grady, eds. *Clinical Hypnosis with Children*. Brunner/Mazel, 1991. 272p. LC 90-15157. ISBN 0-87630-605-9. $32.95.

Hypnosis, which has been used for relief of physical and psychological symptoms since ancient times, is especially effective with children, who are quite responsive to suggestive therapy. This handbook on hypnosis examines its theoretical and experimental foundations, specialized induction techniques, and therapeutic applications; the narrative includes case histories that illustrate the moment-to-moment progress of a hypnotic encounter. In introduction, the text covers developmental considerations in using hypnosis, hypnotic responsiveness in children, and special considerations in using hypnosis with very young children. Psychological applications, including treatment for childhood trauma, sexual abuse, and habits, behavior disorders, anxiety, and learning disorders, are reviewed. Its use in treating medical conditions such as nausea and vomiting, pain management, and enuresis/encopresis is also presented.

Wiener, Jerry M. *Textbook of Child and Adolescent Psychiatry*. American Psychiatric, 1991. 668p. bibliog. index. LC 91-4548. ISBN 0-88048-296-6. $95.00.

Health care professionals with various specializations will find in this clinically focused textbook the state of the art and science of the field of child and adolescent psychiatry. Chapters on developmental, schizophrenic, anxiety, eating, tic, and behavior disorders include *Diagnostic and Statistic Manual of Mental Disorders DSM-III-R* (American Psychiatric Association, 1987) criteria from the clinical findings, differential diagnosis, epidemiology, etiology, clinical course, and prognosis. In addition to a detailed review of clinical disorders, the text includes an introduction to the field and a description of assessment and diagnostic procedures including interviews, classification, psychological testing, and how to present the results to parents and the patient. Special issues such as AIDS, sexual abuse, suicide, gender identity confusion, and forensic psychiatry are addressed, as are various treatment approaches.

Winnicott, D. W. *Therapeutic Consultations in Child Psychiatry.* Basic Books, 1990. 410p. bibliog. index. LC 90-899. ISBN 0-465-08511-3. $34.95.

A standard, first published in 1971, that explores the application of psychoanalysis to child psychiatry, this casebook guides therapists using a single interview program of therapy with their clients. Winnicott describes the "squiggle game" method of exchanging drawings that may quickly illustrate the source of a child's emotional or behavioral problem. Twenty-one case studies that illustrate the therapeutic method are presented, with the first group introducing its use with basic cases, the second covering more complex situations, and the third presenting cases of children with antisocial tendencies, particularly stealing. The children's drawings, in counterpoint to those of the therapist, demonstrate clearly the insights available via this technique.

Zimet, Sara Goodman, and Gordon K. Farley. *Day Treatment for Children with Emotional Disorders.* Plenum, 1991. Vol. 1. *A Model in Action.* 274p. bibliog. index. LC 91-2086. ISBN 0-306-437743-0. $42.50. Vol. 2. *Models Across the Country.* 230p. bibliog. illus. index. LC 91-2086. ISBN 0-306-43744-9. $39.50.

Despite its relatively recent history of 50 years, day treatment for psychological difficulties is increasingly in demand. To assist in the development of the field, two staff members at a program operating at the University of Colorado Health Sciences Center explain what is required to set up a day treatment program, discuss how to design the program, explore theoretical models, and provide treatment components. The first volume profiles the UC program; reviews the clinical and educational programs, such as intake, home visits, "standby" system, and academic skills development; analyzes funding and staff roles; and describes program evaluation and research projects. The second volume describes how to start a program and applies a number of theoretical perspectives to six model programs operating throughout the United States. A lengthy bibliography provides detailed annotations of the existing literature on day treatment.

PROFESSIONAL TITLES: JOURNALS

Adolescent Psychiatry. University of Chicago Press. 1971. A. ISSN 0065-2008. Price varies.

Scholarly reviews of critical issues in adolescent development, psychopathology, and psychotherapy are compiled in this annual series from the American Society for Adolescent Psychiatry. Clinical issues in intensive psychotherapy, as opposed to biological or short-term therapies, are the primary focus of papers presented here. Their depth makes these volumes references for both students and practitioners. Contributors from a variety of disciplines address broad social, cultural, and political concerns as well as specific treatment issues related to the adolescent stage of life. Past topics have included identity, substance abuse, and the Chestnut Lodge program.

Annual Progress in Child Psychiatry and Child Development. Brunner-Mazel. 1968. A. ISSN 0066-4030. Price varies.

Prominent scholars Stella Chess and Margaret Hertzig select significant articles of current interest that have the potential to be of enduring scholarly importance for inclusion in this annual state-of-the-art review. Six major areas of interest are addressed in each volume. A past volume included reviews of development, epidemiology, family issues, clinical issues, treatment, and psychosocial concerns. Articles chosen are generally of two types: original work that promises to advance the study of children and review articles that give a comprehensive picture of the state of knowledge in a key area of research. Each is reprinted in its entirety. In addition, the editors provide an analytical introduction to each section that highlights the significance of each piece.

Behavioral Disorders Journal. Council for Exceptional Children. 1976. 4/yr. ISSN 0198-7429. $54.00.

The Council for Children with Behavioral Disorders, a division of the Council for Exceptional Children, publishes this quarterly journal directed to educators, therapists, and parents concerned with the well-being of children with these disorders. Papers published here are either reports of original research or theoretical discussions of relevant topics in the education of children and adolescents with emotional or behavioral problems. Topics covered in this refereed journal have included response to stimulant medication in children with ADHD, aggression replacement training with adolescents, and vocational training.

Brown University Child Behavior and Development Letter. Manisses Communications. 1984. M. ISSN 0885-7261. $97.00.

Providing "monthly reports on the problems of children and adolescents growing up," this eight-page newsletter publishes commentaries, information on social policy, book reviews, research annotations, and handouts for professionals in child care fields to distribute to parents. Each issue contains a special supplement that is a lengthier discussion of programs such as Head Start and the challenge model approach to children at risk.

Child and Family Behavior Therapy. Haworth. 1978. Q. ISSN 0731-7107. $132.00.

Empirical research with clinical applications for the treatment of children and adolescents with behavioral disorders is the focus of this refereed journal. Review articles, brief case studies, and book reviews are also included for an audience of psychologists, social workers, psychiatrists, and educators. Works published address classroom settings, residential treatment, and psychological counseling. Issues have focused on the effects of family violence on children's behavior disorders, cognitive intervention in enuresis, and good behavior reinforcement in preschoolers.

Child Psychiatry and Human Development. Human Sciences. 1970. Q. ISSN 0009-398X. $175.00.

The official journal of the American Association of Psychiatric Services for Children, this scholarly title has an interdisciplinary and international focus. Insights from psychiatry, pediatrics, psychology, and development are integrated to provide a forum for a diverse professional audience interested in the developing child and adolescent in health and in conflict. In each issue, five or six scholarly articles examine such issues as rage, stealing, post-disaster play and adjustment, and the relation between temperament and behavioral disorders.

Elementary School Guidance & Counseling. American School Counselor Association. 1965. 4/yr. ISSN 0013-5976. $30.00.

Published by the American School Counselor Association (ASCA), a division of the American Counseling Association, this quarterly journal is a source of practical information on techniques for group and individual counseling, program development and evaluation, guidance in the classroom, and applications from research studies. Articles in a past issue addressed empowering homeless children, counseling Hispanic American children, using children's literature in classroom guidance, and transforming at-risk educational practices.

Families in Society: The Journal of Contemporary Human Services. Family Service America. 1920. 10/yr. ISSN 1044-3894. $35.00.

Directed to human service professionals, this journal publishes practice-oriented articles on family, group, and individual counseling and therapy. Theoretical and advocacy issues are also covered. One issue focused on fathers, examining fathers' involvement in Head Start, roles of African American fathers from an ecological perspective, and the paternal presence.

Infant Mental Health Journal. Clinical Psychology. 1980. Q. ISSN 0163-9641. $90.00.

Original research, review articles, program descriptions, clinical studies, and book reviews on infant psychology and psychiatry are published in this interdisciplinary refereed journal. Among the topics covered are infant emotional and social development, interactions between infants and their care givers, cultural influences on infant development, and circumstances that put infants at risk of inadequate development. The journal is the official publication of the International Association for Infant Mental Health (IAIMH) and the World Association for Infant Psychiatry and Allied Disciplines (WAIPAD).

Journal of Abnormal Child Psychology. Plenum. 1973. B-M. ISSN 0091-0627. $225.00.

Empirical studies on the etiology, assessment, treatment, prognosis and follow-up, epidemiology, and ecology of behavioral pathology in childhood and adolescence are emphasized in this refereed journal. Reports of original research, theoretical studies, significant case studies, and brief reports of important ongoing programs are published. The articles accepted address delinquency, neurotic and organic disorders, psychosomatic conditions, and behavioral problems in mental retardation. The journal is the official publication of the Society for Research in Child and Adolescent Psychopathology.

Journal of Child and Adolescent Psychiatric and Mental Health Nursing. Lippincott. 1988. Q. ISSN 0897-9685. $35.00.

Child and adolescent psychiatric and mental health nurses will find original research on issues relevant to their practice and education in this refereed journal. Psychosocial care of youth and their families, social policy factors related to the delivery of care to this population, environmental factors that affect the mental health of children and youth, and the impact of nursing care on cognitive, social, or emotional growth of children and youth are concerns of the journal. Commentary, legislative updates, interviews, and conference news round out the coverage.

Journal of Child & Adolescent Psychotherapy. Human Sciences. 1984. Q. ISSN 1053-0800. $25.00.

Articles published in this interdisciplinary journal for practitioners who work with emotionally disturbed children and adolescents meet editorial standards for relevance, practicality, methodological soundness, and potential to improve services in the field. Research reports, theoretical discussions, critical reviews, program descriptions, position papers, and case studies are published, as are funding opportunities, abstracts of current literature, book and software reviews, and news from associations. Issues have addressed time-out use in public schools, strategic therapy with children, attachment in children with asthma, and a report on the Single-Parent Family Project.

Journal of Child Psychology & Psychiatry & Allied Disciplines. Pergamon. 1960. 4/yr. ISSN 0021-9630. $275.00.

Empirical research, critical reviews, and clinical studies on child and adolescent development, developmental psychopathology, and developmental disorders are combined in this international refereed journal. Research notes, commentaries, occasional book supplements, and news notes about international conferences are also published. New to the journal is a series of "Practitioner Reviews," which draws out practical lessons from a research area. With editorial introductions that highlight articles with the greatest clinical relevance, these reviews make the journal's contents more accessible to the clinician.

Journal of Clinical Child Psychology. American Psychological Association. 1972. Q. ISSN 0047-228X. $120.00.

The official journal of the Section on Clinical Psychology of the American Psychological Association's Division on Clinical Psychology, this title covers child advocacy and professional practice and training in clinical child psychology. In spite of its status, the journal encourages contributions from consumers, students, and practitioners in allied disciplines. Articles presenting diverse viewpoints as well as reports of original research and topical reviews are published here. Among the topics covered in past issues are body image, child abuse, depression, substance use, attention deficit hyperactivity disorder, and the validation of various scales and models.

Journal of Experimental Child Psychology. Academic. 1964. B-M. ISSN 0022-0965. $265.00.

This scholarly journal publishes reports of original research that significantly expands knowledge of the psychology of the child. Other kinds of articles, such as critical reviews, theoretical analyses, and brief reports on methodologies or innovative techniques, are published only to the extent that they stimulate empirical research in the field. Investigations with special needs children as subjects are also published.

Journal of Pediatric Psychology. Plenum. 1976. B-M. ISSN 0146-8693. $250.00.

Research, theory, and professional practice in pediatric psychology, including health, illness, and physical and mental development of children and adolescents are the focus of this scholarly journal. Papers that explore the relationship between psychological and physical health through assessment, intervention, evaluation, and treatment are published, as are pieces that assess the role of psychology in pediatric medicine, health promotion, and illness and injury prevention.

Psychology in the Schools. Clinical Psychology. 1964. Q. ISSN 0033-3085. $30.00.

Research and opinion articles describe practical applications for school psychologists, teachers, and administrators. Articles on evaluation and assessment, educational practices and problems, strategies in behavioral change, and related subjects were published in a past issue. Books received are listed and book reviews published.

School Counselor. American Association for Counseling and Development. 1953. 5/yr. ISSN 0036-6536. $37.50.

In this journal, the American Association for Counseling and Development (AACD) provides a forum for theoretical, philosophical, and empirical articles, commentaries, practice descriptions, and reviews of resources of current interest on school guidance and counseling. Practice guidelines from AACD are published. Reducing stress in gifted students, contemporary counseling approaches, legal liability and student suicides, and support for transfer students were covered in past issues.

DIRECTORY

American Academy of Child and Adolescent Psychiatry (AACAP)

3615 Wisconsin Avenue, N.W., Washington, DC 20016
(202) 966-7300 Fax (202) 966-2891 Toll-free (800) 233-7636
Virginia Q. Anthony, Executive Director
Founded: 1953
Former Name: American Academy of Child Psychiatry
Mission/Goals: To encourage and promote medical advances in the knowledge and treatment of psychiatric illnesses in children
Audience/Clientele: Physicians who have completed an additional five years of residency training in child and adolescent psychiatry
Education and Outreach: Publishing
Publications: *Journal of the AACAP*, bimonthly; *American Academy of Child Psychiatry—Newsletter*, quarterly newsletter covering research updates, statistics, and employment opportunities; *Membership Directory*, periodic
Programs: Annual conference

American Association of Children's Residential Centers (AACRC)

440 First Street, N.W., Suite 310, Washington, DC 20001

(202) 638-1604 Fax (202) 638-4004
Claudia C. Waller, Executive Director
Founded: 1957
Members: 225 individuals, 95 agencies
Mission/Goals: To maintain and enhance sound clinical practice, research, and innovation in children's residential treatment; to provide an annual forum where practitioners may share experiences, exchange ideas, and learn about recent developments in the field, such as therapeutic living experiences, individual educational programs, individual and group therapy, and parent and family therapy
Audience/Clientele: Physicians, psychologists, clinical social workers, child care workers, nurses, state departments of health and human services, others with an interest in children's residential care
Staff: 2 professionals, 18 volunteers
Budget: $130,000 Funding: Fees for services or products, donations, dues
Services: Residential facility, lobbying, advocacy
Awards: Albert E. Trieschman Award for outstanding child care worker in residential setting; Bruno Bettelheim Award to honor a major contributor to the field; Fellow and Life Memberships
Education and Outreach: Seminars, database development, publishing
Publications: *Residential Treatment News*, bimonthly newsletter covering research, governmental policy, book reviews, and calendar; *Contributions to Residential Treatment*, annual proceedings; *Journal of Residential Treatment for Children and Youth*, quarterly; *AACRC Organizational Directory*, annual
Programs: Annual conference

American Counseling Association

5999 Stevenson Avenue, Alexandria, VA 22304
(703) 823-9800 Fax (703) 823-0252 Toll-free (800) 347-6647 TTY/TDD (703) 370-1943
Dr. Theodore J. Remley, Jr., Executive Director
Founded: 1952
Members: 56,000
Affiliates: 53 state groups
Former Name: American Association for Counseling and Development
Mission/Goals: To provide a variety of programs and services that support the personal, professional, and program development goals of the membership
Audience/Clientele: Counselors in a variety of mental health settings, including school counselors, career counselors, mental health counselors, marriage and family counselors
Budget: $9,000,000 Funding: Dues, fees for services or products
Services: Lobbying, insurance
Education and Outreach: Continuing education courses, seminars, library, archives, publishing
Publications: *Counselor Education and Supervision*, quarterly; *Elementary School Guidance and Counseling Journal*, quarterly; *Journal of Counseling and Development*, bimonthly; *Journal of*

Mental Health Counselors, quarterly; *Measurement and Evaluations in Counseling and Development*, quarterly; *School Counselor*, 5/yr; and other scholarly journals related to career and employment counseling

Council on Accreditation of Services for Families and Children

520 8th Avenue, Suite 2202B, New York, NY 10018
(212) 714-9399
David Shover, Executive Director
Founded: 1977
Mission/Goals: To encourage improvement in the quality of social and mental health services by establishing standards for effective performance and a process for measuring compliance to those standards
Audience/Clientele: Providers of any of over 40 human services programs and members of the public needing those services
Staff: 4 professionals, 6 nonprofessionals, 3 volunteers
Budget: $1,100,000 Funding: Fund-raising, fees for services or products, dues
Education and Outreach: Accreditation reviews, publishing
Publications: *Standards for Agency Management and Service Delivery*; *Manual for Agency Accreditation*; *Guidelines for Accreditation*

Division of Family Psychology

3900 E. Camelback Road, #200, Phoenix, AZ 85018
(602) 912-5300 Fax (602) 957-4828
Ronald P. Levant, President
Founded: 1984
Members: 1,800
Mission/Goals: To promote human welfare through the development, dissemination, and application of knowledge about the dynamics, structure, and functioning of families
Audience/Clientele: Professionals and students concerned with family psychology
Funding: Dues
Services: Lobbying, fund-raising, compiling statistics
Awards: Family Psychologist of the Year for outstanding, sustained contributions; Distinguished Service Award; Certificate of Appreciation; Student Research Award
Education and Outreach: In-service programs, continuing education courses, seminars, database development, publishing
Publications: *Division 43 Bulletin: The Family Psychologist*, quarterly; *Journal of Family Psychology*, periodic
Programs: Annual conference held in conjunction with American Psychological Association (APA); Mid-Winter Meeting held in conjunction with APA Divisions of Psychotherapy and Independent Practice

National Academy of Counselors and Family Therapists, Inc. (NACFT)

8038 Camellia Lane, Indianapolis, IN 46219
(317) 898-3211
Anthony T. Palisi, Ed.D., Executive Director
Founded: 1972

Members: 800
Affiliates: 7 regional groups
Former Name: National Alliance for Family Life/American College of Counselors
Mission/Goals: To support the growth and development of human beings within a stable family unit; to strengthen the marriage relationship as the matrix that best fosters values that enrich human growth and development
Audience/Clientele: Professionals who have an interest in marriage and the family from an educational, clinical, or behavioral standpoint, including psychologists, social workers, pastoral counselors, and physicians
Staff: 4 volunteers
Funding: Dues
Services: Counseling, referral
Education and Outreach: In-service programs, continuing education courses, seminars, publishing
Publications: *Family Letter*, 8/yr; *Directory*, biennial; *Newsletter*, quarterly
Programs: Semiannual conference

Society for Behavioral Pediatrics (SBP)

241 E. Gravers Lane, Philadelphia, PA 19118
(215) 248-9168
Noreen M. Spota, Administrative Director
Founded: 1982
Members: 500
Mission/Goals: To improve the health care of infants, children, and adolescents by promoting research and teaching in developmental and behavioral pediatrics; to encourage research in developmental and behavioral pediatrics, with an emphasis on psychosocial issues arising in the context of health care; to promote education in this subject; to raise questions and respond to issues that affect research, teaching, or program development; to promote an understanding of, and particular interest in, the social, educational, and cultural influences on children
Audience/Clientele: Professionals, including pediatricians, child psychiatrists, pediatric nurses, and pediatric social workers, who are committed to research, teaching, and clinical excellence in developmental and behavioral pediatrics as it affects the health care of infants, children, and adolescents
Staff: 1 professional
Budget: $115,000 Funding: Fees for services, donations, dues, royalties, interest
Awards: Irving B. Harris Lectureship, which recognizes a career of excellence in developmental or behavioral pediatrics
Education and Outreach: Continuing education courses, publishing
Publications: *Journal of Developmental and Behavioral Pediatrics*, bimonthly
Programs: Annual conference and workshops

Society for Pediatric Psychology (SPP)

c/o Suzanne Bennett-Johnson, Ph.D., University of Florida, Health Sciences Center, Box J234, Gainesville, FL 32610

(904) 392-3611 Fax (617) 735-PHAX
Suzanne Bennett-Johnson, Ph.D., President
Founded: 1968
Mission/Goals: To encourage the development of theory, research, training, and professional practice in pediatric psychology; to support the application of psychiatric principles to medical and psychological problems of children, youths, and their families; to support legislation benefiting children's health and welfare
Audience/Clientele: Psychologists working in children's hospitals, developmental clinics, and pediatric group practices
Awards: Distinguished Professional Contributions; Research Contributions; Student Research Awards
Education and Outreach: Continuing education courses, seminars, publishing
Publications: *Journal of Pediatric Psychology*, quarterly, includes research reports, literature and book reviews, and case studies; *Newsletter of the Society for Pediatric Psychology*, 3/yr, with abstracts, association news, and employment opportunities
Programs: Annual conference, held in conjunction with the American Psychological Association

Society of Professors of Child and Adolescent Psychiatry (SPCAP)

3615 Wisconsin Avenue, N.W., Washington, DC 20016-3007
(202) 966-7300
Jean De Jarnette, Administrative Assistant
Founded: 1969
Members: 160
Mission/Goals: To provide a forum for discussion and exchange of ideas among child psychiatry program directors in medical schools in order to enhance growth of child psychiatry as a discipline, strengthen graduate and postgraduate medical education, patient care, and research in this subject; to provide a liaison between individuals and organizations concerned with the study and practice of child psychiatry

Audience/Clientele: Professors of child and adolescent psychiatry
Staff: 1 nonprofessional
Budget: $16,000 Funding: Dues
Services: Managed care
Education and Outreach: Continuing education courses, seminars, publishing
Publications: *Newsletter*, periodic
Programs: Annual conference

Youth Emotions Anonymous (YEA)

P.O. Box 4245, St. Paul, MN 55104-0245
(612) 647-9712 Fax (612) 647-1593
Martha Bush, Coordinator
Founded: 1971
Affiliates: 19 state groups
Mission/Goals: Via a 12-step program, to help youths ages 13 to 19 develop healthy emotions and acquire and practice positive habits and attitudes and eliminate negative ones; to aid them in finding solutions to their problems or learning to live at peace with problems they cannot solve
Staff: 1 professional, 5 nonprofessionals, 4 volunteers
Budget: $325,000 Funding: Fees for services, donations
Services: Support group
Education and Outreach: Pamphlets for group organizers
Programs: Annual conference, held in conjunction with Emotions Anonymous

REFERENCE

1. Carolyn S. Schroeder and Betty N. Gordon, *Assessment and Treatment of Childhood Problems: A Clinician's Guide* (New York: Guilford, 1991), 24–25.

CHAPTER

Health Care, Safety, and Death

The average child gets approximately six colds,
or upper respiratory infections, each year.
Marianne Neifert. Dr. Mom

To bring up our children to have healthy attitudes
toward health, we should focus our concern not on
the injuries and diseases that threaten them, but
on preserving their good feelings toward their bodies,
toward themselves as people, and toward us as parents.
Benjamin Spock. Dr. Spock on Parenting

Consulting diagnostic guides that distinguish minor ailments treatable at home from those requiring professional or even emergency attention and practicing a regular routine of preventive care through immunizations, well-baby care, and dental checkups help parents ensure their children's good health. Manuals similar in scope, but with a different level of coverage, are available for the clinician who cares for children.

Children succumb to a number of minor infectious diseases every year. The annual incidence of repeated ear infections per 100 children from birth to age 4 is 16; for children ages 5 to 11, the annual incidence of repeated tonsillitus is 8.5 per 100 children.[1] Without routine immunizations and pediatric care, the incidence of infectious diseases such as measles surges. A record number of cases, 27,786 in 1990, continued a trend started in 1989 after a decade of few reported cases.[2] Regular care is also important in the prenatal period, as low birth weight and premature delivery claim 110.2 and 186 children per 100,000 live births, respectively.[3]

Equally important is protecting children's safety. From purchasing a safe crib and baby-proofing a toddler's environment to teaching bicycle safety to school-age children and safe use of alcohol to adolescents, protecting children from accidental injury or death is essential. For children 18 and under, 20,116,000 injuries were reported in 1985–87.[4] For children 1 to 4 years in age, accidents and adverse effects are the highest cause of death, claiming 17.3 lives per 100,000 children, and homicide is the fourth highest cause, claiming 3.5 lives per 100,000. For children ages 5 to 14 and youths ages 15 to 24, accidents and adverse effects continued as the highest cause of death at rates of 10.4 and 43.9 per 100,000, respectively.[5] Homicide and suicide, the source of 1.5 and .8 deaths per 100,000 children and 19.9 and 13.2 deaths per 100,000 youths,[6] are often related to firearm use, as 72.5 percent of homicides and 55 percent of suicides in children ages 10 to 14 resulted from firearms. The figures are even higher for youths ages 15 to 19: 81.7 and 67.3 percent, respectively.[7]

An asterisk (*) indicates specially recommended titles.

POPULAR TITLES: BOOKS

Adams, David W., and Eleanor J. Deveau. *Coping with Childhood Cancer: Where Do We Go from Here?* New rev. ed. Kinbridge, 1993. 306p. bibliog. illus. index. LC 87-95226. ISBN 0-969-3233-02. $21.95.

> Rather than providing medical information, this handbook by a pediatric social worker and oncology nurse helps parents

understand the emotional and behavioral aspects of childhood cancer. It deals with everyday issues in managing family life, with special emphasis on single parents and adolescents. The text proceeds logically from coping with the shock of diagnosis, with special help for single parents, to dealing with emotional issues in early remission and continued treatment toward remission, long-term survival, or relapse. The authors examine children's knowledge of death, how to prepare for death, and how to survive death through grief and mourning. A reader's guide after the preface directs parents to sections addressing stages of the disease and specific information such as the child's behavior in the hospital, how to help other children during remission, and funerals. Appendixes cover side effects of chemotherapy and provide additional resources.

Brace, Edward R., and John P. Pacanowski; updated by Ed Weiner. *Childhood Symptoms: Every Parent's Guide to Childhood Illnesses.* Rev. ed. Harper-Perennial, 1992. 338p. index. LC 91-55391. ISBN 0-06-271532-1. $30.00. ISBN 0-06-273078-9 pbk. $15.00.

This concise encyclopedia divides childhood disorders into two categories, both of which are organized alphabetically: (1) diseases, disorders, and conditions and (2) complaints, concerns, and problems. The diseases section covers congenital problems such as pigeon chest, deafness, and spina bifida; infectious diseases such as AIDS, strep throat, and Lyme disease; psychological problems such as panic attacks; injuries; orthopedic problems; allergies; and other conditions such as SIDS. The section on complaints addresses such concerns as backache, breath holding, compulsive behavior, headache, incest, lice, sibling rivalry, suicide, and Type A behavior. Informative appendixes provide norms and values, descriptions of specialists and other health care practitioners, a list of poison control centers and toll-free numbers, and a glossary.

Clayman, Charles B., ed. *Your Child's Health.* 144p. Reader's Digest, 1993. The American Medical Association Home Medical Library Series. photog. illus. index. LC 92-38562. ISBN 0-89577-492-5. Price not available.

Brief but heavily illustrated with colorful drawings and clinical photographs, this guide, sponsored by the American Medical Association, covers the basics on child health and health care in easily understandable prose. Information about trends in child health, checkups and immunizations, developmental milestones, and safety is provided, as is advice on how to care for a sick child. Much of this guide is devoted to symptoms and treatments for common childhood disorders.

Dailey, Barbara A. *Your Child's Recovery: A Reference for Parents.* Facts on File, 1991. 172p. LC 90-13973. ISBN 0-8160-2347-6. $22.95.

Dailey, the author of this psychological guide for parents serving as the primary care giver for a seriously ill child, is a pediatric oncology nurse and researcher. She examines the parent's role in the child's recovery, or adjustment in the event of chronic illness, focusing on how illness affects children's behavior and developmental growth. Issues covered include telling the child about the disorder, understanding age-specific reactions, helping the child cope through play therapy, and easing his or her adjustment to the stresses of intensive care,

e.g., close supervision, noise, lack of privacy, and sleep deprivation. The impact of a child's illness on siblings, friends, and family is also explored. Dailey has written a comprehensive and readable reference book for parents adjusting and helping their child cope with a life-threatening illness. Additional readings and resources are provided.

Davis, Deborah L. *Empty Cradle, Broken Heart: Surviving the Death of Your Baby.* Fulcrum, 1992. 231p. LC 90-42662. ISBN 1-55591-063-7. $12.95.

Based on data gathered for the author's dissertation, this sourcebook for parents, families, and clinicians explores the wide range of emotions that occurs after the loss of a baby and strategies for coping with this loss. Case studies and research reports are sources of information on the loneliness of grieving, emotional recovery through grieving, physical healing, affirming the baby's existence, negative feelings associated with grieving, and stages in the resolution of grief. The effect of a baby's death on other family members, support networks, subsequent pregnancies, raising subsequent children, and moving on are aspects of loss that are also covered. Additional resources for parents are listed in the appendix, as is advice for care givers to improve their sensitivity about the issues of perinatal loss.

Elliott, Joanne. *If Your Child Has Diabetes: An Answer Book for Parents.* Perigee, 1990. 192p. bibliog. index. LC 89-29041. ISBN 0-399-51610-7. $9.95.

Preparing parents for the physical and psychological realities of juvenile onset diabetes is the focus of this comprehensive guide. Coverage includes specific instructions on control of blood sugar levels, food plans, and the mechanics of insulin injections and reactions. Other chapters explore the implications of diabetes for school, camp, exercise, and traveling; the particular issues it raises in the very young and in teens; and research developments. The material, which is presented in question-and-answer format, is easily accessible through the index. Appendixes display injection sites, symptoms of diabetic emergencies, and resources for the parent.

* Fancher, Vivian Kramer. *Safe Kids: A Complete Child-Safety Handbook and Resource Guide for Parents.* Wiley, 1991. 209p. bibliog. index. LC 90-21700. ISBN 0-471-52973-7. $12.95.

Arranged in a workbook format, the information in this guide helps parents prepare their children for safe experiences with child care, transportation, school, time alone at home, and sports. Drugs are excluded from coverage. Fancher offers practical tips on identification, street smarts, child-proofing homes, telephone use, and other specific concerns. Many additional references and a list of resource organizations add to the information provided.

Foley, Denise, et al. *The Doctors Book of Home Remedies for Children.* Rodale, 1994. 450p. index. LC 93-5854. ISBN 0-87596-183-5. $27.95.

Tips from a variety of health care professionals are compiled in this single-volume encyclopedia of home remedies for common health problems of children from birth to age 12. A companion to *The Doctors Book of Home Remedies* published in 1990, this guide provides first aid information as well as advice about circumstances in which parents should contact a physician. Quotations from numerous physicians, nurses, dietitians, and other health care professionals provide parents with advice on handling minor ailments such as acne, bedwetting, black eyes, colds, croup, motion sickness, hiccups, nosebleeds, and refusal to go to school.

Freeman, John Mark, Eileen P. B. Vining, and Diana J. Pillas. *Seizures and Epilepsy in Childhood: A Guide for Parents.* Johns Hopkins University Press, 1990. 287p. illus. index. LC 90-4616. ISBN 0-8018-4049-X. $18.95.

Staff at the Pediatric Epilepsy Center of the Johns Hopkins Medical Institutions have compiled a comprehensive guide to the etiology, diagnosis, treatment, and effects of epilepsy and seizures on children and their families. A positive counseling approach is used to emphasize what a child can do as the means for parents and children to gain a broader perspective on accepting and coping with epilepsy. Concise but comprehensive explanations cover the source of seizures in brain functioning, indications of epilepsy, medical treatment, medical emergencies, how to cope with the single seizure, methods for controlling anxiety, how to live with epilepsy, and support services. A glossary defines medical terminology for parents.

Grollman, Earl A. *Talking about Death: A Dialogue between Parent and Child.* 3rd ed. Beacon, 1990. 118p. LC 89-46061. ISBN 0-8070-2364-7. $14.95.

Now in its third edition, this guidebook for parents on acknowledging and discussing death with their children includes information about children's understanding of and reactions to death, as well as advice on how to guide them to a true understanding of its real meaning. Grollman also discusses how children react to specific kinds of death, such as death of a parent or suicide, how to cope with adult grief, and when to seek professional help. A read-along section helps parents communicate with young children, and a section on resources provides access to service agencies, reading materials for children and adults caring for children, and films appropriate for children.

Haerle, Tracy. *Children with Tourette Syndrome: A Parents' Guide.* Woodbine, 1992. 340p. bibliog. index. LC90-50766. ISBN 0-933149-44-1. $14.95.

Tourette syndrome (TS), a physical disorder of the brain that causes involuntary movements and vocalizations, affects all areas of life for an afflicted child and his or her family. Written by parents and professionals, this guide helps parents and their children cope with a diagnosis of TS by explaining its symptoms, onset, associated disorders, emotional adjustment, modification and behavioral treatment, techniques for managing daily life, and life in the community. Developmental, educational, and legal issues are also covered. These informative chapters are supplemented by quotes from parents and a final section written by an adult with TS about his adjustment to the disease and its lifelong impact. Resources and a glossary provide more detailed data.

Huntley, Theresa. *Helping Children Grieve.* Augsburg, 1991. LC 91-12631. ISBN 0-8066-2549-X. $6.95.

Compiled by a pediatric nurse with many years of experience working with terminally ill children, this handbook for par-

ents explains children's understanding of death as they mature, how to talk to children about death, common behaviors of grieving children, and how to help them in the grieving process. Huntley reviews how to use educative moments at home or at school to teach children about death. The final chapters provide advice about children's reactions to a terminal illness, their concerns and fears, and how to provide supportive care for dying children. Numerous references to related materials and a reading list that focuses on handling the deaths of different relations are given in the concise text.

* Lansky, Vicki. *Baby Proofing Basics.* Bookpeddlers, 1991. 147p. illus. index. ISBN 0-916773-28-0. $5.95.

An index provides access to hundreds of practical tips on how to promote children's safety in the home, outdoors, or when traveling. Advice is linked to hazards common at each developmental stage, and home safety tips are listed room by room. Special advice is given about protecting children during holidays, child-proofing clothing, and preventing poisoning. According to the author, accidents are the major cause of death in children under the age of four, with the most common ones being car accidents, drownings, burns, falls, and choking/poisoning. Following the instructions in this handy guide should help parents protect their children by avoiding many common hazards.

Likowski, Alice Duncan. *Your Healthy Child: Guide to Natural Health Care for Children.* Tarcher, 1991. 294p. LC 90-19848. ISBN 0-87477-619-8. $10.95. ISBN 0-87477-620-1 pbk. $9.95.

Likowski's guide to natural remedies for childhood complaints details nutritional, homeopathic, herbal, and acupuncture/acupressure treatments that have been tested by the author, a doctor of chiropractic, on her own child and others. The major portion of the text is devoted to entries on over 100 conditions such as colds, coughs, bruises, muscle cramps, rabies, and hives; information provided includes a definition and brief explanation of the problem, symptoms, standard medical procedures, natural treatments, and indicators that a condition is severe enough to seek medical treatment. Detailed appendixes include homeopathic remedies and where to obtain them, information on nutritional supplements, a glossary of herbs, acupressure point diagrams, and additional readings.

McNicol, Jane. *Your Child's Food Allergies: Detecting and Treating Hyperactivity, Congestion, Irritability, and Other Symptoms Caused by Common Food Allergies.* Wiley, 1992. 160p. bibliog. index. LC 91-34661. ISBN 0-471-55801-X. $9.95.

Results of an experimental investigation of the hyperactivity test diet at Alberta Children's Hospital in 1980 revealed that behavior of half of the 24 children studied and sleep patterns in most improved after three weeks on this diet plan. For parents who want to assess the relationship of their child's allergies to diet before consulting a pediatrician, McNicol summarizes the food content of the diet, explains how to chart reactions, and suggests menus and recipes. The text also reviews how to cope with finicky or sick children, work around special occasions, and reintroduce problem foods. Appendixes include an explanation of how to adapt the menus to adult diets, an approved food list, and a nonfood, problem product list.

Miller, Jeanne E. *The Perfectly Safe Home*. Fireside, 1991. 284p. bibliog. index. LC 91-4711. ISBN 0-671-70580-6. $9.95.

Miller, a child safety expert, has written a detailed guide to safety considerations at home, in the yard and outdoors, and while traveling. The introduction describes safety as a combination of common sense, knowledge of what to watch for and avoid, planning and attention to detail, and constant vigilance. Child-proofing the home, including the nursery, bathroom, and kitchen, is covered in the first section. The second examines home safety, including safe furniture and toys, fire safety, poisons and first aid, and guidance for baby-sitters. Focusing on safety outside the home, the final section discusses preparing a travel safety kit, among other topics. Appendixes provide supplemental information, including lists of harmful plants and household products, vital statistics, and additional readings.

Novick, Nelson Lee. *Baby Skin: A Leading Dermatologist's Guide to Infant and Childhood Skin Care*. Crown, 1991. 180p. index. LC 91-10265. ISBN 0-517-58422-0. $13.00.

Intending this text as a handbook to answer parents' questions and alert them to problems that need attention, the author, a professor of dermatology, reviews the basics of proper skin care, such as choosing soaps, lotions, and diapers; using powders, and protecting skin from the sun. In nontechnical language, but without illustrations, he covers common skin conditions such as diaper rashes, eczemas, insect bites, blood vessel birthmarks, and hair problems. Conditions that may be serious or life-threatening are also addressed.

Pantell, Robert H. *Taking Care of Your Child: A Parent's Guide to Medical Care*. 3rd ed. Addison-Wesley, 1990. 525p. LC 89-38916. ISBN 0-2015-1803-1. $16.95.

To help parents keep their children healthy, this guide provides a concise overview of child growth and development, nutrition, behavior, learning, and health in the first section. In the second section, specific guidance, including decision charts on when to seek medical attention, is presented for the most common medical problems of childhood. Charts for measuring growth and keeping medical records make up the third section.

Pringel, Terry. *This Is the Child*. Southern Methodist University Press, 1991. LC 91-52776. ISBN 0-87074-335-X. $19.95. ISBN 0-87074-332-5 pbk. $9.95.

Written by a father, this is an autobiographical account about his family's struggle with a young boy's treatment for and death from leukemia. The father's approach is deeply introspective and honest, noting, for example, that his son's contraction of leukemia meant the end of normalcy for the family and criticizing, in anger and frustration, the impersonal and sometimes ignorant treatment by physicians, technicians, and other health care personnel. Robert Coles wrote a foreword for the book.

Schiff, Harriet Sarnoff. *The Bereaved Parent*. Penguin, 1978. LC 78-16098. ISBN 0-14-00-5043-4. $2.95.

This text by a mother who lost her son at age 10 is a self-help guide for parents whose child has died and who may not be able to hear or benefit from the advice of others who have not experienced this pain. Schiff offers both understanding and advice to convince bereaved parents that not only will they

survive their loss, they will learn to get on with living. The author also invokes the comments of others in counseling parents about getting through the funeral, grieving, coping with guilt and powerlessness, and taking steps to maintain their marriage, guide their children, communicate with family, friends, and colleagues, and simply function. She acknowledges the value of the book is to provide a thoughtful, knowing, supportive approach to a tragic topic.

Schleichkorn, Jay. *Coping with Cerebral Palsy: Answers to Questions Parents Often Ask*. 2nd ed. Pro-Ed, 1993. 250p. bibliog. illus. index. LC 92-27296. ISBN 0-89-79-576-2. $24.00.

Now in its second edition, this no-frills handbook about cerebral palsy in children, youth, and adults is detailed and comprehensive. When it is important to acquaint parents with specialized concepts, medical terminology is used; otherwise, the material is presented in a clear, easy-to-understand format. The author, a physical therapist and educator, draws on professional experience, discussions with parents, and the research literature to advise parents, social service, and health care professionals on causes, prevention, and diagnoses of cerebral palsy; growth and development; medical and surgical problems; treatment and therapy; psychological, social, and education concerns; and practical considerations of daily life, such as respite care, financial assistance, and sex education. Lists of appropriate videotapes and books; sources for specialized equipment, toys, and clothing; parental support organizations and a glossary supplement the question-and-answer sections.

* Schoemaker, Joyce M., and Charity Y. Vitale. *Healthy Homes, Healthy Kids: Protecting Your Children from Everyday Environmental Hazards*. Island, 1991. 221p. bibliog. index. LC 91-21975. ISBN 1-55963-057-4. $19.95. ISBN 1-55963-056-6 pbk. $12.95.

Written by a microbiologist and a biologist who are also parents, this primer on environmental hazards in or near the home advises parents on children's vulnerability to their toxic effects, clarifies how children are exposed, and explains what actions parents may take to reduce their dangerous effects. The text provides up-to-date information on many hazards, including lead paint and dust, radon, toxic art materials, pesticides in the yard and on foods, food additives, harmful gases, electromagnetic fields, and biological wastes. Resources include lists of products, services, and additional sources of information. The clear writing style makes detailed scientific findings accessible as well as interesting to parents.

Shapiro, Burton L., and Ralph C. Heusnner, Jr. *A Parent's Guide to Cystic Fibrosis*. University of Minnesota Press, 1990. 124p. bibliog. photog. illus. index. LC 90-11033. ISBN 0-8166-1488-1. $14.95.

Parents can refer to this guide to cystic fibrosis for information about the disorder, community resources they may draw on for assistance, and caring for their child at home. Readers will also gain a better understanding of the disorder and a basic vocabulary for communicating about it with health care professionals. The content includes the nature and cause of the disease; physical effects, particularly on the respiratory and digestive systems; diagnosis; therapy; complications; and effects on family and school life. An extensive glossary is included. A final chapter on research approaches acknowledges the hope for better treatment or a cure, noting that the mean age for survival increased from 4 in 1955 to 27 today.

Stanton, Marietta. *Our Children Are Dying: Recognizing the Dangers and Knowing What to Do.* Prometheus, 1990. 217p. bibliog. LC 90-8910. ISBN 0-87975-609-8. $18.95.

In this examination of death in children, Stanton looks at causes by age group, societal factors that increase risks of dying, the roles of support services and the government in preventing death, and how parents can minimize risks by understanding their child's development. The author, a former nurse, examines major causes of death in infants from birth to one year, children ages 1 to 14, and adolescents from 15 to 19, organizing the data in this manner because the risks cluster according to age. For both children and adolescents, accidents cause the highest number of deaths, with motor vehicle accidents the major cause; suicide and homicide are the second and third major causes for adolescents. Congenital defects, SIDS, prematurity, and low birth weight claim the lives of infants. Concluding with a plea for advocacy for children, this text provides practitioners and parents with an easily accessible summary of mortality data and a better understanding of risks to children in their care.

Stevens, Maryann. *Breathing Easy: A Parent's Guide to Dealing with Your Child's Asthma.* Prentice Hall, 1991. 221p. illus. index. LC 90-25564. ISBN 0-13-083692-3. $9.95.

A mother of three children who had severe asthma presents numerous practical techniques for managing daily routines with an asthmatic child. Based on a class Stevens developed to teach parents and their children about asthma control, the text covers the primary questions parents ask, selection of a pediatrician, hospitalization and medications, finances, and advocacy. The majority of the text addresses daily life concerns, such as creating a healthy environment; communicating with the school; family, friends, and care givers; asthma in adolescence; and involvement in sports. Personal anecdotes, quotations from her children, and success stories of prominent people with asthma add to the supportive, practical approach used.

* Wootan, George, and Sarah Verney. *Take Charge of Your Child's Health: A Guide to Recognizing Symptoms and Treating Minor Illnesses at Home.* Crown, 1992. 320p. illus. index. LC 91-38761. ISBN 0-517-57365-2. $18.00.

Wootan, a forthrightly opinionated M.D., and Verney instruct parents on how to conduct physical examinations in this handbook. Other concerns they address in this guide are creating a healthy physical and emotional environment for a child, treating common health problems of childhood, and interacting with the family's physician. The major points of each chapter are summarized in a checklist, and footnotes to the scientific literature are provided. When the authors' opinions differ from commonly accepted beliefs (e.g., promoting a family bed, avoiding solid foods until eight months), and they often do, they say so. Parents who are willing to weigh options and take responsibility for their children's well-being will find this a convenient, readable, occasionally controversial guide.

POPULAR TITLES: JOURNALS

American Health. RD Publications. 10/yr. ISSN 0730-7004. $17.94.

Child safety and health care are the focus of selected feature articles, book reviews, and a regular column in this popular guide to medicine, wellness, nutrition, fitness, and mental health. Issues have addressed such topics as treating pain in children, fluoridation and children, and genetic disorders.

Health. Hippocrates. 1992. 6/yr. ISSN 1059-938X. $18.00.

Tips on topics of interest to parents, such as breastfeeding, nutrition, and disabilities, are found in this magazine, whose focus is health and well-being of adults.

Pediatrics for Parents. Pediatrics for Parents. 1980. M. ISSN 0730-6725. $15.00.

Parenting tips related to health care, diseases, treatments, prevention, and wellness; brief how-to pieces on these topics; and more detailed feature articles are written in nontechnical language by health care professionals for this monthly newsletter. Reviews, editorials, and sources for free or low-cost materials for parents are also provided. One issue addressed at some length the topics of newborn exams, sore throats, and criteria for toy selection and contained many brief articles on such topics as diabetes, sun damage, and violence. This journal is well-written but not illustrated.

PROFESSIONAL TITLES: BOOKS

Anderson, Gary R., ed. *Courage to Care: Responding to the Crisis of Children with AIDS*, Child Welfare League of America, 1990. 416p. LC 90-2085. ISBN 0-87868-401-8. $15.95.

Social service and health care providers will find detailed descriptions of a continuum of programs to serve children with HIV, from family support day care, residential care, and foster care programs. Introductory chapters outline the epidemiology of HIV/AIDS in children, the course of the syndrome, and medical management of pediatric AIDS. AIDS education for child care workers, family care services, care giver support groups, counseling after testing, and grief education are among the training issues discussed. Nearly 100 pages of supplementary information, including a glossary, instructional resources, a directory, a bibliography, and reprinted articles from the American Academy of Pediatrics, reinforce this text's purpose as a resource guide for practitioners.

Barnes, Lewis A. *Manual of Pediatric Physical Diagnosis.* 6th ed. Mosby-Year Book, 1991. 306p. illus. index. LC 91-15458. ISBN 0-8151-0494-4. Price not given.

The pediatric physical exam is distinguished from the adult exam by special techniques for physical examination and great variation in what is normal due to differences in development and the rate of growth. Barnes emphasizes that no routine exam process exists for pediatric physicians because each exam must be individualized to the needs of the child. Using a clinical approach, the author advises pediatricians on how to establish rapport with the child and the parents and instructs readers on how to examine the skin, lymph nodes and general appearance, chest, abdomen, head and neck, and extremities. Chapters also cover standard measurements and physical examination of the newborn. A sample patient record and growth scales are supplied in the appendix.

Bearison, David J. *They Never Want to Tell You: Children Talk about Cancer.* Harvard University Press, 1991. 194p. bibliog. LC 90-49945. ISBN 0-674-88370-5. $19.95.

Using a clinical ethnographic approach to children's experiences with cancer, Bearison presents the narratives of eight children who have the disease. In introducing the material, he reviews the methodology, selection of participants, and goals for the study: to learn better ways to support children with cancer through a clearer understanding of what they feel. The first section presents the narratives in the edited words of the eight subjects. Additional comments are woven into the second section in chapters devoted to the common themes that emerged. These themes include: why me?; God and prayer; fears of cancer; hair loss; advice for others with cancer; friends and family relations; how cancer has changed them; and the experience of talking about cancer.

Brett, Edward M., ed. *Pediatric Neurology.* 2nd ed. Churchill Livingstone, 1991. 895p. photog. index. LC 90-1629. ISBN 0-443-03788-4. $135.00.

Targeted to pediatricians, this detailed reference to neurologic disorders and neurologic aspects of systemic disorders in children assists doctors in making an accurate diagnosis to treat conditions that may be cured and reduce the symptoms of others, such as epilepsy, for which there is no cure. The coverage is comprehensive, including neuromuscular disorders, neurometabolic brain diseases, cerebral palsy, spinocerebellar degeneration, mental retardation, tumors, vascular disorders, and many other syndromes. Extensive photographs enhance basic material on normal development, neurological examination, genetics, and psychological assessment. New to this edition are chapters on acute encephalography and imaging in childhood, as well as a chapter on clinical electromyography, which according to the editor provides technical and clinical guidance not available elsewhere.

Caring for Our Children: National Health and Safety Performance Standards: Guidelines for Out-of-Home Child Care Programs. American Public Health Association and American Academy of Pediatrics, 1992. 410p. bibliog. photog. illus. index. ISBN 0-87553-205-5. $50.00.

Jointly compiled by the American Public Health Association and American Academy of Pediatrics in a lengthy consultative process, this handbook provides standards and rationales with commentary for operating child care services. Among the aspects addressed are staffing and administration, developmental activities, health protection and promotion, infectious disease control, nutrition and food service, and licensing considerations. While mainstreaming children with moderate disabilities is one of the many assumptions behind these guidelines, there is a section on caring for children with severe disabilities. Nearly 40 appendixes provide such information as qualifications for staff, record-keeping forms, equipment standards, an immunization schedule, and food components.

Clunn, Patricia. *Child Psychiatric Nursing.* Mosby-Year Book, 1991. 483p. bibliog. index. LC 90-13310. ISBN 0-8016-0363-3. $23.95.

Clunn presents a current clinical manual for psychiatric nurses caring for children in all settings. The text is divided into four parts: foundations for practice; intellectual, developmental, and behavioral disorders; physical, social, and emotional disorders; and treatment. Within this framework, contributors address the history of child psychiatric nursing, legal and ethical issues, the nursing process, child development, crisis intervention, play therapy, residential programs, and group therapy. Specific disorders, such as disruptive behavior, gender and sexual identity disorders, emotional consequences of chronic physical pain, and anxiety, are also examined in detail.

Cooper, Antonya, and Valerie Harpin. *How Parents Experience the Medical World.* Oxford University Press, 1991. LC 90-14176. ISBN 0-19-261899-7. $14.95.

To help readers understand how parents cope with a child who is ill or one who dies, this anthology, coedited by a parent and a pediatrician, includes parents' accounts. These stories of chronic disorders such as cystic fibrosis and Down syndrome, medical emergencies such as prematurity and placenta previa, and terminal illness such as leukemia and neuroblastoma reveal how parents' sense of self is challenged when they must forfeit care giving to professionals or to death. While the text is intended to help health professionals develop greater awareness of parents' need for concrete information and respect for parents' role in caring for an ill or dying child, the material presented here will also assist parents in similar circumstances to develop a new psychological mind-set for coping with their altered lives.

Corr, Charles A., et al., eds. *Sudden Infant Death Syndrome: Who Can Help and How.* Springer, 1991. 262p. bibliog. index. LC 91-4616. ISBN 0-8261-6720-9. $29.95. ISBN 0-00-003712-5 pbk. $28.95.

Sudden infant death syndrome, or SIDS, is the leading cause of death in infants older than one month, but its cause has eluded researchers who have examined such diverse factors as the pregnancy, respiratory factors, and cardiac arrhythmias. After establishing a historical and theoretical framework, the contributors to this collection examine the loss and grief that result from SIDS and their effects on the parents, siblings, and extended family. The text provides specific guidelines for emergency care providers, counselors, and the professional community in general to follow in helping SIDS survivors acknowledge and resolve their grief. In the final section, service trends are reviewed and information is compiled on relevant books, audiovisuals, and organizations.

Fernbach, Donald J., and Theresa J. Vietti, eds. *Clinical Pediatric Oncology.* 4th ed. Mosby-Year Book, 1991. 720p. LC 90-13368. ISBN 0-8016-3306-0. $89.00.

Providing practical information to aid clinicians in diagnosing and treating children with cancer, this text includes background data on incidence and epidemiology, clinical diagnosis and prognosis, molecular oncology, pathology and immunology, imaging and surgery, radiation and chemotherapy, bone marrow transplantation, and supportive care principles. New to the fourth edition is a chapter on ethical and legal issues; however, all chapters have been extensively revised since the previous edition and 22 of 33 are by new authors. The second half of the book is devoted to specific disorders, such as Hodgkin's disease, myeloproliferative disorders and acute myeloid leukemias, retinoblastoma, nephroblastoma and other renal tumors, and bone sarcomas. The final chapter addresses long-term follow-up.

Green, Morris, and Robert J. Haggerty, eds. *Ambulatory Pediatrics IV.* 4th ed. Saunders, 1990. 605p. bibliog. index. LC 90-8505. ISBN 0-7216-4240-3. $69.16.

The fourth edition of this reference book is organized around the concept of adaptation, which encompasses prevention, health promotion, treatment, and rehabilitation of the child and his or her parents within the social, developmental, psychological, biological, and environmental conditions of their lives. In the section on factors influencing adaptation, contributors examine childhood morbidity and mortality, social and emotional development, life events and crisis, quality of parental care, adolescent pregnancy and risk taking, and related stressors with which children must cope. The second section, on prospective adaptation, addresses such concerns as prenatal visits, pediatric screening tests, immunizations, and injury prevention. The section on concurrent adaptation addresses acute conditions such as poisoning, fainting, and bereavement, and the section on rehabilitative adaptation covers chronic or handicapping disorders such as cerebral palsy, AIDS, sexual abuse, and learning disorders. The final section advises clinicians on the organization and operation of a pediatrics practice.

Grossman, Moses, and Ronald A. Dieckman, eds. *Pediatric Emergency Medicine: A Clinician's Reference.* Lippincott, 1991. 732p. LC 90-6033. ISBN 0-397-51017-9. $49.95.

Using a concise, problem-oriented format, this text provides emergency room physicians with a desk reference to medical emergencies in children. Content includes cardiovascular and pulmonary emergencies, toxicology, trauma, infectious diseases, psychosocial emergencies, and a summary of organ system disorders. Advice on organizing emergency room services and responding to nonemergency complaints, a quick reference guide, and a guide to emergency drugs are also provided. Each chapter in these broadly defined sections is organized in a similar manner, providing, when appropriate, information on etiology and pathophysiology, clinical findings, ancillary data, treatment, disposition, outcome, complications, and a current bibliography.

Hamilton, Persis M. *Basic Pediatric Nursing.* 6th ed. Mosby-Year Book, 1991. 631p. bibliog. photog. illus. index. LC 90-6198. ISBN 0-8016-5869-1. $23.95.

Hamilton presents an introduction to child development, medical care of children, and common childhood disorders for entry-level nurses. Numerous photographs with detailed notes illustrate the narrative. Now in its sixth edition, the text has been completely revised to reflect changes in pediatric practice and health care delivery. Sections on ambulatory care of children, child abuse, and addictive substances have been enlarged. To aid the student, material is presented in nursing process format, illustrated by typical care plans, and numerous pedagogical aids, such as vocabulary, summary outlines, and key concepts, reinforce learning.

Hendee, William R., ed. *The Health of Adolescents: Understanding and Facilitating Biological, Behavioral, and Social Development.* Jossey-Bass, 1991. 562p. illus. index. LC 90-15627. ISBN 1-55542-308-6. $65.00.

This text is intended as a guide and resource for professionals in all fields who work with adolescents. An introduction addressing present demographic characteristics and trends in adolescent health is followed by a section on normal adolescent growth and development, physical and psychological, and a discussion of influences on adolescent health of factors such as the family, social setting, economic status, and lifestyle. Detailed reviews of adolescent health issues, such as substance abuse, sexually transmitted diseases, pregnancy, chronic illness, depression, suicide, and abuse, are provided. Access to health care and services to improve adolescent health are also covered.

Illingworth, Ronald S. *The Normal Child: Some Problems of the Early Years and Their Treatment.* 10th ed. Churchill Livingstone, 1991. 450p. bibliog. illus. index. LC 90-2614. ISBN 0-443-04455-4. $50.00.

Now in its 10th edition, this handbook for pediatricians by a pediatrician (now deceased) reviews in detail normal child development, including normal variations and their causes, to provide doctors with a baseline against which to measure the diseased and abnormal. Information on eating, growth, sleep, crying, and behavior is included, as are data on the normal development of bodily organs and systems. New to this edition are 300 current references, as well as additions to the chapters on breastfeeding; extensive discussion of infant colic; rewritten chapters on physical growth, sleep problems, travel problems, and prevention of infection and accidents; and new chapters on child health surveillance and helping children achieve their potential. Clearly understanding normal development and its variations helps pediatricians allay the concerns of parents, avoid unnecessary tests and treatment, and recognize abnormal conditions when they present themselves.

Jones, Douglas M., Christine A. Gleason, and Susan V. Lipstein. *Hospital Care of the Recovering NICU Infant.* Williams and Wilkins, 1991. 262p. index. LC 90-13158. ISBN 0-683-04476-1. $40.00.

The focus of this anthology is treatment for hospitalized infants when they are moved to the step-down nursery for recovery and are being cared for by personnel who are not neonatal specialists. Although their condition is improving, such infants are not healthy and must be watched for medical conditions or disorders that frequently appear, including apnea, brachycardia, postnatal anemia, retinopathy of prematurity, chronic lung disease, and hearing loss. The content also covers discharge planning, interaction with the family, assessment of risk for developmental disabilities, and surgical management. Charts of laboratory values, growth parameters, and miscellaneous standard measures are available in the appendixes.

Krugman, Saul. *Infectious Diseases of Children.* 9th ed. Mosby-Year Book, 1991. 646p. illus. ISBN 0-8016-5754-7. $69.95.

Now in its ninth edition, Krugman's standard handbook on infectious diseases of children retains its concise, handy format as a source of practical information through extensive revision of the information segments on each disease and disorder covered. Information on new diseases of current interest, such as Haemophilus influenzae and Kawasaki disease, has also been incorporated into the text. Among the topics covered are infant botulism; AIDS; viral hepatitis types A, B, C, D, and E; sepsis in the newborn; sexually transmitted diseases; tick-borne infections; tuberculosis; and other common infectious disorders. Appendixes list antimicrobial drugs and immunization schedules.

Krusinski, Paul A., and Franklin P. Flowers. *Handbook of Pediatric Dermatology.* Year Book, 1990. 407p. photog. illus. index. LC 89-22455. ISBN 0-8151-5203-5. $34.95.

For the practitioner, this concise handbook covers common dermatologic conditions in children, including eczematous diseases, tumors, pustular diseases, disorders in pigmentation, photodermatoses, and ulcerations. The chapter for each disease entity covers symptoms, clinical history, physical and laboratory findings, therapy, differential diagnosis, and complications. Introductory chapters discuss taking a history, the physical examination, and considerations in therapy.

Morgan, John D., ed. *The Dying and the Bereaved Teenager.* Charles Press, 1990. 159p. LC 90-35058. ISBN 0-914783-44-0. $16.95.

Aimed at a diverse professional audience of clergies, social workers, counselors, nurses, administrators, and teachers, this text advises on how to care for the seriously ill or dying teen, help the bereaved adolescent grieve, and set up programs in the schools for helping teens cope with deaths among their classmates. Contributors examine the impact on adolescent development of a parent's, sibling's, or peer's death, cancer support groups, and prevention of multiple suicides.

Neinstein, Lawrence S. *Adolescent Health Care: A Practical Guide.* 2nd ed. Urban & Schwarzenberg, 1990. 1089p. bibliog. illus. index. LC 90-12058. ISBN 0-8067-1352-6. $45.00.

Until fairly recently, the adolescent years were viewed as healthy ones, but adolescents today are subject to such adult health care problems as substance abuse, sexually transmitted diseases (STDs), HIV infection, and suicide. To aid clinicians, Neinstein has written a practical guide in a format accessible for day-to-day consultation. After a survey of general considerations such as growth, development, interviewing and health screening, and nutrition, the author, a pediatrician and director of hospital adolescent health care services, systematically reviews health problems according to the bodily system or function affected, including endocrine, cardiovascular, and neurological disorders; sexuality, family planning, and STDs; psychosocial disturbances such as eating disorders; and substance use. Two appendixes list references, services, and other resources on adolescent health.

Nott, Sandra R., Susan Rowen James, and Arlene M. Sperhas. *Nursing Care of Children and Families.* 2nd ed. Addison-Wesley, 1990. 2000p. bibliog. photog. illus. index. LC 89-18353. ISBN 0-201-1292-3. $66.75.

The second edition of this textbook continues to provide a comprehensive overview of child health nursing from a holistic perspective that integrates the family into all aspects of nursing care. Increased emphasis on patient/family teaching, home care, and pathophysiology is a feature of this edition, as are enhanced illustrations, pedagogical aids, and consistent use of the nursing process to frame discussions. Topics covered include an overview of theory, influences on growth and development, and development by chronological age; child/family assessment; preventive nursing; conditions that put the family or child at psychosocial risk; impact of illness on the child and family; and caring for the ill child. Appendixes provide baseline data on growth, lab values, and clinical decision making.

Pizzo, Philip A., and Catherine M. Wilfert, eds. *Pediatric AIDS: The Challenge of HIV Infection in Infants, Children, and Adolescents.* Williams & Wilkins, 1991. 813p. bibliog. photog. illus. index. LC 90-12675. ISBN 0-683-06894-6. $79.00.

Current information on the management and prevention of HIV infection in children and adolescents is gathered in this practical guide for a wide range of health care professionals. Prepared as a state-of-the-art review that will serve as a base for future strategies, this anthology covers AIDS epidemiology among youth, biology, pathogenesis and transmission characteristics, advances, prenatal diagnosis, and other diagnostic issues. The content also includes clinical manifestations, both infectious complications and organ-specific complications, treatment modalities, and prevention, education, and public policy issues. The text provides information on specialized concerns such as nursing management, issues in foster care, psychosocial support for children with AIDS, legal issues, and child advocacy.

Remington, Jack S., and Jerome O. Klein, eds. *Infectious Diseases of the Fetus and Newborn Infant.* 3rd ed. Saunders, 1990. 1122p. bibliog. LC 89-24301. ISBN 0-7216-2434-0. $185.00.

The medical, social, and economic impact of infections in the fetus and newborn are examined in this comprehensive textbook intended for a broad audience of health care practitioners and students. Each chapter is devoted to a specific disorder or type of infection, and each comprises a historical review, microbiology, epidemiology, pathogenesis and pathology, clinical signs and symptoms, diagnosis, treatment, prognosis, and prevention. Content includes rubella, toxoplasmosis, herpes simplex, enteroviruses, chlamydia, fungal infections, protozoan and helminth infections, hepatitis, and tuberculosis. New to the third edition are chapters on HIV and breastfeeding.

Schwartz, M. William. *Pediatric Primary Care: A Problem-Oriented Approach.* 2nd ed. Year Book Medical, 1990. 974p. bibliog. photog. illus. index. LC 89-22577. ISBN 0-8151-7733-X. $49.95.

Contemporary pediatric care is characterized by office treatment rather than hospitalization, parental involvement, quality of life and wellness, behavioral issues, environmental hazards, and adolescent health care. Intended for physicians and nurses who provide office-based care, this handbook covers many aspects of well-child care, including interviewing; cultural awareness; the impact of TV, day care, AIDS, and divorce; and assessment of signs and symptoms. Illness, injury, developmental disabilities, and behavioral problems are also covered. New to this edition is information on pain management, child abuse, epilepsy, and Lyme disease. The final section of this basic care manual addresses communicating with parents and with subspecialists.

Strasburger, Victor C. *Basic Adolescent Gynecology: An Office Guide.* Urban & Schwarzenberg, 1990. 243p. bibliog. photog. illus. LC 90-11977. ISBN 0-8067-4001-9. $45.00.

Pediatricians specializing in adolescent medicine review clinical aspects of reproductive health care for adolescents in this handbook for practitioners. Because adolescents are maturing more rapidly than in previous generations, and because their sexual activity may put them at risk, pediatricians need to be able to prescribe contraceptives, treat infections or irritations, perform routine exams, and assess, diagnose, and treat abdominal pain, menstrual disorders, and breast conditions. This succinct introduction to adolescent reproductive health serves as a starting point for pediatricians beginning to provide these services to their patients. Chapters on consent and confidentiality issues and adolescent sexuality provide a context for the clinically focused material.

Strasburger, Victor C., and Robert T. Brown. *Adolescent Medicine: A Practical Guide.* Little, Brown, 1991. 569p. bibliog. illus. index. LC 90-63728. ISBN 0-316-81872-0. $45.00.

Strasburger and Brown's concise guide provides a quick overview, practical treatment plan, and references for more information on common health problems in adolescents for the physician new or inexperienced at treating this group of patients. The authors review the source of problems commonly encountered in growth and development, sexuality, chronic and acute illness, sports medicine, psychology, and substance use and advises on how to manage them. For those physicians new to adolescent medicine, the text also includes advice on conducting the individual visit, confidentiality, consent, abortion, and contraception.

Stuber, Margaret L. *Children with AIDS: Clinical Issues for Psychiatrists.* American Psychiatric Press, 1991. 226p. bibliog. LC 91-4581. ISBN 0-88048-199-4. $28.50.

Providing an overview of AIDS in children is the focus of this handbook, intended for a wide audience of health care, neuroscience, and legal professionals. The first section reviews the epidemiology of HIV infection and AIDS in African American and Latino children, in adolescents, and in youths with hemophilia; the process of vertical transmission in infants is also covered. Specific issues of concern for infected children are covered in the second section, including family considerations and right to an education. The final section addresses psychotherapeutic issues, clinical care of pediatric HIV patients, community resources, and coordination of children's care.

Thompson, Sharon W. *Emergency Care of Children.* Jones and Bartlett, 1990. 327p. bibliog. photog. illus. index. LC 89-71617. ISBN 0-86720-417-6. $50.00.

A primer for all health care personnel who may be called on to provide emergency care services to children, this text covers child development and ways in which children are physically different from adults, as well as childhood symptoms, illnesses, and injuries that may lead to the need for emergency treatment. Guidance on taking a history and carrying out a physical examination is provided, as is advice on recognizing and treating social illnesses such as physical abuse, substance abuse, SIDS, and suicide. The focus of the text is on the etiology, pathophysiology, assessment, intervention, and evaluation of symptoms such as diarrhea and shock, emergency illnesses such as meningitis, trauma such as airway obstruction and reactions to insect stings, and health-related illnesses.

Tinkelman, David G., and Charles K. Naspitz. *Childhood Rhinitis and Sinusitis: Pathophysiology and Treatment.* Dekker, 1990. 284p. bibliog. photog. illus. index. LC 90 2861. ISBN 0-8247-8228-3. $79.95.

This sourcebook for practitioners provides an overview of current and past research on disorders of the nose and sinuses, covering the mechanism of allergic reactions, process of inflammation, diagnosis, and treatment. Other topics covered include allergens, effect of air pollution on the upper respiratory tract, nasal obstruction and facial development, the relationship between rhinitis/sinusitis and asthma, and detection and management of nonallergic rhinitis. Extensive references, figures, and photographs supplement the text.

Touloukian, Robert J., ed. *Pediatric Trauma.* Mosby-Year Book, 1990. 553p. bibliog. illus. index. LC 90-6234. ISBN 0-8016-5067-4. $84.00.

Comprehensive coverage and extensive references support the editor's goal of making this textbook the standard reference on childhood injuries for clinicians. Heavily illustrated, the text provides an overview of trauma in children, noting that nearly half the deaths of children ages 1 to 14 are due to trauma, compared to 1 in 12 in the general population. General considerations, such as prehospital resuscitation and treatment, evaluation and initial management of breathing and head injuries, metabolism and nutrition in severe injury, respiratory failure, anesthesia for the trauma patient, imaging of trauma, birth injury, and battered child syndrome, are presented in the first section. The second section addresses specific injuries, including head and spinal cord injury, abdominal and urinary tract injury, insect and spider bites, burns, and sports injuries.

Whaley, Lucille F., and Donna L. Wong. *Nursing Care of Infants and Children.* 4th ed. Whaley, 1991. 2004p. bibliog. photog. illus. index. LC 90-13695. ISBN 0-8016-5378-9. $62.95.

Revised three times since 1979, this thorough textbook and clinical manual is the leading resource on pediatric nursing. The material is presented in two parts, the first covering age- and stage-specific data in a developmental context, including care of common health problems and the nurse's role in prevention, and the second, more serious disorders requiring hospitalization. Due to the increasing complexity of many specialty areas, the authors have enlisted the assistance of 30 experts, but have revised and in some cases reorganized their contributions to preserve the continuity of the text. The extensive reference lists have information on injuries, gay and lesbian families, development of body image, sleep problems, dental care, and more. Numerous pedagogical aids, such as chapter outlines, parent guidelines, key points, questions and controversies, chapter glossaries, and nursing tips, assist the student or practitioner, and ancillary products aid the instructor.

Wilson, Modena Hoover, et al. *Saving Children: A Guide to Injury Prevention.* Oxford University Press, 1990. 247p. bibliog. illus. LC 90-7279. ISBN 0-19-506115-2. $37.95.

Staff of the Johns Hopkins Injury Prevention Center present a multidisciplinary approach to the prevention of injuries to children through safety instruction, environmental modification, media appeals, and, for younger children, improved supervision. Divided into four sections, the text covers the roadway, home, and school/recreation environments. Each chapter provides factual data, developmental considerations from gestation through early adolescence, specific techniques for protection, and considerations for schools and child care centers, health care providers, public agencies, legislators and regulators, law enforcement professionals, and the mass media; each also provides references and additional sources of information.

Yogev, Ram, and Edward Connor, ed. *Management of HIV Infection in Infants and Children.* Mosby-Year Book, 1992. 639p. bibliog. photog. illus. index. LC 91-34896. ISBN 0-8016-5653-3. $59.00.

Pediatricians, many of whom are still unfamiliar with AIDS in children, need to be able to identify patients at risk, diagnose the condition, maintain general health and well-being in their charges, and work in conjunction with specialists, as is done for children with other chronic illnesses. To help practitioners reach this goal, the editors have organized a comprehensive review of HIV and AIDS in infants and children. The content includes epidemiology, organization and delivery of health care services, HIV and the developing immune system, transmission in children, natural history and prognosis, laboratory tools for monitoring HIV, clinical symptoms, and antiviral treatment. Issues of daily living and occupational risks and responsibilities are also covered. The appendixes provide additional information on Centers for Disease Control surveillance, classification of symptoms in children under the age of 13, information sources, centers conducting clinical trials, and demonstration grants.

PROFESSIONAL TITLES: JOURNALS

Adolescent Medicine. Hanley & Belfus. 1990. 3/yr. ISSN 1041-3499. $63.00.

Compiled in collaboration with the American Academy of Pediatrics' Section on Adolescent Health, this triannual publication provides primary care physicians with practical peer-reviewed clinical information compiled by experts for immediate use. The first issue, on the at-risk adolescent, reviewed the field of adolescent health care with emphasis on problems such as teen pregnancies, sexually transmitted diseases, accidents, drug use, and suicide. Subsequent issues covered AIDS, sports medicine, office-based treatment, dermatology, and chronic medical disorders. The editor-in-chief, Donald E. Greydanus, is the author of a recent popular handbook on adolescent health, *Caring for Your Adolescent: Ages 12 to 21.* These handsomely illustrated hardbound issues are also available individually.

Advances in Pediatrics. Mosby-Year Book. 1942. A. ISSN 0065-3101. $59.95.

Detailed scholarly reviews on a variety of topics of current interest to practitioners are presented in this annual series. Among the topics covered in a past volume are children's vulnerability to maltreatment, neonatal screening programs, acute otitis media, obstructive sleep apnea, Lyme disease, and pharmacological treatments for attention deficit hyperactivity disorder. This is an important reference for primary health care providers.

American Journal of Asthma & Allergy for Pediatricians. Slack. 1987. Q. ISSN 0899-7411. $55.00.

Refereed articles by practicing physicians that provide practical advice on the clinical aspects of pediatric asthma and allergy are the focus of this publication. Authors are encouraged to provide patient tips, guidelines for parents, patient education materials, photographs, and other helpful information to accompany their articles. In addition to original articles, practical tips, and patient education materials, the journal publishes book reviews, editorials, insights into controversial issues, and abstracts of studies in regular departments.

American Journal of Diseases of Children. American Medical Association. 1911. M. ISSN 0096-8994. $51.00.

Published by the American Medical Association, this journal reports current clinical information on pediatric diagnosis and treatment in a variety of formats. Included are original research articles, commentaries and letters reporting the results of investigations, cases of the month, pictures of the month, review articles, controversial perspectives, educational interventions, and "From Research to Relevance," a column that reports significant research likely to have practical applications. Legal issues and sports medicine are regularly reviewed, and classical articles occasionally are reprinted with contemporary commentary. A past issue addressed disorders with an impact on bone development.

American Journal of Pediatric Hematology/Oncology. Raven. 1979. Q. ISSN 0192-8562. $108.00.

Since 1981, the American Society of Pediatric Hematology/Oncology has provided a forum for reports on advances in the diagnosis and treatment of cancer and blood diseases in children. The purpose of the refereed journal is to foster research, provide education, and promote interdisciplinary cooperation among pediatric surgeons, radiologists, pathologists, hematologists, and oncologists involved in patient care.

Core Journals in Pediatrics. Elsevier Science. 1978. 11/yr. ISSN 0376-5040. Dfl. 332.00.

By providing brief annotations of significant clinical articles within four to six weeks of original publication, this publication reduces the time that busy pediatricians must devote to keeping up with the literature in their specialty. The "Core Abstracts" section contains abstracts from a dozen of the most important pediatric journals, and the five leading medical titles are summarized in the "Coreview" section.

Issues in Comprehensive Pediatric Nursing. Hemisphere. 1976. B-M. ISSN 0146-0862. $77.00.

Information on the health care needs of children and their families reported from the perspective of nurses and other care givers is the focus of this refereed journal. Among the approaches employed by the journal are reports of original research and state-of-the-art interventions, administrative studies, and theoretical reviews. Occasional theme issues address such topics as family-centered community level care for children with special health care needs.

Journal of Adolescent Health. Elsevier Science. 1980. 8/yr. ISSN 0154-139X. $220.00.

From the Society for Adolescent Medicine comes this interdisciplinary journal, which publishes original research on the unique physical, psychological, and social characteristics of adolescents and their health care problems and needs. With contributions from anthropologists, psychologists, and sociologists, as well as data on acute, chronic, and preventive medical problems of adolescents, this journal has practical interest for a wide variety of professionals working with adolescents.

Journal of Dentistry for Children. American Society of Dentistry for Children. 1933. B-M. ISSN 0022-0353. $65.00.

A professional journal for pediatric dentists, this title covers topical issues in caring for children in the areas of preventive dentistry, child behavior, the dental marketplace, professional and governmental relations, dental education, care for specialized populations, and ethics and social responsibility. Advocating for children, guiding practitioners through changes in professional practice, and encouraging their development are the overriding concerns of this official publication from the American Society of Dentistry for Children. To aid the busy reader, each issue begins with abstracts of all articles published therein.

Journal of Pediatric Health. Mosby-Year Book. 1987. M. ISSN 0891-5245. $26.00.

Health care policy, issues of professional training and practice, and clinical concerns in providing ambulatory care, home health care, school health care, and inpatient nursing services are concerns addressed in this journal. Brief articles on growth and development, pediatric pharmacology, case studies, and professional issues of a controversial nature are also published in regular departments. The periodical also includes news on actions of the National Association of Pediatric Nurse Associates and Practitioners, letters to the editor, national and state legislative updates, and hints on managing patient relations. Twice a year reviews of patient education materials and commercially available products are published.

Journal of Pediatric Nursing. Saunders. 1986. B-M. ISSN 0882-5963. $73.00.

Practical articles on nursing practice with children and families, views on nursing education, international studies, reviews of books and videos, abstracts of current research, and information about equipment are published in this refereed journal. A regular series on research methodology for pediatric nursing studies provides how-to information for nurse researchers. Information on conferences, letters from readers, and news about social policy are also part of the journal's content.

Journal of Pediatrics. Mosby-Year Book. 1932. M. ISSN 0022-3476. $70.00.

Original research, clinical and laboratory observations, and critical reviews of topics covering all aspects of pediatrics are featured in this publication. Each issue provides a comprehensive review on a special topic, approximately 10 full-length research articles, and many brief reports grouped under the broad headings of clinical observations, fetal and neonatal medicine, and pharmacology and therapeutics. An unusual pediatric case is profiled each month.

Journal of Perinatology. Appleton & Lange. 1982. Q. ISSN 0743-8346. $50.00.

The official journal of the National Perinatal Association since 1989, this title reports on the results of clinical research, social and behavioral studies, ethical issues, technology, case studies, and news items about the association. Issues have addressed such topics as reliability of the neonatal oral-motor assessment scale, ethical dilemmas in the neonatal intensive care unit, and magnetic resonance imaging in infants with repetitive focal seizures.

Journal of School Health. American School Health Association. 1930. M. ISSN 0022-4391. $80.00.

Published since 1930 by the American School Health Association, this periodical addresses health promotion in school settings from preschool through high school for a broad audience of educators and health care professionals. Articles provide program and curriculum descriptions, research reports, commentaries, teaching techniques, and health service applications. Special issues are published, such as the topical issue on adolescent sexuality. Other issues addressed such topics as HIV instruction, medication compliance, celebrity advocacy, safety belt incentives, and perception of body weight.

Maternal-Child Nursing Journal. University of Pittsburgh, School of Nursing. 1972. Q. ISSN 0090-0702. $21.00.

Research reports, case studies, and literature reviews on the nursing care of mothers and children are published in this scholarly journal. Written by and for nurse researchers, the articles published cover such topics as oral feeding time in premature infants, infant gender influences on mother separation anxiety, and nurse-parent interactions following the birth of a child with Down syndrome.

Neonatal Intensive Care. Goldstein and Associates. 1988. 6/yr. ISSN 1062-2454. Price not given.

For practitioners in the field, this refereed journal examines diagnostic techniques, research results, and clinical syndromes in the neonatal and perinatal stages after birth. Ethical, legal, and social issues relating to neonatal intensive care practices are also addressed.

Pediatric AIDS & HIV Infection: Fetus to Adolescent. Mary Ann Liebert. 1990. B-M. ISSN 1045-5418. $75.00.

This independent journal includes research and review articles, brief reports, and commentaries covering all aspects of HIV and other retroviral infections in the pregnant mother, child, and adolescent. The journal is multidisciplinary and international in scope, publishing works that deal with community needs, prevention, legal issues, and psychosocial concerns as well as epidemiology, virology, pathology, clinical presentation, and diagnosis and treatment. Among the topics addressed are breastfeeding and HIV infection, development of language in HIV-infected but not ill children, and HIV seroconversion during pregnancy.

Pediatric Asthma, Allergy & Immunology. Mary Ann Liebert. 1987. Q. ISSN 0883-1174. $120.00.

Critical reviews, research reports, and case studies on issues related to clinical management of allergy, asthma, and related immunological concerns in children make up this journal. The social impact of these disorders on children and their families is covered, as well as the medical considerations involved. Issues have examined pediatric anaphylaxis, exercise-induced asthma, and clinical applications for cytokines. Manuscripts are peer-reviewed at the author's request.

Pediatric Clinics of North America. Saunders. 1954. B-M. ISSN 0031-3955. $63.00.

For clinicians, this journal publishes theme issues on topics of current interest, such as asthma, emergency medicine, neurology, and genetics. Each issue includes a preface that summarizes the significance of the technical articles that follow.

Pediatric Nursing. Anthony J. Jannetti. 1975. B-M. ISSN 0097-7805. $21.00.

Reflecting trends, practice, policies, and research in pediatric nursing, this scholarly refereed journal publishes articles on timely or controversial topics not yet covered in the literature. Practicing nurses will also find updates on legislation, products, drugs, home care, health promotion, and critical care. Each issue contains a continuing education series of articles that confers continuing education contact hours; topics have included pediatric liver disease, childhood poverty, and death and dying.

Pediatrics. American Academy of Pediatrics. 1948. M. ISSN 0031-4005. $42.00.

Technical articles, either reports of original research or unusual clinical findings, are reported in this official journal from the American Academy of Pediatrics. Timely information on such diverse health care concerns as smoking, day care center policies, young mothers and child maltreatment, and lead exposure and motor development make this title of interest to a wide audience of professionals who work with children. Policy statements from academy committees, conference announcements, and letters providing practical advice are also published.

Problems in Pediatrics. Mosby-Year Book. 1970. M. ISSN 0045-9380. $60.00.

Pediatricians will find in-depth treatments of selected topics in this monthly journal. Each issue opens with a brief introduction to the contents, a provocative piece on new developments in the field, a lengthy feature article, and a collection of clinical facts and curiosities. In a past issue, the main article featured a review of orthopedics in the pediatrician's practice.

Year Book of Pediatrics. Mosby-Year Book. 1933. A. ISSN 0084-3954. $51.95.

Significant articles selected annually from among the most important journals are reprinted with critical commentaries in this yearbook. Nearly 300 articles are included, covering the subjects of infectious disease and immunology, nutrition and metabolism, child development, psychiatry, therapeutics

and toxicology, oncology, and many others pertaining to clinical practice. Commentaries by the editors and reviewers note the significance of the findings, explain how they relate to trends in the field, and provide advice for clinicians and occasional light humor. A list of journals scanned is included.

DIRECTORY

Ambulatory Pediatric Association (APA)
6728 Old McLean Village Drive, McLean, VA 22101
(703) 556-9222 Fax (703) 556-8729
Marge Degnon, Executive Director
Founded: 1960
Members: 1,300
Affiliates: 10 regional groups
Mission/Goals: To improve health care for children; to improve children's health through research and by improving patient care, teaching, and formulating policy Audience/Clientele: Health professionals and associations concerned with the health of children
Staff: 2 professionals
Budget: $200,000 Funding: Donations, dues
Services: Networking
Education and Outreach: Continuing education courses, publishing
Publications: *Newsletter*, 3/yr, covering ongoing activities of the association; *Educational Guidelines*, a series of guidelines for the education of medical students and pediatric residents
Programs: Annual conference

American Academy of Pediatric Dentistry (AAPD)
211 E. Chicago Avenue, Suite 1036, Chicago, IL 60611
(312) 337-2169
Dr. John A. Bogert, Executive Director
Founded: 1947
Former Name: American Academy of Pedodontics
Mission/Goals: To advance the specialty of pediatric dentistry through practice, education, and research
Audience/Clientele: Dentists, teachers, and researchers involved with pediatric dentistry
Awards: Graduate student pediatric dentistry award program
Education and Outreach: Publishing
Publications: *American Academy of Pediatric Dentistry— Newsletter*, bimonthly, with calendar, research updates, obituaries; *American Academy of Pediatric Dentistry—Membership Roster*, annual; *Pediatric Dentistry*, bimonthly; various pamphlets
Programs: Annual conference

American Academy of Pediatrics (AAP)
141 Northwest Point Boulevard, Elk Grove Village, IL 60009-0927
(708) 228-5005 Fax (708) 228-5097
James E. Strain, M.D., Executive Director
Founded: 1930
Members: 43,000

Affiliates: 59 state groups
Mission/Goals: To ensure for all young people the attainment of their full potential for physical, emotional, and social health; to support professional education, advocacy for children, representation of pediatricians, public education, access to health care, and service to children to achieve these ends
Audience/Clientele: Pediatricians and other professionals who care for or are concerned about children
Staff: 75 professionals, 140 nonprofessionals, 2,000 volunteers
Budget: $28,000,000 Funding: Federal government, fund-raising, fees for services or products, donations, grants, dues
Services: Referral, lobbying, fund-raising, compiling statistics
Education and Outreach: Continuing education courses, publishing
Publications: *Pediatrics*, monthly; *Pediatrics: A Review*, 10/yr; *AAP News*, monthly, with social, economic, and professional aspects of pediatric care; *Fellowship List*, annual
Programs: Annual conference

American Diabetes Association (ADA)

1660 Duke Street, Alexandria, VA 22314
(703) 549-1500 Fax (703) 836-7439 Toll-free (800) ADA-DISC
John H. Graham IV, Chief Executive Officer
Founded: 1941
Members: 11,000 professional, 265,000 general
Affiliates: 54 state groups, 800 local groups
Mission/Goals: To support discovering the means to prevent and cure diabetes; to provide information and support to the millions who have the disease; to educate health professionals and the general public about the seriousness of this chronic disease
Audience/Clientele: People with diabetes and their families, health professionals and scholars
Staff: 13 professionals and nonprofessionals, numerous volunteers
Budget: $56,300,000 Funding: Fund-raising, fees for services or products, donations, dues
Languages: Spanish
Services: Support group, summer camps for children, fund-raising
Awards: Scientific awards and volunteer recognition awards
Education and Outreach: Continuing education courses, seminars, library, research support, publishing
Publications: *Diabetes*, monthly; *Clinical Diabetes*, bimonthly newsletter covering current information on diabetes for physicians not specializing in its treatment; *Diabetes '91*; *Diabetes Spectrum*, bimonthly; *Diabetes Forecast*, monthly magazine for families
Programs: Annual conference with workshops

American Juvenile Arthritis Organization (AJAO)

1314 Spring Street, N.W., Atlanta, GA 30309
(404) 872-7100 Fax (404) 872-0457 Toll-free (800) 283-7800 Membership (800) 933-0032
Patricia Harrington, Vice President
Founded: 1981

Members: 1,100
Mission/Goals: To serve as an advocate for and work to improve the quality of life for children with rheumatic diseases and their families; to do so by working toward improved medical care and providing collective and individual advocacy, stimulating research, guiding education, and providing support
Audience/Clientele: Parents, health professionals, and all interested in childhood arthritis
Staff: 5 professionals, 50–100 volunteers
Funding: Federal government, fund-raising, donations, dues
Services: Referral
Awards: Kathy Angel Award for Parent Leadership; Dawn Hafeli Award for Youth Leadership; Earl Brewer Award for Health Care Professionals
Education and Outreach: Library, seminars, publishing
Publications: *AJAO Newsletter*, quarterly, with current information on issues for children with rheumatic diseases; *Directory of Pediatric Rheumatology Services*; *Educational Rights for Children with Arthritis: A Manual for Parents*; *Understanding Juvenile Rheumatoid Arthritis*, a manual for use by health care professionals in patient education; various books and pamphlets
Programs: Annual conference

The American Pediatric Gastroesophageal Reflux Association, Inc. (APGERA)

23 Action Street, Watertown, MA 02172
(617) 926-3586
Sharon Tiano, President
Founded: 1987
Members: 300
Mission/Goals: To support all families with children suffering with GI reflux, all types of intestinal dysmotility, and experiencing long-term monitoring with cardiac/apnea monitors; to support reflux babies who outgrow the condition by one year; to support children whose condition is chronic; to offer awareness, understanding, education, and support to families and health care professionals
Audience/Clientele: Families whose children suffer from GI reflux
Staff: 3 volunteers
Budget: $10,000 Funding: Fund-raising, donations
Services: Support group, referral, lobbying, fund-raising, compiling statistics
Education and Outreach: In-service programs, continuing education courses, seminars, library, publishing
Publications: *APGERA Newsletter*, quarterly; educational videos; compiling parent questionnaire
Programs: Annual conference for parents and health professionals

American School Health Association (ASHA)

P.O. Box 708, 7263 State Route 43, Kent, OH 44240
(216) 678-1601 Fax (216) 678-4526
Dana A. Davis, Executive Director
Founded: 1927

Former Name: American Association of School Physicians
Mission/Goals: To provide school physicians, nurses, health educators, and public health workers with assistance and information; to promote programs in school health, including the teaching of health, health service, and promotion of a healthful school environment
Audience/Clientele: School personnel concerned with children's health care
Services: Referral, placement, compiling statistics
Awards: William A. Howard Award for distinguished service in school health
Education and Outreach: Teaching aids, research, publishing
Publications: *ASHA Newsletter*, periodic; *Journal of School Health*, monthly; *The Pulse*, quarterly; *Topical Index from the Journal*, annual; *School Health in America*, survey data; various other books
Programs: Annual conference

American Society of Dentistry for Children (ASDC)

211 E. Chicago Avenue, Suite 1430, Chicago, IL 60611
(312) 943-1244 Fax (312) 943-5341
Carol Teuscher, Assistant Executive Director
Founded: 1927
Members: 10,000
Mission/Goals: To provide general practitioners and specialists interested in dentistry for children with information
Audience/Clientele: Pediatric dentists
Services: Placement service
Education and Outreach: Continuing education courses, research, speakers' bureau, publishing
Publications: *ASDC Newsletter*, bimonthly, with news about children's dental health concerns and legislative updates; *Journal of Dentistry for Children*, bimonthly; *Directory of the Membership of the American Society of Dentistry for Children*, annual
Programs: Annual conference

American Society of Pediatric Hematology/Oncology (ASPHO)

King/Drew Medical Center, 12021 S. Wilmington Avenue, Los Angeles, CA 90059
(213) 603-3850 Fax (213) 603-3108
Carl Pochedly, M.D., Secretary-Treasurer
Founded: 1981
Members: 850
Mission/Goals: To improve the understanding and management of disorders of the blood and cancer in children; to improve the total care of children with these diseases, promote education, and foster all relevant clinical and basic research; to promote interdisciplinary cooperation in education, patient care, and research, as well as to establish meaningful relationships with other specialty societies and professional organizations
Audience/Clientele: Pediatric hematologists, oncologists, specialists in related disciplines, other affiliated members
Budget: $50,000

Education and Outreach: Continuing education courses, seminars, publishing
Publications: *American Journal of Pediatric Hematology/Oncology*, quarterly; *Membership Directory*, annual; *PH/O News*, bimonthly newsletter
Programs: Annual conference, periodic symposia

Association for the Care of Children's Health (ACCH)

7910 Woodmont Avenue, Suite 300, Bethesda, MD 20814
(301) 654-6549 Fax (301) 986-4553
William Sciarillo, Executive Director
Founded: 1965
Former Names: American Association for the Care of Children in Hospitals; Association for the Care of Children in Hospitals
Mission/Goals: To investigate the emotional needs of children in medical settings; to foster their well-being; to develop programs of comprehensive care that support these children and their families; to foster high standards for training and practice in all professions working within the pediatric setting
Audience/Clientele: Pediatric child life/activity specialists, nurses, pediatricians, parents, child psychiatrists, psychologists, social workers
Services: Research grants
Awards: Awards for Innovation and Media; Book Awards
Education and Outreach: Publishing
Publications: *ACCH Network*, quarterly; *ACCH News*, bimonthly; *Child's Health Care*, quarterly; *Conference Proceedings*, annual; *Directory of Psychosocial Policy and Programs*, periodic; various bibliographies and pamphlets
Programs: Annual conference

Association of Maternal and Child Health Programs (AMCHP)

1350 Connecticut Avenue, N.W., Suite 803, Washington, DC 20036
(202) 775-0436 Fax (202) 775-0061
Catherine A. Hess, M.S.W., Executive Director
Founded: 1944
Former Name: Association of Directors of State and Territorial Maternal and Child Health and Crippled Children's Programs
Mission/Goals: To provide public health programs addressing the needs of women in their reproductive years, children, and their families in order to ensure the health of all mothers, children, and families; to inform policymakers about the needs of mothers and children and recommend programs that ensure their health; to develop linkages with related national organizations to promote state programs, provide state organizations with information, and foster exchange of ideas among these groups; to study and report on the health of and health services for mothers, children, and families; to develop models, standards, and guidelines and provide technical assistance to promote effective state programs

Audience/Clientele: Decision makers in the public and private sector, staff of state maternal and child health programs, maternal and child health professionals at the state and local levels, and others interested in maternal and child health

Staff: 6 professionals, 2 nonprofessionals

Budget: $750,000 Funding: Federal government, state government, grants, dues

Services: Lobbying, compiling statistics

Awards: John C. MacQueen Lecturer Award, given annually at AMCHP meeting to a distinguished professional in the field

Education and Outreach: Publishing

Publications: *AMCHP Updates*, bimonthly newsletter dealing with Title V maternal and child health programs; various fact sheets and position statements

Programs: Annual conference

Children's Healthcare Is a Legal Duty (CHILD)

P.O. Box 2604, Sioux City, IA 51106

(712) 948-3500 Fax (712) 948-3500 TTY/TDD (712) 948-3500

Dr. Rita Swan, President

Founded: 1983

Members: 330

Mission/Goals: To promote the legal rights of children to medical care; to oppose religious exemptions from parental duties of care; to oppose religiously based neglect and abuse of children

Staff: 4 volunteers

Budget: $14,000 Funding: Donations, dues

Services: Support group, search services, referral, lobbying

Publications: *Newsletter*, quarterly; *The Law's Response When Religious Beliefs against Medical Care Impact on Children*, monograph; *Cry the Beloved Children*, booklet on preventable deaths

The Compassionate Friends

P.O. Box 3696, Oak Brook, IL 60522-3696

(708) 990-0010 Fax (708) 990-0246

Therese Goodrich, Executive Director

Founded: 1978

Affiliates: 655 chapters

Former Name: Society of the Compassionate Friends

Mission/Goals: To provide parents and bereaved siblings with friendship and understanding; to support and aid parents in the positive resolution of grief upon the death of their child; to foster the physical and emotional health of bereaved parents and siblings

Audience/Clientele: Parents and siblings in families in which a child has died

Funding: Private sources, fund-raising, donations, grants

Languages: Spanish

Services: Support group

Education and Outreach: Publishing

Publications: *National Newsletter*, quarterly; *Sibling Newsletter*, quarterly; books, brochures, videos, and other resources

Programs: Annual conference, semiannual regional meetings

Cystic Fibrosis Foundation (CFF)

6931 Arlington Road, No. 200, Bethesda, MD 20814

(301) 951-4422 Fax (301) 951-6378 Toll-free (800) 344-4823

Robert J. Beall, Ph.D., President and CEO

Founded: 1955

Mission/Goals: To provide medical care for patients with cystic fibrosis through care centers; to sponsor research and professional education on the disorder

Audience/Clientele: Physicians

Services: Medical treatment, postgraduate fellowships

Education and Outreach: Accreditation, continuing education courses, publishing

Publications: *Commitment*, 3/yr ; *Annual Report*

Programs: Annual conference

Intensive Caring Unlimited, Inc. (ICU)

910 Bent Lane, Philadelphia, PA 19118

(215) 368-5804 or (609) 799-2059 Fax (215) 233-5795

Helene Duckett, President

Founded: 1978

Mission/Goals: To provide support, information, and referrals to parents of babies who have medical or developmental problems, those going through high-risk pregnancies, and bereaved parents

Audience/Clientele: Parents whose infants have medical or developmental problems, whose infants die, or who have high-risk pregnancies

Budget: $75,000 Funding: Private sources, fund-raising, fees for services or products, donations, grants

Services: Counseling, support group

Education and Outreach: Library, publishing

Publications: *Intensive Caring Unlimited*, quarterly newsletter; information packets; regional resource lists

International Child Health Foundation (ICHF)

Century Plaza, No. 325, 10630 Little Patuxent Parkway, Columbia, MD 21044

(301) 596-4514 Fax (410) 992-5641

Charlene B. Dale, Executive Vice President

Founded: 1985

Former Name: International Child Health and Diarrhoeal Disease Foundation

Mission/Goals: To address medical and related social causes of the majority of illnesses and deaths of children in the United States and abroad; to save the greatest number of children's lives at the lowest possible cost

Audience/Clientele: Health care providers in community outreach programs, families at greatest risk in rural and urban poverty areas

Staff: 3 professionals, 3 nonprofessionals, 25 volunteers

Budget: $250,000 Funding: Private sources, donations, grants

Services: Social service/case management

Education and Outreach: In-service programs, library, database development, publishing

Publications: *International Child Health Foundation Newsletter*, quarterly; *ORT Symposium*; *Cholera Book*; *Annual Report*; brochures

Programs: Video conferences, symposia

Mail for Tots (MFT)

P.O. Box 8699, 25 New Chardon Street, Boston, MA 02114
(617) 242-3538 Fax (617) 242-3538
Edmund Burns, President
Founded: 1975
Members: 2,052
Mission/Goals: To direct cheerful mail to the terminally ill or lonely
Audience/Clientele: Any persons interested in volunteering and any children who would enjoy happy letters
Staff: 2 part-time support staff, numerous volunteers
Funding: Private sources, fund-raising, donations
Services: Letters to ill children
Education and Outreach: Publishing
Publications: Lists of ill persons; *Newsletter*, periodic
Programs: Annual conference

Make-a-Wish Foundation of America (MAWFA)

100 W. Clarendon Avenue, Suite 2200, Phoenix, AZ 85004
(602) 279-9474 Fax (602) 279-0855 Toll-free (800) 722-WISH
Stephen E. Torkelsen, DSW, Executive Director
Founded: 1980
Affiliates: 78 state groups
Mission/Goals: To ensure that wishes are granted to children in the United States with terminal illnesses or life-threatening medical conditions creating the probability the children will not survive beyond their 18th year; to provide resources to fulfill these children's wishes, including trips to Disneyland, computers, pets, visits with the Pope, shopping trips, and visits with celebrities, for qualified children and their families
Audience/Clientele: Children under the age of 18 with terminal or life-threatening illnesses
Staff: 10 professionals, 7 nonprofessionals
Budget: $2,000,000; Funding: Private sources, fund-raising, donations, grants, Combined Federal Campaign (CFC)
Services: Recreation
Education and Outreach: In-service programs, publishing
Publications: *Annual Report*; *Newsletter*; various brochures

Medical Network for Missing Children (MNMC)

67 Pleasant Ridge Road, Harrison, NY 10528
(914) 967-6854 Fax (914) 337-4006
Peter S. Liebert, M.D., Director
Founded: 1984
Mission/Goals: To educate health professionals concerning the problem of missing children and to involve them in recognizing and reporting those children; to promote safety information for parents and children to prevent abductions and molestation; to provide a database of health information for missing children
Audience/Clientele: Health professionals, parents and children in general, and parents of missing children
Staff: 15 volunteers
Funding: Private source
Services: Search services
Education and Outreach: Seminars, database development, publishing

Publications: *Safety Advice for Parents and Children*

National Association of Pediatric Nurse Associates and Practitioners (NAPNAP)

1101 Kings Highway, N., No. 206, Cherry Hill, NJ 08034
(609) 667-1773 Fax (609) 667-7187
Mavis McGuire, Executive Director
Founded: 1973
Mission/Goals: To improve the quality of health care for infants, children, and adolescents; to do so by making health services more accessible and improving the education of parents
Audience/Clientele: Pediatric, school, and family nurse practitioners and others interested in child health
Services: Advocacy, certification, compiling statistics
Education and Outreach: Database development, research, publishing
Publications: *Pediatric Nurse Practitioner*, bimonthly; *Journal of Pediatric Health Care*, bimonthly; brochures
Programs: Annual conference

National Association of School Nurses (NASN)

P.O. Box 1300, Lamplighter Lane, Scarborough, ME 04074
(207) 883-2117 Fax (207) 883-2683
Beverly Farquhar, Executive Director
Founded: 1969
Mission/Goals: To promote health services for schoolchildren; to promote the interests of children to the nursing and medical communities and the general public
Audience/Clientele: School nursing, medical and nursing professionals, educators, general public
Services: Supports research, certification
Education and Outreach: Seminars, publishing
Publications: *NAS Newsletter*, quarterly; *School Nurse*, quarterly magazine; school nursing program guidelines
Programs: Annual conference

National Center for Education in Maternal and Child Health (NCEMCH)

2000 N. 15th Street, Suite 701, Arlington, VA 22201-2617
(703) 524-7802 Fax (703) 524-9335
Rochelle Mayer, Ed.D., Director
Founded: 1982
Former Name: National Clearinghouse for Human Genetic Diseases
Mission/Goals: To provide information, prepare publications, and conduct conferences on maternal and child health, including women's health, infant, child, and adolescent health, nutrition, injury prevention, chronic diseases and disabling conditions, children with special health needs, genetic services, and public health programs and services
Audience/Clientele: Maternal and child health professionals, students, educators, general public
Staff: 24 professionals, 3 nonprofessionals
Funding: Federal government, grants
Services: Referral
Education and Outreach: Library, archives, database development, publishing

Publications: *Reaching Out: A Directory of Organizations Related to Maternal and Child Health*, annual; *Starting Early: A Guide to Federal Resources in Maternal and Child Health*; *Abstracts of Active Projects*, annual; *MCH Bureau Active Projects: An Annotated Listing*, annual; *MCH Program Interchange*, monthly
Programs: Topical symposia and conferences

National Children's Eye Care Foundation (NCECF)
P.O. Box 795069, Dallas, TX 75379-5069
(214) 407-0404 Fax (214) 407-0616
Suzanne C. Beauchamp, Executive Director
Founded: 1970
Former Name: Children's Eye Care Foundation
Mission/Goals: To conduct research on children's eye care; to promote public and professional education and service in the field; to sponsor public information campaigns for parents, teachers, and children that emphasize early detection and treatment
Audience/Clientele: Ophthalmologists and other health care professionals, parents, teachers, children
Services: Postresidency fellowships, research grants
Education and Outreach: Publishing
Publications: *Annual Report*; *National Children's Eye Care Foundation Newsletter*, annual; various brochures
Programs: Annual conference, biennial symposium

National Coalition for School Bus Safety (NCSBS)
P.O. Box 781, Skokie, IL 60076
(708) 679-2694
Laura G. Schwartz, Treasurer
Founded: 1985
Members: 1,000
Affiliates: 30 state groups
Former Name: National Coalition for School Bus Seat Belts (NCSSB)
Mission/Goals: To disseminate information about school bus safety and safe transportation for children
Audience/Clientele: Parents, educators, health professionals, legislators
Staff: 8 volunteers
Budget: $2,000 Funding: Fees for services or products, donations, dues
Languages: French, Spanish
Services: Support group, lobbying
Education and Outreach: In-service programs, seminars, publishing
Publications: *Yellow Book*, a compilation of pro-school bus seat belt information; *Newsletter*; various brochures

National Maternal and Child Health Clearinghouse (NMCHC)
8201 Greensboro Drive, Suite 600, McLean, VA 22102-3810
(703) 821-8955 ext. 254 Fax (703) 821-2098
Linda Cramer, Project Director
Founded: 1983
Mission/Goals: To provide information to health care policymakers and providers and to consumers covering the broad topic of maternal and child health; to transfer information from maternal and child health researchers to the field; to respond to information requests from professionals and consumers about a broad range of topics; to distribute publications developed by the Maternal and Child Health Bureau, Department of Health and Human Services, and to provide referral to other information sources
Audience/Clientele: Health care professionals, consumers
Funding: Federal government
Education and Outreach: Library, publishing
Publications: *Infant Care*, *Healthy Foods*, *Healthy Baby*, and similar brochures for consumers

The National MPS Society, Inc.
17 Kraemer Street, Hicksville, NY 11801
(516) 931-6338
Marie Capobianco, President
Founded: 1974
Members: 800
Mission/Goals: To act as a support group for families of MPS (mucopolysaccharidoses) and other related disorders; to increase professional and public awareness of the disorder and to raise funds to further research on MPS and related disorders
Audience/Clientele: Family and friends of an MPS patient, health care professionals, general public
Budget: $100,000 Funding: Private sources, fund-raising, donations, grants, dues
Services: Support group, referral, research support
Education and Outreach: Library, database development, publishing
Publications: *Courage*, quarterly newsletter; various pamphlets, brochures, and posters
Programs: Semiannual conference

The National Neurofibromatosis Foundation, Inc. (NNFF)
141 Fifth Avenue, Suite 7S, New York, NY 10010
(212) 460-8980 Fax (212) 529-6094 Toll-free (800) 323-7938 TTY/TDD (212) 460-8980
Peter Bellerman, President
Founded: 1978
Members: 31,000
Affiliates: 25 state groups
Mission/Goals: To sponsor research and public awareness of neurofibromatosis (NF); to promote development of clinics and diagnostic and management protocols; to assist patients with information, support groups, and medical referrals
Audience/Clientele: Patients with NF and their families, physicians and other health care providers
Staff: 8 professionals, 6 nonprofessionals, 4 volunteers
Budget: $1,472,844 Funding: Private sources, fees for services or products, donations, grants, dues
Languages: Spanish, German, Portuguese, Italian
Services: Support group, referral, fund-raising
Awards: NNFF Public Service Award and NNFF Institutional Public Service Award presented to individuals and organizations who have provided ongoing support to NNFF; Von Recklinghausen Award presented to scientists or physicians

for their work in NF; Courtemanche Award presented to individuals for outstanding service to NNFF
Education and Outreach: In-service programs, continuing education courses, seminars, library, publishing
Publications: *National Neurofibromatosis Foundation Newsletter*, quarterly; *Neurofibromatosis Research Newsletter*, quarterly; *A Handbook for Parents*, and similar brochures; *Conference Series Monographs*; *NF: A Brighter Tomorrow* video
Programs: Annual conference, symposia

National Safe Kids Campaign (NSKC)
111 Michigan Avenue, N.W., Washington, DC 20010-2970
(202) 939-4993 Fax (202) 939-4838
Herta Feely, Executive Director
Founded: 1988
Mission/Goals: To provide a long-term, nationwide effort to prevent injury, the number-one cause of death and disability in children; to carry out grassroots campaigns, such as a bike helmet awareness campaign to increase helmet use among children, a scald burn prevention campaign, a residential fire detection campaign to increase use of working smoke detectors, and a child safety seat program
Audience/Clientele: Parents, care givers, injury prevention professionals, medical professionals, and educators
Staff: 12 professionals, 8 nonprofessionals, 2 volunteers
Funding: Federal government, private sources, fund-raising, fees for services or products, donations, grants
Services: Lobbying
Education and Outreach: Seminars, library, publishing
Publications: *Campaign Update*, bimonthly newsletter; *Childhood Injury Prevention Quarterly*; *Bicycle Helmet and Bike Safety Strategy*, *Scald Burn Prevention Strategy*, and similar educational books and videos in their areas of interest
Programs: Annual conference

National SIDS Resource Center
8201 Greensboro Drive, Suite 600, McLean, VA 22102
(703) 821-8955 Fax (703) 821-2098
Olivia Coredrill, Project Director
Founded: 1980
Former Name: National Sudden Infant Death Syndrome Clearinghouse
Mission/Goals: To provide information and educational materials on sudden infant death syndrome (SIDS) and related problems; to develop and distribute materials concerning SIDS, grief, apnea, and apnea monitoring
Audience/Clientele: Health care professionals, community service workers, health educators, parents, and the general public
Education and Outreach: Library, database development, publishing
Publications: *National Sudden Infant Death Syndrome Clearinghouse Information Exchange*, quarterly newsletter; fact sheets and grief counseling bibliographies

Neurofibromatosis, Inc. (NF, Inc.)
8855 Annapolis Road, Suite 110, Lanham, MD 20706-2924

(301) 577-8984 Fax (301) 577-0016 (call first) Toll-free (800) 942-6825 TTY/TDD (410) 461-5213
Paul Mendelsohn, President
Founded: 1988
Affiliates: 10 state groups
Mission/Goals: To support individuals and families affected by neurofibromatosis (NF) by providing coordinated educational, support, clinical, and research programs; to promote national, state, and local community involvement
Audience/Clientele: Individuals with NF, families, physicians, nurses, genetic counselors, researchers, social workers, educators, general public
Staff: 35 volunteers
Budget: $300,000 Funding: Donations
Services: Counseling, support group, search services, referral, research support
Education and Outreach: In-service programs, seminars, library, archives, database development, publishing
Publications: *Neurofibromatosis Inc*, periodic newsletter with research summaries, chapter news, symposia information; various brochures
Programs: Periodic symposia

Parent Care (PC)
9041 Colgate Street, Indianapolis, IN 46268-1210
(317) 872-9913 Fax (317) 872-5464
Sarah Killion, Administrative Director
Founded: 1982
Former Name: Parents of Premature and High-Risk Infants International
Mission/Goals: To support parents of premature and high-risk infants; to increase public awareness of the special needs of these families
Audience/Clientele: Perinatal professionals, parent groups, parents of high-risk or premature infants Education and Outreach: Seminars, library, database development, speakers' bureau, publishing
Publications: *Guiding Your Infant through Preterm Development*; *Parents of Prematures Resource Directory*, annual; *News Brief*, quarterly newsletter
Programs: Annual conference

Parents of Murdered Children and Other Survivors of Homicide Victims (POMC)
100 E. Eighth Street, B-41, Cincinnati, OH 45202
(513) 721-5683 Fax (513) 721-5685
Nancy Ruhe, Executive Director
Founded: 1981
Members: 33,000
Affiliates: 35 chapters, 300 contact people
Mission/Goals: To provide crisis counseling, comfort, understanding, and information to those who have lost a loved one to murder; to organize support groups where survivors meet and comfort one another, exchange information, and learn to help themselves through the process of grieving
Audience/Clientele: Survivors of homicide victims

Budget: $120,000 Funding: Private sources, fund-raising, donations, grants
Languages: Spanish
Services: Counseling, support group, referral, fund-raising, compiling statistics
Awards: Lisa Hullinger Memorial Award to individual who best personifies the ideals of POMC; Dorothy Lobes Memorial Award to POMC chapter that best exemplifies the ideals of the organization
Education and Outreach: Seminars, database development, publishing
Publications: *Survivors*, newsletter 3/yr; *Thanks for Asking . . .*, a book written by survivors; brochures in English and Spanish; *Path through the Criminal Justice System*, also in English and Spanish
Programs: Annual conference

RTS Bereavement Services
1910 South Avenue, LaCrosse, WI 54601
(608) 791-4747 Fax (608) 785-2181 Toll-free (800) 362-9567
Brenda Jorgenson, Administrator
Founded: 1982
Former Name: Resolve through Sharing
Members: 7,000 counselors, 800 coordinators
Affiliates: 50 state groups
Mission/Goals: To provide perinatal bereavement training conferences across the nation; to provide support materials to meet the needs of bereaved families
Audience/Clientele: Nurses, physicians, midwives, clergy, funeral directors, bereaved parents
Staff: 13 professionals, 5 volunteers
Funding: Fees for services or products
Languages: Spanish
Services: Referral
Education and Outreach: In-service programs, continuing education courses, seminars, library, publishing
Publications: *Counselor Connection*, quarterly newsletter; training materials for organizing and conducting seminars
Programs: Biennial training conference

SHARE: Pregnancy and Infant Loss Support, Inc.
St. Joseph Health Center, 300 First Capitol Drive, St. Charles, MO 63301-2893
(314) 947-6164 Fax (314) 947-7486
Catherine Lammert, Executive Director
Founded: 1977
Members: 10,000
Affiliates: 250 state groups
Former Name: SHARE (Source of Help for Airing, Resolving Experiences)
Mission/Goals: To serve those who are touched by the tragic death of a baby through miscarriage, stillbirth, or infant death; to provide, through mutual self-help groups, a strong, supportive atmosphere where members can share their experiences and feelings

Audience/Clientele: Bereaved parents, families, children, friends, employers, members of the congregation, care givers, and others in a supportive role
Staff: 1 professional, 30 volunteers
Budget: $130,000 Funding: Private sources, fees for services or products, donations, dues
Services: Support group, search services, referral
Education and Outreach: In-service programs, seminars, library, database development, publishing
Publications: *SHARE Newsletter*, bimonthly, with listing of books and resources, calendar, announcements of new groups; manual on starting a local SHARE group; *Thumpy's Story*, in book, video, and audiocassette format, about children's grief; *International Perinatal Support Groups Listing*, also a listing of parents willing to help others; perinatal bereavement bibliography
Programs: Periodic grief retreats

Shriners Hospitals for Crippled Children (SHCC)
2900 Rocky Point Drive, Tampa, FL 33631-3356
(813) 281-0300 Fax (813) 281-8174 Toll-free (800) 237-5055
Lewis K. Molnar, Executive Vice President
Founded: 1922
Members: 22 hospitals
Mission/Goals: Using the facilities of 19 hospitals providing orthopedic care and 3 providing treatment for burns, to offer treatment to save children's lives and restore their bodies; to conduct research into orthopedic and burn care; to educate physicians and other health care professionals in the care of orthopedic disabilities and burn injuries
Audience/Clientele: Children with severe burns or orthopedic disabilities, up to their 18th birthday, who have conditions whose treatment would pose a financial hardship for their parents and conditions that Shriners Hospitals for Crippled Children could improve
Staff: 1,000 professionals, 3,000 nonprofessionals
Budget: $305,000,000 Funding: Private sources, fund-raising, donations, grants, dues
Languages: Spanish
Services: Emergency medical care, inpatient/outpatient specialty care
Education and Outreach: In-service programs, medical residency, research, publishing
Publications: *Between Us*, newsletter published 3 times per year; fact sheets, pamphlets, and brochures
Programs: Annual conference, with seminar

SIDS Alliance (NSIDSF)
10500 Little Patuxent Parkway, No. 420, Columbia, MD 21044
(410) 964-8000 Fax (410) 964-8009 Toll-free (800) 221-SIDS
Thomas L. Moran, President
Founded: 1991
Former Names: Mark Addison Roe Foundation, National Foundation for Sudden Infant Death, National Sudden Infant Death Syndrome Foundation

Mission/Goals: To provide assistance to bereaved parents who have lost a child to SIDS; to assist families and professionals to care for infants at risk due to respiratory or cardiac problems; to support research and increase public knowledge of SIDS and its causes

Audience/Clientele: Health care professionals, concerned citizens, and parents whose child died of SIDS

Services: Referral

Education and Outreach: Archives, publishing

Publications: *Annual Report*; *Directory*, annual; *The Leaflet*, quarterly newsletter with research updates and news; brochures and reprints of SIDS literature

Programs: Annual conference, periodic regional meetings

Society for Adolescent Medicine (SAM)

19401 E. 40 Highway, Suite 120, Independence, MO 64055

(816) 795-TEEN

Dr. M. Susan Jay, Executive Secretary-Treasurer

Founded: 1968

Mission/Goals: To improve the quality of health care for adolescents; to promote research on normal growth and development during adolescence as well as on diseases that affect adolescents; to foster communication among health care professionals who care for adolescents

Audience/Clientele: Physicians, psychiatrists, social workers, nurses, and other health professionals who work with adolescents

Education and Outreach: Research, publishing

Publications: *Journal of Adolescent Health Care*, bimonthly

Programs: Annual conference

Society for Pediatric Research (SPR)

P.O. Box 675, 141 Northwest Point Boulevard, Elk Grove Village, IL 60009-0675

(708) 427-1205 Fax (708) 427-1305

Debbie Anagnostelis, Executive Director

Founded: 1936

Members: 2,142

Mission/Goals: To encourage investigation of a broad range of areas involving the health and well-being of children; to facilitate this by providing a forum for interchange of ideas and opportunities for young pediatric investigators to present their research

Audience/Clientele: Academicians and researchers who have interests in all areas of pediatric research

Staff: 5 professionals

Budget: $500,000 Funding: Dues, fees for services or products

Services: Research grants

Awards: Young Investigator Award, National Student Award, House Officer Award, Fellow Awards

Education and Outreach: Publishing

Publications: *Pediatric Research Journal*

Programs: Annual meeting

Spina Bifida Association of America (SBAA)

4590 MacArthur Boulevard, N.W., Suite 250, Washington, DC 20007

(202) 944-3285 Fax (202) 944-3295 Toll-free (800) 621-3141

Steve Laubacher, Executive Director

Founded: 1972

Members: 6,000

Affiliates: 82 state groups

Mission/Goals: To provide information related to spina bifida, including progress in the areas of medical, educational, legislative, and financial support; to help fund research and medical facilities; to encourage training of individuals involved in treatment

Audience/Clientele: Parents and other members of families having children born with spina bifida, individuals with the disorder, medical and allied health professionals who work with them

Staff: 5.5 FTE professionals

Services: Support group, referral, lobbying

Education and Outreach: Library, publishing

Publications: *Spina Bifida Insights*, bimonthly newsletter on developments in medicine and policy, with information on new products; *Introduction to Spina Bifida*; *Children with Spina Bifida*; various other books and pamphlets; information sheets covering hip stability and ambulation, kidney care, genetics, and other topics of interest; *SB—A Lifetime Challenge* and other videos; audiotapes of conference proceedings; *Annual Report*

Programs: Annual meeting

Teens Teaching AIDS Prevention (Teens TAP)

3030 Walnut, Kansas City, MO 64108

(816) 561-8784 Fax (816) 531-7199 Hotline (800) 234-8336

Ina R. Pope, Director of Education

Founded: 1985

Mission/Goals: A project of Good Samaritan Project, to assist persons with AIDS and their loved ones to live with HIV by providing education, information, and emotional, financial, legal, and physical support; to assist the community to understand the nature of HIV and its prevention

Audience/Clientele: HIV-infected adolescents and their loved ones

Staff: 4 professionals, 10 nonprofessionals, 400 volunteers

Budget: $646,107 Funding: Federal government, state government, local government, private sources, fund-raising, donations, county government, grants, dues

Languages: Sign language, Spanish

Services: Counseling, support group, social service/case management, fund-raising, compiling statistics

Education and Outreach: In-service programs, seminars, library, publishing

Publications: Brochures and manuals for group leaders

REFERENCES

1. *Incidence and Impact of Selected Infectious Diseases in Childhood.* Vital and Health Statistics, Series 10: Data from the National Health Interview Survey, no. 180. U.S. Department of Health and Human Services, National Center for Health Statistics, 1991, 10.

2. William L. Atkinson et al., "Measles Surveillance—United States, 1991," *Morbidity and Mortality Weekly Report* 41(SS-6) (November 20, 1992): 1.

3. "Annual Summary of Births, Marriages, Divorces, and Deaths: U.S., 1991," *Monthly Vital Statistics Report* 40, no. 13 (September 30, 1992): 22.

4. *Types of Injuries by Selected Characteristics: United States, 1985–87.* Vital and Health Statistics, Series 10: Data from the National Health Survey, no. 175. U.S. Department of Health and Human Services, National Center for Health Statistics, 1990, 38.

5. "Advance Report of Final Mortality Statistics, 1990," *Monthly Vital Statistics Report* 41, no. 7 supp. (January 7, 1993): 21.

6. Ibid.

7. Lois A. Fingerhut, "Firearm Mortality among Children, Youth, and Young Adults 1–34 Years of Age, Trends and Current Status: United States, 1985–90," *Advance Data*, no. 231 (March 23, 1993): 7.

C H A P T E R

18

. × × × × × ×

Nutrition and Fitness

*Feeding is more than getting food on
the table. It is the whole nurturing environment that the child care provider sets up around food.*
Christine Berman and Jacki Fromer. *Meals without Squeals*

It's just as important to grow up fit as it is to grow up smart.
Kenneth Cooper. *Kid Fitness*

A nutritious diet and appealing menu choices promote children's well-being as well as their growth. The decision to breastfeed or bottle feed, even after weighing the relative advantages of each, is a difficult one for new parents. Less than one-third of new mothers breastfed their infants in 1955, compared to nearly two-thirds in 1982 and just over one-half in 1992, according to a comparison of two longitudinal studies on the topic.[1] Other dietary considerations involve when to add solid foods, how to prevent food allergies, and how to avoid unsafe foods, such as raw carrots, which may cause choking. Children's eating habits are the basis of lifelong patterns, so providing a healthy diet high in complex carbohydrates is essential.

The manner in which a parent handles feeding colors a child's perception of what to expect from life. Food battles with a newly independent toddler may violate a child's recent sense of self-control. Christine Berman and Jacki Fromer emphasize that ". . . children have the responsibility of deciding how much—and even whether—they will eat."[2] Parents are left to decide what is eaten and when and where it is consumed.

One of the more challenging aspects of contemporary parenting is setting a good physical fitness example for children. A recent study revealed that only 39.4 percent of currently married men and 38 percent of currently

married women either exercised or played sports regularly.[3] Interesting a child in exercise, finding developmentally appropriate activities, and avoiding injury from overtraining or poor safety precautions are important concerns for both parents and physical education professionals. In 1992, 5,370,525 high school students participated in organized sports activities.[4] Continuing these activities into adulthood will reduce stress, enhance recreation, and improve health.

An asterisk (*) indicates specially recommended titles.

POPULAR TITLES: BOOKS

Avella, Douglas G., and Theresa Foy DiGeronimo. *Raising a Healthy Athlete*. British American, 1990. 326p. bibliog. illus. LC 90-1608. ISBN 0-945167-36-9. $19.95. ISBN 0-945167-32-6 pbk. $8.95.

The emphasis of this concise sourcebook on participation in organized sports is the parent's role in preventing and caring for sports injuries. The authors, one a pediatric orthopedist, note that prevention is possible because most injuries are caused by negligence. They stress that proper nutrition and rest, body conditioning, and a preseason medical exam are essential to preventing injuries in young male and female athletes. Ways to avoid injuries in 14 popular sports by using proper equipment, practice sessions, correct playing techniques, and conditioning exercises are covered. The text also examines symptoms, treatment, and rehabilitation for specific injuries and ailments.

Behan, Eileen. *Microwave Cooking for Your Baby and Child: The ABC's of Creating Quick, Nutritious Meals for Your Little Ones.* Villard, 1991. 233p. illus. index. LC 90-50221. ISBN 0-394-58419-8. $13.95.

Cooking infant and toddler foods in the microwave has the advantages of being fast, preserving nutrients, retaining moisture and soft texture, and avoiding kitchen mess and cleanup, according to Behan, a registered dietician and mother of two. Her knowledge, experience, and research form the basis for a detailed, comprehensive nutrition text that emphasizes food safety and allergy prevention and explains when to introduce a variety of foods and how to avoid health hazards such as obesity, high cholesterol, and cravings for salty or sweet foods. Basic techniques for food preparation are summarized and a nutrition and cooking profile for 100 of the foods most often served is provided. Behan presents recipes in age-specific categories and covers special topics such as nutritious desserts and snacks, food to pack for travels, healthy breakfasts, and foods for all children.

Berman, Christine, and Jacki Fromer. *Meals without Squeals: Child Care Feeding Guide and Cookbook.* Bull, 1991. 240p. illus. LC 91-4498. ISBN 0-923521-10-0. $14.95.

Information about nutrition, advice on feeding and understanding eating behaviors, and healthy recipes are featured in this food guide for child care centers. Prepared by a registered dietician and child care provider, the content includes establishing a policy on feeding children with input from parents; understanding the link between children's development and nutritional needs; planning how and what to feed children; running an efficient, safe kitchen; and addressing environmental concerns such as saving water and energy, recycling, and using nontoxic cleaning products. Healthy recipes, which were tested in large as well as small quantities, and sample menus are also presented. The authors briefly examine special concerns about allergies, diabetes and other illnesses, dental health, constipation, junk food, obesity, pesticides, and similar topics in an appendix, along with basic concepts of nutrition.

* Cooper, Kenneth. *Kid Fitness: A Complete Shape Up Program for Birth through High School.* Bantam, 1991. 367p. bibliog. illus. index. LC 90-9024. ISBN 0-553-07332-X. $20.00.

Written for parents, this book addresses nutrition and exercise for children from the preschool years through adolescence. Acknowledging the importance of parents' involvement, the author, a well-known physician and fitness expert, illustrates how parents can guide, motivate, monitor, and serve as role models for their child's fitness. Topics covered include fitness testing, diet and recipes, stress reduction, and evaluation of sports programs for safer participation. Winner of a *Child* magazine award for excellence in family issues. A foreword by Arnold Schwarzenegger introduces the book.

Graham, Janice. *Breastfeeding Secrets and Solutions.* Pocket, 1993. 95p. index. LC 93-3879. ISBN 0-671-74963-3. $10.00.

Graham's guide for new and expectant mothers who have decided to breastfeed answers common questions clearly and in detail. The book also proposes workable solutions to nursing problems. The author tells what to expect during first nursings and gives facts concerning fears about milk supply, remedying breast soreness, solving difficult breastfeeding behaviors, going back to work, introducing solid food, and weaning. Graham discusses and discredits common breastfeeding myths and indicates how likely it is that specific problems will occur. Her effort is reassuring, and her tone is appealingly supportive without being either overly solicitous or patronizing. An appendix lists resources for mothers who are nursing twins, triplets, etc., or babies with special needs.

Hess, Mary Abbott, Anne Alise Hunt, and Barbara Motenko Stone. *A Healthy Head Start: A Worry Free Guide to Feeding Young Children.* Holt, 1990. 324p. illus. index. LC 90-33523. ISBN 0-8050-1329-6. $19.95.

This recipe book combines information on nutrition and advice on feeding behavior with healthy recipes that emphasize a variety of tastes and textures. The initial chapters address taste bud training, the hunger mechanism and eating schedules, the parents' role in children's food acceptance and regulation, basic nutritional concepts, and what the authors term the "headline-making stuff," such as fat and cholesterol, salt intake, sugar and sweetness, fiber, and food additives. Over 200 recipes provide appealing and flavor-rich ideas for soups, egg dishes, breads, cheese, salads, vegetables, meat, poultry, seafood, and sauces, among others. The authors, a registered dietician, home economist, and professional developer of recipes, consulted parents for real-life feeding experiences and questions. As a result, the final section of recipes for low-sugar and reduced-fat sweets and desserts is the longest chapter.

Huggins, Kathleen. *The Nursing Mother's Companion.* Rev. ed. Harvard Common, 1991. 220p. bibliog. photog. illus. index. LC 90-38863. ISBN 1-55832-025-3. $16.95.

Now in its second edition, this manual by a lactation consultant and perinatal nurse is designed to instruct today's mother in how to breastfeed her child and to serve as a reference throughout the nursing period. It summarizes advantages of breastfeeding, physiology of milk production, and nursing during the first week, the second month, the sixth month, and thereafter. Each chapter features a survival guide that highlights solutions to problems, both small and common and serious and rare, that may be encountered during that time period. Appendixes provide a list of references for nursing mothers and a review of the safety of various drugs during lactation. Numerous illustrations supplement the text.

Jones, Carl. *Breastfeeding Your Baby: A Guide for the Contemporary Family.* Macmillan, 1993. 211p. illus. index. LC 92-26321. ISBN 0-02-080401-6. $10.00.

This thorough account of the advantages, physiology, and techniques of breastfeeding and how to resolve problems associated with it also provides information for the working mother. Those mothers whose babies require special treatment, such as premature infants, twins, ill or hospitalized babies, and those delivered by cesarean, will find chapters devoted to their concerns. The text also explores the role of the father in successful breastfeeding. Such concerns as building and maintaining a milk supply, the mother's self-care, and getting the right start are discussed. The most useful chapter in this helpful and informative text describes seven steps that assure successful breastfeeding to the contemporary mother and her family; the steps include learning about breastfeeding, creating a support system, and selecting both a birthing place and health care providers who are supportive of breastfeeding.

Kimmel, Martha, and David Kimmel, with Suzanne Goldenson. *Mommy Made and Daddy Too: Home Cooking for a Healthy Baby and Toddler.* Bantam, 1990. 308p. LC 89-18244. ISBN 0-553-34866-3. $13.95.

The Kimmels, whose academic backgrounds are in child development and culinary arts, have organized this text after the syllabus of a baby food preparation course that they developed and taught in New York City. Appealing in its layout and illustration, the book covers how to introduce a baby to solid food, principles of child nutrition, allergy detection techniques, food preparation, storage and handling, purchasing information, suggestions for traveling, and food preparation. Numerous recipes used as the basis for their line of fresh baby food products are included. An inventory of kitchen equipment needed to prepare baby food that is fresher, more flavorful, and diverse than comparable store-bought products is included.

* Kitzinger, Sheila. *Breastfeeding Your Baby.* Knopf, 1989. 159p. photog. illus. LC 88-27225. ISBN 0-679-72433-8. $14.95.

Believing that breastfeeding is at its most basic a way to communicate intimately with another human being, the author describes the process in sensuous, imaginative terms. The warm, encouraging, emotional tone is augmented by lovely photographs that illustrate nursing positions and latching techniques and hint at the mutual satisfaction of a successful breastfeeding relationship. Kitzinger, a well-known childbirth educator, also troubleshoots problems such as sleepy or overexcited babies, sore breasts, and expressing milk and explores the mother's relationship with her child and the child's integration into the family. Besides practical advice, this text provides encouragement and support that enhances a new mother's confidence and satisfaction in nursing her child.

Kleinman, Ronald E., and Michael S. Jellinek, with Julie Houston. *Let Them Eat Cake! The Case against Controlling What Your Children Eat.* Villard, 1994. 281p. bibliog. LC 93-16008. ISBN 0-679-41259-X. $19.95.

Practical, down-to-earth advice on controversies such as sugar's influence on children's behavior, the safety of pesticides and additives, vitamin supplements, fiber requirements, and the relationship between television and obesity in children is combined with concise information about growth, nutrition, and fitness. The authors of this handbook, the chief and associate chief of pediatric nutrition at Massachusetts General Hospital and a professional writer respectively, also address feeding interactions and conflicts over food, such as mealtime battles, junk food conflicts, and food tensions at transition stages, as well as food-related problems such as overweight or thin children, eating disorders, and food allergies. Their no-nonsense, calm approach to children's nutrition is based firmly on the scientific literature; they even include a chapter on how to evaluate media reports about food, diet, and nutrition. Among their guiding principles, highlighted in italics throughout the text, are the ideas that growth indicates that a child is getting the food he or she needs, food habits are not fixed in child-

hood, erratic eating patterns are normal in children, no foods are "bad," and foods don't have an impact on behavior.

Kraemer, William J., and Steven J. Fleck. *Strength Training for Young Athletes.* Human Kinetics, 1993. 214p. illus. index. LC 92-22624. ISBN 0-87322-396-9. $16.95.

Strength training for children is supported by professional groups, including the American Academy of Pediatrics, because it increases muscular strength and endurance, improves performance capacity, and prevents injury during sports or recreation. To advise in developing programs that are safe and effective, the authors cover proper program design, competent supervision, and instruction on proper form for exercises. More than 100 resistance exercises for all muscle groups are described and illustrated, then organized into basic training programs for 16 popular sports, including swimming, volleyball, basketball, baseball, and ice hockey. The authors, two fitness professionals with Ph.D.s in physiology, emphasize safety concerns throughout the text.

* La Leche League. *Womanly Art of Breastfeeding.* 5th ed. Viking, 1991. 446p. photog. illus. index. LC 91-15005. ISBN 0-452-26623-8. $10.95.

La Leche League, one of the first self-help parenting groups in the United States, explores in detail techniques, advantages, and challenges of breastfeeding within the context of general child care, such as nurturing, nutrition, and discipline. In this fifth edition of their standard handbook, the league also examines the impact of working on the mother-child relationship; how fathers contribute to successful breastfeeding; breastfeeding under special conditions, such as multiple or cesarean births; and approaches to weaning. Quotations from participants enliven and personalize the text, which is illustrated largely with photographs rather than instructional drawings. La Leche views support for breastfeeding from other mothers as the secret of success.

Lambert-Legace, Louise. *Feeding Your Child.* 2nd ed. Surrey, 1991. 200p. illus. LC 90-24147. ISBN 0-640625-37-7. $10.95.

Good eating habits are influenced by a diet of quality foods and a pleasant eating atmosphere during the first years of life according to the author, a registered dietician. Lambert-Legace relied on personal philosophy, interview data, and the results of scientific research in preparing this comprehensive guide to nutrition, eating, and diet from pregnancy through toddlerhood. Charts and diagrams are used to present food composition, growth, and other key concepts. Menus and recipes for mothers and infants are provided. Content includes the nutritional advantages of breastfeeding, choosing infant formulas, using supplements, introducing solid foods, and preparing homemade baby foods.

Lebow, Michael D. *Overweight Children: Helping Your Child Achieve Lifetime Weight Control.* Insight, 1991. 219p. LC 91-23195. ISBN 0-306-43961-1. $22.95.

Techniques for managing children's weight through diet and exercise are the focus of this practical handbook from the director of the Manitoba Obesity Clinic. Discussions of the causes of obesity and its effects—disease, discomfort, disability, and despair—are based on research reports, clinical experience, and case studies. Social and cultural consequences of being overweight are also explored. LeBow emphasizes positive reinforcement and building self-esteem as important features of a manageable program for weight reduction and control in youth. The final chapter advises obese parents on how to lose weight through the program.

Micheli, Lyle J., with Mark D. Jenkins. *Sportswise: An Essential Guide for Young Athletes, Parents, and Coaches.* Houghton Mifflin, 1990. 300p. bibliog. LC 90-34257. ISBN 0-395-56408-8-5. $9.95.

This primer on childhood sports comprehensively covers fitness programs, injury prevention, nutrition, preparation for participation, and other matters of concern to parents whose children participate in organized athletics. Because one of the authors is an orthopedic surgeon specializing in sports medicine who is also a parent, the text benefits from the perspective that many years of experience in the field brings. The text covers such topics as overuse injuries, the female athlete, stress and psychological injuries, substance abuse in sports, and the value of sports for all children, including those with chronic illness or a disabling condition. The warm, sympathetic tone of the text is underscored by an opening chapter with answers to common questions parents ask, personal anecdotes, and a strong message on the importance of character and enjoyment in sports participation. An appendix lists additional resources for parents.

Moore, Carolyn E. *Keys to Children's Nutrition.* Barron's, 1991. 183p. illus. LC 91-308. ISBN 0-8120-4675-7. $5.95.

Moore's concise encyclopedia guides parents in understanding basic nutrition concepts and food components, planning their children's diet and buying foods, avoiding diet-related health problems, and coping with a variety of special circumstances, such as eating in fast-food restaurants, planning meals for an ill child or one who is involved in sports, and eating disorders. The book provides authoritative information from nutrition professionals. The "key" format of brief chapters makes the material easily accessible for browsing and for reading in short segments. Basic information on growth and food groups is provided, requirements of the school breakfast and lunch programs reviewed, and the safety of supplements, additives, and substitutes considered. Appendixes give helpful tips on reducing fat and sugar and increasing fiber in recipes.

Nursing Mother's Council of the Boston Association for Childbirth Education. *Breastfeeding Your Baby.* 3rd ed. Avery, 1991. 96p. bibliog. photog. illus. index. LC 89-387. ISBN 0-89529-387-0. $3.95.

Detailed step-by-step instructions on preparing to breastfeed; learning about basic nursing skills and normal feeding behavior; avoiding common problems, such as engorgement and sore nipples; managing nutrition and diet; and weaning and solid foods are given in this guide. The text also addresses special circumstances that affect breastfeeding, including nursing after a cesarean birth, premature delivery, multiple births, and work and nursing. While the treatment is brief, there is careful attention to detail; in the discussion of diet, vegetarian diets are covered, and the chapter on breastfeeding after a ce-

sarean birth includes a section on breastfeeding after a repeat cesarean. An index allows easy access to the material covered, and drawings and photos illustrate techniques. A list of additional readings, support organizations, sources of breastfeeding aids, and a bibliography supplement the data provided in the text.

* Satter, Elly. *Child of Mine: Feeding with Love and Good Sense.* Bull, 1991. 463p. bibliog. index. LC 91-3632. ISBN 0-923521-14-3. $14.95.

The social, physical, and psychological aspects of feeding and the basics of a wholesome diet are the focus of this nutrition manual for parents with children up to three years of age. The material, presented in a clear, reassuring manner, is enlivened by personal confidences from the author, a registered dietician, and case histories from her clients. The history of infant feeding is briefly summarized, and calories and normal growth, breastfeeding, the introduction of solid foods, feeding toddlers, regulation of food intake and weight, obesity, the feeding relationship of parent and child, and eating disorders are explored in a folksy manner backed up by scientific references and professional expertise.

Schwarzenegger, Arnold. *Arnold's Fitness for Kids Ages Six to Ten.* Doubleday, 1993. 121p. bibliog. photog. illus. LC 92-28577. ISBN 0-385-42267-9. $15.00.

This workbook, designed for use by parents with their school-age children, attempts to make fitness fun for both groups. Appealing photos of Arnold instructing and exercising with children, as well as homespun tales of Arnold as a youth in Austria, accompany practical advice for making fitness part of family life. Other topics discussed include eating smart, getting the most from school fitness programs and fitness camps, organized sports, and community programs. The remaining chapters address the basics of aerobics, flexibility, strength, and muscular endurance, with specific exercises illustrated for each.

Sears, William, and Martha Sears. *Keys to Breastfeeding.* Barron's, 1991. 172p. illus. index. LC 90-20688. ISBN 0-8120-4540-8. $5.95.

Many years devoted to counseling breastfeeding mothers, personal experience as a couple in which the woman breastfeeds her child, and enthusiasm guide popular parenting authors William and Martha Sears in compiling this brief source of practical advice on the whys and hows of breastfeeding. In very short topical chapters, accessible via an index, the authors present information on preparing to breastfeed; breastfeeding advantages for the mother as well as for the baby; breastfeeding the premature, ill, adopted, or cesarean baby; avoiding or treating problems such as engorgement, sore nipples, and breast infections; determining whether the baby is getting enough milk; increasing the milk supply; and many other matters of concern to the nursing mother. This practical how-to manual uses drawings to illustrate breastfeeding positions.

Watson, Susan. *Sugar-Free Toddlers: 125 Sugarless Recipes Plus Sugar Rating for Hundreds of Store-Bought Products.* Williamson, 1991. 170p. index. LC 91-19860. ISBN 0-913587-57-8. $10.95.

Because toddlers consume such a small amount of food, much of it in the form of snacks, what they eat must have high nutritional content without the empty calories that refined sugar provides. The author, whose credentials are not given, offers more than 100 recipes for naturally sweetened foods that also appeal to toddler tastes and are convenient to prepare and use. Artificial sweeteners and high-caloric sugar substitutes such as molasses, brown sugar, honey, and maple syrup are also eliminated from the recipes for main courses, beverages, snacks, breads, desserts, and sauces compiled here. The sugar content of many commonly available foods is also supplied. As the author attests, the recipes appear adaptable to adult tastes. In light of warnings about the prevalence of salmonella bacteria in poultry products, the use of a raw egg in eggnog is questionable.

Woessner, Candace, Judith Lauwers, and Barbara Bernard. *Breastfeeding Today: A Mother's Companion.* 2nd ed. Avery, 1991. 238p. LC 91-15434. ISBN 0-89529-469-9. $9.95.

Written for the contemporary woman who is an informed consumer well read on matters of health care, this detailed and practical handbook on how to breastfeed also provides current information on the advantages of breastfeeding, nutrition, and how to cope with postpartum adjustment, as well as advice on feeding one's baby outside the home. Techniques for working mothers and mothers of twins, premature babies, or babies delivered by cesarean section are also covered. In the revised edition of a popular guide, the authors advise mothers on how to plan and establish a breastfeeding pattern, ways to overcome temporary obstacles such as engorgement and nipple soreness, family adjustment, and sources of additional support to make the breastfeeding experience a rewarding as well as healthy one for both mother and child. Each chapter concludes with a summary that may be used as a ready-reference. Appendixes list sources of breastfeeding aids and resource groups for mothers.

POPULAR TITLES: JOURNALS

New Beginnings. La Leche League International. 1958. B-M. ISSN 8756-9981. $15.00.

Available as a benefit of membership in La Leche League International (LLLI), this newsletter includes practical information, personal accounts, poems, and commentaries on breastfeeding for parents of nursing infants. Information about new publications, advice on balancing breastfeeding with other activities, and news about LLLI are also included in this helpful publication.

PROFESSIONAL TITLES: BOOKS

Duff, John F. *Youth Sports Injuries: A Medical Handbook for Parents and Coaches.* Macmillan, 1992. 366p. illus. index. LC 91-37789. ISBN 0-02-013691-9. $12.00.

Introductory material on the safety of sports, how to determine whether a child should participate in organized sports, what organized sports are all about, and participation for the young athlete with a disability is provided in the first section of this handbook. How to reduce the risk of injuries through a pre-sports exam, proper nutrition, and safety factors is reviewed, as are how to recognize and treat injuries at home and how to obtain good care by coaches and medical personnel. The long-term consequences of an injury, including its psychological impact, are also covered. The second half of the text covers sports injuries, including a brief explanation of how they occur, anatomy of the injured body part, injury evaluation and causes, prevention, and treatment of specific injuries. The appendixes contain resource material such as definitions of locker room jargon and lists of professional associations.

Endres, Jeanette, and Robert Rockwell. *Food, Nutrition and the Young Child.* 4th ed. Merrill, 1994. 376p. bibliog. photog. index. LC 93-25602. ISBN 0-02-333721-4. Price not set.

Now in its fourth edition, this text provides up-to-date information on food and nutrition for children from birth to age eight who are cared for in home day care, preschool, or full-day day care facilities. What foods to give children, when to provide them, how to encourage nutritious eating, food and nutrition problems common to each age group, and strategies for involving parents are among the topics covered in this easy-to-read textbook suitable for parents as well as child care providers. Among the subjects new to this edition are the Food Guide Pyramid and its application to diet planning for various age groups, expanded information on the benefits to mother and child of breastfeeding, identifying children at risk of developing nutrition problems, successful ethnic menus, and low-fat diets for children. The text is supplemented by discussion questions, numerous references, and several appendixes providing sample feeding charts and parent report forms; agendas for planning, conducting, and evaluating a family workshop; a sample letter to parents; and a listing of the nutritive values of edible parts of foods.

La Leche League. *The Lactation Consultant's Topical Review and Bibliography of the Literature on Breastfeeding.* La Leche League International, 1990. 188p. LC 90-61943. ISBN 0-912500-39-5. $25.95.

Lactation consultants and other health practitioners working with breastfeeding women are the audience for this bibliography and guide to scholarly books and articles on all aspects of lactation. Organized into 45 chapters, the information covered includes citations on anatomy of the breast, physiology of lactation, and biochemistry and immunology of human milk; prenatal preparations and first breastfeedings; course of lactation and common problems; breastfeeding infants with birth defects; relactation and induced lactation; the effects of breast cancer and other illnesses on breastfeeding; and breast pumps and techniques. Each chapter begins with a brief abstract of important issues, learning goals, a study guide useful for lactation consultants preparing to take the International Board of Lactation Consultants Examiners' certification exam, and, in some cases, a list of materials appropriate for use by clients. The chapter concludes with references to related information in other sections. Most of the sections were compiled between 1985 and 1987, but some were updated through 1989, and older citations are included when they are still authoritative. The most important materials are marked with an asterisk.

Concluding chapters cover the research process, ethical considerations of research, statistical analysis, and how to evaluate research studies.

Livshitz, Fima, Nancy Moses, and Jere Ziffor Livshitz. *Children's Nutrition.* Jones and Bartlett, 1991. 591p. illus. index. LC 91-7011. ISBN 0-86720-186-X. $50.00.

A pediatrician, a nurse, and a registered dietician wrote this comprehensive handbook for health care professionals, but the writing style is appropriate for a lay audience as well. Nutrition and diet from conception through adolescence are covered, and many diagrams, tables, and footnotes supplement the text. The nutritional requirements of the pregnant woman, nausea and vomiting, teen pregnancy, water retention, and effects of alcohol, caffeine, and dietetic foods are described. The authors also address how to measure children's nutritional status, nutritional needs of normal infants, breastfeeding, children and adolescents, and low birth weight babies. The nutritional needs of children with specific health problems, such as obesity, cancer, food allergies, and failure to thrive, are reviewed. The final section covers enteral, parenteral, and home nutrition therapy as well as the ethics of nutritional support.

McLaren, Donald S., ed. *Textbook of Pediatric Nutrition.* Churchill Livingstone, 1991. 616p. bibliog. photog. illus. index. LC 90-2680. ISBN 0-443-04090-7. $95.00.

This scholarly nutrition textbook is a resource for health practitioners. The first section covers the relationship between nutrition and development from conception to adolescence. Clinical manifestations of nutritional disorders such as low birth weight infants, food allergies, diabetes, renal disease, vitamin deficiency and toxicity, and obesity, are detailed in the second and fourth sections, while the third section examines nutritional support through enteral and parenteral feeding. The final section looks at pediatric nutrition from a community perspective, examining the nutritional status of all the world's children, the influence of childhood diet on adult disease, and the integration of nutritional assessment in primary care. A substantial number of references, diagrams, charts, and photographs further inform the reader.

Rowland, Thomas W. *Exercise and Children's Health.* Human Kinetics, 1990. 356p. bibliog. photog. illus. index. LC 89-71708. ISBN 0-87322-282-2. $22.95.

Rowland, physician and editor of *Pediatric Exercise Science,* advocates greater pediatrician responsibility for their patients' fitness because of widespread concern about the fitness of American children; development of new sports medicine concerned with diet, assessment, and injury prevention as well as treatment; replacement of free play by organized sports; emergence of the elite prepubertal athlete; and application of exercise as a therapeutic modality. The book is organized to provide basic information on development and children's response to exercise, the scientific basis for exercise as a way to improve and maintain health, and specific techniques for increasing physical activity in children. Patient guidelines for exercises such as walking, running, and swimming are covered in the appendix.

Sullivan, Andy, J., ed. *The Pediatric Athlete.* American Academy of Orthopedic Surgeons, 1990. 266p. bibliog. photog. index. LC 90-080002. ISBN 0-8920-3033-X. $19.00.

The text is based on the curriculum of a seminar on youth sports organized by the American Academy of Orthopaedic Surgeons in 1988 to review current research on pediatric athletics and reach consensus on issues in areas where the research literature is scant. Contributors review conditioning and its role in training, nutritional requirements, weight control and supplements, and participation in sports by children with chronic illness. Psychological considerations, overuse syndromes, rehabilitation, musculoskeletal injuries, and protective equipment are also examined.

PROFESSIONAL TITLES: JOURNALS

Journal of Human Lactation. Human Sciences. 1984. Q. ISSN 0890-3344. $90.00.

Information on breastfeeding is presented in a variety of formats in this official publication of the International Lactation Consultant Association. Original research, case studies, and critical reviews on issues related to human lactation, breastfeeding behavior, services to nursing mothers and their children, and management of the business aspects of lactation consulting are published. Issues have addressed such topics as inactivation of HIV Type I virus in human milk, support for the father of a breastfeeding infant, application for provider status with insurance companies, and anti-infectives in breast milk. Book and video reviews and brief annotations are also published.

Journal of Pediatric & Perinatal Nutrition. Haworth. 1987. S-A. ISSN 8756-6206. $45.00.

Information to guide the nutritional management of children receiving medical care is provided in this refereed journal. Articles address normal as well as therapeutic needs.

Journal of Pediatric Gastroenterology & Nutrition. Raven. 1982. 8/yr. ISSN 0277-2116. $150.00.

This journal is the official publication of the North American Society for Pediatric Gastroenterology and Nutrition and the European Society of Pediatric Gastroenterology and Nutrition. The publication focuses on reporting on nutritional issues in general and the results of original research on topics related to normal and abnormal functioning of the digestive system and its organs, molecular or cellular studies of the gastrointestinal tract, and clinical studies that examine diseases and their treatment. Review articles and short communications are also published.

Leaven. La Leche League International. 1984. B-M. ISSN 8750-2011. $15.00.

Leaven is a bimonthly newsletter published for La Leche League International support group leaders, trained volunteers who have breastfed their own babies. Information helpful to organizing and conducting support group activities, news from the league, a calendar of local conferences, and up-to-date health care data are included.

Pediatric Exercise Science. Human Kinetics. 1989. Q. ISSN 0899-8493. $36.00.

> Original research, review articles, excerpts, book reviews, and editorials address the effects and importance of exercise in children and adolescents in this multidisciplinary journal. The role of exercise in the treatment of chronic disease, prevention of illness, and sports safety are major concerns of this title.

Scholastic Coach. Scholastic. 1931. M. ISSN 0036-6382. $23.95.

> Practical articles on drills, techniques, and conditioning for basketball, track, baseball, soccer, volleyball, football, and hockey are published in this magazine for high school and college coaches and athletic directors. Communication, psychological dimensions, and ethical issues are also covered, as is news on conferences, new products, and books. Interviews, humor, and information specific to women's participation in organized sports are also included.

DIRECTORY

Direction Sports, Inc.
600 Wilshire Boulevard, Suite 320, Los Angeles, CA 90017-3215
(213) 627-9861 Fax (213) 627-7704
Tulley N. Brown, Executive Director
Founded: 1968
Members: 500
Affiliates: 5 state groups, 3 local groups
Mission/Goals: To provide an athletic program designed specifically to serve the educational and attitudinal needs of youth; to improve learning skills, self-concept, and motivation to learn; to prevent recidivism; to employ community teenagers and college youth to discuss issues and supervise team sports in programs that also include discussions with psychologists
Staff: 3 professionals, 42 nonprofessionals, 7 volunteers
Funding: Local government, private sources, fees for products or services, donations, grants
Services: Counseling, recreation
Awards: Free week at Catalina Island Camp for all summer graduates
Education and Outreach: In-service programs, continuing education courses, seminars, publishing
Publications: *Direction Sports,* semiannual newsletter; audiovisuals and clips from local and network television
Programs: Semiannual meeting, with training seminars

The Human Lactation Center, Ltd.
666 Sturges Highway, Westport, CT 06880
(203) 259-5995 Fax (203) 259-7667
Dana Raphael, Ph.D., Director
Founded: 1975
Mission/Goals: To promote international research and education on human lactation and child abuse
Audience/Clientele: Health professionals, nutritionists, lactation consultants, nursing mothers

Funding: Federal government, private sources, fees for services or products, donations
Education and Outreach: Research, museum, library, publishing
Publications: *The Lactation Review,* periodic; pamphlets
Programs: 3 conferences per year

International Lactation Consultant Association
201 Brown Avenue, Evanston, IL 60202-3601
(708) 260-8874
Linda Kutner, President
Founded: 1985
Members: 2,500
Affiliates: 33 regional groups
Mission/Goals: To provide a means of communication and networking between lactation consultants and lactation consultant organizations around the world; to provide support and education for lactation consultants and other health workers interested in breastfeeding and lactation; to support and encourage the development of high standards of ethical practice, promote certification, stimulate research, and create an understanding of breastfeeding as an important preventive health measure; to work toward the worldwide implementation of the International Code of Marketing Breast Milk Substitutes, as interpreted by the World Health Assembly
Audience/Clientele: Lactation consultants and others interested in human lactation and breastfeeding
Staff: 12 members of board of directors
Funding: Fund-raising, dues
Services: Counseling, support group, lactation consulting
Awards: Cecily Williams Award to deserving international person who has done much to support breastfeeding in his or her country
Education and Outreach: In-service programs, continuing education courses, seminars, publishing
Publications: *Journal of Human Lactation,* quarterly; *ILCA Membership Directory,* annual; *Annual Syllabus of Conference*
Programs: Annual conference

La Leche League International (LLLI)
P.O. Box 1209, Franklin Park, IL 60131-8209
(708) 455-7730 Fax (708) 455-0125 Hotline (800) LA-LECHE
Mary Lawrence, Executive Director
Founded: 1956
Members: 40,000
Mission/Goals: To provide nursing mothers with practical information and moral support on breastfeeding; to aid individuals interested in establishing breastfeeding resource centers in areas without leaders or groups
Audience/Clientele: Breastfeeding mothers and families, health care providers
Staff: 20 professionals, 24 nonprofessionals
Budget: $30,000 Funding: Federal government, private sources, fund-raising, fees for services or products, donations, grants, dues

Services: Counseling, support group, networking
Education and Outreach: Continuing education courses, seminars, library, archives, database development, accreditation reviews, publishing
Publications: *New Beginnings*, bimonthly magazine with inspirational stories, practical hints, book reviews, and breastfeeding information; *Womanly Art of Breastfeeding*; 20 other books; 200 information sheets and pamphlets; *La Leche League Directory*, annual; *Breastfeeding Abstracts*, quarterly; *Leaven*, bimonthly
Programs: Seminars on Breastfeeding for Physicians, annual; Lactation Specialists Workshops, several annually

REFERENCES

1. Alan S. Ryan et al., "A Comparison of Breast-feeding Data from the National Surveys of Family Growth and the Ross Laboratories Mothers Surveys," *American Journal of Public Health* 81, no. 8 (August 1991): 1050.

2. Christine Berman and Jacki Fromer, *Meals without Squeals: Child Care Feeding Guide and Cookbook* (Palo Alto, CA: Bull, 1991), 4.

3. *Health Promotion and Disease Prevention: United States, 1990*. Vital and Health Statistics, Series 10: Data from the National Health Survey, no. 185. U.S. Department of Health and Human Services, National Center for Health Statistics, 1993, 40.

4. *National Federation Handbook, 1992–93* (Kansas City, MO: National Federation of State High School Associations, 1992), 54.

PART

5

THE PARENTS'
RESPONSIBILITIES

CHAPTER

Discipline and Guidance

*Because I'm the parent and making decisions of this
sort is my responsibility: Son of "Because I said so."*
John K. Rosemond. *Parent Power!*

Forming families is serious business.
Marian Wright Edelman. *The Measure of Our Success*

Bringing up children—guiding their moral, intellectual,
emotional, and social development—is the focus of discipline. Despite the difficulties they may have in setting
limits, guiding behavior, and punishing misbehavior, most
parents believe that they are doing a good job at these
tasks. According to a recent Gallup poll, 54 percent of
parents surveyed gave themselves a B, while 31 percent
considered their efforts at discipline to be worthy of an
A. When it comes to strictness, again most parents (62
percent) are satisfied with how strict they are with their
own children; however, a great majority (81 percent) think
other parents are not strict enough.[1] While John Bradshaw
considers not setting limits to be abusive,[2] and many authors consider the need to punish a child to be evidence
that disciplinary techniques have failed, others focus on
discipline, especially spanking, as punishment. Nearly half,
or 40 percent, of the parents responding to a *Better Homes
and Gardens* survey sometimes spanked their children,
compared to 44 percent who rarely did, and only 12 percent who never spanked their children.[3]

An asterisk (*) indicates specially recommended titles.

POPULAR TITLES: BOOKS

* Arent, Ruth P. *Parenting Children in Unstable Times.* Fulcrum,
1993. 336p. bibliog. index. LC 93-23064. ISBN 1-55591-132-
3. $14.95.

Unstable environments are as commonplace as the disruption
that a second child brings to a tranquil family, as probable as
divorce or relocating, or as dramatic as illness, abuse, and unemployment. In this empathetic sourcebook, the author, a child
development specialist and social worker, gives advice on 72
potentially disruptive situations that enables parents to carry
out effectively their roles as family managers by achieving mutual respect, healthy self-esteem, and stability. This insightful
text is a particularly reassuring guide for parents facing such
crises as unemployment, chronic illness, learning disabilities,
or physical rehabilitation.

Balter, Lawrence, with Peggy Jo Donahue. *Not in Front of the
Children: Helping Your Child Handle Tough Family Matters.* Viking, 1993. 223p. index. LC 92-50400. ISBN 0-670-84110-
2. $20.00.

Most parents are concerned about finding ways to discuss tough
topics like sex, death, or divorce without harming their children. In this handbook by a psychologist and columnist for
Ladies' Home Journal, parents learn about practical techniques,
or "new moves," that will help them address such anxiety-
producing situations as arguing, nudity, serious illness, divorce,
substance abuse, or job loss. The discussion of each topic describes the child at various developmental stages, common
mistakes made by parents, and recommended approaches for
handling various problems. Factors that affect the parents' perspectives, such as memories of their own childhood and the
impact of the child's temperament and normal developmental
capabilities, are also explored.

Craig, Judi. *Little Kids, Big Questions: Practical Answers to the
Difficult Questions Children Ask about Life.* Hearst, 1993. Good

Housekeeping Parent Guide Series. 204p. bibliog. index. LC 92-36928. ISBN 0-688-11933-6. $12.00.

The author of this second installment in a new series from *Good Housekeeping* emphasizes communication style, approach, and attitude in discussing sensitive or controversial issues such as violence, prejudice, sickness, divorce, addictions, or disaster. Other topics addressed are friendship, love, sex, ethics, and spirituality. Each chapter provides an overview of a single topic, followed by typical questions kids ask and appropriate answers, concluding with additional suggestions for responding to a child's concerns. The author, a San Antonio psychologist, differentiates between answers for young children as opposed to answers for those who are old enough to know something about the issue.

Crary, Elizabeth. *Without Spanking or Spoiling.* 2nd ed. Parenting Press, 1993. 126p. LC 92-85497. ISBN 0-943990-87-4. $19.95. ISBN 0-943990-74-2 pbk. $12.95.

Elizabeth Crary, a prolific author of books about parenting, gives in this handbook a formal, rather formidable method for setting limits on children's behavior. She acknowledges the impact that developmental level, temperament, environmental factors, and parents' expectations have on toddlers' and preschoolers' behavior. She also covers steps in problem solving, how to avoid problems, increasing appropriate and decreasing inappropriate behavior, and teaching new behaviors through exercises and examples. The techniques recommended by the author are based on parent effectiveness techniques, behavior modification, transactional analysis, and Adlerian-Dreikurs psychology.

Cutright, Melitta. *Growing Up Confident: How to Make Your Child's Early Years Learning Years.* Doubleday, 1992. 224p. LC 91-23964. ISBN 0-385-41589-3. $20.00. ISBN 0-385-41590-7 pbk. $12.00.

The author, a former officer of the national PTA, advises parents on teaching preschool children in the home. Linking children's curiosity and confidence in learning to their sense of self-esteem rather than to formal instruction, the author explores how parents can ensure that their children get the proper stimulation, affection, and skills to prepare them for lifelong learning. The text emphasizes the importance of talking, reading, and playing with children; outlines what to expect from quality day care; reviews preschool options and controversies; and advocates better conditions for all children. To stimulate their curiosity and encourage a sense of mastery, Cutright recommends teaching children through activities they enjoy, such as nature walks, art, music, dance, and fantasy play. Acknowledging the importance of self-esteem in a child's ability to learn is an important lesson well presented to parents who are concerned with development rather than achievement in their preschool-age children.

Dumas, Lynne S. *Talking with Your Child about a Troubled World.* Fawcett Columbine, 1992. 335p. bibliog. LC 91-72952. ISBN 0-449-90623-X. $18.00.

The combined wisdom of 120 pediatricians, child psychiatrists, psychologists, and educators on how to present troubling issues to children is compiled in this concise handbook for par-

ents. Written by a former teacher, the text will serve as a resource for parents who must discuss sensitive issues such as AIDS, homelessness, racism and prejudice, drugs and alcohol, cancer, sexual abuse, natural disaster, and job loss with children whom they may consider too young to understand these adult problems. Each chapter opens with a case history in which a topic is introduced, followed by a summary of facts and figures, specific advice on discussing the issue with children, sample questions and answers, helpful resources available, and reading lists for both parents and children. The first chapter is a guide to structuring discussions with children, including how to listen to children, understanding the child's ability to understand, and rules of thumb, such as creating an open living environment, respecting feelings, being honest, and establishing good eye contact—all of which improve the quality of a discussion.

* Edelman, Marian Wright. *The Measure of Our Success: A Letter to My Children and Yours.* Beacon, 1992. 97p. LC 91-42743. ISBN 0-8070-3102-X. $15.00. LC 95-54846. ISBN 0-06-097546-6 pbk. $9.00.

A brief set of essays from Edelman, founder and president of the Children's Defense Fund, this collection is both a gift to parents, in the form of 25 principles by which to raise their children, and an eloquent exhortation to them to extend this love and nurturing to all of America's young. Born and raised in the segregated South by a family who stressed education, service, and, above all, never giving up, Edelman translates her upbringing into advice such as taking parenting and family life seriously, not being afraid of hard work, choosing friends carefully, remembering one's roots, and being confident that one person can make a difference. A preface by her second son Jonah emphasizes that these principles are helpful ones to live by and introduces three autobiographical sections on Edelman's childhood, her parents' legacy to her, and her own letter to her sons.

Eyre, Linda, and Richard Eyre. *Teaching Children Values.* Fireside, 1993. 256p. index. LC 92-39038. ISBN 0-671-76966-9. $11.00.

A firm philosophical base underlies the age-specific methods given here for teaching values to children. Linda and Richard Eyre are the authors of such popular texts as *Teaching Children Joy* (Ballantine, 1986) and hosts of the cable program *Families Are Forever!* In this book they give a warm, noncynical approach to each of 12 values presented by using anecdotes involving their own children, giving general guidelines, and describing methods that work for preschoolers, school-age children, and adolescents. Among the values covered are honesty, courage, peacefulness, self-discipline, and fidelity—all values of being. Values of giving that the authors explore are love, respect, kindness, justice, and loyalty.

* Feiden, Karyn. *Parents' Guide to Raising Responsible Kids: Preschool through Teen Years.* Prentice Hall, 1991. 216p. LC 90-47778. ISBN 0-13-650813-8. $9.95.

Written in a cool, readable style that combines empathy and information, this text from the Children's Television Workshop Family Living Series, with an introduction by Bill Cosby, reviews what constitutes responsibility and the parents' role in developing it. To help children develop a strong sense of empathy, internalized notions of right and wrong, good judgment, awareness of consequences, and willingness to contribute their fair share, parents are advised to model, foster independence, build self-esteem, and set reasonable limits. The book also provides facts and strategies for helping parents address problems in day-to-day interaction, friendships and peer groups, school, and the world at large, in addition to more general advice on instilling values that will endure.

Field, Doug. *Too Old, Too Soon.* Harvest House, 1991. 238p. LC 90-23651. ISBN 0-89081-848-7. $7.95.

The author, a Christian youth minister, explores the sources of pressure on children to act like adolescents and adolescents to act like adults by living up to parents' expectations and external messages regarding money, appearances, substance abuse, and sexual relations. He provides specific, commonsense advice on handling each problem in a positive way; for example, to reduce the negative impact that TV has, he suggests tallying the positive and negative messages heard during viewing, limiting viewing, discussing programs, banning TV, and complaining to the FCC. The final portion of the text addresses five principles that can alleviate pressure on children and improve the quality of parenting: modeling, encouragement, humor, positive memories, and unconditional love. Backed by a solid review of the literature, this handbook gives a balanced view of parenting and offers helpful insights, practical advice, and much support for parents seeking to understand, nurture, protect, and encourage their children in preparation for life in the world today.

Freedman, Marc. *The Kindness of Strangers: Adult Mentors, Urban Youth, and the New Volunteerism.* Jossey-Bass, 1993. 162p. bibliog. index. LC 93-1676. ISBN 1-55542-557-7. $24.95.

This unusual text tells the story of concerned adults who mentor disadvantaged youth one-on-one in a variety of programs throughout the United States. Every chapter concludes with an account by mentors of what their efforts mean, bringing home the reality that each youth faces on a daily basis. Among the issues covered are the history of mentoring, its mythology, its value and limitations, and how to close the gap between motivation and action and encourage the involvement of the middle class in the lives of urban youth.

Golant, Susan K., and Mitch Golant. *Getting Through to Your Kids.* Lowell House, 1991. 180p. LC 91-20356. ISBN 0-929923-47-2. $19.95.

Intended as a practical guide to achieving peace in the family, this text examines obstacles to communication between parents and their children, how to resolve conflicts in particularly difficult situations, and communication tools that assure that each family member is heard. Among the obstacles to communication the Golants, a psychologist and a writer, examine are limitations in the development of children, variations in personality and thinking styles, and attempts to control children's behavior rather than their emotions. Difficult situations, such as power struggles, temper tantrums, bedtime battles, and sibling fights, require the use of effective communication skills. The authors recommend establishing trust, using logical consequences, developing cooperativeness, and communicating through play and humor.

Greven, Philip J. *Spare the Child: The Religious Roots of Punishment and the Psychological Impact of Physical Abuse.* Knopf, 1990. 263p. LC 90-53171. ISBN 0-394-57860-0. $22.45.

Because of the negative psychological consequences of physical punishment in childhood, the author advocates a new commitment to nonviolent punishment in the next generation of parents. He traces the religious roots of physical punishment in the proverbs of the Old Testament, the fear of eternal damnation, a perceived need to break the child's will, and final salvation during the apocalypse but notes the absence of any injunction from Jesus to punish or beat children. Punishment's secular roots in the court, education, and behaviorism are also examined, and the myriad of psychological consequences of punishment, such as anxiety, fear, depression, anger, dissociation, sadomasochism, and domestic and societal violence are thoroughly reviewed. The author's plea for nonviolence, especially directed to those moderates who use physical punishment as a last resort, is a logical conclusion to this detailed and disturbing treatise.

Hausner, Lee. *Children of Paradise: A Nine-Step Program for Successful Parenting in Affluent Families.* Tarcher, 1990. 279p. LC 90-40676. ISBN 0-87477-591-4. $18.95.

Drawing on years of experience as a psychologist in the Beverly Hills school system, Hausner reaffirms the love that affluent or celebrity parents have for their children but also outlines in some detail how qualities that can bring career success are detrimental to a happy family life and the development of competent children with high self-esteem. Her solution, a nine-point plan that directly addresses improving self-esteem and encouraging self-motivation, spending as much time together as possible, improving communication skills, disciplining through consequences, and handling money issues, is practical advice, thoughtfully presented. While only affluent families may have to deal with the effects of taking money for granted, the impact of not making family time a priority and the consequences of unreasonable expectations are issues that parents in all economic situations must deal with. References and a reading list for parents are included.

* Kitzinger, Sheila, and Celia Kitzinger. *Tough Questions: Talking Straight with Your Kids about the Real World.* Harvard Common, 1991. 303p. LC 90-27149. ISBN 1-55832-033-4. $19.95. ISBN 1-55832-032-6 pbk. $12.95.

Trying to raise children by following often complicated, contradictory instructions in how-to books is like using multiple cookbooks to make a souffle, according to this mother and daughter team. In a well-researched and well-written text, the Kitzingers explore the values that mothers hold most important in their lives, how they communicate these values in practice, and where they succeed and fail. By encouraging children's questions on such difficult topics as sex and birth, death, religion, politics and prejudice, and aggression and violence, mothers can share their values and prepare children for life by preparing them to face and deal with reality. Drawing from the results of a survey in a popular British parenting magazine, interviewees' memories of childhood experiences, and cross-cultural studies, the authors also address communicating values about such parental concerns as good behavior, obedience and autonomy, lies and secrets, and friends.

Leach, Penelope. *Children First: What Our Society Must Do—and Is Not Doing—for Our Children Today.* Knopf, 1994. 303p. bibliog. index. LC 93-35476. ISBN 0-679-42133-5. $22.00.

Prominent parenting author Leach (*Your Baby and Child: From Birth to Age Five* and *Babyhood: Infant Development from Birth to Two Years*) broadens her scope from relationships in the individual family to the impact of economic and social policies on our nation's children in her latest work. More an advocate's manifesto than a parenting guide, the text explores which modern trends are harmful to children, how they influence practice and policy in ways contradictory to known parent and child needs, and practical approaches for doing better. In the first part, Leach looks at the impact of work on family life, and, in the second, she examines the influence of gender differences on parenting, the transition to parenthood, day care choices, child development and discipline, and the unrecognized importance of the latency period between ages 6 and 12. The final section presents solutions for putting children first, both at the societal level of human rights and poverty and at the family level of adequate parenting education.

Leman, Kevin. *Keeping Your Family Together When the World Is Falling Apart.* Delacorte, 1992. 336p. LC 91-24479. ISBN 0-385-29944-3. $18.00.

Marriage counselor and prolific author (*Making Children Mind without Losing Yours, The Birth Order Book, Smart Kids, Stupid Choices,* and many others) advocates the use of "reality discipline" to keep a marriage and family intact in this homespun guide to family life. As a consistent, decisive, and respectful way to relate to family members, reality discipline is based on letting children face the consequences of their actions. Seven principles, adapted to the age, development, and ability of each child, guide the practice of this approach: recognizing that the whole is more important than its parts, having values and living by them, putting one's spouse first, balancing responsibility with forgiveness and love, sticking to one's guns, keeping responsibility where it belongs, and treating people like people, not things. Using a cheerful, humorous tone and nontechnical language, Leman focuses on understanding worldly conditions that make an active and thoughtful approach essential, "saving" the marriage, and enabling children to learn responsibility.

Levine, Katherine Gordy. *When Good Kids Do Bad Things: A Survival Guide for Parents.* Norton, 1991. 267p. index. LC 91-8580. ISBN 0-393-03019-9. $19.95.

Avoiding dogmatic recitation of family values and punishments for unacceptable behavior in favor of caring and interventions, the author, a social worker and former foster parent, outlines how to correct bad behaviors in preadolescents and teens ages 10 to 16. Much of her basically sound advice on how to handle confrontations over attire, friendships, academic problems, substance abuse, risk taking, lying, running away, or sexual liaisons involves changing the parents' perspective as well as the child's behavior. The author defines the caring response as

acting promptly to confront unwanted behavior, understand it, consider options, and negotiate a solution, sustaining throughout a loving relationship. She advocates using the caring intervention after several attempts to modify the child's behavior have been unsuccessful. Readable and realistic, this practical text gives parents an essentially assertive approach to use in restricting unexpected and unpleasant behavior. A section on clues to genuine psychopathology as opposed to defiance or poor judgment will help parents determine when to seek outside assistance for their offspring.

Light, Lynn. *Raising Sexually Healthy Children: A Loving Guide for Parents, Teachers, and Care-givers.* Avon, 1988. 284p. illus. index. LC 87-42794. ISBN 0-380-70857-4. $10.00.

Light advises parents to reinforce the values that express their beliefs and improve their communication skills in order to guide children's sexual development from the first moments after birth through adolescence. She provides a 75-item questionnaire on sexuality to help parents determine just what their values are. The text covers bonding, self-esteem, and communicating emotions with an infant, guidelines for healthy touch, preschool sexual dilemmas such as nudity and toilet training, and struggles to define sexual identity and adjust to physical changes such as menstruation in adolescence. Issues in friendship, love, sexual intercourse, and virginity are explored, as are harmful elements of sexuality, including AIDS, sexual abuse, and the impact of divorce on sexual identity.

Lindsay, Jeanne Warren, and Sally McCullough. *Teens Parenting: Discipline from Birth to Three.* Morning Glory Press, 1991. 192p. ISBN 0-93934-54-7. $9.95.

Teaching self-control rather than attempting to control through punishment is the focus of this practical guide to discipline written for teenage parents. The author looks at discipline strategies and concerns important at various developmental stages, such as crying and thumb sucking in the first weeks of life, crawling and eating solid food, walking and exploring, and toilet training. There is also advice on coping with stress, relating to each other, avoiding child abuse with help, and effective sharing of discipline with grandparents. With quotations and case material, the text speaks directly to parents' feelings of frustration as they deal with active toddlers who have not developed the ability to remember instructions from day to day.

Rubin, Theodore Isaac. *Child Potential: Fulfilling Your Child's Intellectual, Emotional, and Creative Promise.* Continuum, 1990. 299p. LC 90-38666. ISBN 0-8264-0489-8. $17.95.

Viewing an "enabler" as a strong, resourceful person who maintains an unshakable sense of self in the process of guiding a child's self-realization, Rubin outlines the dos and don'ts of motivating healthy children to fulfill their intellectual, emotional, and creative potential. In doing so, he defines these concepts, as well as the notion of self-esteem, and explores the assets and liabilities that parents may encourage in their children, the damages that parents may inflict through insensitivity or ignorance, and the techniques parents can use to avoid, minimize, or undo these damages. Constructive forces and inner resources such as curiosity, respect for differences, sense of humor, integrity, and long attention span are assets that parents may encourage in their children; poor self-esteem, hostility, stinginess, self-effacement, addiction, and overwhelming materialism are liabilities that detract from quality of life. Damaging actions such as silence, verbal abuse, overprotection, favoritism, and damning with faint praise undermine a child's potential, whereas enablers like stability, communication, appropriate expectations, and expressions of love boost it. This book is the 30th one from the popular psychoanalyst.

Salk, Lee. *Familyhood: Nurturing the Values That Matter.* Simon & Schuster, 1992. 206p. index. LC 92-8195. ISBN 0-671-72936-5. $21.00.

Well-known parenting author and psychologist Lee Salk wrote columns on "You and Your Family" that ran for nearly 20 years in *McCalls.* This text, published posthumously, consists of a series of thoughtful essays on nurturing the family and on the values that strengthen it, such as emotional support, respect, and responsibility. Dr. Salk defines family as a unit ". . . based on the emotional human needs and responsibilities of a group of people who are sharing each other's lives." He draws on the results of a national survey conducted in the late 1980s for Massachusetts Mutual Life Insurance Company and on his experience as a counselor and researcher to support his advice on home time, discipline, day care, grandparents, blended families, family life during times of stress, and related concerns. The warm tone, sage advice, and supportive focus make this thought-provoking guide an appealing and useful contribution to the field.

* Shalov, Jeanette, et al. *You Can Say No to Your Teenager: And Other Strategies for Effective Parenting in the 1990s.* Addison-Wesley, 1991. 224p. LC 90-41388. ISBN 0-201-57002-5. $16.95.

This book advises parents on how to clarify their values and guide their adolescent children in developing their own identities and beliefs, as well as providing advice on discipline. By maintaining limits that express their values, parents learn when to say no and how to enforce that decision with their teenagers, and, equally important, when to say yes to encourage their teens' continued growth. While no particular techniques are prescribed, the text is thought provoking as an approach to living rather than simply solving behavior problems.

Siegler, Ava L. *What Should I Tell the Kids? A Parent's Guide to Real Problems in the Real World.* Dutton, 1993. 324p. index. LC 93-13413. ISBN 0-525-93648-3. $20.00.

Modern life, with its violence, drugs, AIDS, environmental disasters, and other hazards, affords children very little opportunity for youth and innocence. Ways to tell children about the world in which they live, why it is necessary that they be told, and how and when to tell them are covered in this helpful handbook by a *Child* magazine columnist and psychologist. Parents are advised about how to use "plain talk" to become protective parents. They learn how to avoid overexposing their children or underprotecting them, how to talk about tough topics, and how to provide a cushion of safety against common fears. Many sample dialogues serve as models for parental compassion, communication, comprehension, and competence in dealing with the issues of sexuality and love, illness, disease and death, anger and envy, separation and divorce, and tobacco and drugs.

* Smith, Dian G. *Parents' Guide to Raising Kids in a Changing World: Preschool through Teen Years.* Prentice Hall, 1991. 248p. LC 90-47779. ISBN 0-13-650821-9. $9.95.

Taking into account contemporary society in guiding parents to help their children grow and become self-sufficient, Smith reviews children's basic needs and the basic functions of a family. She covers the history of family life in three sections that examine who we were, who we are, and where we are going. Among the important issues examined are functioning in new family structures, judging outside child care, discussing media messages, avoiding crime and personal violence, and building a family network. In addition to reflecting on the antecedents of today's social conditions, Smith emphasizes the evolution of values that guide parents' actions. Additional readings are well integrated into the narrative and are also annotated in lists directed to adults and children.

Somers, Leon, and Barbara C. Somers. *Talking to Your Children about Love and Sex.* New American Library, 1989. 178p. bibliog. illus. index. LC 88-29266. ISBN 0-453-00651-5. $16.95.

This handbook instructs parents about children's sexual development from birth through adolescence and explores the forms that love takes as children mature. The authors advise parents on how to talk comfortably with their children about love, sex, and safety by presenting sample dialogues focusing on the types of questions kids ask at different ages. The first chapter helps parents explore their own sexual beliefs and understand their own sexual history. Subsequent chapters address starting to talk with children by naming body parts, revealing where children come from with young children, reinforcing values with children ages 6 to 8, instructing about bodily changes and guiding emotional development in preteens, and teaching adolescents about sexual decision making, contraception, AIDS, abortion, sexual abuse, rape, and homosexuality. Throughout this guide the authors emphasize building trust and modeling intimacy through the process of teaching children about love and sex.

Strasburger, Victor. *Getting Your Kids to Say "No" in the Nineties When You Said "Yes" in the Sixties: Survival Notes for Baby Boom Parents.* Fireside, 1993. 286p. index. LC 92-38023. $11.00.

Using a familiar tone and a practical approach, the author, a pediatrician specializing in adolescent medicine, presents parents with ideas to consider about how they are parenting their early adolescents and about pitfalls to watch out for in their own behavior as parents. Pitfalls include such problems as panicking, not letting go, failing to respect teenagers' privacy, depriving them of easy symbols of adolescence, and succumbing to pressure from their own peers. The section on the impact of television is particularly good because of its thorough coverage of such specific areas as aggressive behavior, commercialization, stereotyping, sexuality, alcohol and cigarettes, and school performance. Other chapters address sex, drugs, and contemporary stresses; support systems for difficult teens; and parenting in the 1990s.

Weston, Denise Chapman, and Mark S. Weston. *Playful Parenting: Turning the Dilemma of Discipline into Fun and Games.*

Tarcher, 1993. 269p. bibliog. photog. LC 92-44229. ISBN 0-87477-734-8. $14.95.

The authors, who are child and family therapists with specializations in using play as a therapeutic tool, present a method for "putting the fun back into the fundamentals of parenting." They provide techniques and fun ideas as well as activities to help resolve common behavior problems of children. Early chapters review the basics of positive discipline as well as effective contemporary child behavior management techniques such as logical consequences, family council, modeling, ignoring, and the think chair (another name for time-out). A final chapter advises on how to use children's literature to address behavior problems. The bulk of the text provides easy-to-follow "recipes" that define the problem, identify skills and solutions, present mutually accepted goals, illustrate practice and play, and describe how to review and recognize efforts.

Williamson, Peter A. *Good Kids, Bad Behavior: Helping Children Learn Self-Discipline.* Simon & Schuster, 1990. 256p. LC 90-32180. ISBN 0-671-70220-3. $19.95.

Written by a child and adolescent psychologist, this guide helps parents understand the causes of children's misbehavior and accept discipline as a tool to teach self-control and social mastery. Rather than providing a number of practical techniques that may or may not work with the individual child, the author explains how children use misbehavior to learn to regulate themselves, to understand others, and to test the limits of their boundaries, as well as how each child's temperament, cognitive style, and degree of extroversion make him or her unique and provide insights into effective discipline techniques. Williamson explores the value of positive reinforcement, the need for punishment, and ways that parents' attention can encourage or extinguish misbehavior. Theories of child development and approaches to discipline are combined to form a logical and general problem-solving program that encourages parents to use routines to prevent misbehavior and deal with a child who is out of control rather than willfully misbehaving. Finally, the author advises parents on when they need outside help and how to obtain it. Because it does not provide a quick fix to specific problems but rather approaches discipline as a way to teach young people self-control, the book may be viewed as complex, but it provides an essential background for parents to manage daily living as well as to evaluate the techniques advocated by others.

* Windell, James. *Discipline: A Sourcebook of 50 Failsafe Techniques for Parents.* Collier, 1991. 206p. bibliog. LC 90-23903. ISBN 0-02-029931-1. $9.95.

The 50 discipline techniques summarized in Windell's book make a comprehensive program that parents can learn and effectively apply to instruct, guide, and direct their children. Those techniques that do not work, such as coercing, yelling, nagging, and shaming, and those that probably will not work, such as spanking, criticizing, or embarrassing, are excluded. Drawing upon years of experience as a juvenile corrections counselor, Windell outlines a cumulative, step-by-step program that works by providing practical ways to set rules, prevent problems from developing, encourage self-control, correct behavior, and determine when outside help is needed. Examples demonstrate how to apply these techniques.

Windell, James. *Eight Weeks to a Well-Balanced Child: A Failsafe Program for Toddlers through Teens.* Macmillan, 1994. 239p. index. LC 93-23914. ISBN 0-02-630235-7. $20.00.

This handbook by an experienced parent training instructor translates his eight-week course into written format for wider distribution. Complete with homework assignments, the text emphasizes consistent and precise practice of such techniques as giving praise and attention; providing rewards and privileges; using reminder praise, reprimands, and time-outs; and removing rewards or privileges. In addition, advanced techniques for difficult discipline problems such as drug abuse or stealing are covered, as are behaviors for parents to practice that help maintain better behavior by their children. Why children develop behavior problems is also discussed.

Wyckoff, Jerry, and Barbara C. Unell. *How to Discipline Your Six-to-Twelve Year Old without Losing Your Mind.* Doubleday, 1991. 239p. LC 90-34324. ISBN 0-385-26047-4. $9.95.

Treating discipline as a goal for parents as well as their children, the authors compile options for coping with social and school problems, irresponsibility and disorganization, poor self-image, and "noise," e.g., swearing, complaining, or being demanding. They rely heavily on the token system of assigning chores when rules are broken and emphasize the need for choice and responsibility in helping adolescents develop orderliness and self-control.

Younger, Frances. *Five Hundred Questions Kids Ask about Sex and Some of the Answers: Sex Education for Parents, Teachers, and Young People Themselves.* Thomas, 1992. 212p. bibliog. index. LC 91-47078. ISBN 0-398-05789-3. $27.75.

Compiled by a retired counselor and sex education instructor, this sourcebook on sexuality presents in question-and-answer format information on conception, pregnancy, childbirth, sexual relationships, birth control, and sexually transmitted diseases. The text, which is intended for use by parents, teachers, and teens themselves, emphasizes frank, unambiguous answers to actual questions posed by teens. The author promotes a permissive philosophy about sexuality by declaring that any sexual behavior is acceptable if it does not hurt or offend oneself or another, but the answers also emphasize responsibility, commitment, and the consequences of sexual actions. Related information on sexual maturation and heredity is also provided here.

PROFESSIONAL TITLES: BOOKS

Sabatino, David A. *A Fine Line: When Discipline Becomes Child Abuse.* TAB, 1990. 228p. LC 90-36459. ISBN 0-8306-3566-1. $12.95.

Sabatino presents rational discipline as training that teaches children positive values on which to base their lives and promotes self-control. Rational discipline teaches children respect for rules and for others through the parent modeling responsible adult behavior. Punishment, if used at all, should be used in support of discipline. In contrast, traditional notions of discipline are largely based on punishment or retribution for past acts, e.g., "just desserts" for breaking societal rules, and appeal to parents because they satisfy their need for control and unwillingness to spend as much time as will be needed to instruct or train a child. In situations where life conditions are stressful, when the family adds a further burden or either a parent or the marriage is unstable, the desire to put the parents' needs first may result in abusive parenting. A lengthy, sobering review of the causes and conditions of physical abuse, sexual abuse, and neglect underscores how different from punishment discipline really is.

DIRECTORY

Boy Scouts of America (BSA)
P.O. Box 152079, 1325 W. Walnut Hill Lane, Irving, TX 75015
(214) 580-2000 Fax (214) 580-2502
Jere B. Ratcliffe, Chief Scout Executive
Founded: 1910
Members: 5 million
Affiliates: 390 state groups, 127,000 local groups
Mission/Goals: To serve others by helping to instill values in young people and to prepare them to make ethical choices during their lifetimes; to help youths reach their full potential through organization and cooperation with other community agencies
Audience/Clientele: Local religious, educational, civic, fraternal, and other community organizations that seek to use the programs of the Boy Scouts of America to serve boys beginning at the first grade and young men and women of high school age and their families
Staff: 3,500 professionals, 1.3 million volunteers
Funding: Private sources, fund-raising, donations, grants, dues
Services: Comprehensive youth development
Education and Outreach: In-service programs, continuing education courses, seminars, library, archives, database development, accreditation reviews, publishing
Publications: *Boy Scouts of America—Annual Report to Congress*; *Boys' Life*, monthly magazine covering activities of interest to scouts; *Exploring Magazine: The Journal for Explorers*, quarterly, covering hobbies, entertainment, and outdoor recreation; *Scouting Magazine: A Family Magazine*, bimonthly; handbooks and manuals, merit badge pamphlets, other program items
Programs: Biennial conference

Boys' and Girls' Clubs of America (BGCA)
12330 W. Peachtree Street, N.W., Atlanta, GA 30309
(404) 815-5700
Thomas G. Garth, Director
Founded: 1906
Members: 1,100 clubs
Former Name: Boys' Club Federation of America, Boys' Clubs of America
Mission/Goals: To promote health, social, educational, vocational, and character development of youth; to provide guidance and activities related to health, citizenship, leadership development, youth employment, juvenile justice

Audience/Clientele: Youth, primarily in urban environments
Services: Recreation
Education and Outreach: Seminars, publishing
Publications: *Connections*, quarterly magazine; *Executive Newsletter*, bimonthly; *Annual Report*; *How-to-Do-It*, quarterly; pamphlets, manuals, and booklets
Programs: Annual conference

Children's Creative Response to Conflict (CCRC)
P.O. Box 271, Nyack, NY 10960
(914) 358-4601 Fax (914) 358-4924
Priscilla Prutzman, Program Director
Founded: 1972
Affiliates: 18 state groups
Mission/Goals: To help teachers and others who work with young people to learn creative conflict resolution skills, including cooperation, communication, affirmation, problem solving, mediation, and bias awareness
Audience/Clientele: Teachers, parents, students, young people, and others who work with young people
Staff: 12 professionals, 1 nonprofessional, 10 volunteers
Budget: $111,000 Funding: Federal government, state government, local government, private sources, fund-raising, fees for services or products, donations, grants
Languages: Spanish, French
Services: Support group, residential facility
Education and Outreach: In-service programs, continuing education courses, seminars, library, publishing
Publications: *Friendly Classroom for a Small Planet*; *Children's Songs for a Friendly Planet*; *Sharing Space*, newsletter; *Look Around* audiotapes; various reprints; mediation packet; peace packet
Programs: Periodic conferences

City Kids Foundation
57 Leonard Street, New York, NY 10013
(212) 925-3320 Fax (212) 925-0128
Laurie Meadoff, President
Founded: 1984
Mission/Goals: To ensure the survival of today's youth; to empower young people and ensure that their voices are heard in the most powerful arenas possible; to promote positive values and creativity via programs focusing on self-esteem, education, environmental awareness, AIDS, drugs, crime, health and global issues; to work in conjunction with social service organizations, state and local governments, the entertainment industry, and business to accomplish these goals
Audience/Clientele: Youths between the ages of 13 and 22
Staff: 6 professionals, 15 volunteers
Funding: Private sources, fees for services or products, donations
Services: Counseling (religious), substance abuse treatment, lobbying
Education and Outreach: In-service programs, seminars, performances, publishing
Publications: Fact sheets; *Monthly Letter*

Girl Scouts of the U.S.A. (GSUSA)

420 Fifth Avenue, New York, NY 10018-2702
(212) 852-8000 Fax (212) 852-6517
Mary Rose Main, Executive Director
Founded: 1912
Members: 3,500,000
Affiliates: 333 local groups
Mission/Goals: To meet the special needs of girls; to enable girls to reach their potential as happy persons able to contribute to the functioning of their homes and communities; to promote ethical conduct through the Girl Scout promise and law; to encourage self-awareness, interaction, growth of values, and service to society; to provide girls with opportunities to expand personal interests, learn new skills, and explore career opportunities
Audience/Clientele: Girls ages 5 to 17, adult volunteers, social service professionals
Services: Counseling, international exchange programs
Education and Outreach: Seminars, library, archives, publishing
Publications: *Girl Scout Leader: For Adults in Girl Scouting*, quarterly magazine covering programs, troop activities, health and safety, and news about scouting; *Girl Scouts of the U.S.A.—Annual Report; GSUSA News*, monthly newsletter for Girl Scout Councils; *Environmental Scanning Report*, providing data about demographics, lifestyles, education, and related topics
Programs: Triennial conference

Girls, Inc.

30 E. 33rd Street, New York, NY 10016
(212) 689-3700
Margaret Gates, Director
Founded: 1945
Members: 250,000
Former Name: Girls' Clubs of America
Mission/Goals: To provide girls with information on career choices, life decisions and skills, health and sexuality, leadership and community, sports and adventure
Audience/Clientele: Girls and young women ages 6 to 18
Services: Scholarships, contests in photography, writing, and citizenship
Education and Outreach: Resource center, publishing
Publications: *Voice for Girls*, 3/yr, newsletter covering information of interest to young girls and women; *Annual Report*
Programs: Annual conference

National Council of Young Men's Christian Associations of the United States of America (YMCA/YWCA)

101 N. Wacker Drive, Chicago, IL 60606
(312) 977-0031 Fax (312) 977-9063
Leslie Cohn, Contact Person
Founded: 1851
Members: 14,400,000
Former Name: National Council of the Young Men's Christian Associations of the United States of America, Young Men's Christian Associations of the United States of America

Mission/Goals: To meet the developmental needs of people of all ages, incomes, races, and religions; to strengthen families, develop leadership skills, promote healthy lifestyles, and support community development
Audience/Clientele: General public, families
Services: Counseling, support group, recreation, child care, job training, refugee settlement, placement service, compiling statistics
Education and Outreach: Seminars, archives, library, publishing
Publications: *Young Men's Christian Associations of the U.S.A.—International Notes*, quarterly newsletter; *Young Men's Christian Associations of the U.S.A.—Personnel Notes*, quarterly; *Annual Report; Yearbook and Official Roster; YMCA Directory*, annual; *Discover YMCA*, periodic
Programs: Biennial conference, general assembly every 4–5 years

Toughlove, International

P.O. Box 1069, Doylestown, PA 18901
(215) 348-7090 Fax (215) 348-9874 Toll-free (800) 333-1069
Teresa Quinn, Executive Director
Founded: 1977
Affiliates: 2,000 local groups
Former Name: Toughlove
Mission/Goals: Through support groups, to encourage parents to work together to bring about positive behavior changes in young people in trouble; to encourage young people to stay in and complete high school
Audience/Clientele: Parents of teenagers, professionals who work with teens
Services: Support group, counseling
Education and Outreach: Seminars, speakers' bureau, publishing
Publications: *Toughlove/Notes*, quarterly; *Update to Group*, monthly; *Toughlove: A Self-Help Manual for Kids in Trouble; Toughlove: A Self-Help Manual for Parents Troubled by Teenage Behavior*
Programs: Periodic workshops and training sessions

Young Women's Christian Association of the United States of America (YMCA-YWCA)

726 Broadway, New York, NY 10003
(212) 614-2700 Fax (212) 677-9716
Gwendolyn Calvert Baker, Executive Director
Founded: 1858
Members: 4,000,000
Mission/Goals: To provide support and information in the areas of education, human sexuality, self-improvement, citizenship, emotional and physical health, and others
Audience/Clientele: Women and girls over the age of 12 and their families
Services: Counseling, clubs, recreation, compiling statistics, advocacy
Education and Outreach: Seminars, archives, publishing

Publications: *Young Women's Christian Association of the U.S.A.—Annual Report*; *Young Women's Christian Association of the U.S.A.—Directory*; *YMCA Interchange*, quarterly newsletter; informational and instructional brochures, promotion packets, manuals, and guides
Programs: Triennial conference

REFERENCES

1. George H. Gallup Jr. and Frank Newport, "Virtually All Adults Want Children, but Many of the Reasons Are Intangible," *The Gallup Poll Monthly* 297 (June 1990): 19, 12.

2. John Bradshaw, *Creating Love: The Next Great Stage of Love* (New York: Bantam, 1992), 207.

3. Kate Greer, "Today's Parents: How Well Are They Doing?" *Better Homes and Gardens* 64, no. 10 (October 1986): 40.

CHAPTER

20

Education and Learning

Children are born learners.
Thomas Armstrong.
Awakening Your Child's Natural Genius

Public education works best when parents work with it.
Carol A. Ryan and Paula A. Sline.
How to Get the Best Public School Education for Your Child

Through formal schooling, children acquire basic skills such as mathematics, writing, and reading. Education introduces children to topical studies in science, the fine arts, literature, and social studies, but it also teaches them values such as self-discipline, cooperativeness, and appreciation for cultural diversity. Parents are the primary teachers of their children, particularly in the early years, and the home environment stimulates learning from the first days of life. Conditions at home may also increase children's risk of school failure. In 1988, nearly 500,000 children were born to teenage mothers, and nearly 50 percent of mothers ages 18 to 19 had completed less than 12 years of school. Almost 2 million students were identified as limited in their English proficiency in 1989. Between 1985 and 1989, 19 percent of children lived in households below the poverty level.[1] A survey of teachers indicated that nearly half believed significant family problems were seriously hindering learning in 20 percent of their students.[2]

Education is viewed as most successful when parents and teachers work closely together in providing proper schooling for the children in their care.[3] Hindrances to teachers, such as heavy work loads, negative attitudes of parents and the general public,[4] limited influence in shaping the curriculum, and required courses they may feel unqualified to teach,[5] have a significant influence on children's success in school, just as home factors do. Choosing a good school is a key decision for parents, and many guides to help with the decision are available. Despite the use of measurable criteria, the choice may not be an easy one—"recognizing a good school is like recognizing an ideal mate; we may know one when we see one, but it isn't easy to define."[6] A small percentage of parents, whether for religious or educational reasons, choose to educate their children at home.

An asterisk (*) indicates specially recommended titles.

POPULAR TITLES: BOOKS

* Armstrong, Thomas. *Awakening Your Child's Natural Genius.* Tarcher, 1991. 268p. photog. index. LC 90-21074. ISBN 0-87477-623-6. $22.95. ISBN 0-87477-608-2 pbk. $12.95.

   A handbook, resource manual, and inspirational guide to learning, this text is intended for parents who want their children to become more than successful students in school. Based on articles Armstrong published in *Parenting* magazine from 1987 to 1991, the innovative text tells parents how to support a child's intrinsic drive for learning by developing interests in reading, math, science, and history, and encouraging learning via play, arts, and computers. In addition to an overview of the approach, these chapters provide practical suggestions for implementing it. Armstrong also examines educational systems, such as Montessori and super-learning, that work, and reviews how to maintain the uniqueness of children who are not average. A resources section directs parents to additional books, journals, and organizational sources of learning tools. Many photographs are included, most from *Parenting* magazine. An introduction by Shari Lewis is included.

Berla, Nancy. *The Middle School Years: A Parents' Handbook.* National Committee for Citizens in Education, 1989. 92p. LC 89-62932. ISBN 0-934460-35-3. $6.95.

Berla's brief handbook to middle school education suggests ways in which parents can help their children reach their potential. The content includes recognizing normal behavior of 10- to 14-year-olds, preparing children to solve problems and refine basic skills, identifying qualities of a good middle school and improving a poor school, and ensuring equitable treatment for children. Techniques for parents seeking to become involved in their child's education, both at home and in school, are reviewed, as are obstacles to parental involvement.

* Bloom, Jill. *Parenting Our Schools: A Hands-On Guide to Education Reform.* Little, Brown, 1992. 313p. LC 91-41533. ISBN 0-316-09984-8. $19.95.

How parents can understand their local school system, get involved in its workings, and make real changes for the greater good of their communities is the focus of this text. Bloom outlines the skills involved in parent advocacy, looks at parents' rights and how the legal system guarantees them, and reviews the history, structure, and financial organization of public schools in the first part. Next, she covers issues in four basic areas of concern: teachers and administrators, curriculum and instructional materials, legal rights, and special cases. The final section covers the choice of a school, school-based management, and advocacy. Parents are advised about areas for advocacy, such as curriculum decisions, teaching, hiring and firing, fund raising, school board elections, and links between schools and the business community. Numerous checklists and examples of successful programs reinforce the narrative.

Bradway, Lauren, and Barbara Albers Hill. *How to Maximize Your Child's Learning Ability: A Complete Guide to Choosing and Using the Best Games, Toys, Activities, Learning Aids and Tactics for Your Child.* Avery, 1993. 272p. index. LC 92-32397. ISBN 0-89529-579-9. $9.95

With the goal of helping children become happy, self-confident, and academically successful, this handbook provides parents with techniques for identifying their child's personal style of learning. The guide counsels parents in avoiding conflicts concerning homework and in tailoring play, interpersonal interactions, and activities to build on their children's strengths and help them improve in their weaker areas. The authors, a speech pathologist and a writer (*Baby Tactics*), describe three learning styles—Looker, Listener, and Mover—and describe through case studies how these modes affect daily life. They trace cognitive development from infancy through adolescence, comparing and contrasting children whose dominant learning styles differ, focusing on issues particular to the child's age, and presenting games, toys, and other activities relevant to learning at each stage of development. A separate chapter addresses special learning problems and includes definitions, evaluation and testing, and treatment and therapy. Recommended readings and a list of sources for toys are provided.

Cogen, Victor. *Boosting the Underachiever: How Busy Parents Can Unlock Their Child's Potential.* Plenum, 1990. 328p. LC 90-40668. ISBN 0-306-43569-1. $21.95.

Written by an education consultant, this how-to book outlines a practical step-by-step program to improve a child's academic performance. With "learning how to learn" as its guiding principle, the program emphasizes listening, test taking, reading skills, motivational techniques, and other learning methods. Also covered are how to identify whether a child is in fact an underachiever; the causes of poor performance, such as fear of failing, unpleasant or stressful experiences, or being too bright; and how to work with the teacher.

Dunn, Rita Stafford. *Bringing Out the Giftedness in Your Child: Nurturing Every Child's Unique Strengths, Talents, and Potential.* Wiley, 1991. 209p. bibliog. LC 91-13185. ISBN 0-471-52803-X. $19.95.

Careful attention is given to providing opportunities and activities that nurture any child's natural talents in this parenting handbook. Parents are encouraged to question, observe, and learn how to recognize evidence of giftedness in their children and take practical steps to increase their child's interests and productivity. By nurturing learning in the home, choosing the right teachers and conferring with them, promoting problem solving, selecting appropriate games and activities, restricting TV, and, most importantly, identifying the child's learning style and creating the best learning environment, parents can develop the particular kinds of intelligence that suit their child. An appendix provides additional readings, instruments for diagnosing learning styles, resources to help parents apply their knowledge, and a list of associations concerned with learning styles.

Gould, Toni S. *Get Ready to Read: A Practical Guide for Teaching Young Children at Home and in School.* Rev. ed. Walker, 1991. 166p. bibliog. illus. index. LC 91-22623. ISBN 0-8027-1172-3. $22.95. ISBN 0-8027-7361-3 pbk. $12.95.

A revised edition of *Reading, the Right Start* (1988), this guide for parents explains how to teach children to read using the structural reading method, which emphasizes insight, the structure of the written word, and the correspondence of sounds and letters. The approach provides a step-by-step instructional sequence that takes children from readiness activities to learning specific sound-letter links to actual reading. Many games and activities are included in the book. The author, a reading consultant who developed the course on which this text is based, cautions that this approach is for parents who want to encourage their children in all areas without pressuring them to perform.

Greene, Lawrence J. *1001 Ways to Improve Your Child's Schoolwork: An A to Z Guide to Common Problems and Practical Solutions.* Dell, 1991. 345p. illus. LC 92-131462. ISBN 0-440-50265-9. $12.00.

Information on common academic and school challenges children face, including dyslexia, fear of failure, grammar, listening in class, peer pressure, spelling problems, and working independently, is provided in this one-volume encyclopedia. Entries are arranged alphabetically, with cross-references to related topics and suggested corrective strategies for school and home interventions. When appropriate, the material is coded for grade level. Content also includes recommendations for parents on communicating with the school, evaluating special education programs, participating in parent-teacher conferences, and dealing with teacher-child conflict. A resource list provides references, keyed to the text, on alternate teaching strategies, language arts, learning disabilities, math, phonics, and other academic issues.

Guterson, David. *Family Matters: Why Homeschooling Makes Sense.* Harcourt Brace Jovanovich, 1992. 245p. bibliog. LC 92-7877. ISBN 0-15-193097-X. $22.95.

Guterson's book is a thoughtful introduction to the homeschooling movement and the goals sought by parents who teach their children at home. The author addresses such philosophical issues as the challenge to democracy that homeschooling represents and what an education means, as well as the advantages, academic, social, and political, that homeschooling brings. Guterson also addresses the financial impact of a spouse staying at home and the importance of flexibility in attuning teaching styles to learning theory. The text, by a secondary school English teacher in Washington State who paradoxically homeschools his own children, is an articulate statement on what often is regarded as a fringe movement of the religious right.

Howlett, Bud. *How to Choose the Best School for Your Child: The Long-Awaited Solution to the Dilemma of Finding the Right School.* Gulf, 1991. 221p. photog. illus. LC 90-24844. ISBN 0-87201-217-4. $11.95.

Written by an educator and administrator, this text presents parents with a clear, concise approach to understanding the issues involved in choosing a school for their child from among public, private, and homeschooling options. Howlett advises parents to examine what qualities they wish their child to develop and to assess their needs before beginning the search. Information about learning styles, a checklist for evaluating schools, growth and learning expectations for each grade, and ways to identify an effective teacher are included. Also reviewed are how to gather information and get the child into the school chosen.

Lenn, Peter D. *Active Learning: A Parent's Guide to Helping Your Teen Make the Grade in School.* Penguin, 1993. 167p. bibliog. LC 92-34814. ISBN 0-1401-7653-5. $10.00.

Based on information presented in Active Learning parent seminars, this text provides techniques and advice for parents to help their teens learn study and self-management skills that enhance their ability to succeed at school and in life. The author, founder of Active Learning, focuses on school because it serves as adolescents' full-time job and is the source of much frustration, discouragement, self-doubt, and defiance when progress is poor. He covers major obstacles to good performance in school, such as resistance, lack of learning skills, and low self-confidence. He also discusses achieving mastery in learning, communicating clearly, and being an encouraging parent. Practical matters such as tutoring tips, books and other supplies, and ways to work with the school are also addressed. This positive approach to improving school performance encourages increased effectiveness in the adult world as well.

* Leonhardt, Mary. *Parents Who Love Reading, Kids Who Don't: How It Happens and What You Can Do about It.* Crown, 1993. 238p. index. LC 93-16655. ISBN 0-517-59164-2. $20.00.

A lengthy, annotated list of books arranged by genre and selected by the author's students is one of many highlights of this refreshing, open-minded approach to getting kids to read and to love doing it. Providing easy and completely engrossing reading material, such as comic books, *Mad* magazine, or "bodice-rippers," creating a reading-friendly home, limiting access to television, and, when possible, selecting a reading-friendly school where diverse styles of learning are supported are among the techniques recommended here. Information given on the stages of reading, from leafing through magazines to selecting books to read, and on ways to help poor readers cope with school guides parents in encouraging this essential skill in their children.

Lickona, Thomas. *Educating for Character: How Our Schools Can Teach Respect and Responsibility.* Bantam, 1991. 478p. bibliog. index. LC 91-16853. ISBN 0-553-07570-5. $22.50.

Lickona, a developmental psychologist and a professor of education, outlines a 12-step process for teaching universal moral values such as honesty, fairness, tolerance, prudence, self-discipline, and, in particular, respect and responsibility in elementary school. Drawing on experience, research, and numerous case studies, he describes in detail the practical aspects of each step of the process, including cooperative learning, teaching values through the curriculum, encouraging moral reflection, addressing controversial issues, and teaching children how to solve conflicts. Strategies at a schoolwide level for creating a positive moral culture, sex education, and parental involvement are also covered. Introductory material explores the need for values, education, and what comprises good character.

* Maeroff, Gene I. *The School-Smart Parent.* Holt, 1990. 434p. bibliog. LC 90-33810. ISBN 0-8050-1380-6. $12.95.

This education writer and researcher urges parents to become advocates and guides for their children because the public elementary school system provides few safeguards for children whose parents are not. Maeroff addresses such issues as the increasing competitiveness of the educational system, choosing a school, preparing for preschool, building a foundation for reading, finding child care that best meets children's developmental needs, and preparing for kindergarten. Also covered are school policies and educational philosophies; ways to work with school staff; children with disabilities; the roles of computers and television; following the child's progress in the arts, social studies, and other subjects; mathematics; reinforcement of learning at home; and learning outside the home. Accessible language and detailed coverage make this a useful introduction to elementary schooling in the United States.

Miller, Mary Susan. *Save Our Schools: 66 Things You Can Do to Improve Your School without Spending an Extra Penny.* Harper San Francisco, 1993. 163p. LC 92-56416. ISBN 0-06-250733-8. $8.00.

Without negating the importance of an appropriate level of funding, this text focuses on no-cost or low-cost methods that parents may use to improve the school itself rather than just the child's experience of it. Numerous tips are presented on what parents can do, how to make students a part of the solution, how to strengthen teaching and administration, and how to involve the community in school improvement. Each suggestion includes a rationale for its usefulness as well as ideas for implementing it. Among the clever techniques suggested are involving children in community service; encouraging learning through discovery and independent study projects; making site visits to other schools; implementing evaluation of teachers by their students; creating a parents' space in the school; and establishing year-round school.

Miller, Mary Susan. *The School Book: Everything Parents Should Know about Their Child's Education from Preschool through Eighth Grade*. St. Martin's, 1991. 382p. index. LC 90-49811. ISBN 0-312-05578-1. $24.95. ISBN 0-312-05508-0 pbk. $14.95.

With no introduction, the author plunges into a review of education and schooling from the parents' perspective. Using a question-and-answer format, she covers everything from parents as teachers and whom to contact when the child has a problem at school to choosing a school, getting the preschool child started in school, and meeting the needs of elementary and junior high students.. The content also includes advice on communication with teachers, children, and other parents; questions about the curriculum; grading; homework; educational play; and extracurricular activities. Discussions of problems to anticipate at various grade levels, educational needs of special children, peer relationships, school safety, and parental fears conclude the text.

Pride, Mary. *Big Book of Home Learning*. 3rd ed. Crossway Books, 1990. 286p. illus. index. LC 89-81254. ISBN 0-89107-548-8 pbk. $15.00.

Now in its third and much expanded edition, this reference manual for home schoolers and others provides a perspective on home learning; an explanation of learning styles; annotations for catalogs, books, and magazines; and sources for school supplies. Pride defines homeschooling, describes major styles of homeschooling, lists reference materials, and includes a buying guide and a directory of homeschooling organizations in the United States and worldwide. A wry wit is evident in the annotations, as is a decided philosophical viewpoint on the value of homeschooling. A suppliers index is also provided.

Rimm, Sylvia B. *How to Parent So Children Will Learn*. Apple, 1990. 279p. bibliog. illus. LC 89-84190. ISBN 0-937891-02-9. $15.00.

In this practical handbook for parents, Rimm, an educational psychologist, explores the elements of child rearing and academic achievement that are influenced by parental attitudes and home life circumstances. She examines the implications of parental praise and power in children's behavior, the importance of a united front, homework and study habits that encourage academic accomplishment, and how parents may model and support achievement. The text, illustrated with cartoons and case studies, provides a substantial amount of practical advice with simple techniques and clear rationales for their effectiveness.

* Ryan, Carol A., and Paula A. Sline, with Barbara J. Lagowski. *How to Get the Best Public School Education for Your Child.*

Walker, 1991. 196p. bibliog. index. LC 90-28695. ISBN 0-8027-1156-1. $21.95. ISBN 0-8027-7355-9 pbk. $12.95.

According to the authors, an elementary school principal and a counselor, public school education works best when parents are involved. To aid parents in increasing their participation, the authors highlight the advantages of public school education, demystify the bureaucracy, identify the qualities of a good school, explore the home-school transition, and examine socialization of the child in school play. Ways to interact with teachers and obtain services for special needs children are also reviewed. Trends in public education, such as increased parental choice in school selection, school-based community resource centers, teacher development, extended school year, and earlier intervention, all indicate a growing demand for parental participation in school functions.

* Sonna, Linda Agier. *The Homework Solution*. Williamson, 1990. 185p. LC 90-34235. ISBN 0-913589-52-7. $9.95.

The highly structured homework program outlined here teaches children to accept responsibility for their assignments, reduces conflicts, contributes to good study skills and habits, and enhances motivation. While at the outset the decisions, monitoring, and communications involved require a good deal of parental time, a steadfast enforcement of the rules regarding study time soon brings compliance along with academic improvements. The program, developed by a clinical psychologist, is suitable for students of all ages and at every level of capability. Specific strategies for children with special needs are described. Forms needed for the parents' progress journal and parent-teacher communications are provided in the appendixes.

Spietz, Heidi Anne. *Modern Montessori at Home: A Creative Teaching Guide for Parents of Children Six through Nine Years of Age*. American Montessori Consulting, 1989. 156p. bibliog. photog. illus. index. LC 89-14870. ISBN 0-929487-92-8 pbk. $9.95.

Montessori principles for guiding learning in school-age children are updated for the 1990s in this teaching guide for parents. Sample lesson plans covering phonics, reading, spelling, English grammar, composition, foreign languages, vocabulary building, nutrition, biology, geography, geology, and history are grouped for first and second graders and third and fourth graders, and the advantages of the Montessori method and instructions on preparing stimulating lesson plans are provided. Readers are advised on techniques for creative lesson planning, including defining the objective, taking the child's ability into account, and building in flexibility.

Spietz, Heidi Anne. *Modern Montessori at Home II: A Creative Teaching Guide for Parents of Children 10 through 12 Years of Age*. American Montessori Consulting, 1990. 156p. bibliog. index. LC 90-834. ISBN 0-92987-10-9. $9.95.

Montessori principles for guiding learning in school-age children are updated for the 1990s in this teaching guide for parents. The majority of the text comprises sample lesson plans covering science, health, social science, the humanities, and English for fifth, sixth, and seventh graders. An introduction to the advantages of the Montessori method and instructions on preparing stimulating lesson plans are provided. Readers are advised on techniques for creative lesson planning, including defining the objective, taking the child's ability into account, and building in flexibility.

Unger, Harlow G. *How to Pick a Perfect Private School.* Facts on File, 1993. 218p. index. LC 92-24176. ISBN 0-8160-2753-6. $21.95.

The first three chapters of this detailed handbook provide a reliable guide for parents who are questioning whether their child should attend a private school, what type of education will best meet their child's needs, or which school is the right choice. They paint a rosy picture of private education as more focused on academics and less on discipline, but otherwise they objectively consider such factors as cost, location, special needs, and long-term goals for a child's academic and career success. Apart from a summary chapter, the remainder of the book addresses criteria for evaluating schools and reviewing them "on paper" to decrease the size of the pool of choices and describes site visits to further narrow the pool to include finally only those to which the parents will apply. The text recommends when it is advisable for younger children to be involved in selecting a school. Several appendixes, including a detailed evaluation form, a list of member schools of the National Association of Independent Schools (NAIS), and sources of financial aid, supplement the text.

Unger, Harlow G. *What Did You Learn in School Today?: A Parent's Guide for Evaluating Your Children's Schools.* Facts on File, 1991. 168p. illus. index. LC 90-21724. ISBN 0-8160-2510-X. $18.95.

Unger's handbook guides parents in evaluating their child's current or prospective curriculum, teacher, principal, superintendent, school board, and school facilities. The first section explores how to evaluate each area and the issues in each that should concern parents. "Report cards" or checklists for parents covering school profile, facilities, faculty, policies, and decision making are provided in the second section. The last section presents appropriate academic curriculum for each grade, K through 12. Slim in size but imposing in the demands it makes on concerned parents, this guide gives parents a set of standards to judge schools where no national standards for curricula, personnel, or governing boards exist.

Vaccus, Florence. *It's Fun to Be Smart: A Parent's Guide to Stress-Free Early Learning from Birth through Age 5.* Vade Mecum, 1991. 280p. LC 91-2174. ISBN 0-945847-04-1. $14.95.

The author reviews numerous techniques for stimulating early learning in children from birth to age five in a warm, stress-free manner. Based in part on the author's professional background as a schoolteacher and counselor and in part on her experiences as a parent, the text provides a rationale for early learning, emphasizing the importance of a positive attitude, and examines the importance of stimulation and focusing in making learning pleasurable and exciting. Other topics covered include teaching children how to speak, read, and understand mathematics and other subjects and taking advantage of opportunities for learning in daily outings.

Weininger, Otto, and Susan Daniel. *Playing to Learn: The Young Child, the Teacher, and the Classroom.* Thomas, 1992. 204p. bibliog. index. LC 91-40974. ISBN 0-398-05771-0. $38.75.

By two educators, this text offers a blueprint for teaching language skills, which are the essence of education, through playing, peer relationships, and relationships with parents and teachers. After exploring what education is and what it must become, the authors examine how playing teaches children about the world, techniques for developing language competency through play, and the diagnosis of depression, developmental disabilities, or abuse.

Wiener, Harvey S. *Any Child Can Read Better.* Bantam, 1990. 242p. bibliog. illus. index. LC 90-35985. ISBN 0-553-34773-X. $9.95.

Practical strategies for parents to help their child become a critical reader while learning the basic reading techniques in school make up this book. Wiener cautions parents against actually teaching reading because it is hard to do properly, the child will learn the rudiments without the parents' help, and there is a risk of becoming less than a parent when one becomes an instructor. Instead, he advocates creating a home environment where works are valued and reading is enjoyed and shared. Determining the denotative and connotative meanings of words, previewing techniques, using visual aids to understand, noting inferences, predicting outcomes, and generalizing are strategies parents may use to improve their child's ability to read well. The final chapter is an annotated bibliography of good books for children by age group from preschool to fifth grade and beyond.

POPULAR TITLES: JOURNALS

Growing without Schooling. Holt, 1977. B-M. ISSN 0745-5305. $25.00.

A newsletter for parents who choose to educate their children at home, *Growing without Schooling* provides testimonials and rationales promoting homeschooling as well as tips and techniques for individualized education. Legislative updates, interviews, reviews of books and videos, and resources that provide new opportunities for learning through doing are covered. A directory of subscribers who are willing to provide assistance to other parents is published annually. An annual list of teachers, lawyers, psychologists, school districts, professors, and others who support home schooling is also provided.

Home Education Magazine. Home Education, 1984. B-M. ISSN 088-4633. $24.00.

Feature articles in this journal for homeschooling parents focus on practical matters such as teaching techniques, curriculum suggestions, socialization, and rationales supporting home education. Regular columns look at learning, news, resources, and personal stories. Book excerpts, how-to guides, humor, inspirational pieces, letters, and interviews are published. Past issues have addressed math instruction, stamp collecting and herbs as educational tools, and the grandparent's role in homeschooling.

PROFESSIONAL TITLES: BOOKS

Bowers, C. A., and David J. Flinders. *Culturally Responsive Teaching and Supervision: A Handbook for Staff Development.* Teachers College, 1991. 51p. LC 90-25463. ISBN 0-8077-3078-5. $9.95.

Written by two educators, this concise handbook presents a model of teaching that views the classroom as an ecology of students' language and cultural patterns. The text provides a brief overview of the conceptual foundations (an in-depth review of the rationale can be found in the authors' *Responsive Teaching: An Ecological Approach to Classroom Patterns of Language, Culture, and Thought,* Teachers College Press, 1990), what cultural patterns to look for, and a recommended process for using this handbook. Eleven practical guidelines for recognizing and responding to common culturally influenced beliefs and behaviors in the classroom are provided. They cover important aspects of the ecology of the classroom including lesson structure, culturally stereotyped values, nonverbal patterns of communication, and culturally appropriate participation patterns.

Essa, Eva L., and Penelope Royce Rogers. *An Early Childhood Curriculum: From Developmental Model to Application.* Delmar, 1992. 323p. bibliog. photog. illus. index. LC 91-7521. ISBN 0-8273-4717-0. $25.95.

In use since the mid-1970s, the self-concept curriculum developed by the authors is a comprehensive tool for curriculum plans designed to be developmentally based, relevant to preschoolers, orderly, sequential, adaptable, and socially oriented. The curriculum explores the dimensions of the child, home and family life, friends and school, and community in the context of eight subjects: identity, roles and relationships, environment, movement, safety, health, food, and communications. The text presents an overview of basic child education principles, use and adaptation of the curriculum, lessons within its scope, and case studies.

Feeney, Stephanie, Doris Christensen, and Eva Moravcik. *Who Am I in the Lives of Children: An Introduction to Teaching Young Children.* 4th ed. Maxwell Macmillan, 1991. 460p. bibliog. index. LC 90-20260. ISBN 0-675-21320-7. $27.75.

Students and practitioners will find in this textbook an overview of early childhood education, covering programs from birth to age eight, but concentrating on activities for children ages three to five. The authors emphasize the importance of training, experience, and personality in becoming a good teacher. The text covers five major areas: foundations of early childhood education, including values of the teacher and history of early childhood education; how to understand and evaluate children's development and play; the impact of the environment on teaching and interacting with children; the curriculum for arts appreciation, cognitive development, and language ability; and working with special needs children and with families. New to the fourth edition are chapters on play, a health and safety curriculum, and expanded discussions of the role of the family and increasing professionalization of the field. Appendixes provide additional resources and a review of ethical cases.

Garlington, Jocelyn A. *Helping Dreams Survive: The Story of a Project Involving African-American Families in the Education of Their Children.* National Committee for Citizens in Education, 1991. 167p. bibliog. photog. illus. LC 91-62795. ISBN 0-934460-38-8. $24.95.

Under the auspices of the nonprofit National Committee for Citizens in Education, the With and for Parents project worked with 15 low-income minority families with incoming sixth graders to increase the parents' role in preventing their children from dropping out. This text, a guide but not a formal guidebook for educators, recounts through journal accounts and first-person narratives the successes and challenges faced by program staff. The content includes interaction with the neighborhood, making contact, parents' concerns, students' beliefs, the impact of meetings and written materials, school considerations, and collaborative relationships with other organizations committed to the community. As the summary indicates, the program achieved a moderate degree of success when data from the comparison group of families are reviewed.

Greene, Ellin. *Books, Babies, and Libraries: Serving Infants, Toddlers, Their Parents, and Caregivers.* American Library Association, 1991. 187p. index. LC 91-17050. ISBN 0-8389-0572-2. $25.00.

This primer by a well-known library educator on providing library services to infants and toddlers and information on their care to parents is based on a graduate course she developed as director of the New York Public Library's Early Childhood Project. The text describes the library's current and historical roles in servicing this clientele, reviews early childhood development and learning theories, and summarizes the emergent literacy literature. A detailed list of recommended books, journals, and audiovisuals for an infant and toddler collection is provided, as is a list of 150 retrospective titles to initiate a parenting collection. Sections on program planning, networking and outreach, and planning, implementing, and evaluating services also include appendixes that list organizations, suppliers, and other pertinent information. The course goals, syllabus, and a reading list are included, along with information from the 1989 invitational conference on early childhood education in New York.

Hargreaves, Margaret Barnwell. *Learning under Stress: Children of Single Parents and the Schools.* Scarecrow, 1990. 118p. bibliog. illus. index. LC 90-36579. ISBN 0-8108-2287-3. $20.00.

A study conducted by Women's Action Alliance revealed that children from single-parent families are at greater risk for academic problems than children from two-parent families. Based on census data, literature reviews, and interviews with experts, parents, children, and elementary school children, this report outlines strategies for schools to increase teachers' sensitivity to the single-parent family, develop systems to provide early warning of academic problems, organize support groups for single parents and their children, and collaborate with local communities to provide child care. Appendixes give detailed suggestions for implementing these goals and list additional resources for educators.

* Hildebrand, Verna. *Guiding Young Children*. 5th ed. Macmillan, 1994. 441p. bibliog. photog. LC 93-18438. ISBN 0-02-354518-6. Price not available.

Now in its fifth edition, this undergraduate textbook follows a developmental approach and emphasizes opportunities for interaction with children in the training of early childhood care givers and teachers. It offers guidance in understanding the behavior of young children; suggestions for guiding children through such routines as eating, dressing, and toileting; and strategies for presenting the typical curriculum of art, music, science, literature, language, and play. The first part covers specific routines, and the second part addresses general considerations in child guidance such as appreciating positive behavior, mainstreaming children with disabilities, and communicating with parents. New to this edition are a chapter on promoting self-esteem in children and photos from day care centers throughout the country.

Hildebrand, Verna. *Introduction to Early Childhood Education*. 5th ed. Macmillan, 1990. 591p. photog. LC 90-33465. ISBN 0-02-354535-6. $28.50.

Currently in its fifth edition, this textbook provides theoretical grounding and program-planning ideas for professionals and students working with young children from infancy through age six. Professional concerns, including parent-teacher relations, are also covered, but the primary emphasis is on specific learning activities in the curriculum. Outdoor, creative art, science, perceptual-motor, and dramatic play activities for infants and for toddlers have been added in recognition of the increasing importance of child care services for these age groups. Topics are approached from a developmental perspective. Appealing photographs illustrate the text, and numerous study aids, including discussion questions, projects, additional readings, and lists of videotapes, enhance learning. A lab workbook is available.

Irvine, Jacqueline Jordan. *Black Students and School Failure: Policies, Practices, and Prescriptions*. Praeger, 1991. 146p. bibliog. illus. index. LC 91-3033. ISBN 0-275-94094-2. $14.95.

After a review of the grim statistics on dropout rates, vocational emphasis, the impact of teen parenthood, and other indicators of academic problems experienced by black students, the author examines sources of these problems. Specifically, she looks at the influence of school practices, such as tracking, that conflict with ideals of equality; the influence that a lack of cultural synchronization between teachers and students has; and the effects of low teacher expectations for performance. To improve black students' academic achievement, she proposes policies for reorganizing schools, communicating with parents, and improving staff development and training. Results and methodology of the author's original research on teachers' verbal communications with students by race, gender, and grade level are also provided.

Kobrin, David. *In There with the Kids: Teaching in Today's Classrooms*. Houghton Mifflin, 1992. 256p. illus. LC 91-26600. ISBN 0-395-50083-4. $19.95.

Using a concrete, thought-provoking approach to instructing teachers about teaching, this text explores the experiences of two fictional teachers in realistic high school and elementary school classroom scenarios. The chapters are organized to illustrate pedagogical principles, each beginning with a brief review of the issues, followed by observation of the students and teachers in the classroom, and then a summarizing discussion. Among the practical issues addressed are determining who's in charge, teaching a lesson, deciding what to teach, enhancing presentation skills, handling questions, critical thinking, and motivating students to care about their schoolwork. The text illustrates for new and experienced teachers how to reach students and ultimately teach them one by one.

Lawler, S. Dianne. *Parent-Teacher Conferencing in Early Childhood Education*. National Education Association, 1991. 111p. bibliog. LC 91-13090. ISBN 0-8106-0356-X. $11.95.

Lawler, an educator, proposes a model for teachers to effectively communicate and build partnerships with parents through structured meetings. After outlining her approach to organizing conferences, which includes locating records, arranging a comfortable environment, working toward a partnership, listening, evaluating the conference, and responding to parents' concerns, she applies it to a number of settings. How to deal with conflict and conferences that go awry is covered, as is background information on improving communications, promoting partnerships, understanding parental attitudes and interactions, and the changing family structures. Numerous case examples illustrate the "Lawler model" in action.

Mendler, Allen N. *Smiling at Yourself: Educating Young Children about Stress and Self-Esteem*. Network Publications, 1991. 145p. LC 89-13288. ISBN 0-941816-90-7. $14.95.

Current theory about stress and self-esteem in young children is translated into practical applications in this handbook of activities parents and teachers may use to help children. Techniques for helping children through age 10 like themselves, relax their bodies and minds, get rid of unpleasant feelings without hurting anyone, get along better with others, and cope with the big problems affecting youth today are covered. Written by an educator and psychologist, the text explains each concept, suggests words parents may use with their children, and advises parents on helping children get the greatest benefit out of each activity. Additional readings are provided.

Procidano, Mary E., ed. *Contemporary Families: A Handbook for School Professionals*. Teachers College, 1992. 325p. LC 92-9352. ISBN 0-8077-3166-8. $26.00.

Compiled as a resource and theoretical framework to aid school professionals in understanding and working with individual children and their parents, this handbook reviews the impact of family configuration, ethnic and cultural diversity, environmental stresses, and individual vulnerability on children's school performance. Among the topics addressed are dual-wage and single-parent families, stepfamilies, poverty, illness, divorce, and Hispanic, African American, and Asian ethnicity. Each chapter includes background information, empirical findings on relevant experiences, their effects on children's adjustment to school, and advice on specific applications for the classroom. This anthology will help school professionals of all types avoid misunderstandings due to stereotypes, inexperience, and anecdotal information.

Riechel, Rosemarie. *Reference Services for Children and Young Adults*. Shoe String, 1991. 219p. LC 91-31973. ISBN 0-208-02290-2. $35.00.

Public and school librarians were surveyed to identify current reference service practices, policies, obstacles, and deficiencies in this study. Barriers to providing quality reference services for children and young adults are examined in the opening chapter; these include staffing, hours, attitudes, collection development decisions, and fees. Present services in public and school libraries, including budgets, referral services, programs, automated resources, and telephone reference services, are summarized and case studies presented in subsequent chapters. The author concludes this text with suggestions for improving services targeted to public and school librarians and professionals in school library media centers. The appendixes present detailed survey results, the text of the questionnaire, and a brief bibliography of sources for providing and keeping up with automated reference resources.

Simmons-Matlin, Audrey Ann, and Karen Glover Rossi. *Parents and Teachers: Partners in Language Development*. Alexander Graham Bell Association for the Deaf, 1990. Centennial Language Series. 386p. LC 90-81334. ISBN 0-88200-167-1. $25.95.

The first half of this sourcebook for stimulating language skills outlines the rationale for the practical techniques that are listed in chart format in the second section. The authors, specialists in educating the hearing-impaired child, examine early childhood development; the parent's role in language acquisition; how the child learns to listen, understand meanings, and speak; what the teacher can do to assist; and what the child must know in order to learn language. They follow this up with dozens of specific suggestions for parents and teachers on nurturing children and tuning into their needs; talking to, for, and with children; encouraging awareness of sound and speech; hearing aid use; and structuring the environment for ease in listening.

Spodek, Bernard, and Olivia N. Spodek. *Dealing with Individual Differences in the Early Childhood Classroom*. Longman, 1994. 402p. bibliog. photog. index. LC 92-35209. ISBN 0-8013-0451-2. $23.95.

The focus of this book is advice for elementary school teachers who are integrating children with disabilities and children who are at-risk or who are gifted into a single classroom. Background information, including a historical perspective and description of the characteristics of these children, is covered in the first part. Identifying these children's educational needs, assessing and developing individual educational programs, and working with parents are topics addressed. Also included are planning an integrated classroom; supporting social learning, educational play, and creative expression; and teaching language arts, reading, social studies, and math. Strategies for continuing professional development are presented in the final section.

Swap, Susan McAllister. *Developing Home-School Partnerships: From Concepts to Practice*. Teachers College, 1993. 213p. bibliog. illus. index. LC 92-40877. ISBN 0-8077-3231-1. $48.00. ISBN 0-8077-3230-3 pbk. $17.95.

This guide, written for educators, describes numerous ways in which teachers may build effective collaborative partnerships with parents in order to boost children's performance in school. After a review of the literature documenting the salutary effect of parent involvement, the author explores the obstacles (e.g., demographic change, school norms and limited resources, and parental inexperience) that prevent the easy development of collaborative relationships. Various models and their goals, assumptions, and strategies are considered in the ensuing chapters. Tips on establishing two-way communication are given, as is advice on enhancing children's learning, providing mutual support, and making joint educational decisions. The final chapter describes three "paths" to partnership programs.

Valencia, Richard R., ed. *Chicano School Failure and Success: Research and Policy Agendas for the 1990s*. Falmer, 1991. 353p. illus. index. LC 90-46288. ISBN 0-85000-862-0. $58.00. ISBN 1-85000-863-9 pbk. $24.00.

Based on presentations prepared for a 1989 conference on the education of Mexican-American students, this anthology examines the Chicano educational experience from a variety of perspectives and proposes culturally sensitive strategies to reduce the dropout rate, enhance bilingual education, involve parents to a greater extent, and improve assessment techniques. The contributors provide an overview of Chicano schooling conditions, a historical review of segregation and failure, bilingual education, family influence, cultural factors, educational testing, and broader social and economic factors in Mexican-American school failure.

Waxman, Hersholt C., ed. *Students at Risk in At-Risk Schools: Improving Environments for Learning*. Corwin, 1992. 275p. bibliog. index. LC 91-38882. ISBN 0-8039-4003-3. $32.95.

To help students at risk of dropping out, school conditions must change and become more supportive. After an introduction to theory, the majority of the text covers strategies for improving conditions that alienate the students and their teachers; factors that contribute to low standards and quality of education; the danger of differential expectations for students; and schools that have high noncompletion rates, are unresponsive to students, or have high truancy and discipline problems. Leadership and training programs for educational improvement are also covered in this practical sourcebook for classroom teachers and educational leaders.

PROFESSIONAL TITLES: JOURNALS

Childhood Education. Association for Childhood Education International. 1924. 5/yr. ISSN 0009-4056. $65.00.

A regular publication of the Association for Childhood Education International, this scholarly journal publishes the results of empirical and observational research, case studies, and cross-cultural investigations. An annual theme issue provides in-depth coverage of a specialized topic. The journal has a practical approach, with reviews, news items, and readers' comments. Issues have addressed such topics as developing civic discourse, developing writers in the intermediate grades, preventing low-level lead toxicity, and promoting ecological awareness in children.

Creative Child and Adult Quarterly. National Association for Creative Children and Adults. 1976. Q. ISSN 0098-7565. $55.00.

The National Association for Creative Children and Adults (NACCA) seeks to encourage positive values, appreciation for the arts, and improved schooling in order to help creative individuals reach their potential. This journal is its primary vehicle. It contains research reports, interviews, book reviews, announcements and news about the association, and practical tips for parents and educators. One issue addressed parental support of gifted/talented/creative development through encouragement of independence; a second topic covered was cultural comparisons of creative experiential styles of learning and thinking.

Early Education and Development. Psychology Press. 1989. Q. ISSN 1040-9289. $85.00.

Scholarly papers on infant and preschool development, child care, and intervention/assessment with children from birth to age eight are published in this journal. Additional areas of interest include social and emotional adjustment in school, preschool programming, family life, at-risk children, and children with special needs. The types of articles published are research reports, literature reviews, program evaluations, theoretical papers, and brief reports that address promising approaches to research, program development, intervention, or assessment.

Elementary School Journal. University of Chicago Press. 1900. B-M. ISSN 0013-5984. $49.00.

Articles that emphasize practical applications in elementary schools are the focus of this journal. Research reports, literature reviews, and theoretical analyses are included in the title's scope. This journal concentrates on the scholarly analysis of classroom instruction, also reporting research findings that have applications for teachers. Occasional special issues, such as an issue on middle schools, are published.

First Teacher. First Teacher. 1979. M. ISSN 0744-7434. $24.00.

With a topical approach, this newsletter provides preschool teachers with curriculum ideas, tips, news, project plans, and multicultural food recipes. A past issue focused on creating a learning environment with a positive and healthy attitude toward cultural diversity with suggestions for field trips; universal themes such as music, storytelling, or cooking; recommended readings, and other practical information teachers may apply in the classroom.

Journal of Classroom Interaction. College of Education, University of Houston. 1965. S-A. ISSN 0749-4025. $13.50.

This refereed journal is a scholarly forum for classroom research. Theoretical and empirical articles that emphasize implications for student-teacher interaction are featured. Thematic issues, such as one on communication styles of teachers and student-teacher supervisors, are occasionally published. Other topics regularly addressed are assessment techniques, teacher behavior, perceptions of student behavior, and classroom routines.

Journal of Research in Childhood Education. Association for Childhood Education International. 1986. S-A. ISSN 0256-8543. $65.00.

The education of children from infancy through adolescence is the focus of this scholarly journal. Multicultural and international in scope, this publication from the Association for Childhood Education International contains empirical research, theoretical articles, and ethnographic and case studies conducted in a variety of settings. Issues have covered such topics as stress in kindergarten, using the family as a focus for early education reform, links between research and classroom practice, and ecology of parent-child communications about daily experiences in preschool.

Middle School Journal. National Middle School Association. 1970. 5/yr. ISSN 0094-0771. $35.00.

Parents, teachers, administrators, and other professionals concerned with the educational and developmental needs of youths ages 10 to 15 will find practical, readable articles based on experience in this news magazine. Articles, occasionally organized into theme issues, address curricula, communication and group process, and psychological growth. One theme issue addressed the transition to middle school. Regular columns present advice from teacher to teacher, topical summaries of recent research, and editorials.

School Social Work Journal. Illinois Association of School Social Workers. 1976. S-A. ISSN 0161-5653. $20.00.

Published by the Illinois Association of School Social Workers, this refereed journal provides educators and practitioners with research, reviews, position papers, assessment and intervention methodologies, and program models that contribute to improving services in the schools. Trends in social work practice, innovative approaches, licensure, and social work education are also covered.

Young Children. National Association for the Education of Young Children. 1944. B-M. ISSN 0044-0728. $25.00.

The official journal of the National Association for the Education of Young Children (NAEYC), *Young Children* focuses on providing informally written but nonetheless scholarly articles on research results and theory regarding classroom practice. Some issues feature topical groupings on curricula, such as creative math, social studies, and Native American studies. Regular departments on research in review, care givers' tips, public policy news, information about NAEYC, professional book reviews, and reviews of children's books, videos, and recordings round out each issue.

DIRECTORY

American Montessori Society (AMS)
150 Fifth Avenue, Suite 203, New York, NY 10011
(212) 924-3209 Fax (212) 727-2254
Michael Eanes, Director
Founded: 1960
Members: 12,000
Mission/Goals: To respond to the growing interest in the Montessori approach to early education; to assist in establishing Montessori schools; to set standards for Montessori teacher-training programs in the United States; to provide school consultation and accreditation services

Audience/Clientele: Teachers, parents, non-Montessori educators, school affiliates, and others interested in this educational approach

Services: Accreditation, placement service, compiling statistics

Education and Outreach: Library, exhibit, archives, research, publishing

Publications: *Montessori Life*, quarterly magazine; *School Directory*, annual; *Teacher Training Directory*, annual; papers, books, pamphlets, and bibliographies

Programs: Annual conference, seminannual regional conferences

Association for Childhood Education International (ACEI)

11501 Georgia Avenue, Suite 315, Wheaton, MD 20902

(301) 942-2443 Fax (301) 942-2443 Toll-free (800) 423-3563

Gerald Odland, Executive Director

Founded: 1892

Members: 17,000

Former Names: Merger of International Kindergarten Union and National Council of Primary Education

Mission/Goals: To promote good practices in educating children from infancy through early adolescence; to promote the inherent right to education of all children; to raise standards for teacher preparation; to encourage continuous professional growth of educators; to inform the public of the educational needs of children and the ways in which programs may be adjusted to fit these needs

Audience/Clientele: Parents, teachers, other adults

Services: Lobbying, advocacy

Education and Outreach: Seminars, travel-study tours, publishing

Publications: *ACEI Exchange*, monthly; *Childhood Education*, 5/yr; *Journal of Research in Childhood Education*, biennial; various books and booklets

Programs: Annual study conference, regional conferences

Center for the Study of Parent Involvement

John F. Kennedy University, 370 Camino Pablo, Orinda, CA 94563

(510) 254-0110 Fax (510) 254-4870

Daniel Safran, Ph.D., Director

Founded: 1974

Mission/Goals: To increase understanding of the social and psychological relationship between parents and their children's schools; to study the impact of parent involvement on children's academic achievement and emotional development; to strengthen awareness of institutional, organizational, and cultural factors that obstruct home-school partnerships

Audience/Clientele: Parents, educators, educational policymakers, administrators, researchers, legislators, community and parent groups

Staff: 1.5 FTE professionals, 1.5 FTE nonprofessionals

Budget: $150,000 Funding: Fees for services or products, grants

Services: Advocacy

Education and Outreach: In-service programs, seminars, library, research, publishing

Publications: Newsletter being developed, as are monographs

National Association for the Education of Young Children (NAEYC)

1509 16th Street, N.W., Washington, DC 20036

(202) 232-8777 Fax (202) 328-1846 Toll-free (800) 424-2460

Dr. Marilyn M. Smith, Executive Director

Founded: 1926

Members: 73,000

Former Name: National Association for Nursery Education

Mission/Goals: To identify the needs and rights of young children and to act on their behalf, emphasizing the provision of educational services and support

Audience/Clientele: Teachers and directors of preschool and primary schools, kindergartens, child care centers, church schools, play groups, early childhood education and child development professors, researchers

Services: Accreditation

Education and Outreach: Public service campaigns, publishing

Publications: *Early Childhood Research Quarterly*; *Young Children*, bimonthly; various books, brochures, and posters

Programs: Annual conference

National Committee for Citizens in Education (NCCE)

900 Second Street, N.E., Suite 8, Washington, DC 20002

(202) 408-0447 Fax (202) 408-0452 Toll-free (800) NET-WORK

Former Name: National Committee for Support of the Public Schools

Mission/Goals: To promote participation in all aspects of education by citizens and parents

Audience/Clientele: Parents, teachers, general public

Services: Lobbying

Education and Outreach: Seminars, research, publishing

Publications: *NETWORK for Public Schools*, 6/yr; handbooks and pamphlets for parents on educational issues

National Elementary School Center (ESC)

2 E. 103rd Street, New York, NY 10029

(212) 289-5929 Fax (212) 289-6019

Allan Shedlin Jr., Executive Director

Founded: 1985

Former Name: Elementary School Center

Mission/Goals: To improve the quality of education; to increase public and professional awareness of the effects that elementary schooling has on children's lives; to encourage communication and cooperation among groups working with children; to articulate elementary and middle school practices that can strengthen children's education at all levels

Audience/Clientele: Educators, school board members, parents, pediatricians, psychologists, social workers, and other professionals interested in the development of elementary school age children

Services: Compiling statistics

Education and Outreach: Seminars, symposia, study groups, summer institutes, research, library, speakers' bureau, publishing

Publications: *Conference Proceedings*, 2 or 3 per year; *Focus*, periodic; *The School as Locus of Advocacy for All Children*; other books

Programs: Annual conference

National Head Start Association (NHSA)

201 N. Union Street, Suite 320, Alexandria, VA 22314

(703) 739-0875 Fax (703) 739-0878

Sarah M. Greene, Chief Executive Officer

Founded: 1973

Members: 8,000

Mission/Goals: To upgrade the quality of Head Start services; to integrate activities of the four membership divisions to present cohesive policies, positions, and statements to parents; to increase the number of Head Start programs

Audience/Clientele: Members of Head Start Parent Association, National Head Start Directors Association, National Head Start Staff Association, and National Head Start Friends Association, others interested in the program

Education and Outreach: Seminars, in-service programs, speakers' bureau, publishing

Publications: *NHSA Newsletter*, quarterly; *Tell the Head Start Story*

Programs: Annual conference

National PTA—National Congress of Parents and Teachers

330 N. Wabash Street, Suite 2100, Chicago, IL 60611-3604

(312) 670-6782 Fax (312) 670-6783

Kathryn Whitfill, President

Founded: 1897

Members: 7,000,000

Former Names: National Congress of Mothers and Parent-Teacher Associations; National Congress of Parents and Teachers

Mission/Goals: To unite the family, school, and community on behalf of the education of children and youth; to work for legislation benefiting children and youth

Audience/Clientele: Parents, teachers, students, principals, and other administrators

Services: Lobbying

Awards: Phoebe Apperson Hearst Outstanding Educator of the Year

Education and Outreach: Resource center, cultural arts competition for students, publishing

Publications: *National PTA Directory*, quarterly; *PTA in Focus: A Combined Newsletter from the Three Commissions on Education, Health, and Welfare, and Individual and Organizational Development*, 3/yr; *PTA Today*, 7/yr; *What's Happening in Washington*, bimonthly newsletter; *PTA Handbook*

Programs: Annual conference

Parents Rights Organization

12571 Northwinds Drive, St. Louis, MO 63146

(314) 434-4171

Mae Duggan, President

Founded: 1967

Members: 3,000

Former Name: Parents Rights, Inc.

Mission/Goals: To obtain legal recognition for the right of parents to direct and control their children's education; to secure for parents true freedom in choosing how to educate their children, including alternatives to government-established school systems; to pursue court action in order to achieve these goals; to publish documents that awaken the public to the denial of these rights

Audience/Clientele: Parents who seek alternatives to public schools, teachers, school administrators, groups, churches

Awards: Parents Rights Award for contributions to a better understanding of the rights of parents in education

Education and Outreach: Seminars, continuing education courses, research, speakers' bureau, publishing

Publications: *Parents Rights Newsletter*, quarterly; research papers, legal briefs, books, and monographs

Programs: Annual conference

REFERENCES

1. *State Education Indicators, 1990* (Washington, DC: Council of Chief State School Officers, 1991), 7.

2. *Condition of Teaching: A State-by-State Analysis, 1990* (Lawrenceville, NJ: Princeton University Press, 1990), 21.

3. Carol A. Ryan and Paula A. Sline, *How to Get the Best Public School Education for Your Child* (New York: Walker, 1991), 3.

4. *Status of the American Public School Teacher, 1990/91* (West Haven, CT: National Education Association, 1992), 69.

5. *State Education Indicators, 1990*, 37–38.

6. Ryan and Sline, 38.

C H A P T E R

21

Special and Gifted
Education Needs

Learning disabilities are often so
subtle it is difficult to diagnose them.
We are asking children with
learning disabilities to perform tasks without
giving them the tools they need to accomplish them.
Carol A. Ryan and Paula A. Sline.
How to Get the Best Public School Education for Your Child

Special education programs are designed to provide students with special needs, whether those needs indicate a physical impairment, learning disability, behavioral disorder, or giftedness, with instruction targeted to meet those special requirements. Particularly since passage of Public Law 94-142, the Education for All Handicapped Children Act of 1975, school systems have worked with parents to diagnose special needs and design individual education programs, or IEPs, to give an appropriate public education in the least restrictive environment possible for these children.[1] Approximately 40 percent of children ages 3 to 5 and 6 to 11 with disabilities were served by a resource room in comparison to 29 percent of the children ages 3 to 5 and 21 percent of those ages 6 to 11 who required a separate classroom.[2]

Learning disorders are common, with 48.5 percent of disabled youths presenting symptoms in 1990, but the causes are often unknown.[3] For example, one study concluded children born in May, June, or July are nearly three times more likely to have the reading problems associated with dyslexia than other children. Researchers believe this is because the mothers of these children were more likely to have caught the flu during the second trimester, the time at which the nervous system devel-

ops.[4] Obtaining the educational program that best helps their child is a responsibility that parents must, often with great difficulty, assertively pursue.

An asterisk (*) indicates a specially recommended title.

POPULAR TITLES: BOOKS

Bain, Lisa J. *A Parent's Guide to Attention Deficit Disorders.* Dell, 1991. 216p. bibliog. index. LC 91-24652. ISBN 0-385-30031-X. $10.00.

> With a foreword by C. Everett Koop, this handbook provides insights and information for parents to understand and obtain the best treatment for their child diagnosed with attention deficit hyperactivity disorder, or ADHD. Working with a multidisciplinary team of health care professionals affiliated with the Children's Hospital of Philadelphia, the author, a medical writer, examines the symptoms of ADHD, its causes and diagnosis, sources of support, medical management, behavior management, educational placement, and family therapy. Bain reviews how best to live with the disorder on an ongoing basis and what the future may be like for affected children and their families.

* Bloom, Jill. *Help Me to Help My Child: Sourcebook for Parents of Learning Disabled Children.* Little, Brown, 1990. 324p. LC 89-12854. ISBN 0-316-09982-1. $9.95.

In this rather academic digest of research on learning disabilities, the author addresses the feelings that parents and children have about a learning problem and provides information about specific disorders and remedial techniques. Learning disabilities are defined, and criteria for diagnosis and the source of these problems are examined. Bloom covers evaluation types and tests, home life, and how parents can obtain an individualized education program for their child. State and national special needs organizations, support groups, guides and directories, and an extensive bibliography make this book a thorough guide for parents whose child has a learning disability.

Fowler, Mary Cahill. *Maybe You Know My Kid: A Parent's Guide to Identifying, Understanding, and Helping Your Child with Attention-Deficit Hyperactivity Disorder*. Carol, 1990. 222p. illus. index. LC 93-35870. ISBN 1-55972-022-0. $18.95. ISBN 1-55972-097-2 pbk. $12.00.

Fowler, a parent, outlines for parents what attention deficit hyperactivity disorder is and what actions they may take to manage it in their child. Symptoms in infants, toddlers, and preschool-age children are described. The first part of each chapter on signs and symptoms includes anecdotes from the author's personal experience, and the second part reviews current research, clinical knowledge, and, where possible, treatment options. The same arrangement is used to discuss the disorder in elementary school children, adolescents, and adults with ADHD. Appendixes provide additional information on national support organizations, special education, and civil rights of handicapped individuals.

Garber, Stephen W., Marianne Daniels Garber, and Robyn Freedman Spizman. *If Your Child Is Hyperactive, Inattentive, Impulsive, Distractible: Helping the ADD (Attention Deficit Disorder) Hyperactive Child*. Villard, 1990. 235p. bibliog. illus. index. LC 90-35992. ISBN 0-394-57205-X. $19.95.

What distinguishes ADHD children from other children is the number of impulsive behaviors they have, the length of time these behaviors continue, and the extent to which they are noticeable, according to the authors (psychologists specializing in behavior control) of this guide to a home-based behavior management program for parents. How to tell whether a child really has ADHD, explain the condition, gain support from friends and relatives, and motivate a child with positive reinforcement techniques is covered. The majority of the text is devoted to describing practical techniques for training children to be calm and control impulses, ignore distractions, stretch attention span, and control aggression. The author also describes ways to build a child's self-esteem. Appendixes focus on support groups, where to obtain copies of the fill-in charts used in the text, and suggested readings.

Huston, Anne Marshall. *Common Sense about Dyslexia*. 2nd ed. Madison, 1990. 300p. LC 90-34364. ISBN 0-8191-7804-7. $24.95.

The author, a university professor specializing in reading problems, covers the three types of dyslexia—visual, auditory, and the two combined—in a practical handbook designed to assist parents and teachers in understanding dyslexia. In four sections she covers what dyslexia is and factors in its incidence,

its characteristics as a disconnection in language, diagnosis of dyslexia and the history of our understanding of the concept, and treating its manifestations in adolescents and adults. The tone is commonsense, and the approach to diagnosis and labeling cautious but realistic. Appendixes provide specialized information on errors caused by incorrect phonics instruction, twin studies, and a multisensory approach to learning new reading and spelling words. There is an extensive bibliography as well.

Johnston, Robert B. *Attention Deficits, Learning Disabilities, and Ritalin: A Practical Guide*. 2nd ed. Singular, 1991. 178p. bibliog. illus. index. LC 91-4802. ISBN 1-879105-12-8. $24.50.

The lighthearted tone of this text, written and revised by an M.D., belies the seriousness of its message: educating the public and health care professionals about the effective use of Ritalin in the treatment of learning and attentional disorders. The four principal issues addressed are demystification of the physician's role, dynamics of an effective team approach, the impact of neurological factors, and the need to see learning and attentional disorders as more than a medical issue. Specific contents include defining and identifying these disorders, medical and neurological assessments, medication, and controversial therapies. Several appendixes list resources and address elements of the medical examination and case report.

McCarney, Stephen B., and Angela Marie Bauer. *The Parent's Guide to Attention Deficit Disorders: Intervention Strategies for the Home*. Hawthorne Educational Services, 1991. 125p. ISBN 1-878372-01-7. $13.00.

Prepared by special education specialists, this reference guide lists simple, commonsense strategies for parents to use to redirect inattention, impulsive, or hyperactive behavior in their child. The solutions proposed for such problems as needing questions and directions repeated, interrupting others, or being unable to remain seated are appropriate for preventing problems, reducing problem behavior, increasing the child's self-control, or instructing the child in more acceptable behaviors.

McCarney, Stephen B., and Angela Marie Bauer. *The Parent's Guide to Learning Disabilities: Helping the LD Child Succeed at Home and School*. Hawthorne Educational Services, 1991. 200p. ISBN 1-878372-05-X. $13.00.

Methods for improving learning and correcting behavior problems in children with learning disabilities are described in this guide. The authors address specific problems, such as not hearing all of what is said, not completing homework, losing the place when reading, and not understanding the concept of time. Discussions are organized in several subject categories, which include memory, organization, and following directions; general academics, reading, written/expressive language, and speech; math; handwriting; and self-control. The appendix suggests a broad array of general techniques, such as posted rules, schedules, behavior contracts, and flash card study aids, to assist parents working with their child.

Novick, Barbara Z., and Maureen Arnold. *Why Is My Child Having Trouble at School? A Parent's Guide to Learning Disabilities.* Villard, 1991. 259p. illus. index. LC 90-28508. ISBN 0-394-58509-7. $18.50.

In this handbook, two psychologists specializing in treating learning disabilities explain how inefficiencies in brain functioning cause these disorders. The authors devote several chapters in the first section to the brain and its functions; early sensory-perceptual, motor, linguistic, and cognitive development; learning in school; and psychosocial development, detailing how neurological inefficiency affects these abilities. In the second section, parents will find advice on recognizing the signs of learning difficulties, finding the right professional to evaluate their child, making treatment decisions, and coping with the diagnosis. The third section covers the nature of learning; the core abilities of sensory perception; motor function; memory; language and speech; attention; reading, writing, and arithmetic; and how neurological functioning affects these abilities. The fourth section consists of a summary chapter, followed by appendixes that provide resources for parents about learning disorders and their treatment.

Saunders, Jacquelyn, with Pamela Espeland. *Bringing Out the Best: A Resource Guide for Parents of Young Gifted Children.* Free Spirit, 1991. 234p. bibliog. photog. index. LC 90-24625. ISBN 0-915793-30-X. $12.95.

Saunders provides detailed information on giftedness and practical strategies to help parents meet the needs of a child who has advanced general intellectual ability, advanced academic aptitude, or ability in the visual and performing arts. The authors, an educator and an editor of children's books, present parents with a commonsense approach to determining whether a child is gifted, describe the challenge of giftedness for parents, and suggest enjoyable ways to enhance brain development, toys, and other learning activities. The authors guide parents in coping with the school system by providing a checklist for evaluating preschools, advice on interpreting the results of a school screening test, issues to consider in early entrance, and support for child advocacy. Additional resources for learning about giftedness are listed in the final section.

* Silver, Larry B. *The Misunderstood Child: A Guide for Parents of Learning Disabled Children.* 2nd ed. TAB, 1991. 256p. LC 91-28978. ISBN 0-8306-2954-8. $17.95. ISBN 0-8306-2837-1 pbk. $9.95.

An unusually thorough handbook, this guide to learning disabilities breaks disorders down into functional types and covers associated emotional, social, and family problems children and adolescents with these disabilities face. Evaluation and diagnosis are covered in detail, with separate chapters devoted to attention deficit hyperactivity disorder, treatment for associated emotional and family treatment, and controversial therapies. Parent support organizations are listed in an appendix.

Taylor, John F. *Helping Your Hyperactive Child.* Prima, 1990. 483p. LC 89-39849. ISBN 1-55958-013-5. $19.95.

Parents whose child has attention deficit hyperactivity disorder will find a current, comprehensive guide to diagnosis, medication, control of exposure to chemicals, academic techniques,

and behavior control in children who exhibit this puzzling disorder. The author, a well-known clinical psychologist specializing in treating hyperactivity, emphasizes the effect that coping with this disorder has on the family, covering parents' reactions, marital stress, sibling stress, and joining or starting a support group. This text puts special emphasis on biochemical treatment. Appendixes provide additional information on diagnosis using the Taylor checklists, support groups, offending chemicals, chemical exposure studies, and recommended readings.

Tuttle, Cheryl Gerson, and Penny Paquette. *Parenting a Child with a Learning Disability: A Practical, Empathetic Guide.* Lowell House, 1993. 188p. bibliog. index. glossary. LC 93-1646. ISBN 1-56565-082-4. $29.95.

This handbook helps parents caring for children with learning disabilities in several ways: it explains in everyday language the various types of learning disabilities and provides specific guidance for each type; it describes the purpose of different educational tests administered to children, thereby encouraging parents to be assertive regarding their child's educational rights; and it helps parents work through their feelings of denial, anger, helplessness, and fear. Introductory chapters explain how learning styles differ from learning disabilities, how learning disorders typically affect a child's self-esteem, what special considerations are appropriate in structuring home life, and the importance of being an active part of the child's professional team as well as the primary advocate for the child. Among the disorders covered are attention deficit disorders; language, speech, and writing disabilities; dyslexia; and math disorders. The text concludes with follow-up information on testing and evaluation and finding the right college. The book contains a glossary and appendixes that list state directors of special education, parent training programs, and resource organizations.

POPULAR TITLES: JOURNALS

Gifted Children Monthly. Gifted and Talented Publications, 1980. M. ISSN 8750-684X (0279-4756). $25.00.

This newsletter addresses curricula, emotional development and well-being, parenting concerns, and other issues relating to educating and parenting the gifted child today. Toy, game, and book reviews are provided, along with a pull-out section of games, puzzles, contests, and other activities to interest the gifted child.

Preventing School Failure; for Special Class Teachers and Parents of the Handicapped. Heldref, 1976. Q. ISSN 1045-9884. $52.00.

A publication supported by the Helen Dwight Reid Educational Foundation, this journal for parents and educators of students with special needs publishes issues organized around a theme. Past issues, each of which opened with an editorial summarizing the contents and significance of the articles contained therein, focused on multiculturalism, putting school reform into practice, curriculum-based measurement, and relevance/meaningful learning. Practical information on curriculum planning, test scoring, and instructing multilingual students is also provided.

PROFESSIONAL TITLES: BOOKS

Ariel, Abraham. *Education of Children and Adolescents with Learning Disabilities.* Merrill, 1992. 624p. bibliog. photog. illus. index. LC 92-2871. ISBN 0-675-20544-1. $45.00.

Useful both as a sourcebook for educators, counselors, and other professionals working with children with learning disabilities and as a textbook for students training for the field, this book gives a current overview of theories, curricula, teaching techniques, and intervention approaches. The specific instructions provided to guide classroom management, teaching methods, and design and implementation are based on clinical observations and empirical evidence and illustrated with anecdotes and detailed case studies. The text opens with a detailed introduction to the history of learning disabilities, their definitions, characteristics, and etiology.

Barnett, David W., and Karen T. Carey. *Designing Interventions for Preschool Learning and Behavior Problems.* Jossey-Bass, 1992. 469p. LC 91-38009. ISBN 1-55542-409-0. $39.95.

The process of psychosocial change rather than developmental stages provides the theoretical basis for this handbook of interventions for educators and psychologist who work with preschool children. The text is organized according to intervention design and potential roles for care givers, covering basic interventions for managing severe problem behaviors, development of new behaviors and modification of existing ones, family and home interventions, and school-based approaches. Introductory material reviews assessment practices, parent-teacher consultation, observation techniques, and practical advice on designing interventions. Issues in providing clients with accountable and ethical services are also reviewed.

Bos, Candace S., and Sharon Vaughan. *Strategies for Teaching Students with Learning and Behavior Problems.* 2nd ed. Allyn and Bacon, 1991. 475p. bibliog. photog. illus. index. LC 90-23623. ISBN 0-205-12970-6. $40.00.

For professionals and students working in special education, this textbook provides an overview of the foundations of the field and detailed descriptions of methods for teaching specific subjects. The authors also cover strategies for classroom management consultation and communication with parents and other professionals. After an introduction of the foundations of special education, the text provides background information and strategies for teaching and learning oral language, reading, writing, content subject areas, social skills, and mathematics, as well as using computers to reinforce learning. The second edition is updated with the results of new intervention research and practice, most notably in the chapters on teaching, reading, and social skills, and the section on consultation and communication is expanded.

Cordoni, Barbara. *Living with a Learning Disability.* Rev. ed. Southern Illinois University Press, 1990. 174p. bibliog. LC 89-48902. ISBN 0-8093-1667-6. $19.95. ISBN 0-8093-1668-4 pbk. $14.95.

Methods for dealing with interpersonal and social areas of life are the focus of this practical handbook on educating, parenting, and communicating with children and adolescents with learning disabilities. Developing and sustaining relationships, testing, finding humor and support in daily life, and parenting skills are addressed. Now in its second edition, the text includes an expanded introduction to the realities of daily life, a discussion of language-learning disabilities, and a new chapter on legal rights mandated by the Education for All Handicapped Children Act of 1975. The author is the founder of the Southern Illinois University Achieve Program, a support system for college students that has been operating since 1978. Cordoni's work with learning disabled students and her experience as a mother of two children with learning disabilities are the source of the many case histories and practical strategies presented here.

Dane, Elizabeth. *Painful Passages: Working with Children with Learning Disabilities.* National Association of Social Workers, 1990. 220p. bibliog. index. LC 90-6463. ISBN 0-87101-175-1. $17.95.

Learning disabilities play a role in truancy, dropping out, and family crises, yet historically social workers have lagged in providing services to affected children and their families. To give social workers with a systematic understanding and knowledge for practice in this complex area, the author compiles information from a variety of disciplines on the specific characteristics of learning disabilities; professional, organizational, and political issues that guide how needs are formulated; and the design of services for children with learning disabilities. The content includes evaluation of disability, development of a supportive environment, the impact of learning disorders on psychosocial development, the effect on families of developmental stages in children with learning disabilities, and a review of federal legislation, principally the Education for All Handicapped Children Act of 1975. The author, a social work educator and consultant who focuses on social work roles with children with learning disabilities and their families, proposes a broader view of intervention for future social work practice.

Hallahan, Daniel P., and James M. Kauffman. *Exceptional Children: Introduction to Special Education.* 6th ed. Prentice Hall, 1994. 581p. bibliog. photog. illus. index. LC 93-27213. ISBN 0-13-293333-0. Price not available.

Now in its sixth edition, this introductory text on exceptionality and special education has new emphases on mainstreaming, cultural diversity, working with families, and the transition to the work force or college life. The primary focus of the text is on classroom practices for children with the major exceptionalities: mental retardation, learning disabilities, emotional/behavioral disorders, communication disorders, hearing or visual impairment, physical disabilities, and giftedness. Two introductory chapters include definitions, legal requirements, history and development of special education, and discussion of major current issues, such as normalization and integration. The text is illustrated with photographs and reproductions of paintings and fiber arts created by participants associated with Very Special Arts or the Creative Growth Art Center. Numerous supplementary pedagogical aids, such as an annotated instructor's manual, IBM storyboard software for the creation of transparencies, and an audio/video library, are available.

Haring, Norris G., and Linda McCormick, eds. *Exceptional Children and Youth: An Introduction to Special Education.* 5th ed. Merrill, 1990. 658p. bibliog. photog. illus. index. LC 89-62922. ISBN 0-675-21178-6. $36.95.

The fifth edition of this textbook comprises a current overview of education for children with major disabilities, such as hearing and vision impairments, behavior problems, learning disabilities, mild retardation, moderate to severe physical handicaps, and communication disorders. Information is also included on educating the gifted, working with the families of exceptional children, acknowledging cultural diversity, and easing the transition to work and community living. Chapters begin with learning objectives and conclude with study questions and tips for helping exceptional children. Boxed information, photographs, charts, and other illustrations provide a state-of-the-art review in an attractive format.

Irons-Reavis, Donna. *Educational Interventions for the Student with Multiple Disabilities.* Thomas, 1992. 127p. bibliog. illus. index. LC 92-2608. ISBN 0-398-05793-1. $28.75.

A primer of practical techniques for the teacher who instructs children with multiple severe disabilities, this text reviews general principles on classroom organization and behavior management, including how to physically manage students. The author also examines using adaptive equipment methods for teaching students social and communication, eating, and independent living skills, and gives advice on teaching infants and preschoolers.

Johnson, Lawrence J., and Anne M. Bauer. *Meeting the Needs of Special Students: Legal, Ethical, and Practical Ramifications.* Corwin, 1992. 79p. bibliog. LC 92-4572. ISBN 0-8039-6021-2. $13.00.

The tips in this book are intended to help school administrators become more familiar with statutes and case law related to special education. The authors examine expulsion or discipline of special education students, related services that must be provided, and language and medical issues. Strategies for helping these children succeed in the classroom, methods for controlling inappropriate behavior, collaborative approaches, and examples of and solutions for students who challenge the system are covered. The final chapter is a troubleshooting guide that refers readers to answers in the text to commonly posed questions.

Jones, Carroll J. *Social and Emotional Development of Exceptional Students: Handicapped and Gifted.* Thomas, 1992. 201p. bibliog. index. LC 91-43960. ISBN 0-398-05781-8. $33.75.

Viewed as a guide for parents as well as teachers, this text covers obstacles to the emotional and social development of exceptional children, who are at greater risk for problems than is the population at large. After an introduction to normal development, separate chapters address special considerations for students who have vision, hearing, or communication impairments; behavioral or learning disorders; or physical impairments, as well as students who are mentally retarded or gifted/talented. Each chapter begins with a brief overview of cognitive and academic learning problems, followed by a detailed

discussion of social and emotional learning problems, feelings of personal control, and self-concepts. Appendixes list indicators of healthy development from the sensorimotor stage through adolescence.

Lewis, Timothy. *Teaching Students with Behavioral Disorders: Basic Questions and Answers.* Council for Exceptional Children, 1991. 37p. bibliog. LC 91-12022. ISBN 0-86586-205-2. $7.50.

Answers to the most pressing questions posed by teachers preparing to or currently working with students with behavior disorders are provided in this concise handbook. Organized into three sections, the text covers student assessment, intervention strategies to change academic and social behaviors, and collaborations with parents, administrators, community agencies, and other teachers. Many additional readings are suggested.

Lovinger, Sophie L., Mary Ellen Brandell, and Linda Seestedt-Stanford. *Language Learning Disabilities: A New and Practical Approach for Those Who Work with Children and Their Families.* Continuum, 1991. 180p. bibliog. glossary. LC 90-26001. ISBN 0-8264-0530-4. $18.95.

Written by a team of authors bringing audiology-, psychology-, and speech pathology-influenced perspectives to the problem of language learning disability, this handbook focuses on assessment and remediation techniques. These are presented within the context of normal audiologic, speech-language, cognitive, and emotional development, with an exploration of the issues that youngsters with this disability present to their families. Concrete suggestions for parents and teachers are included in the appendixes, and there is a glossary of terminology familiar to specialists but not to parents or teachers.

Milgram, Roberta M., ed. *Counseling Gifted and Talented Children: A Guide for Teachers, Counselors, and Parents.* Ablex, 1991. 581p. LC 91-9372. ISBN 0-89391-724-9. $45.00.

Even with their special abilities, gifted children have the same basic needs as other children and require continual guidance and counseling to reach their potential. This anthology provides an integrated conceptual framework for guiding gifted children. Developed by the editor, the approach emphasizes personal and social development as well as academic achievement. Contributors examine the role of teachers in counseling gifted children, the major part that parents play in their development, and career education and guidance. Counseling gifted girls, disadvantaged gifted children, gifted children with learning disabilities, and preschool-age gifted are other topics covered. How to adapt to learning styles and developmental needs of gifted children is addressed.

Moores, Donald F., and Kathryn P. Meadow-Orlans, eds. *Educational and Developmental Aspects of Deafness.* Gallaudet University Press, 1990. 451p. illus. LC 90-14014. ISBN 0-930323-52-1. $39.95.

This anthology is the first major source to address applied research in the educational and developmental aspects of deafness. Divided into two parts, it covers the deaf child in school and at home. The editors, founders of the Center for Studies in Education and Human Development at Gallaudet University, note significant progress in educational and vocational opportunities for deaf children over the past two decades, much as a result of advocacy and new legislation. Contributors representing a number of disciplines provide a state-of-the-art assessment of such issues as early literacy development, school placement, cultural considerations, intellectual assessment, classroom communication, parenting, the impact on the family, directiveness in mother-infant interaction, mastery and attachment behaviors, and expressions of affect.

Morgan, Sharon R., and Jo Ann Reinhart. *Interventions for Students with Emotional Disorders.* Pro-Ed, 1991. 212p. bibliog. index. LC 89-29103. ISBN 0-89079-296-8. $32.50.

Morgan and Reinhart's text is a guide to practical methods for teachers to use in working with children with a broad spectrum of emotional disorders. The authors advocate an "empathic" approach to these students and illustrate their model with concrete examples of how empathy affects the way teachers organize the environment, manage instruction, respond to the feelings and emotional well-being of their students, and express related interpersonal qualities. Many references supplement the information presented.

Myers, Patricia I., and Donald D. Hammill. *Learning Disabilities: Basic Concepts, Assessment Practices, and Instructional Strategies.* 4th ed. Pro-Ed, 1990. 593p. bibliog. index. LC 89-29044. ISBN 0-89079-225-9. $41.00.

Professionals working in the field of learning disabilities will find here a current review of strategies for classroom management and curriculum design for students with severe learning disabilities. Now in its fourth edition, this sourcebook presents a comprehensive discussion of the concept of learning disabilities, the scope of remediative techniques available, and the effectiveness of each technique. Introductory chapters cover the history of the field and major types of learning disabilities. Assessment practices are reviewed, as are adjunct therapies that affect instruction. The majority of the text is devoted to remedial techniques for specific disorders, including hyperactivity and disorders that relate to listening and speaking, reading and writing, and math.

Patton, James R., et al. *Exceptional Children in Focus.* 5th ed. Maxwell Macmillan, 1991. 267p. photog. LC 90-41335. ISBN 0-675-21285-5. $13.50.

A readable, concise introduction to special education, this text provides basic descriptions, fundamental concepts, current issues, and major trends for children with a broad range of exceptional conditions. Among the topics covered are learning disabilities, behavior disorders, mental retardation, severe physical handicaps, hearing and visual impairments, and chronic disorders, as well as giftedness and cultural diversity. Photographs, exercises, and case material illustrate the information provided. The final chapters offer a perspective on exceptionality during early childhood and adolescence and review the development of the field of special education.

Rosenberg, Michael S., et al. *Educating Students with Behavior Disorders.* Allyn and Bacon, 1992. 440p. bibliog. illus. index. LC 91-27920. ISBN 0-205-13136-0. $45.00.

The authors have compiled a practical handbook of suggestions for teachers working with children with mild to severe behavioral disorders. In the first section, the authors review definitions and theories of high and low incidence of behavioral disorders including hyperactivity, aggression and rule breaking, autism, and pervasive developmental disabilities. The section on assessment covers standardized instruments and direct, systematic observation. The third section, on managing and teaching students, offers practical suggestions, illustrated with case material on managing the disorders noted above. In addition, guidelines for teaching students with mild to severe behavioral disorders and developing individual plans of study for these students are presented.

Schwarz, Judy. *Another Door to Learning: True Stories of Learning Disabled Children and Adults, and the Keys to Their Success.* Continuum, 1992. 197p. bibliog. illus. LC 91-22731. ISBN 0-8264-0547-9. $18.95.

Eleven case studies compiled by the director of Another Door to Learning, a learning disabilities clinic in Tacoma, Washington, reveal how individuals with language or spatial perception difficulties overcome their handicaps. Promoting the belief that every person can learn, the author explores various symptoms, the development of individualized instructional techniques, and the success of new pathways to learning targeted to individual needs. The tone throughout is inspirational and supportive of the value of differences among individuals.

Silver, Archie A., and Rose A. Hagin. *Disorders of Learning in Childhood.* Wiley, 1990. 683p. bibliog. illus. LC 89-28492. ISBN 0-471-50828-4. $65.00.

This sourcebook on disorders of learning brings together data from a variety of disciplines to support treatment decisions appropriate to the child's total needs. To assist psychiatrists, psychologists, and educators who work with children with learning disorders, the authors provide a clinically based definition of disorders; offer general and specific principles of diagnosis and treatment drawn from biological, psychological, educational, and sociological research; and describe the most common syndromes seen in clinics and classrooms. Specific topics addressed include prevalence, drug management, prevention, effects of poverty, Tourette's syndrome, and future directions for service and research.

Silver, Larry B. *Attention-Deficit Hyperactivity Disorder: A Clinical Guide to Diagnosis and Treatment.* American Psychiatric, 1992. 164p. bibliog. index. LC 91-4868. ISBN 0-880-509-4. $23.50.

Silver offers practitioners a clinical guide to the etiology of attention deficit hyperactivity disorder and associated syndromes and reviews multimodal treatments. He examines the history of nomenclature and concepts and describes clinical problems as well as differential diagnosis of ADHD and associated disorders, including learning disabilities and emotional, social, and family problems. The basic components of multimodal treatment, individual and family education about ADHD as a life disability and its frequent persistence into adulthood, individual and family counseling, behavior modification strategies, and treatment with medications, are reviewed.

In a chapter on nonmedication treatments, the author critically examines evidence for nutritional treatment via defined diets, restrictions on refined sugar and artificial sweeteners, and the role of allergic reactions to diet in ADHD. Selected references are provided in the appendix.

Simpson, Richard L. *Conferencing Parents of Exceptional Children*. 2nd ed. Pro-Ed, 1990. 441p. bibliog. index. LC 89-39434. ISBN 0-89079-210-0. $32.00.

How educators, including classroom teachers, can aid parents and families in coping with the impact of an exceptional child is the focus of this text. The first section reviews the family's needs, the effect of an exceptional child on family life, cultural considerations, age factors, and special issues of single-parent or recombined families. In the second section, technical skills and strategies are examined, including listening skills, development of trust, the initial contact, and training family members in treatment techniques. The final section addresses ongoing activities such as legal and legislative changes, progress reports, unplanned conferences, and group conferences, as well as ways to resolve conflicts between parents and educators. The appendixes include materials for practicing various types of conferences through role-playing.

Simpson, Richard L., et al. *Social Skills for Students with Autism*. Council for Exceptional Children, 1991. 22p. bibliog. LC 91-9006. ISBN 0-86586-202-8. $7.50.

Because social skill deficits are the most significant disability associated with autism, this brief guide for practitioners attempts to identify and review methods and procedures to promote appropriate interpersonal interactions between autistic children and other youths. The content covers four methods of promoting the development of social skills: direct skill instruction, antecedent prompting procedure, peer-initiation strategies, and peer tutoring. Special emphasis is given to factors related to the success of social interaction programming for children with autism, such as reducing problem behaviors before introducing the program, matching programs to students' needs and settings, providing ongoing instruction and monitoring, educating tutors about autism, and maintaining acquired skills. The material presented here is referenced to a lengthy bibliography.

Swanson, H. Lee, and Steven R. Forness. *Handbook on the Assessment of Learning Disabilities: Theory, Research, and Practice*. Pro-Ed, 1991. 438p. bibliog. index. LC 89-13458. ISBN 0-89079-406-5. $35.00.

This text is a sourcebook for graduate students and practitioners of current research on the theoretical bases for diagnosis of learning disabilities. Divided into three parts, the book reviews current perspectives on assessment, assessment models and areas assessed, and the intervention component of assessment. Experts cover specific topics such as behavioral assessment, reading disabilities, diagnosis and assessment of social cognition, assessment of temperament, and the role of standardized tests in planning academic instruction.

Zabel, Mary Kay. *Teaching Young Children with Behavioral Disorders*. Council for Exceptional Children, 1991. 23p. bibliog. LC 91-8465. ISBN 0-86586-200-1. $7.50.

In 1991, a federal law mandating a free, appropriate public education for children ages three to five went into effect. To guide teachers in recognizing behavior disorders or serious emotional disturbances in children of this age group, Zabel's concise handbook summarizes the current literature on intervention, public awareness campaigns, teaching techniques, behavior modification, and development of social skills. Recommendations for in-service training and textbooks are also provided.

PROFESSIONAL TITLES: JOURNALS

Exceptional Child Education Resources. Council for Exceptional Children. 1969. Q. ISSN 0160-4309. $75.00.

Abstracts of books, journal articles, dissertations, and nonprint resources dealing with all aspects of disabled and gifted child education are published in this quarterly index. Targeted to educators, administrators, researchers, and psychologists, the publication aids in identifying current research, public policy, innovative curricula, new programs, and effective classroom techniques.

Exceptional Children. Council for Exceptional Children. 1934. B-M. ISSN 0014-4029. $40.00.

Issues in professional practice and empirical research on the education and development of exceptional children from infancy to adolescence are the focus of this scholarly journal. Special issues on such topics as educating African American exceptional youth and delivery of special education services to Hispanic youth are published annually. The editor provides an analytical preview or preface to the contents of each issue.

Focus on Exceptional Children. Love. 1969. M. ISSN 0015-5114. $27.00.

Each issue of this newsletter is a single article devoted entirely to a specialized aspect of educating or caring for children with special needs. Issues have addressed characteristics of dysfunctional families in which there is a child with special needs, the process of curriculum development for inclusive classrooms, and emotionality in exceptional children. These scholarly but practical articles are written by clinical or educational psychologists, most working in an academic setting.

Gifted Child Quarterly. National Association for Gifted Children. 1957. Q. ISSN 0016-9862. $45.00.

This magazine is targeted to parents as well as teachers interested in educational policy, curricula, and creativity development in gifted children. Among the topics covered are long-range effects of gifted programs, evaluation studies, programs for the gifted in arts and humanities, support for vocational talents, preschool identification and education programs, advocacy, and parent and community roles in nurturing the gifted. The journal emphasizes theory, research, development, and evaluation.

Gifted Child Today. GCT. 1978. B-M. ISSN 0892-9589. $30.00.

Topical issues, including state-of-the-art programs, state and federal policies, new tests to identify nontraditional gifted children, mentoring, and educational acceleration, are featured in this practical news magazine for teachers and parents. Each issue provides regular columns on parenting, recreational activities, and psychological issues.

Journal for the Education of the Gifted. Association for the Gifted. Q. ISSN 0162-3532. $32.00.

The official journal of the Association for the Gifted of the Council for Exceptional Children, this periodical emphasizes the exchange and analysis of information, including different points of view, relevant to educating gifted or talented children. The editors seek original research, theoretical position papers, program descriptions based on accepted educational models, and historical reviews that critically analyze important topics of current interest.

Journal of Learning Disabilities. Pro-Ed, 1968. 10/yr. ISSN 0022-2194. $90.00.

The *Journal of Learning Disabilities* publishes articles on practice, research, and theory written from a variety of disciplinary perspectives. One section of each issue, the "Special Series," is topically focused, with the remainder of the issue covering interventions, research reports, and correspondence. In one issue, articles on academic functioning in children who survive in-hospital cardiac arrest and resuscitation, psychoeducational characteristics of children with insulin-dependent diabetes, and school performance in children with asthma were presented under the topic of pediatric chronic illness.

Learning Disabilities: A Multidisciplinary Journal. Learning Disabilities Association, 1989. S-A. ISSN 1046-6819. $25.00.

This official publication is a forum for providing information on research, theory, practice, issues, and trends regarding learning disabilities. Among the topics addressed are advocacy, assessment, adults, families, law, mental health, social work, public policy, and technology. The journal encourages authors to submit papers expressing nontraditional points of view. Opinion pieces or descriptions of diagnosis and treatment procedures are not included.

Learning Disabilities Research and Practice. Division for Learning Disabilities. 1985. S-A. $32.00.

The "Practice" section of this official journal of the Council for Exceptional Children's Division for Learning Disabilities publishes articles that present validated approaches to service, teacher education, intervention, assessment, and placement. In the "Research" section, basic and applied research using experimental, observational, historic, or ethnographic approaches is presented. The journal also publishes policy analyses, position papers, and critical reviews on specific aspects of learning disabilities. To supplement this two-pronged approach to increasing knowledge and improving service, reviews of diagnostic tests, educational materials, software, and new books are included.

Learning Disability Quarterly. Council for Learning Disabilities. 1978. Q. ISSN 0731-9487. $40.00.

Research, review, theoretical, and procedural articles addressing learning disabled populations and settings for the education of children with learning disabilities are published in this journal. Techniques for identification and assessment of learning disabilities, programming for students with learning disabilities, critical reviews of the literature, evaluations of training and professional resources, practical tips, information on public policy, and position papers outlining trends are published here.

Roeper Review: A Journal on Gifted Children. Roeper City and Country School. 1978. Q. ISSN 0278-3193. $30.00.

Published by the Roeper City and Country School, this scholarly journal provides a forum for all approaches, including philosophical, psychological, and moral, to the education of gifted children. Articles that translate research and theory into classroom, home, and community practice are published. Most of the material is covered in issues with a thematic focus, such as assessment, exceptionally gifted youth, and longitudinal studies in gifted education. Regular departments address family issues, social policy at the state level, recent research and doctoral dissertations, book reviews, and test reviews.

Teaching Exceptional Children. Council for Exceptional Children. 1968. Q. ISSN 0040-0599. $25.00.

This journal focuses on providing practical information to classroom teachers of children who have disabilities or who are gifted. Articles that describe materials, techniques, equipment, or procedures are featured, as are comments and views of practitioners in the field. Issues have addressed phonics instruction, spelling lessons, and functional assessment applications.

DIRECTORY

Children and Adults with Attention Deficit Disorder (CHADD)

499 N.W. 70th Avenue, Suite 308, Plantation, FL 33317
(305) 587-3700 Fax (305) 587-4599
Jack McAllister, Executive Director
Founded: 1987
Former Name: Children with Attention-Deficit Disorders
Members: 8,000
Mission/Goals: To provide support to parents of children with attention deficit disorder (ADD); to act as an information resource about ADD; to ensure that the best possible educational opportunities are available to children with ADD so that their specific problems are identified and appropriately managed within educational settings
Audience/Clientele: Parents and professionals with an interest in attention deficit disorders
Services: Support group, advocacy
Education and Outreach: Seminars, speakers' bureau, publishing
Publications: *Chadder*, 2/yr, newsletter; *The Chadder Box*, 8/yr, newsletter; booklets, brochures, teachers' guides, slide presentation
Programs: Annual conference

Conference of Educational Administrators Serving the Deaf (CEASD)

c/o Ken Rislov, Arizona School for the Deaf and Blind, P.O. Box 5545, Tucson, AZ 85703-0545
(602) 770-3700
Dr. Ken Rislov, President
Founded: 1868
Former Names: Association of Superintendents and Principals of American Schools for the Deaf; Conference of Executives of American Schools for the Deaf
Mission/Goals: To coordinate research on educational problems related to deafness
Audience/Clientele: Executive heads of public, private, and denominational schools for the deaf in the United States and Canada
Services: Compiling statistics
Awards: Award of Merit for meritorious contributions in the field of deafness; Edward Allen Fay Award for a significant publication related to deafness
Education and Outreach: Research, publishing
Publications: *American Annals of the Deaf*, 5/yr; *Newsletter*, bimonthly
Programs: Annual conference

Convention of American Instructors of the Deaf (CAID)

c/o Carl Kirchner, TRIPOD, Burbank Unified School District, 2901 N. Keystone Street, Burbank, CA 91504
(818) 972-2080 Fax (818) 972-2090
Founded: 1850
Members: 1,200
Mission/Goals: To promote the harmonious union of all engaged in the education of children or adults who are deaf or hard-of-hearing
Audience/Clientele: Teachers of students who are hearing impaired
Staff: 1 professional, 40 volunteers
Funding: Private sources, fund-raising, fees for services or products, donations, dues
Languages: American sign language
Services: Recreation, referral, legislative representations, fund-raising
Awards: Quigley Award for greatest contribution; Outstanding Teacher; Outstanding Service Provider; Outstanding Administrator
Education and Outreach: In-service programs, continuing education courses, seminars, accreditation reviews, research, publishing
Publications: *American Annals of the Deaf*, 5/yr; *Proceedings of the Convention*; *News 'n' Notes*, quarterly newsletter; brochures, stickers, and certificates
Programs: Biennial conference

Council for Children with Behavioral Disorders (CCBD)

c/o Council for Exceptional Children, 1920 Association Drive, Reston, VA 22091-1589
(703) 620-3660 Fax (703) 264-9494 TTY/TDD (703) 620-3660
Dr. Joann Webber, President
Founded: 1962
Members: 8,500
Mission/Goals: To contribute to the education and welfare of children and youths with behavioral and emotional disturbances; to promote professional growth and research in order to achieve a better understanding of the problems of these children
Audience/Clientele: Members of the Council for Exceptional Children concerned with behavioral disorders in children
Awards: Carl Fenichel Memorial Award for outstanding graduate student paper
Education and Outreach: Seminars, publishing
Publications: *Behavioral Disorders*, quarterly; *CCBD Newsletter*, quarterly, with information on division activities; *Monographs*, annual
Programs: Annual conference, held in conjunction with Council for Exceptional Children, also annual topical conference

Council for Exceptional Children (CEC)

1920 Association Drive, Reston, VA 22091-1589
(703) 620-3660 Fax (703) 264-9494
J. George Ayers, Executive Director
Founded: 1922
Members: 54,000
Mission/Goals: To promote the rights of all exceptional children, including those who are mentally gifted or mentally retarded, those with hearing or vision impairments, those with physical disabilities, and those with behavioral disorders and learning disabilities, to take advantage of educational opportunities and equal employment opportunities; to provide information to parents, teachers, and others interested in the education of exceptional children
Audience/Clientele: Teachers, school administrators, teacher educators, parents, and others concerned with the education of children who require special services or teachers with special qualifications
Services: Lobbying, advocacy
Education and Outreach: In-service programs, seminars, research, database development, publishing
Publications: *ERIC Clearinghouse on Handicapped and Gifted Children*; *Exceptional Child Education Resources*, quarterly; *Exceptional Children*, quarterly; *Teaching Exceptional Children*, quarterly magazine with classroom-oriented information; research reprints, books, and other materials for teaching exceptional children; audiotapes and videocassettes
Programs: Annual conference

Council for Learning Disabilities (CLD)

P.O. Box 40303, Overland Park, KS 66204
(913) 492-8755 Fax (913) 492-2546
Kirsten McBride, Executive Secretary
Founded: 1967
Members: 4,500
Affiliates: 14 state groups
Former Name: Division for Children with Learning Disabilities

Mission/Goals: To promote the education and welfare of children with learning disabilities; to accomplish this by improving teacher preparation programs and local special education programs

Audience/Clientele: Professionals interested in the study of learning disabilities

Education and Outreach: Seminars, publishing

Publications: *Teaching Writing to the Learning Disabled* and other similar videos; *Research into Practice*; *Journal of Learning Disabilities*; *The Journal of Special Education*

Programs: Annual conference

Council of Administrators of Special Education (CASE)

615 16th Avenue, Albuquerque, NM 87104

(505) 243-7622 Fax (505) 247-4822 CASE.NEWS electronic bulletin board

Dr. Jo Thomason, Executive Director

Founded: 1951

Members: 4,700

Mission/Goals: To promote professional leadership in special education; to support research on problems common to the field; to disseminate information that will contribute to the development of improved services for exceptional children

Audience/Clientele: Administrators, directors, supervisors, or coordinators of programs, schools, or classes of special education for exceptional children, college faculty and graduate students; individuals with an interest in special education

Education and Outreach: Continuing education courses, speakers' bureau, publishing

Publications: *CASE Newsletter*, 5/yr, covering council activities and news; *CASE in Point*, 3/yr, newsletter concerned with programs and issues in the special education field; program management packets; topical monographs

Programs: Several conferences per year, with seminars, held in conjunction with the Council for Exceptional Children

Division for Early Childhood (DEC)

c/o Council for Exceptional Children, 1920 Association Drive, Reston, VA 22091

(703) 620-3660 Fax (703) 264-9494 TTY/TDD (703) 620-3660

Dr. Philippa Campbell, President

Founded: 1973

Members: 7,000

Mission/Goals: To promote education for infants and young children with special needs; to design programs that involve parents in their children's education; to encourage collaboration among groups concerned with early childhood education; to disseminate information and research findings about early childhood

Audience/Clientele: Teachers, students, program administrators, parents, and others interested in the development of children with disabilities

Education and Outreach: In-service programs, seminars, publishing

Publications: *Division for Early Childhood—Communicator*, quarterly newsletter; *Journal of Early Intervention*, quarterly

Programs: Annual conference, in conjunction with Council for Exceptional Children

Gifted Child Society (GCS)

190 Rock Road, Glen Rock, NJ 07452-1736

(201) 444-6530 Fax (201) 444-9099

Gina Ginsberg Riggs, Executive Director

Founded: 1957

Members: 4,000

Mission/Goals: To provide educational enrichment and support for gifted children through national advocacy and educational programs, specifically the Saturday Workshop Program and Summer Super Stars; to train educators to work with gifted children; to provide parents with assistance in facing the challenges of raising gifted children; to seek public recognition of the special needs of gifted children

Audience/Clientele: Educators, parents, and gifted children

Services: Support group, clinical services, testing, competitions

Education and Outreach: Seminars, continuing education courses, library, speakers' bureau, publishing

Publications: *Directory*, periodic; *History*, biennial; *Newsletter*, semiannual; *How to Help Your Gifted Child*; advocacy packets

Programs: Annual conference

Learning Disabilities Association of America (LDA)

4156 Library Road, Pittsburgh, PA 15234

(412) 341-1515 Fax (412) 344-0224

Jean S. Peterson, National Executive Director

Founded: 1963

Members: 60,000

Affiliates: 48 state groups, 600 local groups

Former Names: Association for Children with Learning Disabilities; Association for Children and Adults with Learning Disabilities

Mission/Goals: To advance the education and well-being of children with learning disabilities arising from perceptual, conceptual, or subtle coordinative problems, including those accompanied by behavior difficulties; to disseminate information to the public on learning disorders

Audience/Clientele: Parents of children with learning disabilities, educators, physicians, social workers, administrators, lawyers

Staff: 1 professional, 3 nonprofessionals, numerous volunteers

Budget: $600,000 Funding: Private sources, fund-raising, donations, dues

Services: Support group, referral, lobbying, fund-raising

Awards: Statesmanship Award, for congressperson who promotes legislation for individuals with learning disabilities

Education and Outreach: Seminars, library, publishing

Publications: *Learning Disabilities: A Multidisciplinary Journal*, semiannual; *LDA Newsbriefs*, bimonthly newsletter

Programs: Annual international conference

National Association for Creative Children and Adults (NACCA)

8080 Springvalley Drive, Cincinnati, OH 45236
(513) 631-1777
Ann F. Isaacs, Chief Executive Officer
Founded: 1974
Members: 1,500
Mission/Goals: To support individuals in ways related to research on creativity; to stimulate a positive approach to using leisure time; to foster appreciation of the arts as a means of nurturing creativity
Audience/Clientele: Individuals dedicated to fostering the creativity of gifted children and adults
Services: Consulting, competitions
Education and Outreach: In-service programs, seminars, research, library, speakers' bureau, publishing
Publications: *The Creative Child and Adult Quarterly*; *Newsletter*, periodic; *Proceedings of the Annual Conference*, includes directory; books, brochures, and monographs
Programs: Annual conference

National Association for Gifted Children (NAGC)

1155 15th Street, N.W., No. 1002, Washington, DC 20005
(202) 785-4268
Peter Rosenstein, Executive Director
Founded: 1954
Members: 7,000
Mission/Goals: To improve the education of gifted children; to enhance their potential creativity; to educate teachers, parents, and others about the development of gifted children
Audience/Clientele: Teachers, librarians, university personnel, administrators, parents
Education and Outreach: Continuing education courses, seminars, publishing
Publications: *Gifted Child Quarterly*; *National Association for Gifted Children—Communique*, quarterly newsletter with legislative updates, information on educational needs of gifted children, and association news
Programs: Annual conference

National Association of Private Schools for Exceptional Children (NAPSEC)

1522 K Street, N.W., Suite 1032, Washington, DC 20005
(202) 408-3338 Fax (202) 408-3340
Sherry L. Kolbe, Executive Director
Founded: 1971
Members: 200
Affiliates: 12 state groups
Mission/Clientele: To promote excellence in private special educational settings for exceptional children
Audience/Clientele: Private schools that serve the exceptional population, state associations or individuals who join the association as affiliate members
Staff: 3 professionals, 13 volunteers
Budget: $225,000 Funding: Fund-raising, fees for services or products, donations, dues

Services: Placement service, referral, lobbying
Education and Outreach: Seminars, publishing
Publications: *NAPSEC News*, quarterly newsletter; *National Issues Service*, monthly legislative publication; *NAPSEC Directory*, biennial; brochure covering "least restrictive environment"
Programs: Annual conference

National Center for Learning Disabilities (NCLD)

381 Park Avenue, Suite 1420, New York, NY 10016
(212) 687-7211
Shirley C. Cramer, Contact Person
Founded: 1977
Members: 4,000
Former Name: Foundation for Children with Learning Disabilities
Mission/Goals: To promote public awareness of learning disabilities, neurological disorders, and other deficits that can interfere with children's learning
Audience/Clientele: Professionals working with people with disabilities, parents
Services: Referrals, lobbying
Education and Outreach: Seminars, publishing
Publications: *Their World*, annual magazine

National Foundation for Children's Hearing Education and Research (CHEAR)

928 McLean Avenue, Yonkers, NY 10704
(914) 237-2676
Philip B. Miller, President
Founded: 1969
Members: 4,000
Former Name: International Foundation for Children's Hearing Education and Research
Mission/Goals: To improve education and educational facilities for the deaf and hearing impaired; to increase public awareness of hearing impairment and its effects on schooling and learning
Services: Research support
Education and Outreach: Publishing
Publications: *Hearing Research Developments*, quarterly; various reprints

The Orton Dyslexia Society (ODS)

Chester Building, Suite 382, 8600 LaSalle Road, Baltimore, MD 21204-6020
(410) 296-0232 Toll-free (800) ACCD-123
Rosemary F. Bowler, Ph.D., Executive Director
Founded: 1949
Members: 9,500
Affiliates: 43 branches
Mission/Goals: To enable all individuals to reach their potential through strengthening learning abilities and removing social, educational, and cultural barriers to language acquisition and use; to promote effective teaching approaches and related clinical educational intervention strategies for dyslexics; to sup-

port and encourage study and research on the causes and early identification of dyslexia

Audience/Clientele: Educators, parents, dyslexics, psychologists, speech-language pathologists

Staff: 10 professionals and nonprofessionals, 3 volunteers

Budget: $1,000,000 Funding: Fund-raising, donations, dues

Services: Support group

Education and Outreach: Seminars, publishing

Publications: *Perspectives on Dyslexia*, quarterly newsletter; *Annals of Dyslexia*, annual; pamphlets

Programs: Annual conference

REFERENCES

1. Charles R. Callanan, *Since Owen: A Parent-to-Parent Guide for Care of the Disabled Child* (Baltimore: Johns Hopkins University Press, 1990), 240–50.

2. *Statistical Abstract of the United States*, 12th ed. U.S. Department of Commerce, Bureau of the Census, 1992, 157.

3. Ibid.

4. Dan Hurley, "Dyslexia Found More Often in Kids Born from May to July," *Chicago Sun-Times*, April 23, 1993, 9.

C H A P T E R

Play, TV, and Recreation

Some information is best presented through play.
Steven P. Shelov, ed. *Caring for Your Baby and Young Child*

If there is one single way for
countering the impact of television . . . it is
by helping your child get used to going to the library.
Gene I. Maeroff. *The School-Smart Parent*

An increasingly popular way for parents to spend more time with their children is through shared recreational pursuits. Biking, boating, running, camping, visits to dude ranches, and other outdoor activities are readily available for parents and their children to enjoy. Mail-order catalogs supply parents with products that support an active family lifestyle, and many resorts, cruise lines, and hotels actively seek families with children as their customers. A recent estimate attributes 80 percent of all vacation travel in the United States to family vacations.[1]

One form of recreation that is common if not active is viewing television. *Trends in Viewing* reported that children devoted an average of three hours and 18 minutes per day to watching television in 1990.[2] Whether or not TV harms intellectual or moral development of children is widely debated, as is its impact on the physical health of children. Controlling TV viewing time and programming content will become even more challenging for parents when plans for direct broadcast satellite video are realized, as it will bring an estimated 150 to 500 new channels into the home.[3]

Purposeful play aids the cognitive and motor development of children. According to the American Academy of Pediatrics, "Young children learn a tremendous amount through play, especially when with parents."[4] Playing stimulates children's curiosity and creativity and provides parents with enjoyable activities to share with their children.

An asterisk (*) indicates a specially recommended title.

POPULAR TITLES: BOOKS

Arp, Claudia. *Beating the Winter Blues: A Complete Survival Handbook for Moms.* Nelson, 1991. 208p. LC 91-17234. ISBN 0-8407-3318-6. $9.95.

The theme of activities for children confined to home during inclement winter weather is used as an approach to child rearing and guidance. The author, a parenting support group leader, emphasizes building positive family relationships, teaching responsibility, and developing spiritual values through creative activities, sports, and appreciation for the beliefs behind the winter holidays. Her writing style is humorous and accessible, and her many suggestions for shared, meaningful leisure reflect a practical approach to raising children.

Bennett, Steve, and Ruth Bennett. *365 Outdoor Activities You Can Do with Your Child.* Bob Adams, 1993. 433p. illus. LC 94-177465. ISBN 1-55850-260-2. $6.95.

The authors of *365 TV-Free Activities You Can Do with Your Child* have responded to reader requests by providing parents with numerous outdoor activities for summer and also by reviving traditional games popular when they were children. Putting safety first, they emphasize games that foster a love of learning; promote a sense of family, neighborhood, and community; and present a balance among sports, education, and artistic activities. The games themselves are arranged alphabetically, with indexes by type of activity (such as gardening or group play), by location (such as the beach or backyard), and by season (e.g., summer, fall).

Butler, Arlene Kay. *Traveling with Children and Enjoying It: A Complete Guide to Family Travel by Car, Plane, and Train*. Globe Pequot, 1991. 284p. photog. illus. index. LC 90-28547. ISBN 0-87106-316-6. $11.95.

Butler's book is a compilation of commonsense suggestions for making travel more enjoyable for parents and their children. Beginning with planning, packing, and accommodations, the text also covers eating while traveling, plane and train ride comfort tips, and activities, games, and songs for entertaining kids on the road. Discipline strategies for various ages, health and safety tips, and suggestions for adjusting to the return home conclude the book. Checklists for each topic may be photocopied for use.

Harrison, David, and Judy Harrison. *Canoe Tripping with Children: Unique Advice to Keeping Kids Comfortable*. ICS, 1990. 142p. bibliog. photog. illus. LC 90-30901. ISBN 0-934802-60-2. $9.95.

For families who have an elementary knowledge of canoeing, the Harrisons have written a practical guide to canoeing vacation planning basics, which covers food, clothing, equipment, first aid, safety, canoeing skills, diversions, wildlife, and recording the adventure. Its low cost and appropriateness for a range of athletic abilities make canoeing a wise choice for parents who want to get their families working and playing together as a team.

Jeffrey, Nan. *Best Places to Go: A Family Destination Guide*. Foghorn, 1993. 323p. bibliog. illus. index. LC 92-43694. ISBN 0-935701-75-3. $14.95.

Detailed information about areas throughout the world that are suitable for family adventure travel is provided in this text, with level of experience, budgetary constraints, season of travel, and children's ages being among the factors the authors take into account in making recommendations. The introduction talks about the nuts and bolts of family travel. The final section on resources provides information on tourist bureaus, consulates, and national airlines and supplies suggested readings and useful maps. The remainder of the text consists of entries arranged by destination. Information provided includes a general description of the location, terrain, culture, lifestyle, and climate, followed by practical concerns such as political conditions, language, travel documents, health, food, and shopping. Finally, facts about transportation, accommodations, and points of interest are supplied.

Kaye, Evelyn. *Family Travel: Terrific New Vacations for Today's Families*. Blue Penguin Publications, 1993. Blue Penguin Travel Resource Guides Series. 202p. bibliog. illus. index. LC 93-090008. ISBN 0-9626231-4-8. Price not available. ISBN 0-9626231-3-X pbk. $19.95.

Traveling with children, especially on such active and adventurous vacations as kayaking, hiking, skiing, trips to dude ranches, or trips with an environmental emphasis, requires thorough preparation and advance planning, says the author, a well-known travel writer. One hundred parents who were interviewed in person or via telephone offer help to parents

who seek interesting, educational, and affordable vacations in the United States and abroad. General advice on being flexible, budgeting, identifying enjoyable activities for the entire family, meal planning, entertainment en route, materials needed, and sample trips help parents develop a realistic outlook on vacations with their children. Attractive line drawings and informative personal accounts add to the appeal of this resource guide.

Kaye, Peggy. *Games for Learning: Ten Minutes a Day to Help Your Child Do Well in School—From Kindergarten to Third Grade*. Noonday, 1991. 251p. bibliog. illus. LC 90-28507. ISBN 0-374-27288-3. $24.95. ISBN 0-374-52286-3 pbk. $10.95.

This sourcebook for simple learning games for children ages 5 to 10 emphasizes having fun while improving learning skills such as information gathering through eyes and ears, handwriting coordination, logical thinking, vocabulary building, sounding out words, writing, reading comprehension, counting, and arithmetic functions. Each game is coded according to suggested grade level and requires no more than 10 minutes to complete. Appendixes include a list of titles that children in this age group should know and books that are particularly good for reading aloud.

Lansky, Vicki. *Games Babies Play from Birth to Twelve Months*. Book Peddlers, 1993. 97p. illus. ISBN 0-916773-32-9. $12.95. ISBN 0-916-773-33-7 pbk. $8.95.

Veteran child care author Vicki Lansky has compiled and organized by developmental stage dozens of infant games in this concise handbook. Play is a way for parents to encourage their child's development, to learn about the self and others, and to show love to their offspring. Games such as peekaboo, so-o-o big, puppet play, hide-and-seek, and pat-a-cake teach parents about their child's attention span, abilities, and nonverbal communication, as well as the joys of touching and social interaction. Contemporary parents will appreciate that traditional rhymes have been revised with nonsexist language.

McCabe, Allyssa. *Language Games to Play with Your Child*. 2nd ed. Insight, 1992. 275p. bibliog. index. LC 92-19084. ISBN 0-306-44320-1. $24.95.

Now in its second edition, this book of games to encourage language development in children from birth through 11 years of age helps parents to draw attention to rules in language, identify times and topics for conversations, and give their children many opportunities to practice language skills. Games are organized by age range, but their applicability depends on the level of language ability the child has achieved rather than his or her age. The author, a developmental psychologist, provides the purpose, props needed, a description of the game, variations, and advice on recognizing readiness for each game.

* Morin, Virginia K. *Messy Activities and More*. Chicago Review, 1993. 126p. bibliog. illus. index. LC 92-41453. ISBN 1-53652-173-1. $9.95.

A variety of types of low-cost games, all focused on interaction between parent and child and requiring little in the way of equipment, are presented in this sourcebook. A thoughtful foreword by Ann M. Ternberg, clinical director of the Theraplay Institute in Chicago, points out the advantages of exuberant play with children and provides rules for making play sessions effective. Activities presented here are appropriate for home, classroom, and therapeutic settings, even parties. They include throwing games, ball games, outside activities, music, sensory stimulation, playground rides, body awareness, eating, and other active games.

Mungic, Evelyn Moats, and Susan Jane Bowdon. *Beyond Peek-a-Boo and Pat-a-Cake: Activities for Baby's First Twenty-Four Months*. 3rd ed. New Win, 1993. 376p. illus. LC 93-1421. ISBN 0-8329-0504-6. $14.95.

Appealing line drawings illustrate this guide to age-appropriate activities for infants and toddlers. The text covers infant behavior in easy-to-understand terms; guides parent-child interaction through structured games, songs, and activities; and suggests solutions to frustrations that new parents may encounter. Each chapter focuses on a single month from birth to two years and lists numerous suggestions for games; suggests ways to make routines such as dressing or bathing stimulating; describes a child's reactions to parents, friends, and admirers; and advises new mothers on how to take care of themselves. Now in its third edition, this handbook helps parents become sensitive observers of their children.

Ocone, Lynn, with Eve Pranis. *The National Gardening Association Guide to Kids' Gardening*. Wiley, 1990. 148p. illus. index. LC 89-48993. ISBN 0-471-52092-6. $9.95.

Attractively illustrated, this text is a comprehensive guide to planning a garden, developing the site, and designing the layout. Written by professionals affiliated with the National Gardening Association, the text provides over 70 experiments, tests, and other instructive and enjoyable activities. Portraits of successful programs are presented in the words of their coordinators. Suggestions for overcoming obstacles and tips for indoor and container gardening are also included.

Peel, Kathy. *A Mother's Manual for Schoolday Survival*. Focus on the Family, 1990. 92p. photog. illus. LC 90-36126. ISBN 0-929608-88-7. $7.99.

Hundreds of techniques to help parents master the routines of the school year and foster an atmosphere of learning, love, and creativity in the home are outlined in this how-to manual. From tips on making chauffeuring less onerous to strategies for organizing a child's time home alone after school, Peel's recommendations will help busy parents. Scheduling, communicating, using informational resources, teaching, and simply having fun are discussed. Of special interest are ideas for dads, suggestions for entertaining sick children, and ways to avoid small frustrations of daily life.

Peel, Kathy, and Julie Byrd. *A Mother's Manual for Holiday Survival: Family Fun for Every Special Occasion*. Focus on the Family, 1991. 135p. bibliog. photog. illus. LC 91-32573. ISBN 1-56179-040-0. $9.99.

Creative tips and easy recipes provide an inexpensive means for parents to make both holidays and everyday celebrations memorable. Peel and Byrd's manual describes how to add fun to any holiday, special tips for seasonal events, and ways to reduce frustration and increase enjoyment of everyday celebrations such as birthday parties, family reunions, unexpected visits, and holiday travel.

Perry, Susan K. *Playing Smart: A Parent's Guide to Enriching, Offbeat Learning Activities for Ages 4 to 14*. Free Spirit, 1990. 211p. bibliog. illus. index. LC 90-40224. ISBN 0-915793-22-9. $12.95.

The quirky suggestions for educational fun in this collection are applicable for all age groups up through adult. While they are not designed to improve children's reading, writing, thinking, or calculating skills, such activities as photography, visiting a cemetery, keeping a journal, gardening, and learning about diverse cultures will enhance children's academic abilities. Each chapter concludes with a lengthy list of references to books and games for parents and children who want to further pursue an activity.

* Singer, Dorothy G., and Jerome L. Singer. *The House of Make-Believe: Children's Play and the Developing Imagination*. Harvard University Press, 1990. 339p. LC 90-35503. ISBN 0-674-40874-8. $29.95.

Empirical research, childhood accounts, and theory are synthesized in this exploration of the source and expression of imagination in childhood and early adolescence. The authors, codirectors of the Yale University Family Television Research and Consultation Center, psychologists, and grandparents, examine how imaginative play begins in infancy with peekaboo games and develops in childhood through social pretend play and imaginary friends. The Singers look at the use of play in healing, the impact of television on the imagination, and the creation of an environment supportive of imaginative play. This comprehensive account is intended for mental health and education professionals as well as for parents.

Singer, Dorothy G., Jerome L. Singer, and Diana M. Zackerman. *A Parent's Guide: Use TV to Your Child's Advantage*. Acropolis, 1990. 207p. illus. index. LC 90-34758. ISBN 0-87491-964-9. $9.95.

A substantive handbook for parents, this volume links the results of research on children's TV viewing to practical suggestions for developing critical thinking, reading and writing skills, and creativity through the use of television. The authors, codirectors of the Family Television Research and Consultation Center at Yale University and a former research assistant, review the advantages and disadvantages of TV viewing, viewing habits, special effects, and the television industry. They examine fantasy versus reality, stereotypes, violence, and advocacy. Each chapter includes a glossary, reading list, and activities for children that reinforce the information presented. Appendixes provide sources of television-related materials, guidelines for parents, and tips for critiquing children's advertising.

Sprafkin, Joyce, Kenneth D. Gadow, and Robert Abelman. *Television and the Exceptional Child: A Forgotten Audience*. L. Erlbaum, 1992. 213p. bibliog. index. LC 92-7974. ISBN 0-8058-0787-X. $49.95.

This scholarly review for researchers, educators, and parents focuses on how learning disabled, emotionally disturbed, mentally retarded, and gifted children view, process, and react to television. The opening chapter summarizes 40 years of research on children and TV. Empirical studies of the specialized audiences noted above are relatively few, despite the ubiquity of television viewing among children today. Exceptional children's TV viewing habits, their perceptions of the realism of TV content, their comprehension of programs and commercials, the effects of parental involvement, and the impact of TV on behavior are among the topics examined here in detail. Guidelines for parents and teachers are presented in the final chapter.

Starr, Richard. *Woodworking with Your Kids*. Taunton Press, 1990. 205p. photog. illus. LC 90-39848. ISBN 0-942391-61-6. $14.95.

For parents who want to instruct their children in woodworking, Starr describes techniques for projects appropriate for children as young as five. Methods rather than plans are provided for such projects as bookcases, toy figures, tables, spoons, stools, games, cars, and various types of boxes. The introduction addresses expectations and safety concerns and the final chapter covers tools and techniques. Written by an elementary school teacher who has taught woodworking to children for 20 years, the text is handsomely illustrated with photographs and drawings that will attract children to a pastime that offers them creative challenge, tangible reward, and the opportunity to learn discipline.

POPULAR TITLES: JOURNALS

Children's Video Report. Great Mountain Productions. 1985. B-M. $35.00.

Selected and reviewed by experts in child development and media, most videos included here are also shown to "the toughest critics of all—kids." Each title is judged on the appropriateness and appeal of its story and quality of the overall production. The journal identifies a source for purchasing the titles covered, Upbeat Video in Brooklyn. One issue reviewed titles that addressed some aspect of the Arthurian legend.

Family Fun. Walt Disney Magazine Publishing Group. 1991. B-M. ISSN 1056-6333. $9.95.

Feature articles on getaways, celebrations, road trips, vacations, and fun in the backyard emphasize creative, enjoyable activities at economical prices. Regular departments cover sports, toys and games, "home cooking" recipes, family computing ideas, reminiscences, reviews, and a family almanac of recreational tips. Lovely photographs illustrate practical text. In addition to information, advice, and tips, this magazine encourages an interest in the arts and a respect for nature as part of its overall emphasis on learning through recreation.

Parents' Choice: A Review of Children's Media. Parents' Choice Foundation. 1978. Q. $18.00.

A not-for-profit publication, this newsletter for parents consists of critical evaluations of books, videos, computer programs, television programs, magazines, toys, and recordings. Recently added were evaluations of CD-ROM programs and a column reviewing Spanish items of particular interest to Latino families. Reviews are submitted by over 400 parents, children, librarians, experts, and other well-informed critics nationwide.

PROFESSIONAL TITLES: BOOKS

Abrams, Berenda, and Nancy Kauffman. *Toys for Early Childhood Development: Selection Guidelines for Infants, Toddlers, and Preschoolers*. Center for Applied Research in Education, 1990. 217p. LC 90-2218. ISBN 0-87628-924-3. $22.95.

Information on the role of play in development and numerous suggestions for selecting age- and stage-specific toys make up this guide. Age-specific chapters on toys for infants, toddlers, and preschoolers describe qualities of toys that enhance sensory awareness, balance and big movements, dexterity and hand-eye coordination, vision, space/time awareness, socialization, language, and creativity development in children. Each chapter also contains a chart that rates typical toys against these dimensions. Introductory chapters address why children play, how children develop, and how to select toys that offer high play value and low safety and health concerns.

Garvey, Catherine. *The Developing Child*. 2nd ed. Harvard University Press, 1990. 184p. LC 90-036281. ISBN 0-674-67364-6. $29.00.

Now in its second edition, this text surveys current research on play in areas that are of practical concern to parents and teachers, such as smiling, play with motion, language, objects and social interaction, play with rules, and ritualized play. Learning how to play and the way play influences a child's cognitive and social development are topics new to this edition.

Gustafson, Marilee A., Sue K. Wolfe, and Cheryl L. King. *Great Games for Young People*. Human Kinetics, 1990. 138p. illus. index. LC 90-38917. ISBN 0-87322-299-7. $11.00.

Over 70 games are presented in this sourcebook by three physical education teachers, who devised the text they wished they had had to assist in children's physical, social, and intellectual development. The description for each game outlines its objectives, number of players, equipment needs, teaching strategies, and safety tips. The authors note that each game has been tested to provide low organizational time, minimum or universal equipment, and applicability to large-group instruction. A reference grid lists all the games with guidelines for ages, group sizes, gross motor rating, and skills involved.

Hughes, Fergus P. *Children, Play, and Development*. Allyn and Bacon, 1991. 255p. bibliog. photog. illus. index. LC 90-926. ISBN 0-205-12644-8. $17.25.

Hughes's state-of-the-art review of play and development links the current literature to theoretical perspectives. The author, a clinical psychologist, traces the history and theory of play, reviews cultural and ethnological variations, and examines the characteristics of play in children ages two through adolescence. Gender differences and the effect of mental, physical, or emotional disabilities are covered, as are social, therapeutic, and intellectual considerations in play. Not a how-to book, this text provides the necessary background for clinicians who choose to develop applications.

Lear, Roma. *More Play Helps: Play Ideas for Children with Special Needs*. Heinemann Medical, 1990. 212p. LC 90-183701. ISBN 0-433-00106-2. $35.00.

International contributors supplied the author with ideas for toys that children with disabilities could enjoy. These toys have low technology requirements and are of three types: instant, quick, and long-lasting. After an initial review of how to hang toys, keep them in children's hands, and plan a play session, the remainder of the text is devoted to categories of toys, arranged alphabetically, that would be appropriate for use by children with different disabilities. For example, toys with an aroma are likely to engage children with autism, who often approach objects by smelling them. The international focus of this British author presents readers with a few unfamiliar terms.

Lynch-Fraser, Diane. *Playdancing: Discovering and Developing Creativity in Young Children*. Princeton, 1990. 122p. bibliog. photog. index. LC 90-53357. ISBN 0-87127-153-2. $20.95. ISBN 0-87127-152-4 pbk. $12.95.

Lynch-Fraser promotes expressive movement or dancing as a means of enhancing young children's ability to communicate and solve problems creatively. Written primarily for teachers, but also applicable to parents, the text covers activities and ideas for movement and learning in young children three to eight. The initial chapters review the link between movement and creativity, describe the playdancing program, and review developmental stages in childhood.

Signorielle, Nancy. *A Sourcebook on Children and Television*. Greenwood, 1991. 199p. LC 90-47502. ISBN 0-313-26642-5. $45.00.

Recent research is summarized in a readable manner also appropriate for parents in this survey of television's effects and impact on children. Written by a communications professor who is advocacy-minded, the text covers the history of children's programming, policy issues, formal attributes of television as a medium, and content of children's TV. The author also looks at the impact of gender role messages, violence, and advertising; how children use TV; and its effects on their academic achievement. The appendix includes a detailed review of specific children's programs and videotapes.

Van Evra, Judith Page. *Television and Child Development*. Erlbaum, 1990. 239p. bibliog. index. LC 90-35064. ISBN 0-8058-0575-3. $44.00. ISBN 0-8058-0858-2 pbk. $22.00.

Readers of this textbook will find a comprehensive synthesis of the diverse literature on the role of television viewing in a child's cognitive development. The first section explores children's cognitive processing of television information, what material affects them, and how television information is extracted by children according to age, gender, family background, and other variables. In the second section, the impact of television, including advertising, on the social and emotional development and behavior of children is examined. The final section reviews and integrates theoretical perspectives from the psychology and communication fields. An added feature is the markedly fluid writing style.

DIRECTORY

American Camping Association (ACA)
5000 State Road 67 North, Martinsville, IN 46151-7902
(317) 342-8456 Fax (317) 342-2065
Ruth Lister, Communication Director
Founded: 1910
Members: 5,500
Mission/Goals: To enhance the quality of the camp experience for youth and adults; to promote professional practices in camp administration; to interpret the values of camp to the public
Audience/Clientele: All segments of the camp movement, including agencies serving youth and adults, independent camps, church organizations, and public/municipal agencies
Staff: 30 professionals, numerous volunteers
Budget: $3,500,000 Funding: Fund-raising, fees for services or products, donations, grants, dues, planned giving
Education and Outreach: In-service programs, continuing education courses, seminars, library, archives, accreditation reviews, publishing
Publications: *Camping Magazine*, 7/yr, with association news, book reviews, calendar, legislative news, new product information; *Guide to Accredited Camps*, annual; *How to Choose a Camp*
Programs: Annual conference

American Family Association (AFA)
P.O. Drawer 2440, Tupelo, MS 38803
(601) 844-5036
Donald E. Wildmon, Executive Director
Founded: 1977
Former Name: National Federation for Decency
Mission/Goals: To foster the biblical ethic of decency in American society with primary emphasis on television and other media; to encourage letter-writing campaigns to networks and sponsors protesting programs that promote violence, immorality, profanity, and vulgarity and encouraging programming that is family oriented and wholesome
Audience/Clientele: Parents, families, general public
Services: Compiling statistics, advocacy
Education and Outreach: Speakers' bureau, publishing
Publications: *AFA Journal*, monthly

National Council for Families and Television (NCFT)
3801 Barham Boulevard, Suite 300, Los Angeles, CA 90068
(213) 876-5959
Tricia McLead Robin, President
Founded: 1977
Former Name: National Council for Children and Television
Mission/Goals: To improve the daily life of families and children by improving the contents of prime-time television programming
Audience/Clientele: Television producers, writers, programming executives, advertisers, educators, child development and family life specialists, pediatricians, and psychologists

Services: Consulting
Education and Outreach: Seminars, symposia, publishing
Publications: *NCFT Information Service Bulletin*, monthly;
Television and Families, quarterly
Programs: Annual conference

USA Toy Library Association (USA-TLA)
2530 Crawford Avenue, Suite 111, Evanston, IL 60201
(708) 864-3330 Fax (708) 864-3331
Judith Q. Iacuzzi, Executive Director
Founded: 1984
Members: 880
Mission/Goals: To provide a networking system answering all
those interested in play and play materials; to provide a national
resource to toy libraries, family centers, public libraries, schools,
institutions serving families with special needs, and other groups
or individuals involved with children; to promote the establishment of toy libraries; to join with corporations and individuals
to promote the importance of appropriate toys and play
Audience/Clientele: Toy librarians, child development
experts, toy makers, play therapists, parents, teachers, others
interested in toys

Staff: 1 professional, 1 nonprofessional (both part-time)
Budget: $20,000 Funding: Fund-raising, donations
Services: Referral
Education and Outreach: Seminars, publishing
Publications: *Child's Play*, quarterly newsletter
Programs: Periodic conferences

REFERENCES

1. Eileen Ogintz, "Courting Kids the Inn Thing to Do," *Chicago Tribune*, January 24, 1992, sec. 3, p. 2.
2. *Trends in Viewing*, Television Bureau of Advertising, 1991, 7.
3. "150-Channel Alternative to Cable Set to Be Launched," *Hammond Times*, August 25, 1993, sec. F, p. 1.
4. Steven P. Shelov, ed., *Caring for Your Baby and Young Child: Birth to Age Five* (New York: Bantam in association with American Academy of Pediatrics, 1990), xxiii.

CHAPTER

Religious Training

*Spiritual development is the
growth of the child's view of the world.*
David Heller. *Talking to Your Children about God*

*Children learn spiritual awareness and
sensitivity from being part of a loving community.*
Sheila Kitzinger and Celia Kitzinger. *Tough Questions*

Religion provides children with a spiritual guide and a mission.[1] Religious training encourages children's faith in a greater power and gives them guidance for ethical decision making and daily conduct. Strong beliefs assist parents in making a multitude of decisions that define their child's life, from disciplinary practices to educational and recreational choices. Over 75 percent of the men and women born between 1946 and 1964 want their children to receive religious training; 70 percent of those interviewed were members of a synagogue or church.[2]

An asterisk (*) indicates a specially recommended title.

POPULAR TITLES: BOOKS

Bajema, Edith. *Worship: Not for Adults Only.* CRC Publications, 1990. 95p. bibliog. LC 90-36668. ISBN 0-930265-89-0. $6.50.

Six discussion activities appropriate for Christian parenting groups are included, along with insights and advice on making worship more appealing to children in this concise handbook. Activities were designed to emphasize understanding of a child's view of worship and introduce numerous creative and practical approaches to increase children's interest and participation in worship at home and in church. A review of the meaning of worship and its history provides background information in preparation for the more applied sections on worship practices.

Bell, Roselyn, ed. *The Hadassah Magazine: The Jewish Parenting Book.* Avon, 1990. 376p. LC 89-7746. ISBN 0-02-913-460-9. $13.50.

Reprints of the best of the "Parenting" column published in the *Hadassah Magazine* are collected in this volume of elegantly crafted essays. The essays are organized topically, with the first section covering the Jewish parenting life cycle, followed by sections on providing a Jewish education within and outside the home, linking the family to the community, responding to children's difficult questions, facing the challenges of contemporary life, and passing the family legacy on to the children. Without being prescriptive or rigid, the essays offer practical, commonsense approaches to the many responsibilities and concerns Jewish parents face today.

* Berends, Polly Berrien. *Gently Lead: How to Teach Your Children about God while Finding Out for Yourself.* Harper Collins, 1991. 172p. illus. LC 90-55526. ISBN 0-06-016489-1. $18.95.

This compilation of poems, stories, and personal anecdotes presents a nondenominational approach to nurturing spiritual development in a child. The collection is also a record of the spiritual growth process of Berends, the author of *Whole Parent/Whole Child,* and her children. Among the topics she addresses are God, worship, death, faith, love, and other spiritual issues that children and their parents confront.

Chapin, Alice Zillman. *Building Your Child's Faith.* Nelson, 1990. 156p. LC 90-32644. ISBN 0-8407-3134-5. $8.95.

A Christian educator and writer, Chapin drew upon suggestions from participants in her "How to Share Your Faith with Your Children" seminars to enable parents who lack a detailed knowledge of scripture or a gift for eloquence to succeed in educating their children about God. She provides practical techniques for choosing a Bible, teaching a child to pray, organizing family worship, carrying out a reading plan, and leading a child to accept Christ. When a child is most receptive to various tenets is reviewed in an extensive list of additional readings.

Diamant, Anita. *The New Jewish Baby Book: Names, Ceremonies, Customs*. Jewish Lights, 1993. 288p. bibliog. illus. index. LC 93-25870. ISBN 1-879045-28-1. $15.95.

This guide helps new Jewish parents make their first decisions, which include planning the ceremony to welcome their child into the covenant and community of Judaism and selecting a suitable name. Written by a journalist, the book presents, in a lively manner, well-informed historic, religious, culinary, and literary traditions linked to the birth of a child. Special topics, such as adoption and interfaith families, are covered as well. Sample Brit Milah and Brit Bat ceremonies, advice for Simcha (parties), and a directory of Jewish resources add to the usefulness of this guide.

Fay, Martha. *Do Children Need Religion? Parents, Children, and Religion in a Secular Age*. Pantheon, 1993. 237p. bibliog. LC 92-50475. ISBN 0-679-42054-1. $21.00.

Though not widely acknowledged, new parents feel an obligation to think about their religious beliefs and how they want to convey them to their children, even during times when organized religion appears to have disappeared as a concern. In this thoughtful essay, the author explores Christian parents' difficulty in handling the "big questions" about the existence of God, Heaven, and Jesus when their children innocently and eagerly pose them. Because the most fervent wish of parents is that their children be good, their role as the source of their offspring's morality is a solemn one, with or without the aid of religious faiths. Even if they accept the loss, metaphysical and moral, to children not raised in a particular religion, most parents view being deprived of any religion's rituals, symbols, poetry, magic, and stories as an emotional and cultural loss.

* Fitzpatrick, Jean Grasso. *Something More: Nurturing Your Child's Spiritual Growth*. Viking, 1991. 237p. LC 90-50516. ISBN 0-670-83706-7. $18.95.

In the view of the author, a Christian parenting writer, spirituality is an awareness of humans' sacred connection to all life, and spiritual nurture is a journey of discovery, as opposed to religious or moral instruction. She examines the nature of spirituality in the initial chapters, then looks at spirituality in daily life and in childhood, the role of community and the natural world, acknowledgment of pain, death, and prayer through play. Each chapter is divided into two parts, the first part covering parenting issues from a spiritual perspective and the second consisting of practical suggestions to use to support the child's development. An appendix suggests books and music for the child that express spiritual themes. Chapter 9, on responding to difficult questions, was serialized in *Parents Magazine*.

Furnish, Dorothy Jean. *Experiencing the Bible with Children*. Abingdon, 1990. 139p. bibliog. LC 89-49188. ISBN 0-687-12425-5. $12.95.

With the goal of helping Christian children experience the Bible's content and discover its meaning in their lives today, this handbook reviews what the Bible is, how children develop, and specific techniques for teaching children about the Bible. The text combines and updates two earlier works from Abingdon Press, *Exploring the Bible with Children* (1975) and *Living the Bible with Children* (1979), done in response to requests from Christian education directors, seminary professors, and church schoolteachers who have attended the author's workshops on the topic. The specific content includes history of the Bible and perspectives on its meaning, child development and today's children, and instructions for using creative drama, storytelling, dance, and dialogue to teach children. The appendix is a case study applying the information and methods described here.

Gruzen, Lee F. *Raising Your Jewish-Christian Child: How Interfaith Parents Can Give Children the Best of Both Their Heritages*. Dodd Mead, 1987. 270p. bibliog. index. LC 89-13818. ISBN 1-55704-059-1. $10.95.

Noting the increased incidence of interfaith marriages and the relative homogeneity of the husband and wife in terms of education, economic background, and occupational status, the author, a Christian woman married to a Jewish man, challenges outmoded beliefs that such marriages will fail. To research this book, she interviewed a large number of participants, both spouses and children, in interfaith marriages and drew on her personal experiences as well. The chapters cover children's religious beliefs and practices from preschool age to adolescence, negotiation, faith and organized religion, cultural heritage and family legacy, religious choices, God, ceremonies, and celebrations. Gruzen identifies and discusses the issues involved in interfaith marriages, using case studies, often her own, to illustrate, and provides recommendations and practical advice in an approach that is informative without being prescriptive. For example, she observes that contemporary parents may find God a more difficult topic than sex to discuss with their children, and that they should permit their children to proceed at their own pace in understanding God. She also advises parents to acknowledge the difference between Christ and God, offer children images of God that the parents love and stories that they value, and build their faith through open discussion and exploration rather than simple instructions. An index simplifies use of the information, and a bibliography provides additional information as well as materials to use in guiding children's level of religious faith.

Heller, David. *Talking to Your Children about God*. Bantam, 1988. 167p. index. LC 88-47644. ISBN 0-553-05325-6. $12.95.

This book is written for parents who hope to instill spiritual awareness in their children but who may feel uncomfortable responding to their children's questions or confused about their own beliefs. Among the issues addressed are creating a healthy spiritual environment, knowing one's own spiritual beliefs, talking to children about God, discussing children's notions of God, and discussing the nature and purpose of religion. Information about individual major religions such as Islam, Buddhism, and Judaism is also included. A chapter on interfaith families addresses the special concerns of this group.

Hromas, R. P. *52 Simple Ways to Teach Your Child to Pray*. Oliver-Nelson, 1991. 144p. LC 91-9894. ISBN 0-8407-9590-4. $7.95.

Daily prayer, even prayer "without ceasing," provides a child with the means to communicate with God and grow in his or her spiritual relationship with God according to this Christian guide. To best teach a child to pray, the author, a grandmother, advises parents to pray themselves. She provides numerous approaches to prayer in individual chapters, each organized around a theme, which open with appropriate scripture, provide a background and rationale, and conclude with the text of the prayers themselves. The content is diverse, including prayers for forgiveness, when entering and leaving the house, before a big event, for family members or for a loving heart, and for help in a new place.

Kageler, Len. *Teen Shaping: Positive Approaches for Disciplining Your Teens*. Revell, 1990. 224p. LC 90-35618. ISBN 0-8007-5359-3. $7.95.

This Christian approach to disciplining adolescents is guided by New Testament models of teaching good behavior rather than the Old Testament's emphasis on punishing wrongdoing, as well as the results of a survey on discipline effectiveness administered nationally to Christian college students. Kageler describes common parenting styles, explains why parents use them, and examines how they work or fail in helping parents effectively guide their children ages 11–19 to respect authority, be accountable, and exercise self-control, in other words, to self-discipline. Advice for parents on how to modify their style is practical and theoretical as well as behavioral: pray, set specific goals, and role-play. A helpful handbook for parenting groups as well as individuals, the book also addresses how to regain control and how to discipline children with special problems.

Lucas, James Raymond. *The Parenting of Champions: Raising Godly Children in an Evil Age*. Wolgemuth and Hyatt, 1990. 288p. LC 90-30179. ISBN 0-943497-85-X. $13.95.

This primer of practical techniques for Christian parenting outlines the author's vision, based on scripture, to raise a child who is a champion, a winner in the race to God, and a defender of the faith. Components of the vision include high expectations, open communication, counseling, and modeling. To put this approach into practice requires faith, integrity, stability, holiness, confidence, and balance, as well as practical methods such as family rights, praise, and memories. How to circumvent common obstacles is also reviewed. The author, a management consultant, minister, and parent, develops and defends in this text an aware and realistic approach to Christian parenting that has applicability for non-Christians as well in its emphasis on communication, modeling, and parental goals.

Phillips, Benny, and Sheree Phillips. *Raising Kids Who Hunger for God*. Chosen, 1991. 251p. LC 91-7367. ISBN 0-8007-9181-9. $7.95.

Essays by a Christian minister and his wife, an author and speaker on parenting, explore in alternate chapters basic parenting issues such as discipline, encouraging respect for authority and a sense of responsibility, and fathering in this

practical guide book. The authors first analyze the crisis in contemporary American family life, examining how such problems as a faulty spiritual foundation and misguided priorities affect Christian families. Using scriptural quotations and anecdotes from their own family experiences, they present practical methods for strengthening Christian faith and practices in daily life.

* Reuben, Steven C. *Raising Jewish Children in a Contemporary World: The Modern Parent's Guide to Creating a Jewish Home*. Prima, 1993. 228p. bibliog. index. LC 91-30144. ISBN 1-55958-319-3. $12.95.

This handbook by a Reconstructionist rabbi is a guide to raising children with a positive Jewish self-image, children who understand the key concepts and values of Judaism. It provides parents with an early, accessible approach to incorporating elements of Jewish heritage, ethics, ritual, and culture in a personal lifestyle, as well as helping them instill in their children a sense of belonging to a larger community. Rabbi Reuben covers in a down-to-earth, nonjudgmental fashion such key concerns as finding meaning in holidays and the Shabbat, the role of Israel and the impact of anti-Semitism on the lives of Jews, and recognizing prominent Jewish people as role models. He approaches Judaism as an evolving religious civilization and in this articulate text makes it meaningful for today's parents, particularly those facing the challenge of interfaith marriages. The final chapter contains an extensive bibliography of additional readings organized by chapter.

Shelley, Marshall, ed. *Keeping Your Kids Christian: A Candid Look at One of the Greatest Challenges Parents Face*. Vine Books, 1990. 280p. LC 90-37963. ISBN 0-89283-667-9. $8.95.

Popular Christian authors advise parents on the parent's role in keeping the family Christian, personalizing faith, shaping children and teens, and teaching Christian behavior in a series of brief essays, most of which are original to this anthology. Specific content includes discussions of building family traditions, helping siblings love each other, providing the right role model, teaching kids to give, helping teens handle their anger, teaching children about sex, and coping with drugs and alcohol. Developing roots in Christian beliefs, actions, and being is the focus of the essays included in this anthology.

Wolpe, David J. *Teaching Your Children about God: A Modern Jewish Approach*. Holt, 1993. 254p. bibliog. index. LC 93-2294. ISBN 0-8050-2616-9. $22.50.

Spiritual and religious questions commonly posed by children and youths between the ages of 4 and 14 are explored in this eloquent text for Jewish parents. Origins and explanations of God, where to look for God, God's love and law, dealing with difficult questions such as the existence of evil, and explaining death to children are among the topics examined. Exercises given help parents explore these concerns with their children in a comfortable, natural manner, as do the chapter introductions and summary questions. Rabbi Wolpe also explores in this insightful account the way in which children see the world and what their parents may learn from children's views of the world.

POPULAR TITLES: JOURNALS

Christian Parenting Today. Good Family Magazines. B-M. ISSN 1040-8088. $18.97.

Aimed at a broad spectrum of Christian parents, this upbeat magazine provides feature articles and practical tips based on current research and Bible verses. Book excerpts, humor, inspirational statements, health care information, reviews, and developmental updates provide up-to-date advice on parenting in the '90s. Regular columns address single parenting and the father's role and provide readers with an opportunity to exchange parent-tested tips. Some of the topics covered have been reacting to children's sex play, celebrating Easter week, and reducing conflict among siblings.

Christianity Today. Christianity Today. 1956. 15/yr. ISSN 0009-5753. $24.95.

Subtitled "a magazine of evangelical conviction," this periodical addresses religious training, moral guidance of children, Christian education, and the impact of media on family values.

Your Child. United Synagogue of Conservative Judaism. 1974. Q. ISSN 0044-1007. $3.00.

For parents of young Jewish children, this newsletter provides practical advice on daily living from a conservative perspective. Such topics as helping children grow up, defining what it means to be Jewish, selecting or making Jewish toys, and finding children's books with religious themes were covered in one issue.

PROFESSIONAL TITLES: BOOKS

Coles, Robert. *The Spiritual Life of Children.* Houghton Mifflin, 1990. 351p. bibliog. illus. index. LC 90-40097. ISBN 0-395-55999-5. $22.95.

In this concluding volume of writing on children's perceptions, Coles explores through psychoanalytic observations and interviews with 500 ethnically diverse children what children believe about God and religion. After describing linkages between psychoanalysis and religion and his methodology, he analyzes in a lucid, jargon-free style psychological themes, philosophical reflections, and visionary moments in the children's accounts. He looks at the ways children represent God, including many of their drawings with the text, and explores their understanding of the central messages of Christianity, Judaism, and the Islamic faith. Issues explored by children who do not profess formal religious beliefs are contrasted with those of children who do.

Hyde, Kenneth E. *Religion in Childhood and Adolescence: A Comprehensive Review of the Research.* Religious Education, 1990. 529p. bibliog. index. LC 90-42006. ISBN 0-89135-076-4. $18.95.

Empirical research on the psychology of religion in children and adolescents is the subject of this review. The author organizes a disparate field, covering the history of religious think-ing; children's ideas about God and how they are influenced by parental images; the development of religious beliefs; the impact of teaching styles on religious understanding; religious attitudes, experience, and practices; the religious influence of schools; and religion in adolescence. Substantive appendixes address difficulties in defining religion and measuring attitudes with numerical scales, dimensions of religiousness, extrinsic versus intrinsic beliefs, and religious understanding versus belief. Hyde presents a comprehensive sourcebook for anyone involved in religious education, youth ministry, or the study of the psychology of religion.

DIRECTORY

Association of Jewish Family and Children's Agencies, Inc. (AJFCA)
P.O. Box 248, 3086 State Highway 27, Suite 11, Kendall Park, NJ 08824
(908) 821-0909 Fax (908) 821-0493 Toll-free (800) 634-7346
Bert J. Goldberg, Executive Vice President
Founded: 1972
Members: 145 agencies
Mission/Goals: To support member agencies' service to Jewish families and children by providing information, problem solving, recruitment assistance, research, planning, and other support services; to foster quality of service, coordinate national services and programs, promote understanding of the importance of services to Jewish families and children, and address public policy issues affecting these clients; to accomplish this mission by working with individual agencies and local communities, providing forums for volunteer and professional leaders, and speaking on behalf of the needs of Jewish families and children
Audience/Clientele: Jewish family and children's service agencies
Staff: 4 professionals, 3 nonprofessionals
Budget: $542,000 Funding: Private sources, fees for services or products, combined federal campaign
Education and Outreach: Seminars, resource center, publishing
Publications: *Bi-Monthly Bulletin; Professional Opportunities Bulletin; Resettlement, Acculturation, and Integration Bulletin*
Programs: Annual conference

REFERENCES

1. William Sears, *Christian Parenting and Child Care* (Nashville: Nelson, 1991), 51.

2. George Gallup Jr. and Frank Newport, "Baby-Boomers Seek More Family Time," *The Gallup Poll Monthly* 307 (April 1991): 23–34.

PART

6

CHILDREN IN CRISIS

C H A P T E R

Child Abuse

Child abuse is ineffective parenting in the extreme.
David Sabatino. *A Fine Line*

Right away . . . say "I believe you."
Caren Adams and Jennifer Fay.
Helping Your Child Recover from Sexual Abuse

Contemporary interpretations of child abuse define it as harm to a child through mistreatment or neglect, principally physical abuse and emotional neglect. In 1991, an estimated 2,694,000 children were victims of abuse; the rate of abuse per 1,000 children was 42. From 1985 to 1991, the number of reports of child abuse or neglect rose 40 percent.[1] Child abuse is rarely premeditated; rather, it occurs when parents lose self-control while disciplining a child. According to David Sabatino, "Many parents continue to believe that there is an inherent moral lesson, and therefore intrinsic value, in teaching children to realize that punishment follows rule-breaking."[2] Other influences, those that act to unsettle a family, increase its isolation, or increase the stress the parents must endure, raise the risk of abuse. Parents who have been abused themselves, who have low self-esteem, or who are immature and ignorant about children may become abusive.[3]

Sexual abuse of children is particularly horrifying to contemplate and yet alarmingly common. Denial that incest and other acts of sexual abuse occur across all classes of society is strongest when boys are the victims of assault.[4] Parents help their children recover from sexual abuse by first and foremost believing the charge, then acknowledging the anger, grieving the loss, and rebuilding self-esteem. Reestablishing a sense of safety and self-control and communicating a healthy sexuality to a child

hurt by abuse are also responsibilities that parents must bear.[5]

An asterisk (*) indicates a specially recommended title.

POPULAR TITLES: BOOKS

Adams, Caren, and Jennifer Fay. *Helping Your Child Recover from Sexual Abuse.* University of Washington, 1988. 176p. LC 88-37877. ISBN 0-295-96806-0. $12.95.

When talking about sexual abuse with a child who has been victimized, parents can use this book as a guide. Written to help parents find a role in their child's recovery, the text covers discovery of the abuse, requirements of the legal system, family and friends, responses, the child's reaction, grieving, rebuilding self-esteem, healthy sexuality, self-protection, and long-term adjustment. The material is organized so that information for parents is presented on the left-hand page and suggestions for what parents may say to the child are on the opposite page.

Hillman, Donald, and Janice Solek-Tefft. *Spiders and Flies: Help for Parents and Teachers of Sexually Abused Children.* Lexington, 1988. 198p. bibliog. index. LC 87-38062. ISBN 0-669-17982-5. $29.95. ISBN 0-669-17983-3 pbk. $12.95.

This handbook seeks to provide parents, teachers, and school counselors with specific techniques for aiding children who they suspect or discover have experienced sexual abuse. Drawing from their clinical practice, scholarly research, and parent training classes, the authors examine myths about sexual abuse, review normal sexual development and stage-specific effects of abuse, and examine the nature of abusive encounters, including the context, factors affecting severity, and abuser ploys. Effects of abuse, both short term and long term, assessment of the child's and offender's credibility, actions to take in cases of abuse, the dynamics of abuse, and ways to prevent it from occurring are all explored in a detailed but readable manner. Information on reactions of abused children, treatment goals, counseling skills, and characteristics of perpetrators enhances the coverage of this text. Appendixes provide bibliographies of audiovisual materials, materials for children, and resources for parents and trainers.

Smith, Margaret. *Ritual Abuse: What It Is, Why It Happens, and How to Help.* HarperSanFrancisco, 1993. 213p. bibliog. LC 92-56420. ISBN 0-06-250214-X pbk. $12.00.

The results of several studies of survivors of ritual abuse practiced by violent cults, including a study conducted by the author, inform this guide to the nature of such abuse, its common link to multiple personality disorder and therapy for its survivors. Drawing also on personal experience, the author describes ways in which cults brainwash and program their members; typical characteristics of the abusers; physical, sexual, and emotional abuse of children; beliefs, practices, and structure of various cults; and ways to escape and recover from cult participation. The contents are graphic and horrifying, yet the tone of empathy and respect for the lifelong struggles of survivors make this a compassionate guide for family and friends and an essential tool for therapists who need to acquaint themselves with the circumstances of ritual abuse and the issues it raises for those who have been victimized by such practices.

PROFESSIONAL TITLES: BOOKS

Ackerman, Robert J., and Dee Graham. *Too Old to Cry: Abused Teens in Today's America.* TAB, 1990. 266p. LC 90-43539. ISBN 0-8306-3407-X. $9.95.

Adolescent abuse may not be recognized because teens are perceived as capable of self-defense or flight, but they are likely victims because of their emotional dependence on and submissiveness to their parents. Drawing on research, case material, and professional experience, the authors, a sociologist and journalist, review the causes of abuse, signs of abuse and neglect and their effects, and how to cope with and prevent adolescent abuse. They review specific steps individuals may take to intervene in suspected abusive situations, including resolving immediate family conflicts.

Ammerman, Robert T., and Michel Hersen, eds. *Children at Risk: An Evaluation of Factors Contributing to Child Abuse and Neglect.* Plenum, 1990. 314p. bibliog. LC 90-7228. ISBN 0-306-43437-7. $45.00.

Identifying which children are at risk is a key element of modern research and practice in child abuse prevention. In this anthology, contributors review the status of research on risk factors of abuse and assess progress in preventing its occurrence. The first section includes an introduction to research on risk and guidelines for future empirical investigation. It is followed by sections that address critical areas of maltreatment,

primary risk factors, prevention and treatment techniques, and an agenda for future investigations. Specific contents include a review of the epidemiology of abuse and neglect; discussion of the impact of social variables, parental characteristics, and child characteristics on risk; and a summary of important new treatment techniques.

Barth, Richard P., and David S. Derezotes. *Preventing Adolescent Abuse: Effective Intervention Strategies and Techniques.* Lexington, 1990. 222p. bibliog. index. LC 90-30978. ISBN 0-669-20903-1. $26.95.

Reporting on the first systematic project to describe and analyze prevention programs for adolescent abuse, a two-year study sponsored by California's Office of Child Abuse Prevention, the authors go beyond their evaluation of results to provide a theoretical framework for understanding and focusing these services. The text, which is written for a diverse audience of child care professionals, reviews current research describing adolescent abuse, examines previous programs, analyzes the outcomes obtained in California and elsewhere, and proposes strategies for redesigning curricula on prevention.

Faller, Kathleen Coulborn. *Understanding Child Sexual Maltreatment.* Sage, 1990. 251p. bibliog. index. LC 90-8632. ISBN 0-8039-3841-1. $17.95.

A lot of the data presented here are compiled from the author's work with the University of Michigan's Interdisciplinary Project on Child Abuse and Neglect. The text orients the mental health professional to the incidence, prevalence, indicators, and types of sexual maltreatment in the first section, then goes on to cover protective services (the police, courts, and attorneys) and how to interact with them and diagnosis and case decision making. Content includes how to decide whether abuse has occurred and guidelines for judging its severity. In the final section, sexual abuse in three special situations, divorce, foster parenting, and day care, is explored in detail. All professionals who work with abused children are the intended audience.

Friedrich, William N., ed. *Casebook of Sexual Abuse Treatment.* Norton, 1991. 327p. bibliog. index. LC 91-2548. ISBN 0-393-70113-1. $34.95.

Clinical experts proceed step-by-step through the therapeutic process in the diverse child abuse cases compiled here. Each chapter covers the therapist's theoretical perspective, a brief description of the case, psychological assessment, progress of the therapy (in phases), outcome of treatment, obstacles to treatment, other service systems required, mistakes, and therapist's reaction to the case. Several themes appear regularly in these difficult accounts: no one treatment program exists, the therapist must be "tough and tender" and generally take an advocacy role that continues after termination, and abused children require long-term treatment involving regular consultation with social service agencies. In addition, the cases are linked by the editor's introduction, which identifies special techniques, notes important issues, and raises questions that contribute to the reader's comprehension of the material.

Friedrich, William N. *Psychotherapy of Sexually Abused Children and Their Families.* Norton, 1990. 318p. LC 90-32204. ISBN 0-393-70079-8. $34.95.

Friedrich's down-to-earth, pragmatic review of psychotherapy with abused children is written from the therapist's perspective and even includes a chapter addressing personal needs, goals, and beliefs of the therapist. The author examines the impact of sexual abuse on the child, developmental factors that mediate the abuse, evaluation of the child, and treatment planning. He looks at results obtained with individual psychotherapy, group therapy, and hypnotherapy. Practical advice on case management and managing the sexualized behavior evident in many abused children is provided.

Gelles, Richard J., and Claire Pedrick Cornell. *Intimate Violence in Families*. Sage, 1990. 159p. bibliog. index. LC 90-31861. ISBN 0-8039-3718-0. $19.95. ISBN 0-8039-3719-9 pbk. $9.95.

Prominent author Gelles and collaborator Cornell provide an overview of family violence, its historical context and contemporary incidence, causes, prevention, and treatment in this concise text. Additional chapters look at violence toward children, women, and the heretofore hidden victims of intimate violence—siblings, adolescents, parents, and the elderly. Myths of family violence, e.g., that it is rare or a symptom of mental disorder, are critiqued, as are the theories explaining its causes. The text provides a basic understanding of the issues involved for those in the helping professions.

Gil, Eliana. *The Healing Power of Play: Working with Abused Children*. Guilford, 1991. 210p. bibliog. illus. index. LC 90-6706. ISBN 0-89862-560-2. $35.00. ISBN 0-89862-467-3 pbk. $17.95.

Detailed clinical examples of the therapeutic treatment of children who had been severely neglected or sexually abused, suffered multiple traumas, or been hospitalized constitute half of this clinical guide for psychotherapists who work with abused children. The account of each case covers referral information, social and family history, clinical impressions, treatment phases, and discussion of the results. To provide a context for this data, the author, a psychologist who treats abused children, reviews current research on treatment and play therapy, examines factors involved in making treatment decisions, and looks at issues affecting the clinician, such as countertransference, self-care, and safety.

Goldman, Renitta L, and Richard M. Gargiulo, eds. *Children at Risk: An Interdisciplinary Approach to Child Abuse and Neglect*. Pro-Ed, 1990. 267p. bibliog. photog. illus. index. LC 89-10984. ISBN 0-89079-220-8. $29.00.

Intended for the social service professional and edited by two special education professors, this anthology presents an interdisciplinary approach to child abuse. Selections from an attorney, obstetrician/gynecologist, and social worker address prosecution of child molesters, medical evaluation of the sexually abused child, and family case management, respectively. Two introductory chapters cover history, incidence, identification, characteristics of victims and victimizers, reporting laws, and an educator's perspective. The final chapters review strategies to encourage community involvement and approaches to conducting sound and therefore useful research.

Grubman-Black, Stephen D. *Broken Boys/Mending Men: Recovery from Childhood Sexual Abuse*. TAB, 1990. 182p. bibliog. LC 90-33024. ISBN 0-8306-3562-9. $12.95.

The purpose of this frank discussion of male sexual victimization is to awaken parents, teachers, and psychologists to the reality and effects of an alarmingly common situation in order to better understand and prevent it. The text is divided into two parts. The first part, on broken boys, covers the assault on image, identity, feelings, and behavior that accompanies sexual assault. The second part focuses on the healing process of talking, listening, reevaluating, and letting go of the hurt. The final chapter is a practical and concise guide to signs and symptoms of abuse. Because it is written in the first person, the candid accounts reported here are particularly moving as well as instructive.

Hobbs, Christopher J., Helga G. I. Hanks, and Jane M. Wynne. *Child Abuse and Neglect: A Clinician's Handbook*. Churchill Livingstone, 1993. 325p. bibliog. photog. illus. index. $79.95.

This guide for physicians presents information on recognizing, assessing, managing, and treating the major forms of child abuse such as sexual abuse, neglect, burns and scalds, emotional maltreatment, and failure to thrive. Case material, photographs, and line drawings help provide a thorough introduction to difficult-to-diagnose conditions that physicians may encounter in children.

Hooper, Chrisan, and Deborah Minshew. *The Adoptive Family: The Healing Resource for the Sexually Abused Child*. Child Welfare League of America, 1990. ISBN 0-87868-360-7. $14.95.

Social service professionals can use this training manual to prepare adoptive families to effectively parent sexually abused children. The authors emphasize the parents' role as the primary source of therapy for these children, who need to learn that they are worthy of love and that adults may be trusted. The training covers the dynamics of sexual abuse, keeping and sharing secrets, the impact and effects of abuse, and parenting skills for adoptive parents of these special needs children. Background information, consisting of a literature review, history of the program and results obtained, case studies, and recommendations for further research, supplement the course outline, data, and rationale.

Hudson, Pamela S. *Ritual Child Abuse: Discovery, Diagnosis, and Treatment*. R&E, 1991. 100p. illus. LC 90-64424. ISBN 0-88247-867-2. $11.95.

Compiled by a caseworker and ritual child abuse consultant, this manual for professionals working with severely abused children reviews symptoms and allegations identified from a number of cases throughout the United States to aid in diagnosis of ritual abuse. The author also covers treatment considerations specific to the effects of ritual abuse, such as disillusionment, alienation, disassociation, and multiple personality disorder. The appendix includes an extensive bibliography, list of associations, children's drawings, and the text of the Idaho State Law identifying certain aspects of ritual abuse as illegal.

Hunter, Mic, ed. *The Sexually Abused Male*. 2 vols. Lexington, 1990. LC 90-6352. Vol. 1. 352p. ISBN 0-669-21518-X. $39.95. Vol. 2. 320p. ISBN 0-669-25005-8. $39.95.

The cultural context of child sexual abuse is analyzed in the first volume of this sourcebook, and practical treatment information is provided in the second. In the first volume, contributors examine the politics of sexual abuse, initial and long-term effects, prevalence, and factors mediating its impact. They also review the female offender and assessment issues, such as the medical examination and assessment interviews. In the second volume, experts whose primary professional responsibility is treating sexually abused males provide a framework for understanding the victim's reactions and recovery process, general treatment considerations, and specific treatment strategies. This sourcebook for a broad audience of therapists combines material on adult survivors with data on male child and adolescent victims.

Iverson, Timothy, and Marilyn Segal. *Child Abuse and Neglect: An Information and Reference Guide*. Garland, 1990. 220p. LC 89-71495. ISBN 0-8240-7776-8. $34.00.

This survey provides a general overview of child abuse and neglect in the United States and resources available for helping professionals to promote adaptive parenting and prevent abusive practices in the future. The history of child abuse, theoretical perspectives, definitions, and methods for studying child abuse are discussed. The characteristics of parents who mistreat their children and of children who are abused are described, as are factors that influence poor parenting and its effect on the child's development. The authors also give information on reporting and intervention requirements. Appendixes supplement the text with a list of national resources for training and information and a state-by-state list of reporting regulations.

Jorgenson, E. Clay. *Child Abuse: A Practical Guide for Those Who Help Others*. Continuum, 1990. 220p. bibliog. photog. index. LC 89-25267. ISBN 0-8264-0454-5. $16.95.

Practical counseling techniques to make active intervention in child abuse cases easier for care givers in the helping professions are the focus of this introductory handbook. Suitable also as a source of supplementary readings for undergraduates, the text describes the nature of emotional abuse, working with the child, strategies that support healing, working with parents, how parents cope, and therapy for parents and children. Sexual abuse is not addressed. The tone is empathetic, particularly in the presentation of case material drawn from the author's clinical practice.

Krivacska, James J. *Designing Child Sexual Abuse Prevention Programs: Current Approaches and a Proposal for the Prevention, Reduction, and Identification of Sexual Misuse*. Thomas, 1990. 362p. LC 89-20589. ISBN 0-398-05653-6. $64.75.

Drawing on current theories and research on child development, the author spells out the essential components of an effective child abuse prevention program. These components include promotion of normal childhood sexuality, enhancement of social competency, and age-appropriate instruction in child abuse concepts. As he outlines in his PRISM (Prevention, Reduction, Identification of Sexual Misuse) program, this approach is in contrast to the usual one that transfers adult understanding and concepts to children. The text covers the history and theory of prevention programs and reviews educational programs that work, the dynamics of sexual abuse, program specifics of PRISM, and ways to implement abuse prevention programs.

Levy, Barrie, ed. *Dating Violence: Young Women in Danger*. Seal, 1991. 315p. bibliog. index. LC 90-24538. ISBN 1-87806-703-6. $16.95.

Adolescent dating relationships are vulnerable to violence by virtue of the peer pressure, sex role stereotypes, intense emotionality, and lack of experience the young partners feel. In this sourcebook, compiled by a therapist and consultant, a review of research on dating violence, an analysis of the social context of dating, observations of professionals who work with young abused women, and letters, stories, and interviews with young women are combined to give readers a multidimensional view of the problem. Intervention strategies, education projects, and prevention programs provide additional information for a diverse audience of caring professionals.

Ludwig, Stephen, and Allan E. Kornberg, eds. *Child Abuse: A Medical Reference*. 2nd ed. Churchill Livingstone, 1991. 563p. bibliog. photog. illus. index. LC 91-36285. ISBN 0-443-08722-9. $59.00.

For pediatricians, emergency room personnel, and other health care professionals who encounter children in their practices, this clinical reference reviews how to recognize different types of physical, sexual, or psychological abuse and neglect. The book covers epidemiology and history of medical treatment, records, and treatment of injuries. Heavily illustrated, the text emphasizes recognition of abuse through ophthalmologic, dental, and tissue trauma; burn injuries; and other physical manifestations. New to the second edition is a chapter on the biomechanics of abuse. Forensic issues, such as testimony and forensic pathology, are also covered. Appendixes provide resource material on state laws, an autopsy protocol, diagnostic imaging guidelines, and baseline data on normal growth and development.

Malciodi, Cathy A. *Breaking the Silence: Art Therapy with Children from Violent Homes*. Brunner/Mazel, 1990. 214p. LC 90-1466. ISBN 0-87630-578-8. $29.95.

Malciodi's practical manual for art therapists, social workers, and other professionals who work with disturbed children covers the use of art therapy techniques to help children in a crisis situation, such as a domestic violence shelter. The author explains how to carry out art therapy evaluations and interventions with physically and sexually abused children, how to do short-term therapy and termination in a crisis intervention setting, strategies for developing programs, and applying for grants to fund the programs in shelters. Drawings by abused children are used to reinforce the discussion of symbols of molestation that present themselves in artwork.

Murdock, Rosamond L. *Suffer the Children: A Pediatrician's Reflections on Abuse*. Health, 1992. 186p. LC 91-35371. ISBN 0-929173-09-0. $19.95.

Case material from the files of a pediatrician with 20 years of experience in public health departments and private practice illustrates the forms and extent of child abuse in contemporary society and throughout history. She reviews the impact of sexual abuse, prenatal abuse and neglect, medical and physical neglect, and physical and emotional abuse, as well as the abusive antecedents of running away or suicide in adolescents. Community, governmental, and individual responsibilities for intervening in and preventing abuse are reviewed.

Wiehe, Vernon R. *Sibling Abuse: The Hidden Physical, Emotional, and Sexual Trauma*. Lexington, 1990. 186p. LC 90-31408. ISBN 0-669-24362-0. $29.95.

Personal accounts of emotional, physical, and sexual abuse shared by voluntary respondents to a survey reveal largely hidden problems of sibling abuse. The text, which is written for professionals working in the field of domestic violence and students preparing for these careers, explores using content analysis of the victims' feelings, emotions, and experience of abuse; their parents' reactions; and the effects of abuse on the victims. A theoretical framework for understanding sibling abuse, criteria for distinguishing normal interactive behavior between siblings from abusive behavior, and strategies for preventing abuse are presented. The details of the research methodology and data analysis are reviewed in a separate chapter.

PROFESSIONAL TITLES: JOURNALS

CDF Reports. Children's Defense Fund. 1951. M. ISSN 0276-6531. $29.95.

The monthly newsletter of the Children's Defense Fund (CDF), this journal covers national policy and legislative action, program models, and data on the status of children for a broad audience of child care professionals. Congressional voting records on key pieces of legislation, basic tips for child advocacy, children's sabbaths, child poverty, and news about conferences and publications of the CDF are some of the topics that have been covered in past issues.

Child Abuse and Neglect: The Information Journal. Pergamon. 1977. B-M. ISSN 0145-2134. $180.00.

Taking an international, multidisciplinary perspective, this scholarly refereed journal examines all aspects of child abuse, neglect, and sexual abuse. The official title of the International Society for Prevention of Child Abuse and Neglect, this periodical publishes theoretical and research-focused articles emphasizing prevention and treatment issues. Case comments, brief communications, letters, and announcements are also carried. Special issues, such as the issue on clinical recognition of sexually abused children, are published occasionally.

Child and Youth Services. Haworth. 1977. S-A. ISSN 0145-935X. $160.00.

This journal publishes two theme issues per year on topics relevant to the welfare of children and adolescents. Past issues have addressed the application of a conceptual scheme for child residential care and assessment of false allegations in child maltreatment. Essentially monographs published within the journal format, these issues bring theory, research, commentary, and practice together on topics of current interest.

Child Welfare: Journal of Policy, Practice, and Program. Child Welfare League of America. 1920. B-M. ISSN 0009-4201. $60.00.

The official publication of the Child Welfare League of America, this journal addresses all aspects of caring for children from the practitioner's perspective. Especially important are articles that contribute new information on services to children, administration, casework, community organization, and group work. Other topics of interest are social policy issues that relate to the welfare of children and their families and interdisciplinary studies. Current developments in the field, book reviews, and program reports are covered to aid a variety of professionals concerned with the welfare of children.

Children and Youth Services Review. Pergamon. 1979. B-M. ISSN 0190-7409. $230.00.

Practical and scholarly articles on the problems faced by children and adolescents and service programs designed to address these needs make up this widely indexed interdisciplinary journal. The scope includes sexual abuse, youth unemployment, children's rights, psychiatric services, drug treatment, juvenile justice programs, adoption, and foster care. Reports of current research, policy notes, book reviews, and full-length articles are published.

Children Today. Office of Human Development Services, Department of Health and Human Services. 1954. B-M. ISSN 0361-4336. $14.00.

Brief, easy-to-read articles on a wide range of topics such as pediatric AIDS, after-school child care, and foster care are published in this news magazine for professionals working with children and their families. The issues also include book reviews and reports on programs, all illustrated with numerous photographs.

Children's Legal Rights Journal. Hein. 1979. Q. ISSN 0278-7210. $58.00.

Two to four practical articles dealing with child custody, child support, foster care, special education, child abuse, advocacy, and other related matters regulated by the law are published in each issue of this journal. Editorials and news items are occasionally included. Past issues addressed child fatality review teams, children abducted by a parent, kinship foster care, and support for young mothers.

Journal of Child Sexual Abuse. Haworth. 1992. Q. ISSN 1053-8712. $48.00.

This refereed interdisciplinary journal covers issues of child sexual abuse, treatment, and recovery. Original research, clinical articles, case studies, commentaries, and brief reports are published about children who have been abused, the offenders, and adult survivors. Ritual child abuse, the role of the mother in sexual abuse, medical findings, and cultural considerations in assessing and treating abuse are topics that have been covered in the past.

Journal of Family Violence. Plenum. 1986. Q. ISSN 0885-7482. $110.00.

Clinical reports and original research on all forms of domestic violence, including child abuse, sexual abuse of children, and family conflict, are published in this multidisciplinary journal. The primary focus is on investigations using group comparisons and single-case consultations, but the journal also publishes case studies that utilize innovative techniques for evaluation or intervention. Past issues addressed such topics as patterns of influence and response in abusing families and a model for using time-out as an intervention strategy.

Youth and Society. Sage. 1969. Q. ISSN 0044-118X. $106.00. The socialization of children and adolescents is the subject of this multidisciplinary journal. Empirical and theoretical research with applications for social policy, program development, and institutional operations is published. Past issues examined the effects of age and gender on parental control, sexual coercion attitudes among high school students, and the social psychology of adolescents' role identities as athletes and scholars.

DIRECTORY

American Humane Association Children's Division
63 Inverness Drive East, Englewood, CO 80112-5117
(303) 792-9900 Fax (303) 792-5333 Toll-free (800) 227-5242
Patricia Schene, Ph.D., Director
Founded: 1877
Members: 1,500
Former Name: American Association for Protecting Children
Mission/Goals: To work to improve services to vulnerable children and their families through training and education to child protection agencies, consultation and technical assistance to public and private agencies, publications, and research
Audience/Clientele: Primarily public and private child protection agencies, also mental health professionals, medical personnel, court personnel, educators
Staff: 16 professionals, 4 nonprofessionals
Budget: $1,000,000 Funding: Federal government, fees for products or services, donations, grants, dues
Education and Outreach: In-service programs, library, publishing
Publications: *Protecting Children*, quarterly; *Child Protection Leader*, bimonthly; *Helping in Child Protective Services: A Casework Handbook, Understanding the Medical Diagnosis of Child Maltreatment: A Guide for Non-Medical Professionals*, and similar educational texts; books and pamphlets, leaflets, and other publications
Programs: Annual conference

Athletes and Entertainers for Kids
P.O. Box 191, Building B, Gardena, CA 90248-0191
(310) 768-8493 Fax (310) 768-8307 Toll-free (800) 933-KIDS
Elise Kim, Executive Director
Founded: 1986
Former Name: Athletes for Kids
Mission/Goals: To address the most critical needs of today's youth with athletes and entertainers; to be the most responsive and comprehensive children's charity addressing the critical needs of underprivileged and disadvantaged youth from all walks of life; to give each child a fighting chance for a happy life

Audience/Clientele: High-risk children, particularly in areas overlooked or shunned, such as gang members, juvenile felons, homeless children, pregnant teen mothers, and others
Staff: 2 professionals, 2 nonprofessionals, 400 volunteers
Funding: Private sources, fund-raising, donations, grants
Services: Counseling, support group, placement service, referral, support services
Education and Outreach: In-service programs, continuing education courses, seminars, publishing
Publications: *Financial Report*, annual; *Newsletter*, quarterly

Believe the Children (BTC)
P.O. Box 77, Hermosa Beach, CA 90254
(213) 379-3514
Leslie Floberg, President
Founded: 1986
Mission/Goals: To heighten public and professional awareness of child abuse occuring outside the family; to assist parents of physically, emotionally, sexually, or ritually abused children
Audience/Clientele: Parents of abused children, medical and social work professionals, law enforcement officers, lobbying, support group
Services: Advocacy
Education and Outreach: Research, publishing
Publications: *Believe the Children Newsletter*, annual; various brochures

Child Find of America, Inc.
P.O. Box 277, New Paltz, NY 12561
(914) 255-1848 Fax (914) 255-5706 Toll-free (800) I-AM-LOST (800) A-WAY-OUT
Carolyn Zogg, Executive Director
Founded: 1980
Former Name: Child Find Inc.
Mission/Goals: To bring missing children home; to prevent child abduction; to locate missing children through investigation, photo distribution, mediation, and public information, at no fee
Audience/Clientele: Parents of missing children, local social service agencies, media personnel concerned with the problem of missing children
Staff: 9 professionals
Funding: Private sources, donations, grants
Services: Counseling, search services, referral
Education and Outreach: Publishing
Publications: *Child Find News*; brochure

Child Welfare Institute (CWI)
1365 Peachtree Street, Suite 700, Atlanta, GA 30309
(404) 876-1934 Fax (404) 876-7949
Thomas D. Morton, Executive Director
Founded: 1983
Mission/Goals: To provide organizational development and training services to ensure that the needs of children and families at risk are met competently
Audience/Clientele: Voluntary child welfare agencies, general public

Staff: 14 professionals and nonprofessionals
Budget: $1,800,000 Funding: Federal government, state government, local government, fees for services or products, county government, grants
Education and Outreach: In-service programs, seminars, publishing
Publications: *Ideas in Action*
Programs: Annual conference

Child Welfare League of America (CWLA)
440 First Street, N.W., Suite 310, Washington, DC 20001
(202) 638-2952 Fax (202) 638-4004
David S. Liederman, Executive Director
Founded: 1920
Members: 700
Affiliates: 5 regional groups
Mission/Goals: To improve care and services for deprived, dependent, or neglected children, youth, and their families
Audience/Clientele: Social service agencies and staffs
Services: Placement service, mailing list, consultation, advocacy, standards
Education and Outreach: Research, surveys of agencies and communities, library, publishing
Publications: *Child Welfare: Journal of Policy, Practice, and Program*, bimonthly; *Children's Voice*, 9/yr, newsletter; *CWLA Directory of Member Agencies*, biennial; *Washington Social Legislation Bulletin*, semimonthly; books, monographs,videotapes
Programs: Annual conference

Childhelp USA
6463 Independence Avenue, Woodland Hills, CA 91367
(818) 347-7280 Fax (818) 593-3257 Toll-free (800) 422-4453 Hotline (800) 4-A-CHILD
Sarah O'Meara, Chairman of the Board
Founded: 1959
Members: 1,300
Affiliates: 11 state
groups
Former Names: International Orphans, Inc.; Children's Village USA
Mission/Goals: To contribute to the prevention, treatment, and research of child abuse
Audience/Clientele: Victims of child abuse, adult survivors of child abuse
Staff: 12 professionals, 224 nonprofessionals, 1,400 volunteers
Budget: $9,700,000 Funding: Federal government, state government, private sources, fund-raising, donations, county government, grants, dues
Services: Counseling, support group, social service/case management, residential facility, search services, referral, fund-raising
Awards: For the Love of a Child Award for individuals in the categories of corporate, media, individual, legislative, and lifetime achievement for outstanding contributions to the fight against child abuse and neglect

Education and Outreach: In-service programs, seminars, library, archives, database development, publishing
Publications: *Childhelp Newsletter*, quarterly; *Child Abuse and You . . .* and other pamphlets; *Report*, annual
Programs: Annual conference

Children of the Night, Inc.
14530 Sylvan Street, Van Nuys, CA 91411
(818) 908-4474 Fax (818) 908-1468 Toll-free (800) 551-1300
Dr. Lois Lee, Executive Director
Founded: 1979
Mission/Goals: To provide effective intervention in the lives of children ages 11 to 17 who are sexually exploited and coerced into prostitution or pornography
Audience/Clientele: Children ages 11 to 17 involved in prostitution or pornography
Staff: 6 professionals, 30 nonprofessionals, 25 volunteers
Funding: Private sources, fund-raising, donations, grants
Languages: Spanish
Services: Counseling, support group, social service/case management, residential facility, referral
Education and Outreach: In-service programs, publishing
Publications: Informational pamphlets and brochures

Children's Defense Fund (CDF)
25 E Street, N.W., Washington, DC 20001
(202) 628-8787 Fax (202) 783-7324 Hotline (800) CDF-1200
Marian Wright Edelman, President
Founded: 1973
Former Name: Children's Defense Fund of the Washington Research Project
Mission/Goals: To provide systematic, long-range advocacy on behalf of the nation's children; to conduct research and public education, monitor federal agencies, litigate, draft and testify on legislation, and provide assistance to state and local groups and communities in the areas of child welfare, child health, adolescent pregnancy prevention, child care, family services, and child mental health
Audience/Clientele: Policymaking bodies, social service and health care providers, children, families, general public
Services: Lobbying, advocacy, community organizing, referral, fund-raising, compiling statistics
Education and Outreach: Research, publishing
Publications: *CDF Reports*, monthly newsletter covering child care, health, education, foster care, and other issues relating to children and adolescents; *Adolescent Pregnancy Prevention Clearinghouse Reports*, monographic series; *The Health of America's Children*; *Maternal and Child Health Data Book*; *The State of America's Children*

Clearinghouse on Child Abuse and Neglect Information
P.O. Box 1182, Washington, DC 20013-1182
(703) 385-7565 Fax (703) 385-3206 Toll-free (800) 394-3366

Caroline Hughes, Project Director
Founded: 1975
Mission/Goals: To provide information on the prevention, identification, and treatment of child abuse and neglect; to collect, store, organize, and disseminate information on all aspects of child maltreatment; to promote cooperation and coordination among organizations working to end child maltreatment
Audience/Clientele: Researchers, practitioners, policymakers, libraries, clearinghouses, government officials, students, concerned citizens
Funding: Federal government
Services: Search services, referral
Education and Outreach: Library, database development, publishing
Publications: *Quarterly Bulletin*; *Parents Information Network* available on America Online; grant profiles, monographs, directories, literature reviews, national statistical studies, fact sheets, and posters

Covenant House (CH)

346 W. 17th Street, New York, NY 10011-5002
(212) 727-4000 Fax (212) 989-7586 Toll-free (800) 999-9999
Sr. Mary Rose McGeady, D.C., President and CEO
Founded: 1972
Mission/Goals: To provide, via a crisis center, immediate, short-term care for youths under 21 years of age, including counseling, food, shelter, clothing, medical treatment, and legal assistance
Audience/Clientele: Homeless youth, young mothers and their children, youths who are HIV positive Services: Counseling, medical treatment, residential facility, lobbying, advocacy
Education and Outreach: Research, speakers' bureau

Find the Children

11811 W. Olympic Boulevard, Los Angeles, CA 90064
(310) 477-6721 Fax (310) 477-7166
Judi Sadowsky, Executive Director
Founded: 1983
Mission/Goals: To help locate missing children; to assist searching parents to develop strategies to find their missing children; to act as a liaison between searching parents and law enforcement; to disseminate photos of missing children locally and nationally; to provide a resource for counseling services for recovered children and their families
Audience/Clientele: Parents of missing children
Staff: 2 professionals, 1 nonprofessional, 36 volunteers
Budget: $150,000 Funding: Donations, grants
Services: Social service/case management, referral
Education and Outreach: Publishing
Publications: *Directory of Missing Children*, annual; *Find the Children*, brochure

International Society for Prevention of Child Abuse and Neglect (ISPCAN)

1205 Oneida Street, Denver, CO 80220
(303) 321-3963 Fax (303) 329-3523
Richard D. Krugman, President
Founded: 1977
Members: 1,800
Mission/Goals: To reduce the incidence of child abuse and neglect, including sexual abuse; to provide a forum for sharing information and experiences
Audience/Clientele: Parents, social service agencies, general public
Education and Outreach: Publishing
Publications: *Child Abuse and Neglect: The Information Journal*, quarterly
Programs: Biennial international congress

Missing Children . . . HELP Center

410 Ware Boulevard, Suite 400, Tampa, FL 33619
(813) 623-5437 Fax (813) 623-5430 Toll-free (800) 872-5437 Hotline (800) USA-KIDS
Ivana DiNova, Executive Director and Founder
Founded: 1982
Mission/Goals: To establish good working relationships with law enforcement agencies throughout the United States in order to ensure protection of all children; to serve as the coordinating agency among missing children, their parents, law enforcement, government agencies, and other interested parties; to promote public awareness through crime prevention and education programs, including a voluntary fingerprinting program; to distribute vital information and photos of missing children nationwide
Audience/Clientele: Parents, parent groups, crime watch programs, school psychologists, law enforcement personnel
Services: Support group, search services, referral, lobbying, compiling statistics, fingerprinting, legal assistance, speakers' bureau
Education and Outreach: Seminars, publishing
Publications: Information packets, brochures, posters of missing children, fingerprint cards

National Committee to Prevent Child Abuse (NCPCA)

332 S. Michigan Avenue, Suite 1600, Chicago, IL 60604-4357
(312) 663-3520 Fax (312) 939-8962
Anne Harris Cohn, Executive Director
Founded: 1972
Affiliates: 67 local groups
Former Name: Family Life Achievement Center
Mission/Goals: To enhance public awareness of the incidence, origins, nature, and effects of child abuse; to serve as an advocate to prevent the neglect and physical, sexual, and emotional abuse of children; to facilitate communication, public policy,

research, and improved cooperation among groups working in the area of prevention

Audience/Clientele: Parents, social service workers, law enforcement personnel

Services: Advocacy, media campaigns

Education and Outreach: Seminars, research, publishing

Publications: *Monthly Memorandum*; various books, brochures, and booklets

Programs: Annual leadership conference

The National Court Appointed Special Advocate (CASA) Association (NCASAA)

2722 Eastlake Avenue East, Suite 220, Seattle, WA 98102

(206) 328-8588 Fax (206) 323-8137

Beth Waid, Executive Director

Founded: 1977

Members: 1,100

Affiliates: 40 state groups, 485 local groups

Mission/Goals: To advocate for the best interests of abused and neglected children; to support the development, growth, and continuation of programs that recruit and train volunteers to serve as court-appointed special advocates for abused and neglected children in juvenile dependency proceedings

Audience/Clientele: Local court-appointed special advocates (CASA) program staffs and volunteers, abused and neglected children

Staff: 7 professionals, 5 nonprofessionals

Budget: $1,000,000 Funding: Federal government, private sources, fees for services or products, donations, grants, dues

Services: Referral, fund-raising, compiling statistics, consulting

Awards: Juvenile Court Judge of the Year; Kappa Alpha Theta Program Director of the Year; G. F. Bettineski Child Advocate of the Year

Education and Outreach: In-service programs, seminars, publishing

Publications: *Connection*, quarterly newsletter; *Annual Report*; *Speak Up!*, volunteers' newsletter; various brochures, manuals, internal bulletins, PSAs, and posters

Programs: Annual conference, regional training seminars

The National Exchange Club Foundation for the Prevention of Child Abuse

3050 Central Avenue, Toledo, OH 43606

(419) 535-3232 Fax (419) 535-1989

George Mezinko, Foundation Director

Founded: 1979

Members: 40,000

Affiliates: 65 local abuse prevention programs

Mission/Goals: To eliminate child abuse in all its forms via parent aid, parent support groups, and parenting education

Audience/Clientele: Agencies and individuals interested in child abuse prevention

Staff: 3 professionals, 2 nonprofessionals

Budget: $500,000 Funding: Private sources, fund-raising, donations, dues

Services: Social service/case management, search services, referral, program development and evaluation

Education and Outreach: In-service programs, seminars, library, publishing

Publications: *Foundation Focus*, newsletter; training materials; pamphlets on child abuse prevention

Programs: Annual symposium

National Network of Runaway and Youth Services (NNRYS)

1319 F Street, N.W., Suite 401, Washington, DC 20004

(202) 783-7949 Fax (202) 783-7955 Hotline (800) 878-2437

YOUTHNET electronic bulletin board

Della M. Hughes, Executive Director

Founded: 1975

Members: 900

Affiliates: 30 state groups, 600 local groups

Mission/Goals: To challenge the nation and ourselves to provide positive alternatives to youths in high-risk situations and their families; to accomplish this mission through advocacy and public education, development and dissemination of information and educational materials, an annual symposium, and model programs; to provide training and technical assistance

Audience/Clientele: Runaway, homeless, and other youths in high-risk situations, youth service agencies, state and regional networks, social service departments, local, state, and national governments

Staff: 11 professionals, 1 nonprofessional, 2 volunteers

Budget: $850,000 Funding: Federal government, private sources, fund-raising, fees for services or products, donations, grants, dues

Languages: Spanish, French, sign language

Services: Referral, lobbying, compiling statistics

Awards: National Leadership Awards to individuals or agencies that have made outstanding contributions in the field of youth services

Education and Outreach: Seminars, library, archives, database development, publishing

Publications: *Network News*, quarterly organization newsletter; *Policy Reporter*, 8/yr, focusing on national legislation and policy; *Safe Choices Guide on HIV and AIDS*, *Youth-Reaching-Youth Implementation Guide*, and other trainers' manuals; *How to Be an Effective Advocate* and other informational booklets

Programs: Annual symposium

Orphan Foundation of America

1500 Massachusetts Avenue, N.W., Suite 448, Washington, DC 20044-4261

(202) 861-0762 Fax (202) 223-9079 Toll-free (800) 950-4673

Eileen McCaffrey, President

Founded: 1981

Former Name: Orphan Foundation

Mission/Goals: To help youths too old for adoption who are in institutions or temporary foster care families until legally too

old to remain in the system by providing the education and support that is normally provided by a child's family; to bring the plight of these children to the nation's attention
Audience/Clientele: Foster children, foster parents, social service workers
Services: Support group, residential facility, provision of clothing and other supplies
Awards: Vocational and college scholarships for youths
Education and Outreach: In-service programs, publishing
Publications: *Newsletter*, quarterly

Parents Anonymous (PA)

520 S. Lafayette Park Place, Suite 316, Los Angeles, CA 90057
(213) 388-6685 Fax (213) 388-6896 Toll-free (800) 421-0353
Curtis Richardson, President
Founded: 1970
Former Name: Mothers Anonymous
Mission/Goals: To foster the prevention and treatment of child abuse; to provide parents who become abusive with help
Audience/Clientele: Parents
Services: Counseling, support group
Education and Outreach: Seminars, speakers' bureau, publishing
Publications: *Insider*, quarterly

Parents United International (PU)

232 E. Gish Road, San Jose, CA 95112
(408) 453-7616 Fax (408) 453-9064 Hotline (408) 279-1957
Henry Giaretto, Executive Director
Founded: 1972
Mission/Goals: To provide assistance to families affected by incest and other types of child sexual abuse by providing crisis and long-term support
Audience/Clientele: Individuals and families who have experienced child sexual molestation
Services: Counseling, support groups, legal counseling, compiling statistics
Education and Outreach: Speakers' bureau, publishing
Publications: *The PUN*, quarterly newsletter; various videotapes and brochures
Programs: Annual conference

Paul and Lisa

P.O. Box 348, Westbrook, CT 06498
(203) 399-5338 Fax (203) 399-4428
Susan Breault, Assistant Program Director
Founded: 1980
Mission/Goals: To prevent the sexual exploitation of youth through programs in prevention and intervention, street work outreach, transitional living, and professional training
Audience/Clientele: Junior and senior high school students, social and mental health personnel, civic and religious organizations, concerned individuals, missing, homeless, abducted, runaway, and exploited youth

Staff: 6 professionals, 4 nonprofessionals, 10 volunteers
Budget: $380,000 Funding: Federal government, private sources, fund-raising, fees for services or products, donations, grants
Services: Counseling, support group, social service/case management, residential facility, emergency medical care, referral, lobbying, fund-raising, compiling statistics
Education and Outreach: In-service programs, seminars, publishing
Publications: *The P & L Connection*, quarterly newsletter; description of organization and programs

The Roberta Jo Society, Inc. (RJS)

P.O. Box 916, Circleville, OH 43113
(614) 474-5020
Robin A. Steely, President
Founded: 1979
Members: 144,000
Affiliates: 49 state groups, 70 local groups
Mission/Goals: To make America aware of the huge volume of child abductions throughout the United States every year; to seek attitude changes that aid victims rather than abductors; to improve the general future of these children by finding them so that they can be with their own families; to collect and store data on missing children and issue a missing child report
Audience/Clientele: Parents, general public
Budget: $576,000 Funding: Private sources, fund-raising
Services: Counseling, support group, search services, referral, fund-raising, compiling statistics
Education and Outreach: In-service programs, continuing education courses, database development, publishing
Publications: *Roberta Jo Society—Newsletter*, weekly; *Brochure*, quarterly

Runaway Hotline

Governor's Office, P.O. Box 12428, Austin, TX 78711
(512) 463-1980 Hotline (800) 231-6946
Jill Gardner, Director
Founded: 1973
Mission/Goals: To provide information and referral for runaways and troubled youths; to provide shelter, counseling, legal and medical services, and transportation; to provide a personal and confidential message relay service between runaways and their families
Audience/Clientele: Runaways, potential runaways, and troubled teens ages 11 to 17, parents of such youths
Staff: 3 professionals, 2 nonprofessionals, 150 volunteers
Budget: $210,000 Funding: Federal government
Services: Referral
Education and Outreach: Publishing
Publications: Brochures, files on available shelters, medical and legal aid offices, transportation and counseling services

Society for Young Victims, Missing Children's Center (SYV/MCC)

66 Broadway, Paramount Plaza, Newport, RI 02840
(401) 847-5083 Fax (401) 846-7810 Hotline (800) 999-9024 (sightings only)

June Viasaty, Executive Director

Mission/Goals: To assist families in the search for and recovery of missing children; to provide advice and assistance to parents whose children have been abducted or retained in connection with child custody disputes; to distribute flyers and photos of missing children, organize search teams, fingerprint children, and encourage better communication between police and families of victims

Audience/Clientele: Family and friends of missing children and adults; police departments, welfare departments, district attorneys

Staff: 14 professionals, 25 volunteers

Budget: $120,000 Funding: Private sources, fund-raising, fees for services or products, donations, grants

Languages: Sign language

Services: Counseling, support group, social service/case management, search services, referral, fund-raising, compiling statistics

Education and Outreach: In-service programs, seminars, library, database development, speakers' bureau, publishing

Publications: *The Society for Young Victims Newsletter*, monthly; various brochures

Programs: Annual conference

Vanished Children's Alliance (VCA)

1407 Parkmoor Avenue, Suite 200, San Jose, CA 95126

(408) 971-4822 Fax (408) 971-8516 Hotline (800) 826-4743 (sightings only)

Georgia K. Hilgeman, Executive Director

Founded: 1981

Mission/Goals: To work toward the prevention of abduction and recovery of missing or abducted children

Audience/Clientele: Custodial parents of missing children, law enforcement agencies, other missing children organizations

Staff: 5 professionals, 3 nonprofessionals, 10 volunteers

Budget: $427,000 Funding: Federal government, state government, private sources, fund-raising, donations, grants, dues

Services: Counseling, support group, social service/case management, search services, referral, fund-raising, compiling statistics

Education and Outreach: In-service programs, continuing education programs, seminars, database development, publishing

Publications: *VCA Directory*, annual; *Safety Packet*; brochures and posters

REFERENCES

1. *Current Trends in Child Abuse Reporting and Fatalities: The Results of the 1991 Fifty State Survey* (Chicago: National Committee to Prevent Child Abuse, 1992), 4, 14, 2.

2. David A. Sabatino, *A Fine Line: When Discipline Becomes Child Abuse* (Blue Ridge Summit, PA: TAB, 1991), 40.

3. Robert J. Ackerman and Dee Graham, *Too Old to Cry: Abused Teens in Today's America* (Blue Ridge Summit, PA: TAB, 1990), 55.

4. Stephen D. Grubman-Black, *Broken Boys/Mending Men: Recovery from Childhood Sexual Abuse* (Blue Ridge Summit, PA: TAB, 1990), vii.

5. Caren Adams and Jennifer Fay, *Helping Your Child Recover from Sexual Abuse* (University of Washington Press, 1992), vii–viii.

CHAPTER

Substance Abuse

No one forces kids to start; kids choose to start.
Ronald C. Main and Judy Zervas. *Keep Your Kids Straight*

A strong family support system is clearly an important
preventive strategy in reducing alcohol abuse by adolescents.
John W. Santrock. *Adolescence*

Alcohol is a substance most teens have tried; although most are not heavy users, many use it regularly. In 1991, only 12 percent of high school seniors had never tried alcohol; 54 percent had used it within the previous 30 days.[1] Younger children are aware that alcohol is available to them if they want to try it; 42 percent of the sixth graders and 34 percent of the seventh graders questioned in 1989 said they could obtain alcohol at their schools.[2] Often perceived by parents as less harmful than illegal drugs, alcohol was implicated in 32.3 percent of traffic fatalities in youths ages 16 to 24.[3]

When children and adolescents do use marijuana, cocaine, and other controlled substances, good communication helps parents warn children about the hazards of use, identify initial signs of use, or intervene when use becomes heavy. The question of drug and alcohol use in American society is a complex one; many adolescents mimic their parents' use patterns, accept the glamorous images of use in the media, consider using to be a harmless adolescent rite of passage, or are simply interested in experimenting with a "high."[4] Peer pressure, lack of control, poor stress management, and addiction are less benign reasons for sampling substances that all children learn in school are harmful.

An asterisk (*) indicates a specially recommended title.

POPULAR TITLES: BOOKS

Becnel, Barbara Cottman. *Parents Who Help Their Children Overcome Drugs.* CompCare, 1990. 199p. bibliog. index. LC 90-191700. ISBN 0-89638-218-4. $9.95.

This personal account of a sibling's drug dependence and the author's codependent, or enabling, response illustrates for parents the complexity of the issues involved in a child's drug abuse. In addition to her personal story, the author, a former police analyst who now is a consultant on programs for troubled youth, cites case studies to illustrate the healing process from initial denial through codependency, real assistance, treatment options, and recovery. Appendixes provide references and treatment center data.

Bell, Tammy L. *Preventing Adolescent Relapse: A Guide for Parents, Teachers, and Counselors.* Herald House/Independence, 1990. 184p. bibliog. LC 90-4841. ISBN 0-8309-0571-5. $12.95.

Intended for counselors, therapists, and parents, Bell's text on adolescents' recovery from chemical dependence proposes a model that incorporates addiction symptoms, normal adolescent development, and an understanding of mental disorders to improve outcomes. Diagnosis of chemical dependence, warning signs of relapse, and advice to parents are also covered.

Daley, Dennis C., and Judy Miller. *A Parent's Guide to Alcoholism and Drug Abuse: Practical Advice for Recovery and Relapse Prevention.* Edgehill, 1990. 100p. bibliog. index. LC 89-83896. ISBN 0-926028-01-4. $6.95.

Written by two social workers, this resource guide offers information, support, and practical advice to parents whose child is chemically dependent and in recovery. The authors draw upon their experience, research reports, and results of interviews to examine what chemical dependency is, to what degree the dependent child is affected, the impact of chemical dependency on the family and on parents, and recovery and relapse prevention in parent and child. Several of the chapters contain inventories and questions intended to help the reader relate to what is covered in a personal way. Suggested readings and a list of publisher/distributors of recovery material are also provided.

Dorris, Michael. *The Broken Cord.* Harper and Row, 1989. 300p. bibliog. illus. LC 88-45893. ISBN 0-06-016071-3. $18.95.

Dorris, an anthropologist and formerly single father, recounts the story of the long and slow discovery of the symptoms of fetal alcohol syndrome (FAS) in his adopted son Adam. After rejecting the prognosis of developmental and learning disabilities for many years, a chance encounter with three FAS children on a South Dakota Indian reservation marked the beginning of a lengthy search for scientific data on the causes, symptoms, and prognosis of FAS, most of which are reported here. A frank, moving introduction by Louise Erdrich, attesting to the difficulties of living day in and day out with a child disabled by FAS, provides an emotional context for what follows. The epilogue, Adam's autobiography, illustrates the thoughts and feelings of a child who struggles with the effects of this disorder.

* Main, Ronald C., and Judy Zevas. *Keep Your Kids Straight: What Parents Need to Know about Drugs and Alcohol.* TAB, 1991. 144p. bibliog. LC 90-21674. ISBN 0-8306-7681-3. $7.95.

This how-to handbook outlines strategies for parents to deal with a child's drug and alcohol use, from experimentation through determined use. The authors, a secondary school educator and a chemical dependency counselor, give concrete advice about teaching kids refusal skills, recognizing warning signs, confronting them with signs of abuse, avoiding enabling the use, reacting in a loving but assertive manner, and obtaining outside help. The material is organized to reflect the progression from suspicion to discovery of heavy use.

Sager, Carol. *Drug-Free Zone.* TAB, 1992. 228p. LC 91-14618. ISBN 0-8306-3363-4. $17.95. ISBN 0-8306-2033-8 pbk. $9.95.

Parents will find in this sourcebook tips and techniques for evaluating and improving the effectiveness of anti-drug programs in their child's school. The author, a therapist and counselor, describes the extent of the drug crisis, who the principal players in the school system are, and barriers to change. She explores how parents can promote the success of a drug-free program by becoming involved and by encouraging staff training, prevention education, heightened activities for students, and community support. To support her arguments, Sager provides a "power tool kit" of samples of anti-drug materials and practical advice on instituting and maintaining a drug-free program.

Scott Newman Center. *Straight Talk with Kids: Improving Communication, Building Trust, and Keeping Your Children Drug Free.* Bantam, 1991. 146p. LC 90-21680. ISBN 0-553-29352-4. $4.50.

Here is a brief guide to preventing and intervening in adolescent drug use through improved communication between parents and teens. The content includes building strength of character, avoiding drug use by coping with peer pressure, finding alternatives to drugs, understanding the link between drug use and sex, becoming better role models, recognizing signs of drug use, confronting the child, and seeking professional treatment. The appendix summarizes information on common drugs, including alcohol, and their effects.

Vogler, Roger E., and Wayne R. Bartz. *Teenagers and Alcohol.* Charles, 1992. 147p. LC 91-38965. ISBN 0-91478-57-2. $9.95.

Parents who want to increase their influence over teen drinking may follow the nine practical steps outlined in this handbook to better understand, take action, and prevent problems with alcohol. Tips for maximizing influence through identifying goals, sharing time together, listening, and permitting mistakes, combined with a clear understanding of blood alcohol levels, tolerance, and alcohol's effect on health prepare parents to work effectively with their teens. Recommended strategies are helping teens abstain, teaching sensible drinking, dealing with abuse, preparing preteens, and changing societal views of drinking. An appendix contains charts for estimating blood alcohol levels depending on weight, sex, and amount consumed.

PROFESSIONAL TITLES: BOOKS

Brounstein, Paul J. *Substance Use and Delinquency among Inner City Male Adolescents.* University Press of America, 1990. 140p. bibliog. LC 90-11970. ISBN 0-87766-449-8. $27.25. ISBN 0-87766-475-7 pbk. $12.50.

Based on a study of 387 minority adolescent males in Washington, DC, this report has applications for educators, community organizations, and parents concerned with preventing and intervening in substance abuse. According to the results obtained, sellers differed from users, youths who both used and dealt, and those who did neither. Because of these important differences, education and intervention strategies should be tailored and targeted to specific characteristics of the youth groups involved.

Fiegleman, William. *Treating Teenage Drug Abuse in a Day Care Setting.* Praeger, 1990. 140p. bibliog. index. LC 89-26538. ISBN 0-275-93379-2. $39.95.

The first study published to evaluate teen nonresidential treatment for substance abuse, this monograph describes the adolescent population likely to seek, complete, and benefit from day care drug therapy. The subjects, drawn from a sample of white male patients at the Manhasset Community Day Center in Nassau County, New York, were interviewed three to eight years after their release; urine samples and driving records were also obtained. Researchers examined social factors affecting the completion of care, posttreatment adaptation, and correlates of continuing drug use. Only 14 percent of those admitted, primarily older adolescents with families able to meet the behavioral requirements of the plan, were able to complete the program. Appendixes provide data on coding clinical files, information on the interview schedule, and a summary of results obtained.

Nowinski, Joseph. *Substance Abuse in Adolescents and Young Adults: A Guide to Treatment.* Norton, 1990. 246p. index. LC 89-70965. ISBN 0-393-70097-6. $29.95.

Recognizing that substance abuse may be an adolescent's primary problem and designing treatment programs specifically for this age group are two contemporary breakthroughs in the substance abuse treatment field. In this handbook, practical advice based on a synthesis of developmental theory and twelve-step program precepts is presented to guide clinicians in diagnosing and treating adolescents and their families. The text covers patterns of abuse, causes, assessment techniques, counseling, recovery, and relapse prevention. Case material and checklists contribute to the practical approach.

Petersen, Robert C. *Childhood and Adolescent Drug Abuse: A Physician's Guide to Office Practice.* Rev. ed. American Council for Drug Education, 1991. 69p. LC 87-70131. ISBN 0-942348-20-6. $3.00.

For the practicing physician, this concise handbook provides a brief overview of the "drug scene" and essentials of drug use prevention, diagnosis, and referral. The content includes detection of substance use, behavioral signs, discussions of use with patients and parents, and treatment alternatives. Alcohol, nicotine, marijuana, cocaine, and other substances are examined in individual chapters.

Schinke, Steven Paul, Gilbert J. Botvin, and Mario A. Orlandi. *Substance Abuse in Children and Adolescents: Intervention and Evaluation.* Sage, 1991. 98p. LC 90-9242. ISBN 0-8039-3748-2. $25.00. ISBN 0-8039-3749-0 pbk. $12.95.

This slim handbook reviews the scope of the problem of substance abuse in children and adolescents; current theory and research on causes, risk factors, and prevention; and alternative intervention strategies. The text guides readers on how to evaluate intervention programs in all settings and communicate their efficacy. Programs designed to prevent substance use by children and adolescents are emphasized.

Todd, Thomas C., and Matthew D. Selekman, eds. *Family Therapy Approaches with Adolescent Substance Abusers.* Allyn and Bacon, 1990. 334p. LC 90-842. ISBN 0-205-12505-0. $39.95.

Interdisciplinary techniques for treating adolescent substance abuse make up this sourcebook, aimed at clinicians practicing in chemical dependency, psychotherapy, and family therapy. The contributors present case examples, a thorough review of the current literature, and an emphasis on controversial issues in their discussion of such approaches as Purdue brief family therapy, MRI brief therapy, contextual family therapy, strategic inpatient family therapy, and other brief systemic approaches to adolescent substance abuse.

PROFESSIONAL TITLES: JOURNALS

Journal of Adolescent Chemical Dependency. Haworth. 1989. Q. ISSN 0896-7768. $42.00.

The intended audience for this journal consists of prevention and treatment specialists and chemical dependency clinicians who work with adolescents with drug and alcohol abuse problems. The journal presents practical information on clinical issues, treatment modalities, and specific applications, emphasizing a how-to approach to treating the adolescent and the family. Prevention and intervention strategies in community- or school-based programs are featured.

DIRECTORY

American Council for Drug Education (ACDE)
204 Monroe Street, Suite 110, Rockville, MD 20850
(301) 294-0600 Fax (301) 294-0603 Toll-free (800) 488-DRUG
William Current, Executive Director
Founded: 1977
Members: 1,500
Mission/Goals: To educate the public about the health hazards of drugs
Audience/Clientele: Parents, children, educators, professionals, teens, employers, physicians, community leaders, the media
Staff: 4 professionals, 2 nonprofessionals, 3 volunteers
Budget: $726,211 Funding: Private sources, fees for services or products, donations, grants, dues
Services: Referral, compiling statistics
Education and Outreach: Library, publishing
Publications: *The Drug Educator*, quarterly newsletter addressing the behavioral and psychological effects of marijuana, cocaine, and other psychoactive drugs; brochures, audiovisual materials, conference proceedings, scientific monographs

National Families in Action (NFA)
296 Henderson Mill Road, Suite 300, Atlanta, GA 30345
(404) 934-6364 Fax (404) 934-7137
Sue Rusche, Executive Director
Founded: 1977
Former Names: DeKalb Families in Action, Families in Action, Families in Action Drug Information Center, Families in Action National Drug Information Center
Mission/Goals: To educate parents, children, and the community about the use of drugs; to counteract social pressures that condone and promote drug use; to stop drug use
Audience/Clientele: Parents and other adults concerned about preventing drug use
Services: Lobbying, community organizing
Education and Outreach: Telephone reference service, drug information center, database development, publishing

Publications: *Drug Abuse Update*, quarterly newsletter; *How to Form a Family Action Group in Your Community*; provides Office of Substance Abuse Prevention Information through CompuServe

National Family Partnership (NFP)
11159 B South Town Square, St. Louis, MO 62123
(314) 485-1933
Betty Herron, Contact Person
Founded: 1980
Former Name: National Federation of Parents for Drug-Free Youth
Mission/Goals: To educate parents, adolescents, children, and others about the dangers of marijuana and other mind-altering drugs; to promote, encourage, and assist in the formation of local parent groups throughout the United States; to curtail the use of alcohol and other addictive substances by children and adolescents
Audience/Clientele: Parents, parent groups
Services: Lobbying
Education and Outreach: Seminars, speakers' bureau, publishing
Publications: *NFP News*, quarterly; various manuals and books
Programs: Annual conference

National Parents' Resource Institute for Drug Education (PRIDE)
50 Hurt Plaza, Suite 210, Atlanta, GA 30303
(404) 577-4500
Dr. Thomas J. Gleaton, President
Founded: 1977
Former Name: Parent Resources and Information on Drug Education
Mission/Goals: To promote drug abuse prevention through education; to provide current research information on drug abuse and to facilitate the organization of parent peer groups, parent-school teams, and community action groups to reduce adolescent drug abuse

Audience/Clientele: Parents, educators, youth groups, law enforcement officials, community groups
Services: Recreation, compiling statistics
Education and Outreach: In-service programs, library, speakers' bureau, publishing
Publications: *PRIDE Quarterly*; various pamphlets and books
Programs: Annual conference

Straight, Inc. (SI)
3001 Gandy Boulevard, St. Petersburg, FL 33702
(813) 576-8929 Fax (813) 576-5635 Toll-free (800) 733-8929
Bernadine Braithwaite, Executive Director
Founded: 1976
Mission/Goals: To treat substance using adolescents via an intensive, highly structured, progressive therapeutic process; to reconstruct and revitalize the family system; to provide aftercare support to individuals who have completed the program
Audience/Clientele: Adolescent drug users and their families, substance abuse workers
Services: Counseling, substance abuse treatment, residential facility
Education and Outreach: Publishing
Publications: *Straight Talk*, quarterly newsletter; videotapes, brochures, and pamphlets

REFERENCES

1. *Sourcebook of Criminal Justice Statistics, 1991*. U.S. Department of Justice, 1992, 344.

2. Ibid., 311.

3. Terry S. Zobeck et al. *Trends in Alcohol-Related Fatal Traffic Crashes, U.S.: 1979–90*, Alcohol Epidemiologic Data System Surveillance Reports, no. 22 (National Institute on Alcohol Abuse and Alcoholism, 1992), 27.

4. Donald E. Greydanus, *Caring for Your Adolescent: Ages 12 to 21* (New York: Bantam in association with American Academy of Pediatrics, 1992), 93–95.

PART

7

REFERENCE TOOLS

CHAPTER

Print and Nonprint Reference Materials

*Many parents want their children to have
the satisfying experiences subscriptions can bring.*

Selma K. Richardson. *Magazines for Children*

Indexes, encyclopedias, statistical compilations, book reviews, and other reference tools guide parents and teachers, librarians, child care workers, and other professionals who work with children and adolescents to sources for materials to entertain and educate their charges. At present, the parents' reference shelf, as opposed to their stockpile of reading material and current information resources, is nearly an empty one.

POPULAR TITLES: BOOKS

Cella, Catherine. *Great Videos for Kids: A Parent's Guide to Choosing the Best.* Carol, 1992. 157p. index. LC 92-31006. ISBN 0-8065-1377-2. $7.95.

Brief annotations and evaluative comments provide parents with advice on selecting quality videos for their children that contain little or no violence, racial stereotyping, or gender bias. In addition, each of the titles selected met professional standards for audio and video production, was appealing to the author and the panel of children who screened the videos, and was currently available. Following a discussion of the merits of using videos to develop children's media literacy and critical thinking, the bulk of the text is devoted to entries organized by type. Animated videos, those based on books, educational titles, folk and fairy tales, how-to videos, music, and videos on family topics and holidays are among the types covered.

Chadwick, Bruce A., and Tim B. Heaton, eds. *Statistical Handbook on the American Family.* Oryx, 1992. 312p. bibliog. index. LC 91-44175. ISBN 0-89774-687-2. $59.50.

Drawing on vital statistics, census data, Gallup polls, scholarly survey research, and other statistical sources, this handbook provides a statistical portrait of contemporary American families. Detailed data on marriage, quality of marriage and family life, divorce, children, sexual attitudes and behavior, living arrangements, working women, mothers, family violence, and elder care are included.

*Franck, Irene M. *The Parent's Desk Reference.* Prentice Hall, 1991. 615p. LC 90-27359. ISBN 0-13-649989-9. $29.95.

Brief information on topics concerning parents, such as pregnancy and childbirth, infant care, child development, genetic and other common disorders of childhood, education and special education, and key social problems relating to children is arranged alphabetically in the first section of this one-volume encyclopedia. Each entry has a brief description of the issue, cross-references, a directory of related agencies, and a sampling of recent publications. Many also include sidebars covering scientific data, parenting tips, and other practical advice. The remainder of the book consists of a special help section, a parent's bookshelf, and a kid's bookshelf (both with unannotated entries). The "desk reference" is a way for parents to obtain basic data about a topic and a quick referral to more detailed information and sources of further help.

Franck, Irene, and David Brownstone. *What's New for Parents: The Essential Resource to Products and Services, Programs and Information.* Prentice-Hall, 1993. 232p. bibliog. photog. index. LC 92-39944. ISBN 0-671-85036-9. $12.00.

Prolific reference book authors Franck and Brownstone (*The Parent's Desk Reference*) examine publications, products, and organizational resources new in the 1990s. They cover four areas: fun and games, family health and safety, education and learning, and parenting resources. Brief annotations, photographs, and addresses provide additional information on such topics as children's magazines, guidelines for parent coaches, travel aids, Prodigy, baby proofing, immunization and vaccines, steroids, testing, portfolio assessment, dinosaurs, volunteering, and consumerism. This digest of current news and research is simultaneously a shopping guide.

Freeman, Judy. *Books Kids Will Sit Still For: The Complete Read-Aloud Guide.* 2nd ed. Bowker, 1993. 600p. bibliog. illus. index. LC 90-2373. ISBN 0-8352-3010-4. $34.95.

Presented as a "manual for fooling around with books," this guide contains more than 2,000 kid-tested favorites for reading aloud. Each entry provides full bibliographic information, up to five subject headings, a simple plot statement, and advice on how to share the book with children, the number of sittings required to complete it, and related titles of interest. The author's criteria for inclusion are exciting characters, tight plots, true-to-life dialogue, creative story lines, and a fluid style of writing. The first 100-plus pages serve as a textbook on using books in the classroom; the remainder of the book is devoted to age-graded, subject-focused lists of recommended titles.

Friedes, Harriet. *The Preschool Resource Guide: Educating and Entertaining Children Aged Two through Five.* Plenum, 1993. 247p. bibliog. illus. index. LC 92-41250. ISBN 0-306-44464-X. $27.50.

This reference book for parents and professionals provides descriptions of and comments on educational materials for children two to five years of age. Each of the books, magazines, software programs, videos, and toys presented here was reviewed favorably by an expert in the field. In addition, book clubs and audio recordings are evaluated. The second half of this guide reviews books, journals, professional associations, and free or inexpensive materials for adults who care for and educate children in this age group. The final chapter lists 105 criteria for evaluating readiness for kindergarten, and the appendix talks about the safety of toys. Criteria for judging each format of material reviewed are an important feature of this guide.

Hardy, Dawn. *Bargains-by-Mail for Baby and You: Where to Buy for Your Baby, Nursery, Playroom and Yourself: At Mail-Order Discount Prices.* Prima, 1991. 413p. LC 91-21125. ISBN 1-55958-112-3. $14.95.

The emphasis of this directory of mail-order catalogs and their products is on companies that provide high quality as well as low prices. Companies are listed in alphabetical order, and symbols indicate what type of products are offered. The descriptions for each company are detailed and evaluative. The introduction advises readers on how to avoid pitfalls and make the best use of mail order shopping. A product index is included.

Lansky, Bruce, and Barry Sinrod. *The Baby Name Personality Survey.* Simon & Schuster, 1990. 222p. LC 88-27142. ISBN 0-88166-164-3. $6.95.

Lansky and Sinrod present survey-based information about the image of a name, the supposed personality and imagined looks of people with a particular name, and notable namesakes to assist parents in choosing names that express the qualities they value, such as intelligence, friendliness, creativity, or self-assurance. An alphabetical list of 1,400 names includes traditional information such as derivation, literal meaning, and famous namesakes in addition to the results of the image/personality survey conducted by the Sinrod Marketing Group. Selected names are listed under personality or physical characteristics in a "first impressions" section.

McCullough, Virginia. *Testing and Your Child: What You Should Know about 150 of the Most Common Medical, Educational, and Psychological Tests.* Viking, 1992. index. LC 92-53540. ISBN 0-452-26840-0. $12.00.

Parents who do not understand why a test is prescribed, the context in which it is administered, the consequences of the results, or the importance of testing will not be able adequately to guide their child's development. With the view that parents have the right to know everything, to have the final say about using a test, to ask questions, and to see children's school records, this resource provides profiles of common medical, developmental, educational, and psychological tests. Each profile includes the name and edition of the test, permissions needed to administer it, what is being tested, preparations required, how the test is performed and what to expect during the procedure, how the test is scored and how scores are interpreted, and diagnostic uses. An extensive glossary for the fields covered is included. As the author notes, testing is a process most parents take for granted until an unexpected test is prescribed for their child.

Olson, Stan, and Ruth Kovacs, eds. *National Guide to Funding for Children, Youth, and Families.* 2nd ed. The Foundation Center, 1993. 1028p. bibliog. index. LC 93-168720. ISBN 0-87954-491-9. $135.00.

With entries for over 3,400 foundations and 200 direct corporate-giving programs, this directory provides a convenient starting point for applicants seeking funds for programs whose focus is children, youth, and families. Detailed information, such as purpose and activities, field of interest, qualifying distributions, types of support, limitations, publications, application information, and recent grants awarded, is provided for each agency listed. Numerous indexes, including donors, geographic location, types of support, subject of giving programs, subject of grants awarded, and name of giving programs, provide access to relevant foundations, which are listed alphabetically by name within each state.

Rothman, Barbara Katz, ed. *Encyclopedia of Childbearing: Critical Perspectives.* Oryx, 1993. 472p. bibliog. photog. index. LC 92-14975. ISBN 0-89774-648-1. $74.50.

Entries on all aspects of pregnancy, childbirth, and motherhood, written by experts in the field, comprise the contents of this fascinating exploration of a traditional topic only recently emerging as a focus for scholarly research. Contributors from disciplines as diverse as art history, anthropology, physical therapy, psychology, medicine, nursing, law, history, women's studies, theology, and literature address the theme that childbearing is a social construction with imagery, practices, and technology that emerge from this social base. Among the specific topics addressed are maternity clothes, lactation, breastfeeding, teenage childbearing, the apgar test, parenting with a disability, miscarriage, sudden infant death syndrome, and fathers at birth. The length of the articles varies depending on the complexity of the topic. Cross-references to related topics and recommended readings enhance the usefulness of the text as a whole.

Starer, Daniel. *Who to Call: The Parent's Source Book*. Morrow, 1992. 550p. LC 91-28612. ISBN 0-688-10044-9. $30.00. ISBN 0-688-11729-5 pbk. $15.00.

Starer has compiled a guide to the maze of self-help, governmental, and professional organizations that compile data of potential use to parents. Arranged topically, the directory covers all aspects of parenting, including pregnancy, health, safety, education, recreation, and consumer goods. Each section provides a brief synopsis of the topic, references to other chapters for related concerns, and briefly annotated agency entries. Many of the organizations listed do not have children as their focus but do provide information that parents may need, such as the Center for Disease Control, which distributes pamphlets on AIDS. This sourcebook provides convenient, one-stop shopping for directory information and advice on how best to obtain what is needed quickly via telephone.

PROFESSIONAL TITLES: BOOKS

Richardson, Selma K. *Magazines for Children: A Guide for Parents, Teachers, and Librarians*. 2nd ed. American Library Association, 1990. 139p. index. LC 90-45152. ISBN 0-8389-0552-8. $19.95.

Over 100 of the highest-quality magazines for children up to age 14 or the eighth grade are reviewed in this guide by Selma Richardson, a well-known library educator. Titles included are evaluated according to contents, subject scope, graphics, and format; exclusions are also fully articulated in a substantive introduction on how to use the publication. The entries are arranged alphabetically, with subject access via an index. Religious titles are listed in an appendix, as are editions for visually impaired youth, age and grade level recommendations, and circulation data.

PROFESSIONAL TITLES: JOURNALS

Book Links. Booklist. 1991. B-M. ISSN 1055-4742. $18.00.

Bibliographies, bibliographic essays, and topical reviews of retrospective titles are among the features of *Book Links*, an American Library Association publication for a broad audience concerned with educating children from preschool through the eighth grade. The editors are responsive to their readers, soliciting suggestions for authors and illustrators to feature and comments on placement of articles, indexing, features, and general content. They view the journal's focus as supportive of such trends as using trade books in the classroom, the curricular role of the library media center, and the heavy demand for children's books in day care programs. An-

notations are detailed, indicating reading level and degree of controversy.

Children's Book Review Index. Gale. 1976. A. ISSN 0147-5681. $95.00.

Reviews of children's books, periodicals, and books-on-tape are compiled in this subset of *Book Review Index*. Materials selected are for children age 10 or younger and have been recommended by at least one reviewer. Multiple indexes, including author, title, and illustrator, provide access to the works reviewed.

Children's Literature Abstracts. Children's Literature Association. 1973. Q. ISSN 0306-2015. $30.00.

Recent articles, books, and pamphlets about children's literature are abstracted in this index. Coverage includes authors and illustrators, awards and prizes, collections, exhibitions and libraries, and curriculum, instruction, and bibliotherapy. Other topics addressed are illustration, design, comics, poetry, historical and sociological studies, and folklore, myth, and storytelling. This title is sponsored by the International Federation of Library Associations' Children's Libraries Section and Round Table of Children's Literature Documentation Centers.

Children's Magazine Guide. Bowker. 1948. 9/yr. ISSN 0743-9873. $35.00.

This irregular publication (monthly August through March, bimonthly April and June), the only subject index to articles in children's magazines, indexes a cross section of titles that are commonly found in public library collections or appropriate for elementary and junior high curricula. Demand, usefulness for reference, appealing format, and appropriate level of writing are among the criteria used for selection. Regional, special interest, and promotional titles are excluded. Information on new magazines is compiled, and selected titles directed to educators or librarians are covered in the professional index.

El-Hi Textbooks and Serials in Print. Bowker. 1969. A. ISSN 0000-0825. $109.95.

The catalogs of nearly 1,000 elementary and high school textbook publishers were scanned to create the database produced here. Materials selected include classroom textbooks, reference books, periodicals, maps, teachers' manuals, tests, and programmed learning texts in print format. The volume provides access to the materials cited via six indexes: subject, author, title, series, serials subject, and serials title. Publishers' information is also provided in a separate listing.

The Five Owls. Five Owls. 1986. B-M. ISSN 0892-6735. $18.00.

The best books, those that are intelligently written, attractively illustrated, and appealing to their audience, are reviewed in this bimonthly journal. Each issue contains a feature article, a topical annotated bibliography, suggestions for educators on how to include reading and books in the curriculum, and an interview with a prominent author. Nicely illustrated with black-and-white drawings and photographs, this publication will appeal to librarians, educators, editors, and parents involved with children's literature. Past issues examined Native American literature, picture books for older children, and electoral politics.

ELECTRONIC RESOURCES ON PARENTING AND CHILD CARE

Professionals working with children have long relied on electronic access to the literature of their fields through computerized indexing and abstracting services such as *ERIC, PsycINFO, Medline,* or *Social Work Abstracts* to keep current with scholarship and practice. Today practitioners and the general public alike have end-user access to these services as well as a diverse array of electronic bulletin boards and discussion groups, library online catalogs across the nation, electronic journals and newsletters, data archives, software programs, and media, sound, and full-text images, most accessible from a home or office workstation. These new electronic resources are available through the Internet or commercial services such as CompuServe, Prodigy, or America Online.

Electronic Indexing and Abstracting Services

Gaining entry to the scholarly literature cited in *ERIC, Medline,* or *PsycINFO* required the assistance of a trained intermediary when these databases first appeared in the late 1960s. Since then, these major disciplinary tools have been supplemented by numerous specialized files focusing on discrete topics or products. Currently available databases relating to parenting and child care are listed below.

Many of these files, such as *PsycINFO* and *Medline,* are available to institutions in CD-ROM or datatape formats by subscription from vendors such as SilverPlatter. Licensing CD-ROM files to load on a local area network provides multiple users with simultaneous access. More important, time spent searching the files or compiling and printing topical bibliographies is limited only by limitations on access to workstations, not by the cost of connect time or citation charges. Organizations that have these files on local area networks can also offer user-friendly interfaces, simplified documentation, and other search aids to improve access by professionals or the general public.

ABLEDATA. Newington Children's Hospital, producer. Available from BRS Information Technologies.

Information on therapeutic, educational, sensory, vocational, and technical aids and rehabilitation products for people with disabilities is contained in this database. Both current and discontinued products are included. The *ABLEDATA Thesaurus* (National Rehabilitation Information Center, 1993) provides a search aid. Updated monthly.

Birth Defects Encyclopedia Online. Center for Birth Defects Information Services, producer. Available from BRS Information Technologies.

Leading experts on specific conditions write the entries for this encyclopedia, which provides comprehensive coverage of the biomedical sciences relating to birth defects. Special emphasis is given to patient care applications. Current information only. Updated monthly.

Consumer Drug Information Database. American Society of Hospital Pharmacists, producer. Available from BRS Information Technologies.

Pediatric dosages, pregnancy and breastfeeding cautions, and food and drug interactions are reviewed in this full-text database of comparative consumer drug information for 90 to 95 percent of all drugs prescribed in the United States. Information on uses, undesired effects, dosages, and precautions is also provided. Reloaded annually, with updates as required.

ERIC (Educational Resources Information Center). ERIC Processing and Reference Facility, producer. Available from BRS Information Technologies and DIALOG Information Retrieval Service.

ERIC is a national database sponsored by the U.S. Department of Education that contains research reports, journal articles, program descriptions and evaluations, and curricular materials on all aspects of education. The *Thesaurus of ERIC Descriptors* (12th ed., Oryx, 1990) serves as a search aid. Coverage is 1969 to date. Updated monthly.

Exceptional Child Education Resources. Council for Exceptional Children, producer. Available from BRS Information Technologies.

Print and nonprint materials included in this database address the development and education of people of all ages who have a variety of exceptionalities, from giftedness, talent, or creativity to visual and hearing impairments, mental retardation, developmental disabilities, special health problems, learning disabilities, and behavior disorders, as well as victims of child abuse and neglect. The *Thesaurus of ERIC Descriptors* (12th ed., Oryx, 1990) provides a search aid. Coverage is from 1966 to date. Updated monthly.

Family Resource Database. National Council on Family Relations, producer. Available from DIALOG Information Retrieval Service and BRS Information Technologies.

Print and nonprint resources and programs dealing with the study of or services for the family are listed in this database. The *NCFR/Family Resources Database Subject Index* (National Council on Family Relations) and *Family Resources Database Guide* (National Council on Family Relations) are search aids. Coverage began with 1970 imprints. Updated monthly.

Health Periodicals Index. Information Access Company, producer. Available from BRS Information Technologies and DIALOG Information Retrieval Service.

Nonmedical professionals as well as medical practitioners and scholars are the intended audience for this database. Coverage of health-related articles in general publications began in 1976. The scope includes nutrition and fitness as well as health and medicine. Search aids include *Subject Guide to IAC Databases* (Information Access Co., 1995). Updated weekly.

Linguistics and Language Behavior Abstracts. Sociological Abstracts, producer. Available from DIALOG Information Retrieval Service.

> Selective access to current literature on such topics as hearing, hearing and speech physiology, learning disabilities, mental retardation, special education, psycholinguistics, and related topics is available through this database. Coverage is 1973 to date. Updated quarterly.

Medline. National Library of Medicine, producer. Available from DIALOG Information Retrieval Service and BRS Information Technologies.

> *Medline* covers all aspects of biomedicine, including clinical medicine, biological and physical sciences, and health-related information from the humanities and information science. Coverage began in 1966. Updated weekly.

Mental Health Abstracts. IFI/Plenum Data Co., producer. Available from DIALOG Information Retrieval Service.

> *Mental Health Abstracts* provides access to all aspects of mental health. Domestic and international sources for articles, books, research reports, and program data on child development, crime and delinquency, psychiatry, psychology, and epidemiology are included. Coverage is 1969 to date. Updated monthly.

Nursing and Allied Health (CINAHL). CINAHL Information Systems, producer. Available from BRS Information Technologies and DIALOG Information Retrieval Service.

> Scholarly literature on all aspects of nursing and allied health, including health education, emergency service, physical therapy, and social services in health care is the focus of this database. Consumer health and biomedicine are given selective coverage. The *Nursing & Allied Health (CINAHL) Database Search Guide* (Glendale Adventist Medical Center, 1993) provides assistance in searching. Coverage is 1983 to date. Updated monthly.

PsycINFO. American Psychological Association, producer. Available from DIALOG Information Retrieval Service and BRS Information Technologies.

> *PsycINFO* covers the scholarly literature in psychology and related fields. Coverage includes psychiatry, sociology, education, physiology, and linguistics, as well as applied psychology, personality, psychometrics, sports psychology, and treatment. Search aids include *PsycINFO User Manual* (American Psychological Association, 1992) and *Thesaurus of Psychological Index Terms* (7th ed., American Psychological Association, 1994). Coverage began in 1967. Updated quarterly.

Sport Database. Sport Information Resource Centre, producer. Available from BRS Information Technologies and DIALOG Information Retrieval Service.

> Sport, including recreation, exercise physiology, physical fitness, sports medicine, training, conditioning, coaching, and related subjects, is the focus of this database. The *SPORT Thesaurus* (Sport Information Resource Center, 1994) serves as a search aid. Selective retrospective coverage began in 1969. Updated monthly.

Internet

The explosion of resources available via the Internet has benefited professionals concerned with children. The Internet is commonly defined as a worldwide network comprised of many interconnected networks. Many new users of the Internet begin with electronic mail. Corresponding with colleagues at other institutions or with students reveals the convenience of electronic communications. Neophyte users soon learn to enter BITNET discussion groups through LISTSERVS and to identify additional relevant lists (discussion groups) for their participation. The following lists are representative of the resources on child care and parenting available to the Internet traveler.

> *EDTECH.* Sponsored by the University of North Dakota. LISTSERV%OHSTVMA.BITNET@VM1.NODAK.EDU
>> *EDTECH* provides a forum for practitioners, faculty, and students interested in education technology.
>
> *FAMILYSCI.* Sponsored by the Department of Family Studies, University of Kentucky. LISTSERV@UKCC.UKY.EDU
>> The Family Service Network addresses issues in family sociology, marriage and family therapy, behavioral aspects of family medicine, and related topics in family science.
>
> *PEDIATRIC-PAIN.* Sponsored by Dalhousie University. MAILSERV@AC.DAL.CA
>> Discussion of any topic related to pain in children by any professional or parent is the focus of this list.

LISTSERVs are indexed by subject in the Association for Research Libraries' *Directory of Electronic Journals and Newsletters* (ISSN 1057-1337, Michael Strangelove, ed.). Other sources include the *Directory of Scholarly Electronic Conferences*, a regularly updated electronic directory produced by Diane K. Kovacs at Kent State University. A complete catalog of LISTSERV lists is available by sending the command "list global" to LISTSERV@bitnic.educom.edu. Newsgroups, a resource similar in content to LISTSERVs, addressing parenting and child care are available on USENET, which exists solely to offer "NEWS," a collection of topical forums for exchange of information. Among the active newsgroups related to parenting are K12.chat.teacher, misc.kids, sci.psychology, misc.handicap, and alt.feminism. A useful source of information about the organization of the Internet and how to locate relevant LISTSERVs, newsgroups, and other resources is *Internet Connections: A Librarian's Guide to Dial-Up Access and Use.*[1]

In addition to these regularly appearing resources, the Internet provides access to a remarkable collection of documents, reports, media, graphic images, software, digitized sound recordings, and library online catalogs. To gain access to the millions of files at anonymous FTP (file transfer protocol) sites throughout the world, telnetting to Archie indexing allows users to scan FTP servers and search by keyword for files on any topic of interest.[2] The "Yanoff List" at yanoff@csd4.csd.uwm.edu provides a topical list of telnet addresses, gopher servers, and FTP sites. Gophers provide access to FTP sites as well as to other sources of information. One gopher site that is a convenient starting point from which to search for resources on child care and parenting is "Information by Subject Area!" at RICEINFO.RICE.EDU.[3] The World-Wide Web (WWW) provides hypertext access to information resources held anywhere on the Internet using gopher, FTP, or other interfaces to locate information.[4] For example, the *WWW Virtual Library* listing for "Education" includes a subcategory for "Educational Technology," which in turn gives access to the U.S. Department of Education [16] WWW server containing education research, statistics, and information about the department and its programs.

Locally held resources may be searched remotely by telnetting to individual library online catalogs and following the instructions to gain access and conduct subject, title, or author searches. The LIBS program (for UNIX and VMS users only) simplifies connecting to a remote location by offering a menu from which to select a remote library and presenting instructions on how to search individual catalogs before establishing the connection.[5]

Commercial Online Networks

CompuServe, Prodigy, and America Online are commercial online networks that provide the general public with electronic information services and resources similar to those described above for the Internet. In addition to electronic mail, CompuServe includes *Grolier's Academic American Encyclopedia*, updated quarterly, as well as *HealthNet*, a medical reference source, and numerous other services for a standard monthly fee. Special-interest forums, such as *Attention Deficit Disorder Forum, Disabilities Forum*, and *Health & Fitness Forum* are available for an additional cost that is determined by connect time and modem speed. *Knowledge Index*, labeled a "premium extended service" in promotional literature, provides citations and full-text document delivery for over 50,000 items indexed in over 100 databases, among them *ERIC, PsycINFO, Medline*, and *SPORT*. Access to these files is available through an agreement with DIALOG Information Retrieval Services.

America Online features *Compton's Encyclopedia*. The service also offers the Parent's Forum, a discussion group, which includes the Parent's Newstand, a source for such journals as *Education Week* and *Education News*. The forum contains "folders" on parenting topics, including working moms, single parents, adolescents, and potty training. Other forums address divorce, relationships, and management of anger. A discussion group specifically for teens is also available. In comparison, Prodigy includes a discussion group for parents called the Home Life Bulletin Board. The topic list includes adoption issues; being a terrific dad; parenting children from birth to age 5 and ages 6 to 12; parenting multiples, teens, or children with special needs; single parents; working parents; and day care. Prodigy also offers access to *Grolier's Encyclopedia*. The service charges a single fee per month, but printing and in some cases downloading cost extra. In contrast, America Online's fee is based on connect time, but there are no printing or downloading fees.

OTHER COMMERCIAL RESOURCES

Mail-order catalogs have long functioned as an easy way to obtain children's books, infant supplies, and clothing for all ages. One catalog with special appeal is produced by Chinaberry Book Service. According to the most recent issue, Chinaberry's philosophy is to encourage "conscious parenting" by offering materials that support families attempting to raise "children with love, honesty, and joy to be reverent, loving caretakers of each other and the earth."[6] This catalog provides detailed annotations for books to read to young children, books for young readers, as well as music selections, story tapes, videos, and parenting books. Adult "good reads" and games, toys, and "other stuff" add to the usefulness of this 100-plus–page guide to children's books. To obtain a catalog, contact Chinaberry at 2800 Via Orange Way, Suite B, Spring Valley, CA 91978 or (800) 776-2242.

Another helpful catalog, one that lists multicultural dolls and children's books as well as parenting books that address adoption, special needs, and children's self-esteem, is available from Adoptive Families of America. To obtain their parenting resource catalog, contact Adoptive Families at 3333 Highway 100 N. Minneapolis, MN 55422 or (612) 535-4829.

The Essence of Parenting is a biweekly parenting correspondence course, available on a semiannual (12 lessons) or annual (24 lessons) basis. Each brief lesson builds on the previous ones. The course begins with a lesson on self-discipline and love as motivating factors for parents' behaviors, followed by lessons on taking care of one's own needs, becoming conscious of how parents affect their children, noticing the impact of sensory experiences, and allowing kids to feel their feelings. Other issues addressed include reasons why children misbehave, positive discipline, state of mind versus techniques in discipline, and guilt management. The lessons themselves are light, warm, and supportive. For additional information or to subscribe, contact The Essence of Parenting at P.O. Box 25, Lake Mills, WI 53537 or (800) 873-2640.[7]

REFERENCES

1. Mary E. Engle et al., *Internet Connections: A Librarian's Guide to Dial-Up Access and Use* (Chicago: American Library Association, 1993), 4, 17, 113, 114, 136.

2. Ibid., 85.

3. Loss Pequeno Glazier, "Internet Resources for English and American Literature," *College and Research Libraries News* 55, no. 7 (July/August 1994): 417–22.

4. Engle, 95.

5. Ibid., 101.

6. *Chinaberry: Books and Other Treasures for the Entire Family.* (Spring Valley, CA: Chinaberry Book Service, Autumn 1994) 3.

7. Vic Goodman and Anne Johnson, *The Essence of Parenting Correspondence Course* (Lake Mills, WI: The Essence of Parenting, 1993).

APPENDIXES

APPENDIX

Popular and Professional Videotapes

GENERAL GUIDES TO PARENTING

Introduction to Parenting. The Family Formula: Video Basics of Parenting. VHS, 15 min., with reproducible worksheets. Cambridge Educational. CDFAM102V. 1992. $98.00.

This program introduces students, both as parents and as teens, to basic concepts of parenting styles.

Introduction to the Family. The Family Formula: Video Basics of Parenting. VHS, 15 min., includes reproducible worksheets. Cambridge Educational. CDFAM100V. 1992. $98.00.

Basic concepts of family communication to students, both as parents and as teens, are presented in this video.

Ten Ways to Be a Better Parent. Cambridge Parenting Series. VHS, 25 min., with teacher's instruction manual. Cambridge Career Products. CCP0069SV. 1991. $79.95.

Methods to improve parenting skills are presented in this video, along with methods for building self-esteem, encouraging emotional expression, and establishing consistent guidelines for behavior.

MOTHERING

A New Mother's Feelings. David Lee Miller. VHS, 30 min. Kinetic, Inc. VB400V. 1992. $39.95.

New mothers will find this program helpful for coping with the many emotions associated with the birth of their first child. Covered are the crying baby, postpartum blues, bonding, the baby's appearance immediately after birth, and the father's feelings. Commentary by new and experienced mothers is included.

FATHERING

For Dads Only. VHS, 39 min. Athena Productions. AE300V. 1990. $39.95.

This program instructs fathers in the proper procedures for daily care of infants, such as feeding and burping, diaper changing, bathing, entertaining baby, and stopping a baby's crying. Information is presented in a light, humorous manner.

FAMILY ORGANIZATION

Juggling Your Work and Family. American Management Association. VHS, 30 min. 1990. $79.95.

Working parents and concerned experts address challenges of balancing needs of work and home in a businesslike approach targeted to young professionals.

Parents with Careers: Practical Ways to Balance Career and Family. Active Parenting, Inc. VHS, 32 min., with guide, parent's action plan, leader's guide, promotional posters, and brochures. 1990. $149.00.

Using a practical approach, this video covers challenges faced by contemporary parents, including locating reliable, quality child care, balancing home and career, and sharing household responsibilities.

Working Parents: Balancing Kids and Careers. VHS, 25 min. Learning Seed. #149VHS. 1992. $89.00.

Real parents discuss solutions to managing the dual demands of work and family, including part-time work, telecommuting, family leave, shared jobs, and flextime scheduling. Innovative corporate programs that address this dilemma are profiled.

CHILD CARE

Safe and Sound: Choosing Quality Child Care. Narrated by Meredith Baxter-Birney. U-Matic, VHS, 30 or 56 min., with parent's guide. Carle Medical Communications. 1991. $195.00 (30 min.), $250.00 (56 min.).

This video guides parents through the process of visiting and choosing a child care provider. The contents include a review of in-home care, family day care, and child care centers; quality of personal interactions among children and adults in the program; educational activities; safety and health concerns; communications with parents; licensing and accreditation; special needs; separation and attachment; staff turnover; and group size. Awards: Silver Award, Houston International Film Festival; Runner-up, National Council on Family Relations Media Festival.

Selecting Day Care for Your Child. VHS, 70 min. Sperling Video and Film. Distributed by Aylmer Press. 1991. $59.00.

Tips on evaluating child care centers, in-home care, and family day care and choosing among these options are provided in this video.

Techniques in Childcare: Planning and Operating a Quality Family Day Care. VHS, 49 min. Day Care Video Program. 1990. $69.95.

Prepared by a licensed independent clinical social worker, this production contains interviews with experienced providers that cover setting up contracts, obtaining insurance, planning activities, planning for safety and health, and communicating with parents.

INFANTS

Baby Talk: The Videoguide for New Parents. VHS, 60 min., with reference booklet and poster. Polymorph Films. 1992. $24.95.

Prepared by clinicians to help parents find answers to common questions about infant care, this guide covers newborn appearance, diapering, breastfeeding and bottle feeding, sleep and wake patterns, crying and colic, personality and development, illness, and when to visit the doctor. One section addresses how new parents can take care of themselves too.

Caring for Baby. Two videos, each VHS, 30 min. Chip Taylor Communications. 1990. $159.00 total.

Health care practitioners, including a nurse, a psychiatrist, and a physician, discuss and demonstrate newborn care with parents. Contents include bathing, taking a temperature, breastfeeding, diapering, and other aspects of care of a healthy infant.

Newborn Basics. VHS, 72 min. Cambridge Career Products. CCP0073V. 1991. $39.95.

This video covers the first months of infant care, addressing such basic concerns as how to hold a baby, feeding methods, baby hygiene, temperature taking, home safety, and proper health care, including determining when to visit a doctor.

Parenting the Growing Preemie. Parent Tape #2. VHS, 9 min. Polymorph Films. 1991. $175.00

Prepared for parents of babies in neonatal intensive care, this video provides an overview of preemie development and advice on how to handle and interact with their hospitalized infant.

What's a Parent to Do? VHS, 52 min. MPI Home Video. 1991. $29.95.

Hosted by John Stossel, this video includes parents, clinicians, infants, and toddlers demonstrating techniques for infant and child care. Contents include establishing a loving relationship, helping baby sleep through the night, handling temper tantrums and terrible twos, and other aspects of child development.

TODDLERS AND PRESCHOOLERS

It's Potty Time. Barbara J. Howard. VHS, 25 min. Learning Through Entertainment. LTE100V. 1990. $29.95.

Developed by the Child Development Unit of the Duke University Medical Center Department of Pediatrics, this video helps parents teach their children in a positive manner to use the toilet. With an entertaining approach to model behavior, the production covers all the steps of using the toilet correctly.

SCHOOL-AGE CHILDREN

For Parents of School Age Children. Parent Talk: The Art of Parenting, vol. 2. VHS, 53 min., with teacher's guide. Program Source International. Distributed by Instructional Video. 1989. $69.95.

The contents include 37 parenting tips for raising school-age children, related to topics such as homework, self-care, grades, allowances, effects of TV, fighting, whining, sibling rivalry, self-esteem, and lying.

Solutions to Ten Common Parenting Problems. Cambridge Parenting Series. VHS, 30 min., with instruction manual. Cambridge Career Products. CCP0068V. 1992. $79.95.

Provides simple and practical solutions to minor problems, such as thumb sucking, TV watching, and hyperactive behavior, commonly experienced by parents of young children.

ADOLESCENTS

Active Parenting of Teens Discussion Program. Two videos, VHS, 158 min. total, with leader's guide, parent's guide, drug prevention booklet, illustrated poem, course promotion guide, and starter kit of promotional material, including 2 posters and 24 parent brochures in a vinyl case. Active Parenting. 1990. $295.00.

These videos cover the critical issues and circumstances that make interactions with adolescents so challenging, such as drugs, peer pressure, and sexuality.

Dealing with Teens: A Guide to Survival. VHS, 52 min. Films for the Humanities and Social Sciences. RG-2721. 1990. $159.00.

Provides suggestions for dealing with teens and preteens concerning substance abuse, dating and sexuality, and moods and feelings. This video also provides a list of warning signs to differentiate normal from disturbed adolescent behavior.

For Parents of Teenagers. Parent Talk: The Art of Parenting, vol. 3. VHS, 53 min., with teacher's guide. Program Source International. Distributed by Instructional Video. 1990. $69.95.

This video provides practical information for teachers, counselors, and parent group discussion leaders on a variety of topics, including manners, curfews, jobs, the silent treatment, alcohol usage, skin problems, boredom, suicide, and stepfamilies.

Kids Having Kids: Teenage Pregnancy. Growing Up Fast: A Guide to Unplanned Parenthood. VHS, 30 min. Cambridge Educational. CCP0086V. 1992. $79.95.

The reasons why so many teens get pregnant are addressed in this documentary. Interviews with young women, their boyfriends, parents, counselors, teachers, and other professionals demonstrate the impact of pregnancy, parental obligations, open communication, and realistic decision making.

Kids Raising Kids: Teenage Parenthood. Growing Up Fast: A Guide to Unplanned Parenthood. VHS, 30 min. Cambridge Educational. CCP0087V. 1992. $79.95.

For teens who intend to continue their pregnancies, a positive and responsible attitude is essential, whether they choose marriage or single parenthood. This video covers how to choose the right doctor, proper prenatal care, and the benefits of a good diet, regular exercise, and childbirth instruction. Other topics, such as adjusting to the baby, continuing education, finding help, and managing finances, are addressed through interviews with teenage parents of infants and toddlers.

Pressure-Cooked Kids. VHS, 28 min. Films for the Humanities and Social Sciences. RG-2891. 1991. $149.00.

This video examines how to help teens cope with stress as youths to prepare them to balance work and family life as adults.

Project Future: Teen Pregnancy, Childbirth, and Parenting. Three videos, VHS, each 46–61 min. Vida Health Communications. 1991. $650.00.

This comprehensive video focuses on the needs of adolescent parents-to-be. Discussions with a diverse group of teens are used to present the issues, including the effects of alcohol on newborns as well as normal progression of pregnancies.

Suicide: The Parent's Perspective. VHS, 26 min. Films for the Humanities and Social Sciences. DE-2352. 1990. $149.00.

This video alerts parents to the symptoms of serious trouble and helps them listen to their teenagers. Parents are also counseled about their limits; while parents are urged to do their best, their efforts may not be enough to prevent suicide.

Teenage Mothers: Looking Back . . . Moving Ahead. VHS, 35 min., with study guide. Menninger Video Productions. 1992. $99.00.

Three young women who provide positive role models for teenage mothers who choose to keep their babies are profiled in this video. The contents focus on setting realistic goals in facing the challenges of pregnancy.

CHILD DEVELOPMENT NORMS

Raising America's Children—A Video Series. Thelma Harms and Debby Cryer. 10 videos, VHS, 30 min. each, with study guide and instructor's guide. Delmar. 1990. $85.00 each, $749.00 for set of 10.

Each of the videos in this set addresses a specific aspect of child development, including a secure beginning, relating to others, playing and learning, listening and talking, and coping with stress, experienced by children from infancy through five years. The videos show children at home with their parents or in group settings such as family day care homes, child care centers, half-day preschool programs, and kindergartens. Children with special needs are included in each video, with one program focusing entirely on the educational options for children with special needs.

DEVELOPMENTAL DISABILITIES

The Special Child: Maximizing Limited Potential. VHS, 26 min. Films for the Humanities and Social Sciences. DE-1812. 1991. $149.00.

Screening for developmental problems should begin at three to four months if doubts exist about a child's mental and physical coordination. Topics covered include Down syndrome, autism, problems of neurological control, and speech problems.

PSYCHOLOGICAL DEVELOPMENT

Childhood-Adolescent Disorders: Simulated Evaluations. VHS, 47 min. Health Sciences Consortium. 900-VI-003. 1990. $250.00, $125.00 for members.

To guide professionals in developing skills in observation and assessment of the symptoms of psychosocial disorders in children and adolescents, this program presents three psychiatric case studies illustrating conduct disorder, oppositional defiant disorder, and separation anxiety disorder.

Developing a Positive Self-Esteem in Young Children. VHS, 16 min. Chip Taylor Communications. 1991. $140.00.

Treating self-esteem as a learned rather than innate quality, one that depends on perception of accomplishment rather than the actual achievements themselves, this video instructs care givers in ways to enhance children's level of self-esteem.

How Do I Tell You I Like You? VHS, 20 min. Self Dimensions, Inc. 1990. $79.95.

This program instructs students in ways to communicate with children to foster the growth of positive self-esteem. Techniques covered include active listening, eye-level communication, positive self-talk, and encouragement.

HEALTH CARE, SAFETY, AND DEATH

Adolescents: At Risk for HIV Infection. The CWLA Video Training Series. VHS, with discussion guide. Child Welfare League of America. 4549. 1991. $59.95.

Viewers will find in this video information to make HIV and AIDS more understandable and less threatening to discuss. The focus is on behaviors that put teens at risk for contracting HIV, strategies for helping teens prevent the infection, and considerations related to counseling, HIV testing, and follow-up services.

Caring for Infants and Toddlers with HIV Infection. The CWLA Video Training Series. VHS, 21 min., with discussion guide. Child Welfare League of America. 4522. 1991. $59.95.

The daily life of three families caring for infants and toddlers with HIV infection is explored in this video. Support parents may provide to each other is demonstrated.

Caring for School-Age Children with HIV Infection. The CWLA Video Training Series. VHS, with discussion guide. Child Welfare League of America. 4530. 1991. $59.95.

This production examines the day-to-day life of three families who care for older children who are infected with HIV. Among the issues covered are talking with the infected child, caring for noninfected siblings, and coping with community discrimination.

Cerebral Palsy: What Every Mother Should Know. VHS, 19 min. Films for the Humanities and Social Sciences. DE-2230. 1990. $149.00.

Causes and symptoms of cerebral palsy, along with therapies for treating it, are discussed in this video. Animation is used to illustrate the area of the brain that is damaged in patients with cerebral palsy. Causes such as maternal infections during pregnancy, complications during childbirth, and infant head injuries are covered, as is the use of selective posterior rhizotomy surgery in reducing spasticity in certain patients.

A Challenge for Parents: Eczema in Pre-school Children. Karin Chuoke. VHS, 13 min. Health Sciences Consortium. (B30)911-VI-059. 1992. $195.00.

Educating parents about atopic dermatitis, which occurs in approximately 10 percent of newborns and infants, helps prevent the disease from interfering in the development of the parent-child relationship. The contents include a definition of eczema, trigger factors which may bring on an outbreak, and methods for treatment and prevention. Parents of children with this disorder share their experiences and concerns.

A Child Dies. VHS, 29 min., with study guide. Hospital Satellite Network. Distributed by American Journal of Nursing Co. 1991. $275.00.

Interviews with families who have experienced the death of a child, with discussions led by two nursing professionals, are featured in this video. Grieving is portrayed as a lifelong process that each person experiences individually. Practical advice for nurses who help grieving parents is provided.

Child Safety at Home. VHS, 30 min. Kidsafety of America. KID100V. 1992. $39.95.

With dramatic enactments and checklists, this video educates parents about safety problems in the home, including information about choking, burns, shock, bleeding, drowning, poisoning, fire safety, convulsions, and emergency phone calls. Definitions, causes, and safeguards are given for each.

Childhood Asthma. VHS, 19 min. Films for the Humanities and Social Sciences. DE-2649. 1990. $149.00.

Bronchial and allergic asthma and the diagnosis and treatment of childhood allergies are the focus of this video. Contents cover attack triggers, such as allergies, respiratory infections, exercise, and emotional stress. Animation is employed to show how the bronchial tubes of asthmatics become inflamed and constricted during an attack. Early diagnosis and treatment are emphasized.

Children Die, Too. VHS, 26 min. Films for the Humanities and Social Sciences. DE-2374. 1990. $149.00.

Various approaches to coping with childhood death, including discussions with families who lost a child, comments from a psychiatrist on how members of grieving families can help each other, and what assistance a cancer treatment team can give families, are addressed in this video.

Common Childhood Illnesses. VHS, 45 min. Cambridge Career Products. CCP0049V. 1991. $79.95.

Common childhood illnesses, their symptoms, and possible at-home and medical treatments are covered in this video, along with advice on when to consult a doctor. Children who have experienced diseases such as ear infections, common colds, mumps, tonsillitis, chicken pox, fever, asthma, and measles discuss how they felt, what they looked like, and how they were treated. Awards: Gold Apple, National Educational Film and Video Festival.

A Cradle Song: The Families of SIDS. Dennis Spalsbury. VHS, 29 min. Fanlight Productions. BV-063. 1990. $225.00.

In this video, parents share their pain, anger, and sadness at the death of their children from SIDS.

I'm Just Your Mother—Ethical Dilemmas in the NICU: The Parents' Perspective. Winifred J. Pinch and Charles Lenosky. VHS, 30 min. Health Sciences Consortium. (B23)901-VI-084. 1990. $345.00, $241.50 for members.

Health professionals will find this video helpful for understanding the parents' perspective in making treatment decisions for premature infants. The story of one family's fears, frustrations, and confusion when faced with the reality of a premature infant is portrayed, along with the accompanying medical complications.

Letting Go. VHS, 29 min. AJN Videos. 4307S. 1991. $285.00.

The stories of two families who recently lost a child illustrate the experiences of parents, children, and nurses who have lived through such an ordeal.

Living with Loss: Children and HIV. The CWLA Video Training Series. VHS, 26 min., with study guide. Child Welfare League of America. 4824. 1991. $59.95.

This video explores positive ways of coping with the loss that all who are in contact with a child feel after the child's death. The course of the disease from diagnosis through sick and well periods to death is covered, along with methods for coping with the grieving that occurs throughout each stage.

The Newly Diagnosed Family. Issues in Cystic Fibrosis Series. VHS, 30 min. Health Sciences Consortium. 891-VI-041. 1990. $395.00, $276.50 for members.

Targeted to health professionals, this program stimulates discussion about how to skillfully meet the needs of parents whose children have cystic fibrosis. Excerpts from a discussion between a group leader and members of two families describe impact of the diagnosis, interactions with health professionals, and particularly how information on the disorder was conveyed.

The Ouchless House: Your Baby Safe Home. VHS, 30 min., with poster. Cambridge Career Products. CCP0071V. 1992. $59.95.

How to create a home that is safe for children to explore, avoid unnecessary injuries, and be prepared for quick action if an accident occurs are covered in this video.

Parenting the Acutely Ill Infant. Parent Tape #1. VHS, 14 min. Polymorph Films. 1991. $175.00.

Intended for parents whose infants have been admitted to the NICU, this video explains what happens there in an attempt to help parents adjust to the new and frightening environment, become more actively involved, and ultimately be better able to care for their child's needs.

The Prevention and Treatment of Childhood Injuries. VHS, 50 min., with softcover book. Cambridge Educational. ACV300V. 1991. $39.95.

Primary causes of injuries, advice on prevention, and first-aid treatment are presented through reenactments in this video for child care providers. Contents include drowning, choking, burns, traffic safety, poisoning, fractures, sprains, bites and stings, and other hazards for parents, teachers, and baby-sitters to be aware of when caring for children.

Recently Bereaved Parents—Part I. Issues in Cystic Fibrosis Series. VHS, 28 min. Health Sciences Consortium. N891-VI-046. 1990. $395.00, $276.50 for members.

This video is the first part of a facilitated group interview with parents of children who recently died from cystic fibrosis. Topics addressed include the decision to bring the child home to die and how to raise a terminally ill child as normally as possible.

Recently Bereaved Parents—Part II. Issues in Cystic Fibrosis Series. VHS, 28 min. Health Sciences Consortium. N891-VI-047. 1990. $395.00, $276.50 for members.

A continuation of part 1, the discussion addresses how parents, their dying child, and the child's care givers dealt with the dying-at-home phase of cystic fibrosis. Parents reflect on their memories of their child's last days and what they gained in loving a terminally ill child.

Siblings. Issues in Cystic Fibrosis Series. VHS, 30 min. Health Sciences Consortium. 891-VI-051. 1990. $395.00, $276.50 for members.

The effect that a chronic illness in one child has on the entire family is explored in this video. Excerpts from an interview in which family members discuss the impact of cystic fibrosis (CF) on their lives, such as the amount of attention a CF child requires, facing the facts, disruption of family plans, fear during acute attacks, fear of being a carrier, coping with the child's death, and dealing with anger and lack of understanding from the outside world, are presented.

When to Call the Doctor If Your Child Is Ill. VHS, 45 min. Cambridge Career Products. CCP0048V. 1991. $79.95.

Because it is difficult or impossible for infants and children to communicate "what hurts," parents must learn what symptoms to look for in deciding whether medical care is needed or whether self-help methods will suffice. Scenarios using common illnesses, warning signs, and possible treatments illustrate concepts.

NUTRITION AND FITNESS

Breastfeeding: A Special Relationship. VHS, 25 min. Eagle Video Productions. 1991. $79.00.

How to successfully breastfeed by reading a baby's signals and recognizing the responses of the mother's body is covered in this program. Covered are choosing positions, latching on, solving minor problems, and going back to work.

Family Fitness One. VHS, 40 min. Crazy Legs Productions. Distributed by Threshold Marketing. 1992. $29.95.

Exercise suggestions for the entire family are presented here using demonstrations by parents and children.

More Than Child's Play: Kids, Parents, and Sports. VHS, 25 min. Films for the Humanities and Social Sciences. DE-2380. 1990. $149.00.

The pros and cons of youth sports, the role of parents and coaches, and how to make youth sports a positive experience for all involved are explored in this video. The presentation includes comments by professional athletes and prestigious coaches.

Nutritional Aspects of Breastfeeding. VHS, 15 min. Health Sciences Consortium. (B30)900-VI-044. 1990. $195.00.

This program is a guide to infant nutrition for the breastfeeding mother. The stages of breast milk production, benefits of breastfeeding for child and mother, caloric needs and proper selection of foods for the mother, factors that affect milk production, and techniques for storing and freezing breast milk are discussed. $195.00.

DISCIPLINE AND GUIDANCE

Basic Parenting Skills. VHS, 55 min. Cambridge Career Products. CCP0033V. 1990. $89.95.

In a parenting group, young parents, frustrated with parenting young children, explore strategies for building discipline, communication, and stability in their children's lives. In the discussion, discipline is presented as a system for teaching and reinforcing desirable behavior, with practical techniques for dealing with tantrums and other undesirable behavior. How to set reasonable expectations, establish limits, and apply them firmly is explained.

Helping Your Child Succeed. Common Sense Parenting Series. VHS, 50 min. Father Flanagan's Boys Home. 1992. $39.95.

The video demonstrates to parents how to prepare children for new or difficult situations they will encounter in daily life.

Also covered are solving problems, reducing peer pressure, and increasing self-esteem.

How to Raise Happy, Confident Kids. VHS, 80 min. Career Track Publications. 1990. $39.95.

Simple skills for stopping misbehavior, winning a child's co-operation, improving communication, setting fair limits, reducing the number and severity of conflicts, and asserting one's rights as a parent are demonstrated in this video.

Managing Difficult Behavior in Young Children. VHS, 45 min. Modern Learning Production, 1992. $64.95.

An educator presents practical techniques, based on temperament, for preventing and stopping misbehavior in children, such as logical consequences and cooling off.

Negotiating within the Family! You and Your Child Can Both Get What You Want. Boy's Town Parenting Series. VHS, 15 min., with booklet. Father Flanagan's Boys Home. 1990. $29.95.

The technique of using a written agreement to help children identify and achieve realistic personal goals is described.

1-2-3 Magic. VHS, 120 min. Child Management. 1990. $39.95.

This video provides parents with a strategy developed by a clinical psychologist for disciplining children ages 2 to 12 without arguing, yelling, or spanking. How to avoid falling prey to manipulation and how to ensure that children do what they are instructed to do are also covered.

Take Time to Be a Family! Holding Successful Family Meetings. Boy's Town Parenting Series. VHS, 15 min., with booklet. Father Flanagan's Boys Home. 1990. $29.95.

Parents are instructed in how to use a weekly get-together to build children's decision-making skills and enhance their sense of responsibility.

Teaching Responsible Behavior. Common Sense Parenting Series. VHS, 50 min. Father Flanagan's Boys Home. 1992. $39.95.

This video demonstrates for parents how they may correct children's misbehavior. Advice is offered on how to help children accept responsibility for homework and household chores, and how to set and achieve realistic goals.

The Video SOS! Help for Parents. VHS, 65 min., with leader's guide, reproducible handouts, and illustrated handbook for parents and professionals. Parents' Press. 1991. $150.00.

For counselors, educators, churches, and social service professionals as well as parents and parent groups, this video presents child management skills and concepts with practical applications. Among the techniques covered are rewards for good behavior, including social, activity, and material rewards; active ignoring; scolding; time-out; logical consequences; punishment; being a good role model; and many others.

When I Was Your Age: Discipline in the Family. The Family Formula: Video Basics of Parenting. VHS. Cambridge Educational. CDFAM110V. 1992. $79.00.

Introduces basic concepts to new parents for disciplining young children.

You Can Be a Better Parent in 30 Minutes. VHS, 30 min., with free subscription to the *Family America Society Newsletter,*

bumper sticker, and refrigerator magnet. Cambridge Career Products. FAS100V. 1992. $29.95.

The problems parents face in obtaining proper behavior from their children and disciplining them when they misbehave are covered in this program, as are practical solutions with immediate applicability. Contents include following directions, behaving in public, accepting no, and doing chores, along with more reflective concerns, such as recognizing and praising good behavior, avoiding comparisons among children, and understanding the consequences of poor disciplinary techniques.

EDUCATION AND LEARNING

Parent-Teacher Conferences: Resolving Conflicts. VHS, 37 min., with discussion guide. Menninger Video Productions. 1992. $135.00.

Teachers who view this video will learn how to involve parents in decisions and promote home-school collaboration. Using a step-by-step conferencing process, teachers learn to negotiate differences, find common ground, and arrive at creative solutions. Interviews and dramatizations illustrate the instructions given.

Why Do These Kids Love School? Dorothy Fadiman. VHS, 60 min. Pyramid Film & Video. 1991. $95.00.

Tom Peters introduces this program, which consists of visits to secondary schools that have students who excel. Common characteristics of the schools are parental involvement, facilitating principals, and autonomous teachers.

SPECIAL EDUCATION NEEDS

All about Attention Deficit Disorder, Part I: Symptoms, Development, Prognosis, and Causes. VHS, 108 min. Child Management. 1991. $29.95.

The first part of this two-volume set addresses the symptoms of attention deficit disorder (ADD); its impact on home, school, and social life; the developmental course of the disorder; prognosis; and theories about its causes. The format is a lecture by a physician whose child also has ADD, with commentaries by parents, children, and teachers on how the disorder has affected them.

All about Attention Deficit Disorder, Part II: Diagnosis and Treatment. VHS, 85 min. Child Management. 1991. $29.95.

Diagnostic considerations and treatment options, including medication and counseling, are covered in the second part of this two-volume set. Lectures by a physician whose child has ADD and discussions by families and teachers who are affected by the disorder are included.

The Attention Dimension. VHS, 10 min. Health Sciences Consortium. (B30)901-VI-019. 1990. $195.00.

Dramatizations and interviews with K-12 students illustrate the variety of attention problems in existence, ways to understand them, and how to give or seek help in solving them.

Dyslexia: Diagnosis and Prognosis. VHS, 26 min. Films for the Humanities and Social Sciences. DE-2348. 1990. $149.00.

This program provides an overview of the various disorders labeled dyslexia, symptoms in preschool and school-age children, the probable source of the dyslexic's learning disabilities, types of diagnostic testing, and effective learning assistance to enable dyslexics to develop their intelligence and their potential.

Homework and Learning Disabilities: A Common Sense Approach. VHS, 35 min. Menninger Video Productions. 1991. $99.00.

Practical methods parents may use to help children with learning disabilities study are demonstrated in this video. Strategies for teachers that foster home-school cooperation and maximize children's learning are also presented.

TEACCH: Program for Parents. Eric Schopler. VHS, 45 min. Health Sciences Consortium. (B30)901-VI-082. 1990. $195.00.

For parents, this video introduces the TEACCH program for treating and educating autistic children. The method, developed with parents' input, emphasizes understanding the child's condition, dealing effectively with special needs, and encouraging as normal a life as possible for the child.

PLAY, TV, AND RECREATION

Roughhousing. VHS, 30 min. Cambridge Career Products. AF100V. 1992. $39.95.

A guide to safe and fun physical play for children is presented to parents and teachers in this video. Both theoretical and practical approaches for roughhousing for preschoolers, school-age children, and families, along with guidelines for safety, are presented.

CHILD ABUSE

Childhood Physical Abuse. VHS, 26 min. Films for the Humanities and Social Sciences. DE-2350. 1990. $149.00.

For professionals who work with abused children and their families, this video covers the kinds of adults likely to abuse their children, signs of abuse, methods for dealing with abuse, how abusive parents may stop abusing, what happens to children when the legal system is involved, and whether and how abuse can be prevented.

Childhood Sexual Abuse. VHS, 26 min. Films for the Humanities and Social Sciences. EB-2349. 1990. $149.00.

This program examines how sexually abused women learn to work out the problems caused by abuse and what measures they may take to protect their own children from a recurrence of the pattern. Psychiatrists, social workers, and law enforcement officers explain how the pattern of abuse spreads throughout a family, why children can be manipulated into silent acceptance of abuse, signs and symptoms, the reliability of children as witnesses, teaching preventive skills to children, and under what circumstances treatment of abusers can be effective.

Date Rape: It Happened to Me. VHS, 30 min. Bellis/Carpenter Production. Distributed by Pyramid Films. 1991. $395.00.

Featuring male and female narrators, this dramatization focuses on the rape of one high school girl by her steady boyfriend. Issues are explored through testimony of actual rape survivors, expert advice from rape counselors, and advice from police.

Heart on a Chain: The Truth about Date Violence. VHS, 17 min. MTI Film. 1991. $350.00.

Through dramatization of several high school relationships, this video examines issues involved in physical and emotional abuse. A narrator explains how abuse begins, where it can lead, and that it is always wrong.

SUBSTANCE ABUSE

Adolescent Alcoholism: Recognizing, Intervening, and Treating. 11 videos, VHS, 5–25 min. each, each with pamphlet; study guide with set, also available for $19.95 if tapes purchased individually. Health Sciences Consortium. 1990. $1,995.00 for series, $997.50 for set for members; $195.00 for individual programs, $97.50 for individual programs for members.

This series provides a framework for increasing awareness of health care providers about teenage alcoholism and substance abuse. Factual information, trends in current thinking regarding factors, and models of alcoholism are presented, with emphasis being on the disease model. The series is also intended as a trigger for discussions between parents and their adolescents in prevention and treatment programs.

A P P E N D I X

Statistical Data

Statistical data reveal the circumstances of children living in the United States today in a graphic way that no how-to guide, popular or professional, can approximate. The data compiled here present a portrait of the conditions of contemporary childhood, demonstrating family structure, who provides children's daily care, health and safety hazards children must confront, incidence of disabilities, threats of abuse and substance abuse, and leading causes of death. While admittedly the data present a challenging, even bleak, story of life for today's children and youths, they also illustrate and confirm trends and patterns that might otherwise be viewed as exaggerated or denied entirely. The tables themselves are organized following the topical arrangement of this sourcebook.

Federal agencies and departments, especially the Department of Commerce, Bureau of the Census, are dependable sources for reliable, valid data on children and youths and are the sources for many of the tables presented here. In addition to the decennial *Census of Population and Housing*, which includes the *Census of Population, General Population Characteristics*, the bureau publishes *Current Population Reports, Population Characteristics Series P-20* and *Series P-23*; *Current Population Reports Special Studies Series P-23*; *Current Population Reports, Household Economic Studies P-70*; and the *Statistical Abstract of the United States*. The Department of Justice produces the annual *Sourcebook of Criminal Justice Statistics*.

The Department of Health and Human Services, National Center for Health Statistics, is a primary source for data on health care, safety, disabilities, morbidity, mortality, natality, and fertility. Among the significant resources compiled by the department are *Vital and Health Statistics, Series 10: Data from the National Health Survey; Monthly Vital Statistics Report; Morbidity and Mortality Weekly Report; Advance Data;* and *Health United States*. The *Digest of Education Statistics* is produced by the National Center for Education Statistics.

Individual researchers and private agencies such as the Gallup Poll Monthly, Children's Defense Fund, Phi Delta Kappa, and Population Reference Bureau are sources for statistical, attitudinal, and behavioral data, often for narrowly defined groups. The Annie E. Casey Foundation produces the *Kids Count Data Book*, a convenient annual compilation of data addressing the well-being of children. A text synthesizing data on children and families is *Statistical Handbook on the American Family*, edited by Bruce A. Chadwick and Tim B. Heaton (Oryx Press, 1992). A complete citation to the source of the data presented accompanies each table. Many are drawn from more complex tables covering the population as a whole or presenting additional demographic variables.

HIGHLIGHTS

Depending on their race or ethnic background, children under 18 years of age constituted from approximately 23 to 35 percent of all persons in their racial group in the United States in 1990 (see Table B-1). Nearly 47 percent of all married couples had children under the age of 18 in contrast to 61 percent of the woman-only households (see Table B-2). Most children under 6 years of age whose parents were ages 15 to 24 or over 65 lived with their mother only, in contrast to those children whose parents were 25 to 64 years old. Only when parents were 30 years or older did the majority of children ages 6 to 11 live with both parents (see Table B-3). The lowest rate of household discontinuation, involving a change of family members, occurred for white married couples with children when only the husband worked; the lowest rate for African American or Hispanic married couples was observed when both worked (see Table B-4). Recent projections predict that married couples without children will be the largest family group in 1995 and 2000, a change from 1970, when married couples with children were the most numerous (see Table B-5). The majority of children of all races live with both parents. Of those who live with one parent, that parent is usually the mother (see Table B-6).

Who is taking care of young children? Mothers who are employed full-time are more likely to use care in another home than are mothers who work part-time; they are also more likely to select organized child care facilities than mothers employed part-time (see Table B-8). Even children ages 13 or 14 spent relatively few hours per week (1.1–2.0 hours) caring for themselves (see Table B-9) according to a recent Bureau of the Census report, a figure that contradicts the popular image of lonely "latch-key" children.

Threats to health and safety vary with the age of the child. A high percentage of homicides and suicides in children and youths result from firearms, with the lowest percentage of homicide deaths by firearms (45.2 percent) in white girls ages 10 to 14 and the highest (90.9 percent) in African American boys ages 15 to 19 (see Table B-10). Over 2 million children lived with orthopedic impairments in 1992 (see Table B-11), and over 1 million had a speech impairment. The rate of orthopedic impairments per 1,000 children was 35.3 in 1986–88. Nearly 32 boys per 1,000 persons had an orthopedic impairment (39 percent for girls), and 24 boys per 1,000 persons had a speech impairment, compared to 12 per 1,000 persons for girls (see Table B-12).

Children under 17 years living with their mother and stepfather had the highest incidence of accidents and injuries, frequent headaches, and chronic enuresis (see Table B-13) of children in all types of households, whereas children living with their never-married mother and no father had the lowest incidence of these complaints. The annual injury rate for girls under 18 years was 27.5 per 100 persons, compared to a rate of 36.1 per 100 persons for boys of that age (see Table B-14). Among the most common sources of injuries were doors, walls, beds, tables, chairs, and, at the top of the list, bicycles (see Table B-15).

For all children and youths ages 1 to 24, accidents were the leading cause of death in 1990. Other significant hazards were congenital anomalies, malignant neoplasms, diseases of the heart, and, for youths ages 15 to 24, suicide (see Table B-16). A more detailed breakdown of causes of death is presented in Table B-17. Over 14 percent of infant deaths were due to Suddent Infant Death Syndrome (SIDS) in 1988, an increase of 2 percent since 1980 (Table B-18).

Proper nutrition and physical fitness prepare children for healthy lives as adults. Over half of the children included in the National Health Survey in 1990 were breastfed, and nearly one-quarter were breastfed for longer than six months (see Table B-19). Thousands of children participate each year in organized sports, with the most popular sports being football, basketball, and baseball for boys and basketball, track, and volleyball for girls (see Table B-20).

School life today reflects problems that children bring to the classroom as well as those that occur in their pursuit of an education. While fewer than 26 percent of the teachers surveyed by the Carnegie Foundation for the Advancement of Teaching considered lack of parental support, abused or neglected youths, poor health among students, or absenteeism to be serious problems at their schools, well over 50 percent of the respondents considered these hazards to be somewhat of a problem (see Table B-21). Nearly 90 percent of new teachers surveyed after their first year in the classroom thought that many children bring such difficult family problems to school with them that they have difficulty learning (see Table B-22).

Other sources have presented data that indicate that the rate of child abuse reporting increased from 1988 to 1991; 42 reports per 1,000 U.S. children were received in 1991 compared to 35 per 1,000 in 1988 (see Table B-23). The type of maltreatment most often reported from 1976 to 1986 was deprivation of necessities. The average age of the abused child was 7, with incidence divided nearly equally between boys and girls; the average age of the abusers was 31. The majority of the abusers over the years covered were women (see Table B-24). Abuse is self-inflicted where alcohol, marijuana, and other drugs are concerned. Nearly 33 percent of the high school seniors questioned in a recent survey had used marijuana at least once (see Table B-25). In comparison, 88 percent of all seniors had used alcohol at least once during that same time period (see Table B-26).

TABLE B-1

DISTRIBUTION OF U.S. CHILDREN IN 1990

Summary	All Children Male	Female	White Male	Female	African American Male	Female	Hispanic Origin Male	Female
Under 5 years	9,392,409	8,962,034	7,004,481	6,645,009	1,408,495	1,377,407	1,218,194	1,169,330
5–9 years	9,262,527	8,836,652	6,990,531	6,625,737	1,350,265	1,320,844	1,118,733	1,075,119
10–14 years	8,767,167	8,347,082	6,606,726	6,246,832	1,314,408	1,287,182	1,023,383	978,234
15–19 years	9,102,698	8,651,317	6,845,571	6,497,132	1,342,263	1,316,230	1,083,893	970,064

Percent Distribution	All Children Male	Female	White Male	Female	African American Male	Female	Hispanic Origin Male	Female
Under 5 years	7.7	7.0	7.2	6.5	9.9	8.7	10.7	10.7
5–17 years	19.1	17.3	17.9	16.2	24.3	21.2	24.2	23.9
Total under 18 years	26.9	24.3	25.1	22.7	34.2	29.9	34.9	34.5

Males per 100 Females	All Children	White	African American	Hispanic Origin
Under 5 years	104.8	105.4	102.3	104.2
5–17 years	105.1	105.8	102.5	105.3
Total under 18 years	105.0	105.7	102.4	104.9

Note: Persons of Hispanic origin may be of any race. "All Children" includes persons of races other than African American and white or persons of Hispanic origin.

Source: *1990 Census of Population, General Population Characteristics: United States*. U.S. Department of Commerce, Bureau of the Census, 1992, pp. 23–24.

TABLE B-2

CHARACTERISTICS OF U.S. FAMILIES WITH CHILDREN IN 1991
(Numbers in thousands)

	White	African American	Hispanic Origin	All Races
Married Couples				
Total Families	47,014	3,569	3,454	52,147
With children under 18	21,531	1,884	2,273	24,397
Percent of all families	45.8%	52.8%	65.8%	46.8%
Total own children under 18	40,285	3,583	4,949	45,882
Average no. children per family with children	1.87	1.90	2.18	1.88
Women-Headed Families (no male present)				
Total Families	7,512	3,430	1,186	11,268
With children under 18	4,337	2,294	799	6,823
Percent of all families	57.7%	66.9%	67.4%	60.6%
Total own children under 18	7,134	4,348	1,630	11,864
Average no. children per family with children	1.64	1.90	2.04	1.74

(continued on p. 228)

TABLE B-2 (continued)

CHARACTERISTICS OF U.S. FAMILIES WITH CHILDREN IN 1991
(Numbers in thousands)

Men-Headed Families
(no female spouse present)

Total Families	2,276	472	342	2,907
With children under 18	925	202	131	1,181
Percent of all Families	40.6%	42.8%	38.3%	40.6%
Total own children under 18	1,384	314	217	1,777
Average no. children per family with children	1.50	1.55	1.65	1.50

Note: Persons of Hispanic origin may be of any race; figures for whites and African Americans include persons of Hispanic origin.
Source: *Digest of Education Statistics, 1992*. National Center for Education Statistics, 1992, p. 26.

TABLE B-3

LIVING ARRANGEMENTS OF CHILDREN UNDER 18 YEARS BY AGE OF PARENT, 1992
(Numbers in thousands)

	15–19 Years	20–24 Years	25–29 Years	30–34 Years	35–39 Years	40–44 Years	45–49 Years	50–54 Years	55–59 Years	60–64 Years	65 and Beyond
Children under 6 Years											
Living with both parents	56	1,160	3,616	5,523	3,896	1,705	505	111	73	25	15
Living with mother only	402	1,557	1,815	1,124	511	172	45	13	11	14	19
Living with father only	15	142	245	185	91	55	9	11	4	10	5
Total	473	3,859	5,676	6,832	4,498	1,932	559	135	88	49	39
Children 6–11 Years											
Living with both parents	—	113	1,215	3,973	4,875	3,591	1,415	398	192	72	20
Living with mother only	1	223	1,379	1,611	1,200	571	190	59	15	11	1
Living with father only	1	14	73	172	200	108	58	18	11	7	11
Total	2	350	2,667	5,756	6,275	4,270	1,663	475	218	90	32
Children 12–17 Years											
Living with both parents	—	15	179	1,063	3,369	4,610	2,919	1,167	491	190	86
Living with mother only	3	3	138	1,049	1,442	1,172	586	197	34	19	10
Living with father only	4	1	6	70	149	230	149	54	43	11	20
Total	7	19	323	2,182	4,960	6,012	3,654	1,418	568	220	116
Total Children											
Living with one or both parents	482	3,227	8,465	14,771	15,733	12,213	5,876	2,029	875	358	186

Source: *Marital Status and Living Arrangements: March 1992*. Current Population Reports, Series P20-468.
U.S. Department of Commerce, Bureau of Census, 1992, pp. 29–32.

TABLE B-4

HOUSEHOLD DISCONTINUATION RATES FOR TWO-YEAR PERIODS, MID-1980S
(Percent discontinued)

	White		African American		Hispanic Origin	
	With Children %	Without Children %	With Children %	Without Children %	With Children %	Without Children %
Married-Couple Households						
Both worked	7.1	6.6	8.6	5.7	8.8	11.2
Husband only worked	6.7	6.3	17.5	5.2	9.3	15.0
Wife only worked	12.9	9.7	15.7	12.4	(B)	(B)
Neither worked	14.5	13.4	21.8	22.1	13.1	12.0
Female-Headed Households						
Householder worked	27.1	37.7	15.8	23.3	14.6	(B)
Householder didn't work	27.7	29.2	10.9	18.0	16.3	16.3

(B) Base less than 200,000

Note: Persons of Hispanic origin may be of any race. Percents do not equal 100 because all household types are not included.
Source: *Studies in Household and Family Formation: When Households Continue, Discontinue, and Form.* Current Population Reports, Special Studies P-23, no. 179. U.S. Department of Commerce, Bureau of the Census, 1992, p. 12.

TABLE B-5

PROJECTED FAMILY COMPOSITION IN THE UNITED STATES, 1970–2000

Type of Family	1970	1990	1995	2000
Married Couple without children	37.1%	41.7%	41.8%	42.8%
Married Couple with Children	49.6%	36.9%	36.2%	34.5%
Female Head with Children	5.7%	10.2%	10.0%	9.7%
Male Head with Children	.07%	1.8%	2.2%	2.7%
Other Families	6.9%	9.4%	9.8%	10.3%
Total Families (in millions)	51.2	64.5	68.0	71.7

Note: Rates for 1990 are also projections.
Source: Dennis A. Ahlburg and Carol J. DeVita, "New Realities of the American Family," *Population Bulletin* 47, no. 2 (August 1992): 7.

TABLE B-6

LIVING ARRANGEMENTS OF CHILDREN UNDER 18 YEARS, 1992
(Numbers in thousands)

	All Races	White	African American	Hispanic Origin
Living with Both Parents	46,638	40,635	3,714	4,935
Living with Mother Only				
Married Spouse Absent	3,790	2,465	1,218	673
Divorced	5,507	4,266	1,040	633
Never Married	5,410	2,016	3,192	757
Widowed	688	503	156	104
Total	15,396	9,250	5,607	2,168
Living with Father Only				
Married, Spouse Absent	491	372	72	66
Divorced	932	795	96	66
Never Married	594	432	122	115
Widowed	165	122	38	33
Total	2,182	1,721	327	279
Total Children Living with One or Both Parents	64,216	51,606	9,648	7,382

Note: Persons of Hispanic origin may be of any race. Numbers may vary due to rounding.
Source: *Marital Status and Living Arrangements: March 1992*. Current Population Reports, Population Characteristics, Series P20-468. U.S. Department of Commerce, Bureau of the Census, 1992, pp. 29, 33, 37, 41.

TABLE B-7

ADOPTIONS BY RELATIONSHIP OF PETITIONER, 1970–86

	1986	1982	1975	1970
Total Adoptions	104,088	141,861	129,000	175,000
Relatives	52,931	91,141	81,300	85,800
Unrelated Petitioners - Total	51,157	50,720	47,700	89,200
Public Agency	20,064	19,428	18,600	29,500
Private Agency	15,053	14,549	18,100	40,100
Independent	16,040	16,743	11,000	19,600

Source: *Statistical Abstract of the United States*. U.S. Department of Commerce, Bureau of the Census, 1992, p. 373.

TABLE B-8

PRIMARY CHILD CARE ARRANGEMENTS USED BY WORKING MOTHERS FOR CHILDREN UNDER 15 YEARS, 1988
(Numbers in thousands)

	Mother Employed Part-Time	Mother Employed Full-Time	Total
Care in Child's Home	2,577	2,582	5,158
By father	1,751	1,155	2,906
By grandparent	247	523	770
By other relative	228	443	671
By nonrelative	351	460	811
Care in Another Home	1,241	3,082	4,323
By grandparent	286	744	1,060
By other relative	230	393	623
By nonrelative	725	1,915	2,640
Organized Child Care Facilities	754	2,223	2,977
Day/group care center	452	1,479	1,931
Nursery school/preschool	301	744	1,045
School-Based Activity	105	256	361
Kindergarten/Grade School	5,047	10,785	15,832
Child Cares for Self	172	309	481
Mother Cares for Child at Work	713	442	1,155

Note: Figures for mothers who care for children while at work include mothers who work at home. Numbers may vary due to rounding.
Source: Martin O'Connell and Amara Bachu, *Who's Minding the Kids?: Child Care Arrangements: Fall 1988*. Current Population Reports, Household Economic Studies P70-30. U.S. Department of Commerce, Bureau of the Census, 1992, p. 23.

TABLE B-9

AVERAGE WEEKLY HOURS OF CHILD CARE USED BY EMPLOYED MOTHERS, 1988

		Hours per Week			
	Number of Children	Spent by Mother at Work	Child in After-School Care	Child in Non-School Arrangement	Child Cares for Self
Summary:					
Under 5 years	9,483	33.6	.3	29.7	—
5–14 years	20,804	34.7	18.7	7.0	0.7
Total	30,287	34.4	12.9	14.1	0.5
Detailed:					
Under 1 year	1,523	32.9	—	29.9	0.1
1 year	1,979	33.8	0.1	30.0	—
2 years	1,945	33.6	0.1	30.3	—
3 years	2,022	33.4	—	29.7	—
4 years	2,014	34.0	1.4	28.5	—
5 years	2,144	33.7	10.8	17.3	—
6 years	2,050	33.6	18.3	8.9	0.1
7 years	2,128	34.2	19.2	7.7	0.1
8 years	2,024	34.5	19.9	7.3	0.1
9 years	2,160	34.8	20.1	6.0	0.3
10 years	2,037	34.4	19.1	5.3	0.6
11 years	2,148	35.7	20.2	5.2	1.0
12 years	2,003	35.3	20.0	5.0	1.5
13 years	2,063	35.9	20.0	3.6	1.1
14 years	2,045	35.2	19.5	3.2	2.0

Note: School includes kindergarten and school-based activities.
Source: Martin O'Connell and Amara Bachu, *Who's Minding the Kids?: Child Care Arrangements: Fall 1988*. Current Population Reports, Household Economic Studies P70-30. U.S. Department of Commerce, Bureau of the Census, 1992, p. 8.

TABLE B-10

PERCENT OF HOMICIDES AND SUICIDES RESULTING FROM FIREARMS, 1990 [AGES 10–19 YEARS]

	Percent Homicides Due to Firearms	Percent Suicides Due to Firearms
Age 10–14 years	72.5	55.0
White		
Male	80.3	53.7
Female	45.2	56.1
African American		
Male	85.2	71.4
Female	66.1	62.5
Age 15–19 years	81.7	67.3
White		
Male	76.7	69.4
Female	54.8	57.3
African American		
Male	90.9	76.4
Female	67.0	65.4

Source: Lois A. Fingerhut, "Firearm Mortality among Children, Youth, and Young Adults 1–34 Years of Age, Trends and Current Status: United States, 1985–90," *Advance Data*, no. 231 (March 23, 1993): p. 7.

TABLE B-11

INCIDENCE OF IMPAIRMENTS IN CHILDREN AND YOUTH UNDER 18, 1992
(Numbers in thousands)

Condition	Number
Visual impairment	694
Color blindness	309
Cataracts	63
Glaucoma	55
Hearing impairment	997
Tinnitus	76
Speech impairment	1,388
Absence of extremities	37
Paralysis of extremities	222
Deformity or orthopedic impairment	2,190
Back	795
Upper extremities	156
Lower extremities	1,318

Note: Data are based on household interviews of the civilian noninstitutionalized population.
Source: *Current Estimates from the National Health Interview Survey, 1992*. Vital and Health Statistics, Series 10: Data from the National Health Survey, no. 189. U.S. Department of Health and Human Services, National Center for Health Statistics, 1994, p. 95.

TABLE B-12

RATE OF CHRONIC DISABLING CONDITIONS IN CHILDREN AND YOUTH UNDER 18, 1986–88
(Rates per 1,000 persons)

Condition	Total	Male	Female
Vision impairments	10.5	14.1	6.6
Hearing impairments	17.7	19.1	16.2
Speech impairments	18.3	24.4	11.9
Orthopedic impairments	35.3	31.9	38.9

Source: *Prevalence of Selected Chronic Conditions: United States, 1986–88.* Vital and Health Statistics, Series 10: Data from the National Health Survey, no. 182. U.S. Department of Health and Human Services, National Center for Health Statistics, 1993, p. 10.

TABLE B-13

PERCENT OF CHILDREN UNDER 17 TREATED FOR HEALTH PROBLEMS IN THE PAST 12 MONTHS BY FAMILY TYPE, 1988
(Numbers in thousands)

	Total Children	Accident or Injury	Chronic Asthma	Frequent Headaches	Speech Defect	Chronic Enuresis
All Children	63,569	14.0	4.2	2.8	2.6	2.4
Biological Mother and Father	38,999	13.4	3.9	2.5	2.3	2.3
Formerly Married Mother and No Father	6,945	17.4	5.9	4.1	3.2	2.9
Never-Married Mother and No Father	4,752	9.1	5.0	2.3	4.3	2.3
Mother and Stepfather	5,818	17.7	4.8	5.0	2.4	3.0

Source: *Family Structure and Children's Health: United States, 1988.* Vital and Health Statistics, Series 10: Data from the National Health Survey, no. 178. U.S. Department of Health and Statistics, 1991, pp. 17, 18, 19, 20, 21.

TABLE B-14

AVERAGE ANNUAL NUMBER OF SELECTED INJURIES AND RATE PER 100 PERSONS UNDER 18 YEARS OF AGE, 1985–87
(Numbers in thousands)

	Male		Female	
	Number of Injuries	Rate per 100 Persons	Number of Injuries	Rate Per 100 Persons
All Injuries	11,632	36.1	8,484	27.5
Fractures				
Skull/intracranial injuries	520	1.6	165	0.5
Neck, trunk, upper limbs	1,076	3.3	567	1.8
Lower limbs	236	0.7	253	0.8
Sprains	1,609	5.0	1,347	4.4
Dislocations	156	0.5	167	0.5
Open wounds/lacerations	3,980	12.3	1,853	6.0
Superficial injuries	752	2.3	753	2.4
Contusion (with intact skin surface)	1,719	5.3	1,539	5.0
Burns	145	0.4	241	0.8
Toxic effects (nonmedicinal)	215	0.7	185	0.6
All other injuries	1,102	3.4	1,330	4.1

Note: Data are based on household interviews of the civilian noninstitutionalized population. Not all injuries tabulated are included in the table.
Source: *Types of Injuries by Selected Characteristics: United States, 1985-1987.* Vital and Health Statistics, Series 10: Data from the National Health Survey, no. 175. U.S. Department of Health and Human Services, Center for Health Statistics, 1990, pp. 20, 21.

TABLE B-15

INJURIES ASSOCIATED WITH SELECTED CONSUMER PRODUCTS, 1991 [AGES 0–24 YEARS]

Product	Number of Injuries Reported in Survey	Age Distribution		
		0–4 Years	5–14 Years	15–24 Years
House				
Doors	7,045	23.5	23.3	16.1
Windows	3,263	11.1	17.2	29.7
Walls/ceilings	5,460	18.3	27.3	22.5
Porches/balconies	2,329	18.0	18.4	13.9
Stairs/steps	2,363	14.4	11.5	16.3
Handrails	997	18.3	26.6	13.8
Appliances				
Refrigerators	598	9.3	10.7	18.0
Freezers	103	11.6	2.3	13.9
Heaters	225	36.3	16.7	14.9
Microwave ovens	153	13.9	21.6	15.2
Ovens	246	36.3	3.3	11.3
Water				
Bathtubs	3,150	22.3	11.0	10.1
Hot water	1,130	27.7	14.8	15.3
Radiators	476	51.9	19.8	7.7
Sinks	475	27.3	13.9	9.9
Furniture				
Beds	6,322	37.0	15.3	5.8
Tables	7,703	49.9	16.0	7.1
Chairs	5,346	29.7	14.2	7.7
Desks, chests, etc.	2,270	29.9	26.7	10.2
Cabinets	2,433	23.5	18.5	11.6
Sofas/couches	2,319	46.3	16.1	9.0
Play				
Bicycles	13,523	8.9	58.4	14.6
Swimming pools	1,204	14.0	42.6	19.6
Toys	1,649	49.1	26.0	6.4
Baby Care				
Walkers	752	96.2	1.6	0.5
Strollers	400	89.8	4.3	2.2

Note: Data are from a sample of hospital emergency rooms participating in the National Electronic Injury Surveillance System (NEISS).

Source: *Product Summary Report, All Products, 1991.* Consumer Product Safety Commission, 1992, pp. 5–20.

TABLE B-16
TEN LEADING CAUSES OF DEATH IN 1991 [AGES 1–24 YEARS]

	1–4 Years	5–14 Years	15–24 Years
Unintentional injuries	1	1	1
Congenital anomalies	2	4	7
Malignant neoplasms	3	2	4
Homicide/legal intervention	4	3	2
Diseases of heart	5	5	5
Suicide	—	6	3
Pneumonia/influenza	6	7	8
Chronic obstructive pulmonary disease	—	8	10
Conditions originating in perinatal period	8	—	—
Human immunodeficiency virus infection	7	9	6
Cerebrovascular diseases	—	10	9
Septicemia	9	—	—
Benign neoplasms, carcinoma in situ, unspecified neoplasms	10	9	—

Note: Based on death rates per 100,000 population in group specified.
Source: *Health United States 1993*. U.S. Department of Health and Human Services, National Center for Health Statistics, 1994, p. 99.

TABLE B-17

DEATHS FROM SELECTED CAUSES IN 1990 [AGES 0–24 YEARS]

	Under 1 Year	1–4 Years	5–14 Years	15–24 Years
All Causes	38,351	6,931	8,436	36,733
Intestinal infections	98	13	6	2
Whooping cough	11	1	—	—
Meningococcal infection	50	38	18	32
Septicemia	267	100	46	84
Measles	11	29	4	7
Other infectious diseases	370	222	192	728
Malignant neoplasms	90	513	1,094	1,819
Diabetes mellitus	4	7	24	115
Nutritional deficiencies	16	4	1	9
Anemias	29	51	51	124
Meningitis	197	81	37	29
Cardiovascular diseases	963	335	401	1,224
Cerebrovascular diseases	148	45	73	234
Acute bronchitis	75	18	6	5
Pneumonia and influenza	634	171	134	231
Chronic obstructive pulmonary disease	55	55	115	178
Hernia/abdominal obstruction	87	23	27	22
Chronic liver disease	16	7	7	44
Nephritis	151	24	20	57
Congenital anomalies	8,239	896	468	491
Conditions originating in perinatal period	17,482	134	29	5
Symptoms, signs, ill-defined conditions	6,409	270	123	711
Accidents/adverse effects	930	2,566	3,650	16,241
Suicide	—	—	264	4,869
Homicide/legal intervention	332	378	512	7,354

Note: Rates per 100,000 population in specified group. Data for some causes are not tabulated here.
Source: Brenda S. Gillum and Bettie L. Hudson, "Advance Report of Final Mortality Statistics, 1990," *Monthly Vital Statistics Report* 41, no. 7 Supplement (January 7, 1993): 22–23.

TABLE B-18

MORTALITY RATES AND RATIO FROM SUDDEN INFANT DEATH SYNDROME (SIDS)

	1988		1980	
	Rate per 100,000 Births	Proportion of Deaths	Rate per 100,000 Births	Proportion of Deaths
United States				
White	123.7	14.5	128.3	11.7
African American	226.2	12.8	280.0	13.1
Total	140.1	14.1	152.5	12.1

Source: "Variations in the Incidence of Sudden Infant Death Syndrome (SIDS), U.S., 1980–88." *Statistical Bulletin* 74, no. 1 (January/March 1993): 12, 16.

TABLE B-19
PERCENT OF CHILDREN UNDER 4 YEARS OF AGE WHO WERE BREASTFED, 1990

	Ever Breastfed	Breastfed 6 Months or More
Total Children	52.1	24.0
Age		
Under 1 year	54.5	22.4
1 year	50.1	22.4
2 years	51.0	23.6
3 years	54.4	26.2
4 years	50.1	24.9
Gender		
Male	52.5	23.6
Female	51.6	24.5
Race/Ethnicity		
White	56.4	26.4
African American	24.6	9.7
Hispanic Origin	50.6	19.6

Note: Persons of Hispanic origin may be of any race.

Source: *Health Promotion and Disease Prevention United States, 1990.* Vital and Health Statistics, Series 10: Data from the National Health Survey, no. 185. U.S. Department of Health and Human Services, National Center for Health Statistics, 1993, p. 13.

TABLE B-20
MOST POPULAR SPORTS FOR HIGH SCHOOL STUDENTS IN 1993–94

	School Programs	Boys Participating	School Programs	Girls Participating
Basketball	16,451	530,068	16,016	412,576
Football	13,029	903,971	70	334
Track and Field (outdoor)	14,192	419,758	14,027	345,700
Baseball	13,962	438,846	80	353
Soccer	7,445	255,538	5,463	166,173
Cross Country	10,693	162,188	10,142	124,700
Golf	10,605	131,207	4,957	36,601
Wrestling	8,538	223,433	220	783
Tennis	9,069	135,702	8,780	136,239
Swimming and Diving	4,595	81,328	4,643	102,652
Volleyball	1,207	26,208	12,403	327,616
Softball (fast pitch)	62	1,228	10,243	257,118
Softball (slow pitch)	16	198	1,925	41,118
Field Hockey	1	1	1,452	53,747

Source: Reprinted with permission from *National Federation Handbook, 1993–94.* National Federation of State High School Associations, 1994, in press.

TABLE B-21

TEACHERS' PERCEPTIONS OF SCHOOL PROBLEMS IN 1990
(N=21,389)

	Serious Problem at My School %	Somewhat of a Problem at My School %	Not a Problem at My School %
Absenteeism	19	64	17
Disruptive Behavior in the Classroom	16	70	14
Student Apathy Toward School	30	56	14
Student Turnover	13	55	31
Lack of Parental Support	25	62	13
Alcohol Use (*Secondary teachers only)	24	60	16
Drug Use (other than alcohol)	7	43	50
Abused/Neglected Youth	19	70	11
Poor Health Among Students	6	61	33
Undernourished Youth	7	56	38

Source: *Condition of Teaching: A State-by-State Analysis, 1990*. Carnegie Foundation for the Advancement of Teaching, 1990, pp. 23, 24. ©1990, The Carnegie Foundation for the Advancement of Teaching. Reprinted with permission.

TABLE B-22

NEW TEACHERS' PERCEPTIONS OF PARENTS, STUDENTS, AND FAMILY LIFE IN 1991
(N = 1,007)

	Agree			Disagree		
	Strongly %	Somewhat %	Total %	Strongly %	Somewhat %	Total %
Effective teachers need to work well with their students' parents.	85	13	98	—	2	2
Too many parents treat their children's schools and teachers as adversaries.	14	57	71	4	24	28
Health and social problems should be addressed by other agencies outside the school. A school's job is to teach children.	4	21	25	30	44	74
Many children come to school with so many problems that it's very difficult for them to be good students.	47	42	89	3	8	11
I can really make a difference in the lives of my students.	68	30	98	—	1	1

Source: Reprinted with permission from *Metropolitan Life Survey of the American Teacher, 1991: New Teachers' Expectations and Ideals: A Survey of New Teachers Who Completed Their First Year of Teaching in Public Schools in 1991*. Metropolitan Life Insurance Co., 1991, pp. 5, 11.

TABLE B-23

CHILD ABUSE REPORTING AND FATALITIES, 1988–91

	1991	1990	1989	1988
Estimated number of reported child victims	2,694,000	2,537,000	2,407,000	2,243,000
Rate per 1,000 U.S. children	42	39	38	35
Reported abuse-related fatalities	1,033	1,145	1,114	1,021
Total projected fatalities nationwide	1,383	1,253	1,230	1,181
Abuse-related fatality rate per 100,000 U.S. children	2.15	1.95	1.92	1.89

Note: Reported fatalities include only confirmed cases. Abuse-related fatality per 100,000 children based on 1989 census data.
Source: Reprinted with permission from *Current Trends in Child Abuse Reporting and Fatalities: The Results of the 1991 Fifty State Survey.* National Committee to Prevent Child Abuse, 1992, pp. 4, 14.

TABLE B-24

CHARACTERISTICS OF CHILD ABUSE REPORTS

	1986	1985	1984	1976
Number of children reported	2,086	1,928	1,727	669
Rate per 10,000 children	328	306	273	101
Type of maltreatment				
Deprivation of necessities	54.9	53.6	54.6	70.7
Minor physical injury	13.9	17.8	17.7	18.9
Sexual maltreatment	15.7	13.8	13.3	3.2
Emotional maltreatment	8.3	11.5	11.2	21.6
Other	21.6	13.8	16.5	11.2
Characteristics of child				
Average age (years)	7.2	7.2	7.2	7.7
Sex				
Male	47.5	47.6	48.0	50.0
Female	52.5	52.4	52.0	50.0
Characteristics of abuser				
Average age (years)	31.7	31.6	31.5	32.3
Sex				
Male	44.1	44.1	43.0	39.0
Female	55.9	55.9	57.0	61.0

Source: *Statistical Abstract of the United States, 1992.* U.S. Department of Commerce, Bureau of the Census, 1992, p. 186.

TABLE B-25

REPORTED MARIJUANA AND COCAINE USE BY HIGH SCHOOL SENIORS IN 1992
(N=15,000)

	Never Used %	Ever Used %	Used within Last 30 Days %	Used within Last 12 Months but Not Last 30 Days %	Used but Not within Last 12 Months %
Marijuana					
All seniors	67.4	32.6	11.9	10.0	10.7
Sex					
Male	63.7	36.3	13.4	11.0	11.9
Female	71.4	28.6	10.2	8.7	9.7
College plans					
None or under 4 years	58.2	41.6	15.0	12.5	14.3
Complete 4 years	71.2	28.8	10.4	9.0	9.4
Cocaine					
All seniors	93.9	6.1	1.3	1.8	3.0
Sex					
Male	93.0	7.0	1.5	2.2	3.3
Female	94.9	5.1	0.9	1.5	2.7
College plans					
None or under 4 years	90.0	10.0	2.3	2.8	4.9
Complete 4 years	95.3	4.7	0.8	1.6	2.3

Source: *Sourcebook of Criminal Justice Statistics, 1992*. U.S. Department of Justice, 1993, p. 327.

TABLE B-26

ALCOHOL USE REPORTED BY HIGH SCHOOL SENIORS IN 1992
(N=15,000)

	Never Used %	Ever Used %	Used within Last 30 Days %	Used within 12 Months but Not Last 30 Days %	Used but Not within Last 12 Months %
All Seniors	12.5	87.5	51.3	25.5	10.7
Sex					
Male	12.4	87.6	55.8	21.4	10.4
Female	12.4	87.6	46.8	29.4	11.4
College Plans					
None or under 4 years	9.8	90.2	54.9	24.8	10.5
Complete 4 years	13.1	86.9	50.0	25.9	11.0

Source: *Sourcebook of Criminal Justice Statistics, 1992*. U.S. Department of Justice, 1993, p. 326.

AUTHOR INDEX

TITLE INDEX

SUBJECT INDEX

by Janet Perlman